Cyclopedia of World Authors II

A-Dav

CYCLOPEDIA of WORLD AUTHORS II

VOLUME ONE—A-DAV

Edited by

FRANK N. MAGILL

Salem Press
Pasadena, California   Englewood Cliffs, New Jersey

∞ The paper used in these volumes conforms to the American National Standard for Permanence of Paper for Printed Library Materials, Z39.48-1984.

Library of Congress Cataloging-in-Publication Data
Cyclopedia of world authors II / edited by Frank N. Magill.
p. cm.
Includes bibliographical references.
ISBN 0-89356-512-1 (set)
1. Literature—Bio-bibliography. 2. Literature—Dictionaries. 3. Authors—Biography—Dictionaries. I. Magill, Frank Northen, 1907- . II. Title: Cyclopedia of world authors 2. III. Title: Cyclopedia of world authors two.
PN451.C93 1989
809—dc20
[B] 89-10659
CIP

ISBN 0-89356 512-1 (set)
ISBN 0-89356 513-x (volume 1)

PRINTED IN THE UNITED STATES OF AMERICA

PUBLISHER'S NOTE

CYCLOPEDIA OF WORLD AUTHORS II provides brief introductions to the lives and works of 705 important modern writers. It includes more than eighty percent of the authors whose works are covered in the twenty-six volumes of the *Masterplots II* series, and thus forms a useful companion to that series. This four-volume set, arranged alphabetically by author, includes individuals who were still active at the time that the revised edition of the first *Cyclopedia of World Authors* was published, in 1974, as well as those who required new treatment as the result of posthumous publication and further scholarship; however, the vast majority of authors covered in these volumes—eighty percent—are new. The current publication thus forms a much-needed companion set to the original *Cyclopedia*.

In addition to well-known fiction writers, poets, and dramatists, this set recognizes men and women whose principal works fall under genre headings as varied as literary criticism, science fiction, linguistics, theology, autobiography, mystery/detective fiction, and politics. Although the genres of their works are wide-ranging, the authors selected share the distinction of having had a significant impact on international letters; in the case of authors whose writing is, for the most part, nonliterary, their work has had considerable influence outside their particular disciplines. While the set covers English-language authors extensively, writers from countries as diverse as Japan, Nigeria, the Soviet Union, and Brazil, as well as the Western European nations, are also represented.

The articles, all signed by respected scholars, are designed to provided quick overviews of the authors in roughly one thousand words. Following the format established in the first *Cyclopedia of World Authors*, ready-reference data at the top of each entry include birth and death information and a listing of principal works, categorized by genre and ordered chronologically by year of publication. (Plays are listed by their original date of appearance: if that date was a first performance, "pr."; if a first publication, "pb.") The body of the article covers highlights of the individual's biography and briefly assesses the literary career, tracing the author's development and considering his or her work in a larger context.

A major feature of each article is the narrative bibliography at the end, which offers accessible references for additional study. This select listing identifies for the student key books and articles on these figures. All efforts have been made to include the most comprehensive and up-to-date source materials of use to general readers and students alike.

Volume 4 contains an index of the authors covered, including cross-reference listings of major pseudonyms or other names by which they may have been known.

CONTRIBUTING REVIEWERS

Michael Adams
Wagner College

Patrick Adcock
Henderson State University

Bland Addison, Jr.
Worcester Polytechnic Institute

Jacob H. Adler
Purdue University, West Lafayette

Anthony M. Alioto
Columbia College

Joseph A. Alvarez
Central Piedmont Community College

Anu Aneja
Pennsylvania State University, State College

Andrew J. Angyal
Elon College

Raymond M. Archer
Indiana University at Kokomo

Stanley Archer
Texas A&M University

Christopher M. Armitage
University of North Carolina at Chapel Hill

Dorothy B. Aspinwall
University of Hawaii at Manoa

Bryan Aubrey
Maharishi International University

Ehrhard Bahr
University of California, Los Angeles

James Baird
University of North Texas

Thomas P. Baldwin
Western Kentucky University

Stanislaw Baranczak
Harvard University

Dan Barnett
California State University, Chico

Thomas F. Barry
University of Southern California

Melissa E. Barth
Appalachian State University

Thomas O. Beebee
Pennsylvania State University

Rebecca Bell-Metereau
Southwest Texas State University

Alfred Bendixen
California State University, Los Angeles

Robert Bensen
Hartwick College

Mary G. Berg
Harvard University

Robert L. Berner
University of Wisconsin—Oshkosh

John B. Beston
Nazareth College of Rochester

Suzann Bick
Antioch College, Yellow Springs

Cynthia A. Bily
Adrian College

Dominic J. Bisignano
Indiana University and Purdue University at Indianapolis

Wayne M. Bledsoe
University of Missouri-Rolla

J. H. Bowden
Indiana University, Southeast

Robert Boyd
St. Louis Community College

Jerry Bradley
New Mexico Tech

Harold Branam
Temple University

Gerhard Brand
California State University, Los Angeles

Philip Brantingham
Loyola University of Chicago

Francis J. Bremer
Millersville University

J. R. Broadus
University of North Carolina at Chapel Hill

William S. Brockington, Jr.
University of South Carolina, Aiken

Alan Brown
Livingston University

Carl Brucker
Arkansas Tech University

Rosanne Brunton
Pennsylvania State University, State College

Hallman B. Bryant
Clemson University

David L. Bullock
Kansas State University, Manhattan

Lori Hall Burghardt
University of Tennessee, Knoxville

Roland E. Bush
California State University, Long Beach

Joanne Butcher
University of Miami

Edmund J. Campion
University of Tennessee, Knoxville

Byron D. Cannon
University of Utah, Salt Lake City

Warren J. Carson
University of South Carolina at Spartanburg

Sonya H. Cashdan
East Tennessee State University

Thomas J. Cassidy
State University of New York, Binghamton

C. L. Chua
California State University, Fresno

John R. Clark
University of South Florida

Greta McCormick Coger
Northwest Mississippi Junior College

William Condon
University of Michigan

Del Corey
Macomb Community College

Laura Cowan
University of Maine

Timothy J. Cox
Pennsylvania State University, State College

Virginia Crane
California State University, Los Angeles

C. Culleton
University of Miami

Walter C. Daniel
University of Missouri, Columbia

Jane Davis
Cornell University

Liselotte M. Davis
Yale University

Susan Davis
Independent Scholar

R. M. Day
East Tennessee State University

Michael P. Dean
University of Mississippi, Oxford

Thomas Derdak
University of Chicago

John Louis DiGaetani
Hofstra University

Bruce L. Edwards
Bowling Green State University

Clifford D. Edwards
Fort Hays State University

Robert P. Ellis
Worcester State College

Nancy L. Erickson
Erskine College

Kathleen M. Ermitage
Loyla University of Chicago

Thomas L. Erskine
Salisbury State University

Thomas H. Falk
Michigan State University, Williamston

Kathy A. Fedorko
Middlesex County College

Donald M. Fiene
University of Tennessee, Knoxville

Edward Fiorelli
Saint John's University, New York

David Marc Fischer
Independent Scholar

David Francis
University of Delaware

CONTRIBUTING REVIEWERS

Margot K. Frank
Randolph-Macon Woman's College

Bruce A. French
University of New Haven

C. George Fry
Saint Francis College

Daniel J. Fuller
Kent State University

Susan VanZanten Gallagher
Calvin College

Helen S. Garson
George Mason University

Jill B. Gidmark
University of Minnesota, Minneapolis

Paul Giles
Portland State University

Jacqueline L. Gmuca
University of South Carolina, Coastal Carolina College

Donald S. Gochberg
Michigan State University, East Lansing

Lois Gordon
Fairleigh Dickinson College

Glenn A. Grever
Illinois State University, Normal

Caroline Nobile Gryta
Kent State University

Jay L. Halio
University of Delaware, Wilmington

William S. Haney II
Maharishi International University

Todd C. Hanlin
University of Arkansas, Fayetteville

Lee Emling Harding
Mississippi College

Natalie Harper
Simon's Rock of Bard College

David M. Harralson
Utica College of Syracuse University

E. Lynn Harris
University of Illinois, Wheaton

Hunt Hawkins
Florida State University, Tallahassee

James Hazen
University of Nevada, Las Vegas

Michael Helfand
University of Pittsburgh, Pittsburgh

Terry Heller
Coe College

Karl Henzy
University of Delaware

Jane Hill
Longstreet Press

Bill Hoagland
Northern Montana College

Eric H. Hobson
University of Tennessee, Knoxville

Michael Hollister
Portland State University

Pierre L. Horn
Wright State University

Christa I. Hungate
East Tennessee State University

David Huntley
Appalachian State University

E. D. Huntley
Appalachian State University

Mary Anne Hutchinson
Utica College of Syracuse University

Allen E. Hye
Wright State University

Archibald E. Irwin
Indiana University, Southeast

Charles M. Israel
Columbia College

Dennis Jackson
University of Delaware

Tommie L. Jackson
Saint Cloud State University

Shakuntala Jayaswal
University of New Haven

W. A. Johnsen
Michigan State University, East Lansing

Chandice Johnson
North Dakota State University, Fargo

D. Barton Johnson
University of California, Santa Barbara

Isaac Johnson
Pacific Union College

Jodi A. Johnson
Los Angeles Pierce College

James T. Jones
Southwest Missouri State University

Albert E. Kalson
Purdue University, West Lafayette

Steven G. Kellman
University of Texas at San Antonio

Martin Kich
Lehigh University

Ann Klefstad
Sun and Moon Press

Wm. Laird Kleine-Ahlbrandt
Purdue University, West Lafayette

Paula D. Kopacz
Eastern Kentucky University

Charles Kraszewski
Pennsylvania State University, State College

Katherine C. Kurk
Northern Kentucky University

John Lang
Emory and Henry College

P. R. Lannert
Independent Scholar

Karl G. Larew
Towson State University

Eugene S. Larson
Los Angeles Pierce College

Donald F. Larsson
Mankato State University

Terry Lass
Columbia College in Missouri

Mary S. LeDonne
State University of New York, Binghamton

Richard M. Leeson
Fort Hays State University

Jordan Leondopoulos
Saint John's University, New York

Leon Lewis
Appalachian State University

Leslie W. Lewis
Indiana University, Bloomington

Terrance L. Lewis
College of Charleston

T. M. Lipman
Independent Scholar

James Livingston
Northern Michigan University

Janet E. Lorenz
Independent Scholar

Michael Loudon
Eastern Illinois University

Perry D. Luckett
United States Air Force Academy

Reinhart Lutz
University of California, Santa Barbara

Annette Peters Lynch
Mount San Antonio College

John O. Lyons
University of Wisconsin—Madison

Janet McCann
Texas A&M University

Arthur F. McClure
Central Missouri State University

C. S. McConnell
University of Calgary, Alberta, Canada

Michael John McDonough
Alfred University

Christopher MacGowan
College of William and Mary

F. K. McHugh
Eastern Michigan University

Louis K. MacKendrick
University of Windsor, Ontario, Canada

Stephen A. McKnight
University of Florida, Gainesville

Alan L. McLeod
Rider College

Marian B. McLeod
Trenton State College

CONTRIBUTING REVIEWERS

Victoria E. McLure
Texas Tech University

David W. Madden
California State University, Sacramento

Paul D. Mageli
University of Chicago

Thomas A. Maik
University of Wisconsin—La Crosse

Martha Manheim
Seina Heights College

Lois A. Marchino
University of Texas at El Paso

Joss Marsh
University of California, Santa Barbara

Charles E. May
California State University, Long Beach

Jean-Pierre Metereau
Texas Lutheran College

Walter E. Meyers
North Carolina State University

Jennifer E. Michaels
Grinnell College

Vasa D. Mihailovich
University of North Carolina at Chapel Hill

Randall M. Miller
Saint Joseph's University

Robert A. Morace
Daemen College

Robert E. Morsberger
California State Polytechnic University, Pomona

Anita Moss
University of North Carolina at Chapel Hill

James V. Muhleman
Hawaii Loa College

Marilyn Mumford
Bucknell University

Marie Murphy
Loyola College

John M. Muste
Ohio State University

William Nelles
Northwestern State University

Reiko Nemoto
Pennsylvania State University—University Park

Emma Coburn Norris
Troy State University, Montgomery

Robert H. O'Connor
North Dakota State University

Steven E. Olson
Central State University

Kathleen K. O'Mara
State University of New York, Oneonta

Thomas O'Toole
Saint Cloud State University

Robert M. Otten
Assumption College

Robert J. Paradowski
Rochester Institute of Technology

John G. Parks
Miami University

David B. Parsell
Furman University

David Patterson
Oklahoma State University, Stillwater

Joseph R. Peden
Bernard M. Baruch College,
City University of New York

William E. Pemberton
University of Wisconsin—La Crosse

Charles A. Perrone
University of Florida, Gainesville

Joseph F. Pestino
Nazareth College of Rochester

Robert B. Pettit
Manchester College

William L. Phillips
University of Washington

Susan L. Piepke
Bridgewater College

Steven L. Piott
Clarion University

Bonnie C. Plummer
Eastern Kentucky University

John F. Povey
University of California, Los Angeles

Marian Price
University of Central Florida

Wade Provo
Rockford College

Charles Pullen
Queen's University, Ontario, Canada

Victor J. Ramraj
University of Calgary, Alberta, Canada

Jennifer L. Randisi
California State University, San Bernardino

Abe C. Ravitz
California State University, Dominguez Hills

John D. Raymer
Indiana University, South Bend

Dennis Reinhartz
University of Texas at Arlington

Rosemary M. Canfield Reisman
Troy State University, Troy

Judith Ricker-Abderhalden
University of Arkansas, Fayetteville

Carl Rollyson
Bernard M. Baruch College, City University of New York

Paul Rosefeldt
University of New Orleans

Joseph Rosenblum
University of North Carolina at Greensboro

Nancy E. Rupprecht
Middle Tennessee State University

Susan Rusinko
Bloomsburg University

Arthur M. Saltzman
Missouri Southern State College

Per Schelde
York College, City University of New York

Barry P. Scherr
Dartmouth College

Thomas C. Schunk
Bellevue College

Barbara Kitt Seidman
Linfield College

Catharine F. Seigel
Rhode Island School of Design

J'nan Morse Sellery
Harvey Mudd College

Richard M. Shaw
North Dakota State University, Fargo

Walter Shear
Pittsburgh State University, Pittsburgh

Richard J. Sherry
Asbury College

John C. Sherwood
University of Oregon

R. Baird Shuman
University of Illinois, Urbana-Champaign

Brandie Siegfried
Brigham Young University

Carl Singleton
Fort Hays State University

Genevieve Slomski
Independent Scholar

Marjorie Smelstor
Ball State University

Clyde Curry Smith
University of Wisconsin—River Falls

Roger Smith
Fairleigh Dickinson University

Ira Smolensky
Monmouth College

James E. Smythe
Pepperdine University

Katherine Snipes
Eastern Washington University

Philip H. Solomon
Southern Methodist University

Isabel B. Stanley
East Tennessee State University

David R. Stefancic
University of Wisconsin—Stout

H. R. Stoneback
State University of New York, New Paltz

Michelle Stott
Brigham Young University

Gerald H. Strauss
Bloomsburg University

CONTRIBUTING REVIEWERS

Mary J. Sturm
University of Chicago

James Sullivan
California State University, Los Angeles

Mary Rose Sullivan
University of Colorado at Denver

David Sundstrand
Citrus College

Charlene Suscavage
University of Southern Maine

Catherine Swanson
University of Oxford

Roy Arthur Swanson
University of Wisconsin—Milwaukee

Susan Swartzlander
Bucknell University

Daniel Taylor
Bethel College

Thomas J. Taylor
Purdue University, West Lafayette

Carolyn S. Terry
Pennsylvania State University, State College

Lou Thompson
New Mexico Tech

Larry W. Usilton
University of North Carolina at Wilmington

Luiz Fernando Valente
Brown University

Peter Valenti
Fayetteville State University

Dennis Vannatta
University of Arkansas at Little Rock

Michelle Van Tine
Columbus State Community College

Jon S. Vincent
University of Kansas, Lawrence

Paul R. Waibel
Trinity College

Steven C. Walker
Brigham Young University

Suzanne Ward
California State University, Sacramento

Clifton L. Warren
Central State University

Judith Anderson Weise
State University of New York, Potsdam

Steven C. Weisenburger
University of Kentucky, Lexington

Thomas Whissen
Wright State University

Duffield White
Wesleyan University

Barbara Wiedemann
Auburn University at Montgomery

Clarke L. Wilhelm
Denison University

John R. M. Wilson
Mid-America Nazarene College

Norma C. Wilson
University of Soth Dakota, Vermillion

Mark Royden Winchell
Clemson University

Michael Witkoski
Independent Scholar

Timothy C. Wong
Ohio State University, Worthington

Paul A. Wood
Villanova University

Karin A. Wurst
Michigan State University, East Lansing

Vincent Yang
Pennsylvania State University, State College

William M. Zanella
Hawaii Loa College

LIST OF AUTHORS IN VOLUME 1

LIST OF AUTHORS IN VOLUME 1

LIST OF AUTHORS IN VOLUME 1

Cyclopedia
of
World Authors II

A-Dav

EDWARD ABBEY

Born: Home, Pennsylvania
Date: January 29, 1927

Died: Tucson, Arizona
Date: March 14, 1989

Principal Works

NOVELS: *Jonathan Troy*, 1954; *The Brave Cowboy*, 1956; *Fire on the Mountain*, 1962; *Black Sun*, 1971; *The Monkey Wrench Gang*, 1975; *Good News*, 1980; *The Fool's Progress*, 1988.

NONFICTION: *Desert Solitaire*, 1968; *Appalachia*, 1970; *Appalachian Wilderness*, 1973; *Slickrock: Endangered Canyons of the Southwest*, 1971; *Cactus Country*, 1973; *The Hidden Canyon: A River Journey*, 1977; *The Journey Home*, 1977; *Abbey's Road*, 1979; *Desert Images*, 1979; *Down the River*, 1982; *Beyond the Wall*, 1984; *Slumgullion Stew: An Edward Abbey Reader*, 1984.

Edward Abbey's work provokes an intensity of response that is singular among writers of the American West. He is best known for his iconoclastic attacks on the forces of modern society that have encroached on the remaining wilderness areas in the United States, in particular the deserts of the Southwest. His condemnation of government in the service of greedy developers, mindless strip mining, and "industrial tourism" is vitriolic and impassioned. To his adherents, he is a voice of truth; to his detractors, he is a troublesome crank out of touch with the modern world. At the center of this continual controversy stands a writer who is at once intensely private and painfully self-revelatory.

Edward Abbey was born and educated in the Allegheny Mountains of Pennsylvania, where he was graduated from high school in 1945. It was during the summer of 1944 while hitchhiking through the western United States that Abbey became entranced with the desert country of the Southwest. He was to return to the East to be drafted into the Army soon after completing high school. The years following his discharge from the Army found him caught between his roots in the East and his growing love for the open spaces of the West. It was during this period that Abbey began writing fiction. His novel, *Jonathan Troy*, published in 1954, is reflective of the schism in Abbey's personal life. The title character is drawn away from the world that he inhabits in the East, and like Abbey, he finds that freedom of spirit is only attainable in untrammeled landscapes of the West.

After completing his B.A. at the University of New Mexico in 1951, he lived as a Fulbright Fellow at the University of Edinburgh. Returning to the United States in 1953, he made an unsuccessful attempt to live and work in the East as a graduate student of philosophy at Yale University, where he stayed for a few weeks before returning to the University of New Mexico. In 1956, Abbey was to produce two works that delineate the central thematic concerns of his work: his thesis, on anarchism and the morality of violence, and the novel *The Brave Cowboy*, which sets its anachronistic hero against the forces of bureaucratic brutality.

Jack Burns, the protagonist of *The Brave Cowboy*, loves the land of the Southwest and the freedom of his life as an itinerant sheep herder. Yet he is a man out of step with the times. He thinks it unnecessary to carry identification because he knows who he is, and his principal mode of transportation is his spirited mare, Whisky, who has trouble sharing space with the newfangled horseless carriage. When Burns is drawn into a confrontation with the technological power of modern law enforcement, he makes a heroic escape only to be run down on the highway by a truck carrying a load of bathroom fixtures. The message is clear. The encroachment of the urban environment into the physical and spiritual landscape of the West becomes a metaphor for the destruction of a way of life characterized by personal freedom, physical labor, and respect for the land. The polarities between the individual and bureaucratic establishment, between the landscape of the wilderness and the contamination of urban life established in *The Brave Cowboy* provide the basic thematic understructure of Abbey's work. Abbey uses these themes again in *Fire on the Mountain*, where the protagonist perishes at the hands of the United States government in defense of his ranch, slated to become a weapons testing site. In this work there is an urgency not present in *The Brave Cowboy*.

The publication of *Desert Solitaire*, a series of reflective essays centered on Abbey's experiences as a park ranger at Arches National Monument, propelled Edward Abbey into public attention and provided a watershed for defenders and detractors. Abbey's prose soars from lyrical paeans to the remaining unspoiled land of the Southwest to vituperative attacks on the forces he believes are participating in its destruction, that is, industrial and commercial development, aided and abetted by government bureaucracy. It is the work for which he is best known and by which he is most frequently defined.

Three more nonfiction books quickly followed: *Appalachian Wilderness*, *Slickrock*, and *Cactus Country*. In these works Abbey supplies the text in conjunction with popular landscape photographers. Although these books are intended for the coffee table, Abbey's message is still present if somewhat muted.

In both his later fiction and nonfiction, Abbey is no longer content to bemoan the destruction of his beloved Southwest. His counsel borders on sedition. In *The Monkey Wrench Gang*, four unlikely comrades roam about the land pulling up survey stakes, burning billboards, and planning the destruction of Glenn Canyon Dam. His fictional creations provide the model for action. The essays collected in *The Journey Home* and *Abbey's Road* angrily urge action before it is too late, and in fact suggest that it may already be too late. The 1980 novel, *Good News*, is set in a dark and grim future where both the land and the individual have fallen victim to the pervasive totalitarianism of power and greed. In *The Fool's Progress*, the dying protagonist joins the *danse macabre*, unable to save himself, much less his beloved wilderness, from the blight of urban death.

Despite Abbey's iconoclastic and frequently enraged stance, his concerns reflect his literary predecessors. Like Henry David Thoreau and John Muir, Abbey finds a spiritual appeal in nature, but unlike them he has seen the continuing encroachment of commerce and industry into what little remains of wilderness land. Abbey is more the direct descendant of Mary Austin, who alone spoke against the building of Boulder Dam at a conference of prominent Southwesterners in 1927. Her voice was prophetic, and Abbey echoes her cry against the sacrifice of the natural environment to the needs of a technological society.

BIBLIOGRAPHICAL REFERENCES: Garth McCann's "Edward Abbey," *Boise State Western Writers Series*, XXIX, edited by Wayne Chatterton and James H. Maguire, though dated, provides a useful discussion of Abbey and his earlier works through 1975. Ann Ronald's *The New West of Edward Abbey*, 1982, is the best unified analysis of the man and his works. *Resist Much, Obey Little*, 1985, edited by James Hepworth and Gregory McNamee, contains essays written especially for this collection by such writers as Wendell Berry, William Eastlake, Gary Snyder, and Barry Lopez. It is also useful for the three personal interviews with Abbey which shed light on the author's attitude toward his work. Finally, Ann Ronald's chapter on Edward Abbey in *A Literary History of the American West*, 1987, edited by Thomas J. Lyon, J. Golden Taylor, et al., provides a cogent commentary on his work and an assessment of its significance. See also William T. Pilkington, "Edward Abbey: Southwestern Anarchist," *Western Review*, III (1966), 58-62; Les Standiford, "Desert Places: An Exchange with Edward Abbey," *Western Humanities Review*, XXIV (1970), 395-398; Delbert E. Wylder, "Edward Abbey and the Power Elite," *Western Review*, VI (1969), 18-22; Sheldon Frank, "Wilderness," *The National Observer*, September 6, 1975, 17; William Marling, "Anarchism and Ecology," *Southwest Review*, I, no. 1 (1976), 108-111; Ted Morgan, "Subvert and Converse," *The New York Times Book Review*, July 31, 1977, 1011; Dennis Drabelle, "Environments and Elitists," *The Nation*, CXXXIV, no. 17 (1982), 533-535; and John N. Cole, "Edward Abbey: A Sage of the Sagebrush," *The Washington Post Book World*, May 30, 1982, 3.

David Sundstrand

KŌBŌ ABE

Born: Tokyo, Japan
Date: March 7, 1924

PRINCIPAL WORKS

NOVELS AND NOVELLAS: *Owarishi michi no shirube ni*, 1947; *Baberu no to no tanuki*, 1951; *Mahō no chōku*, 1951; *Kemonotachi wa kokyō o mezasu*, 1957; *Daiyon kampyōki*, 1959 (*Inter Ice Age 4*, 1970); *Suna no onna*, 1962 (*The Woman in the Dunes*, 1964); *Tanin no kao*, 1964 (*The Face of Another*, 1966); *Moetsukita chizu*, 1967 (*The Ruined Map*, 1969); *Hakootoko*, 1973 (*The Box Man*, 1974); *Mikkai*, 1977 (*Secret Rendezvous*, 1980).

POETRY: *Mumei shishu*, 1947.

PLAYS: *Omae ni mo tsumi ga aru*, pr. 1965 (*You, Too, Are Guilty*, 1978); *Tomodachi*, pr., pb. 1967 (*Friends*, 1969); *Bō ni natta otoko*, pr., pb. 1969 (*The Man Who Turned Into a Stick*, 1975); *Gikyoku zenshu*, pb. 1970.

Kōbō Abe is one of Japan's most prolific postwar writers; his novels, plays, and stories focus on the alienation of contemporary men and women. Born Kimifusa Abe in Tokyo, he lived until the age of sixteen in occupied Mukden, China, where his physician father worked and taught at the Japanese-run Manchurian School of Medicine. The Japanese colony in which his family lived grew with Japan's expansive presence on the Asian continent in the 1920's and 1930's. War with China broke out in 1937, and Abe returned to Tokyo in 1941 to attend school and receive military training. His early interests included insect collecting and mathematics. Following in his father's footsteps, Abe entered the medical school of Tokyo Imperial University in 1943, specializing in gynecology. He interrupted his studies, however, to return to Manchuria. Following his repatriation at the end of the war, he resumed his university courses. He and his wife, Machi, were married while Abe was a student. She was to become an artist and set designer, and her drawings illustrate many of her husband's later literary works.

An indifferent student not really interested in medicine, Abe was permitted to be graduated after he promised his mentors that he would not practice. By this time his father had died, and Abe may have felt released from pressures to become a doctor. A collection of his poems, *Mumei shishu* (poems of an unknown poet), was privately printed in 1947. He received his medical degree in 1948, and his first piece of fiction, *Owarishi michi no shirube ni*, was published the same year in *Kosei*. In this story about a self-imposed exile in Manchuria he explored themes that would continue to provide him with material: human identity and the experience of being separated from one's homeland. "Kabe" (the wall) and "S. Karuma-shi no hanzai" (S. Karuma's crime) together garnered the 1951 Akutagawa Prize; these and other early works—"Dendorokakariya" (1949; dendrocacalia), "Akai mayu" (1950; "The Red Cocoon"), *Baberu no to no tanuki* (a badger in the tower of Babel), and *Mahō no chōku* (the magic chalk)—explored existential concerns and show evidence of his appreciation of the works of Fyodor Dostoevski, Franz Kafka, Martin Heidegger, and Karl Jaspers.

In his early writings, Abe developed a style rooted in realism yet tinged with surrealism and the irrational. His pieces in the period from 1950 to 1955 focused on nameless, often homeless ordinary humans in impersonal cities being transformed into other forms, a motif presaged in Franz Kafka's *Die Verwandlung* (1915; *The Metamorphosis*, 1936) and Eugène Ionesco's *Rhinocéros* (pr. 1959; *Rhinoceros*, 1959). Transformation (into cocoons, plant stalks, walls) could be either a positive force leading to a new way of life or a negative one destroying the psyche. Abe made his 1955 short story "A Stick," a commentary on dehumanization, into a play in 1957; it was later combined with two other short works into a three-act 1969 drama, *The Man Who Turned Into a Stick*. *Kemonotachi wa kokyō o mezasu* (the beasts go homeward) features an autobiographical plot concerning a seventeen-year-old boy abandoned in Manchuria after World War II and his search for his homeland and his identity.

A variation on the theme of identity and place is developed in *The Woman in the Dunes*. Here a male teacher, trapped at the bottom of a sand pit with a woman, struggles with a seemingly pointless existence, as they both strive to keep the hole from filling up with collapsing sand. The protagonist finally accepts the freedom the sand pit gives him, in contrast to his former life in the city; indeed, the sexual liberation he enjoys with the woman is a fulfillment he had not experienced on the outside. This novel won the 1962 Yōmiuri Literature Prize and was made into an award-winning 1964 film by Hiroshi Teshigahara.

Set in the future, *Inter Ice Age 4* deals with the the choices a computer scientist must face as a melting polar ice cap forces him to choose between helping to save the human race through the bizarre application of his scientific work and dealing with the personal consequences of the mutation that threatens his wife and unborn child. Another science-fiction theme is used to explore the concept of identity in *The Face of Another*. In this story, a scientist who has been disfigured in a laboratory explosion has a new face made for himself; using it as a mask, he seduces his own wife, only to lose her when she recognizes him. *The Ruined Map* uses a detective plot to posit that freedom is gained through the dissolution of the self. *The Box Man*, too, is set in the city; its protagonist lives in a cardboard box and has various reactions to the "others" on the outside.

To assure proper interpretation of his pieces, Abe began to direct his own productions at the Abe Studio, which he founded. Among Abe's plays, *Friends* is the most widely performed and appreciated, both in Japan and in the West. An absurdist piece, it depicts a family of eight who take over the apartment of "the Man." Ultimately they shut him in a cage and he dies, victimized by those who ostensibly were assuaging his loneliness. Many of Abe's writings reflect the postwar Japanese intellectual's interest in Marxism and alienation. A leading leftist thinker, he was for a time a member of the Japanese Communist Party but was expelled after writing an unflattering report of his 1956 visit to several Eastern European countries. His writings, however, go beyond the strictly political to wrestle with sociological and psychological issues: the modern sense of rootlessness and of lost identity.

Abe's intellectual debt to Western existentialists has been noted frequently, yet his originality in applying existentialist thought to Japanese culture must be acknowledged as well. Faced with absurdities both humorous and tragic, his characters are caught in dilemmas in which the real and the imagined become hopelessly blurred. Though these characters are often merely sketches and the plot lines are vague, illogical, and dreamlike, Abe's writings have been widely hailed as expressive of the crises faced by human beings in a technological, urbanized society.

BIBLIOGRAPHICAL REFERENCES: Short introductions to Abe's major translated works are available in Alfred H. Marks and Barry D. Bort, *Guide to Japanese Prose*, 1984; some of the published translations also have helpful introductions. "Abe Kōbō," in *Introduction to Contemporary Japanese Literature*, 1972, edited by Kokusai Bunka Shinkokai, gives a brief overview of his works, as does Armando Martins Janeira, *Japanese and Western Literature: A Comparative Study*, 1970. The early Abe and his works of the early 1950's are discussed by Fumiko Yamamoto in "Metamorphosis in Abe Kōbō's Works," *Journal of the Association of Teachers of Japanese*, XV (November, 1980), 170-194. Hisaaki Yamanouchi, "Abe Kōbō and Ōe Kenzaburo: The Search for Identity in Contemporary Japanese Literature," in *Modern Japan: Aspects of History, Literature, and Society*, 1975, edited by W. G. Beasley, is reworked in Yamanouchi's 1978 monograph, *The Search for Authenticity in Modern Japanese Literature*. J. Thomas Rimer has brief references in *Modern Japanese Fiction and Its Traditions: An Introduction*, 1986, and a short study of *The Woman in the Dunes* is included in his *A Reader's Guide to Japanese Literature from the Eighth Century to the Present*, 1988. *The Woman in the Dunes* is analyzed in detail in Arthur G. Kimball, "Identity Found," in *Crisis in Identity and Contemporary Japanese Novels*, 1972, and in William Currie, "Abe Kōbō's

Nightmare World of Sand," in *Approaches to the Modern Japanese Novel*, 1976, edited by Kinya Tsuruta and Thomas E. Swann. Abe's role in modern Japanese theater is discussed in *Modern Japanese Drama: An Anthology*, 1979, edited by Ted T. Takaya. Olof G. Lidin has an interpretive essay, "Abe Kōbō's Philosophy of the Box," in *Transcultural Understanding and Modern Japan*, 1983, edited by Klaus Kracht and Helmut Morsbach. Lidin has also written "Abe Kōbō's 'Mikkai': A Discussion," in *Man and Society in Japan Today*, 1984, edited by Mikolaj Melanowicz; that volume also contains Vlasta Winkelhöferová's essay "Main Themes and Types of Hero in Abe Kōbō's Prosaic Work."

William M. Zanella

PETER ABRAHAMS

Born: Vrededorp, South Africa
Date: March 19, 1919

PRINCIPAL WORKS

NOVELS: *Song of the City*, 1944; *Mine Boy*, 1946; *The Path of Thunder*, 1948; *Wild Conquest*, 1950; *A Wreath for Udomo*, 1956; *A Night of Their Own*, 1965; *This Island Now*, 1966.
SHORT FICTION: *Dark Testament*, 1942.
NONFICTION: *Return to Goli*, 1953; *Jamaica: An Island Mosaic*, 1957.
AUTOBIOGRAPHY: *Tell Freedom*, 1954.

Peter Abrahams is one of the most important South African authors. He was the first nonwhite South African to publish a novel in English since Solomon Plaatje, whose *Mhudi* was published in 1930. Moreover, since his literary career began with the short story collection *Dark Testament* in 1942, Abrahams has established himself as a prolific writer. Abrahams was born in Vrededorp, a mixed ghetto, on March 19, 1919; his father was Ethiopian, and his mother was black. When Abrahams was five, his father died, and he was sent to live with relatives in rural Elseburg. On returning to Johannesburg, he entered school at about age eleven. After a few years, however, his education was interrupted by the Depression, and he was forced to seek work. Working at the Bantu Men's Center, Abrahams was exposed to the works of Afro-American authors, principally W. E. B. Du Bois and such Harlem Renaissance writers as Langston Hughes, Countée Cullen, and Sterling Brown. He would later be influenced by Richard Wright as well.

After working at the Bantu Men's Center, Abrahams began attending St. Peter's Secondary School, one of the best South African schools for nonwhites. There, Abrahams had essential experiences which shaped his vision as a writer. While at St. Peter's, Abrahams had his first contacts with whites, influencing his ideas about the possibility of interracial harmony among certain individuals—a theme that runs through his works. Moreover, he was exposed to left-wing politics. Later, he began a brief flirtation with Marxism; his classic novel *Mine Boy* exhibits this interest in its focus on the possibility that workers could achieve a revolutionary interracial friendship.

After attending St. Peter's, Abrahams left South Africa. He began work as a stoker on a freighter around the time of the beginning of World War II. At the end of two years at sea, he arrived in England, where he lived for much of the next decade. Soon after settling in England, he published his first work, *Dark Testament*. During the 1940's, Abrahams established a reputation as a novelist—with the publication of *Song of the City*, *Mine Boy*, and *The Path of Thunder*—and also as a journalist. As part of his journalism career, for example, he returned to South Africa in 1952 to write about the issue of race relations for the *London Observer*.

After visiting Jamaica to write the history *Jamaica: An Island Mosaic*, published in 1957, Abrahams and his family went to live there in 1959. While his subsequent writings have focused on South Africa, as in *A Night of Their Own*, they have also focused on the West Indies, as in *This Island Now*. Thus, Abrahams has established himself as a truly international writer.

The major themes of Abrahams' works are intraracial and interracial conflict, the possibility for resolution of such conflict, and the chances for the transcendence of racism between blacks and whites. These issues span his literary career. *Mine Boy*, for example, which is considered Abrahams' first major novel, begins in a manner well-known to South Africans: An innocent young man from the country moves to the decadent city. The theme of *Mine Boy*, however, shows that interracial harmony can exist in the midst of a country corrupted by racism. Furthermore, the early *The Path of Thunder* and the later *A Night of*

Their Own not only dramatize the question of intraracial and interracial harmony but also ask whether interracial love could serve to help people reject the rigidly racist system of South Africa. Thus, Abrahams' works explore whether segregation and apartheid can be transcended by interracial relationships among people of goodwill.

Although Abrahams is concerned with racial transcendence, he also consistently writes about those who are corrupted by the racist system. This theme is evident in *The Path of Thunder*, as well as in Abrahams' nonfictional study of South Africa, *Return to Goli*, and in the autobiographical *Tell Freedom*. In considering Abrahams' career, therefore, it is evident that his works present an argument on whether people can transcend the racial discord of their society.

Many critics note Abrahams' idealism in writing of the possibility of resolution of racial discord. Some are critical of this quality, finding Abrahams' handling of the theme overly sentimental, pointing particularly to the books *Mine Boy* and *The Path of Thunder*. This criticism is answered by those who maintain that Abrahams is, in fact, emphasizing the difficulty of finding such a solution. *Mine Boy*, for example, argues that interracial harmony can only be established among a few men of goodwill. Furthermore, *The Path of Thunder* ends violently with the deaths of the black and white lovers and the triumph of racial hatred. There is a strong defense, then, against the charge that Abrahams is a sentimental idealist.

The charge is further refuted by those who note that Abrahams is greatly concerned with the possibility that racial hostility may remain fixed among the various racial groups in South Africa. He is not, therefore, merely a dreamer; in fact, his novels question whether interracial harmony is possible. Abrahams' major concerns are with exploring the negativity of race relations in society, considering whether this negativity can be overcome, and gauging the pressures against such a resolution in the context of a society corrupted by hatred and racism.

BIBLIOGRAPHICAL REFERENCES: Kolawole Ogungbesan, *The Writing of Peter Abrahams*, 1979, contains useful background information and sharp critical insights on Abrahams' works. Michael Wade, *Peter Abrahams*, 1972, includes criticisms of each of Abrahams' works up to and including *This Island Now*. A useful study guide on one of Abrahams' novels is Rodney Nesbitt, *Notes on Abrahams' "Mine Boy,"* 1975. See also "Peter Abrahams," in O. R. Dathorne, *African Literature in the Twentieth Century*, 1974; "The Novel," in Ursula A. Barnett, *A Vision of Order: A Study of Black South African Literature in English (1914-1980)*, 1983; Claude Wauthier et al., "Peter Abrahams," in *Modern Commonwealth Literature*, edited by John H. Ferres and Martin Tucker, 1977; Michael Wade, "South Africa's First Proletarian Writer," in *The South African Novel in English: Essays in Criticism and Society*, edited by Kenneth Parker, 1978; Bernth Lindfors, "Peter Abrahams," in *Contemporary Novelists*, edited by James Vinson, 1972; Christopher Heywood, "The Novels of Peter Abrahams," in *Perspectives in African Literature: Selections from the Proceedings of the Conference on African Literature Held at the University of Ife*, 1971; Kolawole Ogungbesan, "A Long Way From Vrededorp: The Reception of Peter Abrahams' Ideas," *Research in African Literatures*, XI (1980), 187-205; Kolawole Ogungbesan, "The Political Novels of Peter Abrahams," *Phylon*, XXXIV (1973), 419-432; Richard Rive, "Writing and the New Society," *Contrast*, XII, no. 3 (1979), 60-67; and Paul A. Scanlon, "Dream and Reality in Abrahams' *A Wreath for Udomo*," *Obsidian*, VI, nos. 1/2 (1980), 25-32.

Jane Davis

CHINUA ACHEBE

Born: Ogidi, Nigeria
Date: November 16, 1930

PRINCIPAL WORKS

NOVELS: *Things Fall Apart*, 1958; *No Longer at Ease*, 1960; *Arrow of God*, 1964; *A Man of the People*, 1966; *Anthills of the Savannah*, 1987.

SHORT FICTION: *The Sacrificial Egg and Other Stories*, 1962; *Girls at War*, 1972.

POETRY: *Beware, Soul Brother and Other Poems*, 1971; *Christmas in Biafra and Other Poems*, 1973.

ESSAYS: *Morning Yet on Creation Day*, 1975; *The Trouble With Nigeria*, 1983; *Hopes and Impediments*, 1987; *Nigerian Topics*, 1987.

CHILDREN'S LITERATURE: *Chike and the River*, 1966; *How the Leopard Got His Claws*, 1972 (with John Iroaganachi); *The Flute*, 1977; *The Drum*, 1977.

Chinua Achebe is one of the two or three best-known African writers. He was born in Ogidi, in eastern Nigeria, on November 16, 1930. His father, Isaiah, was a Christian church teacher, but other relatives retained the traditional beliefs of their Igbo tribe. Young Achebe was educated at the local mission school, then at Government College, in nearby Umuahia, and finally at the national University College at Ibadan, where he received his B.A. in 1953. Following his graduation, Achebe worked for the Nigerian Broadcasting Corporation for a period of twelve years, rising from Talks Producer in the capital of Lagos to Controller in Enugu to Director of External Broadcasting in Lagos again. During this period he also began to write novels, initially in an effort to correct the picture of Africa given by the English writer Joyce Cary in *Mister Johnson* (1939), which Achebe had read while studying literature in college.

Achebe published his first novel, *Things Fall Apart*, in 1958, two years before Nigerian independence. Set around the turn of the century, the book shows the arrival of the first English missionaries in an Igbo village named Umuofia. Countering the misconception that precolonial Africa was a void, Achebe gives a very complete description of Igbo culture. This description is sympathetic but still quite objective, revealing as it does the factors in the culture (such as cult slaves and the ritual killing of twins) which made some members susceptible to conversion to Christianity, thereby dividing the tribe and rendering it unable to resist the colonial takeover. The hero of the novel, Okonkwo, defends the traditional ways to the point of obsession because his personal status depends on them. Ironically, he goes so far as to violate some of the tribe's rules and thereby harm the very tribal integrity he is attempting to preserve. In the end, he hangs himself when he cannot convince his fellow tribesmen to attack the Europeans. The tragedy of Okonkwo has Greek dimensions, but in his case Fate is the force of European imperialism, which exposes and takes advantage of the weaknesses in his character and his tribe.

Things Fall Apart has been by far Achebe's most successful novel, being translated into more than thirty languages and selling more than three million copies. This success has unfairly led to some undervaluation of Achebe's later novels. In 1960 Achebe published *No Longer at Ease*, a sequel of sorts since its hero, Obi, is Okonkwo's grandson. The time setting is the period from 1955 to 1957, when Nigeria was moving toward self-rule. In *Arrow of God*, published in 1964, Achebe again returned to the past. Set in the 1920's, the book describes the downfall of Ezeulu, the Chief Priest of the god Ulu in the Igbo village of Umuaro, at a time when the British were creating "warrant chiefs" to implement their policy of indirect rule. Achebe's fourth novel, *A Man of the People*, published in 1966, portrays corruption in an unnamed postindependence African country, presumably Nigeria. The book ends with an army coup designed to oust the bribe-taking politicians.

A Man of the People proved prophetic, since it was published in the same month, January, when Major General Johnson Aguiyi-Ironsi, an Igbo, took control of the government and mounted an anticorruption drive. Six months later General Yakubu Gowon from the northern Hausa tribe succeeded in a countercoup, unleashing a wave of anti-Igbo violence. Achebe was forced to leave Lagos and return home. A three-year civil war ensued as eastern Nigeria attempted, and failed, to break away as the independent country of Biafra. During the war Achebe went on several missions to Europe and the United States as a fundraiser for the Biafran cause. He also became associated as a Senior Research Fellow with the University of Nigeria in Nsukka from 1967 to 1972. Following the war, he was a visiting professor in the United States for four years at the Universities of Massachusetts and Connecticut. In 1976 he returned as a professor of English to Nsukka, where he became a professor emeritus in 1985. Since 1986 he has been Pro-Chancellor of Anambra State University of Technology in Enugu, in eastern Nigeria.

During the war and in the years following, Achebe found himself unable to write novels, but he remained productive, publishing a book of short stories, a volume of poetry, several works for children, and two collections of essays. In 1987 he brought out his first novel in more than twenty years. *Anthills of the Savannah* tells the story of three friends in the fictional country of Kangan as they come into conflict against a background of political turmoil and corruption.

Achebe conceives of himself as a political writer. He believes that it is his duty to teach Europeans and Africans themselves about the richness and validity of traditional African culture. The novels in which he does so, *Things Fall Apart* and *Arrow of God*, have sometimes been unfairly criticized as more similar to anthropological treatises than literature. While they are written in a very direct, simple, and conventionally realistic style, they portray their characters with subtlety and complexity.

In order to reach a wider audience, even within his own country, Achebe has deliberately chosen to write in English, but he feels the English language can be shaped to express African reality. That reality is disturbing, and Achebe is unflinching in his depiction of the corruption and violence that trouble contemporary Africa. He blames African leaders for their failures, but he also sees the harmful influence of European countries which continue to manipulate the economies of their former colonies. While bleak, Achebe's outlook is not hopeless. He finds worth in ordinary Africans, in their culture, and in the ability of people to remember and imagine.

Achebe's influence on younger African writers has been enormous. He has been very active as an editor and publisher. Perhaps more important has been his example as a writer. He has established models of certain fictional situations, such as the initial colonial encounter, which have been much imitated. He has set standards of literary quality for others to emulate. Finally, he has shown great personal dedication and perseverance as a writer through turbulent times.

BIBLIOGRAPHICAL REFERENCES: The best critical essays on Achebe have been collected in *Critical Perspectives on Chinua Achebe*, 1978, edited by C. L. Innes and Bernth Lindfors. Overviews of the Achebe works include G. D. Killam, *The Novels of Chinua Achebe*, 1969, revised as *The Writings of Chinua Achebe*, 1977; Arthur Ravenscroft, *Chinua Achebe*, 1969, revised 1977; David Carroll, *Chinua Achebe*, 1970, revised 1980; and Benedict C. Njoku, *The Four Novels of Chinua Achebe: A Critical Study*, 1984. Books which analyze specific works include Kate Turkington, *Chinua Achebe: "Things Fall Apart,"* 1977; A. M. Kemoli, *Notes on Chinua Achebe's "Things Fall Apart,"* 1975; and Peter Mills, *Notes on Chinua Achebe's "No Longer at Ease,"* 1974. An excellent background study is Robert M. Wren, *Achebe's World: The Historical and Cultural Context of Chinua Achebe's Novels*, 1980. General studies of African literature which have substantial sections on Achebe and place him in relation to his fellow writers include the outdated but still useful Gerald Moore, *Seven African Writers*,

1962; Charles R. Larson, *The Emergence of African Fiction*, 1972; James Olney, *Tell Me Africa*, 1973; Emanuel Obeichina, *Culture, Tradition, and Society in the West African Novel*, 1975; and Claude Wauthier, *The Literature and Thought of Modern Africa*, 1979.

Hunt Hawkins

ARTHUR ADAMOV

Born: Kislovodsk, Russia
Date: August 23, 1908

Died: Paris, France
Date: March 16, 1970

PRINCIPAL WORKS

PLAYS: *La Parodie*, pb. 1950; *L'Invasion*, pr., pb. 1950; *La Grande et la Petite Manœuvre*, pr. 1950; *Le Professeur Taranne*, pr., pb. 1953 (*Professor Taranne*, 1960); *Le Sens de la marche*, pr., pb. 1953; *Tous contre tous*, pr., pb. 1953; *Le Ping-Pong*, pr., pb. 1955 (*Ping-Pong*, 1959); *Paolo Paoli*, pr., pb. 1957 (*Paolo Paoli: The Year of the Butterfly*, 1959); *Le Printemps '71*, pb. 1960; *La Politique des restes*, pb. 1966; *M. le modéré*, pb. 1968; *Off Limits*, pb. 1968.
AUTOBIOGRAPHY: *L'Aveu*, 1946.

Together with his contemporaries Samuel Beckett and Eugène Ionesco, Arthur Adamov first drew attention as a practitioner of the nontraditional, antirationalist trend in French drama that Martin Esslin would soon label "the Theater of the Absurd." Like Beckett, an Irishman, and Ionesco, half Romanian, the Russian-born Adamov did not even begin writing plays until around the age of forty, and then in French, an acquired idiom. Before long, however, Adamov would renounce his apparent affinities with Ionesco and Beckett, opting instead for didactic, political theater in the manner of Bertolt Brecht, even going so far as to repudiate the early plays that had made his reputation and upon which much of it still rests. In general, though, Adamov's political, or "epic," plays proved rather less successful than his earlier, "absurdist" ones. In the mid-1960's, Adamov appeared to be attempting a fusion of his two characteristic styles toward the creation of a third. Long in failing health, Arthur Adamov died early in 1970 of a drug overdose, leaving more questions than answers concerning his rightful place in literary or dramatic history.

Born in Kislovodsk in 1908 to the wife of a prosperous oil-well owner, Adamov spent his earliest childhood in the city of Baku, then the capital of the Russian petroleum industry. Despite his privileged circumstances, young Arthur always feared poverty, perhaps anticipating his eventual life on the fringes of Parisian art and culture. The outbreak of World War I in 1914 found the Adamov family on vacation in Germany, from which they managed to escape to Switzerland only with royal intervention. The Russian Revolution caused further disruption in Adamov's family life. The family would move to Mainz, Germany, and then to the outskirts of Paris.

Published as a poet before he turned seventeen, Adamov made many acquaintances among the Surrealists and also cultivated the friendship of Antonin Artaud (1896-1948), later to be recognized among the major theorists of avant-garde theater. Like Adamov, Artaud was a deeply troubled individual prone to mental illness; he was also a visionary, whose radical approaches to dramatic concept and production would appear, years later, in some of Adamov's more memorable plays. Unfortunately Artaud, for all of his demonstrable brilliance as a theorist, was all but incapable of writing plays. Adamov, meanwhile, remained on the fringes of Parisian culture, living off the income of occasional translations and adaptations while he worked on his poetry and on the hallucinative memoir which became *L'Aveu* (confession). In 1941, less than a year after the Nazi occupation of Paris, Adamov was arrested for "comments hostile to the Vichy government" and imprisoned in a concentration camp; his internment, joined to his earlier experience as a "stateless person," seems to have heightened Adamov's political consciousness, until then overshadowed by his own psychological problems.

In 1947, coincidentally the year that he met his future wife Jacqueline Trehet, Adamov turned his attention to the writing of plays, initially as a form of catharsis. *La Parodie* (the parody) was the first to be written, soon followed by *L'Invasion* (the invasion) and *La Grande et la Petite Manœuvre* (the great and small maneuver). Advised by the director Jean Vilar,

Adamov took the unusual step of publishing his first two plays as a book before they were ever performed, in hopes that performance would soon follow; he was not to be disappointed. By the end of that year, 1950, his first and third plays had been performed, with the second soon to follow. His early productions coinciding roughly with those of Ionesco, preceding those of Beckett by at least two years, Adamov found himself at the forefront of a new, vigorous, and newsworthy current in French and world drama, notable for its antirationalism and apparent anarchy. Like Ionesco, Adamov in his early plays evoked both the uselessness of language and the ultimate isolation of the individual. *L'Invasion*, the first of his plays to reach a truly wide audience, describes the woes and eventual death of a man dedicated to saving the writings of his deceased brother-in-law. *Professor Taranne*, perhaps the best known of Adamov's plays, presents the unforgettable spectacle of an apparently distinguished man systematically and symbolically stripped of his identity by the perceptions of society. *Ping-Pong*, in fact a transitional work, portrays the dehumanization and eventual destruction of two men by their fascination with pinball machines.

With *Ping-Pong*, Adamov first crossed the boundary from the personal to the political; while the characters' obsession with inventing the perfect pinball machine harks back to Adamov's earliest efforts, their exploitation by the consortium prepares the way for a full-blown critique of the capitalist system, first expressed in *Paolo Paoli*, set at the turn of the twentieth century; not yet free of his absurdist mode, Adamov here chooses as the business of his capitalist characters a vigorous trade in butterflies and ostrich feathers, essential to women's fashions of the time. Although promising, *Paolo Paoli* proved a bit too long, and long-winded, for most audiences; in such subsequent efforts as *La Politique des restes* (the politics of waste), set in South Africa, and *Off Limits*, set in the United States at the time of the Vietnam conflict, featuring drugged hippies and drunken entrepreneurs, Adamov appeared to have lost not only his perspective but also the irony that had assured the success of such otherwise harrowing plays as *Ping-Pong* and *Professor Taranne*.

Even as he attempted, during the 1960's, to continue the Brechtian tradition of committed, objective theater, Adamov was earning belated recognition in English-speaking countries and elsewhere as a master of absurdist drama, a convention that he had long since renounced. Drinking heavily, dissatisfied with the fortunes of his later efforts, Adamov nevertheless continued to work at a variety of writing projects until he apparently took his own life (as had his father and Artaud before him). Never quite able to equal the power of Brecht in his didactic efforts, he is most likely to be remembered for *Ping-Pong* and *Professor Taranne*.

BIBLIOGRAPHICAL REFERENCES: Martin Esslin, *The Theatre of the Absurd*, 1961, revised 1969, is nearly definitive in his treatment of Adamov's early plays. John H. Reilly, *Arthur Adamov*, 1974, is the first full-length study of Adamov in English, treating all of his plays (and styles) in detail. It also discusses *L'Aveu* and Adamov's other occasional writings. Leonard C. Pronko, *Avant-Garde: The Experimental Theatre in France*, 1962, deals intelligently with Adamov's early plays and some of their possible sources. George E. Wellwarth, *The Theater of Protest and Paradox*, 1964, presents an appreciative survey of Adamov's strengths and weaknesses as a playwright, treating both his absurdist and his polemical periods. See also Margaret Dietemann, "Departure from the Absurd: Adamov's Last Plays," *Yale French Studies*, XLVI (1971), 48-59, and Richard E. Sherrell, "Arthur Adamov and Invaded Man," *Modern Drama*, VII (1965), 399-404.

David B. Parsell

ALICE ADAMS

Born: Fredericksburg, Virginia
Date: August 14, 1926

PRINCIPAL WORKS

NOVELS: *Careless Love*, 1966; *Families and Survivors*, 1974; *Listening to Billie*, 1978; *Rich Rewards*, 1980; *Superior Women*, 1984; *Second Chances*, 1988.

SHORT FICTION: *Beautiful Girl*, 1979; *To See You Again*, 1982; *Return Trips*, 1985.

Alice Boyd Adams was born in Virginia and reared on a farm south of Chapel Hill, North Carolina, where her father, Nicholson Barney Adams, taught Spanish at the university. She was graduated from Radcliffe College with a B.A. in 1945, and she wed Mark Linenthal, Jr., in 1947. After the couple spent time in Paris, where Linenthal studied at the Sorbonne, they settled in California. Linenthal taught English at San Francisco State University and completed doctoral work at Stanford University.

Careless Love was not published until Adams was forty years old, but its self-actualized, adventuresome heroine, Daisy Duke Fabbri, quickly found an eager audience of liberated women. Divorced and eager to experience life, Daisy moves from a weak husband to a lover and a Latin lothario to satisfy her sexuality. The plot offers little more than typical soap opera fare, but the characterization and atmosphere impressed readers.

In *Families and Survivors*, Adams chronicles the post-World War II lives of Louisa Calloway and Kate Flichinger, from their friendship as teenagers to the vicissitudes of marriage and divorce. Through Louisa's hippie daughter, the story comes full circle, for she is as different from Louisa as Louisa was from her own mother. Curiously moving in its romantic interludes, precise detail, and striking character assessments, this novel exhibits the author's unusual stylistic use of parenthetical phrases to suggest future happenings. Her ability to describe the settings—Virginia, New York, California—and to capture the native idiom is exceptional.

In *Listening to Billie*, Adams examines intense psychosexual situations. Evan Quarles, a professor and the husband of the heroine, Eliza, falls in love with "the most beautiful boy in the world," a student in his Cicero class. Unable to cope, Evan becomes a suicide, like Eliza's father. Through several affairs, including an interracial one, Eliza learns to relate to varying social levels. Then both her stepsister Daria and she fall for that same "most beautiful boy in the world," Reed Ashford. Eliza begins to understand her late husband's obsession; later, through association with several feminist women who live together, she recognizes the vulnerability of people when beauty enters into otherwise predictable and dreary lives. The title of Adams' novel refers to Billie Holiday, whose blues music resonates with Eliza's own pain and grief.

By the 1970's, Adams' short stories had found an audience in magazines such as *The New Yorker*, *Redbook*, *Mademoiselle*, and *Cosmopolitan*. Her first collection, *Beautiful Girl*, contains sixteen stories and brought further attention to her as a feminist chronicler of the times. In it, Adams centers on beautiful, intelligent, pained women who examine their pasts and arrive at important conclusions. This collection offers wide-ranging dialogue, with allusions to a score of subjects from Bob Dylan to Delmore Schwartz and Ezra Pound. When Adams recalls her Southern origins, as in the poignant "Verlie I Say unto You," she is at her best.

Daphne Matthiessen is the protagonist and narrator of Adams' fourth novel, *Rich Rewards*. An interior decorator "of sorts," middle-aged, and divorced years ago, Daphne comes to San Francisco to aid her friend Agatha with the renovation of an old house. An Easterner, Daphne views San Francisco's beauty through unjaundiced eyes. Free sexually, Daphne enjoys men. Years later, Daphne and Jean-Paul, a European and a Socialist, are destined to meet again and enjoy "rich rewards" as experienced and worldly-wise lovers.

To See You Again appeared in 1982, and by then Adams' art ranked with that of Joyce Carol Oates and John Updike. All three short-story writers received the O. Henry Award. The nineteen stories in this collection are about the remembrance of things past. "Snow" recalls a skiing weekend in the High Sierras when the narrator, handsome San Francisco architect Graham, and his girlfriend, Carol, meet the tall lesbian lover of his obese daughter Susanah. What appears to Graham to be a threatening weekend becomes, instead, a time of warm friendship and mutual understanding. Continually provocative, Adams urges readers to consider unusual situations by framing them in an acceptable manner.

Perhaps Adams' best-known work, *Superior Women* follows four decades of the lives of five young women who meet at Radcliffe in 1943. The leader of the group is Megan Greene, a straight-A student with "smoldering sexual energy." Other freshmen who surround her are Lavinia, the "ice queen" debutante; Peg, the political activist; Cathy, the masochist, torn between "self denial" and "hunger for life"; and Janet, pretty, feisty, and Jewish. Cataloging the women's jobs and their affairs, the novel is formulaic and bulky. It achieves its aim by asking an age-old question: Are men put off by intelligent, accomplished women? (Adams answers in the affirmative.) *Superior Women* suffers, too, from Adams' frequent problem with tone: Which scenes are satire, and which parallel reality?

The fifteen stories that make up *Return Trips* suggest women on the move. More self-aware with each decade, often married many times, and now alone, these women are driven to discover themselves. Several stories deal with the ending of significant relationships. Most affecting, "Molly's Dog" recounts how Molly and her gay friend Sandy experience a weekend in Carmel, California, argue over a stray dog, and face the disintegration of their long-term friendship.

Second Chances, like *Superior Women*, deals with a group of characters; this time men and women past middle age who live in the hope of changing themselves and their lives. Adams continues to explore extraordinary characters in realistic yet uncommon situations, and in doing so, suggests particularly well the multiple dimensions of independent women.

BIBLIOGRAPHICAL REFERENCES: The majority of critical material on Adams' work is in the form of reviews and interviews. See Patricia Holt, "PW Interviews: Alice Adams," *Publishers Weekly*, CCXIII (January 16, 1978), 8-9; Dean Flower, "Fiction Chronicle," *The Hudson Review*, XXXII (Summer, 1979), 295-296; Daphne Merkin, "Tale of a Woman Writer," *The New Leader*, LXI (March 27, 1978), 21-23; Lois Gould, "Life After Radcliffe," *The New York Times Book Review*, LXXXIX (September 23, 1984), 9; Robert Phillips, "Missed Opportunities, Endless Possibilities," *Commonweal*, CX (March 25, 1983), 188-190. See also Cara Chell, "Succeeding in Their Times: Alice Adams on Women and Work," *Soundings*, LXVIII (Spring, 1985), 62-71.

Clifton L. Warren

RICHARD ADAMS

Born: Newbury, England
Date: May 9, 1920

PRINCIPAL WORKS

NOVELS: *Watership Down*, 1972; *Shardik*, 1974; *The Plague Dogs*, 1977; *The Girl in a Swing*, 1980; *Maia*, 1984; *Traveller*, 1988.

SHORT FICTION: *Sinister and Supernatural Stories*, 1978; *The Iron Wolf and Other Stories*, 1980 (also known as *The Unbroken Web*).

CHILDREN'S LITERATURE: *The Tyger Voyage*, 1976; *The Adventures of and Brave Deeds of the Ship's Cat on the Spanish Maine: Together with the Most Lamentable Losse of the Alcestis and Triumphant Firing of the Port of Chagres*, 1977; *Our Amazing Sun*, 1983; *Our Wonderful Solar System*, 1983; *The Bureaucats*, 1985; *Legend of Te Tune*, 1986.

NONFICTION: *Nature Through the Seasons*, 1975 (with Max Hooper); *Nature Day and Night*, 1978 (with Hooper); *Voyage Through the Antarctic*, 1982 (with Ronald M. Lackley); *A Nature Diary*, 1986.

Richard Adams emerged suddenly and memorably as a writer of imaginative fiction and children's books in the early 1970's. He was born in Newbury, England, on May 9, 1920, the son of Evelyn George Beadon Adams, a surgeon, and his wife, Lilian Rosa (Button) Adams. The youngest of three children, Adams spent his time reading and roaming the family's spacious gardens or the nearby rolling hills of Berkshire. He filled his solitary hours with fanciful games about ruling an imaginary country. After attending boarding and preparatory schools in Berkshire, Adams entered the University of Oxford.

His education was interrupted by service with the British Airborne Forces during World War II. In 1946 he returned to Oxford and took his master's degree in modern history at Worcester College two years later. In 1949 he married Barbara Elizabeth Acland; they had two daughters, Juliet and Rosamond, in 1957 and 1958. Immediately after leaving Oxford, Adams went into public service. He was employed by the Ministry of Housing and Local Government for twenty years in a variety of posts. When Housing and Local Government was incorporated into the Ministry of the Environment, Adams was appointed assistant secretary. For twenty-five years, he lived and worked in London. He read voraciously in the classic works of English and Continental literature but had no literary ambitions.

Adams' daughters Juliet and Rosamond precipitated his literary career. Seeking to amuse them on long drives, Adams invented a story about a warren of Berkshire rabbits forced to flee by a housing development. Dodging automobiles and trains, fighting other rabbits, a small band succeeds in establishing a new home. Juliet and Rosamond suggested additional characters and adventures until the length and complexity demanded that Adams preserve the story in manuscript. He sent the book, now embellished with chapter titles and epilogues, to several publishers and agents, but all refused to consider it. Hearing that a small publisher, Rex Collings, was reprinting novels about animals, Adams submitted his tale, *Watership Down*, which was accepted for a small printing of two thousand copies. A brisk sale attracted a major publisher, and *Watership Down* soon became a best-seller in both England and the United States, with sales of 700,000. Adams' novel followed the path of Robert Louis Stevenson's *Treasure Island* (1883), Lewis Carroll's *Alice in Wonderland* (1865), and A. A. Milne's *Winnie-the-Pooh* (1926): First told to amuse real children, these stories made their way into print and became classics.

Watership Down's success enabled Adams to retire from government service and devote himself to writing. Within five years he published two more books with central animal figures: *Shardik*, about a huge bear, and *The Plague Dogs*, about two canines. *Shardik* is a tale of cruelty and destruction in the imaginary kingdom of Bekla. Its protagonist is fearsome, perhaps demoniac, possibly divine. *The Plague Dogs*, an attack on vivisection, tells how Rowf and Snitter flee an experimental laboratory. Their link to *Watership Down* is Adams' concern for environmental issues and humankind's "uneasy détente" (as Adams calls it) with animals. A decade passed before Adams returned to the genre with *Traveller*, whose narrator is the horse of Robert E. Lee. The commander's steed recounts the Civil War's heroism and horrors as seen through equine eyes.

Adams resists classifying his animal fictions as children's literature. He is the first major writer since Rudyard Kipling to create convincing animal protagonists by attributing human emotions and ideals to them but not giving them greater physical abilities than real animals.

Adams' other prolific publications since 1976 fall into three groups. His children's books, most notably *The Tyger Voyage* and *The Bureaucats*, are tales of fantasy and imagination with animals as central characters. They combine the Aesopian trick of using animal characters to discuss human virtues and vices with a scientific realism that resists sentimentality.

Adams' nonfiction works also display his love of nature and his environmental concerns. Firmly believing that respect for nature depends on accurate knowledge, Adams lures readers of *Nature Through the Seasons* and *A Nature Diary* to seek pleasure in the observation of even the commonest plants, landscapes, and creatures. Adams follows in the tradition of British nature writers such as Gilbert White, who portray the pleasures of rural retirement and reflection.

Adams' two novels written with an adult audience in mind, *The Girl in a Swing* and *Maia*, are erotic stories with strikingly different narrative approaches. *The Girl in a Swing*, gothic in mood and narrative, tells of the passionate courtship and marriage of antiques dealer Alan Desland and a mysterious German girl, Kathë. Their love is haunted and destroyed by a murdered child from Kathë's past. *Maia* returns to the imaginary land first described in *Shardik* to trace the life of a teenage girl. Her descent into the hedonistic life of a courtesan exposes the moral decay undermining an elegant, wealthy civilization.

Watership Down remains the most widely discussed and debated of Adams' works. Marketed as a children's book in England and as an adult novel in the United States, *Watership Down* divides readers, reviewers, and critics. Is it simply an exercise in imagination, a delightful attempt to bridge the gap between human intelligence and animal intelligence? Has it some deeper meaning beneath the deceptively familiar tale of the rabbits' search for a new home? Is it a homily on the struggle between good and evil that goes on literally beneath people's feet? Is it an allegory of the political struggles between ideologies that have ravaged the earth in the twentieth century? Adams' protestations that he intended nothing more than a gripping narrative have not effectively stilled the curiosity of readers inevitably stirred beyond their expectations.

BIBLIOGRAPHICAL REFERENCES: Anyone curious about Adams' life and thought must piece together the few articles that have appeared. *Current Biography Yearbook*, 1978, and *Contemporary Authors, New Revision Series*, Vol. 3, 1981, edited by Ann Evory, provide biographical data and a bibliography of interviews. One of the portraits of Adams is by Timothy Green, "Richard Adams' Long Journey from *Watership Down*," *Smithsonian*, X (July, 1979), 76-82. Adams' own revealing account of his art appears in "Some Ingredients of *Watership Down*," in *The Thorny Paradise: Writers on Writing for Children*, 1975, edited by Edward Blishen. See also Rita Mae Brown's review of *Traveller* in *The New York Times Book Review*, XCIII (June 5, 1988), 13, and the interview by J. F. Baker in *Publishers Weekly*, CCV (April 15, 1974), 6-8.

Robert M. Otten

RENATA ADLER

Born: Milan, Italy
Date: October 19, 1938

PRINCIPAL WORKS

NOVELS: *Speedboat*, 1976; *Pitch Dark*, 1983.

NONFICTION: *Toward a Radical Middle: Fourteen Pieces of Reporting and Criticism*, 1969; *A Year in the Dark: Journal of a Film Critic, 1968-69*, 1969; *Reckless Disregard: Westmoreland v. CBS et al., Sharon v. Time*, 1986; *Politics and Media: Essays*, 1988.

That Renata Adler has been acclaimed both as a journalist and as a novelist would be less surprising were her novels at all realistic in technique. Yet while her novels are not journalistic per se, they are decidedly contemporary. Indeed, it is for her creation of a distinctly contemporary voice that Adler deserves the high praise she has received. Adler was born in Milan, Italy, on October 19, 1938, and was educated at Bryn Mawr College, the Sorbonne, and Harvard University. She later earned a law degree from Yale University as part of her research for her fifth book, *Reckless Disregard*, a work in which Adler's own high standards led her to criticize the Columbia Broadcasting System (CBS) and *Time* magazine for their "reckless disregard" of the truth in their reporting of General William Westmoreland's alleged misconduct during the Vietnam War and Israeli defense minister Ariel Sharon's part in the massacre of Palestinian civilians by Lebanese soldiers in 1983. As one who came of age during the Eisenhower years, Adler sees herself as part of a largely forgotten, seemingly speechless generation, inconspicuous to the point of anonymity. The voice which Adler has developed in her novels (and to a lesser extent her nonfiction) to capture this sense of anonymity is, paradoxically, remarkably distinctive; yet it is similar in certain ways to the minimalism of her contemporaries Leonard Michaels and Joan Didion. Having begun her career as a journalist (much of her work has appeared in *The New Yorker*), Adler served as film critic for *The New York Times* in the late 1960's, and this latter experience helps to account for the cinematic quality of her work.

The cinematically disjunctive style and structure of her novels are designed to reflect an equally disjunctive world, or, rather, an equally disjunctive perception of the world. Her novelistic prose is brittle, and the narrative voice as self-consciously detached and inflectionless as it is anonymous. The landscape, or "mindscape," is lunar—bleak and colorless—and the characters indistinct, rendered merely as roles or names; they appear as little more than black-and-white snapshots glimpsed while absentmindedly thumbing through someone else's photograph album. Scenes are juxtaposed rather than linearly and logically assembled; the reader discovers that the onward march of Adler's relentlessly paratactic sentences leads not to resolution but instead to reversals, returns, and refrains. The effect, however, is not exactly one of despair. In fact, Adler has been a harsh critic of the apocalyptic stridency and unearned nihilism which she believes characterizes so much contemporary fiction, art, and music.

Skeptical of the "seismological" approach adopted by a number of postwar novelists, Adler prefers what she terms the "polygraph" method, which entails the author's focusing on a particular psychological point of view. *Speedboat*, Adler's first novel, is precisely such a work: a polygraph of a life of quiet desperation for which Henry David Thoreau's *Walden* (1854) is no longer a possibility. As the title suggests, this novel deals with motion—flying, driving, boating—but this is motion without any apparent aim and without any evident destination. The problem which the narrator, Jen Fain, faces is one which the novel's reader must face as well: how to transform the fragmentary scenes, situations, and moments into the wholeness of story. The discontinuity of Jen's style of narration does not so much obscure her story as bring her predicament into even clearer focus. Jen remains elusive. In some ways she resembles Adler, but in most respects she remains a mystery, a welding together of opposites. (Thus her name, ambiguous, suggests both preference and falsification.) The one constant that does emerge from her disconcerting narration is her refusal to heed the voice, perhaps her own, which tells her to "forget it . . . throw it away."

The same is true of the narrator-heroine of *Pitch Dark*. Heeding Emily Dickinson's dictum "Tell all the truth/ But tell it slant," Kate tries to make sense of the end of a love affair. More clearly than in *Speedboat*, structure here gives way to voice, sequential plot to imagistic pattern, as the psychological problem of how to live without love becomes the narrative problem of how to tell the story of such a loss. Adler combines sentimental love story with existential angst and postmodern technique. In her art, despair is compounded by blackly humorous self-consciousness and yet offset, at least in part, by the Beckett-like persistence of the main character. Whether dealing with society, politics, and culture (as in *Toward a Radical Middle*), film (*A Year in the Dark*), the media and the courts (*Reckless Disregard*), or the efforts of her two main characters to narrate and thereby make sense of their lives, Adler has shown little concern for what others may consider fashionable. She has earned much praise and caused much confusion. Unable to place her or her work with precision, critics have largely given her more tacit respect than attention.

BIBLIOGRAPHICAL REFERENCES: Adler has gained critical attention primarily in the form of reviews, of which the most extensive if not the most laudatory is Joseph Epstein's discussion of Adler and Joan Didion in "The Sunshine Girls," *Commentary*, LXXVII (June, 1984), 62-67. Other significant reviews include Jacob Brackman, *Esquire*, LXXXIII (March, 1970), 26; Wilfrid Sheed, *The New York Times Book Review*, LXXV (march 19, 1970), 12; Richard Corliss, *National Review*, XXII (April 7, 1970), 369-370; Robert Towers, *The New York Times Book Review*, LXXXI (September 26, 1976), 6-7; Richard Todd, *The Atlantic Monthly*, CCXXXVIII (October 1976), 112-114; Blanche M. Boyd, *The Nation*, CCXXIII (November 6, 1976), 469-470; Peter S. Prescott, *Newsweek*, CII (December 19, 1983), 82; and Roger Shattuck, *The New York Review of Books*, XXXI (March 15, 1984), 3.

Robert A. Morace

JAMES AGEE

Born: Knoxville, Tennessee
Date: November 27, 1909

Died: New York, New York
Date: May 16, 1955

PRINCIPAL WORKS

NOVEL: *A Death in the Family*, 1957.

NOVELLA: *The Morning Watch*, 1951.

POETRY: *Permit Me Voyage*, 1934; *The Collected Poems of James Agee*, 1968.

ESSAYS: *Let Us Now Praise Famous Men*, 1941 (with Walker Evans); *Agee on Film: Reviews and Comments*, 1958.

SCREENPLAYS: *The Red Badge of Courage*, 1951; *The African Queen*, 1952; *The Bride Comes to Yellow Sky*, 1952; *Noa Noa*, 1953; *White Mane*, 1953; *Green Magic*, 1955; *The Night of the Hunter*, 1955; *Agee on Film: Five Film Scripts*, 1960.

SHORT FICTION: *The Collected Short Prose of James Agee*, 1968.

CORRESPONDENCE: *Letters of James Agee to Father Flye*, 1962.

James Rufus Agee was less successful as an inventor of fiction than he was as a recorder of experiences. The event that marked a turning point in his early life was the death of his father, Hugh James Agee, in an automobile accident when Rufus, as his family called him, was six. The victim's widow, Laura Tyler Agee, a self-righteous woman who came from a refined Knoxville family, undoubtedly repeated the details of the accident so often that her son and daughter, Emma, knew the story by heart. The young Agee enshrined the gruesome details in his memory, and they eventually became the basis for his celebrated novel, *A Death in the Family*.

Three years after her husband's death, Laura Agee, a devout Episcopalian, spent part of her summer on the grounds of St. Andrew's School in Sewanee, Tennessee, and in 1919, she took up permanent residence there. James Agee attended the school and came to know Father James Harold Flye and his wife. Flye, who spent the summer of 1925 bicycling through Europe with Agee, remained his friend throughout the author's life. Much of the voluminous Flye-Agee correspondence has been published.

After five years at St. Andrew's, Agee and his mother returned to Knoxville. James attended Knoxville High School for a year before entering Phillips Exeter Academy in Exeter, New Hampshire, where he edited the *Phillips Exeter Monthly* and blossomed as a writer. After graduation in 1928, he entered Harvard University.

When Agee finished Harvard, the Great Depression was at its worst. Jobs were scarce, but Henry Luce, faithful to his alma mater, employed as many promising young Harvard graduates as possible in his publishing empire. Agee—tall, lanky, with unruly dark hair and dancing blue eyes—joined *Fortune* as a reporter. He was married to Olivia Saunders in 1933. Yale University Press published his first book, *Permit Me Voyage*, a collection of poems, as part of its Younger Poet Series. In 1935, Agee took a leave of absence from *Fortune* to pursue his writing.

Agee and his wife then moved to Anna Maria, Florida. A month after Agee returned to *Fortune* in 1936, he was asked to do a story with Walker Evans about tenant farmers in the South. The two gathered information and took photographs in Alabama. Although *Fortune* did not publish the Agee-Evans material, these sketches and photographs provided the basis for Agee's next book, *Let Us Now Praise Famous Men*, a collaboration with Evans.

The book, later recognized as perceptive and well written, was virtually unnoticed at the time of its publication because of the nation's preoccupation with World War II. It failed to bring Agee the initial recognition he deserved. Immediately before the publication of his next book, Agee, now divorced and remarried to Alma Mailman, worked for *Time* as a staff writer.

In 1942, Agee, starstruck since childhood, began to write a film column for *The Nation*. Producing a daunting number of film reviews for both *Time* and *The Nation* between 1942 and 1948, he became thoroughly immersed in the medium, mastering quickly the techniques of film writing. Among Agee's film credits are the screenplays *The African Queen*, *The Bride Comes to Yellow Sky*, *Noa Noa*, and *The Night of the Hunter*.

Film writing helped to solve some of Agee's financial problems. He continued to write autobiographical fiction also. In 1951, *The Morning Watch*, his sensitive novella about a twelve-year-old boy's religious experience in the chapel of a boy's school much like St. Andrew's, was published. Agee began to have heart problems, and on May 16, 1955, riding in a taxicab to his doctor's office in Manhattan, he suffered a fatal heart attack.

At the time of his death, Agee had nearly completed *A Death in the Family*, which was published unfinished in 1957 and earned for him a Pulitzer Prize in 1958. The book, relating a young boy's perception of his father's death in an automobile accident, is the one for which Agee is best remembered. In it, as in *The Morning Watch*, Agee demonstrates his unique ability to penetrate the consciousness of youth and write a sustained account of a crucial experience through which a child has lived.

BIBLIOGRAPHICAL REFERENCES: The preeminent study of James Agee is Laurence Bergreen, *James Agee: A Life*, 1984, which is remarkably well researched and which presents intelligent interpretations of Agee's disparate work. It supersedes both Kenneth Seib, *James Agee: Promise and Fulfillment*, 1968, which is still excellent for its comprehensive bibliography, and Victor Kramer, *James Agee*, 1975. Kramer's "Agee in the Forties: Unpublished Poetry and Fiction by James Agee," *The Texas Quarterly*, XI (1968), 9-55, presents a comprehensive overview of Agee's unpublished work housed in the Humanities Research Center of the University of Texas. David Madden edited *Remembering James Agee*, 1974, which contains somewhat dated but important critical articles by a broad range of scholars. An interesting psychoanalytical study of Agee's work is Mark A. Doty, *Tell Me Who I Am: James Agee's Search for Selfhood*, 1981. Joel Agee, Agee's son by his second wife, provides intriguing insights into the son's relationship with his father—more revealing for what it does not say than for what it does say—in *Twelve Years: An American Boyhood in East Germany*, 1981. Another perceptive family assessment is that of Joel's mother, Alma Neuman, "Thoughts of Jim: A Memoir of Frenchtown and James Agee," *Shenandoah*, XXXIII (1981-1982), 25-36.

R. Baird Shuman

SHMUEL YOSEF AGNON

Born: Buczacz, Galicia
Date: July 17, 1888

Died: Jerusalem, Israel
Date: February 17, 1970

Principal Works

NOVELS AND NOVELLAS: *Hakhnasat kala*, 1931 (*The Bridal Canopy*, 1937); *Bilevav yamim*, 1935 (*In the Heart of the Seas*, 1947); *Sipur pashut*, 1935; *Ore'ah nata lalun*, 1939 (*A Guest for the Night*, 1968); *Shevu'at emunim*, 1943 (*Betrothed*, in *Two Tales*, 1966); *Temol shilshom*, 1945; *Edo ve'Enam*, 1950 (*Edo and Enam*, in *Two Tales*, 1966); *Shira*, 1971; *Bahanuto shel Mar Lublin*, 1974.

SHORT FICTION: *Sefer hama'asim*, 1931; *Beshuva venahat*, 1935; *Elu ve'elu*, 1941; *Samukh venir'e*, 1951; *A Whole Loaf*, 1957; *Twenty-one Stories*, 1970; *Ir umelo'a*, 1973.

RELIGION: *Yamim nora'im*, 1937 (*Days of Awe*, 1948); *Sefer, sofer, vesipur*, 1937; *Atem re'item*, 1959.

CORRESPONDENCE: *Esterlain yekirati: Mikhtavin 684-691 (1924-1931)*, 1983.

Shmuel Yosef Agnon, corecipient of the 1966 Nobel Prize in Literature, is the leading modern writer in Hebrew. Taken as a whole, his works are sometimes called "the modern Jewish epic." Agnon was born Shmuel Yosef Czaczkes on July 17, 1888, in Buczacz, a small town in eastern Galicia, then part of the Austro-Hungarian Empire. His middle-class Jewish parents came from a scholarly Orthodox tradition that Agnon seemed destined to continue. As a child, he was steeped in Jewish folklore and religious teachings, studying in Hebrew school, taking private Talmud lessons, and reading independently in Hasidic literature. His imagination embraced the cozy world of the Eastern European shtetl that would become the main subject of his early fiction and a symbolic focus throughout his work.

In 1907, after making his start as a writer in Hebrew and Yiddish (the everyday language of the shtetl), Agnon emigrated to Palestine. He had been active in Zionist circles, and, in his fiction, to "go up to" the Land of Israel is the ambition of every pious Jew. In Palestine, he continued to work for Zionist organizations and to write short fiction (henceforth only in Hebrew), first in Jaffa, then in Jerusalem. The idealistic young man from Buczacz apparently found Palestine inspiring, but it was also racked by turbulence, violence, and disorientation. Jewish homeland or not, Palestine was the scene of a confused present that contrasted with the orderly past represented by the shtetl. As such, Palestine formed the other symbolic focus of Agnon's imagination.

Agnon's change of surnames marks his suspension between these two places and all they symbolized. His pen surname is derived from the title of his first important story, "Agunot" (1908). *Agunot* is the plural of *aguna*, a Hebrew word for a woman whose husband has left her without granting a divorce; thus she exists in a marital limbo, neither taken nor available. Metaphorically, her state of suspension suggests any divided spiritual state which one can neither change nor escape. Like an *aguna*, Agnon was suspended between the two worlds—one dying and the other waiting to be born—represented by the shtetl culture and Palestine. Agnon's literary mission was to depict, to contrast, and ultimately to bridge those two worlds, using his personal dilemma as a mirror of modern Jewish history.

In 1913, Agnon went to study in Germany, where he was stranded by the outbreak of World War I. Agnon ended up staying in Germany from 1913 to 1924. There he read widely in contemporary European literature, mingled with leading Jewish intellectuals (such as theologian Martin Buber), and gained a patron, Salman Schocken, who became his publisher. He continued to write short fiction that resembled folk tales and also a number of Kafkaesque stories. There he also met Esther Marx, whom he married in 1919; they had a daughter, Emuna, born in 1921, and a son, Hemdat, born in 1922. When their Homburg home burned in 1924, destroying Agnon's valuable collection of books and manuscripts plus an unfinished novel, Agnon and his family moved to Jerusalem.

In the following decade, Agnon produced his long comic masterpiece *The Bridal Canopy* and a novella in a similar vein, *In the Heart of the Seas*. Set in the small towns and villages of Galicia around 1820, *The Bridal Canopy* tells the picaresque story of a pious but poverty-ridden Hasid, Reb Yudel Nathanson, who is on a quest to raise dowries and find husbands for his three ripe daughters. Various commentators, including the Nobel Prize Committee, have referred to *The Bridal Canopy* as a Jewish version of Miguel de Cervantes' *Don Quixote de la Mancha* (1605), complete with a Sancho Panza in Nuta, Reb Yudel's wagon driver. Besides Cervantes, Agnon's narrative technique here—characterized by verbal play, joking, gossip, folklore, scriptural exegesis, rabbinical argument, and short stories embedded within the larger story—also recalls such early masters as François Rabelais and Laurence Sterne. One could hardly find a more entertaining celebration of the old shtetl culture.

Even as Agnon was writing this celebratory work, he was forcibly reminded of the shtetl culture's demise. In 1929, Agnon toured Galicia, and out of his disillusioned return to his hometown came, years later, the novel *A Guest for the Night*. This bleak, autobiographical novel shows the destruction of the shtetl culture after World War I—plus the destruction of one of Agnon's symbolic focuses. Thereafter, his unhappiness expressed itself as growing alienation from a modern world severed from its spiritual roots—a feeling no doubt intensified by the Holocaust (which Agnon does not treat in his writings). This sense of spiritual impotence prevails in his later work, such as the novellas in *Two Tales*. In *A Guest for the Night* and later works, the shtetl culture lingers over Agnon's work only as a ghost: an implied contrast and a symbol of longing.

Agnon's talent as a writer was recognized early in Jewish circles and later honored repeatedly by the state of Israel. An official sign admonishing QUIET, AGNON IS WRITING was posted in his Jerusalem neighborhood, and he was accorded a state funeral when he died of a heart attack in 1970. Yet Agnon's work also has universal appeal. He offers particular insight into the tortured turns of modern Jewish culture and history, but these turns have various types of significance for the rest of the world. For example, Agnon's Modern Jewish Epic has close parallels with the depiction of Appalachian culture in the United States by such writers as novelist Harriette Arnow and poet Jim Wayne Miller. Agnon thus provides another installment of the great modern theme, the development from a traditional society (ordered, religious) to a modern society (confused, secular), and his images of spiritual loss have universal significance.

BIBLIOGRAPHICAL REFERENCES: Arnold Band, *Nostalgia and Nightmare: A Study in the Fiction of S. Y. Agnon*, 1968, though dated, remains a comprehensive and useful critical work on Agnon. Other general studies include Baruch Hochman, *The Fiction of S. Y. Agnon*, 1970, and Harold Fisch, *S. Y. Agnon*, 1975. While concentrating on themes, David Aberbach, *At the Handles of the Lock: Themes in the Fiction of S. J. Agnon*, 1984, also offers psychoanalytical insight into Agnon's characters. While Agnon is discussed only briefly in Robert Alter, *The Invention of Hebrew Prose: Modern Fiction and the Language of Realism*, 1988, this study illumines the context of his work. See also D. Patterson, "S. J. Agnon: The Writer and the Legend," *Ariel*, no. 11 (1965); J. Gross, "The Art of Agnon," *The New York Review of Books*, March 11, 1966; G. Scholem, "Reflections on S. Y. Agnon," *Commentary*, December, 1967; R. Alter, "Agnon's Last Word," *Commentary*, June, 1971; and J. Dan, "Agnon and Celestial Jerusalem," *Forum*, Winter, 1979.

Harold Branam

CONRAD AIKEN

Born: Savannah, Georgia
Date: August 5, 1889

Died: Savannah, Georgia
Date: August 17, 1973

PRINCIPAL WORKS

POETRY: *Earth Triumphant and Other Tales in Verse*, 1914; *Turns and Movies and Other Tales in Verse*, 1916; *The Jig of Forslin*, 1916; *Nocturne of Remembered Spring and Other Poems*, 1917; *The Charnel Rose*, 1918; *Senlin: A Biography and Other Poems*, 1918; *The House of Dust*, 1920; *Punch: The Immortal Liar*, 1921; *Priapus and the Pool*, 1922; *The Pilgrimage of Festus*, 1923; *Priapus and the Pool and Other Poems*, 1925; *Selected Poems*, 1929; *John Deth: A Metaphysical Legend, and Other Poems*, 1930; *The Coming Forth by Day of Osiris Jones*, 1931; *Preludes for Memnon*, 1931; *Landscape West of Eden*, 1934; *Time in the Rock: Preludes to Definition*, 1936; *And in the Human Heart*, 1940; *Brownstone Eclogues and Other Poems*, 1942; *The Soldier: A Poem by Conrad Aiken*, 1944; *The Kid*, 1947; *Skylight One: Fifteen Poems*, 1949; *The Divine Pilgrim*, 1949; *Collected Poems*, 1953; *A Letter from Li Po and Other Poems*, 1955; *Sheepfold Hill: Fifteen Poems*, 1958; *Selected Poems*, 1961; *The Morning Song of Lord Zero*, 1963; *A Seizure of Limericks*, 1964; *Thee: A Poem*, 1967, *Collected Poems 1916 1970*, 1970, *The Clerk's Journal*, 1971.

NOVELS: *Blue Voyage*, 1927; *Great Circle*, 1933; *King Coffin*, 1935; *A Heart for the Gods of Mexico*, 1939; *Conversation: Or, Pilgrim's Progress*, 1940; *The Collected Novels of Conrad Aiken*, 1964.

SHORT FICTION: *Bring! Bring! and Other Stories*, 1925; *Costumes by Eros*, 1928; *Among the Lost People*, 1934; *Collected Short Stories*, 1960.

CHILDREN'S LITERATURE: *Cats and Bats and Things with Wings: Poems*, 1965; *Tom, Sue, and the Clock*, 1966; *A Little Who's Zoo of Mild Animals*, 1977.

PLAY: *Mr. Arcularis*, pb. 1957.

LITERARY CRITICISM: *Skepticisms: Notes on Contemporary Poetry*, 1919; *A Reviewer's ABC: Collected Criticism of Conrad Aiken from 1916 to the Present*, 1958.

AUTOBIOGRAPHY: *Ushant: An Essay*, 1952.

CORRESPONDENCE: *Selected Letters of Conrad Aiken*, 1978.

Conrad Potter Aiken was a central figure in the American Poetry Renaissance of the early twentieth century. He was born in Savannah, Georgia, on August 5, 1889, the son of parents of distinguished New England ancestry. His father, William Ford Aiken, studied medicine at Harvard University and in Europe. His mother, Anna Potter Aiken, was the daughter of William James Potter, a prominent minister in New Bedford, Massachusetts, who left the Unitarian church to cofound the less sectarian Free Religious Association. For his free thinking and rationalism, Potter assumed heroic stature in many of Aiken's works. The key event of Aiken's life occurred when his father shot to death his wife and himself in February, 1901. The tragedy's effects on the development of his personality are analyzed, often through elaborate dream sequences, in much of Aiken's writing. Following the deaths of his parents, Aiken was separated from his two younger brothers and sister to be reared by relatives in New Bedford and Cambridge, Massachusetts. Aiken entered Harvard University in 1907, where he became a close and lifelong friend of T. S. Eliot. As a student, he was deeply influenced by the naturalistic rationalism of George Santayana, who argued that the greatest poetry was philosophical, capable of expressing a coherent worldview based upon a knowledge of contemporary scientific and humanistic thought.

Aiken's first book of poetry, *Earth Triumphant and Other Tales in Verse*, appeared in 1914, and his criticism began to appear in 1915. Between 1914 and 1925, Aiken published ten volumes of poetry and some one hundred critical essays. Aiken's most important works prior to the early 1920's were his five verse "symphonies": *The Charnel Rose*, *The Jig of Forslin*,

Senlin, *The House of Dust*, and *The Pilgrimage of Festus* (published together as *The Divine Pilgrim* in 1949). Alternately musical, fragmented, dreamlike, morbid, and erotic, these long poems were designed to depict progressive stages in the development of consciousness, essentially along Freudian lines, and to tell the story of Aiken's life.

As a critic, Aiken warred with the Imagists and such popular anthologizers and editors as Harriet Monroe, Louis Untermeyer, and Amy Lowell. Because he had no use for nationalistic themes, poetic cliques, manifestos, schools, or prizes, Aiken often distanced himself from many of the popular poetic trends of his time. He repeatedly argued for "scientific" critical standards. Aiken was the first Freudian critic; he praised Walt Whitman and championed Emily Dickinson. In "The Impersonal Poet," he expressed every major tenet of Eliot's seminal essay "Tradition and the Individual Talent" in *The Sacred Wood* (1920). Beginning in the early 1920's, Aiken, in such short lyrics as "Cliff Meeting" and "Sea Holly," began to write in a voice that finally expressed his anguished vision of deterministically fused subjective and objective realms. At the same time, he also turned to the short story, where he proved himself to be a master of psychological realism, particularly in the depiction of compulsive behavior and parent-child relationships, as in "Silent Snow, Secret Snow."

Aiken moved with his wife and children to England in 1921. Isolated and believing himself a failure, he began in 1924 to write *Blue Voyage*, an autobiographical stream-of-consciousness novel that profoundly influenced Malcolm Lowry. *Great Circle*, Aiken's second novel, further explores both his childhood and the breakup of his first marriage. Much like his two first novels, Aiken's most powerful poems, *Preludes of Memnon* and *Time in the Rock*, were written in the period surrounding his first divorce in 1928, his compulsive second marriage in 1930, his suicide attempt in 1932, and his second divorce and third marriage in 1937. In these poems, Aiken analyzes the biological causes and artistic implications of his own compulsive personality.

From the urbane *Brownstone Eclogues* of 1942 until his death in 1973, Aiken's poetry celebrated both his New England ancestry and the American scene. *Sheepfold Hill* contains Aiken's most explicit and nostalgic ancestral memoirs. From 1950 to 1952, he was Poetry Consultant at the Library of Congress, during which time he wrote his postmodernist, highly confessional autobiography, *Ushant*. Despite the quality and quantity of his work, Aiken did not receive the critical recognition afforded to his contemporaries T. S. Eliot, Ezra Pound, Wallace Stevens, or William Carlos Williams. Aiken's early disputes with editors and other poets contributed to his reputation as a loner. By his own admission, much of his earliest verse was derivative and flawed. As a modernist, Aiken sought to be cosmic at the wrong historical juncture. His lifelong quest to develop a workable Darwinian and Freudian theory of the "evolution of consciousness" marks Aiken as one of the most significant American writers of the twentieth century.

BIBLIOGRAPHICAL REFERENCES: Edward Butscher, *Conrad Aiken: Poet of White Horse Vale*, 1988, the first volume of a projected two-volume biography, provides a complete account of Aiken's life and work up to 1925; Butscher's approach is emphatically psychoanalytic. Harry Marten, *The Art of Knowing: The Poetry and Prose of Conrad Aiken*, 1988, presents a general introduction to Aiken's epistemological themes. Ted R. Spivey, *The Writer as Shaman: The Pilgrimages of Conrad Aiken and Walker Percy*, 1986, discusses Aiken, Percy, and the concept of modern cultural crisis. Earlier, still-valuable studies include Jay Martin, *Conrad Aiken: A Life of His Art*, 1962, and Frederick J. Hoffman, *Conrad Aiken*, 1962. Houston Peterson, *The Melody of Chaos*, 1931, though dated, is still important for its influence on subsequent Aiken critics. Reuel Denney's pamphlet *Conrad Aiken*, 1964, remains a good short study of Aiken. Joseph Killorin's introduction and notes to the *Selected Letters* provide key details about Aiken's life. Special journal issues devoted to Aiken include *Wake 11*, 1952; *Studies in the Literary Imagination*, XIII (1980); and *The Southern Quarterly*, XXI (1982), which considers Aiken's prose. Valuable interviews are Ashley Brown, "An Interview with

Conrad Aiken," *Shenandoah*, XV (1963), 19-40, and Robert Hunter Wilbur, "The Art of Poetry IX: Conrad Aiken, an Interview," *The Paris Review*, Fall/Winter, 1972, 59-68. See also Richard P. Blackmur, "Conrad Aiken: The Poet," *The Atlantic Monthly*, December, 1953, 77-82; Calvin S. Brown, "Music and Conrad Aiken," *The Georgia Review*, XXVII (1973), 477-488; Malcolm Cowley, "Conrad Aiken: From Savannah to Emerson," in—*And I Worked at the Writer's Trade: Chapters of Literary History, 1918-1978*, 1978. A complete bibliography is F. W. and F. C. Bonnell, *Conrad Aiken: A Bibliography (1902-1978)*, 1982.

Steven E. Olson

JOANNE AKALAITIS

Born: Chicago, Illinois
Date: June 29, 1937

PRINCIPAL WORKS

PLAYS: *Dressed Like an Egg*, pr. 1977; *Southern Exposure*, pr. 1979; *Dead End Kids*, pr. 1980; *Green Card*, pr. 1986.

JoAnne Akalaitis is recognized for her contributions to performance art and avant-garde drama, particularly with Mabou Mines, the theater company which she helped form in 1969. Akalaitis was born in Chicago, Illinois, in 1937, and she was reared in a Lithuanian Catholic neighborhood. She studied philosophy at the University of Chicago and Stanford University. She later participated in the Actor's Workshop in San Francisco in 1962, working with Ruth Maleczech and Lee Breuer. Together with these and other performers, she formed the theater collective Mabou Mines. She received training from such well-known acting teachers as Bill Hickey, Herbert Berghof, Spalding Gray, and Joyce Aaron.

Akalaitis was awarded financial support from the National Endowment for the Arts and the New York State Creative Artists Public Service Program. Working with Mabou Mines, she contributed to such conceptual collaborations as *Red Horse Animation* (1970) and *The Saint and the Football Player* (1976), which took place first as visual performance pieces in New York's Solomon R. Guggenheim Museum, the Museum of Modern Art, and the Berkeley and Pasadena art museums. Other multimedia events include performances with the 1976 American Dance Festival. Composer Philip Glass was once married to Akalaitis, and he provided music for Mabou Mines in *Dressed Like an Egg* and *Dead End Kids*, significant contributions to New York's burgeoning avant-garde theater.

Akalaitis describes her work as disconnected from the American theater tradition of such artists as Tennessee Williams, Arthur Miller, and Edward Albee, whose work focuses on domestic issues and personal relationships. In distinct contrast, Akalaitis' work with Mabou Mines is more avant-garde and less rooted in typically American themes. Her use of music, art, science, and surrealist and expressionist forms aligns her with the tradition of such European artists as Bertolt Brecht. Her group, Mabou Mines, shocks the audience out of its usual expectations through nontraditional use of props, opening of the stage boundaries, onstage narration, unconventional exchanges of character portrayal among various actors, and set designs and scene changes that call attention to the fact that the play is a staged performance.

Akalaitis' work is highly conceptual, often calling on her background in philosophy. It requires active participation and thought on the part of audience members, who may grope to decipher meanings or form logical patterns out of apparent chaos. Coming from a collaborative theater background, she does not wish to force actors or audiences into a rigid interpretation. Akalaitis and Mabou Mines, therefore, rely on spontaneity in rehearsal and performance, creating a dialectic between past and present, traditional theater and nontheatrical media, individual and collective visions, and rehearsed and impromptu material.

Dressed Like an Egg was her first widely accepted work, performed at the New York Shakespeare Festival (Joseph Papp, artistic director) in May of 1977. This collage piece with ten segments draws on the writings of Colette. Each segment deals in some manner with the issue of gender, with comic scenes focusing audience attention on the concept of the ideal, in sexuality, romance, and intellect. *Dressed Like an Egg* explores sexual ambiguity in visually shocking scenes, perhaps an allusion to Colette's intimate friendships with other women.

Akalaitis often presents historical information, incorporating facts, abstract philosophy, and surreal and absurdist features into her own brand of performance art. *Southern Exposure*, performed at The New Theatre Festival, Baltimore, in 1979, is an exploration of exterior and interior poles. The play offers tribute to early explorers of the Antarctic at the same time that it explores interior, or mental, uncharted territory, areas of the mind untouched by civilization, perhaps seeking the blank spot of pure being, nonbeing, or Nirvana. Past and present both play a role in this play, which demands that audiences superimpose their own definitions of "culture" on empty space. The set, costumes, slides, film, and props point to the relationship between the exploration in art and in the world of the geographical explorer. This juxtaposition of scientific and spiritual realms shows similarities, in that both represent the human impulse to impose order on emptiness or chaos.

The group's most well-known work, *Dead End Kids*, has been noted for its didacticism, but it has also been praised for its innovative stage design and its effectiveness in conveying the horrors of nuclear war and its aftermath. It bears witness to human intellectual curiosity and the self-destructive impulse toward ultimate domination over life itself.

In what some critics consider her most difficult work, *Green Card*, Akalaitis points to the inhumanity of United States immigration policies. The viewpoints of immigrants appear in a random "collage" of characters, revealing information and attitudes of various aliens, from the past to the present. For example, one segment features a Jewish refugee from the turn of the century, and another shows a central American political protestor from El Salvador. As with *Dead End Kids*, the opening occurs as the audience enters, with loudspeaker voices delivering lines relevant to the play's theme. *Green Card* opened in Los Angeles' Mark Taper Forum in 1986. The Los Angeles opening is fitting, in that this metropolis is described within the play as "really a jail." In this play, Akalaitis questions the United States position of instigator and promoter of wars and repressive governments that force new immigrants to enter the United States in the futile hope of refuge.

Critics seem to agree on the virtues and failings of JoAnne Akalaitis' work. Her unconventional methods, timely topics, and cooperative approach all contribute to the vibrancy and relevance of her work. At the same time, these elements may make her work obscure, confusing, or offensive to some audiences. Her refusal to submit to standard theater practices results in a theater whose form follows its function of challenging audiences to think. Whether American mainstream theater is ready for her work remains to be seen.

BIBLIOGRAPHICAL REFERENCES: Debra Cohen's article "The Mabou Mines' *The Lost Ones*," *The Drama Review*, XX (June, 1976), 83-87, offers solid insights into the purposes behind Akalaitis' collaborative work with Mabou Mines. Terry Curtis Fox's "The Quiet Explosions of JoAnne Akalaitis," *The Village Voice*, May 23, 1977, 77, places Akalaitis within the avant-garde theater tradition in New York, as does Richard Lacayo's "Directors Fiddle, Authors Burn," *Time*, CXXV (January 21, 1985), 74, a description of director Akalaitis' run-in with playwright Samuel Beckett over changes in his play. Jonathan Kalb's "JoAnne Akalaitis," interview in *Theater*, XV (Spring, 1984), 6-13, gives good illustrations of her work, along with biographical information. See also *The Theatre of Images*, 1977, edited by Bonnie Marranca; Xerxes Mehta, "Notes from the Avant-Garde," *Theatre Journal*, XXXI (March, 1979), 20-24, and "Some Versions of Performance Art," also in *Theatre Journal*, XXXVI (May, 1984), 165-198; and Sally R. Sommer, "JoAnne Akalaitis of Mabou Mines," *The Drama Review*, XX (September, 1976), 3-16.

Rebecca Bell-Metereau

VASSILY AKSYONOV

Born: Kazan, Soviet Union
Date: August 20, 1932

Principal Works

LONG FICTION: *Kollegi*, 1960 (*Colleagues*, 1962); *Zvezdnyi bilet*, 1961 (*A Starry Night*, 1962; also as *A Ticket to the Stars*); *Apelsiny iz Marokko*, 1963 (*Oranges from Morocco*, 1979); *Pora, moi drug, pora*, 1965 (*It's Time, My Friend, It's Time*, 1969); *Zatvorennaya bochkotara*, 1968 (*Surplussed Barrelware*, 1985); *Stalnaya ptitsa*, 1977 (*The Steel Bird*, 1979); *Poiski zhanra*, 1978; *Zolotaya nasha Zhelezka*, 1979 (*Our Golden Ironburg*, 1986); *Ozhog*, 1980 (*The Burn*, 1984); *Ostrov Krym*, 1981 (*The Island of Crimea*, 1983); *Bumazhnyi peizazh*, 1983; *Skazhi izyum*, 1985 (*Say "Cheese,"* 1989).

SHORT FICTION: *Katapulta*, 1964; *Na polputi k lune*, 1965; *Zhal, chto vas ne bylo s nami*, 1969; *The Steel Bird and Other Stories*, 1979; *Pravo na ostrov*, 1983.

PLAYS: *Vsegda v prodazhe*, pr. 1963; *Potselui, Orkestr, Ryba, Kolbasa . . .*, pb. 1964; *Chetyre temperamenta*, pb. 1967 (*The Four Temperaments*, 1987); *Aristofaniana s lyagushkami*, pb. 1967-1968; *Tsaplya*, pb. 1979 (*The Heron*, 1987).

NONFICTION: *Kruglye sutki: non-stop*, 1976; *V poiskakh grustnogo bebi*, 1987 (*In Search of Melancholy Baby*, 1987).

BIOGRAPHY: *Lyubov k elektrichestvu*, 1971.

MISCELLANEOUS: *Quest for an Island*, 1987.

Vassily Pavlovich Áksyonov is the leading figure among those Soviet writers who came of age following Joseph Stalin's death in 1953. The writers of the new generation dreamed of turning their country away from the nightmare of Stalinism toward a new future—socialism with a human face. Literature became the herald and beacon for the young generation, and Aksyonov as the controversial leader of the "young prose" movement became its spokesman and chronicler.

Aksyonov's parents, both committed Communists, were falsely arrested as "enemies of the people" in 1937. Aksyonov rejoined his freed mother and stepfather, a Catholic doctor-prisoner, in Siberia at age seventeen. Because "it's easier for doctors in the camps," it was decided that Aksyonov would attend medical school in Leningrad, from which he was graduated in 1956. Taking advantage of the "thaw," the young doctor began writing. With the success of his first novel, *Colleagues*, Aksyonov turned to full-time writing. He became a major figure on the cultural scene with *A Ticket to the Stars*, a landmark book that served as the rallying point for the new generation. Soviet readers were not accustomed to sympathetic accounts of youthful alienation and were shocked by the book's racy language and its young heroes' irreverent attitude toward authority. In March, 1963, Nikita Khrushchev called a meeting of Soviet writers at which he half-cajolingly, half-threateningly castigated Aksyonov and his colleagues.

Throughout the rest of the 1960's, Aksyonov succeeded in publishing only two further novels. His many short stories were even more popular: The most famous was "Halfway to the Moon" (1963); the best was "Victory" (1965). As publication became more difficult, Aksyonov turned to the theater, which he saw as a forum for social satire. Between 1963 and 1968, he wrote four plays, but only one, *Vsegda v prodazhe* (always on sale), survived the censor until banned in 1972. Aksyonov also worked on a number of film scripts.

The Steel Bird, written in 1965 but first published more than a decade later in the United States, marks a crucial turning point for Aksyonov both stylistically and thematically. The earlier writings had remained within the limits of realism, and their optimistic themes were more social than political. *The Steel Bird* is a modernist political allegory warning of the return of Stalinism. The major work of the 1970's was *The Burn*, written between 1969 and 1975 but published, again only in the West, in 1980. The long, complex novel is an indictment of the Russian intelligentsia for its moral collapse before the resurgent (if milder) Stalinism of the mid-1960's.

Aksyonov was permitted to accept a one-term appointment as Regents' Lecturer at the University of California at Los Angeles in 1975. The experience is reflected in his second major novel of the 1970's, *The Island of Crimea*, a futuristic fantasy in which Crimea has become an independent capitalist supercivilization reminiscent of Southern California. The novel is also Aksyonov's bitterest indictment of the Soviet Union, for after the free Crimeans' vote for reunification with Mother Russia, that country, unable to grasp the idea, invades. During the late 1970's, Aksyonov and a number of his colleagues boldly undertook to publish *Metropol*, an uncensored literary anthology. Strong government pressure was brought to bear upon the contributors. Aksyonov resigned from the Writers' Union in protest and was, in effect, forced to emigrate. In the months before his emigration, Aksyonov penned his best play, *The Heron*, which he dedicated to his *Metropol* friends. The heron, a symbol of freedom, is killed at the end of the play, although there is hope that, phoenixlike, it may arise from the ashes.

Aksyonov arrived in the West in July of 1980. His major unpublished works of the 1970's, *The Burn* and *The Island of Crimea*, appeared first in émigré Russian editions and then in translation. In the United States, Aksyonov has taught at various universities and has been a Fellow at the prestigious Woodrow Wilson International Center and a resident of Washington, D.C. His most substantial "American" novel, *Say "Cheese,"* is loosely based upon the *Metropol* affair, although the scene is changed to the world of Moscow photographers rather than writers. Aksyonov has been active as a spokesman for Russian culture, making many broadcasts and participating in numerous conferences. He has also proved a prolific journalist in both the émigré and American press. With his departure from the Soviet Union, Aksyonov's works were banned. The advent of Mikhail Gorbachev's *glasnost* has permitted the reappearance of some of Aksyonov's work in his homeland.

Aksyonov's tales often involve a search for some ideal, some goal, whose attainment would resolve all the perplexities of human existence. This ideal goal, never attained, assumes different forms in different works. The young heroes of the "youth prose" period scorn safe, personally advantageous choices and aspire to their "ticket to the stars." The passengers in *Surplussed Barrelware* share a dream that the goal of their journey is to find "the Good Man." A more frequent variant, the mysterious "Unknown Woman," occurs in many of the works. The scientists in *Our Golden Ironburg* seek the mysterious "double fyu." *The Burn*'s artists and scientists all strive toward miraculous creations, as well as the mysterious beauty, Alisa. The much-sought heron in the play of that name (the heron image occurs in other works as well) signifies love, altruism, freedom, and creativity. *The Burn* is the first Aksyonov work to state explicitly the theme at which he had previously only hinted. In the corrupt world of *The Burn*, only one character possesses the moral fiber to oppose unwaveringly the evil of Stalinism—Sanya Gurchenko, a Russian Jew who escapes a labor camp to become a Jesuit theologian in the West. He argues that all men seek God, but they seek God in different ways. Man approaches this ultimate truth only in moments of intuitive, suprarational inspiration. The higher emotions, such as compassion, charity, and the urge for justice are rationally inexplicable. Creativity is similarly trans-rational. Christianity, precisely because it is concerned with such unaccountable human phenomena, offers a basis for moral action.

Aksyonov is a major voice in contemporary Russian literature. He has a great theme, the fate of his country and his generation, and immense technical facility as a writer. Russian modernism traces its roots to Nikolai Gogol (1809-1852) with his love of the absurd and fascination with the play and power of language itself. These aspects of Gogol were emphasized by Andrey Bely, the turn-of-the-century Symbolist, whose *Petersburg* (1913-1914; English translation, 1959) was the first great Russian modernist novel. This tradition, suppressed following the imposition of Socialist Realism circa 1934, has been richly revitalized by the work of Vassily Aksyonov.

BIBLIOGRAPHICAL REFERENCES: A literary biography and bibliography of work by and about Aksyonov may be found in Edward Możejko, Boris Briker, and Per Dalgård, eds., *Vasiliy Pavlovich Aksënov: A Writer in Quest of Himself*, 1986. This collection of essays by various hands provides the best overview of Aksyonov, although later writings such as *The Burn*, *The Island of Crimea*, *Bumazhnyi peizazh*, and *Say "Cheese"* are treated only in passing or not at all. Per Dalgård, *The Function of the Grotesque in Vasilij Aksenov*, 1982, provides a more specialized view of the post-1965 work through *The Burn*. The biographical connections between Aksyonov's *The Burn* and his mother's account of her exile are examined in David Lowe's "E. Ginzburg's *Krutoj maršrut*" and V. Aksenov's "*Ożog*: The Magadan Connection," in *Slavic and East European Journal*, XXVII (Summer, 1983), 200-210. Ellendea Proffer, "The Prague Winter: Two Novels by Aksyonov," in *The Third Wave: Russian Literature in Emigration*, 1984, edited by Olga Matich and Michael Heim, examines *The Burn* and *The Island of Crimea*. On the last, see especially Olga Matich, "Vasilii Aksyonov and the Literature of Convergence: *Ostrov Krym* as Self-Criticism," *Slavic Review*, XXXXVII, no. 4 (1988), 642-651. Also of interest are Greta Slobin, "Aksyonov Beyond 'Youth Prose': Subversion Through Popular Culture," *Slavic and East European Journal*, XXX (1987), 50-64, and D. Barton Johnson, "Vasilij Aksionov's Aviary: *The Heron* and *The Steel Bird*," *Scando-Slavica*, XXXIII (1987), 45-61.

D. Barton Johnson

RYŪNOSUKE AKUTAGAWA
Ryūnosuke Niihara

Born: Tokyo, Japan
Date: March 1, 1892

Died: Tokyo, Japan
Date: July 27, 1927

PRINCIPAL WORKS

SHORT FICTION: *Kappa*, 1927 (English translation, 1970); *Aru ahō no isshō*, 1927 (*A Fool's Life*, 1971); *Rashomon and Other Stories*, 1930, 1952, 1964; *Tales Grotesque and Curious*, 1930; *Hell Screen and Other Stories*, 1952; *Japanese Short Stories*, 1961; *Exotic Japanese Stories: The Beautiful and the Grotesque*, 1964.

MISCELLANEOUS: *Akutagawa Ryūnosuke zenshū*, 1967-1969.

Ryūnosuke Akutagawa was the leading short-fiction writer of the Taishō period (1912-1926). He was born in Tokyo's Tsukiji Foreign settlement. His original surname was Niihara, after his father, Toshizō Niihara, owner of dairy farms serving Tsukiji's foreign residents, and his given name was Ryūnosuke, commemorating his birth in the year of the dragon. Since his parents, according to Japanese superstition, were at ill-omened ages when he was born, Akutagawa, to avoid bad luck, was "abandoned" and handed over to his father's friend and then accepted back into the Niihara family as a "foundling." His mother, Fuku, blaming herself for the death of her eldest daughter from meningitis eight months after her son was born, went insane, an affliction which Ryūnosuke later believed he had inherited. After his mother became incapable of caring for him, he was reared by his mother's elder brother, Michiaki Akutagawa. Two years after his mother's death, he was formally adopted by Michiaki and took the Akutagawa surname. These complicated events left the impressionable child scarred by shame and distrustful of others.

In his youth, much of it spent in the care of his spinster aunt, Fuki, Akutagawa was encouraged in his interests in literature and the arts and avidly read traditional literature, especially illustrated storybooks (*kusazōshi*) of the Edō period (1600-1868) featuring ghost tales. A sickly child prone to convulsions, he nevertheless excelled at school and started writing stories and poems in primary school. In middle school, he was reading widely in Japanese and Chinese literature and among translated European authors. During his years at the Tokyo First High School, where he majored in English literature, his friends thought him kind and considerate, while outsiders considered him aloof. He was graduated second in his class in 1913 and entered the English literature department of Tokyo Imperial University. He published translations from English and "Rōnen" (old age), his first original piece, in the student magazine *Shinshicho* (new thought tides). In 1914, a literary periodical published his stories "Hyottoko" (the comic mask) and "Rashōmon," the tale of a twelfth century Kyoto underling who degenerates into a criminal by stealing the clothes off an old woman. As a university student, he became acquainted with the novelist Natsume Sōseki and attended Thursday Club meetings at his home. Akutagawa first received wide recognition for the humorous 1916 story "The Nose," about a Buddhist priest's preoccupation with the unusual length of his nose.

His student successes caught the eyes of publishers, and established writers such as Sōseki praised his talent. In 1916, the year of his graduation from the university, he published more than a dozen stories, including "Imogayu" ("Yam Gruel"), about sadistic tricks played on a lowly samurai. These showed his gift for transforming grotesque anecdotes into well-crafted stories. While living in Kamakura and teaching English at the naval engineering academy at Yokosuka, he fell in love with a childhood friend, sixteen-year-old Tsukamoto Fumi. They were married in 1918, after she finished school. Aunt Fuki moved in with the newlyweds and became a surrogate but domineering mother-in-law. In 1917, many of Akutagawa's earlier stories were gathered in two collections. The *Osaka Mainichi* newspaper hired him in 1918 under an exclusive contract, and he became a full-time writer in 1919. Major stories that appeared in anthologies and newspapers during this period include "Hankechi" ("A Handkerchief"), "Gesaku Zammai" ("A Life Spent at Frivolous Writing"), "Hōkyōnin no Shi" ("The Martyr"), "Kumo no ito" ("The Spider's Thread"), and "Jigokuhen" ("Hell Screen"). The latter is a macabre story relating a painter's struggle between the demands of his art and life; it is considered one of Akutagawa's finest creations. These works confirmed his reputation as a brilliant stylist adept at turning scenes of degradation and bitter comedy into well-wrought stories.

In 1920, the newspaper sent him to China as a correspondent. Between bouts with illness he was intrigued by China's exotic past. Four months later, back home, his health rapidly deteriorating, he churned out China reports to please his employer. "Nakin no Kirisuto" ("Christ in Nanking"), "Tu Tze-chun," "Shūzanzu" ("The Painting of an Autumn Mountain"), and the famous "Yabu no naka" ("In a Grove"), comparing and contrasting how a young samurai couple and a bandit differently explain the "truth" about a case of rape and murder, are important works from the early 1920's. Akutagawa and his family escaped the great 1923 Kantō earthquake, but from then on insomnia, piles, stomach pains, and other ailments continuously plagued him. Henceforth, thinly veiled autobiographical topics and contemporary themes were featured in his writings as he began eschewing historical and phantasmagoric storytelling in favor of probing his own inner thoughts and emotions. Socialist ideas attracted him in the early 1920's at a time when proletarian literature was in vogue, and in stories featuring the character Horikawa Yasukichi, he flirted with leftist themes. He did not believe in the then-popular "I-novel" (*watakushi shōsetsu*), but he admired the realistic writings of Naoya Shiga, whom he tried to emulate in his self-revealing late works. Through bouts of declining health he engaged in a literary debate with Jun'ichirō Tanizaki over the role of plot structure and lyricism in the writing of fiction. In his last two years, in spite of personal setbacks involving relatives' illnesses and financial difficulties and his own depression and ailments, his creative powers were reinvigorated. In addition to several stories, he produced the novella *Kappa*, a satire of human foibles seen through the underground world of the mythological elfin kappa sprites.

"Haguruma" ("Cogwheel"), a posthumous short story concerning the author's own mental breakdown, horrifically described what was happening to Akutagawa in his last year. Hallucinations and paranoia plagued him, and sleeping potions and opium provided little relief. The suicide of his brother-in-law in January, 1927, and the mental breakdown of a friend in May may have driven him over the edge. During the night of July 24, 1927, he committed suicide by taking a lethal overdose of medicine; he was thirty-five years old. Akutagawa's tragic death deeply affected Taishō writers and symbolized the anxiety of the times. His legacy of about a hundred fine stories is wide in scope, ranging from early works that blend historical scenes from the past with modern psychological insights to later "confessional" writings that reveal his inner torments. The pre-1922 stories, based on foreign ideas and Chinese and Japanese history originals in classical anthologies, though derivative, are ingenious tales exploring the bittersweet dimensions of the bizzare from a modern perspective. While he often pieced together borrowed story ideas and employed predictably manipulative surprise endings, most of his first fiction is infused with haunting touches, making for pleasureable reading. The later writings cannot be divorced from the tragic dimensions of his physical and mental condition, yet they are important not just as autobiographical revelations but as literary witness to the struggle between the life of the writer and the demands of art. Akutagawa ended that struggle in suicide. His late writings, pointing toward that perhaps inevitable end, remain as testaments to his tortured genius.

BIBLIOGRAPHICAL REFERENCES: Beongcheon Yu, *Akutagawa, An Introduction*, 1972, is a major literary biography with notes, chronology, and list of translations. A shorter but equally insightful study is Donald Keene, *Dawn to the West: Japanese Literature in the Modern*

Period (Fiction), 1984. Howard S. Hibbert, "Akutagawa Ryūnosuke and the Negative Ideal," in *Personality in Japanese History*, 1970, edited by Albert Craig and Donald H. Shively, uses the psychological approach to analyze his life and oeuvre. A good brief biography is G. H. Healey's introduction in the Geoffrey Bownas translation of *Kappa*, 1971. A section in Makoto Ueda, *Modern Japanese Writers and the Nature of Literature*, 1976, gives an overview of his writings in the context of the "negation of a negative spirit." A comparison with Naoya Shiga is in Hisaaki Yamanouchi, *The Search for Authenticity in Modern Japanese Literature*, 1978. Arima Tatsuo's chapter "Akutagawa Ryūnosuke: The Literature of Defeatism," in his *The Failure of Freedom: A Portrait of Modern Japanese Intellectuals*, 1969, evaluates his place in Taishō history. Kinya Tsuruta, "Akutagawa Ryūnosuke and the I-Novelists," *Monumenta Nipponica*, XXV (1970), and his "The Theme of Death in Akutagawa Ryūnosuke," *Literature East and West*, XV/XVI (1971/1972), are important analytical essays, complemented by Tsuruta's "Akutagawa's 'In a Grove,'" in *Essays in Japanese Literature*, 1977, edited by Katsuhiko Takeda.

William M. Zanella

EDWARD ALBEE

Born: Virginia
Date: March 12, 1928

Principal Works

PLAYS: *The Zoo Story*, pr. 1959; *The Death of Bessie Smith*, pb. 1959; *The Sandbox*, pb. 1959; *Fam and Yam*, pr. 1960; *The American Dream*, pb. 1960; *Who's Afraid of Virginia Woolf?*, pr., pb. 1962; *The Ballad of the Sad Café*, pr., pb. 1963; *Tiny Alice*, pr. 1964; *Malcolm*, pr. 1965; *A Delicate Balance*, pr. 1966; *Everything in the Garden*, pr. 1967; *Box*, pr. 1968; *Quotations from Chairman Mao Tse-tung*, pr. 1968; *All Over*, pr., pb. 1971; *Seascape*, pr., pb. 1975; *Counting the Ways*, pb. 1976; *Listening*, pr., pb. 1977; *The Lady from Dubuque*, pr. 1980; *Lolita*, pr. 1980; *The Man Who Had Three Arms*, pr., pb. 1982; *Finding the Sun*, pr. 1983; *Marriage Play*, pr. 1987.

No recent American playwright has revealed an anger as sharp and sustained as Edward Albee's; few have imposed such great emotional demands on audiences. When he is compared to such contemporary absurdist playwrights as Jack Gelber, Jack Richardson, Kenneth Brown, and Arthur Kopit, Albee is generally shown to be the most challenging and searching among them. His particular talent lies in writing plays in which human emotions alternate drastically at such breakneck speed that audiences, emotionally drained by what they experience, emerge, nevertheless, with a renewed vision of society.

Edward Franklin Albee was born somewhere in Virginia and, before he was two weeks old, was taken to Washington, D.C., where his parents gave him up for adoption to Reed and Frances Albee of Larchmont, New York. Reed Albee, part owner of Keith-Albee Theaters, was wealthy, so Edward was reared in a privileged atmosphere. One of his early pastimes was attending matinees of Broadway plays. He came into contact, too, with the theater people, who were frequent guests of his adoptive parents.

An indifferent student, Albee attended private schools. He left Trinity College after studying there for one and a half years. For the next decade he lived in Greenwich Village on the income from a small trust fund, supplementing this income with paychecks from menial jobs. While he was working as a Western Union messenger, Albee met W. H. Auden, who encouraged his writing, as had his high-school teachers a decade earlier.

At thirty, Albee reassessed his life and decided that he had to redirect it. He spent three weeks writing *The Zoo Story*, which remains one of his most celebrated plays. It is a minimalist, absurdist drama, simply set, and uses only two characters, Peter and Jerry. Jerry lures Peter into a fight and dies on Peter's knife, ironically a gift from Jerry. The language and sense of confinement the play projects are intense and deliver an impact like that of Jean-Paul Sartre's *Huis-clos* (1944; *No Exit*, 1946).

Albee carried the same minimalist effects into his best-known play, *Who's Afraid of Virginia Woolf?* A couple, George, a history professor, and his wife, Martha—named for George and Martha Washington—entertain a new faculty couple, Nick and Honey, in their living room. Martha's father is president of the college at which George teaches. Nick, whose name has been thought to suggest Nikita Khrushchev, teaches biology at the same college.

Who's Afraid of Virginia Woolf? is a long play whose inner tensions are heightened by the confinement of Albee's set, a living room in which the past (history, a humanistic outlook) is pitted against the future (biology, a scientific outlook). Martha, several years George's senior, seduces Nick but finds him impotent. George extracts secrets from Honey, Nick's slim-hipped, childless wife, while Martha takes Nick to bed.

George and Martha, childless, have invented a son, a blond boy about Nick's age whose imaginary presence pervades the play. As easily as they have created him, however, they dispatch him to serve their nefarious purposes. At the end of Act 2, a messenger arrives with a telegram announcing that the son, the "little bugger," is dead. In this play, Albee exploits Aristotle's unities to create a universal trap in which all modern humankind is caught.

Nick, the biologist, will prevail—but he is emotionless. He married Honey not out of love but because she had a hysterical pregnancy. Albee calls George and Martha's fictional child their little "bumble of joy," a term which may reflect Albee's self-image as a foundling. Nick and Honey are realists who do not have even a fictional "bumble of joy."

The Sandbox and *The American Dream*, one-act plays, have identical casts of characters modeled on Albee's adoptive parents and on his grandmother Cotter. Both plays expose an antiseptic, emotionless society that values appearances only, while the satirical *Fam and Yam* makes interesting comments on modern theater. "Fam" refers to "Famous American" writers, "Yam" to "Young American" writers.

Albee received the Pulitzer Prize in drama for both *A Delicate Balance* and *Seascape*. Also significant is *Tiny Alice*, a Faustian play with a twist. Church administrators barter lay brother Julian's soul, sacrificing Julian to Miss Alice in return for a two-billion dollar gift to the church, reminiscent of Swiss playwright Friedrich Dürrenmatt's *Der Besuch der alten Damen* (1956; *The Visit*, 1958).

Albee adapted Carson McCullers' *The Ballad of the Sad Café* (1951), James Purdy's *Malcolm* (1959), and Vladimir Nabokov's *Lolita* (1955), writing dramatic adaptations to impose upon himself an artistic discipline he believed he needed. The McCullers adaptation was his most successful of the three.

BIBLIOGRAPHICAL REFERENCES: Richard E. Amacher's *Edward Albee*, 1969, a valuable early assessment of Albee, has been updated and strengthened in the 1982 revision. Amacher also produced *Edward Albee at Home and Abroad: A Bibliography*, 1973, a collaboration with Margaret Rule, superseded by the 1986 publication of Richard Tyce's *Edward Albee: A Bibliography*. C. W. E. Bigsby's *Albee*, 1969, offers impressive interpretations and is well supplemented by *Edward Albee: Twentieth Century Views*, edited by Bigsby, 1975, which presents varied insights by other scholars. Michael E. Rutenberg's *Edward Albee: Playwright in Protest*, 1969, makes interesting inroads into understanding Albee's anger and dissonance, as does Foster Hirsch's *Who's Afraid of Edward Albee?*, 1978, which provides political interpretations of Albee's work. Anita Maria Stenz's *Edward Albee: The Poet of Loss*, 1978, provides sharp insights. Gerry McCarthy's *Edward Albee*, 1987, a short, useful introductory volume, offers photographs of scenes from Albee's plays. A diverse overview of Albee's work and its reception is *Critical Essays on Edward Albee*, edited by Philip C. Kolin and J. Madison Davis, 1986. *Edward Albee: An Interview and Essays*, edited by Julian N. Wasserman, 1983, provides a somewhat offhand interview.

R. Baird Shuman

RICHARD ALDINGTON

Born: Portsmouth, England *Died:* Sury-en-Vaux, France
Date: July 8, 1892 *Date:* July 27, 1962

PRINCIPAL WORKS

POETRY: *Images (1910-1915)*, 1915; *The Love of Myrrhine and Konallis, and Other Prose Poems*, 1917; *Images of War: A Book of Poems*, 1919; *Images of Desire*, 1919; *Exile and Other Poems*, 1923; *A Fool i' the Forest: A Phantasmagoria*, 1924; *The Eaten Heart*, 1929; *A Dream in the Luxembourg*, 1930; *The Complete Poems of Richard Aldington*, 1948.

NOVELS: *Death of a Hero*, 1929; *The Colonel's Daughter*, 1931; *Women Must Work*, 1934.

BIOGRAPHY: *Voltaire*, 1925; *The Duke: Being an Account of the Life and Achievements of Arthur Wellesley, First Duke of Wellington*, 1943; *The Strange Life of Charles Waterton, 1782-1865*, 1949; *D. H. Lawrence: Portrait of a Genius But . . .*, 1950; *Pinorman: Personal Recollections of Norman Douglas, Pino Orioli, and Charles Prentice*, 1954; *Lawrence of Arabia: A Biographical Enquiry*, 1955.

SHORT FICTION: *Roads to Glory*, 1930.

LITERARY CRITICISM: *Literary Studies and Reviews*, 1924; *French Studies and Reviews*, 1926; *Introduction to Mistral*, 1956.

TRANSLATIONS: *Fifty Romance Lyric Poems*, 1928; *Remy de Gourmont: Selections for All His Works*, 1928.

AUTOBIOGRAPHY: *Life for Life's Sake: A Book of Reminiscences*, 1941.

Richard Aldington was one of the founders of the Imagist school of poetry and one of the important "warrior" literary figures who emerged out of World War I. He was the son of a lawyer who lived in Portsmouth, England, although the family moved to Dover a few years later. Living in these small port cities gave Aldington an appreciation for the nearby countryside, and he was an avid hiker. Because he lived in Dover throughout his later youth and adolescence, Aldington and his family had ready access to France for short vacations. Aldington would always maintain a deep affection for France and would live there most of his last sixteen years, the last three near the small central French village of Sury-en-Vaux.

Aldington became a part-time sports writer after briefly attending University College; he covered a few events each week on commission and began writing short pieces and poems for the large London periodical market. Living on the fringes of the London literary world, Aldington quickly found other writers who shared his ideals and goals, especially two American poets, Ezra Pound and H. D. (Hilda Doolittle), who would introduce him to a wider literary circle. It was Pound, aided by Aldington and H. D., who founded the Imagist school of poetry. Three of Aldington's poems appeared in the November, 1912, issue of *Poetry*, which had printed in its second issue Pound's statement of the new movement's ideals. Aldington's three poems were the first to be published under the name "Imagist." As the movement grew, it acquired its own periodical, *The Egoist*, in 1913, and Aldington became its literary editor. At this time, H. D. and Aldington were married. (They were separated in 1919 and divorced in 1938.)

In June, 1916, Aldington was accepted into the British army. The experience of fighting on the Western Front was as shocking to Aldington as it was to many others. While he wrote some excellent poetry on the war, such as those found in *Exile and Other Poems*, he is better remembered for his 1929 novel, *Death of a Hero*—like many of the war novels, a semifictional, semiautobiographical portrait of how the Great War affected a generation of men who had fought in the trenches. Although the original work was censored for giving an accurate portrayal of frontline language and life, uncensored versions have been printed since 1965. Aldington followed this work a year later with a collection of short stories about the war, *Roads to Glory.*

In many respects, Aldington reached his greatest literary fame in the early 1930's. He had produced many articles and reviews in British and French periodicals throughout the 1920's, his Imagist poetry was being revived, his current poetry was respected, and more recent works (especially *Death of a Hero*) had made him a well-known literary figure. He would continue to write until late 1957, becoming a respected member of the British literary scene—though not an author well received by the masses.

In the 1950's, Aldington's name again made literary news, this time as the author of three very controversial biographies: *D. H. Lawrence: Portrait of a Genius But . . .*, *Pinorman: Personal Recollections of Norman Douglas, Pino Orioli, and Charles Prentice*, and *Lawrence of Arabia: A Biographical Enquiry.* The first two works greatly upset many within the English literary world, as they challenged the conventional portraits of these men, all of whom had been Aldington's close friends. The biography of T. E. Lawrence, easily the best researched work Aldington ever produced, created an even greater, more widespread furor, as it knocked Lawrence of Arabia off the pedestal on which he had been put during and after World War I. Aldington was attacked by the popular press, and the literary critics in Great Britain and the United States who had been upset with his two earlier works created a wall of silence around his last works.

Aldington, however, remained a well-respected writer in other European countries. The French honored him with the Prix de Gratitude Mistralienne for his 1956 study on the Provençal poet Frédéric Mistral, and he died in 1962 after having completed a three-week tour of the Soviet Union at the invitation of the Soviet Writers' Union.

Richard Aldington was an important British literary figure in the first half of the twentieth century, although he was rarely considered to be in the first rank of writers or poets. The value of his work has become better recognized by literary scholars and cultural historians as the final literary battles he fought recede further from current events and enter the realm of scholarship.

BIBLIOGRAPHICAL REFERENCES: Richard Eugene Smith's *Richard Aldington*, 1977, is easily the most readily available source on Aldington's life and works. *Imagism: A Chapter for the History of Modern Poetry*, by Stanley K. Coffman, 1951, remains a standard starting point for the understanding of the place Imagism had in the first half of the twentieth century, along with J. B. Harmer, *Victory in Limbo: Imagism, 1908-1917*, 1975. For discussions of the place of Aldington's war poetry and fiction, see the standard works on the literature of World War I: *Heroes' Twilight: A Study of Literature of the Great War*, 1965, by Bernard Bergonzi; *The Great War and Modern Memory*, 1975, by Paul Fussell; and Robert Wohl's *The Generation of 1914*, 1979; as well as Norman T. Gates, "Images of War and *Death of a Hero*: Aldington's Twice Used Images," *Modern British Literature*, IV (1979), 120-127. Many of Aldington's letters and manuscripts are at the Southern University of Illinois at Carbondale and are listed by Norman T. Gates in "The Richard Aldington Collection at Morris Library," *ICarbS*, III, 61-68. H. D. wrote an autobiographical novel, *Bid Me to Live*, 1960, giving her side of their marriage and the breakup. A better account can be found in Vincent Quinn's biography *Hilda Doolittle (H. D.)*, 1967. Two other autobiographical works which should be consulted would be that of Aldington's best friend, John Cournos, *Autobiography*, 1935, and of Aldington's lover in the 1930's, Bridget Patmore, *My Friends When Young: The Memoirs of Bridget Patmore*, 1968.

Terrance L. Lewis

BRIAN W. ALDISS

Born: East Dereham, Norfolk, England
Date: August 18, 1925

Principal Works

NOVELS: *The Brightfount Diaries*, 1955; *Non-Stop*, 1958 (revised as *Starship*, 1959); *Equator*, 1958 (also known as *Vanguard from Alpha*); *Bow Down to Nul*, 1960 (also known as *The Interpreter*); *The Male Response*, 1961; *The Primal Urge*, 1961; *Hothouse*, 1962 (also known as *Long Afternoon of Earth*); *The Airs of Earth*, 1963 (revised as *Starswarm*, 1964); *The Dark Light Years*, 1964; *Greybeard*, 1964; *Earthworks*, 1965; *An Age*, 1967 (also known as *Cryptozoic!*); *Report on Probability A*, 1968; *Bearfoot in the Head: A European Fantasia*, 1969; *The Hand-Reared Boy*, 1970; *A Soldier Erect*, 1971; *Frankenstein Unbound*, 1973; *The Eighty-Minute Hour*, 1974; *The Malacia Tapestry*, 1976; *Brothers of the Head, and Where the Lines Converge*, 1977; *A Rude Awakening*, 1978; *Enemies of the System*, 1978; *Life in the West*, 1980; *Moreau's Other Island*, 1980 (also known as *An Island Called Moreau*); *Helliconia Spring*, 1982; *Helliconia Summer*, 1983; *Hothouse*, 1984; *Helliconia Winter*, 1985; *The Year Before Yesterday: A Novel in Three Acts*, 1987, *Ruins*, 1988; *Forgotten Life*, 1988.

SHORT FICTION: *Space, Time, and Nathaniel: Presciences*, 1957; *The Canopy of Time*, 1959 (revised as *Galaxies like Grains of Sand*, 1960); *No Time Like Tomorrow*, 1959; *The Airs of Earth*, 1963; *Best Science-Fiction of Brian W. Aldiss*, 1965 (also known as *Who Can Replace a Man?*); *The Saliva Tree and Other Strange Growths*, 1966; *Intangibles Inc. and Other Stories*, 1969 (revised as *Neanderthal Planet*, 1969); *The Moment of Eclipse*, 1970; *The Book of Brian Aldiss*, 1972 (also known as *Comic Inferno*); *Excommunication*, 1975; *Last Orders and Other Stories*, 1977; *New Arrivals, Old Encounters: Twelve Stories*, 1979; *Foreign Bodies*, 1981; *Seasons in Flight*, 1984; *New Arrivals, Old Encounters: Twelve Stories*, 1986.

NONFICTION: *Cities and Stones: A Traveller's Yugoslavia*, 1966; *The Shape of Further Things: Speculations on Change*, 1970; *The Billion Year Spree: A History of Science Fiction*, 1973; *Science Fiction Art*, 1975; *Science Fiction as Science Fiction*, 1978; *This World and Nearer Ones: Essays Exploring the Familiar*, 1979; *Science Fiction Quiz*, 1983; *The Pale Shadow of Science*, 1985; *The Trillion Year Spree*, 1986 (with David Wingrove).

POETRY: *Pile: Petals from St. Klaed's Computer*, 1979; *Farewell to a Child*, 1982.

PLAY: *Distant Encounters*, pb. 1978.

Although most readers will recognize the British writer Brian W. Aldiss as the creator of popular mainstream science fiction, his list of work encompasses many more interests. His chief concern is with the exploration of human nature, either as he observes it around him or as he extrapolates what it would or should be in an imagined fictive place and time. In addition, he has produced volumes of travel literature, short stories, autobiography, and art and literary criticism. No matter the form or genre, Aldiss is intent on examining what makes people tick.

Aldiss was born in 1925 to Stanley and Elizabeth May Wilson Aldiss. He spent his early childhood in East Dereham, England, and was sent away to boarding school at the age of eight. His father later moved the family to Gorleston-on-Sea in Norfolk, where, Aldiss observes, he first made an acquaintance with American pulp magazines and science fiction. After leaving school in 1943, Aldiss joined the British army and was stationed in the Far East, an experience which he believes had a lasting impact on his life and writing, most especially in his use of lush tropical settings and in his exploration of the themes of isolation and exile.

Aldiss returned home from the war in 1947 and went to work as an assistant in an Oxford bookshop, submitting his first piece of fiction to John W. Campbell's *Astounding Science*

Fiction and beginning work on a still-unpublished novel. His first piece of published writing ran serially for two years as "The Brightfount Diaries" in the magazine *Bookseller* under the pseudonym Peter Pica. In 1955, Faber and Faber published the collected pieces as a novel under Aldiss' name. In 1957 Aldiss went to work as literary editor for the *Oxford Mail*. He also published short stories and worked on *Non-Stop*, which appeared in 1958. This novel, like many that followed, explores the issue of isolation; it tells the story of a failed interstellar mission whose vessel circles Earth.

One feature of Aldiss' science fiction and fantasy that makes it unlike the work of many other, more confirmed writers in the genre is that he places much emphasis on the nature of human feeling and relationships. Aldiss explores these issues in such science fiction and fantasy novels as *The Dark Light Years*, a book that examines the implications of humans' first encounter with aliens; *Moreau's Other Island*, which continues H. G. Wells's *The Island of Doctor Moreau* (1896) assuming that the work on the island continued in an effort to find a creature that would be able to survive World War III; and *The Malacia Tapestry*, a sword-and-sorcery tale of a world caught up in the battle between good and evil magicians.

Besides writing science fiction and fantasy, however, Aldiss is equally at home in novels of the everyday. Much of his mainstream fiction deals with sexuality, often exploring individual preferences from a comic perspective. Two of his early novels, *The Male Response* and *The Primal Urge*, fall into this category. More important is his series chronicling the sexual exploits and maturation of Horatio Stubbs: *The Hand-Reared Boy*, which traces the hero's adolescent adventure, and its sequels, *A Soldier Erect* and *A Rude Awakening*. Because of the relatively conservative temper of the time during which these books were written, Aldiss initially encountered some difficulties in getting a publisher to accept them. The latter two books were favorably received and became best-sellers, despite their blatant treatment of their protagonist's sexual fantasies and adventures. Aldiss' mainstream novels often rely on his own life experiences for their themes, as in the case of *Forgotten Life*, which portrays the lives of two brothers, Clement and Joseph Winter, whose combined careers closely parallel Aldiss' own.

In addition to his novels of real and otherworldly adventures, Aldiss has produced many volumes of short stories that take up the same issues as his longer fiction, including what many critics believe to be his best, *The Moment of Eclipse*, which won for Aldiss the British Science Fiction Association Award. In this volume Aldiss takes his themes and inspiration from such authors as Thomas Hardy and Edgar Allan Poe and from the painter Antoine Watteau.

Aldiss has also written a history of science fiction literature, originally published as *The Billion Year Spree*, updated with coauthor David Wingrove as *The Trillion Year Spree*. This study provides readers with an entertaining and informative chronicle of the genre Aldiss knows best and gives thorough and useful background for those interested in learning about the roots of contemporary science fiction. Finally, Aldiss has published poetry, travel literature, essays, and has served as the editor for collections of science fiction and fantasy short stories.

Brian Aldiss continues to explore new territory and to do so in a variety of genres and styles. His prodigious and varied output offers readers the opportunity to enjoy his capable storytelling without feeling as though they are simply covering familiar territory one more time. Aldiss is also a thought-provoking writer because he crosses generic boundaries, something that is most unusual for writers of standard science-fiction fare.

BIBLIOGRAPHICAL REFERENCES: See Margaret Aldiss, *The Work of Brian W. Aldiss: An Annotated Bibliography and Guide*, 1988; Brian Griffin and David Wingrove, *Apertures: A Study of the Writings of Brian Aldiss*, 1984; Fredric Jameson, "Generic Discontinuities in Science Fiction: Brian Aldiss' *Starship*," *Science-Fiction Studies*, I (1973), 57-68; Richard Mathews, *Aldiss Unbound: The Science Fiction of Brian W. Aldiss*, 1977; and the interview by Charles

Platt in *Who Writes Science Fiction?*, 1980 (republished in the United States as *Dream Makers: The Uncommon People Who Write Science Fiction*, 1980).

Melissa E. Barth

CIRO ALEGRÍA

Born: Sartimbamba, Peru
Date: November 4, 1909

Died: Chaclacayo, Peru
Date: February 17, 1967

PRINCIPAL WORKS

NOVELS: *La serpiente de oro*, 1935 (*The Golden Serpent*, 1943); *Los perros hambrientos*, 1938; *El mundo es ancho y ajeno*, 1941 (*Broad and Alien Is The World*, 1941); *Siempre hay caminos*, 1969; *Lázaro*, 1973; *El dilema de Krause: Penitenciaria de Lima*, 1979.

SHORT FICTION: *Duelo de caballeros*, 1963; *La ofrenda de piedra*, 1969; *Sueño y verdad de América*, 1969; *Siete cuentos quirománticos*, 1978.

NONFICTION: *Gabriela Mistral intima*, 1969; *La revolución cubana: Un testimonio personal*, 1973; *Mucha suerte con harto palo: Memorias*, 1976.

Ciro Alegría, the internationally prominent Peruvian novelist, short-story writer, journalist, and teacher, was born on November 4, 1909, at Hacienda Quilca, his maternal grandfather's estate near Sartimbamba in northern Peru. He was the eldest of the five children of José and Maria Herminia Bazán Alegría. At age seven, he made the long journey to Trujillo to live with his paternal grandmother and attend school at the Colegio Nacional de San Juan, where his teacher was the renowned poet César Vallejo. Alegría contracted malaria and returned to the mountains to recuperate, completing his primary education in the Andean town of Cajabamba. He spent the year of 1923 on his paternal grandfather's estate, Marcabal Grande, before returning to Trujillo for high school. He said later that this yearlong adventure of living and laboring with Indian and mestizo workers was crucial to his later identification with the country dwellers of Peru and with the plants and animals central to their lives.

During his high school years in Trujillo, Alegría wrote stories and poems, and he began to take great interest in political reform movements. He was particularly convinced by the ideas of José Carlos Mariátegui, who advocated major changes which would improve the condition of Indians. Alegría became interested in journalism, began to edit the student newspaper, and started to publish articles in the newspaper *El Norte*. In 1930, he enrolled in the National University of Trujillo and helped to found the American Popular Revolutionary Alliance (APRA) political party. In 1931, Alegría and others were jailed and tortured for their participation in what was deemed a subversive movement. When an APRA-sponsored uprising took control of Trujillo in 1932, Alegría was freed; when the government regained power, he fled and was imprisoned in a Lima penitentiary until freed by an amnesty in 1933.

Jailed again for conspiracy in 1934, Alegría was deported to Chile. In Santiago, he married Rosalia Amézquita, with whom he subsequently had two sons. He won the prestigious Nascimiento publishing house prize for *The Golden Serpent*, a novel about the adventures of the boatmen of Calemar, in an Andean jungle valley, who ferry people and livestock across the treacherous Marañon River. Descriptions of the powerful Marañon unify a series of episodes which involve boatmen, farmers, fishermen, and occasional outsiders such as a young engineer from Lima who dreams of exploiting the mineral wealth of the remote region. Rural rhythms of life and death are described lyrically, and men are seen as heroic in their struggle for existence.

Alegría was hospitalized for tuberculosis between 1936 and 1938. His second novel, *Los perros hambrientos* (starving dogs), was published in 1938. It describes the life of Indian and mestizo inhabitants of the northern Andean area, recounted by an omniscient narrator who is a foreigner to the life he describes and thus explains it as he tells of the ravages of a terrible drought. As in *The Golden Serpent*, the world described is one in which men live in very close relationship with an often-hostile natural world. Men suffer from a harsh physical environment and also from social injustices: The farmers do not own their land, and they are exploited by landlords and by the state. The dogs of the title are the companions of the oppressed peasants and share in their hardships and occasional joys and triumphs. Despite the horrors of drought and the suffering it brings, traditional rural ways of life are celebrated.

In 1940, thanks to the financial support of a circle of Chilean friends, Alegría was able to complete a third novel, *Broad and Alien Is the World*, which was published in 1941 in both Spanish and English. In *Broad and Alien Is the World*, Indian peasants are involved not only in a struggle with nature, as in Alegría's two previous novels, but also in resistance to the landowning oligarchy and the legal and political structures which reinforce economic power. The traditional Indian way of life and its values are depicted sympathetically as Alegría describes the remote community of Rumi.

Alegría soon moved to the United States. He held many jobs, translated screenplays for Metro-Goldwyn-Mayer, wrote and edited for various publications, and lectured at Columbia University in New York. His interest in political reform and in human rights was sustained, and he published many articles on these subjects, although he resigned from the APRA party in 1948. Divorced from Rosalia Amézquita in 1947, he was married to Ligia Marchand in Puerto Rico in 1948. He worked on several novels, and in 1949 he began to teach classes at the University of Puerto Rico. He continued to work on a quartet of novels, only one of which was ever finished: *Siempre hay caminos* (there are always ways); which was published posthumously.

After serving as editor of the magazine *Presente* in 1952, Alegría moved in 1953 to Havana, Cuba, where he wrote for various magazines and worked on the novel *Lázaro*, the incomplete text of which was published after his death. Alegría and Ligia Marchand were separated. He taught at the Cuban Universidad de Oriente, and in 1957, was married to a Cuban poet, Dora Varona. After twenty-three years of exile, Alegría was invited to return to Peru to participate in the Third Festival of the Peruvian Book; he spent three months in Peru, lecturing at the University of San Marcos and traveling to various cities, including Trujillo. Back in Cuba, he witnessed many of the events of Fidel Castro's revolution; Alegría's account would later be published as *La revolución cubana: un testimonio personal* (the Cuban revolution, a personal testimony).

In 1960, Alegría and his family returned to Lima. He was elected a member of the Academia Peruana de la Lengua. In 1961, he joined Fernando Belaunde Terry's Popular Action party and ran for the senate unsuccessfully in the 1962 elections. In 1963, Alegría was elected a National Deputy and resumed active political life serving in the Chamber of Deputies. His collection of short stories *Duelo de caballeros* (duel of gentlemen) was published in 1963 and gathers together many tales that had been published previously in English translation or in small magazines. Set in remote Andean areas, these stories tell of Indian culture and resourcefulness, and of a close alliance between man and nature.

Alegría participated as a writer in many international conferences, and in 1966 was elected President of the National Association of Writers and Artists. He died on February 17, 1967, of a cerebral hemorrhage. His fourth son, with Dora Varona, was born after his death. Varona began to edit and publish the many manuscripts Alegría left, and a series of volumes of novels, stories, and memoirs have appeared posthumously. Alegría is still best known for his three magnificent early novels, which speak eloquently of the Indian and mestizo people of the northern Andean area of Peru.

BIBLIOGRAPHICAL REFERENCES: Eileen Early's *Joy in Exile: Ciro Alegría's Narrative Art*, 1980, is an excellent overview and study of Alegría's major books. It is particularly useful for the English-speaking reader since she explains Alegría's background and references clearly. Other interesting studies include Earl Aldrich's chapter on Alegría and Alcides Arguedas in *The Modern Short Story in Peru*, 1966; Phyllis Rodriguez-Peralta, "Ciro Alegría: Culmination of Indigenist-Regionalism in Peru," *Journal of Spanish Studies Twentieth Century*, VII, no. 3 (1979), 337-352; Francis T. McGourn, "The priest in *El mundo es ancho y ajeno*," *Romance Notes*, IX (1968), 224-233; and Lewis Taylor, "Literature as History: Ciro Alegría's

View of Rural Society in the Northern Peruvian Andes," *Ibero-Amerikanisches Archiv*, X (1984), 349-378. James Higgins provides a very lucid summary of Alegría's novels in *A History of Peruvian Literature*, 1987. For an extensive bibliography, see the chapter on Alegría in David W. Foster, *Peruvian Literature*, 1981.

Mary G. Berg

SHOLOM ALEICHEM
Solomon Rabinowitz

Born: Pereyaslav, Russia
Date: March 2, 1859

Died: Bronx, New York
Date: May 13, 1916

PRINCIPAL WORKS

SHORT FICTION: *Tevye der Milkhiker*, 1894-1914 (*Tevye's Daughters*, 1949); *Ayznban Geshikhtes*, 1911; *Yiddishe Kinder*, 1911 (*Jewish Children*, 1920); *Monologn*, 1935; *Inside Kasrilevka*, 1948; *The Adventures of Menachem-Mendl*, 1969; *The Best of Sholom Aleichem*, 1979.

NOVELS: *Natasha*, 1884; *Die Velt Rayze*, 1886-1887; *Sender Blank*, 1888; *Stempenyu*, 1889 (English translation, 1913); *Yosele Solovey*, 1890; *Der Mabl*, 1907; *Blondzhende Stern*, 1909-1911 (*Wandering Star*, 1952); *Marienbad*, 1911.

PLAYS: *A Doktor*, pr. 1887 (*She Must Marry a Doctor*, 1916); *Yakenhoz*, pr. 1894; *Mazel Tov*, pr. 1904; *Tsuzeyt un Tsushpreyt*, pr. 1905; *Samuel Pasternak*, pr. 1907; *Stempenyu*, pr. 1907; *Die Goldgrebber*, pr. 1908; *Agenten*, pb. 1908; *Az Got Vil, Shist a Bezem*, pb. 1908; *Konig Pic*, pb. 1910; *Shver Tzu Zeyn a Yid*, pb. 1912; *Dos Groyse Gevins*, pb. 1915; *Menshen*, pb. 1919; *Der Get*, pr. 1924; *The World of Sholom Aleichem*, pb. 1953; *Fiddler on the Roof*, pr. 1964.

AUTOBIOGRAPHY: *Funem Yarid*, 1940 (*The Great Fair: Scenes from My Childhood*, 1955).

One of the founders of modern Yiddish literature and the most widely read Yiddish author, Sholom Aleichem was a humorist of the first order. Born Solomon Rabinowitz, he spent much of his youth in the village of Voronko, which would serve as the model of Kasrilevke, the quintessential Jewish shtetl (hamlet) about which he wrote. His father, Nochem Rabinowitz, was fairly wealthy; he ran the general store, supplied beets to sugar refineries, and operated the local post office. A devout Jew, he nevertheless wanted his son to receive a good secular education as well as a religious one.

When the boy was twelve, his father lost most of his money, and the Rabinowitz family was forced to move back to Pereyaslav, where Sholom Aleichem had been born. Despite this financial reverse, Nochem sent his son to the Russian County School, an unusual step for an Orthodox family; Sholom was graduated with highest honors in 1876. Already he had become a prolific writer. His first literary effort was a collection of the Yiddish curses that his stepmother rained down on him. (His mother, Chaya Ester, had died of cholera when he was thirteen, in 1872.) Inspired by the popularity of Abraham Mapu's romantic Hebrew novels, he wrote an imitation called "Bas Tzion" (the daughter of Zion), and a reading of Daniel Defoe's *Robinson Crusoe* (1719) prompted "The Jewish Robinson Crusoe."

After finishing high school with highest honors, Aleichem became a tutor to the thirteen-year-old Olga Loyev at Sofievka, near Kiev, and secretary to her father, Elimelech Loyev. When Elimelech Loyev learned of his daughter's romantic attachment to her tutor, he dismissed Aleichem, but Olga was married to him on May 12, 1883, without her father's permission. Loyev was soon reconciled to the couple and invited them to live on his estate.

After Loyev's death in 1885, Sholom Aleichem and his family moved to Kiev—the Yehupetz of the tales—where he used his inheritance to subsidize the *Yiddishe Folksbibliotek* (popular Yiddish library), an annual he edited to encourage Yiddish literature. Two volumes appeared (1889 and 1890) before he lost most of his money in the collapse of the Kiev stock market. This disaster would contribute to the creation of one of Sholom Aleichem's most enduring characters, Menachem-Mendl, the eternal speculator; it also initiated twenty years of financial hardship. Despite a prodigious literary output—the most comprehensive edition of his works runs to twenty-eight volumes and, even at that length, is incomplete—Aleichem earned a precarious living until 1909, when world Jewry celebrated his twenty-fifth anniversary as a published writer. This recognition led to editions in Polish and Russian and the return to him of profitable copyrights he had earlier sold for a pittance. Thus, in his final years he enjoyed financial security as well as great popularity: His funeral—held in New York in May, 1916—was attended by 150,000 people.

Such a tribute was well deserved, for more than anyone else of his generation Aleichem shaped the course of Yiddish literature. In his autobiography he recalls that when he was a child, people were ashamed to be seen with a Yiddish book because such a book suggested ignorance. In 1888 the Hebrew poet Y. L. Gordon expressed surprise that someone as educated as Sholom Aleichem would write in Yiddish rather than in Hebrew or Russian. For his Yiddish stories Rabinowitz adopted the pseudonym Sholom Aleichem (the common Jewish greeting meaning "peace be with you") to disguise his identity from his father, who loved Hebrew, just as Sholom Jacob Abramovich (1835-1917), who wrote under his own name in Hebrew, had assumed the mask of Mendele Mokher Sefarim ("Mendele the Bookseller") for his Yiddish pieces.

Sholom Aleichem elevated the status of Yiddish. Through the encouragement of the *Yiddishe Folksbibliotek* and, even more significantly, through his example, he turned Yiddish into a sophisticated literary language. Paradoxically, he accomplished this transformation by emphasizing the oral qualities of the language and its roots among the common folk. Claiming to be not the writer but the recorder of stories told to him by his characters Tevye or Menachem-Mendl, he captured the idiom of the Eastern European shtetls even as they were vanishing under the twin pressures of anti-Semitism and modernization.

This world of Sholom Aleichem is not without its darker side. Leyzer, the driver in *Yosele Solovey* (the nightingale), remarks, "It's a wicked world." Yet as Sholom Aleichem writes in his short story "The Lottery Ticket," "I don't like mournful pictures. My muse does not wear a black veil on her face. My muse is a poor—but cheerful one. . . ." Menachem-Mendl never is but always longs to be rich. Tevye loses his money, his daughters, his home. Yet Sholom Aleichem's characters are never defeated. When Kasrilevke burns, the villagers re-create their community on New York's Lower East Side. These stories are comic not only because of the humorous style and ironic contrast between reality and expectation but also because they end with regeneration rather than despair. Thus Sholom Aleichem captures the essence of the Jewish experience, the ability to rise from disaster and the faith in the future.

Such a vision may be condemned as sentimental, and for much of Sholom Aleichem's career it was. He was dismissed as a writer of popular stories for the masses rather than as a literary artist. More recent critics have come to appreciate his sophisticated use of the persona in the manner of Mark Twain (who called himself the American Sholom Aleichem) and his sympathetic treatment of common people.

Sholom Aleichem's works have been translated into most of the languages of Western Europe, and by 1972 more than six thousand books, articles, and reviews dealing with them had appeared. His legacy, maintained by Mordecai Spector, Abraham Reisen, Lamed Shapiro, and Joseph Opatoshu in the early 1900's, has influenced later writers as well, among them the Nobel laureates Saul Bellow and Isaac Bashevis Singer. As long as Jews care about their heritage, as long as people love to laugh—and sometimes cry—Sholom Aleichem's reputation is secure.

BIBLIOGRAPHICAL REFERENCES: Marie Waife-Goldberg wrote the first book-length biography on Aleichem, *My Father, Sholom Aleichem*, 1968. It concentrates on the author's private life rather than on the literature. Joseph and Frances Butwin, *Sholom Aleichem*, 1977, surveys the life and works, as does Sol Gittleman, *Sholom Aleichem: A Non-Critical Introduction*, 1974. Useful chapters appear in Solomon Liptzin, *The Flowering of Yiddish Literature*, 1963; his more recent *A History of Yiddish Literature*, 1972; and Charles A. Madison, *Yiddish Literature: Its Scope and Major Writers*, 1968. Dan Miron, *Sholom Aleykhem: Person, Persona, Presence*, 1972, examines the writer's use of masks; Miron's *A Traveler Disguised: A Study in the Rise of Modern Yiddish Fiction in the Nineteenth Century*, 1973, discusses the role Mendele Mokher Sefarim and Sholom Aleichem played in the flowering of Yiddish literature in the late 1800's. Among the more important articles on Sholom Aleichem are Alfred Kazin's introduction to the Modern Library edition of the *Selected Stories of Sholom Aleichem*, 1954; J. Niger, "The Gift of Sholom Aleichem," *Commentary*, II (August, 1946), 116-123; Shmuel Niger, "The Humor of Sholom Aleichem," in *Voices from the Yiddish: Essays, Memoirs, Diaries*, 1972, edited by Irving Howe and Eliezer Greenberg; Irving Howe, "Sholom Aleichem: Voice of Our Past," in his *A World More Attractive: A View of Modern Literature and Politics*, 1963; and A. Makdonyi, "Sholom Aleichem as a Dramatic Writer," in *Sholom Aleichem Panorama*, 1948, edited by Melech W. Grafstein.

Joseph Rosenblum

YUZ ALESHKOVSKY

Born: Krasnoyarsk, Soviet Union
Date: September 21, 1929

PRINCIPAL WORKS

NOVELS: *Dva bileta na elektrichku*, 1963; *Kysh, dva portfelya, i tselaya nedelya*, 1970; *Kysh i ya v Krymu*, 1973; *Nikolai Nikolaevich*, 1980; *Maskirovka*, 1980 (also known as *Kamufliazh*); *Kenguru*, 1981 (*Kangaroo*, 1986); *Ruka*, 1980 (*The Hand*, 1989); *Sinen kii skromnyi platochek*, 1982; *Kniga poslednykh slov*, 1982; *Karusel*, 1983; *Smert v Moskve*, 1984; *Bloshinoe tango*, 1986.

Since his emigration from the Soviet Union to the United States in 1979 and the publication of his works by American and French publishers (beginning with Ardis' publication of *Nikolai Nikolaevich* in 1980), Yuz Aleshkovsky has become a leading writer among the Russian émigrés. In the Soviet Union, his best-known works are the anti-Stalinist songs he wrote when he was in prison in the early 1950's. These songs have entered into Soviet popular culture and are known by heart by millions of Soviet citizens. Until the spring of 1989, however, when *Novy mir* published a collection of these songs under Aleshkovsky's name, the Soviet public thought of them as anonymous folk songs. The children's stories and novels which Aleshkovsky published while a member of the Writers' Union in the 1960's and 1970's are also quite well known to the general reading public in the Soviet Union. His adult novels, none of which has been published in the Soviet Union, have earned for him both fame and notoriety among the Soviet educated elite. These novels are noted for their comic, earthy, obscene style of narration and their fantastic, picaresque plots in which a roguish hero/narrator tells how he has used his underworld skills to survive the Stalin years, from the late 1920's to the 1950's. As yet, these novels have not been deemed publishable by the Soviet censorship, because of both their obscene style and the biting political satire which they direct against the Soviet state.

Although he was born into an educated Moscow family in which it would be normal to pursue a higher education, young Aleshkovsky rebelled against the conventions he would have had to follow if he had pursued such a course. He left high school in Moscow at the end of World War II after throwing a brick through the school director's window. After working at various factory jobs in the late 1940's, he was drafted into the navy. Yet again, in 1950, he rebelled against the authorities and was sentenced to prison for insubordination (charges included stealing his commanding officer's car). Released from prison a year early during the general amnestying of prisoners after Joseph Stalin's death in 1953, Aleshkovsky became a truck driver and began writing stories for children, publishing his first story in 1955. He became a professional writer and member of the Writers' Union in 1963, writing stories for children and scripts for television and films during the 1960's and 1970's.

At the end of the 1970's, Aleshkovsky collaborated with a number of other Moscow writers to arrange the samizdat publication of *Metropol*, a collection of prose and poetry which had not been approved by the censorship. Soon after the authorities had attacked him for his role in samizdat, Aleshkovsky emigrated, in 1979, to the United States, settling in Middletown, Connecticut, with his wife Irina, a member of the Russian Department at Wesleyan University. He has been a prolific writer since the publication of *Nikolai Nikolaevich* in 1980.

Beginning with *Nikolai Nikolaevich*, Aleshkovsky's novels have been based on the invention of strange and surreal plots which give his picaresque protagonists plenty of room to explore the strange and surreal social realities of Stalinist Russia. In *Nikolai Nikolaevich*, the narrator is a retired pickpocket who, in order to avoid a crackdown against petty theft, takes a job as a sperm donor in a biology lab. This job places him at the center of the Lysenko affair, in which classical Darwinian genetics was discredited by Trofim Lysenko, with Stalin's support, because it did not adequately emphasize the role of environmental determinism in evolution. In *Maskirovka* (camouflage), the narrator is an alcoholic hired by the government to lead a brigade of alcoholics who walk the streets of Moscow as "camouflage" to lull foreign observers into thinking that Soviet society is degenerate and therefore not a military threat to the West. While carrying out his duties for the government, the narrator tells about the institutes and factories which the Soviet government has built secretly under the streets of Moscow and which are producing the most powerful and technologically advanced army in the world.

In *Kangaroo*, the narrator is again a common thief whom the State Security Committee (KGB) picks in 1949 as the subject of its last great show trial (following in the tradition of the public trials of elite members of the military and the Communist party under Stalin). *Kangaroo* describes the mixture of brute force and futuristic terror which the KGB brings to bear upon the narrator to make him lose touch with his simple earthy self and appear on national television with a confession of fabricated crimes against the state. The narrator's strong, physical, sexual sense of self is ultimately victorious in this struggle. Aleshkovsky would say that the positive moral goal of *Kangaroo* is to encourage his Soviet readers to affirm a similar sense of self.

The longest and most politically complex of Aleshkovsky's novels is *The Hand* (or hired killer). Its hero is a KGB agent who, as a child, watched his family being killed by Soviet secret police for resisting the collectivization of agriculture in the early 1930's. Having survived the Stalin era by himself becoming a member of the KGB and a personal bodyguard to Stalin, the narrator uses his position to avenge himself upon the twelve men who had killed his family when he was a child. *The Hand* is composed primarily of the dialogue between the main character and his present victim, the last of these twelve men, to whom he tells his life story as he prepares to torture and kill him. Ending ultimately with the narrator's suicide, *The Hand* starkly poses a complex moral-political problem for the Soviet reader: Those who have survived the Stalinist system may be implicated in it, so to repudiate it may entail some kind of self-negation.

Although the satire which Aleshkovsky directs against the Soviet Stalinist system is often violent as in *The Hand*, his books are normally charged with a loving appreciation for the simple pleasures of life: food, erotic sexuality, and the witty, playful dialogue which his narrators share with their interlocutors. The erotic principle which Aleshkovsky finds embodied in these simple pleasures is for him an absolute metaphysical principle of goodness. In this respect, his fictive heroes follow in the tradition of figures such as Fyodor Dostoevski's Dmitri Karamazov: They are earthy, humanly flawed embodiments of Divine Love. The same Dostoevskian influence can be seen in his plots: He follows Dostoevski in inventing fantastic adventure-filled plots that represent the struggle between good and evil in contemporary reality.

BIBLIOGRAPHICAL REFERENCES: Some of the best material on Aleshkovsky (including interpretations and interviews) is in Olga Matich and Michael Heim, *The Third Wave: Russian Literature in Emigration*, 1983. Edward J. Brown treats Aleshkovsky briefly at the end of his *Russian Literature Since the Revolution*, 1982. Priscilla Meyer has written about his narrative style in "Skaz in the Work of Juz Aleshkovskij," *Slavic and East European Journal*, XXVIII (Winter, 1984), 455-461.

Duffield White

NELSON ALGREN
Nelson Ahlgren Abraham

Born: Detroit, Michigan
Date: March 28, 1909

Died: Sag Harbor, New York
Date: May 9, 1981

Principal Works

NOVELS: *Somebody in Boots*, 1935; *Never Come Morning*, 1942; *The Man with the Golden Arm*, 1949; *A Walk on the Wild Side*, 1956; *The Devil's Stocking*, 1983.

POETRY: *Chicago: City on the Make*, 1951.

SHORT FICTION: *The Neon Wilderness*, 1947; *The Last Carousel*, 1973.

TRAVEL SKETCHES: *Who Lost an American?*, 1963; *Notes from a Sea Diary: Hemingway All the Way*, 1965.

ANTHOLOGY: *Nelson Algren's Own Book of Lonesome Monsters*, 1962.

Nelson Algren is one of the most important American novelists to document the lives of the dispossessed and downtrodden. He was born in Detroit, Michigan, on March 28, 1909, the last of three children of poor native Chicagoans who moved back to Chicago when Algren was three years old. Though he is primarily associated with the Division Street neighborhood of Chicago, he did leave Illinois in 1931, when he was graduated from the University of Illinois with a journalism degree. In the course of his travels throughout the Southwest, also an important setting in his fiction, he worked at several odd jobs and served time in prison before he returned to Chicago, where he renewed his studies of Division Street and began to write in earnest. *Somebody in Boots*, a Depression novel that was revised and reissued as *A Walk on the Wild Side*, appeared in 1935 and was followed in 1942 by *Never Come Morning*, a novel about a Chicago prize fighter. He also wrote some notable short stories.

After a three-year tour in the Army (1942-1945), Algren resumed his writing career and received grants from the American Academy of Arts and Letters and from the Newberry Library to work on *The Man with the Golden Arm*, which received the first National Book Award. His prose-poem, *Chicago: City on the Make*, appeared in 1951. Algren's novelistic career ended, with the exception of the unfavorably reviewed *The Devil's Stocking*, in 1956, and his remaining literary years were devoted to travel books (*Who Lost an American?* and *Notes from a Sea Diary: Hemingway All the Way*) and short stories (*The Last Carousel*). During this period (from 1956 to 1981) he also traveled widely and taught on college campuses, but when he died in Sag Harbor, New York, on May 9, 1981, he was, except to university professors and literary critics, almost unknown to the reading public.

Chicago: City on the Make, an unpopular prose-poem which juxtaposes the old and new Chicago, is Algren's most atypical work in form. In content, however, it is vintage Algren: Readers are exposed to the underside of the Windy City. *The Devil's Stocking*, a thinly veiled fictionalization of boxer Reuben "Hurricane" Carter's life, lacks the intensity and power of Algren's earlier novels but does absorb the reader in Algren's lifelong interest in boxing and in the plight of those whom Leslie Fiedler called Algren's "stumblebums" and derelicts.

Algren's fictional world is circumscribed in terms of geography (Chicago and the Southwest), character (the Depression losers hitherto ignored in American fiction), and theme (entrapment and enclosure). His male protagonists are alone, stunted emotionally (sometimes physically) by their environments, and efforts at escape are futile, usually ending in what seems inevitable death. In fact, Algren portrays his characters as animals caged in prisons, brothels, and cities that he sees as madhouses. Victims of illusory dreams of success, Algren's characters believe in the American Dream; they attempt to act meaningfully and to be "somebody," but they are not real competitors, only passive spectators of their own fates who remain "nobodies." (Frankie in *The Man with the Golden Arm* is "Private Nowhere.")

If they succeed in a battle, it is a transitory, illusory victory that is followed by a defeat and death in the war. (In *Never Come Morning*, Bruno wins his boxing match only to be arrested and executed for a crime he committed earlier.) Not only are the characters trapped by their environment, but they are also tormented by guilt, which only adds to their entrapment and almost prompts them to seek the punishment they believe they deserve. For the most part, the guilt stems from the male protagonist's treatment of a loving, enduring woman (the abandoned and gang-raped Steffi of *Never Come Morning*, the raped Terasina in *A Walk on the Wild Side*). Only in *A Walk on the Wild Side* is there atonement and possible redemption, but that "optimistic" ending follows the protagonist's mutilation.

Although Ernest Hemingway once rated him as second only to William Faulkner as an American novelist, Algren peaked commercially and critically in the 1950's (two of his novels were adapted to the screen), and he seems consigned to the stature of a dated Depression writer whose fame rests on being the first American novelist to write about life's losers. A neo-naturalist with roots in Stephen Crane and Theodore Dreiser, Algren possesses the naturalistic excesses of his literary predecessors: melodrama, romanticism, and heavy-handed animal imagery. Moreover, he has been charged with formlessness, and the fact that his few novels are episodic has led some critics to claim that his real achievement was in the short-story genre. In the 1950's, however, his vision of America appealed strongly to uncertain, alienated, and jaded postwar Americans.

BIBLIOGRAPHICAL REFERENCES: The first full-length treatment of Algren's work is Martha Heasley Cox and Wayne Chatterton, *Nelson Algren*, 1975; the book includes a biography, a bibliography, and a chronology, as well as fairly extended analyses of Algren's major work. Algren materials have been listed in Kenneth G. McCullum's *Nelson Algren: A Checklist*, 1973. Critics who have treated Algren in their books include Blanche Gelfant, *The American City Novel*, 1970; Chester E. Eisinger, *Fiction of the Forties*, 1963; and Alfred Kazin, *Conversations with Nelson Algren*, 1962, which includes biographical and critical information. George Bluestone, in "Nelson Algren," *Western Review*, XXII (Autumn, 1957), 27-44, discusses the role of love and death in Algren's fiction, which he sees as only tangentially naturalistic, and Maxwell Geisman, in "Nelson Algren: The Iron Sanctuary," *College English*, XIV (1953), 311-315, regards Algren as a realistic writer who depicts a world where human beings ironically find prison the only available sanctuary. Laurence Lipton, in "A Voyeur's View of the Wild Side: Nelson Algren and His Reviewers," *Chicago Review Anthology*, Winter, 1957, 31-41, defends Algren's works against reviewers, including Leslie Fiedler and Norman Podhoretz. A more recent study is Mary Ellen Pitt's "Algren's El: Internationalized Machine and Displaced Nature," *South Atlantic Review*, LII (1987), 61-74, which treats the railway as a symbol of entrapment in urban life.

Thomas L. Erskine

WOODY ALLEN
Allen Stewart Konigsberg

Born: Brooklyn, New York
Date: December 1, 1935

PRINCIPAL WORKS

SCREENPLAYS: *What's New, Pussycat?*, 1965; *What's Up, Tiger Lily?*, 1966 (with Frank Buxton, Louise Lasser, Len Maxwell, Mickey Rose, Julie Bennett, and Byrna Wilson); *Take the Money and Run*, 1969 (with Rose); *Bananas*, 1971 (with Rose); *Everything You Always Wanted to Known About Sex* (*but were afraid to ask)*, 1972; *Play it Again, Sam*, 1972; *Sleeper*, 1973 (with Marshall Brickman); *Love and Death*, 1975; *Annie Hall*, 1977 (with Brickman); *Interiors*, 1978; *Manhattan*, 1979 (with Brickman); *Stardust Memories*, 1980; *A Midsummer Night's Sex Comedy*, 1982; *Zelig*, 1983; *Broadway Danny Rose*, 1984; *The Purple Rose of Cairo*, 1985; *Hannah and Her Sisters*, 1986; *Radio Days*, 1987; *September*, 1987; *Another Woman*, 1988; *New York Stories*, 1989 (with Francis Coppola and Martin Scorsese).

SHORT FICTION: *Getting Even*, 1971; *Without Feathers*, 1975; *Side Effects*, 1980.

PLAYS: *Don't Drink the Water*, pb. 1966; *Play It Again, Sam*, pb. 1969; *The Floating Light Bulb*, pb. 1981.

Woody Allen is one of the most highly regarded American screenwriters and humorists. He was born Allen Stewart Konigsberg in Brooklyn, New York, on December 1, 1935, the son of Martin and Nettie Cherry Konigsberg. He grew up in the Flatbush section of Brooklyn while his father went from job to job and his mother kept the accounts in a flower shop. The young Allen spent his childhood playing baseball and basketball, listening to the radio, reading comic books, and teaching himself magic tricks and the clarinet.

When he was fifteen, Allen began sending jokes to gossip columnists Earl Wilson and Walter Winchell under the name Woody Allen, adopting his neighborhood nickname resulting from always being the one who supplied the stick for playing stickball. After his name was mentioned in Wilson's column, he was hired to write jokes attributed to a press agent's clients and later to create material for radio and television performers. After finishing high school and briefly attending New York University and the City College of New York, Allen became a full-time comedy writer for such television programs as Sid Caesar's *Your Show of Shows*.

In 1961, he quit his job with *The Garry Moore Show* to become a stand-up comedian. Allen created the distinctive comic persona of a schlemiel unlucky in love and incompetent in all areas of modern life. His work as a comedian led to an offer from producer Charles K. Feldman to write a screenplay. Allen hated the resulting bedroom farce, *What's New, Pussycat?*, so much that he decided to become a film director so that he could exert more control over his scripts. He first tested his skill as a filmmaker by taking a low-budget Japanese espionage thriller and dubbing it with outrageously incongruous English to create *What's Up, Tiger Lily?* At the same time, Allen expanded his interests to the theater with *Don't Drink the Water* and *Play It Again, Sam* and to the printed page with humorous short stories appearing in such publications as *The New Yorker.* He began his exceptionally prolific career as writer, director, and star of films with *Take the Money and Run*, and his films gradually evolved from extensions of his nightclub routines into insightful studies of male-female relations. Many of these films have been strongly autobiographical and have featured his offscreen love interests: Louise Lasser, Diane Keaton, and Mia Farrow. In 1987, Farrow gave birth to Allen's first child.

Allen's plays have represented his least significant achievement. Only *Play It Again, Sam* is noteworthy, with its hero unsuccessful with women until the spirit of Humphrey Bogart begins giving him romantic pointers. His satirical stories combine sophisticated entertainment with serious observations about love and death. "The Whore of Mensa" is a private-eye parody in which attractive young women are paid to discuss literature and philosophy with men desperate for intellectual stimulation. In "The Kugelmass Episode," an English professor is given a respite from an unsatisfying marriage by having an affair with the heroine of Gustave Flaubert's *Madame Bovary.* Allen's fiction, with its many allusions, delight in wordplay, and juxtapositions of unusual elements, is in the tradition of such American humorists as S. J. Perelman and Robert Benchley. Not mere entertainments, "The Whore of Mensa" and "The Kugelmass Episode" depict the shallowness of most romantic relations, and the latter story illustrates one of Allen's most persistent themes: People rarely get what they want out of love affairs.

The films written and directed by Allen have progressed from parody (gangster movies in *Take the Money and Run*, science fiction in *Sleeper*) to addressing serious topics. The transitional film is *Love and Death*, a spoof of nineteenth century Russian novels which compares the fragility of love with that of life itself. Allen's work evidences his obsession with death; in the Academy Award-winning *Annie Hall*, the hero is so concerned with the possibility of dying that he cannot enjoy life. Allen's character in *Hannah and Her Sisters*, in contrast, completely changes his life after learning that he is not suffering from a fatal illness. To underscore his point about embracing life, Allen has the character miraculously overcome sterility and impregnate his second wife.

Allen's attempts to emulate his cinematic hero, the great Swedish writer-director Ingmar Bergman, with studies of the angst-ridden have not met with the favor of critics or audiences. *Interiors*, *September*, and *Another Woman* have been attacked for the banality of their upper-middle-class characters and the awkwardness of their dialogue, especially in comparison with such a heartfelt seriocomedy as *Manhattan*, generally considered his finest film. Even his best films and stories have been accused of pandering to a limited audience: urban intellectuals with artistic pretensions, especially Jewish New Yorkers. His proponents claim that his works exemplify the essence of contemporary American wit, sophistication and irony blended with an understanding (for a male artist) of women and the intricacies of male-female relations surpassed only by his master, Bergman.

BIBLIOGRAPHICAL REFERENCES: Foster Hirsch, *Love, Sex, Death, and the Meaning of Life: Woody Allen's Comedy*, 1981, is a thorough study of Allen's work. Tom Shales, "Woody: The First Fifty Years," *Esquire*, CVII (April, 1987), 88-95, is an excellent summary of the strengths and weaknesses of Allen's art. Other studies include Eric Lax, *On Being Funny: Woody Allen and His Comedy*, 1976; Maurice Yacowar, *Loser Take All: The Comic Art of Woody Allen*, 1979; Diane Jacobs, *But We Need the Eggs: The Magic of Woody Allen*, 1982; Gerald McKnight, *Woody Allen: Joking Aside*, 1982; Douglas Brode, *Woody Allen: His Films and Career*, 1985; Robert Benayoun, *The Films of Woody Allen*, 1986; and Nancy Pogel, *Woody Allen*, 1987.

Michael Adams

ELECHI AMADI

Born: Aluu, Nigeria
Date: May 12, 1934

Principal Works

NOVELS: *The Concubine*, 1966; *The Great Ponds*, 1969; *The Slave*, 1978; *Estrangement*, 1985.

PLAYS: *Isiburu*, pb. 1973; *"Peppersoup" and "The Road to Ibadan,"* pb. 1977.

NONFICTION: *Sunset in Biafra: A Civil War Diary*, 1973; *Ethics in Nigerian Culture*, 1982.

Born a member of the Ikwerre tribe in Aluu, Nigeria, May 12, 1934, Elechi (Emmanuel) Amadi appears to have been inspired by the spirit which prompted Chinua Achebe to write *Things Fall Apart* (1958): the desire to show that Africa was not one long night of savagery before the coming of the Europeans. Amadi's novels, particularly *The Concubine* (the tale of one woman's effect on a village) and *The Great Ponds* (the recounting of a feud between two villages over fishing rights), are replete with anthropological detail; one learns as much about the Ikwerre from Amadi as one learns about the Ibo from Achebe. Yet whereas Achebe concerns himself with the results of the European contact on a tribal society in his first novel, Amadi sets his first two novels in rural communities that have little or no contact with the outside world. The conflicts are internal and have to do with the villagers themselves.

In a way, Amadi represents the second generation of African authors. Educated in still-colonized Nigeria, Amadi was graduated from University College of Ibadan in 1959 and became a surveyor for the colonial administration, a job that he held until Nigeria's independence in 1960. After independence, he became a science teacher and eventually headmaster of a school in Enugu, Nigeria.

In 1963, Amadi joined the Nigerian army; he rose to the rank of captain and left in 1966. He rejoined in 1968 and served with the Marine Commandos during the Biafran war. From this experience comes his diary, *Sunset in Biafra*, describing his imprisonment in Port Harcourt and his subsequent involvement in bringing order back to the war-torn country. At the end of the war, he was made government divisional officer and senior assistant secretary.

Since Amadi lived most of his adult life in independent Nigeria, it is understandable that his first two novels had nothing to do with colonization. Furthermore, the British colonizing methods had rarely been as culturally imperialist as the French, particularly in Nigeria; hence, there were still remnants of traditional cultures extant—although the overwhelming impact of the West, with its money economy and attractive material goods, ensured that these would not last long. Thus Amadi preserved what he knew of his own culture—that of the Ikwerre—in *The Concubine* and *The Great Ponds*.

During the hiatus between the publication of his first two novels and that of his next one, Amadi served as an administrative officer and produced several plays. A devout Protestant, he also wrote prayer books in Ikwerre and worked on translating the entire Protestant prayer book into his native language.

In 1978, Amadi published *The Slave*, another novel set in the African past. *Estrangement* followed in 1986; it is a portrait of the aftermath of the Biafran war seen through the eyes of four major characters. In this novel Amadi explores in depth and with sensitivity the results of a bitter civil war, particularly its effects on the basic humanity of his characters. There is little of the anthropological detail that one finds in his earlier novels; here the concern with the universal is more apparent, although it was never absent from the earlier works. The exoticism is kept to a minimum so as not to distract the reader from the very real drama and suffering of the people involved.

BIBLIOGRAPHICAL REFERENCES: For an overview of Amadi's work as seen by the author himself, one should look at "Amadi's War Diary," *West Africa*, VIII (October, 1973), 1421-1422. Good analyses of his novels can be found in Geoffrey Finch, "Tragic Design in the Novels of Elechi Amadi," *Critique*, XVII, no. 2 (1975), 5-16. Taiwo Oladele, in his *Culture and the Nigerian Novel*, 1976, compares Elechi Amadi and Onuora Nzekwu in terms of how each author deals with traditional culture. Although he deals only with Amadi's earlier work, Eustace Palmer offers a thoughtful analysis in a chapter on Amadi in his *An Introduction to the African Novel*, 1972.

Jean-Pierre Metereau

JORGE AMADO

Born: Near Ilhéus, Bahia, Brazil
Date: August 10, 1912

PRINCIPAL WORKS

NOVELS AND NOVELLAS: *O país do carnaval*, 1931; *Cacáu*, 1933; *Suor*, 1934; *Jubiabá*, 1935; *Mar morto*, 1936; *Capitães da areia*, 1937; *Terras do sem fim*, 1943 (*The Violent Land*, 1945); *São Jorge dos Ilhéus*, 1944; *Seara vermelha*, 1946; *Os subterrâneos da liberdade*, 1954 (includes *Agonia da noite*, 1961; *A luz no túnel*, 1963; *Os ásperos tempos*, 1963); *Gabriela, cravo e canela*, 1958 (*Gabriela, Clove and Cinnamon*, 1962); *Os vehlos marinheiros*, 1961, includes *A morte e a morte de Quincas Berro D'Agua* (*The Two Deaths of Quincas Wateryell*, 1965) and *A completa verdade sôbre as discutidas aventuras do Comandante Vasco Moscoso de Aragão, capitão de longo curso* (*Home Is the Sailor*, 1964); *Os pastores da noite*, 1964 (*Shepherds of the Night*, 1967); *Dona Flor e seus dois maridos*, 1966 (*Dona Flor and Her Two Husbands*, 1969); *Tenda dos milagres*, 1969 (*Tent of Miracles*, 1971); *Tereza Batista cansada de guerra*, 1972 (*Tereza Batista: Home from the Wars*, 1975); *Tieta do Agreste*, 1977 (*Tieta, the Goat Girl*, 1979); *Farda fardão, camisola de dormir*, 1979 (*Pen, Sword, Camisole*, 1985); *Tocaia Grande: A face obscura*, 1984 (*Showdown*, 1988).

BIOGRAPHY: *ABC de Castro Alves*, 1941; *O cavaleiro da esperança*, 1945.

CHILDREN'S LITERATURE: *O gato malhado e a andorinha sinhá: Uma historia de amor*, 1976 (*The Swallow and the Tomcat: A Love Story*, 1982).

PLAY: *O amor de Castro Alves*, pb. 1947 (also as *O amor do soldado*).

POETRY: *A estrada do mar*, 1938.

TRAVEL SKETCHES: *Bahia de todos os santos*, 1945; *O mundo da paz*, 1950.

Jorge Amado is Brazil's most popular novelist of the twentieth century. He was born in the municipality of Itabuna in the cacao region of southern Bahia. His father was a cacao planter who lost his first plantation in a flood in 1914 but who later managed enough success in the business to send his son to boarding schools, first in the state capital of Salvador and later in the then national capital, Rio de Janeiro. Amado was not a good student—though he liked to read and write—but he eventually managed to complete a law degree, the diploma for which he never bothered to claim. By the time he had completed his studies, in fact, he had already worked for a time as a reporter, joined a bohemian group called the Academy of Rebels, and published two novels.

In his second novel, Amado abandoned the rather pretentious intellectualism of his first work and turned to his memories of life on the cacao plantation as the basis for his fiction. In his third, he portrayed urban slum dwellers in the city of Salvador. These two locales, the lawless frontier of the cacao planters and the milieu of the lower social strata of Brazil's oldest city, are important to his canon. These were neither pretty memories of a childhood gone by nor picturesque glimpses of colorful folk, for Amado was clearly an angry young man, a fact the Brazilian government recognized several times in the 1930's by burning his books in public and sending their author to jail and even into exile. Amado returned to Brazil in 1945 at the end of the dictatorship of Getúlio Vargas. In that same year he was married to Zélia Gattai, with whom he would father two children. He was also elected to the Brazilian Congress that year, running on the ticket of the Brazilian Communist Party.

The Party operated openly and legally only for a brief period, however, and within two years Amado was again in exile, first in Paris and later in Prague, where his daughter Paloma was born. In 1951 he won the Stalin Peace Prize.

Amado's leftist sympathies were largely undisguised in the early works, which display increasing skill in evoking scene and sentiment and progressively more elaborate narrative structures. This political commitment reached its peak in the trilogy *Os subterrâneos da liberdade* (the freedom underground), a work of considerable narrative skill whose art is diluted by a preachy quality which many readers found irritating. The first volume of the work was published in 1954, when Amado returned to Brazil from his exile.

In 1958 he published *Gabriela, Clove and Cinnamon*, which many critics considered a watershed work in his canon. It was a convoluted and dramatic narrative, but it not only lacked but also outright undermined the righteous tone of some of the earlier works. It purported, in fact, to be no more than a "chronicle of a town in the interior," and its narrator appeared to be as bemused by the goings-on as many readers are likely to be. This work was the beginning of the quintessential Amado, a gifted narrative craftsman with a keen eye and a finely tuned ear who turned the minor triumphs and traumas of Brazil's lower social registers into something that might be called high comic melodrama.

Certain features of this "new" Amado were present in even the earliest works, but since 1958 Amado's novels are all essentially comic. They are also all set either in the state of Bahia or in the city of Salvador, whose magical quality Amado exploits in the manner New Orleans writers exploit the special character of their city. Bahia is not only Brazil's oldest city, it is the most African—and it is tropical. The setting means that the scene is exotic even to most Brazilians, and Amado takes full advantage of the otherness implicit in that fact to fashion stories that could have taken place only in such surroundings. Many of his later novels feature direct intervention in events by African deities.

Although the political element seemed to many to have disappeared from the later novels, the ethical bent of the later works was expressed in terms of hostility to propriety and contempt of the establishment. Earlier Amadian heroes and heroines were angry rebels and innocent victims—the later ones were rather more like gleeful subversives. In *Dona Flor and Her Two Husbands* the heroine manages to find happiness by having two husbands—one of them dead, to be sure, but one who nevertheless remains remarkably lusty after death. In *Tieta*, yet another heroine (heroines outnumber heroes in these works) uses money earned in prostitution to save the ecosystem and sagging economy of her hometown, providing lessons on life and love along the way.

After 1952 Amado lived in a charming but unpretentious house in Salvador, though he did much of his writing in the homes of friends in Brazil and Portugal, since his residence became a tourist attraction. Brazil's most prolific writer of bestsellers, he also became something of a rarity in Brazilian society in another sense: He is a writer who lives by writing alone. In 1961 he was seated in the Brazilian Academy of Letters.

Amado has been criticized as being too facile a writer, for his blatant leftism, for his fondness for amoral or even immoral acts and characters, even for being racist and sexist. Not much of this criticism stands up to close scrutiny, however, and some seems inspired solely on the grounds that anybody who sells this many books cannot be worth much as a writer. No author in Brazil offers a serious challenge to his popularity at home, and his works in translation have sold well and at times spectacularly in the forty-odd languages in which they are available. This success may indicate that a well-wrought narrative, whatever malice it may express toward political or moral convention, has appeal to a broad segment of the international reading public. No Brazilian writer of this century has done as much to give new life to the concept of the pleasure of the text, and few writers of any nationality are his rival as an original and productive fabulist.

BIBLIOGRAPHICAL REFERENCES: For a general overview of the complete works, see Jon S. Vincent, "Jorge Amado," in *Latin American Writers*, edited by Carlos A. Solé. For information on the early works in the context of Brazilian literature, see Fred P. Ellison, *Brazil's New Novel*, 1954; Ralph Edward Dimmick, "The Brazilian Literary Generation of 1930," *Hispania*, XXXIV (1951), 181-187; and Samuel Putnam, "The Brazilian Social Novel, 1935-1940," *Inter-American Quarterly*, II (1940), 5-12. A discussion of Amado and other popular writers and their reading public can be found in Jon S. Vincent, "The Brazilian Novel: Some

Paradoxes of Popularity," *Journal of Inter-American Studies and World Affairs*, XIV (1972), 183-199. See also Nancy T. Baden, "Popular Poetry in the Novels of Jorge Amado," *Journal of Latin American Lore*, II (1976), 3-22; Bobby J. Chamberlain, "The *malandro*, or Rogue Figure, in the Fiction of Jorge Amado," *Mester*, VI (1976), 7-10; Fred P. Ellison, "Social Symbols in Some Recent Brazilian Literature," *Texas Quarterly*, III (1960), 112-125; Russell G. Hamilton, "Afro-Brazilian Cults in the Novels of Jorge Amado," *Hispania*, L (1967), 242-252; Claude L. Hulet, *Brazilian Literature*, III (1975), 328-338; and Jon S. Vincent, "Jorge Amado, Jorge Desprezado," *Luso-Brazilian Review*, XV (1978), 11-17.

Jon S. Vincent

ERIC AMBLER

Born: London, England
Date: June 28, 1909

PRINCIPAL WORKS

ESPIONAGE FICTION: *The Dark Frontier*, 1936; *Background to Danger*, 1937; *Epitaph for a Spy*, 1937; *Cause for Alarm*, 1938; *A Coffin for Dimitrios*, 1939; *Journey into Fear*, 1940; *Judgment on Deltchev*, 1951; *The Schirmer Inheritance*, 1953; *State of Siege*, 1956; *Passage of Arms*, 1959; *The Light of Day*, 1962; *A Kind of Anger*, 1964; *Dirty Story*, 1967; *The Intercom Conspiracy*, 1969; *The Levanter*, 1972; *Doctor Frigo*, 1974; *The Siege of the Villa Lipp*, 1977; *The Care of Time*, 1981.

SCREENPLAYS: *The Way Ahead*, 1944 (with Peter Ustinov); *United States*, 1945; *The October Man*, 1947; *The Passionate Friends: One Woman's Story*, 1949; *Highly Dangerous*, 1950; *The Magic Box*, 1951; *Gigolo and Gigolette*, 1951; *The Card*, 1952; *Rough Shoot*, 1953; *The Cruel Sea*, 1953; *Lease of Life*, 1954; *The Purple Plain*, 1954; *Yangtse Incident*, 1957; *A Night to Remember*, 1958; *The Wreck of the Mary Deare*, 1960; *Love Hate Love*, 1970.

ESSAYS: *The Ability to Kill*, 1963.

MEMOIR: *Here Lies*, 1985.

Because Eric Ambler's earliest novels were the first realistic portrayals of international intrigue that adhered to high literary standards, he must be considered the virtual creator of the modern genre of espionage fiction. He was born in London on June 28, 1909, the son of Alfred Percy Ambler and his wife, Amy Madeline Andrews. His parents were music hall artists, and though his father later worked in advertising, his parents' enthusiasm for music and the theater profoundly affected Ambler's early development.

In 1917 he entered Colfe's Grammar School with a scholarship and later studied piano at Blackheath Conservatory. In 1926 he was awarded an engineering scholarship to Northhampton Polytechnic, which later became part of the University of London. He spent most of his two years there reading in the British Museum and attending films, plays, and law court sessions because by this time, influenced by the plays of Henrik Ibsen, he was determined to be a playwright. Ambler's recognition of the Machiavellian aspects of politics and the realities of class struggle were enhanced during the General Strike of 1926, when the London Rifle Brigade, in which he had enlisted as a Territorial, was deputized as "special constables."

In 1928 he left school to take a position as a technical trainee at the Edison Swan Electric Company, but his artistic ambition was still strong. He attempted to write a novel about his father's theatrical life, and when he abandoned this project he and a partner formed Barclay and Ambrose, a music hall comedy team for which Ambler wrote and composed songs. In 1931 he entered the publicity department of the Edison Swan company as an advertisement copywriter; a year later he set himself up as a theatrical press agent, and in 1933 he joined a large London advertising firm. Yet his primary concern throughout this period was still the theater, and he was writing unsuccessful one-act plays.

Ambler's decision to write espionage fiction was made gradually. It developed in part from his profound awareness of the irrational aspects of modern international affairs, which was deepened by his reading of Carl Jung, Friedrich Nietzsche, and Oswald Spengler and by his first encounter with Fascism during a vacation in Benito Mussolini's Italy. It also was the result of his contempt for the work of his predecessors, and his first effort, *The Dark Frontier,* was partially intended as a parody. Set in a fictitious Balkan country and concerned with the development of an atomic bomb with which the villains intended to blackmail the world, it was both prescient about the world's future and implicitly critical of the espionage stories of John Buchan, who was definitely an establishment writer, and of the Bulldog Drummond stories of "Sapper," which were virtually Fascist in their implications. Ambler, though he never participated in left-wing politics, was vaguely Socialist in sentiment, and having written his parody, he saw an opportunity to turn the espionage genre upside-down, in effect, by producing espionage stories which would present their protagonists's predicaments in the light of left-wing assumptions.

With the commercial success of his next novel, *Background to Danger*, Ambler left advertising and went to live in Paris, where he wrote his other prewar novels: *Epitaph for a Spy*, *Cause for Alarm*, *A Coffin for Dimitrios*, and *Journey into Fear.* His method was to present an innocent professional who, caught up in an intrigue, is forced to cooperate with the left-wing forces of good against Fascist villains.

In 1940 Ambler joined the Royal Artillery. In 1942 he was assigned to the British Army's film unit and in 1943 to John Huston's crew during the filming of *The Battle of San Pietro*. This experience led to a highly successful postwar career as a screenwriter, his most distinguished script being that for *The Cruel Sea*, and he spent eleven years in Hollywood. In 1968 he moved permanently to Switzerland.

Meanwhile Ambler had resumed his career as a novelist in 1951. By this time the world had changed radically from what it had been in the 1930's, when the moral issues of international politics were simplified by the menace of Fascism. Because the confusions of the Cold War had changed the espionage genre, the tone of his postwar works was often cynical, and they were usually set on the periphery of the East-West conflict—in the Middle East, the East Indies, Africa, or Central America.

The best of these works, however, set a high standard and are remarkable experiments in the field of espionage fiction. The two novels about Arthur Abdel Simpson, *The Light of Day* and *Dirty Story*, were a departure for Ambler, whose earlier protagonists had been average, reasonable people in extraordinary and often-irrational situations. Simpson is an opportunist who would seem a great scoundrel if only the people with whom he becomes embroiled were not worse, and he is a product of Ambler's belief that "most people are more odious than they think. Not wicked, just odious." Probably Ambler's most distinguished postwar novel is *The Intercom Conspiracy*, which develops the idea that between the intelligence services of the two sides in the Cold War the innocent bystander will find little choice. Finally, *The Siege of the Villa Lipp* is a remarkable experiment in which Ambler translated the methods of modern intelligence agencies into the terms of modern business practice in telling the story of the way illegally acquired funds are "laundered."

Ambler's importance in the development of the modern espionage novel cannot be exaggerated. When he began his career, espionage novels lacked respectability because of their unrealistic plotting and characterization. Ambler proved that they could treat the actual conditions of international intrigue realistically and that they could adhere to the highest formal and stylistic standards. For these reasons, and because his work is an honest reflection of the historical conditions of his time, he must be considered the first significant practitioner of the espionage genre.

BIBLIOGRAPHICAL REFERENCES: One source of information about Ambler's life is an unsigned biographical note, "Eric Ambler," *Wilson Library Bulletin*, XVII (June, 1943), 784. For Ambler's own comments on the espionage genre and on his career, see two interviews: Malcolm Oram, "Eric Ambler," *Publishers Weekly*, CCVI (September 9, 1974), 6-7, and Joel Hopkins, "Interview with Eric Ambler," *Journal of Popular Culture*, IX (Fall, 1975), 285-293. In the absence of a full-length critical study, the following works on the espionage genre are the best critical discussions: Gavin Lambert, *The Dangerous Edge*, 1976; Donald McCormick, *Who's Who in Spy Fiction*, 1977; Hugh Eames, *Sleuths, Inc.: Studies of Problem Solvers*, 1978; LeRoy L. Panek, *The Special Branch: The British Spy Novel 1890-1980*, 1981; and John G. Cawelti and Bruce A. Rosenberg, *The Spy Story*, 1987.

Robert L. Berner

KINGSLEY AMIS

Born: London, England
Date: April 16, 1922

PRINCIPAL WORKS

NOVELS: *Lucky Jim*, 1954; *That Uncertain Feeling*, 1955; *I Like It Here*, 1958; *Take a Girl Like You*, 1960; *One Fat Englishman*, 1963; *The Egyptologists*, 1965 (with Roger Conquest); *The Anti-Death League*, 1966; *I Want It Now*, 1968; *Colonel Sun*, 1968; *The Green Man*, 1969; *Girl, 20*, 1971; *The Riverside Villas Murder*, 1973; *Ending Up*, 1974; *The Crime of the Century*, 1975; *The Alteration*, 1976; *Jake's Thing*, 1978; *Russian Hide-and-Seek*, 1980; *Stanley and the Women*, 1984; *The Old Devils*, 1986; *Difficulties with Girls*, 1988.

SHORT FICTION: *My Enemy's Enemy*, 1962; *Collected Stories*, 1980.

POETRY: *A Frame of Mind*, 1953; *A Case of Samples*, 1956; *A Look Round the Estate*, 1967; *Collected Poems, 1944-1979*, 1979.

NONFICTION: *New Maps of Hell*, 1960; *What Became of Jane Austen? and Other Questions*, 1970.

MISCELLANEOUS: *The James Bond Dossier*, 1965.

A novelist, poet, critic, essayist, and short-story writer, Kingsley Amis is best known as one of England's foremost contemporary satirical novelists, comparable to Evelyn Waugh, H. G. Wells, Henry Fielding, and Samuel Butler. Kingsley Amis was born in London on April 16, 1922, the son of William Robert Amis, an office clerk, and Rosa Annie (Lucas) Amis. From his conservative, lower-middle-class Baptist parents, Amis learned the Protestant virtues of thrift, hard work, and patience. He considered himself a timid and lonely boy and did not gain confidence in himself until he began attending school, first at St. Hilda's College, then at Norbury College, where at the age of eleven he saw his first story, "The Sacred Rhino of Uganda," published in the school magazine. William Amis, to help cultivate his son's abilities, sent Amis to a top private preparatory school, the City of London School. In 1941 Amis went to the University of Oxford, but after one year he was drafted and commissioned as an officer in the Royal Corps of Signals. After three and a half years in Belgium, France, and Germany, during which time he became a lieutenant, Amis returned to St. John's College. In 1947 he earned his B.A. with first-class honors in English. He has two sons and a daughter from his marriage to Hilary Ann Bardwell, which ended in divorce in 1965. His second marriage to Elizabeth Jane Howard, a writer, also ended in divorce, in 1983. Amis was named a Commander of the Order of the British Empire in 1981.

Amis' first novel, *Lucky Jim*, not only attracted favorable attention but also identified Amis with the "Angry Young Men" movement of British working-class writers of the 1950's. The novel's satire and sardonic style impressed reviewers, and the protagonist, Jim Dixon, became a symbol of rebellion against the establishment and one of the most popular antiheroes of modern literature. Though appearing to be a young man's novel, *Lucky Jim* is an extremely humorous and socially significant book that caught the general mood of unrest in England after World War II. Amis denied any affiliation with the emergent group of angry novelists and playwrights; indeed, as his career evolved he began to shock his liberal admirers with his increasing conservatism in politics and social affairs.

The three comic novels that followed *Lucky Jim*—*That Uncertain Feeling*, *I Like It Here*, and *Take a Girl Like You*—are considered by critics as variations on the same theme of rebellious adjustment to established society, though they exhibit progressively more control and competence. Amis spent the year 1958-1959 teaching creative writing at Princeton University. Over the next five years he coedited the science-fiction anthology series *Spectrum* with Robert Conquest. In 1961 he accepted the post as the director of English studies at Peterhouse College, Cambridge. After two semesters as a visiting professor of English at

Vanderbilt University in 1967 and 1968, Amis devoted himself entirely to writing, though without immediately producing a work of popular success. Unlike his previous work, *The Anti-Death League* was part espionage thriller and part love story, its mood somber and fatalistic. By the late 1960's, Amis had alienated the liberal-cultural following of *Lucky Jim*.

In *I Want It Now*, Amis satirized the "trendy Lefty" through its hedonistic hero, a television talk show host opportunist. An admirer of the James Bond series, Amis wrote *Colonel Sun* under the pseudonym Robert Markham, but it suffered in comparison to the earlier Bond books because it "humanized" the hero's macho image. Amis' subject matter varies widely, as evidenced by *The Riverside Villas Murder*, a meticulous period mystery set in the 1930's and portraying an adolescent hero. Critics charged that the book was inconsistent with his earlier work, and they could not determine whether it was a straight detective story or a parody.

Throughout the 1970's and into the 1980's, Amis wrote six more novels that the critics often compared to *Lucky Jim*. *Jake's Thing* portrays an Oxford don undergoing sex therapy to revive his flagging libido, and *Stanley and the Women* portrays a cynical, mid-level executive surrounded by women who undermine his sense of self. Critics consider both novels to be misogynistic. In *The Alteration* and *Russian Hide-and-Seek*, Amis experiments with the science-fiction subgenre of creating alternate worlds, an expression of his growing interest in historical and political fiction. For *The Alteration*, which revises history such that the Protestant Reformation never occurred, Amis won the John W. Campbell Award for science fiction.

Amis has been praised for the compassion he shows for the main characters in his two novels about the trials of growing old, *Ending Up* and *The Old Devils*. *The Old Devils*, which won for Amis the 1986 Booker Prize, Great Britain's highest honor for fiction, is a humane comedy of manners about the relationships of four semiretired couples who are dedicated to drinking as though it were a national pastime. A technical masterpiece, the novel engages the reader with its impressive prose, witty dialogue, and surprising paradoxes. As Anthony Burgess wrote in his review, "There is one old devil who is writing better than he ever did."

While Amis continued to write poetry throughout his career, he has attracted his greatest following with his humorous novels. *Lucky Jim* remains the best-known example of the neo-picaresque comic form. Though some critics find in Amis a creative self-destructiveness, his vitality and comic talent as a satirical writer remains undisputed. He thinks of himself as writing novels in the main tradition of English literature, telling believable stories in a straightforward style, using no modernist tricks. His goal has always been to portray human nature and universal truth.

BIBLIOGRAPHICAL REFERENCES: See Jack Gohn, *Kingsley Amis: A Checklist*, 1976, for the numerous reviews and articles on Amis' work. Also see Dale Salwak, *Kingsley Amis: A Reference Guide*, 1978, for a dated but still-useful bibliography on Amis. An excellent study of Amis' contribution to the mainstream moralist tradition of English literature is John McDermott's *Kingsley Amis: An English Moralist*, 1988. See also Philip Gooden, "Kingsley Amis," in *Makers of Modern Culture*, 1981, edited by Justin Wintle; M. Barber, "Art of Fiction LIX Kingsley Amis," *Authors in the News*, II (1976), 5-14; Dale Salwak, "Interview with Kingsley Amis," *Contemporary Literature*, XVI (Winter, 1975), 1-18; Arthur Waldhorn, "Kingsley Amis," *Dictionary of Literary Biography*, XV (1983), 3-13; Frank McGuinness, "Yawning Chasms," *London Magazine*, December, 1971/January, 1972, 159-162; W. Hutchings, "Kingsley Amis's Counterfeit World," *Critical Quarterly*, Summer, 1977, 71-77; Karl Miller, "The Post-Sexual Revolution," *The Times Literary Supplement*, September 22, 1978, 1043; and David Lodge, "Closing Time," *The New York Review of Books*, XXXIV (March 26, 1987), 15-17.

William S. Haney II

MAXWELL ANDERSON

Born: Atlantic, Pennsylvania
Date: December 15, 1888

Died: Stamford, Connecticut
Date: February 28, 1959

PRINCIPAL WORKS

PLAYS: *White Desert*, pr. 1923; *What Price Glory?*, pr. 1924 (with Laurence Stallings); *Outside Looking In*, pr. 1925; *First Flight*, pr. 1925 (with Stallings); *Three American Plays*, pb. 1926; *Saturday's Children*, pr., pb. 1927; *Gods of the Lightning*, pb. 1928 (with Harold Hickerson); *Gypsy*, pr. 1929; *Elizabeth the Queen*, pr., pb. 1930; *Night over Taos*, pr., pb. 1932; *Both Your Houses*, pr., pb. 1933; *Mary of Scotland*, pr., pb. 1933; *Valley Forge*, pr., pb. 1934; *Winterset*, pr. pb. 1935; *The Masque of Kings*, pb. 1936; *High Tor*, pr., pb. 1937; *Knickerbocker Holiday*, pr., pb. 1938 (lyrics; music by Kurt Weill); *Key Largo*, pr., pb. 1939; *Eleven Verse Plays, 1929-1939*, pb. 1940; *Joan of Lorraine*, pr., pb. 1946; *Anne of the Thousand Days*, pr., pb. 1948; *Lost in the Stars*, pb., pb. 1949 (lyrics; music by Weill); *Barefoot in Athens*, pr., pb. 1951; *Bad Seed*, pr. 1954; *The Day the Money Stopped*, pr., pb. 1958; *The Golden Six*, pr. 1958; *Four Verse Plays*, pb. 1959.

NOVEL: *Morning Winter and Night*, 1952.

POETRY: *You Who Have Dreams*, 1925; *Notes on a Dream*, 1971.

NONFICTION: *The Essence of Tragedy and Other Footnotes and Papers*, 1939; *Off Broadway: Essays About the Theatre*, 1947.

SCREENPLAYS: *All Quiet on the Western Front*, 1930 (with others); *Joan of Arc*, 1947 (with Andrew Solt); *The Wrong Man*, 1956.

James Maxwell Anderson is second only to Eugene O'Neill in the annals of American theater, being perhaps less original than O'Neill but more versatile and commanding in his use of language. He was born near Atlantic, Pennsylvania, on December 15, 1888, the son of Baptist lay minister William Lincoln Anderson and Charlotta Perrimela Stephenson. During the first few years of Anderson's life, the family moved frequently from parish to parish in Ohio and Pennsylvania. He started high school in 1904, but had already begun to receive an informal education through constant reading—a habit that was to stay with him throughout his life. By the time he was graduated from Jamestown High School in North Dakota in 1908, he had discovered John Keats, Percy Bysshe Shelley, William Shakespeare, and other great poets. He had also begun to write poetry, which became a lifelong avocation.

During his ensuing college days at the University of North Dakota, Anderson became increasingly involved in poetic and dramatic studies. He was a charter member of a theatrical group organized by professor Frederick H. Koch, he edited the school yearbook, and he wrote the class play in 1911. These formative experiences prepared Anderson to pursue a theatrical career and, especially, to focus on poetic drama for the modern stage.

After marriage to classmate Margaret Haskett, Anderson began a short-lived career in education as a teacher and high school principal. Graduate study in English at Stanford University, several teaching jobs, and copyediting work with two San Francisco newspapers preceded an offer from *The New Republic* to become a staff writer in New York City. There, from 1919 to 1922, Anderson published numerous poems and essays while working on the editorial staff of two newspapers. He was also cofounder and editor of *Measure*, a monthly poetry magazine that published many of the best poets of the time.

Beginning in 1923, however, Anderson turned his attention to drama. His first produced play was *White Desert*, a verse tragedy about hardship and jealousy on the North Dakota plains. Although it ran for only twelve New York performances, it showed his determination to bring verse to the American stage, as well as his concern over the viability of ideals in modern society. Anderson continued to study the failure of idealism in *What Price Glory?*, a prose play based on war stories told to him by Laurence Stallings and written during evenings at the New York Public Library. It debunked romantic views of warfare that emphasized honor and glory, stressing instead less abstract reasons for fighting, such as the need for survival and commitment to comrades. The play was a critical and financial success, thus allowing Anderson to establish himself and his family in Rockland County, New York, where he dedicated himself to writing as a full-time occupation.

Anderson's works span a remarkable range of forms and subject matter. For example, his penchant for social criticism emerged in *Saturday's Children*, *Gods of the Lightning*, and *Both Your Houses*, which won for Anderson the Pulitzer Prize in drama in 1933. These plays merged strong characters with insightful analysis of contemporary institutions and supple dramatic prose to capture the attention of his audiences. At the same time, however, Anderson was arguing in his essays for a more "exalted" theater—a dramatic experience that depended on heightened emotion and language to lift the audience above ordinary life.

Anderson's focus on language led him to write verse dramas whose flexible iambic pentameter allowed them to be popular on the New York stage. At first, he concentrated on historical tragedies, including *Elizabeth the Queen*, *Mary of Scotland*, and *Valley Forge*. Yet even in these "history" plays, he developed characters with modern sensibilities and confronted complex political realities, which had their counterparts in present-day society. Eventually, Anderson turned his attention to writing verse plays on contemporary themes—generally considered his greatest achievement. *Winterset* and *High Tor*, two plays on modern themes, each ran for more than 170 performances, and both received the Drama Critics Circle Award for dramatic excellence.

In addition to his achievement in social dramas and verse tragedy or comedy, he also wrote two distinguished musicals with composer Kurt Weill. Anderson's most notable musical drama was an adaptation of Alan Paton's novel, *Cry, the Beloved Country* (1948). The adaptation, entitled *Lost in the Stars*, ran for 250 New York performances and won for Anderson the Brotherhood Award from the National Conference of Christians and Jews; it is a sensitive treatment of the apartheid problem in South Africa.

Between 1925 and 1951 Maxwell Anderson became one of the most eminent and exciting playwrights in the United States. His original productions during that period amazed his contemporaries with their versatility and poetic power. He believed that playwrights must celebrate whatever is good and worth saving from the often-confused events of their own time. His high sense of purpose drove him to try to rise above contemporary acclaim—to write plays with the power to move audiences over the ages. According to most critical opinion, the results were impressive even when Anderson fell short of his own high standards. Anderson's moral purpose, facility with language, experimentation, and very real accomplishments across a range of dramatic forms have made him one of the preeminent American playwrights of the twentieth century.

BIBLIOGRAPHICAL REFERENCES: Bibliographies of works by and about Anderson include Martha Cox, *Maxwell Anderson Bibliography*, 1958; *A Catalogue of the Maxwell Anderson Collection at the University of Texas*, 1968, compiled by Laurence G. Avery; and *Maxwell Anderson and S. N. Behrman: A Reference Guide*, 1977, edited by William Klink. Important biographical information is in *Dramatist in America: Letters of Maxwell Anderson, 1912-1958*, 1977, edited by Laurence G. Avery, and Alfred S. Shivers, *The Life of Maxwell Anderson*, 1983. Book-length critical studies include Mabel D. Bailey, *Maxwell Anderson, the Playwright as Prophet*, 1957, and Alfred S. Shivers, *Maxwell Anderson*, 1976.

Perry D. Luckett

ROBERT ANDERSON

Born: New York, New York
Date: April 28, 1917

Principal Works

PLAYS: *Come Marching Home*, pr. 1945; *All Summer Long*, pr. 1953; *Tea and Sympathy*, pr., pb. 1953; *Silent Night, Lonely Night*, pr. 1955; *The Days Between*, pr., pb. 1965, revised 1969; *You Know I Can't Hear You When the Water's Running*, pr., pb. 1967; *I Never Sang for My Father*, pr., pb. 1968; *Solitaire/Double Solitaire*, pr. 1971; *Free and Clear*, pr. 1983.

NOVELS: *After*, 1973; *Getting Up and Going Home*, 1978.

SCREENPLAYS: *Tea and Sympathy*, 1956; *Until They Sail*, 1957; *The Nun's Story*, 1959; *The Sand Pebbles*, 1966; *I Never Sang for My Father*, 1970.

His ability to dramatize the human need for worth and understanding made Robert Woodruff Anderson one of the most popular American playwrights of the 1950's and 1960's. Like most of his characters, he came from a well-to-do family. His father, James Hewston Anderson, was an executive for the United Verde Copper Company and, later, after the 1929 stock market crash, an agent for the Northwestern Life Insurance Company. If by this man Robert Anderson was exposed to the value of competition and economic success, his mother, Myra Ester Griff, instilled in him a love of the arts and the theater.

Anderson attended good schools: a private grade school in New Rochelle, Phillips Exeter Academy in New Hampshire, and Harvard University, from which he was graduated magna cum laude in 1939. While at the university he met his future wife, Phyllis Stohl, a woman ten years his senior, who convinced him that his destiny lay in the writing of drama. He had already written more than twenty one-act and full-length dramas, few of which survive. Yet this output formed his theatrical apprenticeship.

During the war, Anderson served as an officer in the Navy, seeing duty in the South Pacific on board the cruiser *Alaska* for which he was awarded a Bronze Star. While on board ship, he wrote *Come Marching Home*, which won for him an Army-Navy prize for the best drama written by a serviceman. After the war, it was produced at several small theaters. This work and other scripts earned for him a National Theater Conference Fellowship, enabling him and Phyllis Stohl (whom he had wed in 1940) to live in New York, where he devoted himself full-time to playwriting.

Anderson earned extra money by writing radio plays, adaptations of famous American works, and by teaching playwriting. He once remarked that it was teaching that helped him learn how to become a playwright and that working on radio and television scripts made him "a professional writer." Yet it was not until 1953 that he experienced his first real success.

When *Tea and Sympathy* was produced on Broadway, the critics were almost unanimous in praising it as a significant work of theater. The public responded by giving it a run of 712 performances. The play's themes of loneliness and lack of understanding became standard in Anderson's work. In this coming-of-age drama, set in a New England boarding school, a compassionate housemother offers the young hero, who believes himself to be homosexual, salvation through sex. Such an ending might seem implausible, but it works dramatically. Anderson has willingly suspended disbelief through careful plotting and skillfully crafted character development. In a milieu in which little boys are not supposed to cry, Anderson is saying that it is fine to show emotion, that being a man includes tenderness, gentleness, and consideration.

The dramatization of sexuality as a means of communication and regeneration also occurs in *Silent Night, Lonely Night*, in which Anderson further treats marital and midlife crises. His characters reflect the fears and neuroses of their times, each in his own way searching for a meaningful relationship, for someone to love. In *I Never Sang for My Father*, Anderson explores a son's relationship to his father and mother. The plot of this *Bildungsroman* is rather loosely constructed, but its characters are characteristically well drawn. The action, as in his other plays, is frankly autobiographical and presented melodramatically, while remaining universal in appeal nevertheless. The dichotomy between the typical masculine drive for success and the feminine virtues of sensitivity and compassion is again apparent and establishes the basic tension between the main character and his parents. Anderson maintains that a society in which the acquisition of status and wealth determines a person's worth is fundamentally sterile.

Although the subject matter of his plays tends to be repetitious, the structure and tone changes often, from the four comic one-acts contained in *You Know I Can't Hear You When the Water's Running* to the stylistic narrative style of *I Never Sang for My Father* to the allegorical *Solitaire/Double Solitaire*. Anderson's consistent dramatization of marital relationships, pitting an insensitive husband against a more comprehending spouse (Anderson's women appear to be natural creatures of understanding) makes his later plays seem repetitious. They also began to lose the dramatic fire of earlier works in their expository style. Few modern playwrights, however, can match Anderson's display of sympathy and sensitivity for human beings tortured by alienation and self-doubt. In presenting human emotion, he appears taken by the romantic mystique of redemption through love but offers little hope to those already suffering from a lifetime of misunderstanding.

In an emerging age of women's liberation, in which the macho image becomes an amusing stereotype, Anderson's plays might seem irrelevant. Yet critic and scholar Thomas Adler is confident that they will continue to be performed "most especially because of Anderson's humanity and compassion in portraying his distraught and lonely creatures."

BIBLIOGRAPHICAL REFERENCES: The first book-length treatment of Anderson is the fine, perceptive study by Thomas P. Adler, *Robert Anderson*, 1978. For books in which mention of Anderson and his plays appear, see Eric Bentley, *The Dramatic Event: An American Chronicle*, 1954; C. W. E. Bigsby, *Contemporary Dramatists*, 1973; John Gassner, *Theatre at the Crossroads: Plays and Playwrights of the Mid-Century American Stage*, 1960; and Walter Kerr, *How Not to Write a Play*, 1955.

Wm. Laird Kleine-Ahlbrandt

MÁRIO DE ANDRADE

Born: São Paulo, Brazil
Date: October 9, 1893

Died: São Paulo, Brazil
Date: February 25, 1945

PRINCIPAL WORKS

NOVELS: *Macunaíma, o heroi sem nenhum caracter*, 1928 (English translation, 1984); *Amar, verbo intransitivo*, 1927 (*Fräulein*, 1933).

SHORT FICTION: *Belazarte*, 1934; *Contos novos*, 1946.

POETRY: *Há una gota de sangue em cada poema*, 1917; *Paulicéia desvairada*, 1922 (*Hallucinated City*, 1968); *Losango cáqui*, 1926; *Clã do jaboti*, 1927; *Remate de males*, 1930; *Lira paulistana*, 1946; *Poesias completas*, 1955.

LITERARY CRITICISM: *A escrava que não é Isaura*, 1925; *Aspectos da literatura Brasileira*, 1943; *O empalhador de passarinho*, 1944.

MISCELLANEOUS: *Ensaio sobre a música brasileira*, 1928; *Música, doce música*, 1933; *Danças dramáticas do Brasil*, 1959; *Aspectos da música brasileira*, 1965.

Mário Raul de Morais Andrade is regarded as the consummate writer of twentieth century Brazil for the breadth of his creative, critical, and investigatory efforts. With important organizational roles and literary production, he was at the fore of Brazilian modernism because of his spiritual leadership; he has often been called the "pope" of the movement. Andrade was born and died in Brazil's largest city, São Paulo, where he studied, worked, and founded several important cultural institutions. Andrade received a classical Catholic secondary education and took a degree in piano from the São Paulo Conservatory in 1917. The same year he published his first book of poems, which reflect on the pain and suffering of World War I. In the early 1920's, Andrade became an advocate of literary renovation; he was a principal figure in the polemical Week of Modern Art (1922), which officially launched artistic modernism in Brazil. As a collaborator in literary reviews, a creative author, and an essayist, Andrade was essential to the development of the modernist movement, which championed literary use of natural language and national cultural awareness, as well as formal innovation in the light of changes in European literatures. In 1922 he published the combative volume of poetry *Hallucinated City*, an extravagant free-verse collection that celebrated the Brazilian urban experience and mocked staid traditionalists. He formalized his arguments for change in subsequent influential essays.

In 1924, Andrade became professor of musical history at the São Paulo Conservatory, a position he maintained while pursuing literary interests. Andrade took numerous research trips around Brazil, on which he absorbed colonial heritage and explored the vast and rich systems of folk culture in the northern regions of the country. The 1927 collection of poetry *Clã do jaboti* (a tribal clan) reflects the author's characteristic preoccupation with folk traditions and nonacademic, popular language.

The author's broad ethnographic knowledge and his philosophy of "Brazilian-ness" emerge in his most important work, *Macunaíma*. First called a "story," then a "novel," and finally a "rhapsody," this unusual work of fiction is subtitled "the hero with no character." This phrase keys the author's literary concern with Brazilians' multifaceted cultural identity. In the elaboration of this pseudo-epic, Andrade draws upon the legends and myths of Amazonian natives, Afro-Brazilian folklore, and a vivid imagination. Rejecting the spirit of normative linguistic practice, the author blends all manners of speech and parodies the gap between official written Portuguese and the actual forms used by the people, educated and uneducated alike. At the same time, he brings into question the Eurocentric view which dominated New World thinking. Establishment critics were perplexed by the work when it appeared, and it remained unappreciated for many years. Today *Macunaíma* is regarded as a central contribution to Brazilian modernism and as a landmark in modern New World literature.

In the 1930's, Andrade was noted for outstanding achievements in teaching and cultural development. He sat on the commission charged with reforming the National School of Music, where he helped to organize the first congress focusing on the employment of Brazilian Portuguese in erudite vocal music. Andrade's essay on this topic is one of the many studies he published on classical, popular, and folk music. He was director of the Municipal Department of Cultural Affairs of São Paulo, where he created the first children's parks as well as the Municipal Archive of Sound Recordings, an important research source to this day. Andrade also conceived a law establishing the National Service for Historical and Artistic Patrimony, and he declared the first historical monuments in São Paulo in 1936. In the next year, he founded the Brazilian Society for Ethnography and Folklore. His pioneer research and writing have earned for him recognition as the first ethnomusicologist in Brazil. As for academic contributions, Andrade was instrumental in bringing French anthropologist Claude Lévi-Strauss to teach and do research in Brazil. Andrade taught aesthetics in 1938-1939 at the University of the Federal District, Rio de Janeiro, where he was a high-ranking official of the National Book Institute and a major force behind the development of the first encyclopedia of Brazilian affairs.

Andrade undertook further travels around Brazil in the 1940's, but he returned to reside in São Paulo, where he labored indefatigably until his sudden death. He left much research, several critical essays, and many creative pieces unpublished. The collected poems were published in 1955. The complete works (exclusive of letters and journalism) have been published in twenty volumes covering fiction, poetry, literary criticism, art history, musical history, folklore, and even medicine. Given this vast production in different disciplines, Mário de Andrade must be regarded as one of the major forces in Brazilian intellectual history. In literature, he is remembered for his fundamental contributions to technical and thematic renovation of fiction and poetry, as well as for an exemplary attitude toward national language and cultural manifestations.

BIBLIOGRAPHICAL REFERENCES: Portuguese-language criticism of Andrade's literary output is voluminous; there are translated highlights in David W. Foster and Virginia R. Foster, *Modern Latin American Literature*, Vol. 1, 1975. Translations of long studies have appreciable commentary; see Afrânio Coutinho, *An Introduction to Literature in Brazil*, 1969, and Wilson Martins, *The Modernist Idea*, 1970. Following the chapter on Andrade in John Nist, *The Modernist Movement in Brazil*, 1967, further English-language criticism has appeared; see David William Foster, "Some Formal Types in the Poetry of Mário de Andrade," *Luso Brazilian Review*, XX (December, 1965), 75-95; and Thomas R. Hart, "The Literary Criticism of Mário de Andrade," in *Essays in Literary Theory, Interpretation, and History*, 1968, edited by Peter Demetz. For discussion of the major novel and the 1969 film based on it, see Randal Johnson, "Macunaíma as Brazilian Hero: Filmic Adaptation as Ideological Radicalization," *Latin American Literary Review* VII (Fall/Winter, 1978), 38-44, and *Cinema Novo × 5: Masters of Contemporary Brazilian Film*, 1985. For an appreciation of Mário de Andrade the musicologist, see Gerard Béhague, *Music in Latin America*, 1979.

Charles A. Perrone

IVO ANDRIĆ

Born: Dolac, Yugoslavia
Date: October 10, 1892

Died: Belgrade, Yugoslavia
Date: March 13, 1975

PRINCIPAL WORKS

SHORT FICTION: *Pripovetke*, 1924, 1931, 1936; *Priča o vezirovom slonu*, 1948; *Odabrane pripovetke*, 1954, 1956; *Panorama*, 1958; *Anikina vremena*, 1967.

NOVELS: *Travnička hronika*, 1945 (*Bosnian Story*, 1958; better known as *Bosnian Chronicle*); *Na Drini ćuprija*, 1945 (*The Bridge on the Drina*, 1959); *Gospodjica*, 1945 (*The Woman from Sarajevo*, 1965); *Prokleta avlija*, 1954 (*Devil's Yard*, 1962).

POETRY: *Ex Ponto*, 1918; *Nemiri*, 1920; *Šta sanjam i šta mi se dogadja*, 1976.

NONFICTION: *Zapisi o Goji*, 1961.

MISCELLANEOUS: *Sabrana dela*, 1963.

Ivo Andrić is one of the greatest writers in modern Yugoslav literature and the only Yugoslav recipient of the Nobel Prize. He was born in Dolac, a small village near Travnik, in Bosnia, on October 10, 1892. The son of an impoverished silversmith, he spent his early childhood in Sarajevo. After his father's death he went to live in Višegrad, where he finished elementary school. Upon completing high school in Sarajevo, he studied Slavic literature and history at universities in Zagreb, Vienna, Kraców, and Graz. During World War I he was arrested by Austrian authorities as a Yugoslav nationalist, and he spent three years in confinement, almost ruining his health. In prison, Andrić wrote his first literary works, poems in prose collected in *Ex Ponto* and *Nemiri* (restlessness). Upon liberation and unification of his country, he entered diplomatic service in 1921 and served in that capacity in Rome, Bucharest, Madrid, and Geneva; his last post was in Berlin at the time of Germany's attack on Yugoslavia.

Andrić abandoned poetry in the early 1920's and started writing short stories, eventually becoming the leading short-story writer in Yugoslav literature between the two world wars. The main features of his narrative style are already discernible in his first stories, and there is relatively little change in his basic worldview or in his narrative technique during the five decades of his development. Even his early prose poems, as well as his later novels, reveal his predilection for short-story writing. He always remained a storyteller.

The setting for Ivo Andrić's fiction is most frequently Bosnia, with its numerous races, nationalities, and religions. The narrow region of Bosnia, however, widens by implication into the whole country, indeed the entire world. Although Andrić usually concentrates on the Turkish or Islamic element, he often portrays Catholic characters. The third large group, the Orthodox, remains somewhat in the background. Andrić likes to dwell in the distant past. In his treatment of minute detail he is scrupulously faithful to the historical sources, but he gives them artistic form. By making references to the legends of the past, he is trying to solve the riddles of human existence. Yet his constant journeys into the past do not signify escape from present reality, but rather a keen understanding of the unity of time and space in the history of the Bosnian people. In stories which deal with the present he is less successful in creating lasting characters or convincing narratives.

Through the stories of Andrić parade scores of crippled and mentally deranged people, people who carry deep within themselves a heavy burden of guilt. The characters in Andrić's stories display an acute sense of loneliness and have difficulties reaching an understanding with their fellow men. They seem to spend their lives in search of a lost identity. The strong individual is condemned to a futile existence. When his pent-up emotions erupt with passion or frustration, he comes to a tragic end, pulling others into the abyss. Despite such a bleak atmosphere, Andrić is not negating life. He firmly believes that there exists an unknown formula which governs the relationship between joy and sorrow. He sees life as a constant struggle between opposites in nature, especially in the human soul. In man's ability to win that struggle and extricate himself from the oppressing forces lies Andrić's solution of the riddle of life.

Andrić spent World War II in seclusion in Belgrade, writing the three major novels which would earn for him lasting fame. After the war, he occupied various important positions, including those of parliament member and head of the writers' union. In 1961 he received the Nobel Prize "for the epic force with which he has traced themes and depicted human destinies from his country's history." During the interwar years, when he wrote nothing but short stories, he honed his skills for greater achievements. Even though the short story seems to be Andrić's most natural genre, he is equally at home with the novel, mainly because he uses a similar technique of storytelling. Thus, what has been said about his stories applies to his novels as well. Two of his major novels, *Bosnian Chronicle* and *The Bridge on the Drina*, are in essence chronicles, the former covering eight years and the latter four and a half centuries.

Bosnian Story relates the experiences of the French consul in Travnik, then under Turkish administration. Rather than being a straight historical chronicle, however, the novel depicts a contrast between the West, represented by the French and Austrian consuls, and the East, represented by the Turks. The interplay of these forces, the lack of mutual understanding, and the resulting chasm between them form the backbone of the novel. In addition, the psychological penetration of the characters, especially that of the French consul Daville, yields masterly microstudies that make the novel, according to some critics, Andrić's best work.

The Bridge on the Drina is a novel of truly epic proportions. On the most superficial level, it is the story of the famous bridge at Višegrad, from its conception in the middle of the sixteenth century to the beginning of World War I. In essence, however, it is the story of generations of the people living by the bridge and of their struggles against the elements, the Turkish rulers, and one another. In all of their struggles, a desire to live in liberty, peace, and harmony is the guiding force. Since the Drina River was the dividing line between Serbia and Bosnia held by the Turks, the bridge itself became the symbol of bridging the West and the East, of permanence in the world of constant change, and of the hope in a better world.

One other novel by Andrić, *Devil's Yard* is praised by most critics. It is the story of the imprisonment in Istanbul of a young scholar from the Balkans and of his efforts to preserve his dignity against the injustice of his sentence and the cruelty of the warden personifying the quintessential tyrant. As in so many of his works, Andrić uses struggle and suffering to underscore his basic belief in the sanctity of human life. In the last years of his life, which he spent in semiretirement, Andrić was recognized as one of the most important writers in the world.

BIBLIOGRAPHICAL REFERENCES: Celia Hawkesworth's *Ivo Andrić: Bridge Between East and West*, 1984, offers an excellent introduction that is both informative and insightful. Hawkesworth is also the editor of a compendium, *Ivo Andrić: Proceedings of a Symposium Held at the School of Slavonic and East European Studies*, 1985, with several excellent studies by both Yugoslav and foreign scholars. See also Ante Kadić, "The French in *The Chronicle of Travnik*," *California Slavic Studies*, I (1960), 134-169; E. D. Goy, "The Work of Ivo Andrić," *Slavonic and East European Review*, XLI (1963), 301-326; Nicholas Moravcevich, "Ivo Andrić and the Quintessence of Time," *Slavic and East European Journal*, XVI (1972), 313-318; Vasa D. Mihailovich, "The Reception of the Works of Ivo Andrić in the English-Speaking World," *Southeastern Europe*, IX (1982), 19-25; and Želimir B. Juričić, "The Young Ivo Andrić: The Tale of Two Towns," *Serbian Studies*, II (1982), 13-32.

Vasa D. Mihailovich

JERZY ANDRZEJEWSKI

Born: Warsaw, Poland
Date: August 19, 1909

Died: Warsaw, Poland
Date: April 19, 1983

PRINCIPAL WORKS

FICTION: *Drogi nieuniknione*, 1936; *Ład serca*, 1938; *Noc*, 1945; *Popiół i diament*, 1948 (*Ashes and Diamonds*, 1962); *Wojna skuteczna*, 1953; "Złoty lis," 1954 ("The Golden Fox," 1962); *Złoty lis*, 1955; *Kryją ziemię*, 1957 (*The Inquisitors*, 1960); *Bramy raju*, 1960 (*The Gates of Paradise*, 1962); *Idzie skacząc po górach*, 1963 (*A Sitter for a Satyr*, 1965); *Apelacja*, 1968 (*The Appeal*, 1971).

Jerzy Andrzejewski was representative of the group of Polish writers that evolved in postwar Poland. Andrzejewski was born into a middle-class family in Warsaw in 1909. He started a career as a journalist but was writing fiction by the time he was thirty. His first book was a collection of short stories and was published in 1936 under the title *Drogi nieuniknione* (unavoidable roads). In 1938, he published his first novel, *Ład serca* (mode of the heart). The main character of the work is a priest, and the work showed Andrzejewski's early Catholic influence. The novel set the tone for his later work, which was to present individual characters with moral dramatic conflicts. He was given two literary honors for *Ład serca*, including the designation "best young writer" from the Polish Academy of Literature.

The advent of World War II and the invasion of Poland by Nazi Germany interrupted Andrzejewski's early writing career. He stayed in Poland during the war and recorded his experiences and those of his friends in a series of short stories: "Przed sadem" (1941; on trial), "Apel" (1942; roll call), and "Wielki tydzen" (1943; holy week). These stories were published after the war, in 1946, under the title *Noc* (the night). The stories deal with life under the Nazi Occupation, whether as an underground fighter or as an inmate at the death camp in Auschwitz. In these stories, Andrzejewski began to show a dislike for the Polish trait of romantic heroism, which encouraged people to do heroic deeds without thought to their success or failure. A deed was done for the sake of honor alone.

The end of World War II did not bring peace to Poland or Andrzejewski. With the arrival of the Soviet army in Poland, a Communist government was imposed on the country. A civil war between Communist and anti-Communist forces ravaged the country for four years. By using as a backdrop this civil war, Andrzejewski continued his criticism of romantic heroism and created his most memorable work, *Ashes and Diamonds*, first published in 1948. The central figure of the story is Mathew, a member of the underground army who has fought against the Nazis and now the Communists. He is given one final order to assassinate the local party chief. He agonizes over the order since he knows that it will accomplish nothing and all he wishes to do is go home and lead a normal life. Finally, he does carry out the order, because he feels bound by his oath as a soldier. Mathew dies a short time after the assassination when he is shot by accident by a security patrol. The story gives great insight into the Poland of 1945 and has remained a popular book in Poland to this day.

Andrzejewski, as well as other Polish intellectuals, believed that social reform was necessary in order for the people of Poland to lift themselves from their self-destructive mentality. For this reason he joined the Polish Workers' Party in 1949. He became an avid supporter of Socialist Realism and even tried to write in this form. His major attempt at Socialist Realism was the novel *Wojna skuteczna* (an effective war), which was poorly received and gave many the impression that Andrzejewski had sold his soul to the new government. Czeszław Miłosz, in his classic work *Zniewolony umyesł* (1953; *The Captive Mind*, 1953), described Andrzejewski as "Alpha the Moralist."

The year 1953 was an important year for Poland and Andrzejewski because it was the year that Joseph Stalin died and the Communist system began its long thaw. Andrzejewski had already begun to question the usefulness of Socialist Realism, the subordination of the individual for group conformity, even before the revelations about Stalin's system in 1955. In a series of short stories, published under the title *Złoty lis* (the golden fox) in 1955, the author attacked the crushing of individualism by the Socialist system. "The Golden Fox" is the story of a little boy who tries to convince adults of the existence of a fox living in his closet. The adults refuse to believe him and tell him this is impossible, that this fox could not really exist. In the end, the boy is forced to conform to the adult reality and deny the existence of the golden fox. The story is a beautiful parable on the restrictiveness of Socialist Realism. Andrzejewski was to continue his attack on Socialist literature in 1957 with his book *The Inquisitors*, which drew parallels between the Spanish Inquisition and Socialist culture under Stalinism. It was also in 1957 that Andrzejewski decided that the Communist Party was incapable of true social reform and resigned his membership.

In 1960, he published *The Gates of Paradise*, which deals with the children's crusade to the Holy Land in the Middle Ages. Rather than a historical recounting of the crusade, it is more of a self-examination of conscience by the author. In it, he questions the merits of giving oneself over to an ideal hastily. Andrzejewski had found that he had done what he had accused others of doing ever since World War II. He, too, was guilty of romantic heroism.

In the 1960's, Andrzejewski began to attract attention in the West as well as in Poland. After a long stay in Paris, he wrote a comic novel called *A Sitter for a Satyr*, a parody on Pablo Picasso's life. In the 1970's Andrzejewski became actively involved with the political opposition movement in Poland in support of workers and civil rights. He was a founding member of the Workers' Defense Committee (KOR) in 1976. He began to publish outside Poland as more of his works were censored by the government. Andrzejewski continued to write until his death from a heart attack in April of 1983.

BIBLIOGRAPHICAL REFERENCES: For critical assessments of Andrzejewski, see M. J. Krynski, "The Metamorphoses of Jerzy Andrzejewski: The Road from Belief to Skepticism," *Polish Review*, VI (1961/1962), 119-124, and J. Krzyżanowski, "On the History of *Ashes and Diamonds*," *Slavic and East European Journal*, XV (1971), 324-331. For useful background information, see Czesław Miłosz's *The History of Polish Literature*, 1983, and *The Captive Mind*, 1953. See also *An Introduction to Modern Polish Literature*, 1981, edited by Adam Gillou and Ludwik Krzyzanowski; Bolesław Klimaszewski, *Outline History of Polish Culture*, 1983; and *The Modern Polish Mind*, 1964, edited by Maria Kuncewiczowa.

David R. Stefancic

MAYA ANGELOU

Born: St. Louis, Missouri
Date: April 4, 1928

PRINCIPAL WORKS

AUTOBIOGRAPHY: *I Know Why the Caged Bird Sings*, 1970; *Gather Together in My Name*, 1974; *Singin' and Swingin' and Gettin' Merry Like Christmas*, 1976; *The Heart of a Woman*, 1981; *All God's Children Need Traveling Shoes*, 1986.

POETRY: *Just Give Me a Cool Drink of Water 'fore I Die*, 1971; *Oh Pray My Wings Are Gonna Fit Me Well*, 1975; *And Still I Rise*, 1978; *Shaker, Why Don't You Sing?*, 1983.

Maya Angelou is a twentieth century Renaissance woman. As a writer, she is best known for her autobiographies, particularly *I Know Why the Caged Bird Sings*, and her collections of poetry, but she also has gained prominence through her playwriting, directing, acting, dancing, and involvement in civil rights movements. Born on April 4, 1928, in St. Louis, Missouri, she was sent by her mother, upon the breakup of her marriage, to Stamps, Arkansas, where she lived with her paternal grandmother, Ann Henderson. These years are chronicled in the first volume of Angelou's autobiographies, and they include both typical and atypical experiences of growing up, from the time Angelou imposed silence upon herself to the time she was graduated from Lafayette Training School, aware of the racial prejudice which had prevented her from aspiring to more than an education in a vocational school.

After graduation, Angelou moved to San Francisco to live with her mother, give birth to a son, study dance and drama, and begin a career as a performer. In the 1950's she performed in nightclubs in San Francisco and New York and toured Europe and Africa as a member of a company staging the folk opera *Porgy and Bess* (pr. 1935). In the 1960's, at the request of Dr. Martin Luther King, she became the Northern Coordinator for the Southern Christian Leadership Conference. Following this experience, she lived in Ghana, where she was a reporter for the *Ghanian Times*, a writer for Radio Ghana, an editor of the *African Review*, and an assistant administrator at the University of Ghana. In 1970 she published the first, and most famous, of a series of autobiographies.

I Know Why the Caged Bird Sings takes its title from a poem by Paul Laurence Dunbar which includes the following lines: "I know why the caged bird sings, ah me/ When his wing is bruised and his bosom sore. . . ." The poet Dunbar and the autobiographer Angelou both explore the feeling of entrapment, a caged-in experience particular to the black man and woman learning to survive in the twentieth century. Angelou continued to explore these dual realities of slavery and survival in the autobiographies written after *I Know Why the Caged Bird Sings*. Between 1974 and 1986, she wrote four more memoirs—*Gather Together in My Name*, *Singing' and Swingin' and Gettin' Merry Like Christmas*, *The Heart of a Woman*, and *All God's Children Need Traveling Shoes*—and made hundreds of television appearances. In addition, she wrote for the theater, for the cinema, and for televison. In 1981 she was appointed the first Reynolds Professor of American Studies at Wake Forest University.

Angelou's writings reveal the mixture of poetry and prose and drama that characterizes her career as a writer. In addition to this mixture of genres, the works demonstrate a combination of comedy and drama, from anecdotes that reveal humorous incidents associated with childhood experiences to passages that suggest the dramatic intensity of growing up black and female in a racist, sexist South. Like the painter who mixes colors to achieve a unique hue, Angelou's mix results in a particular voice that sings of slavery and survival, of hatred and love, and of darkness and illumination.

Her most significant work, and the one which best demonstrates this unique voice, is *I Know Why the Caged Bird Sings*. Both popular and academic audiences have identified this autobiography as one of the finest of its kind, a memoir that speaks of the unique experience of Maya Angelou while at the same time offering a universal story of maturation. The other autobiographies have not been received so enthusiastically and are sometimes criticized for lacking the complexities and depth of *I Know Why the Caged Bird Sings*. The same criticism is frequently leveled against Angelou's poetry, which, while entertaining, is not always as compelling and complex as the first autobiography. Despite this mixed review of her later works, there is little question that both the quantity and quality of her work, particularly the quality of her first memoir, assure Maya Angelou a place in literary history.

BIBLIOGRAPHICAL REFERENCES: For works about Maya Angelou, the best sources are articles or chapters in books, most dealing with Angelou's first autobiography. Early essays include Sidonie Ann Smith, "The Song of a Caged Bird: Maya Angelou's Quest After Self-Acceptance," *Southern Humanities Review*, VII (1973), 365-375; George E. Kent, "Maya Angelou's *I Know Why the Caged Bird Sings* and Black Autobiographical Tradition," *Kansas Quarterly*, VII (1975), 72-78; and John T. Hiers, "Fatalism in Maya Angelou's *I Know Why the Caged Bird Sings*," *Notes on Contemporary Literature*, VI (1976), 5-7. A collection of essays edited by Mari Evans, *Black Women Writers (1950-1980): A Critical Evaluation*, 1983, includes a brief statement by Angelou about the way she writes as well as two essays and a selected bibliography. Both essays deal with Angelou as autobiographer: Selwyn R. Cudjoe, "Maya Angelou and the Autobiographical Statement," and Sondra O'Neale, "Reconstruction of the Composite Self: New Images of Black Women in Maya Angelou's Continuing Autobiography." Interviews with Maya Angelou are included in *Black Women Writers at Work*, 1983, edited by Claudia Tate, and in *The Black Scholar*, IV, no. 8 (1977), 44-53.

Marjorie Smelstor

JEAN ANOUILH

Born: Cérisole, France
Date: June 23, 1910

Died: Lausanne, Switzerland
Date: October 3, 1987

PRINCIPAL WORKS

PLAYS: *L'Hermine*, pr. 1932 (*The Ermine*, 1955); *Le Voyageur sans bagage*, pr., pb. 1937 (*Traveller Without Luggage*, 1959); *Le Bal des voleurs*, pb. 1938 (*Thieves' Carnival*, 1952); *La Sauvage*, pr., pb. 1938 (*The Restless Heart*, 1957); *Léocadia*, pr. 1940 (*Time Remembered*, 1955); *Le Rendez-vous de Senlis*, pr. 1941 (*Dinner with the Family*, 1958); *Antigone*, pr. 1944 (English translation, 1946); *L'Invitation au château*, pr. 1947 (*Ring Round the Moon*, 1950); *Ardèle*, pr. 1948 (English translation, 1951); *La Répétition: Ou, L'Amour puni*, pr., pb. 1950 (*The Rehearsal*, 1958); *Colombe*, pr. 1951 (*Mademoiselle Colombe*, 1954); *La Valse des toréadors*, pr., pb. 1952 (*Waltz of the Toreadors*, 1953); *L'Alouette*, pr., pb. 1953 (*The Lark*, 1955); *Ornifle: Ou, Le Courant d'air*, pr. 1955 (*Ornifle*, 1970); *Pauvre Bitos: Ou, Le Dîner de têtes*, pr., pb. 1956 (*Poor Bitos*, 1964); *L'Hurluberlu: Ou, Le Réactionnaire amoureux*, pr., pb. 1959 (*The Fighting Cock*, 1960); *Becket: Ou, L'Honneur de Dieu*, pr., pb. 1959 (*Becket: Or, The Honor of God*, 1962); *Le Boulanger, la boulangère et le petit mitron*, pr. 1968; *Cher Antoine: Ou, L'Amour raté*, pr., pb. 1969; *Le Directeur de l'opéra*, pr., pb. 1972 (*The Director of the Opera*, 1973); *L'Arrestation*, pr., pb. 1975; *Le Scénario*, pr., pb. 1976; *Le Nombril*, pr., pb. 1981.

Active as a dramatist for fully half a century, Jean Anouilh was arguably the best known and most performed French playwright of his generation, his work often straddling (and sometimes crossing) the traditional French boundary that separates literary from commercial theater. Pessimistic in their outlook, often dazzling in their presentation, Anouilh's plays were almost always memorable, notable for their consummate "theatricality." Initially recognized and hailed as a "serious" playwright, Anouilh went on to disappoint many of his earliest supporters by appealing to a wider, less sophisticated audience. Anouilh's work also frequently drew controversy because of the author's implied conviction that his art was somehow above politics. Notwithstanding, a number of Anouilh's plays remain in the worldwide dramatic repertory, where they are likely to remain for sometime to come.

Jean-Marie-Lucien-Pierre Anouilh was born June 23, 1910, in Cérisole, near Bordeaux, on the Atlantic coast of France. His father was a tailor, his mother a violinist of presumably modest talent who often played in hotel and casino orchestras. Notoriously secretive about his private life, the mature Anouilh once claimed cryptically that he had "no biography" and was most pleased not to have any. It is clear in any case that Anouilh was attracted to plays and playwriting from adolescence onward. Completing his secondary education in Paris, Anouilh befriended the future director Jean-Louis Barrault, a classmate at the Collège Chaptal; after a year and a half of law school, he worked briefly as a copywriter for an advertising agency, earning extra money writing jokes for motion pictures as he attempted to write plays. In 1931, he succeeded the playwright and scenarist Georges Neveux as secretary to the eminent director Louis Jouvet (1887-1951), who had fostered and developed the playwriting talents of Jean Giraudoux (1882-1944), at the time France's leading playwright and in many ways Anouilh's immediate professional ancestor. It was during his brief tenure with Jouvet that Anouilh wrote *The Ermine*, produced early in 1932 to mixed but generally favorable reviews.

A few lesser plays followed. It was *Traveller Without Luggage*, written during 1936 and performed the following spring, that first established Anouilh as a major playwriting talent. Based on part upon real news stories, drawing also upon Giraudoux's *Siegfried* (pr. 1928) and upon the Oedipus legend, *Traveller Without Luggage* emerged as an eminently playable blend of comic and tragic elements, with a number of memorable scenes. It also continued

Anouilh's presentation of themes such as the impossibility of true love or friendship and the ironic contrast between the real and the ideal in life as it apparently must be lived. Though far from original, Anouilh's characteristic themes escaped banality through the author's lightness of touch, infused by an instinctive sense of theater worthy of Molière or William Shakespeare.

With the success of *Thieves' Carnival*, followed by that of *Dinner with the Family*, two distinctly comic efforts, Anouilh proceeded to advance his own case with nontraditional classifications of his plays as they began to appear in print. In place of the traditional "tragedy" or "comedy," Anouilh's efforts were billed as "black" plays or "pink" plays, later to be augmented by "shining" and "secret" plays. Besides calling attention to the playwright's professed originality, such classifications served to underscore his deep conviction, amply expressed within the plays themselves, that such concepts as tragedy and comedy were quite unthinkable in a world increasingly devoid of meaning. Accordingly, the "black" plays contain many comic moments, and the "pink" plays, although humorous, remain haunted by the author's chronic pessimism.

Antigone, written and first performed during the Nazi occupation of Paris, brought true fame to Anouilh even as it embroiled him in extreme controversy. Like Giraudoux and many other, lesser French playwrights of the interwar and wartime years, Anouilh here used the characters and structure of Greek myth toward the expression of contemporary concerns. The third of his "black" plays, *Antigone* presents a heroine who proceeds toward her death without illusions, sheer obstinacy replacing the faith of her Greek model; Creon, meanwhile, emerges as a tough-minded pragmatist obliged by his position to put politics ahead of personal concerns. Although quite consistent with Anouilh's earlier portrayals of the conflict between the ideal and the real, *Antigone* gave rise to vigorous criticism from those who saw the play as political allegory tilted toward the Vichy government, presumably symbolized in Creon. Anouilh, meanwhile, claimed total disinterest in politics, a most difficult position to maintain under the circumstances.

In addition to provoking political controversy, *Antigone* served also to focus attention, perhaps inappropriately, upon Anouilh as a serious, thought-provoking playwright whose works might be considered alongside those of Jean-Paul Sartre (1905-1980) and Albert Camus (1913-1960), both professional intellectuals who had turned to the theater in order to express their ideas. Anouilh, who had never sought to write anything but playable theater, no doubt felt miscast in such company, and during the decade that followed World War II seems to have gone out of his way to distance himself from the "thinker-playwrights" with increasingly spectacular, at times unabashedly commercial efforts.

During the last quarter-century of his life and career, Anouilh tended to turn out episodic, quasi-autobiographical plays of the sort associated in the United States with Neil Simon, participating increasingly in the planning and execution of their production. Even amid widespread disenchantment with the course that his career had taken, Anouilh's plays continued to attract audiences and occasional favorable criticism. Among his more remarkable later efforts was *L'Arrestation* (the arrest), dealing with the "total recall" of an aging, dying gangster. The play's debut coincided with a memorable Paris revival of Anouilh's *Antigone*.

BIBLIOGRAPHICAL REFERENCES: H. G. McIntyre, *The Theatre of Jean Anouilh*, 1981, embracing nearly all of Anouilh's career, is admirable in its assessment of the author's skills and accomplishments; with regard to the later plays, McIntyre properly discerns continuity where other critics have seen only chaos. Alba Della Fazia, *Jean Anouilh*, 1969, is notable for thematic criticism and for the few bare facts then available concerning the author's life. Leonard Pronko, *The World of Jean Anouilh*, 1961, and Philip Thody, *Anouilh*, 1968, offer good background studies with useful analytical chapters. John Harvey, *Anouilh: A Study in Theatrics*, 1964, provides invaluable insights into the author's distinctly "theatrical" concept and execution, comparing him to previous masters of the stage. See also David I. Grossvogel,

Twentieth Century French Drama, 1961, and Jacques and June Guicharnaud, *Modern French Theatre*, 1967. For perceptive, even exhaustive analysis of particular efforts, John S. Beynon, *Anouilh: "L'Alouette" and "Pauvre Bitos,"* 1984, and W. D. Howarth, *Anouilh: Antigone*, 1983, are highly recommended.

David B. Parsell

MICHAEL ANTHONY

Born: Mayaro, Trinidad
Date: February 10, 1932

PRINCIPAL WORKS

NOVELS: *The Games Were Coming*, 1963; *The Year in San Fernando*, 1965; *Green Days by the River*, 1967; *Streets of Conflict*, 1976; *All That Glitters*, 1981.

SHORT FICTION: *Sandra Street and Other Stories*, 1973; *Cricket in the Road*, 1973; *The King of the Masquerade*, 1974; *Folk Tales and Fantasies*, 1976.

NONFICTION: *Glimpses of Trinidad and Tobago with a Glance at the West Indies*, 1974; *Profile Trinidad: A Historical Survey from the Discovery to 1900*, 1975.

Michael Anthony was born in 1932 in a remote, rural area of southern Trinidad called Mayaro. Later, he went to school in the second largest town in Trinidad, San Fernando, before working in an iron foundry at Pointe à Pierre. In the 1950's, Great Britain called on members of its former colonies to provide cheap labor in the mother country, and Anthony arrived there in 1955. He worked in factories and on the railways before joining Reuters, the international news service.

During this period, Anthony began publishing stories in the literary magazine *BIM*, a West Indian publication produced in Barbados. His first novel, *The Games Were Coming*, was published in 1963, but it was the second, *The Year in San Fernando*, that has received the most critical attention. Even this novel, upon its publication in 1965, had a cool reception from Caribbean critics. There were two reasons for this initial criticism. First, in a society in which education, autonomy, and a sense of cultural history are lacking, it was felt that those who produce art should protest and clearly demonstrate the need to fill these gaps. Second, as the novel is written with such apparent ingenuousness and charm, early critics failed to note the subtle intricacies of its construction. Yet these novels are positive in that they honor the culture of Trinidad and the high level of community involvement of its inhabitants.

The Year in San Fernando tells the story of one year in a young boy's life, when he leaves his tiny village to go to the city. The author himself spent such a year from 1943 to 1944, when, at the age of twelve, he stayed in San Fernando. The novel is written entirely in the first-person voice of the young boy, with absolutely no intrusion of the adult authorial voice. The reader experiences the year as the child does, impressions changing as new information accumulates. Anthony enables the reader to experience the boy's fear, his growing sense of pride at being able to function in "the big city," and the development of his relationship with the people around him. The novel is tightly constructed, taking place in one year, in one house, and with a fixed group of characters. The author draws no large conclusions. Nor does he attempt to show the change from childhood to maturity that is the staple of the *Bildungsroman*. Instead he gives voice to a usually unheard member of society, with extremely sensitive compassion. It is his ability to allow normally silent characters to speak which is the most prominent feature of Anthony's work.

Each of Anthony's books can be read and enjoyed by young adults, who can readily identify with the youthful narrators and understand the clear prose. *The King of the Masquerade*, for example, is a slim volume aimed at the young reader. The novella describes a young boy's secret participation in the annual Carnival in Trinidad, an event scorned by his professional parents. The work demonstrates the artistic and community value of this enormous event, the essentially Trinidadian nature of the spectacle, and mocks the snobbery of people who divorce themselves from their own culture.

Anthony left England in 1968, never having felt the sense of confusion experienced by many writers in exile. In 1970, after having spent two years in Brazil, where he set the novel *Streets of Conflict*, Anthony became an official of the Ministry of Youth, Sports, and Culture in Trinidad. Since this appointment, Anthony has written a number of works on the history and culture of Trinidad and Tobago, including a collection of folk stories, *Folk Tales and Fantasies*.

BIBLIOGRAPHICAL REFERENCES: For criticism that places Anthony's work in its cultural context, see Kenneth Ramchand, *The West Indian Novel and Its Background*, 1970. For further analysis, see Richard I. Smyer, "Enchantment and Violence in the Fiction of Michael Anthony," in *World Literature Written in English*, XXI (1982), 148-159. Other sources include Louis James, *The Islands in Between*, 1968; Paul Edwards and Kenneth Ramchand in their introduction to *The Year in San Fernando*, in *London Magazine*, VII (1967), 117-120; Gareth Griffiths in his introduction to *Cricket in the Road*, 1973, and Anthony's own introduction to *Cricket in the Road*, 1973. Also see Sylvia Wynter's excellent and enthusiastic reviews of *Green Days by the River* and *The Games Were Coming* in *Caribbean Studies*, CXII (1970), 111-118.

Joanne Butcher

AHARON APPELFELD

Born: Czernowitz, Romania
Date: 1932

PRINCIPAL WORKS

NOVELS: *Badenheim, 'ir nofesh*, 1975 (*Badenheim 1939*, 1980); *Tor-ha-pela'ot*, 1978 (*The Age of Wonders*, 1981); *Kutonet veha-pasim*, 1983 (*Tzili: The Story of a Life*, 1983); *Nesiga mislat*, 1984 (*The Retreat*, 1984); *To the Land of the Cattails*, 1986 (also known as *To The Land of the Reeds*); *Bartfus ben ha-almavet*, 1988 (*The Immortal Bartfuss*, 1988); *Al kol hapshaim*, n.d. (*For Every Sin*, 1989).

SHORT FICTION: *'Ashan*, 1962; *Ba-gai ha-poreh*, 1963; *In the Wilderness*, 1965; *Kefor 'al ha-arets*, 1965; *Be-komat ha-karka'*, 1968; *Adne ha-nahar*, 1971; *Ke-me a edim*, 1975; *Shanim ve-sha ot*, 1976.

NONFICTION: *Ke' ishon ha-ayin*, 1973; *Masot be-guf rishon*, 1979.

Aharon Appelfeld is a survivor of the Holocaust whose writing is stamped by a melancholy sense of the doom he managed to elude. His published works in Israel include more than half a dozen novels, several story collections, and a book of essays; many of his novels and short stories have been translated into English. His writing has earned for him a significant and distinctive place in contemporary fiction. None of his texts directly alludes to the Holocaust's appalling reality of suffering and deaths almost beyond reckoning: The horrors to come (or remembered) are a baleful flickering on the horizon of his muted, compressed, austerely understated perspective.

Appelfeld's hometown of Czernowitz, in the province of Bukovina, had belonged within the sprawling Austro-Hungarian Empire until 1918, when it became part of the newly created nation of Romania; it is now in the Soviet Union. Appelfeld was seven years old when German troops occupied Czernowitz. His mother was soon killed, while he and his father were transported to the Ukraine and separately interned. In 1941, the youngster managed to escape from his camp. Being blond, he was able to hide his Jewish identity from both the Germans and the anti-Semitic Ukrainian peasants. For three years, he worked as a shepherd and farmhand, associating mostly with horse thieves and prostitutes. After the armistice, he joined a group of boys who wandered to Southern Italy and from there migrated to British-mandate Palestine in 1946. There he worked on a farm mornings and learned Hebrew afternoons. From 1948 to 1950, he served in the Israeli army.

In 1950, Appelfeld passed the matriculation exam for admission to the Hebrew University in Jerusalem. After obtaining his B.A. and M.A. degrees, he studied briefly in Zurich and Oxford but then returned to Israel, where he would teach Jewish literature at Ben-Gurion University in Beersheba. Married to an Argentine-born woman, he has two sons and one daughter. In 1960, he chanced to see his father's name on a list of immigrants due to arrive from Eastern Europe. Naturally, the son rushed to welcome his father. Just as understandably, the father failed to recognize the twenty-eight-year-old, balding, bespectacled man as his son.

From the late 1950's, Appelfeld began to write, first poems, then stories, and finally short novels. It took him a long time to find his natural voice and subject matter. In a revealing interview with the American author Philip Roth, Appelfeld noted that Franz Kafka's works, which he had discovered in the 1950's, had influenced him more deeply than any other. The best-known of Appelfeld's translated novels is the first one published in the United States, *Badenheim 1939*, whose Hebrew title could more literally be translated as "Badenheim, resort town." Badenheim is a Jewish spa near Vienna, where, in the summer of 1939, the Sanitation Department begins to register all vacationers. In the book's final paragraph, the visitors are moved to a freight train and headed toward their impending doom in the East. In the second translated novel, *The Age of Wonders*, the Holocaust again overtakes a group of bourgeois, assimilated, unwary Jews in an isolated Austrian town. Again, Appelfeld makes no explicit reference to historic events. As in a Kafka text, the overpowering ordeal descends inexplicably, irrationally, irresistibly.

Tzili is a simpler tale than the first two, with the wanderings of a slow-witted, East European Jewish girl an approximate parallel to Appelfeld's own during and after World War II. Tzili survives the Holocaust almost inadvertently: She is a simpleton blessed with animal strength, almost mute, unable to feel profound grief, rage, or resentment over her brutalization. Yet her dull passivity somehow enables her to endure horrors that overwhelm more intelligent and introspective Jews. In *The Retreat*, Appelfeld returns to the provincial Austria of the late 1930's. It is a cool, probing, and unsparing critique of Jewish attempts to assimilate themselves to the dominant gentile culture. The novel concludes flatly and forebodingly, with the reader aware that European Jewry's encounter with tragic history is about to reach its apocalypse.

To the Land of the Cattails is another journey toward doom, with a divorced Jewish mother and her sensitive, adolescent son traveling to her parents' home in Appelfeld's native province of Bukovina. The mother and her parents disappear. The son then joins a cluster of Jews at a railroad station, waiting for the train that will carry them to their grim fate.

The Immortal Bartfuss is the first translated novel to focus on contemporary Israel. The protagonist, Bartfuss, has survived the Holocaust, now lives in Jaffa, and broods through an insular, self-isolated, emotionally numb existence. His wife is embittered, his daughter is mentally handicapped, and his relations with friends and acquaintances are wary and mistrustful. At the end, Bartfuss shows some signs of crossing over from psychosis to fellowship and generosity.

Appelfeld's artistic aim is to produce fiction which meditates somberly and austerely on the precarious course of modern Judaism. He struggles relentlessly with the culture of self-rejection to which all too many Jews succumbed in Eastern and Central Europe. In his flat, controlled, subdued, and fabulistic prose that is never shrill, thundering, or moralizing, he presents scenes that pass a scorching judgment on both Jewish self-hatred and gentile homicide. As a Holocaust writer, he belongs to the company of Elie Wiesel, Jerzy Kosinski, and Primo Levi, and may well be their literary master with his elegiac, dreamlike prose at the service of a stern moral vision. His sadness at man's capacity for victimization and cruelty is expressed in admirably compelling images.

BIBLIOGRAPHICAL REFERENCES: An excellent interview with Philip Roth was published in *The London Review of Books*, X (March 17, 1988), 12-16. Israel Shenker has a chatty, biographical account, "Aharon Appelfeld," in his collection of articles, *Coat of Many Colors: Pages from Jewish Life*, 1985. Among the more thoughtful book reviews are these: Gabriele Annan, review of *Badenheim 1939*, *The New York Review of Books*, XXVIII (1981), 3; Thomas Flanagan, review of *Badenheim 1939*, *The Nation*, CCXXXII (1981), 122; Joel Agee, review of *The Age of Wonders*, *The New York Times Book Review*, LXXXVI (1981), 1; A. Alvarez, review of *The Age of Wonders*, *The New York Review of Books*, XXIX (1982), 33-34; Robert M. Adams, review of *Tzili*, *The New York Book Review of Books*, XXX (1983), 34-36; Vivian Gornick, review of *The Retreat*, *The Village Voice*, XXIX (1984), 51; John Gross, review of *To the Land of the Cattails*, *The New York Times Book Review*, XCI (1986), 31; Patrick Parrinder, review of *To the Land of the Reeds* (British title of *To the Land of the Cattails*), *The London Review of Books*, IX (1987), 16-17; Leonard Michaels, review of *The Immortal Bartfuss*, *The New York Times Book Review*, XCIII (1988), 1-3.

Gerhard Brand

JOHN ARDEN

Born: Barnsley, England
Date: October 26, 1930

Principal Works

PLAYS: *All Fall Down*, pr. 1955; *The Waters of Babylon*, pr. 1957; *Live Like Pigs*, pr. 1958; *When Is a Door Not a Door?*, pr. 1958; *Serjeant Musgrave's Dance: An Unhistorical Parable*, pr. 1959; *The Business of Good Government*, pr. 1960 (with Margaretta D'Arcy); *The Happy Haven*, pr. 1960; *Ironhand*, pr. 1963; *The Workhouse Donkey*, pr. 1963; *Armstrong's Last Goodnight: An Exercise in Diplomacy*, pr. 1964; *Ars Longa, Vita Brevis*, pr. 1964 (with D'Arcy); *Fidelio*, pr. 1965; *Left-Handed Liberty*, pr., pb. 1965; *Friday's Hiding*, pr. 1966 (with D'Arcy); *The Royal Pardon*, pr. 1966 (with D'Arcy); *The Vietnam War-Game*, pr. 1967 (with D'Arcy); *Harold Muggins Is a Martyr*, pr. 1968 (with Cartoon Archetypal Slogan Theater and D'Arcy); *The Hero Rises Up*, pr. 1968 (with D'Arcy); *The Soldier's Tale*, pr. 1968; *The True History of Squire Jonathan and His Unfortunate Treasure*, pr. 1968; *The Ballygombeen Bequest*, pr., pb. 1972 (with D'Arcy); *The Island of the Mighty*, pr. 1972 (with D'Arcy); *Henry Dubb Show*, pr. 1973 (with D'Arcy); *Portrait of a Rebel*, pr. 1973 (with D'Arcy); *The Non-Stop Connolly Show*, pr. 1975 (with D'Arcy); *The Little Gray Home in the West*, pr. 1978 (with D'Arcy; revision of *The Ballygombeen Bequest*); *Vandaleur's Folly: An Anglo-Irish Melodrama*, pr. 1978 (with D'Arcy).

NOVEL: *Silence Among the Weapons*, 1982 (also known as *Vox Pop: Last Days of the Roman Republic*, 1983).

NONFICTION: *To Present the Pretence*, 1977.

John Arden was part of a major theatrical movement of the late 1950's and early 1960's which addressed large political and social issues from the world stage. Along with his colleagues from Great Britain's "fringe" theater, such as Harold Pinter, John Osborne, and Arnold Wesker, Arden reestablished the stage as a forum for collective cultural debates among members of the audience and theater practitioners. Born in a middle-class section of Yorkshire and educated in a private boarding school during World War II, Arden did not share the immediate working-class background of other playwrights of the so-called New Wave. His University of Cambridge education in architecture, together with his love of history and classical literature, gives his work a structure and texture more refined than the rough-cut language and settings of Pinter, Wesker, or Henry Livings. He was no less dedicated to the pacifist ideals of young postwar England, however, from having come to them through intellectual deliberation rather than childhood deprivation, and his most famous work, *Serjeant Musgrave's Dance*, still stands today as the most powerful antiwar play from the period.

Arden's career has taken an odd shape, partly because of his (and London's) indifference to the financial successes by which plays are so often judged and partly because Arden himself has divided his attention, first advocating social reform, then criticizing the exploitation of socialism by the working class (his three "socialism" plays, published in the 1960's but produced before *Serjeant Musgrave's Dance*, are ambivalent in their viewpoint). At the same time, Arden sees the danger to the artist in a socialist state, where conformity is valued above individual freedom of expression.

After a decade of writing realistic plays, Arden began to explore the stage possibilities of the artificiality built into the theatrical language. His work became much more stylized; it is significant that his work is discussed in two separate volumes on modern drama, one on realism and one on expressionism. Without reverting entirely to verse, Arden makes use of an enriched language not only to evoke the sense of historicity but also to enlarge the human dimensions of his characters, two features of his plays that separate him from his peers and add a universality to his message. For example, the trilogy based on the Arthurian legends, *The Island of the Mighty*, which he wrote with his wife, Margaretta D'Arcy, is set in medieval times but speaks directly to the question of the relationship between art and power, in any society. Among the adaptations on which he and his wife have collaborated are reworkings of an early Renaissance satire and Johann Wolfgang von Goethe's *Goetz von Berlichingen* (pb. 1773). This kind of intellectual exercise is outside the dramatic interests of the other British playwrights who constituted the New Wave of drama emerging from the fringe theater of London in the early 1960's.

Overintellectual and overstructured in his approach and lacking the creative dramatic voice of his contemporaries, Arden will always be difficult to classify. Even his "poetry" in such middle works as *Armstrong's Last Goodnight* is countered by a more propagandistic style in later works, especially *The Non-Stop Connolly Show*, a six-part extravaganza produced in 1975 and published in five volumes from 1977 to 1978. His work is performed more often on college campuses than in commercial venues, another clue to the complexity and nonconformist artistic vision of Arden's work. Added to his already confused aesthetic profile is the combative relationship he maintains with the press. His future importance in the study of modern English drama and in theater in general lies in the fascination this same complexity and range of imagination provokes in scholars and readers.

BIBLIOGRAPHICAL REFERENCES: John Russell Taylor's introduction to Arden's *Three Plays*, 1964, is the entry point for any study of Arden's work; John Russell Taylor, *Anger and After: A Guide to the New British Theatre*, 1969, tells the complete story of the rise of the New Wave writers. J. L. Styan, in *Modern Drama in Theory and Practice*, Vols. 1 and 3, 1981, demonstrates the split in theatrical styles in Arden's canon. Ronald Hayman, *British Theatre Since 1955: A Reassessment*, 1979, clarifies the change in Arden's emphasis after entering a working partnership with D'Arcy. Arden's own essay collection, *To Present the Pretence*, 1977, suggests that theme rather than plot was the generating factor in the later work. Ronald Hayman, *John Arden*, 1968, revised 1969, is part of a worthwhile but sometimes hurried series of such works by Hayman on Pinter, Wesker, John Whiting, and others. Finally, Albert Hunt, *Arden: A Study of His Plays*, 1974, discusses the work more thoroughly and through a greater range of Arden's canon.

Thomas J. Taylor

HANNAH ARENDT

Born: Hannover, Germany
Date: October 14, 1906

Died: New York, New York
Date: December 4, 1975

PRINCIPAL WORKS

POLITICAL PHILOSOPHY: *The Origins of Totalitarianism*, 1951; *The Human Condition*, 1958; *Eichmann in Jerusalem: A Report on the Banality of Evil*, 1963, revised 1964; *On Revolution*, 1963; *Men in Dark Times*, 1968.

Hannah Arendt, a German-Jewish refugee from Adolf Hitler and Nazism, devoted her scholarly efforts to the philosophical analysis of the events and conditions that led to the rise of totalitarianism and to a pervasive sense of personal, social, and political alienation in modern times. She was born in Hannover, Germany, on October 14, 1906, the only child of Paul Arendt, an engineer, and Martha (Cohn) Arendt. The family moved to Königsberg when she was young. She received a B.A. degree from the University of Königsberg in 1924. In 1928 she received a Ph.D. from the University of Heidelberg, completing a dissertation on the concept of love in Saint Augustine's writing. Three leading scholars strongly influenced her: Edmund Husserl, Karl Jaspers, and Martin Heidegger.

Nazi anti-Semitism forced Arendt to move to Paris in 1933. There she studied, wrote, and worked with the Youth Aliyah, a relief organization that found homes in Palestine for Jewish orphans. The National Socialist threat to France prompted Arendt's emigration to the United States in 1940. She became a naturalized citizen in 1950 and lived in the United States until her death, in 1975. From 1944 to 1946 Arendt was research director for the Conference of Jewish Relations; she served as chief editor of Schocken Books from 1946 to 1948. In 1952 she received a Guggenheim Fellowship and began to devote more time to research and writing. Despite her excellent training and credentials, she was unable to secure permanent academic appointments until 1963, when she was appointed to the Committee on Social Thought at the University of Chicago. In 1967 she joined the graduate faculty of the New School for Social Research.

Arendt's writings are devoted to the philosophical analysis of the origins and consequences of the major political catastrophes of modern times: totalitarianism, revolution, and war. Her studies carried her beyond the usual boundaries of political science into a philosophical and historical analysis of the destruction of classical political theory, secularization of the Judeo-Christian views of human nature and society, and the rise of political ideology and the distorted understanding of the human condition that characterizes modern mass culture. Her first major publication was *The Origins of Totalitarianism* in 1951. According to Arendt, totalitarianism has it origins in anti-Semitism and in nineteenth century imperialism. Totalitarian leaders control all aspects of public and private life; defend ideologies based on class struggle or racial purity; reduce questions of political order and disorder to pragmatic, utilitarian, and economic considerations; and subordinate individuals and civil rights to the interests of the state. In 1958 she published *The Human Condition*, which attempts to shed light on the present state of personal and social alienation by interpreting it through traditional philosophical categories, for example, the public and private realms, the *vita activa*, and the meaning of labor.

Her best-known and most controversial work is *Eichmann in Jerusalem: A Report on the Banality of Evil*, which appeared first as a series of articles for *The New Yorker* and as a book in 1963. Arendt claimed that too much attention to Eichmann the man obscured the broader intellectual and cultural disorders that allowed the rise of Nazism and permitted the "final solution to the Jewish problem." For Arendt, the Germans who "followed orders" or failed to resist Hitler, the other European governments and peoples, and even the Jews themselves, who passively allowed the spread of the Nazi horror, had to share the blame for what happened. The controversy surrounding the book centered on Arendt's comments about the Jews, which many believed showed little sympathy or understanding of their suffering. Arendt made an effort to reply to her critics, but the controversy followed her for many years.

Her other books were far less controversial. In 1963 she published *On Revolution*, which offers a comparative analysis of the American and French revolutions and criticizes the French intellectual and political leaders for allowing the quest for democratic freedom to degenerate into an anarchic destruction of political order. Her 1968 book, *Men in Dark Times*, did create some controversy because of an essay on Bertolt Brecht which argued that "there is no doubt that Brecht had a high regard for Stalin." At her death she was working on a three-volume work, "The Life of the Mind." She had completed the first volume, "Willing," was writing the third draft of the second volume, and had completed a first draft of the third, "Judging."

William Jovanovich, president of the publishing firm Harcourt Brace Jovanovich, described Arendt as "the outstanding woman thinker of our time." Other well-known political analysts as different as Irving Kristol and Harrison Salisbury have given her similar praise.

BIBLIOGRAPHICAL REFERENCES: Margaret Canovan, *The Political Thought of Hannah Arendt*, 1974, examines the origins of Arendt's political theory. *Hannah Arendt: Recovery of the Public World*, 1979, edited by Melvyn A. Hill, is based on a conference on Arendt's political philosophy. Stephen Whitfield, *Into the Dark: Hannah Arendt and Totalitarianism*, 1980, examines criticisms of Arendt's writings and contains a good bibliography. Bhikhu C. Parekh, *Hannah Arendt and the Search for a New Political Philosophy*, 1981, examines Arendt's criticisms of current political philosophies. Elisabeth Young-Bruehl, *Hannah Arendt: For Love of the World*, 1982, is the definitive biography. Gordon J. Tolle, *Human Nature Under Fire: The Political Philosophy of Hannah Arendt*, 1982, is largely a critique of *The Human Condition*. George Kateb, *Hannah Arendt: Politics, Conscience, Evil*, 1983, treats Arendt's theory as a defense of democracy, and Derwent May, *Hannah Arendt*, 1986, is an intimate biography.

Stephen A. McKnight

AYI KWEI ARMAH

Born: Sekondi-Takoradi, Ghana
Date: 1939

Principal Works

NOVELS: *The Beautyful Ones Are Not Yet Born*, 1968; *Fragments*, 1969; *Why Are We So Blest?*, 1972; *Two Thousand Seasons*, 1973; *The Healers*, 1978.

Ayi Kwei Armah is one of the most acclaimed, yet controversial, West African writers. Born in 1939 to Fante-speaking parents at Sekondi-Takoradi, in the western region of Ghana, Armah received his early education at Achimota College, near Accra. In 1959, Armah traveled to the United States on a scholarship, studying for one year at Groton School in Massachusetts, and later at Harvard University, where he was graduated summa cum laude with a degree in sociology. Armah returned to Ghana in 1964 and worked briefly as a scriptwriter for Ghana Television. In 1967, Armah traveled to the United States on a grant from the Fairfield Foundation to participate in the graduate writing program at Columbia University, New York. Subsequent to his studies at Columbia University, Armah went to Paris and worked as an editor-translator for *Jeune Afrique*. In 1968, Armah returned to the United States and took a teaching post at the University of Massachusetts. Four years later, Armah traveled to Dar es Salaam, Tanzania, where he accepted a teaching job. Armah's works exhibit Western influences, as they show the plight of alienated heroes in search of values in a society seemingly devoid of meaning.

Set in Sekondi-Takoradi, one of Ghana's major port cities, *The Beautyful Ones Are Not Yet Born* chronicles the life of a railway clerk who routinely must make hard choices between easy money that would enable him to provide more adequately for his family and his own conscience, which disallows his acceptance of bribes as a means of getting ahead. Armah considers corruption and opportunism as responsible for the failure of the nationalist movement, since newly elected leaders, once they have risen to power, become no less predisposed than were their colonialist predecessors to secure their own positions through unethical means or at the expense of the masses they were elected to serve.

The despair that results from dashed hopes also pervades Armah's second and third novels. In *Fragments* and *Why Are We So Blest?*, Armah depicts insular individuals, or artist-heroes, whose aspirations are thwarted by a grasping, acquisitive society. The artist-hero Baako Onipa in *Fragments* suffers from guilt because he falls short of familial expectations that he will enrich the lives of family members by supplying them with modern luxuries from abroad. The guilt related to his perceived failure ultimately leads him to a nervous collapse. Armah's *Why Are We So Blest?*, which is set in Algiers, also features an artist-hero, whose spiritual pursuits eventually lead him into self-imposed exile.

Armah's fourth and fifth novels, *Two Thousand Seasons* and *The Healers*, represent a departure from Armah's earlier works. Contrastingly, they are not set in postindependence Africa; instead, they span a number of centuries prior to the colonization of Africa. In fact, the intent of the author is to probe the source of the corruption identified in earlier novels and, in doing so, to provide hope for Africa's redemption. The two novels are therefore more optimistic than the first three, whose artist-heroes are described as islands of virtue in a wasteland of greed and corruption. In *Two Thousand Seasons* and *The Healers*, Armah relies upon the collective wisdom of traditional storytellers, or *griots*, whose solidarity and grounding in communal or traditional values provide an effective antidote to destructive forces.

Criticism of Armah's fourth and fifth novels has been predictable, since it corresponds with earlier criticism of Armah's novels, namely, that his characters too often lack human dimension. The characters in *The Beautyful Ones Are Not Yet Born* were criticized for being mere mouthpieces for the author; that is, politicians were made the epitome of corruption.

Their negative portrayals, combined with what some consider to be Armah's obsession with offal, led them to equate the novel with exaggeration and distortion that reflected the author's own rage at what he considered a betrayal of nationalist hopes. Others have argued that such criticism is unfounded, since it does not stem from a consideration of the work as an art form but, rather, from the work's unpopular views.

Despite, however, the controversy that was sparked with Armah's first novel, the writer remains at the forefront of African literature and has been credited with helping to usher in "the coming of age of the African novel." Unlike his literary predecessors, whose novels were comparable to anthropological treatises detailing the customs of African society, Armah's novels are more carefully crafted and stylized. More important, however, Armah's novels are more introspective. Unlike earlier writers, who were content to dramatize the clash between African and Western cultures, Armah not only delved into the root causes of the conflict but also, in his later novels, succeeded in providing hope for its amelioration.

BIBLIOGRAPHICAL REFERENCES: Robert Fraser, *The Novels of Ayi Kwei Armah*, 1980, is a comprehensive study that treats chronologically and individually Armah's respective novels. Criticism of *The Beautyful Ones Are Not Yet Born* is contained in Shatto Arthur Gakwandi, *The Novel and Contemporary Experience in Africa*, 1977, and Eustace Palmer, *An Introduction to the African Novel: A Critical Study of Twelve Books*, 1972. A discussion of *The Beautyful Ones Are Not Yet Born* is contained in chapter 9 of Charles Larson, *The Emergence of African Fiction*, 1970, and a discussion of *Fragments*, in Oyekan Owomoyela, *African Literatures: An Introduction*, 1979. An analysis of female portrayals in Armah's novels is contained in Abena P. A. Busia, "Parasites and Prophets: The Use of Women in Ayi Kwei Armah's Novels," in *Ngambika: Studies of Women in African Literature*, 1986, edited by Carol Boyce Davies and Anne Adams Graves. See also Harold R. Collins, "The Ironic Imagery of Armah's *The Beautyful Ones Are Not Yet Born*: The Putrescent Vision," *World Literature Written in English*, XX (1971), 37-50; Gareth Griffiths, "Structure and Image in Kwei Armah's *The Beautyful Ones Are Not Yet Born*," *Studies in Black Literature*, II (1971), 1-9; Margaret Folarin, "An Additional Comment on Ayi Kwei Armah's *The Beautyful Ones Are Not Yet Born*," *African Literature Today*, V (1971), 116-129; Kolawole Ogungbesan, "Symbol and Meaning in *The Beautyful Ones Are Not Yet Born*," *African Literature Today*, VII (1975), 93-110; Richard Priebe, "Demonic Imagery and the Apocalyptic Vision in the Novels of Ayi Kwei Armah," *Yale French Studies*, LIII (1976), 102-136; Robert Fraser, "The American Background in *Why Are We So Blest?*," *African Literature Today*, IX (1978), 39-46; Joyce Johnson, "The Promethean 'Factor' in Ayi Kwei Armah's *Fragments* and *Why Are We So Blest?*," *World Literature Written in English*, XXII (1982), 497-510.

Tommie L. Jackson

HARRIETTE ARNOW

Born: Wayne County, Kentucky
Date: July 7, 1908

Died: Ann Arbor, Michigan
Date: March 22, 1986

PRINCIPAL WORKS

NOVELS: *Mountain Path*, 1936; *Hunter's Horn*, 1949; *The Dollmaker*, 1954; *The Weedkiller's Daughter*, 1970; *The Kentucky Trace: A Novel of the American Revolution*, 1974.

NONFICTION: *Seedtime on the Cumberland*, 1960; *The Flowering of the Cumberland*, 1963; *Old Burnside*, 1977.

Harriette Louisa Simpson Arnow chronicled the people and land of rural Kentucky in both fiction and nonfiction. She was born on July 7, 1908, in Wayne County, Kentucky, where she spent her early years. By the time she was of school age, the family had moved to Burnside, Kentucky, high on a hill above the Cumberland River. Her parents, Elias and Mollie Jane Denney Simpson, were both descendants of original Kentucky settlers, so Arnow was reared with a strong sense of roots and a hearty appreciation for the region. Storytelling, too, was part of her early education. In a 1983 interview published in *Appalachian Journal*, Arnow talked about the stories she had heard as a child, adding that by the time she was five or six she was already changing the stories she did not like. An appreciation for this region and its storytelling were to figure prominently in her career as a writer.

Yet the family love of stories did not extend to writing. The plan for young Arnow was far more practical: to finish high school as quickly as possible, then to attend college for two years to prepare for teaching school. For a while, Arnow followed her parents' wishes. She attended Berea College for two years, then took a position in a one-room school in a Kentucky hollow, where life was even more isolated, more rural, and more homespun than in Burnside. Although she left this teaching post after only a year, these were the people whose fictionalized selves would prove to be the most compelling characters in Arnow's stories. *Mountain Path*, published in 1936, was based in part on this early experience.

Arnow returned to school, this time to the University of Louisville, which granted her a B.S. degree in 1930. While she studied primarily math and science at the university, for the first time she found a group of students who were as interested in writing as she, and with them she began to practice her craft. In 1934 Arnow took a decisive step: Saying she "would rather starve as a writer than as a teacher," she quit her job, moved into a furnished room in downtown Cincinnati near the library, and determined to read the great novels and to write. In 1935 she published two stories in small magazines, followed by "The Washerwoman's Day," published in *The Southern Review* during the winter of 1936 and often anthologized. One story, "Two Hunters," was published by *Esquire* magazine under the pseudonym H. L. Simpson.

In 1939 she was married to a Chicago newspaperman, Harold Arnow, and once again writing was relegated to stolen time. The couple moved to a farm in southern Kentucky, and later, during the war years, to Detroit. Arnow was not able to publish another novel until 1949, when *Hunter's Horn* appeared. The novel was a best-seller and widely acclaimed for its realism and powerful characterization. It tells the story of a Kentucky hill country farmer obsessed with an elusive red fox that is creating havoc on his farm.

Arnow's third novel is generally considered her best. *The Dollmaker* depicts the hard struggle for economic, emotional, and artistic survival experienced by a poor white woman during war years. Gertie Nevels reluctantly leaves rural Kentucky to follow her husband to Detroit. The move is a mistake, and Gertie yearns only to return to the rich earth and rural values she left behind. Gertie's husband grasps at the new life, however, looking beyond the tawdry conditions of their wartime housing project to the promises of the new materialism. He buys on time and runs the family into debt. Numerous strikes and walkouts further reduce the family's circumstances. All along Gertie has enjoyed carving, but now her one joy in life is reduced to a matter of production and profits. The dollmaker, no longer an artist, becomes a hawker of painted jumping jack dolls.

Critically acclaimed when published in 1954, *The Dollmaker* once again gained national attention when it aired as a television drama starring Jane Fonda in 1984. The novel warrants reappraisal not only for its realistic depiction of everyday life in an urban melting pot but also for its depiction of the massive social pressures that bear down upon the individual. The novel evidences feminist themes as the strong female battles for individual integrity, family unity, and aesthetic triumph against the male materialist, industrialist complex that Clovis, the husband, readily accepts. Male versus female tensions extend to rural versus urban, art versus materialism, family unity versus disintegration, and individualism versus mass adaptability. The novel is more than a good regionalist work; it drives to the heart of tensions and conflicting values that continue to plague the modern world.

After *The Dollmaker* Arnow turned to writing social history about her native region. *Seedtime on the Cumberland* shows pioneer life as lived by ordinary men and women in the Cumberland Valley, from Kentucky extending to Tennessee. It received an Award of Merit from the Association for State and Local History. *The Flowering of the Cumberland* is described as a companion piece, covering approximately the same years (1780 to 1803) and centering on the middle Tennessee area and its social, as opposed to individual, development. Some fourteen years later, in 1977, she published her last historical work, *Old Burnside*, in tribute to the Burnside that existed before the Army Corps of Engineers radically changed the landscape. These historical works show careful research and attention to the same kind of detail that colors Arnow's novels.

Arnow wrote other novels in the 1970's. *The Weedkiller's Daughter* depicts a teenage girl growing up in an oppressive family in suburban Detroit. *The Kentucky Trace* returns to the American Revolution to portray the upheavals that ordinary people in Kentucky mountain country experienced during this most significant of American wars. Inspired by tales of the revolution handed down to her by grandparents and parents during childhood, *The Kentucky Trace* brings together Arnow's Kentucky roots, her family's love for tales, and the realism and social detail of the serious historian.

Although reassessment of her work began in the 1980's, Arnow still has not received the national recognition she deserves. Considered a regionalist, she nevertheless explores themes and values that are universal. Her sympathy for the individual who holds out for a genuine life of simple values suggests the power of the human being to endure, if not to triumph. At the end of *The Dollmaker*, Gertie realizes that the face of Christ she has vainly sought to free from a cherished block of cherry wood could have been any one of the familiar faces of the neighbors she saw every day in the alleys of the housing project. This compassion for ordinary people is not Gertie's alone; it marks the great artists of the Western tradition; it marks the work of Harriette Arnow.

BIBLIOGRAPHICAL REFERENCES: The best general study is Wilton Eckley's *Harriette Arnow*, 1974. Joyce Carol Oates's afterword to the Avon paperback edition of *The Dollmaker*, 1972, is worth reading, as is Glenda Hobbs's "Harriette Arnow's Kentucky Novels: Beyond Local Color," in *Regionalism and the Female Imagination*, 1985, edited by Emily Toth. Another article by Hobbs, "A Portrait of the Artist as Mother: Harriette Arnow and *The Dollmaker*," appeared in *The Georgia Review*, XXXIII (1979), 851-866. See also Dorothy Lee, "Harriette Arnow's *The Dollmaker:* A Journey to Awareness," *Critique: Studies in Modern Fiction*, XX (1978), 92-98. Barbara Baer provides an overview in "Harriette Arnow's Chronicles of Destruction," *The Nation*, January 31, 1976, 117-120.

Paula D. Kopacz

FERNANDO ARRABAL

Born: Melilla, Spanish Morocco
Date: August 11, 1932

Principal Works

PLAYS: *Pique-nique en campagne*, wr. 1952, pr. 1959 (*Picnic on the Battlefield*, 1960); *Le Tricycle*, pr. 1958 (*The Tricycle*, 1966); *Fando et Lis*, pb. 1958 (*Fando and Lis*, 1962); *La Cimetière des voitures*, pb. 1958 (*The Car Cemetery*, 1960); *La Communion solennelle*, pr. 1958 (*Solemn Communion: Panic Ceremony*, 1967); *Guernica*, pr. 1959 (English translation, 1967); *Le Grand Cérémonial*, pr. 1964 (*The Grand Ceremonial*, 1970); *Cérémonie pour une chèvre sur un nuage*, pr. 1966 (*Ceremony for a Goat on a Cloud*, 1978); *L'Architecte et l'Empereur d'Assyrie*, pr., pb. 1967 (*The Architect and the Emperor of Assyria*, 1969); *Dieu est-il devenu fou?*, pb. 1967 (*Has God Gone Mad?*, 1978); *Le Jardin des délices*, pr., pb. 1969 (*The Garden of Delights*, 1974); *Bestialité érotique*, pr., pb. 1969 (*Erotic Bestiality*, 1978); *Et ils passèrent des menottes aux fleurs*, pr., pb. 1969 (*And They Put Handcuffs on the Flowers*, 1972); *Le Ciel et la merde*, pb. 1972; *Bella Ciao, la guerre de mille ans*, pr., pb. 1972; *Jeunes Barbares d'aujourd'hui*, pr., pb. 1975 (*Today's Young Barbarians*, 1978); *La Tour de Babel*, pr., pb. 1976; *Punk et punk et colégram*, pb. 1978; *La Pastaga des loufs: Ou, Ouverture orang-outan*, pb. 1978; *Le Roi de Sodome*, pr. 1979; *Tormentos y delicias de la carne: Homenaje a la conjura de los necios de John Kennedy Toole*, 1985.

NOVELS: *Baal Babylone*, 1959 (*Baal Babylon*, 1961); *L'Enterrement de la sardine*, 1961 (*The Burial of the Sardine*, 1966); *La Torre herida por el rayo*, 1983 (*The Tower Struck by Lightning*, 1988); *La Reverdie*, 1985; *La Vierge rouge*, 1986.

NONFICTION: *Le "Panique,"* 1973.

MISCELLANEOUS: *Échecs et mythe*, 1984.

One of the founders of the so-called Panic theater movement and one of the most important playwrights to emerge in the 1960's was the Spaniard Fernando Arrabal. He was born in 1932 in Melilla, Spanish Morocco, and his early life was unusual and disturbing. Born during the Spanish Civil War to an officer in the Republican (anti-Franco) army, he saw the war enter his own home when his father was arrested and removed. Arrabal senior was condemned to death by the Franco regime, a sentence later commuted to thirty years of imprisonment.

At age four, Arrabal moved with his mother and siblings to Ciudad Rodrigo in Spain, where he received his first schooling under the supervision of Catholic Fathers. Later he was sent to a preparatory school for the military academy. It became clear that Arrabal was not meant for a military career, and he began instead to study law. While going to the university, Arrabal started writing plays. *Picnic on the Battlefield* was written in 1952, when Arrabal was only twenty. It is a one-act antiwar piece which, although sketchy, is effective and amusing.

A feature of Arrabal's early plays is the presence of childlike characters, both innocent and cruel. In *The Tricycle*, a clown-comedy that evokes Samuel Beckett, the play's four characters center their lives on a park bench and a tricycle they use to give children rides. They talk, sleep, and play games of pride, sexuality, and death. For money, they murder a stranger. Still, they are not evil; indeed, they are not even really aware of what it is they have done. They are pre-social, moral idiots—monsters of the Freudian id. The play, like many of Arrabal's early plays, is perhaps best understood if seen as a metaphor for life itself: people living in a world where morality and decency are unaffordable and unattainable luxuries.

Arrabal moved to Paris in 1955 but had trouble gaining recognition. Not until 1958 did he get a play published. The journal *Les Lettres nouvelles* (the new literature) agreed to publish *Picnic on the Battlefield*. Not long after this, another publisher put out the first volume of

Arrabal plays and roughly at the same time *Picnic on the Battlefield* was produced. Arrabal had arrived.

His plays were now being produced in Paris by small companies but did not create much of a stir. They were still too sterile and formalistic. In the early 1960's, however, Arrabal founded, with the Mexican director Alexandro Jodorowsky and others, the Panic movement, named for the Greek god Pan. The idea was to create something real, a theater at once sacred and profane, poetic and vulgar, jeering and serious. Arrabal was influenced both by the surrealists and by Antonin Artaud, who advocated a ritualized theater where the boundary between actors and audience is removed.

The Panic theater period was fruitful for Arrabal. He wrote prolifically and with more purpose and artistic maturity than in his earlier works. Two of his best works, *The Architect and the Emperor of Assyria* and *The Garden of Delights*, date to this period. The former especially is exemplary of Panic theater and of the more mature Arrabal. The play has, as the title suggests, only two characters. Like all Arrabal characters, they are less psychologically drawn profiles than prototypes. The Emperor survives an airplane disaster and finds himself on a small island with only one inhabitant, the Architect. These two play a Robinson Crusoe/Friday game of civilized and uncivilized, of culture versus nature. Constantly switching roles, they enact a trial where the crimes of the Emperor, who may or may not have been the President of the United States, are judged by the Architect. The verdict is death, and the judge has to consume—literally eat—the corpse after the execution. Thus the two change roles: The Architect becomes the Emperor by absorbing his body and brain. The audience witnesses a rite of transition, or a series of rites, the progression from life to death, from a primitive condition to a civilized condition, from one evolutionary stage to the next. *The Architect and the Emperor of Assyria* was the first of Arrabal's plays to be received with virtual across-the-board critical applause. He had really arrived.

Then came 1968, student revolts, and "guerrilla" theater—street theater with uncompromising political messages. Arrabal was part of the student movement and wrote a number of plays that can be characterized as guerrilla theater. The best of these, perhaps his best play, is *And They Put Handcuffs on the Flowers*, a rousing, moving, disgusting denouncement of political oppression in Spain. The play, which is set in a prison and details the dreams and ugly realities of five political prisoners, could have been written about Argentina, the Soviet Union, Israel, or South Africa—anywhere where political opponents of repressive regimes are jailed and tortured with impunity. In the 1970's, Arrabal seemed to lose some of his belligerence and began to write comedies that the bourgeoisie could appreciate.

Arrabal's theater is at its worst infantile, vulgar, and pointless, but at its best, as in *The Architect and the Emperor of Assyria* and *And They Put Handcuffs on the Flowers*, it has an almost folkloric directness: Arrabal can access his own unconscious and project his dreams and fantasies onto characters and plots that enact universal rituals. His plays have the texture of life, of history. Individuals lose their individuality by multiplication, constantly changing places, constantly transgressing boundaries. Yet they are always locked in the same pattern of absurdity and cruelty, with brief moments of pleasure and, perhaps, love thrown in to give, if not meaning, the semblance of a purpose to life.

BIBLIOGRAPHICAL REFERENCES: The best source of biographical material about Arrabal is Peter L. Podol, *Fernando Arrabal*, 1978; Podol provides a useful chronology and includes chapters on Arrabal's early years. Another excellent work is Thomas John Donahue, *The Theater of Fernando Arrabal: A Garden of Earthly Delights*, 1980; Donahue outlines clearly the artistic, intellectual, and personal influences that helped shape Arrabal's work and gives astute readings and critical assessments of most of Arrabal's plays. A shorter treatment of Arrabal's work can be found in Martin Esslin's *The Theater of the Absurd*, 1961. The Panic theater period in Arrabal's career is the subject of a chapter in a book by Gloria Orenstein, *The Theater of the Marvelous*, 1975; the chapter, "A Surrealist Theatrical Tractate: Fernando

Arrabal," traces the influence on Arrabal from Antonin Artaud, André Breton, and Salvador Dalí. Finally, see Beverly DeLong-Tonelli "Bicycles and Balloons in Arrabal's Dramatic Structure," *Modern Drama*, 1971, 205-209.

Per Schelde

ANTONIN ARTAUD

Born: Marseilles, France
Date: September 4, 1896

Died: Ivry, France
Date: March 4, 1948

PRINCIPAL WORKS

POETRY: *Tric-trac du ciel*, 1923 (*Heavenly Backgammon*, 1965); *L'Ombilic des limbes*, 1925 (*Umbilical Limbo*, 1964); *Le Pèse-nerfs*, 1925 (*The Nerve Scales*, 1968); *Pour en finir avec le jugement de dieu*, 1947.

CRITICISM: *Correspondance avec Jacques Rivière*, 1924 (*Correspondence with Jacques Rivière*, 1965); "À la grande nuit: Ou, Le Bluff surréaliste," 1927 ("In the Dark: Or, The Surrealist Bluff," 1968); *L'Art et la mort*, 1929 (*Art and Death*, 1968); *Le Théâtre et son double*, 1938 (*The Theatre and Its Double*, 1958); *Les Lettres de Rodez*, 1946 (*Letters from Rodez*, 1960).

OTHER NONFICTION: *Les Nouvelles Révélations de l'être*, 1937; *D'un voyage au pays des Tarahumaras*, 1945 (*A Voyage to the Land of the Tarahumara*, 1976); *Van Gogh: Le Suicidé de la société*, 1947 (*Van Gogh: The Man Suicided by Society*, 1949); *Vie et mort de Satan le Feu*, 1953.

NOVEL: *Héliogabale: Ou, L'Anarchiste couronné*, 1934 (*Heliogabalus: Or, The Anarchist Crowned*, 1976).

PLAYS: *Le Jet de sang*, pb. 1924 (*The Jet of Blood*, 1963); *Les Cenci*, pr. 1935 (*The Cenci*, 1969).

Antonin Artaud, a poet, dramatist, and essayist, was a central figure in the European avant-garde movement. An inquisitive student and a voracious reader, he became so deeply depressed at age nineteen that he destroyed all of his early works. His parents committed him to a nearby sanatorium. During the next five years, he was sequestered in several clinics. In 1920 his parents finally sent him to Paris, where he would begin his chosen career in the arts.

Artaud's first collection of poems, *Heavenly Backgammon*, published in 1923, was a slim volume of eight poems written in a mixed style of gothic romanticism and Symbolism—and showing the influence of Charles Baudelaire and Edgar Allan Poe. He later dismissed this work because it followed an established literary tradition. More important during this time was Artaud's preoccupation with the theater. Until 1924, he worked with Charles Dullin's experimental Théâtre de l'Atelier, where he collaborated on set and costume design; he also acted in many of the productions and in the budding film industry.

Artaud's precarious mental and physical states were exacerbated by the laudanum and opium which he had been taking since 1919. It caused him to be erratic and moody, making it impossible for him to sustain personal and professional relationships. Yet Artaud was able to document his experience with pain in the well-received *Correspondence with Jacques Rivière*, the first text to attract wide attention. The year 1924 marked another important beginning for Artaud: his association with the newly formed Surrealist group, led by Andŕe Breton. Attracted by the group's spirit of revolt against bourgeois standards, Artaud became an active contributor to *La Revolution surréaliste*, the official publication of the movement. Artaud's first two important collections, *Umbilical Limbo* and *The Nerve Scales*, come from this period. The style was vastly different, reflecting the fragmented images of a mind in torment. Artaud's association with the Surrealists continued until 1927. For Artaud, the metaphysical rather than the political transformation of the conditions of human existence was the only role for art. The essay "In the Dark: Or, The Surrealist Bluff" articulates these beliefs.

Artaud's first attempt to form an independent theater grew out of his frustration with the theater of the 1920's. The Alfred Jarry Theater provided a place for experimental drama to mix with music, poetry, and painting. Artaud's revolutionary ideas about theater took written form during the 1930's, after he had seen a production of a Balinese theatrical troupe. The experience confirmed his growing belief in the primary importance of physical gesture in the creation of a truly metaphysical theater. He wrote a series of essays on the principles of this new theater, which he called the Theater of Cruelty, and these were published in *The Theater and Its Double*, one of the most important documents in modern theater. Artaud wanted a theater where "violent physical images [would] crush and hypnotize the sensibility of the spectator," where text would be eliminated or subjugated to theatrical language, such as lighting, movement, and scenery, and where the effect would be the release of subconscious and anarchic impulses in the spectators. He wanted a total theater. With Louis Jouvet, Artaud formed the Theatre of Cruelty in 1935. Its only production was *The Cenci*, a tale of incest and murder based on Stendhal and Percy Bysshe Shelley. With music, ritual chanting, and frenzied movement, it was poorly received. Tired of rejection and poverty, Artaud decided to go to Mexico in 1936, where he studied the rites of the Tarahumara Indians.

In the late 1930's, after returning from Mexico, Artaud suffered his most serious breakdown, and he was labeled an incurable schizophrenic. After chemotherapy and shock treatments, which Artaud deeply resented, he nevertheless returned to productivity. He wrote incessantly during his last two years. After seeing a Vincent van Gogh exhibition, he wrote *Van Gogh: The Man Suicided by Society*—a violent, lyrical work. Struck by the similarities in their lives, he attacked modern society, which he believed reduces geniuses to suicide.

In discussing Artaud's contributions, it is almost impossible to separate the man from the work, the madness and the genius from the art. He has been called a visionary and a prophet in his revolutionary view of theater and its relationship to the spectator. He wrote from the conviction that his physical and emotional pains were meaningful experiences with metaphysical repercussions, and he believed that conveying this anguish necessitated new forms of art. His Theatre of Cruelty was a place where man's precarious existence was to be portrayed through varied nonrepresentational dramatic techniques to shock and to awaken the brutalized consciousness of the audience, to make the audience aware of the primal forces operating in all people. These concepts paved the way for the Theatre of the Absurd and other experimental theater.

BIBLIOGRAPHICAL REFERENCES: The best anthology for American readers is *Antonin Artaud: Selected Writings*, edited by Susan Sontag, 1976; the best introductions to Artaud in English are Julia F. Costich, *Antonin Artaud*, 1978, a well-written overview and critique of his works, and Naomi Greene, *Antonin Artaud: Poet Without Words*, 1970, a thorough earlier study. Eric Sellin's *The Dramatic Concepts of Antonin Artaud*, 1968, surveys the major cultural and dramatic influences. See also Bettina L. Knapp, *Antonin Artaud: A Man of Vision*, 1969; Martin Esslin, *Antonin Artaud*, 1976; Albert Bermal, *Artaud's Theatre of Cruelty*, 1977. Noteworthy articles include Mary Ann Caws, "Artaud's Myth of Motion," in *The Inner Theater of Recent French Poetry*, 1972; John D. Lyons, "Artaud: Intoxication and Its Double," *Yale French Studies*, L (1974), 120-129; and Leo Bersani, "Artaud, Birth, and Defecation," *Partisan Review*, XLIII (1976), 439-452.

Lori Hall Burghardt

SHOLEM ASCH

Born: Kutno, Poland
Date: November 1, 1880

Died: London, England
Date: July 10, 1957

PRINCIPAL WORKS

NOVELS: *Dos Shtetl*, 1905 (*The Little Town*, 1907); *Amerike*, 1911 (*America*, 1918); *Mottke Ganev*, 1917 (*Mottke the Thief*, 1917); *Onkl Mozes*, 1918 (*Uncle Moses*, 1920); *Kiddush Hashem*, 1920 (English translation, 1926); *Toyt Urteyl*, 1926 (*Judge Not*); *Khayim Lederers Tsurikkumen*, 1927 (*Chaim Lederer's Return*); *Farn Mabul*, 1927-1932 (*Three Cities*, 1933); *Der Tilim Yid*, 1934 (*Salvation*, 1934); *Three Novels*, 1938 (includes *Uncle Moses*, *Judge Not*, and *Chaim Lederer's Return*); *Der Man fun Notseres*, 1943 (*The Nazarene*, 1939); *The Apostle*, 1943; *Ist River*, 1946 (*East River*, 1946); *Mary*, 1949; *Moses*, 1951; *Der Novi*, 1955 (*The Prophet*, 1955).

SHORT FICTION: *From Many Countries: The Collected Stories of Sholem Asch*, 1958.

ESSAYS: *What I Believe*, 1941; *One Destiny: An Epistle to the Christians*, 1945.

PLAYS: *Tsurikgekumen*, pr. 1904; *Der Got fun Nekome*, pr. 1907 (*The God of Vengeance*, 1918).

Sholem Asch is the most important Yiddish novelist of the early twentieth century. He was born on November 1, 1880, in Kutno, Poland, to Moishe Asch, a businessman, and his wife, Malka Asch. The eleventh of fifteen children, he was educated in the local Hebrew school and later taught Hebrew. In 1896, his first literary sketches, written in Hebrew, were rejected by the publisher to whom he had submitted them.

In 1899, Asch moved to Warsaw, where he became the protégé of the famous Yiddish writer I. L. Peretz. Following Peretz's advice, Asch began to write in Yiddish and was soon publishing in Yiddish newspapers. In 1901, Asch was married to Matilda Spiro, and in 1902, their first child was born. In 1904 Asch brought out his first novel, *The Little Town*, which established his reputation as a major Yiddish writer. That year also saw the successful production of his first play. Three years later, the play *The God of Vengeance* brought him international fame as a dramatist. The powerful story of a Jewish procurer who cannot protect his young daughter from the evil inherent in his own occupation, *The God of Vengeance* was presented in Warsaw, St. Petersburg, Berlin, and New York.

Concerned about the safety of his four young children in troubled Poland, Asch moved in 1914 with his family to New York, where he continued to write and to publish plays and novels, still in Yiddish. It was to be some years before the translations of his works into English would be successfully promoted. Fortunately, Abraham Cahan, the editor of the *Jewish Daily Forward*, had a policy of publishing what he considered the best in Yiddish literature. Beginning with *America*, the tragic story of an immigrant boy who cannot adjust to the United States, for years Cahan serialized every Asch novel before it was circulated in book form worldwide in Yiddish and in German.

Although he had become an American citizen in 1920, Asch decided to make his permanent home in Nice, where he settled in 1925. In 1933, his dream was at last realized: *Three Cities* became the first of his novels to become a best-seller in English translation. By 1938, however, it was becoming clear that even literary merit could not protect a Jew living in Europe, and Sholem and Matilda Asch decided to stay in the United States.

For three decades, Asch had been working on a life of Jesus Christ, a work which he hoped would contribute to greater understanding between Christians and Jews. Cahan urged him to give up the project; however, Asch insisted on publishing the novel. When *The Nazarene* appeared in 1939, it was read and praised by millions of Christians, but the Jewish community, led by Cahan, attacked its author as an apostate. That opposition strengthened when *The Apostle*, the story of Saint Paul, appeared, and *Mary* brought an outcry from

Roman Catholics as well. After Asch and his wife moved to Miami in 1951, he was attacked in the street by Yiddish extremists. Finally, because he had submitted his works to a Marxist paper, the only Yiddish publication which would accept his works, the aging author was called to explain his actions before the notorious House Committee on Un-American Activities. In 1953, he and his wife left the United States to live in England and France. After suffering a stroke during a stay in Israel, Asch died in London on July 10, 1957.

Since his death, Jewish writers and critics have come to new understandings of Asch's intentions. In all of his works, he explored the relationships of Jewish characters to the worlds which they inhabit and to the traditions in which they were reared. Many of the early novels and stories take place in the little Jewish villages which preserve past customs and in the Jewish sections of European cities. Typical of these works is *Mottke the Thief*, the picaresque tale of a spoiled, willful boy who runs away from home, becomes a vagabond entertainer, kills a pimp for his identity papers, sinks into the Warsaw underworld, and finally, turned idealistic, is betrayed by a foolish young girl and sent to prison.

A second group of novels, set in the United States, describes the conflict between the traditional values of the Eastern European Jewish immigrant and the diverse, unconventional environment of New York. *East River*, for example, is the story of a Jewish boy who has fallen in love with a Roman Catholic girl, to the horror of both families. Although critics suggest that Asch's happy ending is implausible, they praise his realistic handling of the psychological problems involved in such a relationship.

The third group of works, published late in Asch's life, consists of those novels in which he placed Jesus and Mary within their Jewish environment, the stories of Paul and of Moses, and the study of Second Isaiah, *The Prophet*. Ironically, these books, which brought him the greatest criticism, particularly from his own people, are those which are probably his most spiritual, written in the tradition of Jewish mysticism.

The two themes which pervade Asch's works are the essence of Judaism: the universal rule of God and the moral obligation of the individual. No one who commits evil deeds can escape God's judgment. Those who try, such as the protagonists in *The God of Vengeance* and in *Mottke the Thief*, will eventually be trapped. Although the innocent and the pious cannot be assured of protection from the violence and bestiality of this world, they can save their souls from pollution. By clinging to God, human beings, whether Christian or Jewish, can attain a spiritual freedom. The fact that Asch's convictions are dramatized in works which are psychologically convincing and intellectually challenging has earned for him a lasting place among the greatest of Yiddish writers, as well as an important ranking among American novelists.

BIBLIOGRAPHICAL REFERENCES: A useful bibliography of Asch's works in English, with information about reprints and editions, is offered by Libby Okun Cohen, "Shalom Asch in English Translation: A Bibliography," *Bulletin of Bibliography*, XXII (January-April, 1958), 109-111. Probably the most balanced biographical and critical work is Ben Siegel, *The Controversial Sholem Asch: An Introduction to His Fiction*, 1976. An interesting article by Asch's son is Nathan Asch, "My Father and I," *Commentary*, XXXIX (January, 1965), 55-64. See also these interviews: "Sholem Asch Speaks," *The Mediator*, XXV (April-June, 1952), 1, and Lewis Nichols, "Talk with Sholem Asch," *The New York Times Book Review*, LX (November 6, 1955), 26. Outstanding critical articles include Oscar Cargill, "Sholem Asch: Still Immigrant and Alien," *College English*, XII (November, 1950), 67-74, and Harry Slochower, "Franz Werfel and Sholem Asch: The Yearning for Status," *Accent*, V (August, 1945), 73-82, reprinted in Harry Slochower, *No Voice Is Wholly Lost: Writers and Thinkers in War and Peace*, 1945.

Rosemary M. Canfield Reisman

ISAAC ASIMOV

Born: Petrovichi, Soviet Union
Date: January 2, 1920

Principal Works

SCIENCE FICTION: *Pebble in the Sky*, 1950; *I, Robot*, 1950; *The Stars Like Dust*, 1951; *Foundation*, 1951; *Foundation and Empire*, 1952; *Second Foundation*, 1953; *The Caves of Steel*, 1954; *The Martian Way and Other Stories*, 1955; *The End of Eternity*, 1955; *The Naked Sun*, 1957; *Earth Is Room Enough: Science Fiction Tales of Our Own Planet*, 1957; *Lucky Starr and the Rings of Saturn*, 1958; *Nine Tomorrows: Tales of the Near Future*, 1959; *Fantastic Voyage*, 1966; *Through a Glass Clearly*, 1967; *Nightfall and Other Stories*, 1969; *The Gods Themselves*, 1972; *Buy Jupiter and Other Stories*, 1975; *The Bicentennial Man and Other Stories*, 1976; *The Complete Robot*, 1982; *Foundation's Edge*, 1982; *The Robots of Dawn*, 1983; *Robots and Empire*, 1985; *Foundation and Earth*, 1986.

SCIENCE: *The Chemicals of Life: Enzymes, Vitamins, Hormones*, 1954; *Inside the Atom*, 1956; *The World of Carbon*, 1958; *The World of Nitrogen*, 1958; *Words of Science and the History Behind Them*, 1959; *Realm of Numbers*, 1959; *The Intelligent Man's Guide to Science*, 1960; *Life and Energy*, 1962; *The Search for the Elements*, 1962; *The Genetic Code*, 1963; *The Human Body: Its Structures and Operation*, 1964; *The Human Brain: Its Capacities and Functions*, 1964; *A Short History of Biology*, 1964; *Asimov's Biographical Encyclopedia of Science and Technology*, 1964; *A Short History of Chemistry*, 1965; *The Neutrino: Ghost Particle of the Atom*, 1966; *Understanding Physics*, 1966; *The Genetic Effects of Radiation*, 1966; *The Universe: From Flat Earth to Quasar*, 1966; *Science, Numbers and I*, 1968; *Electricity and Man*, 1972; *Worlds Within Worlds: The Story of Nuclear Energy*, 1972; *Today, Tomorrow and . . .* , 1973; *Our World in Space*, 1974; *The Collapsing Universe*, 1977; *A Choice of Catastrophes: The Disasters That Threaten Our World*, 1979; *Visions of the Universe*, 1981; *Exploring the Earth and the Cosmos: The Growth and Future of Human Knowledge*, 1982; *The Roving Mind*, 1983; *The History of Physics*, 1984; *Robots: Machines in Man's Image*, 1985 (with Karen A. Frenkel).

MYSTERY AND DETECTIVE FICTION: *Death Dealers*, 1958; *Tales of the Black Widowers*, 1974; *Murder at the ABA: A Puzzle in Four Days and Sixty Scenes*, 1976; *The Key World and Other Mysteries*, 1977; *The Union Club Mysteries*, 1983; *Computer Crimes and Capers*, 1983; *The Disappearing Man and Other Mysteries*, 1985.

HISTORY: *The Greeks: A Great Adventure*, 1965; *The Roman Republic*, 1966; *The Roman Empire*, 1967; *The Egyptians*, 1967; *The Dark Ages*, 1968; *The Shaping of England*, 1969; *Constantinople: The Forgotten Empire*, 1970; *The Shaping of France*, 1972; *The Shaping of North America from Earliest Times to 1763*, 1973; *The Birth of the United States, 1763-1816*, 1974; *Our Federal Union: The United States from 1816 to 1865*, 1975; *The Golden Door: The United States from 1865 to 1918*, 1977.

OTHER NONFICTION: *Asimov's Guide to the Bible*, 1968; *Asimov's Guide to Shakespeare*, 1970; *Extraterrestrial Civilizations*, 1979; *The Annotated "Gulliver's Travels,"* 1980; *Asimov on Science Fiction*, 1980; *The Edge of Tomorrow*, 1985.

AUTOBIOGRAPHY: *In Memory Yet Green: The Autobiography of Isaac Asimov, 1920-1954*, 1979; *In Joy Still Felt: The Autobiography of Isaac Asimov, 1954-1978*, 1980.

Although often singled out for the great number and wide variety of his books, to the general reader Isaac Asimov is best known and most likely to be remembered for his works in science fiction. He was born in Petrovichi, a shtetl (a small, culturally homogeneous Jewish community) about 250 miles southwest of Moscow. Throughout his life Isaac, the first son of Judah and Anna Rachel (Berman) Asimov, has celebrated January 2, 1920, as his birthday, although as a result of lost records and faulty memories the actual date is uncertain.

At the urging of relatives in the "Golden Land" of America, the Asimov family, which had recently added a daughter, left the Soviet Union in 1923 and traveled to the United States, settling in Brooklyn, where another son was born. Judah Asimov did odd jobs, accumulated some money, and in 1926 bought a small candy store, in which he and his wife labored for sixteen hours a day, seven days a week. Isaac, who learned from his father to respect hard work and careful study, helped his parents after school.

Asimov became an American citizen when he was eight years old. By that time, he was already recognized as an exceptionally bright student in the Brooklyn public school he attended. Even before he began school, he had become a voracious reader, a practice that led him in the summer of 1929 to experience his first science fiction in *Amazing Stories*. Because Judah Asimov believed that only bums read the pulps, he initially refused to allow his son to read these magazines in his store's racks, but when *Science Wonder Stories* appeared, the word "science" convinced him of the new publication's value. Soon, Isaac was an avid fan. These magazines interested him not only in science and fiction but also in writing, and by the age of eleven he was composing stories of his own.

In 1935, when he was fifteen, Asimov was graduated from high school and enrolled in Seth Low Junior College, then a part of Columbia University. Following his father's recommendation, he started as a premedical student majoring in zoology, but he switched his major to chemistry in his sophomore year. While in college he continued to write stories, and his father bought him a typewriter to facilitate the process. In the summer of 1938, he completed a story called "Cosmic Corkscrew," whose generating idea was helical time travel. Asimov knew that John W. Campbell edited *Astounding Science Fiction* in New York City, but he was surprised by his father's suggestion that he take his story to Campbell in person, which proved to be more economical since mailing the story would have cost twelve cents whereas the round-trip subway fare was only ten cents. Campbell graciously talked with Asimov for over an hour, and although he turned down the story, he encouraged the young writer to keep trying. Twelve rejections later, Asimov made his first sale, "Marooned off Vesta," to *Amazing Stories* in October, 1938.

After receiving his B.S. degree in 1939, and after failing to get into medical school, Asimov continued at Columbia University in pursuit of a graduate degree in chemistry. Despite these moves toward a career in chemistry, he thought of himself more and more as a science-fiction writer, particularly after Campbell and other editors began regularly publishing his stories. He wrote his most famous story, "Nightfall," in 1941 at the suggestion of Campbell, who, building on an idea of Ralph Waldo Emerson, wondered how human beings would react to the stars if they were visible only once every thousand years.

In the summer of 1941, after obtaining his master's degree, Asimov married Gertrude Blugerman, a union that eventually produced two children, a boy and a girl. During World War II, he worked as a civilian chemist at the Naval Air Experimental Station in Philadelphia, and starting in 1945, he served in the U.S. Army and achieved the rank of corporal. In 1946, following his discharge, he returned to Columbia, where he studied the rates of biochemical reactions. Having received his Ph.D. in 1948, he began postdoctoral studies on nucleic acids at Columbia, before accepting an invitation in 1949 to teach biochemistry at the Boston University Medical School. He became a tenured professor in 1955.

During his years as an academic, Asimov continued to write science fiction in his spare time. In 1950 he published his first novel, *Pebble in the Sky*, in which he used the experiences of an old European immigrant from twentieth century Chicago in a future society where Earth is a backward planet in a Galactic Empire to make pungent comments on racial intolerance and militarism. In several other books written in the 1950's, he introduced many innovative ideas into science fiction. For example, he developed the three basic laws of robotics, which proposed that robots, though they should be self-protective and obedient, have as their chief duty that no human being ever comes to harm. Asimov, who saw these laws as his most likely claim to permanent fame, used them as the basis for more than two dozen short stories and three novels. In one of them, *The Caves of Steel*, he became the first writer to integrate science fiction with the detective novel, and the characters he introduced, Elijah Baley, a New York detective, and his robot partner, Daneel Olivaw, appeared again in *The Naked Sun*, where another murder was solved. Unlike many writers after him, Asimov had a positive attitude toward robots, and he castigated the fear of mechanical intelligence as a "Frankenstein complex."

Another great achievement in the 1950's was Asimov's Foundation series, a group of stories inspired by Edward Gibbon's *The History of the Decline and Fall of the Roman Empire* (1776-1788). Although the term "trilogy" is often applied to the three volumes derived from these stories, it is misleading because Asimov did not plan the nine stories as three unified novels. This collection won the Hugo Award for the most outstanding series of all time in 1966. Though the award reflected the exuberant enthusiasm of science-fiction fans, critics now agree that the series was a milestone in the maturation of the genre. The stories deal with such fundamental issues as the success versus the failure of human (and alien) societies, free will versus determinism, and the individual versus history. The Foundation series remained popular decades after its original publication, having sold more than two million copies.

Asimov quit teaching to become a full-time science writer in 1958. From the late 1950's to the middle 1960's, he became known as America's "Great Explainer" because of his ability to translate scientific jargon into transparent prose without sacrificing accuracy. His popularizations introduced many lay readers to the mysteries of mathematics, astronomy, physics, chemistry, biology, and technology. Although general readers enjoyed these books, scientists and scholars were critical of them as superficial and unscholarly. Asimov replied that it was sufficient for him to know enough about a field to be able to communicate its basic ideas intelligently and interestingly to novices; he conceded that nothing he wrote could enlighten specialists.

During the decade from 1965 to 1975, Asimov began to write on an even wider variety of subjects than in his science books: popular history, the Bible, William Shakespeare, and mystery stories. In the early 1970's, his first marriage ended in divorce. He moved from Boston to New York, and on November 30, 1973, he married Janet Opal Jeppson, a psychiatrist and writer. During this troubled period, he began, after a fourteen-year hiatus, to write science fiction again. In 1972, he published *The Gods Themselves*, which some critics believe is his best novel. Asimov himself has called it his favorite, and it garnered for him both a Nebula Award and a Hugo Award. In this story, which hinges on an exchange of energy between two parallel universes, he explores the idea that scientific knowledge can be a form of ignorance when it comes into conflict with true emotion. In 1982, he published *Foundation's Edge*, a sequel to the Foundation series. Like the series, this novel investigates the nature of free will and the question of historical determinism, but there are also great differences. For example, in the earlier novels Asimov sees rationality as the only trustworthy human trait, whereas in *Foundation's Edge* his characters are mired in complex motivations within motivations, where a failure of imagination can be more important than a computer failure.

In the early 1980's, Asimov continued to write despite serious health problems, and with even greater intensity: It took him nineteen years to write his first hundred books, ten years to write his second hundred, five years to write his third, and an even shorter time for his fourth hundred. According to Asimov, the reason for his acceleration of production is his participation in the game of immortality: He wants to make sure that at least some of his books live after his death.

Asimov once defined science fiction as the branch of literature concerned with the impact of science on human beings. The genre arose after the Industrial Revolution because historical events were forcing people to adapt to a rapidly changing society. By allowing readers, through their imagination, to try on possible changes for size, science fiction becomes not an escape from reality but an escape into reality. A theme common to most of Asimov's writings, both fiction and nonfiction, is the power of reason. He is proud of being a secular humanist, and through his stories and popularizations, he has tried to show how reason can help humankind solve such problems as overpopulation, prejudice, and war. In his fiction, a reasoned rather than emotional approach usually provides the solution to conflicts. Whether writing fiction or nonfiction, Asimov chose themes with validity in the past, present, and future: the economic, political, and religious forces behind the rise and fall of empires; the effects of technology on society; and the human heart in conflict with its mind. As time dates his scientific writings, his science-fiction corpus looms larger. Indeed, his work in this genre helped it to outgrow its birth in the pulps to become an important part of modern fiction.

BIBLIOGRAPHICAL REFERENCES: For extensive bibliographies on Isaac Asimov, see Matthew Tepper, *Asimov Science Fiction Bibliography*, 1970, and Marjorie Miller, *Issac Asimov: A Checklist of Works Published in the United States*, 1972. Asimov's science fiction has been the subject of several book-length studies, the best being Joseph F. Patrouch, Jr., *The Science Fiction of Isaac Asimov*, 1974. George E. Slusser, *Isaac Asimov: The Foundations of His Science Fiction*, 1979, has an excellent analysis of Asimov's style. Jean Fiedler and Jim Mele, *Isaac Asimov*, 1982, devote too much space to plot summary and not enough to critical analysis, though they make some insightful comments on a few of the stories and novels. Several of the essays in *Isaac Asimov*, 1977, edited by Joseph D. Olander and Martin Harry Greenberg, are valuable. Asimov's achievements in science fiction have been discussed in several histories of the genre. Donald A. Wollheim, *The Universe Makers: Science Fiction Today*, 1971, analyzes the relationship between Asimov's science fiction and history in a chapter entitled "The Decline and Fall of the Galactic Empire." Brian Aldiss, *Billion Year Spree: The True History of Science Fiction*, 1976, has integrated Asimov's accomplishments into a good account of how various writers built on the technological developments and social evolution of their times. Patricia S. Warrick, *The Cybernetic Imagination in Science Fiction*, 1980, analyzes a subgenre of science fiction, robot and computer stories, and because of Asimov's importance to this field, she has an extensive investigation of his stories on mechanical intelligence. A representative selection of critical articles begins with the collection in *Fantasy and Science Fiction*, October, 1966, a special issue devoted to Asimov's life and work. See also Damon Knight, "Asimov and Empire," in his *In Search of Wonder: Essays on Modern Science Fiction*, 1967.

Robert J. Paradowski

MIGUEL ÁNGEL ASTURIAS

Born: Guatemala City, Guatemala
Date: October 19, 1899

Died: Madrid, Spain
Date: June 9, 1974

Principal Works

NOVELS: *El Señor Presidente*, 1946 (*The President*, 1963); *Hombres de maíz*, 1949 (*Men of Maize*, 1975); *Viento fuerte*, 1950 (*The Cyclone*, 1967; better known as *Strong Wind*); *El papa verde*, 1954 (*The Green Pope*, 1971); *Los ojos de los enterrados*, 1960 (*The Eyes of the Interred*, 1973); *El alhajadito*, 1961 (*The Bejeweled Boy*, 1971); *Mulata de tal*, 1963 (*Mulata*, 1967); *Maladrón*, 1969.

SHORT FICTION: *Leyendas de Guatemala*, 1930; *Week-end en Guatemala*, 1956; *El espejo de Lida Sal*, 1967.

PLAYS: *Soluna*, pb. 1955; *Teatro: Chantaje, Dique Seco, Soluna, La audiencia de los confines*, pb. 1964.

POETRY: *Sien de alondra*, 1949; *Bolívar*, 1955; *Clarivigilia primaveral*, 1965.

ESSAYS: *Rumania: Su nueva imagen*, 1964; *Latinoamérica y otros ensayos*, 1968.

Miguel Ángel Asturias is unquestionably one of the three most important Latin American writers of his generation (Jorge Luis Borges and Alejo Carpentier are the other two) and one of the two major influences in the twentieth century on the development of the Latin American novel. He was born in Guatemala City, Guatemala, to Ernesto Asturias, a magistrate, and María Rosales, a schoolteacher, on October 19, 1899, a year after the accession to the presidency of the infamous dictator, Manuel Estrada Cabrera. Unable to tolerate the politically vindictive and repressive measures of the Estrada Cabrera regime, Ernesto Asturias moved his family to a small village near the outskirts of Guatemala City. There, and later in Salamá, an even smaller village in the Guatemalan interior, the young Miguel's contact with the magical vision of the indigenous Indian cultures initiated his personal education and stimulated his artistic development.

Travels into the hinterland with his maternal grandfather to oversee the family estates were also a regular part of his early years and subsequently provided the intimate knowledge and experience of Indian languages, life-styles, and traditions which would lead Asturias in later years to first the writing of a thesis (*El problema social del indio*, 1923) on the social problems of the Indian in Guatemala and later, in the mid-1920's, to the formal study (and translation into Spanish) of pre-Columbian literary and mythological texts.

The years from 1899 to 1920, lived under the sternly repressive government of Estrada Cabrera, were decisive in shaping the political and artistic temperament of the writer. As a student activist, Asturias spearheaded the founding of a popular university in 1922, following the overthrow of the Estrada Cabrera dictatorship (an event to which his activities had significantly contributed). As a community project, the popular university was intended to increase the social and political influence of the underprivileged sectors of Guatemalan society through the contributions and active involvement of the middle class in educational and other programs for the poor.

Although granted his law degree in 1923, because he was an editor of a weekly journal called *Tiempos Nuevos* (new times), Asturias was forced into exile when the paper fell into disfavor with the succeeding regime. It was during this first of several exiles in London, and later Paris, that Asturias returned to his diary in a notebook—begun in December of 1917, in response to the great earthquake that leveled Guatemala City—to produce the stories that were subsequently transformed into his first expression of devotion to his country and his first published work, *Leyendas de Guatemala* (legends of Guatemala).

Breaking with the realist and naturalist traditions of Indianist writings of previous generations, Asturias expanded the possibilities of the genre by infusing a conventional narrative style with the mythopoeic language and the oneiric texture and modes of perception found in the *Popol Vuh* (c. 1550) and the *Annals of the Cakchiquels* (sixteenth century). Under the notable influence of these surviving sacred texts of the Maya Quiché and Maya Cakchiquels, his authoritative knowledge derived from five years of literary and anthropological studies at the Musée de l'Homme and the Sorbonne in Paris, and inspired by the theories and techniques of French Surrealism for exploring the unconscious in literature and art, Asturias managed to bring an unprecedented degree of innovation and authenticity to Latin American imaginative writings about Indians.

Although the critical reception accorded his first book was favorable and encouraging, nearly sixteen years separate the stories of *Leyendas de Guatemala* from Asturias' first novel, *The President*. It began as a short story ("Los mendigos politicos," the political beggars) written originally for a literary contest in Guatemala in 1923 but never submitted. Stimulated by personal memories evoked by meetings of exiled writers to discuss and compare anecdotes on Latin American dictatorships they had known, the story evolved over the next two decades from oral speech and tale into what is generally considered to be the author's most important novel. First published in Mexico in 1946, *The President* epitomizes the most characteristic and persistent elements found in Asturias' fiction: the fusion of myth, dream, and magic to establish a specific cultural frame of reference; political portraiture and social criticism; linguistic inventiveness; complexity of narrative structure; and technical experimentation designed to expand the experience of the novel beyond the narrow confines of naturalism and literary regionalism. The themes of man in harmony with nature, man's resistance to economic exploitation, and the evil and cruelty of political corruption are also central to the novel's purpose.

In 1952, Asturias received the Prix International du Livre Français for the French translation of *The President* and, in 1972, the William Faulkner Foundation's Ibero-American Novel Award when the English translation appeared. Although based on incidents of the Estrada Cabrera dictatorship, the novel's events exist in that kind of fantastically timeless dimension and locale intended to evoke the type of "hallucinatory" perception and experience of the world that Asturias associates with the indigenous, pre-Columbian imagination: *realismo mágico*. This "magical realism" became the dominant tendency in Latin American prose fiction of the twentieth century, and Asturias is considered one of its inventors and (along with the Cuban, Alejo Carpentier) its most successful practitioner.

The critical success of *The President* was followed three years later by *Men of Maize*, the novel Asturias identified as his favorite. Based on Indian legends of man's creation by the gods from corn, the novel is much more obscure, much more "Indianist," and much less nightmarish in atmosphere than *The President*.

Asturias returned to Guatemala in 1933 and established a radio news program, "El diario del aire" (daily news on the air). It was the only news commentary program under the right-wing regime of then-president Ubico. Following the 1944 revolution, Asturias was appointed to diplomatic posts in Mexico, Argentina, France, and El Salvador. The years from 1954 to 1959 saw him again in exile. Artistically, these were very productive years. He completed his Banana Trilogy, begun in 1950 with *Strong Wind* and followed by *The Green Pope* and *The Eyes of the Interred*. This trilogy was followed by *The Bejeweled Boy*, *Mulata*, and *Maladrón*, along with several collections of short stories, several volumes of poetry, and numerous journalistic writings.

In 1966, Asturias was awarded the Lenin Peace Prize; in 1967, he became the first Latin American novelist to be awarded the Nobel Prize in Literature; and in 1970, he was made a member of the French Légion d'Honneur. These prestigious awards gave international recognition of his importance. They also contributed greatly to diminishing negative criticism of the author's works because of the pervasive Marxist, anti-American themes explicit in his narratives. Today there is neither question of Asturias' literary achievements nor debate over the significance of his contribution to world literature.

BIBLIOGRAPHICAL REFERENCES: Richard E. Moore, *Asturias: A Checklist of Works and Criticism*, 1979, is still the best compilation of critical literature on the major and minor works of the author. For further study, see Richard J. Callan, *Miguel Ángel Asturias*, 1970, a perceptive Jungian approach to the major novels and plays that contains much helpful biographical information, and Martha Pilon, *Miguel Ángel Asturias: Semblanza para el estudio de su vida y obra con una selección de poemas y prosas*, 1968, published in Guatemala in honor of the writer's Nobel award. Publications which contain lengthy interviews and discussions about Asturias' major works include Luis Harss and Barbara Dohmann, "Miguel Ángel Asturias, or the Land Where the Flowers Bloom," in *Into the Mainstream: Conversations with Latin American Writers*, 1967; Rita Guibert, "Miguel Ángel Asturias," in *Seven Voices*, 1973; and Gunter Lorenz, "*Men of Maize*: An Interview with Asturias," in *Review 75*, 1975. See also Thomas Lyons, "Miguel Ángel Asturias: Timeless Fantasy," *Books Abroad*, Spring, 1968, 183-189; José Vasquez Amaral, "*El Señor Presidente*," in *The Contemporary Latin American Narrative*, 1970; and John S. Brushwood, "From *Todo verdor perecerá* to *El Señor Presidente* (1942-1945)," in *The Spanish American Novel*, 1975.

Roland E. Bush

MARGARET ATWOOD

Born: Ottawa, Ontario, Canada
Date: November 18, 1939

Principal Works

NOVELS: *The Edible Woman*, 1969; *Surfacing*, 1972; *Lady Oracle*, 1976; *Life Before Man*, 1979; *Bodily Harm*, 1981; *The Handmaid's Tale*, 1986; *Cat's Eye*, 1989.

SHORT FICTION: *Dancing Girls*, 1977; *Murder in the Dark*, 1983; *Bluebeard's Egg*, 1983.

POETRY: *Double Persephone*, 1961; *The Circle Game*, 1964; *Talismans for Children*, 1965; *Kaleidoscopes Baroque: A Poem*, 1965; *Speeches for Dr. Frankenstein*, 1966; *Expeditions*, 1966; *The Animals in That Country*, 1968; *The Journals of Susanna Moodie*, 1970; *Procedures for Underground*, 1970; *Power Politics*, 1971; *You Are Happy*, 1974; *Selected Poems*, 1976; *Two-Headed Poems*, 1978; *Snake Poems*, 1983; *Interlunar*, 1984; *Selected Poems II*, 1987.

NONFICTION: *Survival: A Thematic Guide to Canadian Literature*, 1972; *Second Words: Selected Critical Prose*, 1982.

CHILDREN'S LITERATURE: *Up in the Tree*, 1978; *Anna's Pet*, 1980 (with Joyce Barkhouse).

Margaret Eleanor Atwood is Canada's foremost contemporary writer of novels, poetry, and literary criticism. She was born November 18, 1939, in Ottawa, to Margaret Killam Atwood and Carl Edmund Atwood, an entomologist whose university position and scientific research were responsible for his family's dual life, spent both in Toronto and in the bush country of Quebec. After attending public school in Toronto, she enrolled at Victoria College, University of Toronto, where in 1961 she received her B.A. degree in English language and literature and was awarded the E. J. Pratt Medal for *Double Persephone*, a book of poetry.

After intermittent graduate study at Harvard University, where she was profoundly influenced by the myth criticism of Northrop Frye, she returned to Canada, where the acclaimed *The Circle Game* established her as one of Canada's leading poets. While she has continued to publish poetry regularly, she has increasingly turned her attention to fiction, beginning with *The Edible Woman*, a novel that also concerns the male-female relationships she had explored in her poetry. In 1972 she published her second novel, *Surfacing*, perhaps her best fictional work, and *Survival*, a book of literary criticism that not only charted Canadian literary history but also identified survival as the most important Canadian theme, as well as her own predominant theme.

In 1973 she left teaching (she had taught at several Canadian universities), resigned as editor of House of Anansi Press, was divorced from her first husband, moved to Alliston, Ontario (with writer Graeme Gibson), and became a self-supporting writer. During this watershed year she was invited to tour the Soviet Union as part of a cultural exchange program, but she later canceled the trip to protest the Soviet expulsion of Aleksandr Solzhenitsyn. This decision, seen in terms of her Canadian nationalism and her feminist voice, made her a reluctant political figure. She has since traveled widely, received numerous literary awards and honorary degrees, published regularly, and become the Canadian voice in literature (in 1981 she served as chair of the Writers' Union of Canada).

Her work, regardless of genre, is remarkably consistent in theme, subject matter, and tone, though *The Handmaid's Tale*, her most popular novel, did strike reviewers as a bit atypical. The dystopian, futuristic science-fiction novel does, however, have a female protagonist whose survival is threatened by a patriarchal society, and her story, preserved for a later generation of "literary" scholars, itself becomes the vehicle for ridiculing male chauvinism, modern sensibilities, and political totalitarianism.

Atwood's interior landscape, developed early in *The Circle Game* and *The Animals in That Country*, is characterized by critics as violently dualistic. The pervasive doubling of worlds, visions, and cultures has been linked to her childhood, when she switched back and forth from bush country to urban metropolis, and more directly to her view of people living in an "objective" world and shaping that world by how they perceive it. That is, people are simultaneously committed to a civilized world of ostensible order and reason and cowed by their unconscious fears and phobias. According to Atwood, rather than choose to live superficially in the objective world or to retreat into self, people should reject the destructive extremes of polarity and accept duality.

Atwood writes primarily about the present, not the past or the future, and she focuses on domestic relations in banal urban centers. When a woman journeys to the wilderness, as in *Surfacing*, the journey is psychological and mythic as well as geographical, and the goal is redemption and renewal through self-discovery. Unfortunately, men act as obstacles to such journeys because as consumers they exploit, even "devour," women (in *The Edible Woman* the protagonist substitutes a cake for herself). For women to escape the "circle games," they must perceive reality accurately, and Atwood expresses the duality through mirror imagery and multiple points of view (*Life Before Man*, *Two-Headed Poems*). In fact, her later fiction, like her later poetry, has become more experimental, more concerned with narration and voice.

Atwood is at once the most studied, influential, popular, and controversial of Canadian writers, and she has transcended geographical barriers, particularly with *The Handmaid's Tale*, to achieve international status. Moreover, though a self-confessed recluse who does not see herself as a preacher or a politician, she has become, in typically dualistic fashion, a political figure who exercises so much literary authority through her publishing activities and her literary criticism that she has been seen as the high priestess of Canadian literature. Her novels, which depict women as victims in masculine Westernized society, also have inevitably made her, despite her protests, a heroine of the women's movement. As resistant to labels as she is, her work remains both distinctly Canadian and feminist.

BIBLIOGRAPHICAL REFERENCES: Two book-length studies of Atwood's work are Jerome H. Rosenberg's *Margaret Atwood*, 1984, which contains a biography, bibliography, and general overview of Atwood's work; and Sherrill Grace's *Violent Duality: A Study of Margaret Atwood*, 1980, which, limited in scope because of its thesis, nevertheless provides closer analysis of some works. Essays on Atwood's work are collected in *The Art of Margaret Atwood: Essays in Criticism*, 1981, edited by Arnold E. Davidson and Cathy N. Davidson, which contains an exhaustive list of primary and secondary works; *Margaret Atwood: Language, Text, and System*, 1983, edited by Sherrill E. Grace and Lorraine Weir; and *Margaret Atwood: Reflection and Reality*, 1987, edited by Beatrice Mendez-Egle. *The Malahat Review*, no. 41, 1977, edited by Linda Sandler, is a special issue devoted to Atwood and her work.

Thomas L. Erskine

LOUIS AUCHINCLOSS

Born: Lawrence, New York
Date: September 27, 1917

PRINCIPAL WORKS

NOVELS: *The Indifferent Children*, 1947; *Sybil*, 1951; *A Law for the Lion*, 1953; *The Great World and Timothy Colt*, 1956; *Venus in Sparta*, 1958; *Pursuit of the Prodigal*, 1959; *The House of Five Talents*, 1960; *Portrait in Brownstone*, 1962; *The Rector of Justin*, 1964; *The Embezzler*, 1966; *A World of Profit*, 1968; *I Come as a Thief*, 1972; *The Partners*, 1974; *The Winthrop Covenant*, 1976; *The Dark Lady*, 1977; *The Country Cousin*, 1978; *The House of the Prophet*, 1980; *Watchfires*, 1982; *The Book Class*, 1984; *Honorable Men*, 1985; *Diary of a Yuppie*, 1986; *The Golden Calves*, 1988; *Fellow Passengers*, 1989.

SHORT FICTION: *The Injustice Collectors*, 1950; *The Romantic Egoists*, 1954; *Powers of Attorney*, 1963; *Tales of Manhattan*, 1967; *Second Chance*, 1970; *Narcissa and Other Fables*, 1983; *Skinny Island*, 1987.

MEMOIR: *A Writer's Capital*, 1974.

ESSAYS: *Reflections of a Jacobite*, 1961; *Motiveless Malignity*, 1969; *Reading Henry James*, 1975; *Life, Law, and Letters*, 1979.

OTHER NONFICTION: *Richelieu*, 1972; *Persons of Consequence: Queen Victoria and Her Circle*, 1979.

Initially recognized as a younger competitor to John P. Marquand and John O'Hara, two novelists noted for their deft portrayals of business and society in fiction, Louis Auchincloss soon distinguished himself as their equal if not their superior. Auchincloss' name has come to be identified with the tradition of the "novel of manners," as the genre is now called. Acknowledging his debt to Henry James and Edith Wharton, as to Marcel Proust and other European masters of the form, Auchincloss went on during the 1960's to develop the novel of manners in its contemporary mode. Marquand had died in 1960; O'Hara, although resentful of Auchincloss' success, diverted most of his own energies toward shorter fiction until his death in 1970. Thereafter, Auchincloss remained almost alone and unchallenged as the American chronicler of manners.

Louis Stanton Auchincloss was born September 27, 1917, in Lawrence, Long Island, New York, the second son and third child of a successful Wall Street lawyer. The Auchincloss family, of Scottish origin, had grown both numerous and prosperous in the New World, initially engaged in the wool trade. Unlike O'Hara and Marquand, both born to privilege only to lose it soon after, Auchincloss never suffered the decline in family fortunes that was thought to provide both older writers with their inspiration and their ambitions. Notwithstanding, the young Louis Auchincloss grew up both perceptive and observant, developing a keen, analytical view of the Establishment, to which he has belonged since birth.

After graduation from the prestigious Groton School in Massachusetts, Auchincloss went on to Yale University, where he attempted to write novels. Following the rejection of his first novelistic effort, Auchincloss decided to leave Yale after three years and seek admission to a law school where a bachelor's degree might not be necessary for admission. The University of Virginia accepted him in 1938, allowing him to complete his legal studies and actually begin his career several months before his country's entry into World War II. After the bombing of Pearl Harbor in December, 1941, Auchincloss volunteered for commissioned service in the Navy, serving first in the Canal Zone and subsequently in both European and Pacific war theaters. While in the Navy, Auchincloss read voraciously for pleasure, turning back toward the writerly ambitions that he had renounced upon entering law school.

At war's end, after finishing *The Indifferent Children*, Auchincloss returned to his prewar job with the Wall Street firm of Sullivan and Cromwell, devoting his spare time to the writing of short stories and one novel, *Sybil*. Toward the end of 1951 he resigned from Sullivan and Cromwell, resolved to devote all of his time and energy to writing; after publishing a third novel, *A Law for the Lion*, Auchincloss noticed that his furlough from the law had not noticeably improved his writing and sought a return to legal practice. Barred by company policy from returning to Sullivan and Cromwell once he had resigned, Auchincloss was hired in 1954 by the rival firm of Hawkins, Delafield, and Wood. During the late 1950's he published three "professional," or "Wall Street," novels that attracted generally favorable reviews, incidentally competing with novels of O'Hara and Marquand also published at that time. *The Great World and Timothy Colt*, *Venus in Sparta*, and *Pursuit of the Prodigal* all announced the arrival of an extremely talented novelist doubly informed by his "insider" status both as a Wall Street lawyer and as a member in good standing of Manhattan high society. Certain critics deplored the continued use of New York settings, claiming also to find certain characters boring, a criticism that would continue to haunt Auchincloss for the rest of his career. Other critics, however, perceived in Auchincloss' New York a microcosm of upwardly mobile American business and society; indeed, a number of Auchincloss' featured characters are New Yorkers only by adoption, having come to the city in search of fame and fortune, much as their European counterparts might flock to Paris.

Around 1960, Auchincloss began the experiments with viewpoint and with narrative voice that would bring him his greatest measure of success, both with critics and with the reading public. *The House of Five Talents*, ostensibly a memoir written shortly after World War II by an aging, affluent spinster, is both a stylistic tour de force and an authoritative chronicle of New York business and society between the Civil War and World War II. *Portrait in Brownstone* covers much the same territory, yet without repetition. *The Rector of Justin*, dealing with the founder of a New England preparatory school from a multiplicity of viewpoints, is one of Auchincloss' most ambitious and most masterful works, notable both for its documentary interest and for Auchincloss' deft characterization of the various narrators through their "own" words. In his subsequent novel, *The Embezzler*, Auchincloss again blended history with fiction, attributing the well-documented crime of Richard Whitney to one Guy Prime, a wholly fictional character with family, friends, and motivations quite different from Whitney's.

Following *The Embezzler*, Auchincloss continued to turn out well-written, eminently readable novels dealing with his characteristic themes and subjects, particularly the interaction of privilege, responsibility, and power among those in positions of trust. As a rule, however, his later novels failed to meet the high standard that he had set for himself. Some notable exceptions to that rule are *I Come as a Thief*, dealing with a self-corrupting lawyer; *The House of the Prophet*, depicting loosely (but frankly) the life of pundit Walter Lippmann; *Watchfires*, treating crises of conscience during the War Between the States; and *The Golden Calves*, which turns the author's politically watchful eye upon the inner workings of an art museum. Arguably, however, the sheer volume of Auchincloss' later output has tended to hide the true achievement of his middle years, upon which his reputation properly should rest.

BIBLIOGRAPHICAL REFERENCES: Christopher C. Dahl, *Louis Auchincloss*, 1985, presents a solid chronological treatment of Auchincloss' novels, with useful information on the author's possible historical models for his characters. David B. Parsell, *Louis Auchincloss*, 1988, isolates characteristic themes and concerns in Auchincloss' fiction, attempting to re-create the author's fictional "world." For perspectives on Auchincloss' position within the "novel of manners" tradition, see Gordon Milne, *The Sense of Society: A History of the American Novel of Manners*, 1977, and James W. Tuttleton, *The Novel of Manners in America*, 1972.

David B. Parsell

W. H. AUDEN

Born: York, England
Date: February 21, 1907

Died: Vienna, Austria
Date: September 29, 1973

PRINCIPAL WORKS

POETRY: *Poems*, 1930; *The Orators*, 1932; *The Dance of Death*, 1933; *Look, Stranger!*, 1936; *Spain*, 1937; *Another Time*, 1940; *New Year Letter*, 1941 (aso known as *The Double Man*); *Three Songs for St. Cecilia's Day*, 1941; *For the Time Being*, 1944; *The Age of Anxiety*, 1947; *Nones*, 1951; *Mountains*, 1954; *The Shield of Achilles*, 1955; *The Old Man's Road*, 1956; *Homage to Clio*, 1960; *About the House*, 1965; *City Without Walls and Other Poems*, 1969; *Academic Graffiti*, 1971; *Epistle to a Godson and Other Poems*, 1972; *Thank You, Fog: Last Poems*, 1974; *Collected Poems*, 1976; *Selected Poems*, 1979.

PLAYS: *The Dog Beneath the Skin: Or, Where Is Francis?*, pb. 1935 (with Christopher Isherwood); *The Ascent of F6*, pb. 1936 (with Isherwood); *On the Frontier*, pr., pb. 1938 (with Isherwood); *Paul Bunyan*, pr. 1941; *The Rake's Progess*, pr., pb. 1951 (with Chester Kallman); *Elegy for Young Lovers*, pr., pb. 1961 (with Kallman); *The Bassarids*, pr., pb. 1966 (with Kallman).

NONFICTION: *Letters from Iceland*, 1937 (with Louis McNeice); *Journey to a War*, 1939 (with Isherwood); *The Enchafèd Flood: Or, The Romantic Iconography of the Sea*, 1950; *The Dyer's Hand and Other Essays*, 1962; *Secondary Worlds*, 1968; *A Certain World: A Commonplace Book*, 1970; *Forewords and Afterwords*, 1973.

ANTHOLOGIES: *The Oxford Book of Light Verse*, 1938; *Poets of the English Language*, 1952 (with Norman Holmes Pearson); *Nineteenth Century British Minor Poets*, 1966.

One of the most important poets of the twentieth century, Wystan Hugh Auden was born in York, in northern England, a rugged land of cliffs and escarpments that were to figure as part of his poetic landscape. His father was a prominent physician, his mother a former nurse; Auden was thus reared in a cultivated environment, a background that showed itself in his adoption of aristocratic behavior during his undergraduate career at the University of Oxford, 1925 to 1928. Originally intending to become a mining engineer, he abandoned this intention to become a poet, though his interest in science helped forge an intellectual rigor and objectivity that would characterize some of his best poetry. Along with fellow poets and students such as Stephen Spender, Auden became the leader of the so-called Thirties Group, which was to make its mark in that decade. Auden had already met Christopher Isherwood by this time, having attended St. Edmund's School in Surrey with him. With Isherwood, Auden wrote a travel book and three plays.

After receiving his degree from Oxford in 1928, Auden spent more than a year in Berlin with Isherwood and wrote poems which appeared in his first volume, *Poems*. A voracious and catholic reader, he had by this time come into contact with works on psychology and the theories of Homer Lane, a disciple of Sigmund Freud. The clinical nature of much of Auden's poetry of this period, dealing with man's anxiety and his fragmented self, can partly be attributed to the poet's interest in and interpretation of modern psychological theories. By 1930, Auden was teaching school in Scotland. *The Orators*, published in 1932, is an extraordinary collection of poems dealing with man's failings in a repressive society—the Enemy. By 1936, two more volumes followed, and his poetry had taken on what the public regarded then as Marxist tones.

The most eminent poet of his day, Auden emigrated to the United States in 1939, becoming an American citizen in 1946. For the rest of his life, except for brief periods as an Oxford professor, Auden remained a part of the American literary scene, the New York City literary scene in particular. He lectured and taught at a number of American colleges and universities and steadily produced a body of work that established him as one of the foremost poets of the century.

Another Time and *New Year Letter* introduce a less cryptic poet, one more committed to a Christian belief in man's failings and his capacity for redemption. Many of the poems in these volumes are lyrical, showing the influence of William Butler Yeats, and contain an almost existential outlook on Christianity. *The Age of Anxiety* (which won for Auden the Pulitzer Prize), *Nones*, and *The Shield of Achilles* reflect a more quietly ruminative poet, the Christian interpreter of his society. Auden's major themes in these works treat the city as both a symbol for and a creation of man and his civilization. His landscapes are primarily urban and industrial, though some poems, such as the famous "In Praise of Lomestone" (1948), suggesting the rugged northern district of his boyhood in England, describe the natural landscape in symbolic terms, as representing facets of the human personality as well as its spiritual conflicts.

Though some critics see the quality of Auden's work after 1945 as declining, a growing number have reassessed his canon and have come to regard him as a poet who continued to grow creatively throughout his career. Auden is a difficult but rewarding poet. His technical skill, his enormous range and mastery of numerous poetic forms show that, though a modernist, Auden is heir to the great tradition of English poetry. He has written sonnets, odes, epigrams, sestinas, villanelles, pastorals, ballades, satires, and a panoply of other formal types of poetry.

Auden could be viewed as a kind of twentieth century metaphysical poet. For example, his poetic treatment of the worldly and his use of ordinary objects and familiar places serve as points of departure from which witty, metaphorical meanings develop. His poems often have a conversational, colloquial tone. Like the Metaphysical poets of the seventeenth century, Auden enjoyed witty playfulness, associating an abstract, even abstruse idea with a simple, even homely fact. His poems are marked by a keen intelligence that draws upon a wide range of cultural material. As Auden himself declared: Poetry is a game of knowledge.

BIBLIOGRAPHICAL REFERENCES: Edward Mendelson, *W. H. Auden: Nineteen Hundred Seven to Nineteen Hundred Seventy Three*, 1980, is an indispensable source of material on the poet. Mendelson's personal association with Auden and his consequent access to Auden's letters and other personal material make this biography the most authoritative. Mendelson is also the editor of *The Complete Works of W. H. Auden*, the definitive edition of Auden's works, published by Princeton University Press. *Plays and Other Dramatic Writings, 1928-1938*, the first volume of the projected eight-volume edition, was published in 1989. Humphrey Carpenter, *W. H. Auden: A Biography*, 1981, is also thorough. Joseph Warren Beach, *The Making of the Auden Canon*, 1957, sheds light on the meticulousness of Auden's revisions of his work. John G. Blair, *The Poetic Art of W. H. Auden*, 1965, concentrates on the work of Auden's American phase, while Samuel Hynes, *The Auden Generation*, 1972, treats the poet's early development through the 1930's. Monroe Spears, *The Poetry of W. H. Auden: The Disenchanted Island*, 1963, presents a balanced critique of the poet's work by a close analysis of the texts. Despite its age, Richard Hoggart, *Auden: An Introductory Essay*, 1951, is a clear, direct evaluation of Auden's poetry to that time. F. R. Leavis, *New Beginnings in English Poetry*, 1950, presents the view that Auden's poetic quality declined after 1945, while John Bayley, *The Romantic Survival*, 1957, suggests that Auden is the aesthetic heir to Charles Dickens. John Fuller, *A Reader's Guide to W. H. Auden*, 1970, contains a well-researched bibliography.

Edward Fiorelli

ERICH AUERBACH

Born: Berlin, Germany
Date: November 9, 1892

Died: Wallingford, Connecticut
Date: October 13, 1957

PRINCIPAL WORKS

LITERARY CRITICISM: *Dante als Dichter der irdischen Welt*, 1929 (*Dante: Poet of the Secular World*, 1961); *Das französische Publikum des 17. Jahrhunderts*, 1933; *Neue Dantestudien*, 1944; *Mimesis: Dargestellte Wirklichkeit in der abendländischen Literatur*, 1946 (*Mimesis: The Representation of Reality in Western Literature*, 1953); *Literatursprache und Publikum in der lateinischen Spätantik und im Mittelalter*, 1958 (*Literary Language and Its Public in Late Latin Literature and in the Middle Ages*, 1965); *Scenes from the Drama of European Literature*, 1959.

Erich Auerbach was one of the most influential and thought-provoking literary critics of the twentieth century. As a high school student in Berlin, he received a solid education in German, French, and Latin. In 1913, he defended his doctoral dissertation on jurisprudence at the University of Heidelberg. During World War I, he served in the German army. After his return to civilian life, Auerbach decided against practicing law and instead undertook the study of Romance philology. In 1921, he completed his doctoral dissertation at the University of Griefswald on literary techniques in French and Italian short stories from the early Renaissance.

Throughout his long and distinguished academic career, Auerbach maintained a serious interest in philology, stylistics, and the influence of the classical traditions on French and Italian writers. He published important scholarly works in his native language, German, as well as in Italian, French, and English. His mastery of many languages enabled him to make insightful comments on the interrelationships among the literatures of different countries.

In the 1920's, Auerbach worked as a librarian in the Prussian State Library in Berlin. In 1929, he published an important study on Dante, and this book resulted in his appointment to the chair of Romance philology at the University of Marburg, where he taught from 1929 until 1935. In analyzing Dante's writings in Italian and Latin, Auerbach combined a rigorous philological approach with interpretative criticism. Auerbach stressed the dangers of anachronistic explanations of Dante's works. Auerbach showed that one must discover the meanings of key terms and concepts for Dante's learned contemporaries in order not to misjudge Dante's true originality. His research on Dante convinced Auerbach that each period in European literature had developed a unique form of creativity which literary historians needed to recognize and appreciate. Auerbach believed that flexibility and cultural relativism were essential for literary criticism.

Auerbach's intellectual and moral commitment to tolerance would soon be severely tested. In 1935, he and other Jewish professors were dismissed from German universities by the Nazis. In 1936, Auerbach and his family fled to Turkey. For the next eleven years Auerbach taught French and Italian in Istanbul. Although Auerbach accepted this necessary exile with dignity, at first he felt a sense of alienation in Turkey because he did not know its culture or language. He nevertheless learned Turkish and became greatly admired by his colleagues and students there.

Between May, 1942, and April, 1945, Auerbach wrote his critical masterpiece, *Mimesis*. Each of the twenty chapters in *Mimesis* is an extended stylistic and historical analysis of a specific literary passage. Each chapter combines stylistics and historical philology with a thoughtful discussion of the cultural, social, and aesthetic value systems which constituted the unique traits of specific periods in European literary history. The breadth of *Mimesis* is quite extraordinary. Auerbach makes insightful comments on the cultural movements and traditions which produced such diverse writers as Homer, Chrétien de Troyes, François Rabelais, Molière, Friedrich Schiller, Stendhal, and Virginia Woolf. In *Mimesis*, Auerbach demonstrates that flexbility and an acceptance of cultural diversity are essential for meaningful literary criticism.

Auerbach himself realized that his method, which combined stylistics with historical and interpretive criticism, could easily be applied to many important authors and literary movements which he had not discussed in *Mimesis*. The twenty chapters in *Mimesis* made readers more sensitive to the artistry by which writers presented their own perception of reality and defined the basic aesthetic and ethical beliefs of their cultures. *Mimesis* is especially important because it enriched the reader's understanding of the rich diversity and complexity in European literature.

After the Allied forces liberated the concentration camps in 1945, Erich Auerbach became fully conscious of the horrors of the Holocaust. During the last years of his life, he frequently wrote on the conflicts between a commitment to moral values and the destructive power of evil in society. In a 1946 essay titled "The Triumph of Evil," Auerbach discusses Blaise Pascal's affirmation that a society which rejects God and denies the dignity of each individual invariably yields to evil. The relevance of this analysis to Nazi Germany could not have escaped the attention of Auerbach's readers.

In 1947, the Auerbachs emigrated to the United States, where he accepted a position at Pennsylvania State University. Unfortunately, Auerbach suffered from a heart condition, and his inability to pass a medical examination prevented him from receiving tenure at the university. He then spent one year at Princeton University before being named a professor of Romance Languages at Yale University. He taught at Yale from 1950 until his death in Wallingford, near New Haven, on October 13, 1957. During his decade in the United States, Erich Auerbach once again had access to excellent library collections on European literatures. He published extensively on French literature. His posthumously published book *Literary Language and Its Public in Late Latin Literature and in the Middle Ages* encouraged fellow scholars to examine the works of many neglected neo-Latin writers. While indispensable for medievalists, Auerbach's last book never had the broad appeal of *Mimesis*.

Had he not written *Mimesis*, Erich Auerbach would probably be remembered as a very learned Dante and neo-Latin specialist. One should not underestimate the significance of his insightful writings on medieval literature. *Mimesis*, however, enriched all areas of literary criticism because it demonstrated quite eloquently that stylistics and historical, or sociological, criticism complement each other very well. *Mimesis* helped critics to understand that it is not truly significant if a literary text does or does not realistically reproduce historical events. Such ephemeral realism does not interest readers from different cultures. In interpreting literary works, one should rather admire the subtle artistry by which gifted writers both express their own perceptions of reality and make their readers more sensitive to the diversity of the human condition. The first published reviews of *Mimesis* were extraordinarily favorable both in North America and in Europe. Since Auerbach's death in 1957, admiration for *Mimesis* has not abated. This seminal work has enabled generations of readers to appreciate more thoroughly the complex relationships between the study of European literature and the history of European ideas.

BIBLIOGRAPHICAL REFERENCES: Valuable assessments of the importance of *Mimesis* for stylistics and literary theory include Helmut Hatzfeld, *Romance Philology*, II (1949), 333-338, and René Wellek, *The Kenyon Review*, XVI (1954), 299-307. Two very useful studies which compare Auerbach with fellow literary critic and German emigré Leo Spitzer (1887-1960) are Robert Scholes, *Literary Criticism and the Structures of History: Erich Auerbach and Leo Spitzer*, 1982, and Harry Levin, "Two *Romanisten* in America," in *The Intellectual Migration: Europe and America, 1930-1960*, 1969, edited by Donald Fleming and Bernard Bailyn. See also Thomas M. De Pietro, "Literary Criticism as History: The Example of Auerbach's

Mimesis," *Clio*, VIII (1979), 377-387, and W. Wolfgang Holdheim, "Auerbach's *Mimesis:* Aesthetics as Historical Understanding," *Clio*, X (1981), 143-154.

Edmund J. Campion

ISAAC BABEL

Born: Odessa, Russia
Date: July 13, 1894

Died: Siberia, Soviet Union
Date: March 17, 1941

PRINCIPAL WORKS

SHORT FICTION: *Odesskie rasskazy*, 1926 (*Tales of Odessa*, 1955); *Konarmiia*, 1926 (*Red Cavalry*, 1929); *Collected Stories*, 1955; *Izbrannoe*, 1957, 1966; *Lyubka the Cossack and Other Stories*, 1963; *You Must Know Everything: Stories, 1915-1937*, 1969.

PLAYS: *Zakat*, pb. 1928 (*Sundown*, 1935; better known as *Sunset*); *Mariia*, pb. 1935 (*Maria*, 1966).

MISCELLANEOUS: *The Lonely Years, 1925-1939: Unpublished Stories and Private Correspondence*, 1964; *The Forgotten Prose*, 1978.

Isaac Babel, for all the sparseness of his literary output, is generally regarded as the greatest Soviet-Russian writer of short stories. He was born on July 13, 1894, to a middle-class, rather ambitious Jewish family living in a colorful, lower-class section of Odessa known as the Moldavanka. Young Babel spent his first decade in the nearby city of Nikolayev, where he was pushed by his family into fanatical diligence as a student, this being the only hope for escape from political oppression. The terrible pogrom of October, 1905, forced the Babels back to Odessa, where Isaac continued his studies and began to write stories. His first published story, "Old Shloime," about an old man who commits suicide, appeared in 1913 in Kiev, where Babel was a student at the Institute of Finance and Business, no better college being open to him as a Jew.

Obtaining his degree in 1916, he resolved upon a career as a writer and moved (illegally) to St. Petersburg. There, Maxim Gorky the famed "Stormy Petrel" of the Russian Revolution, published two of Babel's stories and thereby earned the young writer's lifetime loyalty. By that time Babel understood that as Jews could hope for nothing from the czarist regime, it was best for them to support the Social Democrats.

In 1918, Babel served in the Red Army, requisitioning grain on the Volga River; he also worked briefly for the Cheka, the first Soviet political police agency. In 1919, he worked for the People's Commissariat for Education, at one point returning to Odessa to wed Evgeniia Gronfein, who would emigrate to France in 1925. In 1920, Babel was assigned as war correspondent and propagandist to General Semyon Budenny's First Cavalry, which fought in the Ukraine and Poland; the Cossack cavalry troops reached the very outskirts of Warsaw before being turned back in September of 1920.

Throughout his years in the Red Army, Babel kept detailed diaries upon which his journalistic pieces and many of his best stories would be based. Three dozen or more sketches and diary excerpts appeared in minor periodicals throughout the period 1917-1920. In 1921, the story "The King" was published in an Odessa magazine. It was the first of Babel's major works and one of the four stories that would appear in *Tales of Odessa* in 1926. Although Babel also published the thirty-five stories that appear in *Red Cavalry* approximately during this same period (1923-1925), the earlier stories lack the truly brilliant touch of the later ones. Regardless, from the time that Babel began publishing his stories in major Soviet periodicals in the early 1920's, he was recognized both nationally and internationally as a unique, powerful, and shocking new writer. Nevertheless, he had his enemies in political ideologues, anti-Semites, and puritans.

The Odessa tales share with the Red Cavalry cycle a rich, rhythmic, colorful style characteristic of the immediately postrevolution period in Soviet literature, labeled "ornamentalism" by critics. Very short works were the rule, and style often dominated content. In *Red Cavalry*, however, Babel achieved a deeply intriguing and above all laconic symbolism that one does not find in "The King" and other stories of the Odessa group. The latter stories, though, were limited in time and place to the prewar Moldavanka quarter with an all-Jewish cast of characters typified by giant stevedores, voluptuous prostitutes, and merry gangsters dressed in raspberry slacks and chocolate-hued shoes. The gangster Benya Krik, protagonist of "The King," appears also in other works, including "Sunset," an unpublished story that served as the basis for a play of the same title published in 1928. It deals with the means used by Benya to seize the throne from his gangleader father.

Babel wrote only one other play, *Maria*—the first part of a projected trilogy about a Russian general's family from the Revolution to the 1930's. It is clear that Babel would have written other dramatic works had his life not been cut short. As it was, he worked on some fifteen or twenty films from 1925 onward. He wrote scenarios and the like, often in collaboration with other writers, because he needed the money—at first to visit his wife and daughter Nathalie (born in 1929 in France) and later to support his mistress and his travels. Later still, Babel needed the money to support his second wife, Antonina Nikolaevna Pirozhkova, to whom he was married in 1935; their daughter Lidiia was born in 1937.

The playfulness of the Odessa tales is largely absent from the Red Cavalry cycle of stories, which, as a unified collection published in 1926, constitute Babel's greatest work. The primary motifs of the collection include the vast irony of a diffident intellectual Jew riding to war with a gang of primitive, murderous Cossacks. The nominally Communist Cossacks, although admirable in many respects, retain a crude Christianity and are anti-Semites. They commit horrors against the Hasidic Jews of Galicia. Yet it is not only Jews who suffer in these stories but also Polish Catholics, who were despised by the Orthodox Cossacks as well. The many victims in these pages are often depicted in imagery suggesting ritual sacrifice—with the further implication that all are reenacting the agony of Christ. Still, the dramatized contrasts between Marxism and religion, death and sexual love, suffering and the life force, are never fully resolved—which accounts for the artistic power of these stories. Through paradox, irony, and epiphanic revelation, Babel achieves an almost biblical or mythic depth in his remarkable Red Cavalry cycle.

Nearly as powerful is the cycle of six "Childhood Stories," never collected as a book. Published between 1915 and 1937, these marvelously sensitive autobiographical tales are stylistically more conventional than those described above, presenting a classical subtlety and precision worthy of Anton Chekhov. Probably the best known of these is "The Story of My Dovecot," which is set in Nikolayev on the terrible day of the 1905 pogrom. It makes flawless use of the literary device of the epiphany.

So prolific in the 1920's, Babel published no more than a dozen stories in the 1930's, using silence as a form of political protest. Babel's last story, "The Trial," was published in 1938. He himself was arrested in 1939 and tried by a closed military court in 1940. He died in a labor camp in 1941. He was officially rehabilitated thirteen years later, at which time a diligent search for all of his diaries, manuscripts, and fugitive published works began. Writing in Russian as a Jew, a Communist, an atheist, and even, in some sense, a Christian, Babel gave to the world some of the most memorable stories of the twentieth century.

BIBLIOGRAPHICAL REFERENCES: Patricia Carden, *The Art of Isaac Babel*, 1972, sees a concern for justice as the fundamental theme of *Red Cavalry.* A perceptive brief work is R. W. Hallet, *Isaac Babel*, 1972, which has a useful chronology. James E. Falen, *Isaac Babel: Russian Master of the Short Story*, 1974, provides an excellent literary biography and perceptive analyses of the major works, including the film scenarios. The books by Falen, Hallet, and Carden are occasionally unreliable, given later Babel scholarship. For more recent studies, see Carol Luplow, *Isaac Babel's "Red Cavalry,"* 1982; Danuta Mendelsohn, *Metaphor in Babel's Short Stories*, 1982; Ephraim Sicher, *Style and Structure in the Prose of Isaak Babel*, 1986; and Milton Ehre, *Isaac Babel*, 1986, a basic text for the general reader by a reliable scholar.

Donald M. Fiene

BERYL BAINBRIDGE

Born: Liverpool, England
Date: November 21, 1933

PRINCIPAL WORKS

NOVELS: *A Weekend with Claud*, 1967, revised 1981; *Another Part of the Wood*, 1968; *Harriet Said*, 1972; *The Dressmaker*, 1973 (also known as *The Secret Glass*); *The Bottle Factory Outing*, 1974; *Sweet William*, 1975; *A Quiet Life*, 1976; *Injury Time*, 1977; *Young Adolf*, 1978; *Winter Garden*, 1980; *Watson's Apology*, 1984; *Filthy Lucre: Or, The Tragedy of Andrew Ledwhistle and Richard Soleway*, 1986.

SHORT FICTION: *Mum and Mr. Armitage*, 1985.

Beryl Bainbridge is one of the most interesting of contemporary English novelists, but she is little known in the United States. She writes about a working-class world whose inhabitants are colorless and ineffectual. She was born in Liverpool on November 21, 1933, the daughter of Richard Bainbridge, a salesman, and his wife, Winifred. Although her father achieved a measure of success, he never forgot his working-class roots. He believed that, despite the illusions of the pleasures of home and family, the working man is alone. When he dies, nothing is left but a few tattered possessions. Even the memories of the poor—the places they were born, their rented flats, their factories—will be swept away by the rich. Thus began the theme of alienation and meaninglessness that seems to permeate Bainbridge's novels.

Bainbridge attended the Merchant Taylor's School, Great Crosby, England. She was an actress, appearing in the Liverpool Playhouse, London's West End theaters, and repertory theaters in Windsor and Salisbury. She also worked in television and wrote and read stories for a children's radio program in Manchester. Bainbridge was married to Austin Davies, an artist, on April 24, 1954, and had three children before her divorce. She has called herself a socialist and "lapsed Catholic." On the dust jackets of her novels, she refers to herself as "something of a recluse." She paints primitives, among them the fictional characters of her novels. She eventually settled in Camden Town, London.

Bainbridge's novels are populated with the lonely, unlucky, and discontented. They look for respectability and acceptance but often end in desperation. As the story of the elderly Jewish woman Shebah is told and retold in *A Weekend with Claud*, the characters betray one another and drift apart rather than finding solace in community. The young boy Roland, one of the few vital characters in *Another Part of the Wood*, is allowed to die of a tranquilizer overdose, alone and forgotten. In *Sweet William*, Ann, a single girl living in Hampstead, interacts with other characters so bland and nondescript that they are hardly discernible.

The characters constantly face alienation and can find no way to escape it. At the end of *Harriet Said*, the girl who has been seduced by the czar is surprised that he has some affection for her. To the girl, his was a meaningless act of little emotion or consequence. Freda and Brenda in *The Bottle Factory Outing* live together in a threadbare flat, sleeping in a double bed with a row of books between them to cut them off from each other. In *A Quiet Life*, Alan's mother leaves the family's flat each evening and sits in a train station because her husband repulses her. After twenty years of marriage, Watson, the emotionless headmaster in *Watson's Apology*, decides to leave his wife.

These novels also have a horrific and comic irony that at times can be inhumanly savage. Freda, who tries to seduce Vittorio and is murdered in *The Bottle Factory Outing*, is propped up in the back seat of a car while her roommate and other coworkers drive through the Windsor Safari Park on the company picnic. The roommate, Brenda, is in shock and chooses not to report the crime, even as the dead Freda is stuffed and pickled in spirits in an old wine barrel to be thrown overboard at sea. All is accepted as normal. After Ira is stabbed in the neck with a pair of scissors in *The Dressmaker* because Nellie is "annoyed" with him, she uses the same pair of scissors to help sew his shroud because it is "the least she can do." *The Quiet Life* is a novel of great domestic anger and frustration, but when Alan's father dies of a heart attack caused by this domestic pressure, Alan relates this event matter-of-factly. In *Injury Time*, Binny and the robbers who have barricaded themselves in her apartment play an imaginary game of Ping-Pong before the window to convince the police outside that all is normal. There are no rules for the Ping-Pong game, or for the lives of the characters. Television, Binny comments, is more real than their lives.

In *Young Adolf*, Bainbridge portrays the young Hitler visiting relatives in Liverpool. He has no clothes except those on his back, and he suffers indignity after indignity. The more Adolf is developed sympathetically, the greater the irony. In *Winter Garden*, Ashburner, a boring, conservative lawyer, tells his wife that he is going to Scotland. Instead, he travels with his mistress to Moscow and loses her soon after they arrive. All of this is told so plainly that the horror and comedy screams at the reader.

Bainbridge is at her best, however, when she describes the trivial and commonplace surrounding her characters. Wet and rusty toilets work sporadically if at all. Shins are painfully skinned on unknown objects in dark hallways. Rubenesque ladies are hot and breathless as they cram themselves in the back seats of cars. Half-smoked cigars are brought home to be cherished and slowly smoked. These fictions are set in worn flats, old bottle factories, and huts in the woods that are uniformly described in flat monotone. Not much happens in the worlds of Bainbridge's characters, except those fleeting moments of horror best forgotten.

BIBLIOGRAPHICAL REFERENCES: Book reviews provide the best access to the Bainbridge canon, some of the best of which are Karl Miller's "A Novelist Worth Knowing," *The New York Review of Books*, May 16, 1974, 24-28, concentrating on four early novels, Diane Johnson's "The Suffering of Young Hitler," *The Times Literary Supplement*, December 1, 1978, 1385; Julia O'Faolain's "Slices of Life and Death," *The New York Times Book Review*, April 13, 1980, 14; and Valentina Yakovleva's, "On Reading Beryl Bainbridge: A Voice from the Public," *Soviet Literature*, XI (1984), 141-149. For reviews of Bainbridge's well-known novel *Harriet Said*, see *The New York Times Book Review*, LXVIII (September 30, 1973), 38; *Ms.*, III (December, 1974), 39; and *The New Yorker*, XLIX (October 29, 1973), 49.

David M. Harralson

MIKHAIL BAKHTIN

Born: Orel, Russia
Date: November 16, 1895

Died: Moscow, Soviet Union
Date: March 7, 1975

PRINCIPAL WORKS

LITERARY CRITICISM: *Problemy tvorchestva Dostoevskogo*, 1929; *Problemy poetiki Dostoevskogo*, 1963 (*Problems of Dostoevsky's Poetics*, 1973, 1984); *Tvorchestvo Fransua Rable i narodnaya kul'tura srednevekov'ya i Renessansa*, 1965 (*Rabelais and His World*, 1968); *Voprosy literatury i estetiki*, 1975 (*The Dialogic Imagination*, 1981); *Estetika slovesnogo tvorchestva*, 1979; *Speech Genres and Other Late Essays*, 1986; *The Architectonics of Answerability*, 1988.

Since the 1970's Mikhail Mikhailovich Bakhtin has emerged from decades of obscurity to be hailed as one of the leading and most original theorists in a remarkably wide variety of disciplines ranging from linguistics and the social sciences to semiotics and literary criticism. Bakhtin was born on November 16, 1895, in the town of Orel, south of Moscow. He studied philology at the University of Odessa and later at Petrograd, after which he began his teaching career, first in a provincial elementary school and subsequently at secondary schools and the teachers' college at Saransk. Three books written in the 1920's—*Freidizm: Kriticheskii ocherk* (1927; *Freudianism: A Marxist Critique*, 1973), *Formal'nyi metod v literaturovedenii: Kriticheskoe vvedenie v sotsiologicheskuyu poetiku* (1928; *The Formal Method in Literary Scholarship*, 1978), and *Marksizm i filisofiya yazyka* (1929; *Marxism and the Philosophy of Language*, 1973)—have been attributed, either in their entirety or in part, to Bakhtin even though signed by his friends and colleagues, V. N. Volosinov and P. N. Medvedev. The political climate in postrevolutionary Russia may have necessitated this deception on the part of a writer whose religious views made him suspect as revolutionary freedom gave way to political repression. In 1929, the year he published the early version of his important study of Fyodor Dostoevski, Bakhtin was sentenced to internal exile and forced to work as a clerk on the Siberian border. He returned to teaching in 1936, but the following years were beset by difficulties. In 1938 chronic osteomyelitis led to the amputation of a leg, and acceptance of his doctoral dissertation on François Rabelais, written and submitted in 1940, was delayed for political reasons until 1952 (and left unpublished until 1965). Although Bakhtin wrote copiously throughout his entire career despite physical infirmities, political difficulties, exile, and a demanding teaching schedule, few of his books appeared under his own name during his lifetime. In his final years his work began to exert its influence on the new generation of Soviet intellectuals. He died in Moscow on March 7, 1975.

At the time of his death, Bakhtin was largely unknown outside the Soviet Union. Within a decade that situation changed dramatically. The reason for this sudden rise to fame had less to do with those critiques of Freudianism, Marxism, structuralism, and the social sciences which Bakhtin either wrote or influenced in the late 1920's than it did with his having articulated many of the same concerns that have become identified with a later period of theoretical inquiry. He formulated precisely the kind of metatheory that more recent theorists have pursued so avidly. Whether Bakhtin's thinking developed over the course of his career, as Michael Holquist has argued, or remained of a piece, as Tzvetan Todorov has claimed, remains in dispute. This much, however, is clear: that his major preoccupations remained remarkably consistent, and these may for convenience be divided into two large and largely overlapping areas: linguistics and literary study.

In linguistics, Bakhtin opposed both the Romantics' view that language is chiefly a matter of individual expression and the structuralists' preference for abstract language over concrete individualized speech (and speech acts). Language, Bakhtin maintains, is essentially dialogic; that is, it is a matter of neither rules nor specific meanings but of relations between, for example, speaker and addressee, or the verbal content of the text and the nonverbalized content of the "intertext" with which any utterance is necessarily in dialogue. The utterance constitutes the basic unit in Bakhtin's linguistics. It is not a statement per se, but the point at which competing "voices" intersect. Such a view leads Bakhtin to claim that language is never uniform (static or "monological"); it is always plural (or fluid—in process—and "dialogical"). He also maintains, however, that in addition to the competing voices present in any given utterance—in addition, that is, to the centrifugal forces driving language toward diversity—there is a counter movement, a centripetal force, driving language toward uniformity. In this way both linguistic chaos and linguistic tyranny are avoided. This provisional equilibrium is necessary because language, as Bakhtin conceives it, is by its very nature social and therefore in search of its own unattainable coherence. Utterance is therefore not a product, or thing, but a process saved from mere relativism by the assumed existence of an addressee, or extratemporal, extraspatial Superaddressee (not unlike the God of Bakhtin's Russian Orthodox church), which stands for the possibility that one's speech will somehow be understood by someone.

Bakhtin's theory of language is the foundation of his valorization of the novel—which, for Bakhtin, is the very "genre of becoming": open, fluid, formless, incomplete, protean, parodic, and anti-canonic. The novel as defined by Bakhtin stands in opposition to the authority and closure that he associates with those more monological genres—poetry, drama, and epic—in which stasis and dogmatic assertion are the rule. Bakhtin finds the fullest expression of the novel's dialogic essence in the works of Dostoevski; in them, the characters and their speech lose the last traces of monological certainty and enter into dialogue—both textual and intertextual)—with one another, with their author, with Dostoevski's other works, and ultimately with the intertextual literary and extraliterary encyclopedia. In *Rabelais and His World*, Bakhtin traces the dialogical novel back to its source, which, he contends, is not the epic but instead folklore in general and popular laughter and carnival in particular. At carnival time and in the carnivalistic pre-novels of Rabelais, the eternal word dissolves and in dissolving becomes the immense pluralism of the present moment. The works of Rabelais and the novels of Dostoevski foreground the plurality of the present that lies at the heart of language, of all human experience, and certainly of Bakhtin's philosophical anthropology, toward the formation of which his linguistic and literary theories played significant parts.

BIBLIOGRAPHICAL REFERENCES: *Mikhail Bakhtin*, 1984, by Katerina Clark and Michael Holquist, is an excellent biography of the man and a penetrating study of his ideas; it includes useful and unusually thorough summaries of Bakhtin's major works, terms, and concepts. Tzvetan Todorov's *Mikhail Bakhtin: The Dialogical Principle*, 1984 (first published in French in 1981), provides a brief but intelligent, topically arranged introduction to Bakhtin and his dialogical theory by a man who is himself a leading twentieth century literary critic. Holquist's "Prologue" to Bakhtin's *Rabelais and His World*, 1984, and his introductions to two collections of Bakhtin's essays, *The Dialogic Imagination*, 1981, and *Speech Genres and Other Late Essays*, 1986, are formidable critical essays in their own right. The introduction to Bakhtin's *Problems of Dostoevsky's Poetics*, 1984, by another major contemporary critic, Wayne C. Booth, is especially important for its analysis of the ways in which Bakhtin's theory challenges many of the assumptions upon which much twentieth century Anglo-American criticism (including Booth's) is based. The pieces collected in *Bakhtin: Essays and Dialogues on His Work*, edited by Gary Saul Morson, 1986, are drawn from the journal *Critical Inquiry*; a similar volume, *Rethinking Bakhtin*, 1988, edited by Morson and Caryl Emerson, includes a previously untranslated text by Bakhtin. Among the many practical applications of Bakhtin's theories to literary works, three representative examples may be singled out here: David Lodge's "Lawrence, Dostoevsky, Bakhtin: D. H. Lawrence and Dialogical Fiction," *Renaissance and Modern Studies*, XXIX (1985), 16-32; Malini Schueller's "Carnival Rhetoric and Extra-Vagrance in Thoreau's *Walden*," *American Literature: A Journey of Literary History,*

Criticism, and Bibliography, LVIII (March, 1986), 33-45; and Robert A. Morace's *The Dialogical Novels of Malcolm Bradbury and David Lodge*, 1989. Finally, Julia Kristeva's seminal essay "Word, Dialogue, and Novel," first published in 1969 and collected in her *Desire in Language: A Semiotic Approach to Literature and Art*, 1980, should not be overlooked by anyone interested in Bakhtin's work.

Robert A. Morace

JAMES BALDWIN

Born: New York, New York
Date: August 2, 1924

Died: St. Paul de Vence, France
Date: November 30, 1987

PRINCIPAL WORKS

NOVELS: *Go Tell It on the Mountain*, 1953; *Giovanni's Room*, 1956; *Another Country*, 1962; *Tell Me How Long the Train's Been Gone*, 1968; *If Beale Street Could Talk*, 1974; *Just Above My Head*, 1979.

SHORT FICTION: *Going to Meet the Man*, 1965.

PLAYS: *The Amen Corner*, pr. 1954; *Blues for Mister Charlie*, pr., pb. 1964.

ESSAYS: *Notes of a Native Son*, 1955; *Nobody Knows My Name*, 1961; *The Fire Next Time*, 1963; *The Devil Finds Work: An Essay*, 1976.

OTHER NONFICTION: *The Evidence of Things Not Seen*, 1985; *The Price of the Ticket*, 1985.

From the immediate critical success of *Go Tell It on the Mountain*, James Baldwin's writings have been well received by the intellectual community, but his fiction, which deals frankly and sympathetically with controversial issues such as civil rights and homosexuality, did not immediately win popular approval. In fact, not until the 1974 publication of *If Beale Street Could Talk* did Baldwin make the best-seller list. In the meantime, this extraordinary man had won awards ranging from a Rosenwald Fellowship in 1948 to a Guggenheim Fellowship in 1954 to election to the National Institute of Arts and Letters in 1964.

Born out of wedlock in Harlem, James Baldwin was the eldest of nine children, a fact that forced him to shoulder much of the day-to-day responsibility for his half brothers and sisters. In addition, his relationship with David Baldwin, his stepfather, was ambivalent at best. A carpenter and storefront preacher, David Baldwin intended to be both a good husband to Baldwin's mother and a real father to young James. Yet Baldwin and his stepfather were never comfortable together, and home became an unbearable place for James, though his baby-sitting responsibilities required him to stay there most of the time.

Young Baldwin fared little better outside the home, where his intellectualism and his physical unattractiveness alienated him from his peers and his blackness alienated him from the rest of society. Baldwin, therefore, turned inward for refuge, first to reading and then to writing. Though writing was not to be an easy escape, Baldwin soon realized that it was his only chance to get himself and his family out of the ghetto. Early aid from Richard Wright helped him secure a Eugene F. Saxton Memorial Award in 1945, and Baldwin also began placing essays in *The Nation*, *The New Leader*, and *Commentary*. By 1948 he had gained enough recognition to win a Rosenwald Fellowship, which allowed him to escape to France, where he worked on his first novel, *Go Tell It on the Mountain*.

Go Tell It on the Mountain, set in the 1930's, deals with the dead-end existence of Harlem blacks. The novel tells the story of four people whose lives center on the Temple of the Fire Baptized, a storefront church like the one in which David Baldwin preached. The characters are desperate to change their fates, to escape Harlem's limitations. Yet the available escapes seem worse then the conditions under which the characters live: Sex is a pleasant but temporary respite, drugs and alcohol relieve the symptoms but impoverish and finally kill their users, and stepping across the line into the white world is the most dangerous of all. Religion, says preacher Gabriel Grimes, provides the only real escape, but through the prayers of the adolescent John Grimes's mother, stepfather, and aunt, Baldwin demonstrates that, ironically, religion may be the worst escape these characters could choose. Adherence to its values assures a long life, but a long life only prolongs their suffering.

Throughout this and his other novels, Baldwin probes the basic theme of isolation. His characters strive to establish an identity and to participate in activities that connect them with others. Society, however, keeps their lives fragmented and meaningless, and the racial stereotypes with which society labels these characters serve to deny them an individual identity by forcing a group identity on them. If "all blacks are alike," then there can be no individual identity.

Sexuality, while it provides no escape, is nevertheless one way Baldwin's characters fight against society's impersonalizing pressures. In Baldwin's works, sex, whether heterosexual or homosexual, is a way to assert one's personhood and to establish individual, personal contact with an other. Baldwin skirts this issue in *Go Tell It on the Mountain*, but he deals with it directly in the controversial *Giovanni's Room* and expands that treatment to its fullest in *Another Country.* There, Baldwin deplores the white culture, whose emphasis on success at any price alienates people by forcing them to compete against one another and by demanding that they conform to a cultural norm, an act that also forces them to deny their own identities. Within this context, sexual contact, whether with a person of the same or the opposite sex, the same or another race, the same or a different class, forces people to expose themselves, to get close to someone, to become vulnerable. Out of such moments, some, but by no means all, of Baldwin's characters manage to build a whole life for themselves, a kind of refuge from the spite and the struggle of so-called normal society.

Baldwin's heroes, therefore, are heroes because they succeed on a personal level, not because they bring about sweeping social change. In fact, in *Tell Me How Long the Train's Been Gone*, Baldwin uses Leo Proudhammer, an actor and civil rights activist, to demonstrate that it is these small successes that really matter, that if they are sustained, they eventually accumulate into a more powerful change than any one individual can bring. Thus, throughout his career, James Baldwin has concentrated on individuals, allowing the social relevance in his novels to emerge as a result of the problems of his characters, rather than building his characters around a social issue. The result is a convincing, humane body of literature.

BIBLIOGRAPHICAL REFERENCES: In an extremely useful and valuable resource, *James Baldwin*, 1980, Carolyn Wedin Sylvander examines the many connections between James Baldwin's life and his works; Stanley Macebuh's *James Baldwin: A Critical Study*, 1973, complements the Sylvander work by providing an analysis of the cultural and historical background of Baldwin's writings. See also W. J. Weatherby, *James Baldwin: Artist on Fire*, 1989. Louis H. Pratt's *James Baldwin*, 1978, is an introductory study with a biographical sketch and an overview of Baldwin's career. *James Baldwin: A Collection of Critical Essays*, edited by Keneth Kinnamon, 1974, presents a helpful collection of critical and personal responses to Baldwin's writings by literary critics, by fellow writers such as Langston Hughes, and by fellow activists such as Eldridge Cleaver. *Critical Essays on James Baldwin*, 1988, edited by Fred L. Standley and Nancy V. Standley-Burt, is also a valuable collection, gathering thirty-six reviews and essays that cover all phases of Baldwin's career. For an extensive interview, see "The Art of Fiction LXXVIII: James Baldwin," *The Paris Review*, XXVI (Spring, 1984), 48-82.

William Condon

J. G. BALLARD

Born: Shanghai, China
Date: November 15, 1930

PRINCIPAL WORKS

SCIENCE FICTION: *The Wind from Nowhere*, 1962; *The Drowned World*, 1962; *The Drought*, 1964 (also known as *The Burning World*); *The Crystal World*, 1966; *The Atrocity Exhibition*, 1969 (also known as *Love and Napalm: Export U.S.A.*); *Crash*, 1973; *Concrete Island*, 1974; *High Rise*, 1975; *The Unlimited Dream Company*, 1979; *Hello America*, 1981.

NOVELS: *Empire of the Sun*, 1984; *The Day of Creation*, 1987.

SHORT FICTION: *The Voices of Time*, 1962; *Billenium*, 1962; *The Four-Dimensional Nightmare*, 1963; *The Terminal Beach*, 1964; *The Impossible Man*, 1966; *The Disaster Area*, 1967; *The Overloaded Man*, 1967; *Vermilion Sands*, 1971; *Chronopolis*, 1971; *Myths of the Near Future*, 1982.

James Graham Ballard is one of the most important postmodern writers in English. Generally categorized as science fiction, most of Ballard's work moves beyond that label to address the impact of technology and American culture on the imagination. The son of James Ballard, a businessman, and his wife, Edna, J. G. Ballard was born on November 15, 1930, in Shanghai, where he lived until 1946.

In his highly autobiographical novel *The Empire of the Sun*, which Steven Spielberg made into a film in 1987, Ballard's protagonist, Jim, is separated from his parents at the outbreak of World War II and spends three years in a Japanese prison camp. There, the boy's contacts to his old world (already a bizarre amalgam of Chinese environment overlaid with the life-styles of Europeans) occur through magazines and the warplanes which the United States sends to the Far East. In a touching scene, Jim clips out the photograph of a couple from an advertisement in *Life* magazine for use as a likeness of his parents. It is not difficult to see how Ballard's fiction becomes obsessed with the icons of America, and why it centers on war, disaster, and imprisonment.

After education at Leys School, and two years of medicine at King's College, Ballard served in the Royal Air Force, where he underwent pilot training in Canada. Back in England, he worked as a science editor and was married to Helen Mary Matthews in 1955; before her death in 1964, they had a son and two daughters.

In 1956, Ballard sold "Prima Belladonna" to *Science Fantasy* magazine and soon became a distinguished literary voice. His short stories are unique in their pictorial evocation of setting and psychological mood. Accordingly, they fascinate less through an intricate plot or a variety of different characters than through the intensity with which they explore places. For example, in "The Garden of Time," Ballard describes a strange garden whose flowers arrest time.

Ballard's longer fiction commenced with his 1962 *The Wind from Nowhere*. It was the first of a quartet of "natural disaster novels" which share a surrealist setting and an emphasis on tableaux, or still scenes. For example, the pool where man-beast Quilter collects his harem of suburban housewives in *The Drought* is a setting which serves as a motif for the state of Western culture.

Ballard's poetic vision became increasingly darker as he focused on the perturbing icons of American culture. In his 1970 masterpiece, *The Atrocity Exhibition*, stylistic radicalism matches images of assassination weapons, atrocity newsreels, and mutilated faces; as with *Crash* in 1973, the first of three "urban disaster" novels (*Concrete Island* and *High Rise* followed), critics failed to see past the overt message that war atrocities and violent car crashes further the "psychosexual health" of the populace. In reality, the apparent message was a mask for the voice of deep moral outrage at the technological and media-inundated world. The novels work out that outrage by carrying their effects to blackly logical excess.

In 1979, Ballard entered a new cycle with *The Unlimited Dream Company*, a pastoral fantasy in which a stranded pilot transforms a London suburb into a tropical aviary and teaches its inhabitants how to fly. In *Hello America*, Ballard once again revels in fantastic tableaux when he conjures up dead freeways and the empty, sand-swept ruins of Las Vegas, once the natural oil has been depleted. *The Empire of the Sun* marks Ballard's entry into mainstream literature, and his 1987 novel, *The Day of Creation*, is further proof that his imagination convinces regardless of genre.

For some time, the literary validity of J. G. Ballard's highly imaginative fiction was not fully recognized. Some critics were unwilling to consider his science fiction seriously; others attacked his inelegant style and failed to see the appropriateness of his language, which consciously employs technical jargon and stark contrasts of metaphors to alienate the reader. There also was concern with the "pessimistic" ending of books such as *The Drowned World*, in which the protagonist does not go northward to escape the ever-increasing heat but decides to go south. Here, the subtle transformation of an apparently realist text into a more metaphorical and poetic work is lost on many readers.

BIBLIOGRAPHICAL REFERENCES: Peter Brigg, *J. G. Ballard*, 1985, is the most exhaustive monograph on Ballard and contains a fine bibliography. David Pringle, *Earth Is the Alien Planet: J. G. Ballard's Four-Dimensional Nightmare*, 1979, gives an overview and discusses literary context, symbolism, and key themes of Ballard's work. James Goddard and David Pringle have edited *J. G. Ballard: The First Twenty Years*, 1976, which is still useful. *Re/Search: J. G. Ballard*, *Re/Search*, Vol. 8, 1984, edited by V. Vale and Andrea Juno, is a flashy publication full of photographic and literary material on and by the author. David Pringle's *J. G. Ballard: A Primary and Secondary Bibliography*, 1984, is the best guide available. See also "The Works of J. G. Ballard," in Colin Greenland, *The Entropy Exhibition*, 1983; Reinhart Lutz, "The Two Landscapes of J. G. Ballard's *Concrete Island*," in *Mindscapes*, 1989, edited by George Slusser; Charles Nicols, "J. G. Ballard and the Limits of Mainstream SF," *Science-Fiction Studies*, III (1976), 150-157; Jonathan Benison, "In Default of a Post of Space: J. G. Ballard and the Current State of Nihilism," in *Just the Other Day*, 1985, edited by Luk de Vos; "J. G. Ballard," in *The Imagination on Trial*, 1981, edited by Alan Burns and Charles Sugnet; Terry Dowling, "Alternative Reality and Deviant Logic in J. G. Ballard's Second Disaster Trilogy," *Science Fiction*, I (1977), 6-18; Anthony Ryan, "The Mind of Mr. J. G. Ballard," *Foundation*, no. 3. (March, 1973), 44-48; Robert L. Platzner, "The Metamorphic Vision of J. G. Ballard," *Essays in Literature*, X (1983), 209-217; Lorenz J. Firsching, "J. G. Ballard's Ambiguous Apocalypse," *Science-Fiction Studies*, XII (1985), 297-310; and Bruce Franklin, "What Are We to Make of J. G. Ballard's Apocalypse?" in *Voices for the Future*, 1979, edited by Thomas D. Clareson, 1979.

Reinhart Lutz

JOHN BANVILLE

Born: Wexford, Ireland
Date: December 8, 1945

PRINCIPAL WORKS

NOVELS: *Nightspawn*, 1971; *Birchwood*, 1973; *Doctor Copernicus*, 1976; *Kepler*, 1981; *The Newton Letter: An Interlude*, 1982; *Mefisto*, 1986.

SHORT FICTION: *Long Lankin*, 1970, revised 1984.

SCREENPLAY: *Reflections*, 1984.

John Banville has emerged in recent years as one of Ireland's most important modern writers. Born in the town of Wexford in the southern part of Ireland, Banville was educated near his home, first at the Christian Brothers School and later at St. Peter's College but did not go on to attend a university. From 1966 to 1967, he lived in Greece. He later moved to Dublin, where, in 1969, he was married to Janet Dunham. The following year he began working as a copy editor for *The Irish Press*, a job which he continued to hold even after his reputation as a writer was well established.

Banville's first book, *Long Lankin*, was published that same year. A collection of short stories and a novella set in modern-day Dublin, the book offers an interwoven portrait of characters trapped in the confusion and bleakness of modern life. Casting a dark shadow over the stories is the English ballad that provides the book with its name; *Long Lankin* is a haunting tale of love and death that serves as the thematic basis for Banville's characters and their lives. The book was greeted with praise from literary critics, who pointed to Banville's fictional debut as a work of exceptional talent and promise.

In 1971, Banville's first novel appeared. *Nightspawn* draws on the author's own sojourn in Greece for its setting and its depiction of the events leading up to that country's 1967 military coup. Its central figure and narrator is Ben White, a character who figured prominently in the *Long Lankin* stories, making *Nightspawn* in some ways a sequel to Banville's earlier work. Ostensibly a thriller, the book blends mythic images with historical events as it explores the functions and limitations of modern literature. The book drew a mixed critical reaction, receiving praise for the beauty of its language and criticism for its convoluted plotting.

In his second novel, *Birchwood*, Banville takes on the traditions of Irish literature with a modern slant. The work is set in a large country house peopled with eccentric, sharply drawn characters. Banville gives this setting a contemporary twist, as his hero, the book's narrator, chronicles his childhood in such a house and his subsequent experiences with a traveling circus, which he joins on his quest for his perhaps imaginary sister. An examination of truth and memory, the story is filled with strange happenings—a death by spontaneous combustion, a band of transvestite revolutionaries—all set against the backdrop of the great potato famine and related with what even Banville's critics admitted was startling originality. The year of the book's publication, Banville received both the Allied Irish Banks prize and the Arts Council of Ireland and Macaulay Fellowship.

In 1976, Banville wrote the first of three novels inspired by Arthur Koestler's *The Sleepwalkers: A History of Man's Changing Vision of the Universe* (1959), a study of several famous astronomers. *Doctor Copernicus* offers a vivid portrait of the chaotic late fifteenth-early sixteenth century world in which the great astronomer lived and worked, blending fiction and fact as it explores the relationship between the Polish scientist's theories and the society which shaped him. Central to Banville's novel are the ties he finds between science and art, with Copernicus' theories helping him to express and define himself. The book received both the Irish-American Foundation Award and the James Tait Black Memorial Prize.

Banville followed *Doctor Copernicus* five years later with *Kepler*, the second of the

Koestler-inspired novels. Perhaps the most accessible of Banville's novels, the book is nevertheless cleverly structured in accordance with its subject's theories of planetary orbits. Banville posits a relationship between Kepler's often unhappy and disjointed personal life and his passion for searching out order in the cosmos. Caught on the cusp between the medieval and modern worlds, Kepler is both superstitious and insightful (one of his tasks is to devise astrological charts). *Kepler*, like *Doctor Copernicus*, was widely praised for its historical narrative and its compelling development of character. The novel received the Guardian Fiction Prize in 1981.

The third novel in the series is *The Newton Letter: An Interlude*. Unlike its two predecessors, however, the book abandons the trappings of the historical novel and returns to its author's fascination with literature and the creative process. Told in the form of letters from an unnamed narrator, the novel chronicles the narrator's efforts to finish a book he is writing on Sir Isaac Newton, a task made increasingly difficult by his growing absorption in the lives of his neighbors. As he studies a letter from Newton detailing the astronomer's own breakdown, the writer himself suffers a similar inability to marshal his thoughts and emotions. Martin Swales, writing in the *London Review of Books*, described *The Newton Letter* as "a compassionate and vibrantly intelligent novel—and also a timely one."

Banville continued his exploration of life and literature in *Mefisto*, a self-reflexive novel in two parts. Its story is the life history of Gabriel Swan, whose reminiscences are an indistinguishable mixture of reality, memory, and imagination. Like many of Banville's characters, Gabriel is on a personal quest, sometimes guided by his own Mephistopheles, the mysterious Felix. With *Mefisto*, Banville once again addresses the rich legacy of Irish literature, drawing on William Butler Yeats, James Joyce, and Samuel Beckett in the book's structure, style, and many literary allusions. It is a novel that continues Banville's ongoing thematic preoccupations and helps solidify his reputation as one of the most challenging and gifted of contemporary Irish writers.

BIBLIOGRAPHICAL REFERENCES: An extensive critical study of Banville's work can be found in a special issue of the *Irish University Review* devoted to Banville, Spring, 1981. *The Irish Novel in Our time*, 1976, edited by Patrick Rafroidi and Maurice Harmon, contains an insightful chapter on Banville, "Be Assured I Am Inventing: The Fiction of John Banville," by Seamus Deane. Among the journal articles focusing on Banville's work are Auberón Waugh's critical "Potato Crop," *The Spectator*, February 10, 1973; reviews of *Doctor Copernicus* by Julian Barnes, *New Statesman*, XCII (November 26, 1976), 766, and Stephen Clark, *The Times Literary Supplement*, December 10, 1976, 1533; Paul Taylor's review of *Kepler*, "Head in the Stars," *The Times Literary Supplement*, January 30, 1981, 107; and Russell McCormmach's "He Remodeled the Cosmos," *The New York Times Book Review*, LXXXVIII (May 29, 1983), 10. Also of interest are Martin Swales's review of *The Newton Letter: An Interlude*, "Creative Affinities," *London Review of Books*, July 15, 1982, 22, and M. Hites's article in *The New York Times Book Review*, XCII (July 19, 1987), 19. For an insightful analysis of *Mefisto*, see Barbara Hardy's "Birdboy," *Books and Bookmen*, September, 1986, 26.

Janet E. Lorenz

AMIRI BARAKA
Everett LeRoi Jones

Born: Newark, New Jersey
Date: October 7, 1934

Principal Works

PLAYS: *A Good Girl Is Hard to Find*, pr. 1958; *The Eighth Ditch*, pr. 1960; *The Toilet*, pr. 1964; *Dutchman*, pr., pb. 1964; *The Slave*, pr., pb. 1964; *The Baptism*, pr. 1964; *Jello*, pr. 1965; *Experimental Death Unit #1*, pr. 1965; *A Black Mass*, pr. 1966; *Arm Yrself or Harm Yrself*, pr., pb. 1967; *Slave Ship: A Historical Pageant*, pr., pb. 1967; *Madheart*, pr. 1967; *Great Goodness of Life (A Coon Show)*, pr. 1967; *Home on the Range*, pr. 1968; *The Death of Malcolm X*, pb. 1969; *Junkies Are Full of (SHHH . . .)*, pr. 1970; *Bloodrites*, pr. 1970; *A Recent Killing*, pr. 1973; *The New Ark's a Moverin*, pr. 1974; *Sidnee Poet Heroical*, pr. 1975; *S-1*, pr. 1976; *The Motion of History*, pr. 1977; *What Was the Relationship of the Lone Ranger to the Means of Production?*, pr., pb. 1979; *At the Dim'crackr Convention*, pr. 1980; *Weimar 2*, pr. 1981; *Money: A Jazz Opera*, pr. 1982; *Primitive World*, pr. 1984.

SCREENPLAYS: *Dutchman*, 1967; *Black Spring*, 1967; *A Fable*, 1971.

NOVEL: *The System of Dante's Hell*, 1965.

POETRY: *Selected Poetry of Amiri Baraka/LeRoi Jones*, 1979.

NONFICTION: *Cubra Libre*, 1961; *Blues People: Negro Music in White America*, 1963; *Home: Social Essays*, 1966; *Black Music*, 1968; *Raise Race Rays Raze: Essays Since 1965*, 1971; *Beginning of National Movement*, 1972; *The Creation of the New Ark*, 1975; *Daggers and Javelins: Essays*, 1984; *The Autobiography of LeRoi Jones/Amiri Baraka*, 1984; *The Artist and Social Responsibility*, 1986.

Amiri Baraka (Everett LeRoi Jones) is one of the most important and most articulate writers of the Black Arts Movement. Born on October 7, 1934, to a middle-class family, he was graduated from high school at fifteen and attended Rutgers University on a science scholarship. After a year, he transferred to Howard University, receiving a B.A. in English in 1954. After serving in the Air Force, Baraka moved to Greenwich Village, plunging into a bohemian life-style that was influenced by the aesthetic protests of the Beat generation. During this period, he was married to a Jewish intellectual with whom he edited *Yugen*, an avant-garde magazine. He gained recognition as a music critic, did graduate work in philosophy at Columbia University and the New School for Social Research, and taught courses at both schools as well as the State University of New York at Buffalo. Although he wrote plays during this period, most have been lost—except *The Eighth Ditch*, which was later incorporated into his novel, *The System of Dante's Hell*. Closed after a few days because of obscenity, the play's aborted production marked the first of Baraka's many conflicts with the law.

The year 1964 was the beginning of a radical shift in Baraka's political and aesthetic beliefs. He increasingly associated himself with the cultural aspirations and standards of the black community. He developed the Black Arts Repertory Theatre/School in Harlem, with the goal of increasing black pride by utilizing theater as a weapon against American racism. In addition, four of his plays that year gained for him both notoriety and fame. In *The Baptism*, a minister and Bohemian homosexual compete for the favors of a young boy seeking baptism. *The Toilet* is set in a high school latrine where a white homosexual is beaten senseless for loving a black gang leader. The racial and sexual ambivalence which runs through these plays is eliminated in *The Slave*, a frankly autobiographical work. A returning black serviceman violently renounces his former life, shooting the husband of his white former wife and watching as their home and his children are destroyed by his black revolutionary forces.

In 1967, LeRoi Jones officially became Imamu (prophet) Amiri (warrior) Baraka (blessed), a minister of the Kawaida faith and an adherent of black cultural nationalism. He returned to Newark, where he founded Spirit House Theatre and became active in local politics. The plays from this period reflect Baraka's antiwhite rage in the form of agitprop theater, designed to shock and to assault. For example, *Madheart* is a morality play in which a black Everyman removes female obstacles—a sexual white woman, an Uncle Tom mother, an assimilationist sister—on his road to black manhood. Many critics believe that *Slave Ship* is Baraka's most significant play from this period. Subtitled *A Historical Pageant*, the play presents the exploitation and victimization of the black man in America. Using music to reinforce his images of black history, Baraka assaults the moderate views of most middle-class blacks and advocates violence as a means of solving racial conflict.

In 1974, Baraka renounced Black Nationalism for Marxist-Leninist-Maoist thought and dropped Imamu from his name. Dismissing most of his sociopolitical ideas of the 1960's, calling them chauvinistic, he began to analyze the problems of blacks in economic rather than racial terms. Three plays particularly reflect this shift in ideology. *S-1*, like the left-wing plays of the 1930's, calls for the overthrow of the capitalist regime, populated by blacks and whites, by the call of the black Communist protagonist: "We fight opportunism, we fight chauvinism. And we fight narrow nationalism too." Generally, these more didactic plays have not met with critical success. Baraka defends his work from this period by insisting that its political philosophy represents a growth of, and not a change in, his previous ideologies. What has remained consistent is his focus on how culture shapes internal and other personal conflict as well as social and political strife.

Although Baraka's critical reputation has been on the decline, his impact on theater cannot be overestimated. Although his best-known works are linked to the violence and radicalism of the late 1960's and early 1970's, Baraka's impact extends beyond that time. He brought to the stage black cultural experiences, rituals, and language as well as anger and the burning need to find a solution to the problems of living in a racist society. His work has paved the way for a whole generation of black playwrights, challenging them with his experimental and cultural models.

BIBLIOGRAPHICAL REFERENCES: See Theodore Hudson, *From LeRoi Jones to Amiri Baraka: The Literary Works*, 1973; Kimberly W. Bentson, *Baraka: The Renegade and the Mask*, 1976; Werner Sollors, *Amiri Baraka/LeRoi Jones: The Quest for a Populist Modernism*, 1978; Lloyd W. Brown, *Amiri Baraka*, 1980; Henry C. Lacey, *To Raise, Destroy, and Create: The Poetry, Drama, and Fiction of Imamu Amiri Baraka (LeRoi Jones)*, 1981; *Amiri Baraka: The Kaleidoscopic Torch*, 1985, edited by James B. Gwynne; Leslie Catherine Sanders, "No One Will Turn to That Station Again," in *The Development of Black Theater in America*, 1987. See also Donald Gibson, *Five Black Writers: Essays on Richard Wright, Ralph Ellison, James Baldwin, Langston Hughes, and LeRoi Jones*, 1970, and *Imamu A. Baraka (LeRoi Jones): A Collection of Critical Essays*, 1978, edited by Kimberley Bentson.

Lori Hall Burghardt

OWEN BARFIELD

Born: London, England
Date: November 9, 1898

PRINCIPAL WORKS

PHILOSOPHY: *Saving the Appearances: A Study in Idolatry*, 1957; *Worlds Apart: A Dialogue of the 1960's*, 1963; *Unancestral Voice*, 1965; *History, Guilt, and Habit*, 1979.

CRITICISM: *History in English Words*, 1926; *Poetic Diction: A Study in Meaning*, 1928; *Romanticism Comes of Age*, 1944, revised 1966; *Speaker's Meaning*, 1967; *What Coleridge Thought*, 1971; *"The Rediscovery of Meaning" and Other Essays*, 1977.

NOVEL: *This Ever Diverse Pair*, 1950.

PLAY: *Orpheus: A Poetic Drama in Four Acts*, pb. 1983.

CHILDREN'S LITERATURE: *The Silver Trumpet*, 1925.

Although largely neglected by students of twentieth century English literature, Arthur Owen Barfield's writings significantly influenced several of the most popular contemporary English authors, especially C. S. Lewis. It is difficult to classify Barfield. His writing reveals a lifelong interest in epistemological questions, especially the roles of language and imagination in the development of human consciousness.

Barfield was born on November 9, 1898, in London, the youngest of four children. His father, Arthur Edward Barfield, was a successful lawyer. His mother, Elizabeth Shoults Barfield, was a zealous feminist, active in the struggle for women's suffrage. They were both lovers of music and books; evenings in the Barfield home were often spent with the parents, playing the piano and singing or reading aloud from some popular book.

Barfield was tutored at home until he was eight years old. At age eight, he was enrolled at Highgate Preparatory School. There he received a classical education centered on the study of Greek and Latin. In December, 1916, he was awarded a scholarship at Wadham College, University of Oxford. His entrance was delayed by military service, as he served with the Royal Engineers from 1917 to 1918. With the end of war, and after recuperating from a wound, he began studies in English literature at Wadham College in October, 1919. He was awarded a B.A. degree in English language and literature, with first-class honors, in 1921. He subsequently earned a B.Litt. degree in 1928, and a bachelor of civil law degree in 1934.

After leaving Oxford, Barfield worked as a free-lance writer and did part-time editorial work for several periodicals, incuding *New Statesman*, *London Mercury*, and *Truth*. In 1925, he published his first book, *The Silver Trumpet*, a fantasy for children. A second book, *History in English Words*, appeared in 1926. In 1928, he published *Poetic Diction*, his most important work.

Barfield was married to Christian Maude Douie in 1923, a dance teacher whom he had met during the early 1920's, when he briefly considered becoming a professional dancer. They adopted two children and became foster parents to a third. By 1930, it was evident that Barfield could not earn enough money from writing to support a family. Hence, he began training for a career as a lawyer and eventually became a partner in his father's law firm in London. From 1930 until his retirement in 1959, Barfield contributed an occasional article to several periodicals and published three books, including an autobiographical novel, *This Ever Diverse Pair*, under the pseudonym G. A. L. Burgeon. Once retired from his law practice, Barfield returned to his first love: writing. He also began lecturing at universities in Canada and the United States. During the 1960's, he held visiting professorships at both Drew and Brandeis universities.

Barfield's writings are heavily influenced by his interest in anthroposophy, a spiritualistic school of philosophy founded in 1912 by Rudolph Steiner, an Austrian philosopher, artist, and scientist. Barfield joined the Anthroposophical Society in 1922. His growing interest in what

C. S. Lewis considered occultism grealty alarmed Lewis. Over the next several years, the two friends carried on a "Great War" through correspondence. Lewis tried to dissuade Barfield from anthroposophy, while Barfield tried to convince Lewis that imagination could be a way to truth. Although Lewis never accepted anthroposophy, and Barfield never became, like Lewis, an orthodox Christian, their dialogue during their "Great War" and their ongoing friendship influenced both men. In his autobiography *Surprised by Joy: The Shape of My Early Life* (1955), Lewis acknowledges Barfield's influence, especially that of his arguments in *Poetic Diction*. Lewis also recommends *Poetic Diction* in his book *Miracles: A Preliminary Study* (1947) and frequently cited it in his lectures at the Universities of Oxford and Cambridge. Barfield was a member of the literary circle known as the Inklings, associated with Lewis during the 1940's. They remained close friends until Lewis' death in 1963.

It is difficult to attempt an analysis of Barfield's writing. As with anthroposophy, which so heavily influenced Barfield's thinking, his books are concerned with esoteric topics such as the evolution of consciousness. According to Barfield, the history of words and their changing meanings is a key to understanding the mind, or human consciousness, and the real world (that is, the nonmaterial, or spiritual, world which the mind helps create and of which the mind originally was a part).

While study of Owen Barfield remains largely a by-product of the ongoing interest in Lewis and other members of the Inklings, there is a small but growing body of scholarship acknowledging the powerful originality of Barfield's work. In the United States, one of Barfield's most outspoken advocates is the novelist Saul Bellow, whose fiction since *Humboldt's Gift* (1975) clearly reveals Barfield's influence.

BIBLIOGRAPHICAL REFERENCES: There is a brief biographical sketch in *The Inklings: C. S. Lewis, J. R. R. Tolkien, Charles Williams, and Their Friends*, by Humphrey Carpenter, 1979; Carpenter also gives much attention to Barfield's relationship with, and influence on, the Inklings. Perhaps the most complete biographical sketch is Marjorie Lamp Mead, "Owen Barfield: A Biographical Note," in the 1986 edition of Owen Barfield's *The Silver Trumpet*. Additional biographical information can be gleaned from "A Conversation with Owen Barfield," *Evolution of Consciousness: Studies in Polarity*, 1976, edited by Shirley Sugerman. For a discussion of the influence of anthroposophy on Barfield, see "Owen Barfield and Anthroposophical Romanticism," in R. J. Reilly, *Romantic Religion: A Study of Barfield, Lewis, Williams, and Tolkien*, 1971, and Patrick Grant, "The Quality of Thinking: Owen Barfield as Literary Man and Anthroposophist," *Seven*, III (1982), 113-125. Lionel Adey, *C. S. Lewis's "Great War" with Owen Barfield*, 1978, reprints letters the two friends exchanged and discusses the key issues they debated. See also Thomas Kranidas, "The Defiant Lyricism of Owen Barfield," *Seven*, VI (1985), 23-33; "Belief in Thinking: Owen Barfield and Michael Polanyi," in Patrick Grant, *Six Modern Authors and Problems of Belief*, 1979; Douglas Sloan, *Insight-Imagination: The Emancipation of Thought and the Modern World*, 1983; Roger S. Jones, *Physics as Metaphor*, 1982; and references to Barfield in the extensive literature on C. S. Lewis.

Paul R. Waibel

DJUNA BARNES

Born: Cornwall-on-Hudson, New York *Died:* New York, New York
Date: June 12, 1892 *Date:* June 18, 1982

PRINCIPAL WORKS

NOVELS: *Ryder*, 1928; *Nightwood*, 1936.
SHORT FICTION: *A Night Among the Horses*, 1929; *Spillway*, 1962; *Smoke*, 1982.
PLAYS: *Three from the Earth*, pr., pb. 1919; *The Antiphon*, pb. 1958.
JOURNALISM: *Interviews*, 1985; *New York*, 1989.
CHILDREN'S LITERATURE: *Creatures in an Alphabet*, 1982.
MISCELLANEOUS: *The Book of Repulsive Women*, 1915; *A Book*, 1923; *A Ladies' Almanack*, 1928; *Selected Works*, 1962.

Djuna Chappell Barnes has been a writer more often praised than read, and more praised than understood. She was, by some accounts, the most important woman writer in the expatriate Paris of the 1920's, and her brilliant novel *Nightwood* has influenced many subsequent writers—William Faulkner and John Hawkes, to name two examples. In her own words, she became "the most famous unknown writer" of her time. *Nightwood* has been in print continuously for more than fifty years; however, it sells only a few thousand copies every year. Barnes is one of the most important American modernist figures. Her readership is small, but it has always been composed of those who matter to literature.

Barnes's upbringing was odd in the extreme and was mined by her for her work throughout her life, particularly for her novel *Ryder* and her play *The Antiphon*. Her father, born Henry Budington, eventually settled on the name Wald Barnes after experimenting with many others. He was an open bigamist, sexually licentious, a somewhat cracked intellectual living a wild, rural, impoverished life on his affluent brother's estate on Storm King mountain in the town of Cornwall-on-Hudson, a country place for Greenwich Village bohemians. He lived with his (perhaps common-law) wife Elizabeth Chappell as well as with a mistress; her father's selfishness and her mother's passive acceptance of victimization angered Barnes throughout her life. She had brothers; all were rather oddly named, like herself.

The actual events of her family life are shrouded and obscure—Barnes was not a willing interview subject. In fact, she was one of the most private of public figures. Not much factual information is known about the circumstances that drove Barnes to hate her father so intensely and distrust her brothers so thoroughly. She received no formal schooling and learned from her family at home. Her grandmother, Zadel Barnes Budington Gustafson, had been a writer and had lived in London, supposedly hosting a literary salon there. She lived with the family and was Djuna's primary teacher and influence. Zadel was an unconventional matriarch, having been divorced and having had a career of her own. She indulged her son Wald Barnes, while understanding both his gifts and his weaknesses. Eventually Djuna became a source of financial support for this unruly family and paid for the care of Zadel in her old age from her earnings as a reporter.

After her parents separated and left the farm, Barnes went to Greenwich Village, attended the Art Students' League briefly, and began working as a free-lance artist and journalist. She worked for many newspapers in New York and Brooklyn, doing interviews and action pieces, some short fiction, and, later, short dramas in a vivid, idiosyncratic style hardly imaginable for journalists today. She became associated with the Greenwich Village bohemian scene and knew many of the literary and artistic lights of that milieu, including the notoriously sleazy self-promoter Guido Bruno, who published Barnes's *The Book of Repulsive Women* in 1915. This short chapbook of poems and drawings on lesbian topics would certainly have been censored if the censors could have imagined what it was about. Barnes was involved with the Provincetown Players, the radical theater group founded in 1916. Several of her plays were produced by them, one of the most important, *Three from the Earth*, in 1919. In the years 1916 to 1923, she wrote many playlets and small dramas that were published in various periodicals, some under the pseudonym Lydia Steptoe.

In 1919 or 1920, she went to Paris, joining the expatriates there, and became friends with James Joyce and his wife, Nora. He had an influence on her, as she had on him—he gave her his annotated manuscript of *Ulysses* (1922) in 1923, and so must have respected her greatly. During this period, she returned to New York from time to time, in 1923 publishing *A Book*, a collection of stories, drawings, and poems.

In 1920, Barnes had met Thelma Wood; after 1923, they were living together. This great love affair, which provided the material for the central events of *Nightwood*, continued for many years, stormily, before ending in the 1930's. *Ryder*, that strange fiction of mixed genres and drawings based largely on her radically strange family, was published in 1928; *Nightwood* appeared eight years later. Between them there was nothing else. *Nightwood* took Barnes years to write—she went through agonies of rewriting and revision. During this period, she moved between Paris, Tangiers, Peggy Guggenheim's house in South Devon (Hayward Hall), and New York. She was not to produce another major work until *The Antiphon* in 1958. *Nightwood* was first published in England by Faber & Faber and edited by T. S. Eliot, who wrote what was to become a much-quoted introduction to the work. The novel was well received in England, garnering many enthusiastic reviews. Its later reception in America was more puzzled. When Barnes finished *The Antiphon*, Eliot again read the manuscript and took it for Faber & Faber, but this time he was perplexed by the work—a response that was typical.

Writing did not come easily to Barnes; the process was slow and painstaking, which can be seen in all of her works. She is not a writer of narrative that flows and "writes itself": She had a difficult time with plot. Her works are like tableaux or collections of emblems. They contain many kinds of language and tend to illuminate a static situation rather than spin out a tale. She used varieties of archaic genres and language: the anatomy for *Nightwood*; for *Ryder* the languages of François Rabelais and Geoffrey Chaucer; in *The Antiphon* the language of William Shakespeare. Barnes's work is Joycean in that it refuses the invisibility of language typical of the supposedly naturalistic novel in favor of an invocation of many means in service of a near-obsessive desire to see, and to understand in a metaphysical way, the inner truths and structures of events and relationships. Her visual art is illustrative of this tendency as well. Her many portraits perform a kind of flaying operation on their subjects and are as formal and abstracting as caricatures, isolating emblematic features of the sitters, sometimes in a way destructive of surfaces, and often destructive of vanity.

In 1939, Barnes sailed to New York, barely escaping Europe in time to avoid the war. When she arrived, she was penniless and prospects were bleak. In 1940, she finally obtained a small apartment in the Village at Patchin Place; she would live there in increasing isolation for forty-one years until her death. There she worked, first on *The Antiphon*, then on poetry, most of which is still unpublished. She survived on a small stipend from Peggy Guggenheim and on royalties from *Nightwood*.

There is an increasing appreciation of Barnes's works, both in America and abroad. Some of her journalism and short fiction has been collected and reappraised, and the Field biography, though not authorized and rather flawed, brought some attention to Barnes's career. She is now seen as the extremely important figure in the development of modernism that she actually was in her day. Moreover, the addition of Barnes to the pantheon of great modernists helps to show that the modernist movement was not so radically different from what is called "postmodernism," as is often supposed, for one finds in her work the manipulation of genre conventions and the fondness for self-reflective structures often identified with the post-modernists.

BIBLIOGRAPHICAL REFERENCES: Douglas Messerli, *Djuna Barnes: A Bibliography*, 1976, is a full and comprehensive bibliography, well annotated, on not only Barnes's own works and Barnes criticism but also the many mentions of Barnes in the books of her contemporaries; it includes a good brief introduction. Andrew Field, *Djuna: The Life and Times of Djuna Barnes*, 1983, is one of the only complete biographies of Barnes. It is colorful and dramatic and informed by Field's great affection and respect for his subject, but it is not authorized and is, at times, perhaps overly speculative. Joseph Frank, *The Widening Gyre: Crisis and Mastery in Modern Literature*, 1963, contains an important interpretation of space and time in *Nightwood*. James Scott, *Djuna Barnes*, 1976, a volume in the Twayne World Authors series, is a good source; he provides a viewpoint in opposition to Frank's. Wallace Fowlie, *Love in Literature: Studies in Symbolic Expression*, 1965, contains a chapter entitled "Woman: *Nightwood* of Djuna Barnes," which has been influential in Barnes studies. See also T. S. Eliot's introduction to *Nightwood*, reprinted in *The Criterion* for April, 1937; the foreword to *Interviews*, 1985, and the introduction to *Smoke*, 1982, both by Douglas Messerli; and Suzanne C. Ferguson, "Djuna Barnes' Short Stories: An Estrangement of the Heart," *The Southern Review*, XXVI (January, 1969), which covers the short fiction of Barnes that had been published up to that time.

Ann Klefstad

JULIAN BARNES

Born: Leicester, England
Date: January 19, 1946

PRINCIPAL WORKS

NOVELS: *Metroland*, 1980; *Before She Met Me*, 1982; *Flaubert's Parrot*, 1984; *Staring at the Sun*, 1986.

MYSTERY AND DETECTIVE FICTION: *Duffy*, 1980; *Fiddle City*, 1981; *Putting the Boot In*, 1985; *Going to the Dogs*, 1987.

By the time his third book was published, Julian Barnes was hailed by critics on both sides of the Atlantic as one of the most accomplished novelists to appear on the scene in years. He was born in Leicester, England, on January 19, 1946, and educated at the City of London School from 1957 to 1964 and at Magdalen College, Oxford, from which he was graduated with honors in 1968. From 1969 to 1972 he worked as a lexicographer for the *Oxford English Dictionary* supplement (a job that may have reflected or contributed to the interest in wordplay that marks his writing). In 1977 Barnes began working as a reviewer and literary editor for British journals and newspapers such as the *New Statesman* and the *New Review.* From 1979 to 1986 he worked primarily as a television critic, first for the *New Statesman* and then for the *London Observer.*

In 1980 Barnes published his first novel, *Metroland*, a first-person account of the maturation of Christopher Lloyd, who rebels against his bourgeois suburban London upbringing and enjoys a bohemian fling in Paris before settling down to middle-class domesticity at home. The novel made an immediate impression, even among those critics who found the conclusion somewhat simplistic. (Lloyd successfully accommodates both his aesthetic ambitions and a publishing career.) The critics admired its remarkably assured tone, its well-turned phrases, and its lively reworking of the traditional apprenticeship story. Two years later, Barnes's second novel, *Before She Met Me*, attracted even more favorable notice. This novel is a witty but chilling depiction of an intelligent man destroyed by his obsessive jealousy. Graham Hendrick, a mild-mannered history teacher, happily remarried after a painful divorce, finds himself unable to stop brooding over the men in his new wife's past. He haunts motion-picture theaters to watch love scenes she played in a brief career as an actress and studies her possessions for clues to former lovers, fantasizing about the violence he would do to them. On the surface the novel depicts the comic entanglement of life with art—a novelist friend, for example, complicates Graham's search for truth by his penchant for putting real people into his fiction—but on a deeper level it depicts the tragic entanglement of reason with emotion in the human psyche, since Graham suspects that his brain is turning into his "own enemy." Although some critics complained of a lack of credibility in characterization, most agreed on the disturbing power of Barnes's portrayal of his protagonist's disintegration.

Barnes's outstanding success came two years later with *Flaubert's Parrot*, which most readers found a dazzling tour de force and many thought reminiscent, in ingenious wordplay, of the work of Vladimir Nabokov. Geoffrey Braithwaite, a retired English doctor and admirer of Gustave Flaubert, believes he owns the stuffed bird that sat on the Master's desk and is dismayed to find that a French museum claims to have the original. He sets out to find the truth, not only about the bird but also about Flaubert. What follows is part biography, part mystery, part essay, demonstrating the elusiveness of "fact" as it reveals truths about the doctor's relationship with his dead wife, who seems a modern counterpart of Flaubert's Emma Bovary. Some critics objected to the mixing of genres and the abundance of epigrams in *Flaubert's Parrot*. (John Updike, for example, found the novel an inventive and erudite "treatise" on Flaubert and an engaging "conversation" with the author, but with too much "artifice" to engage the reader as a novel.) The public, undaunted by the book's convoluted structure—including passages in the form of encyclopedia entries, a bestiary, and examination questions—found it both entertaining and instructive and made it an immediate bestseller.

Barnes's next novel, *Staring at the Sun*, was a radical departure in tone and theme. Jean Serjeant, an ordinary middle-class girl growing up after World War I, persists in asking questions—not, however, about truth, art, and life but merely about the small curiosities of her small world. Despite being exploited for her naïveté, she endures, unembittered and open-minded, to her one hundredth birthday, which occurs in 2021. Machines now exist to answer all questions, but when Jean's son—sixty years old and weary of life—seeks information about whether suicide is acceptable, the computer rejects his questions as "not real." He must turn to his naïve old mother to learn how death relates to life. More subdued in tone and style than its predecessors, *Staring at the Sun* illustrates Barnes's continuing interest in formal experimentation to probe the complex interaction of mind and body and past and present.

Barnes pursued simultaneously a second career as a writer of mystery fiction under the pseudonym Dan Kavanagh. *Duffy*, published in 1980, introduced his eponymous detective hero, a former policeman whose new work as a security specialist keeps him in contact with criminals at all levels of society, and *Fiddle City*, *Putting the Boot In*, and *Going to the Dogs* continued his adventures. Despite their less profound themes, these mysteries share many of the stylistic characteristics, particularly puns and literary allusions, of the serious novels: In *Going to the Dogs*, for example, the title refers not only to the dog track at which Duffy hits on the solution to the crime but also to his view of English society, with its indulgence in drugs and pornography. Even as he parodies classic detective fiction, Barnes skillfully employs all the conventions of the form, in well-constructed plots, credible characters, and tersely witty dialogue.

Barnes's serious novels won for him immediate and unusual recognition at home and abroad. *Metroland* was awarded the Somerset Maugham Award in 1981, and *Flaubert's Parrot*, nominated for the prestigious Booker McConnell Prize for Fiction in 1984, was subsequently awarded the Geoffrey Faber Memorial Prize in England and the Prix Médicis and Prix Gutenberg in France. Barnes also received an American Academy and Institute of Arts and Letters Award in 1986. Critics and the general public have agreed that his fiction is both entertaining in its Nabokovian wit and ingenuity and thought-provoking in its exploration of perennial moral and aesthetic questions.

BIBLIOGRAPHICAL REFERENCES: There are numerous reviews and interviews. See John Updike, "A Pair of Parrots," *The New Yorker*, LXI (July 22, 1985), 86-90; Francine Prose, "Men Who Read Women's Minds (Women in Male Fiction)," *Savvy*, IX (August, 1988), 18; Craig Brown, "Britain's Literary Luminaries," *Harper's Bazaar*, CXXI (February, 1988), 154; D. J. R. Bruckner, "Planned Parenthood and the Novel," *The New York Times Book Review*, XCII (April 12, 1987), 3; Jay Parini, Review of *Metroland*, *The New York Times Book Review*, XCII (May 3, 1987), 26; Gary Krist, Review of *Before She Met Me*, *The New York Times Book Review*, XCI (December 28, 1986), 12.

Mary Rose Sullivan

PETER BARNES

Born: London, England
Date: January 10, 1931

PRINCIPAL WORKS

PLAYS: *The Man with a Feather in His Hat*, pr. 1960 (teleplay); *The Time of the Barracudas*, pr. 1963; *Sclerosis*, pr. 1965; *The Ruling Class: A Baroque Comedy*, pr. 1968; *Leonardo's Last Supper*, pr. 1969; *Noonday Demons*, pr. 1969; *Lulu*, pr. 1970; *The Bewitched*, pr., pb. 1974; *The Frontiers of Farce*, pr. 1976; *Antonio*, pr. 1977 (radio play), 1979 (staged); *Laughter!*, pr., pb. 1978; *Barnes' People I: Seven Monologues*, pr., pb. 1981 (radio play); *Barnes' People No. II: Seven Dialogues*, pr., pb. 1984 (radio play); *Red Noses*, pr., pb. 1985; *The Real Long John Silver and Other Plays: Barnes' People III*, pr., pb. 1986 (radio play).

SCREENPLAYS: *Violent Moment*, 1959; *The White Trap*, 1959; *Breakout*, 1959; *The Professionals*, 1960; *Off-Beat*, 1961; *Ring of Spies*, 1963 (with Frank Launder; also known as *Ring of Treason*); *Not with My Wife You Don't*, 1966; *The Ruling Class*, 1972.

Peter Barnes, one of the most inventive and challenging contemporary dramatists, combines a hatred of the class system with a savage, satirical, and wildly comic style. Born in the East End of London to working-class parents, Barnes was the older of two children. His parents moved to Clacton-on-Sea, a resort area where they operated an amusement park and where Barnes was educated. After leaving school at seventeen, he worked for the Greater London Council before serving in the Royal Air Force from 1949 to 1950.

Upon his return to civilian life, Barnes wrote film reviews for the Greater London Council, resigning in the early 1950's to become a free-lance film critic. In 1956 he joined Warwick Films as a story editor, where he was responsible for selecting material for possible filming by the studio. From 1959 to 1966, Barnes wrote seven screenplays, including *The White Trap* and *Not with My Wife You Don't*, and a television script, *The Man with a Feather in His Hat*. Feeling constrained by these commercial parameters and desiring to express his own ideas freely, Barnes turned to the stage.

The Ruling Class brought Barnes to international prominence. Aiming for a "comic theatre of contrasting moods and opposites, where everything is simultaneously tragic and ridiculous," Barnes satirizes the values, viciousness, perversions, and manipulations of the British ruling class. After *The Ruling Class*, Barnes's view of society becomes even bleaker. In *Leonardo's Last Supper*, the famous artist is brought to a charnel house after having been prematurely declared dead. In the midst of his joy over his second chance to continue his creativity, he is killed by the poor family who need the burial money. In the companion piece, *Noonday Demons*, two fourth century hermits argue about to whom God speaks until the one kills the other. Using a language that combines archaisms and modern slang, Barnes underscores the parallels with contemporary debates about capitalism, religion, and self-interest. The style is comic and vituperative in the manner of Ben Jonson.

Although Barnes left school at seventeen, he has been and is an enthusiastic and disciplined self-educator. As a result, he is not only an unusually literate dramatist but also a prolific adapter of works by those dramatists whom he particularly admires. Since 1970, when he combined two of Frank Wedekind's plays into *Lulu*, he has worked on other adaptions. He is particularly drawn to Jonson's avaricious characters and abundant vulgarity of language and situation. These are qualities that are readily apparent in Barnes's own work.

In *The Bewitched*, Barnes continues his preoccupation with the power of a ruling class, the profit motive, and murder in the name of God. It is a huge play with more than thirty scenes and forty characters. *Laughter!* provoked even more commentary, as Barnes explores in graphic theatrical terms further links between insanity, political power, and comedy. *Red Noses*, set during the black Plague of the fourteenth century, continues Barnes's preoccupation with comedy and social upheaval. The Red Noses are a religious group of entertainers who try to divert the populace; in the process, they discover the revolutionary possibilities of the stage in combating the oppressive forces of the church and state. With the end of the plague, repression is reestablished and Barnes's hope that "laughter linked with revolution might be the best of both worlds" is not yet achieved.

Producers reluctant to stage his plays because of their controversial nature, Barnes has become involved in writing for the British Broadcasting Corporation. *Barnes' People I*, *Barnes' People II*, and *Barnes' People III* are collections of seven short pieces each, exploring the forms of the monologue, the dialogue, and three voices respectively. His vision continues to be bleak, as Barnes explores individuals "unique in their creative energies for good and evil," ordinary people trapped in an unjust and horrifying society.

Opposed to naturalism, Peter Barnes has created a theatrical style all his own, though it reflects those works which have captured his eclectic interests. His plays have been called Baroque and Jacobean, terms which link them to the late Renaissance, a period by which he is admittedly fascinated. His plays mirror the same kind of world in decay, marked by extravagant language, macabre violence, and grotesque verbal and visual images. He has also been influenced by Bertolt Brecht and Antonin Artaud, as his works both reflect and parody epic theater and the theater of cruelty. He is a theatrical playwright whose "artistic signature" consists of juxtaposing comedy, shock effects, music, social commentary, popular culture, and literary allusions to break through the complacency of the audience.

BIBLIOGRAPHICAL REFERENCES: Bernard F. Dukore, *The Theatre of Peter Barnes*, 1981, is a thorough examination of the works of Barnes in the context of the writers who influenced him and in the light of the controversy surrounding his ideas and his theatrical style. It is the first full-length study, written by the critic who would completely dominate Barnes's scholarship in the 1980's. See also John Russell Taylor, *The Second Wave*, 1971; Bernard F. Dukore, "Peter Barnes," in *Essays on Contemporary British Drama*, 1981, edited by Hedwig Bock and Albert Wertheim; Bernard Dukore, "People Like You and Me: The Auschwitz Plays of Peter Barnes and C. P. Taylor," *Essays in Theater*, III (1985), 108-124; Bernard Dukore, "Newer Peter Barnes with Links to the Past," *Essays in Theater*, V (1986), 47-59; Bernard Dukore, "*Red Noses* and *St. Joan*," *Modern Drama*, XXX (1987), 340-351; and Bernard Dukore, "The Author's Play," *Twentieth Century Literature*, XXXIII (1987), 159-178.

Lori Hall Burghardt

PHILIP BARRY

Born: Rochester, New York
Date: June 18, 1896

Died: New York, New York
Date: December 3, 1949

PRINCIPAL WORKS

PLAYS: *A Punch for Judy*, pr. 1921; *You and I*, pr. 1923; *The Youngest*, pr. 1924; *In a Garden*, pr. 1925; *White Wings*, pr. 1926; *John*, pr. 1927; *Paris Bound*, pr. 1927; *Cock Robin*, pr. 1928 (with Elmer Rice); *Holiday*, pr. 1928; *Hotel Universe*, pr., pb. 1930; *Tomorrow and Tomorrow*, pr., pb. 1931; *The Animal Kingdom*, pr., pb. 1932; *The Joyous Season*, pr., pb. 1934; *Bright Star*, pr. 1935; *Spring Dance*, pr., pb. 1936; *Here Come the Clowns*, pr. 1938; *The Philadelphia Story*, pr., pb. 1939; *Liberty Jones*, pr., pb. 1941; *Without Love*, pr. 1942; *Foolish Notion*, pr. 1945; *My Name Is Aquilon* pr. 1949; *Second Threshold*, pr., pb. 1951 (with Robert E. Sherwood).

NOVEL: *War in Heaven*, 1938.

Like a character from his own sparkling plays, Philip Barry had the good fortune to be handsome, clever, and rich. Born into an Irish-Catholic middle-class family (his dying father left him unprovided for in his will), he was fortunate in his opportunities for education, marriage, and the fulfillment of his talent. After finishing public high school in Rochester, New York, Barry was accepted into Yale University in 1913, when he was seventeen. From his freshman year he showed a keen interest in literature; he read avidly and wrote poems and stories for the Yale literary magazine. He spent a year in London as a code clerk for the American embassy during World War I and afterward returned to the United States, receiving a degree from Yale in 1919.

Barry's interest in the theater, evident even in his early teens, now ripened into an ambition that would make him one of the most successful playwrights of his time. He enrolled in George Pierce Baker's Workshop 47 drama course at Harvard University in 1919 and earned Baker's respect and friendship. Baker perceived the authenticity of Barry's talent and gave him the encouragement and knowledge that made the workshop indispensable not only to Barry but also to a generation of American dramatists, including Eugene O'Neill.

Barry's first play, *A Punch for Judy*, was completed at the workshop and produced in 1921. By this time he had met Ellen Semple, a wealthy debutante, and the two were married in July, 1922. For a wedding present the couple was given a house in Cannes, on the French Riviera, and for the rest of his life Barry moved between Broadway and Cannes as his career blossomed.

His first major success was the comedy *You and I*, which ran on Broadway for 170 performances. The play was characteristic of the well-made comedy of manners that became Barry's hallmark: clever, witty dialogue among charming men and women of high society, a romance with its conflicts, and an artfully satisfying resolution.

His next play, *The Youngest*, about the younger generation's conflict with the conventions of family life, established Barry as the foremost American dramatist of the comedy of manners. Yet it was *Paris Bound*, *Holiday*, and, especially, *The Philadelphia Story* that earned for him a significant place in American drama. In these plays, serious themes such as adultery, love sacrificed for career, and divorce were presented in the content of humor and good sense, punctuated by crisp, clever dialogue. They are among Barry's most appealing works.

Not content simply to entertain, however, Barry also wrote plays in which he experimented with darker themes and more serious intentions. *In a Garden* is a thoughtful comedy about a successful dramatist's sense of self. *White Wings* treats the clash of tradition and modernity and the impediment of such a clash to love and romance. *John* explores the religious doubt and disappointment of John the Baptist. *Hotel Universe* is a serious, dreamlike play that brings a group of wealthy people onto a terrace overlooking the Mediterranean in search of life's meaning. Similarly, *Here Come the Clowns* establishes a vaudevillian setting in which the main character, like Job, confronts God on the mystery of evil. Though they contain some of Barry's best writing, these plays only puzzled the public.

Philip Barry died suddenly of heart failure on December 3, 1949. He left behind some twenty plays, ranging from high drawing-room comedy to religious allegory, fantasy, and philosophical explorations on the meaning of life. He is generally remembered, however, as the master of high comedy. At its best, his work in this genre catches the tempo and the temper of a society representing a kind of American royalty, a hierarchy of wealth and privilege, which flourished particularly during the boom years after World War I. Barry's people are monied, cultivated, and charming; the conflicts that stain their lives are the domestic incivilities of adultery, divorce, and shallow materialism. Though such conflicts are resolved by the very qualities of intelligence and benign common sense that mark the characters themselves, his plays manage to suggest the triumph of a value system relevant not only to the Barry men and women but also to humanity at large. His serious plays, though not artistically satisfying, are thoughtful, often-poetic presentations of the doubts and despair inherent in the experience of all intelligent human beings. Despite the workmanlike quality of his plays and their inerrant dramatic technique, only a few of Philip Barry's comedies are still performed. Yet the solidity of his work suggests that he is a playwright who deserves more serious attention.

BIBLIOGRAPHICAL REFERENCES: The general neglect of much of Philip Barry's work is evidenced by the relative scarcity of critical material. Joseph Roppolo, *Philip Barry*, 1965, is one of the few full-length studies of the dramatist and his work. Brendan Gill's copious introduction in *States of Grace: Eight Plays by Philip Barry*, 1975, is the best convenient account and is particularly insightful on the familial, cultural, and social background from which Barry wrote. Jean Gould in *Modern American Playwrights*, 1966, describes the dramatist as the sunny, "Celtic" contrast to the somber Eugene O'Neill, while noting the spiritual concerns in the work of both. *The Theater of Our Times*, by John Gassner, 1954, offers a judicial assessment of Barry's work, as does Arthur Hobson Quinn in his classic *A History of the American Drama from the Civil War to the Present Day*, 1943. *The American Drama Since 1918*, by Joseph Wood Krutch, 1939, 1957, offers a well-balanced account, particularly of Barry's more serious plays. For a discussion of individual plays, see C. W. E. Bigsby, *A Critical Introduction to Twentieth-Century American Drama*, 1982, which treats Barry's *Hotel Universe* and its presentation by the Theater Guild. *The Stage Is Set*, by Lee Simonson, 1932, discusses the particular problems of staging *Hotel Universe*.

Edward Fiorelli

JOHN BARTH

Born: Cambridge, Maryland
Date: May 27, 1930

PRINCIPAL WORKS

LONG FICTION: *The Floating Opera*, 1956; *The End of the Road*, 1958; *The Sot-Weed Factor*, 1960; *Giles Goat-Boy: Or, the Revised New Syllabus*, 1966; *Chimera*, 1972; *Letters: A Novel*, 1979; *Sabbatical: A Romance*, 1982; *The Tidewater Tales: A Novel*, 1987.

SHORT FICTION: *Lost in the Funhouse*, 1968.

LITERARY CRITICISM: *The Friday Book*, 1984.

John Barth, one of the most influential American writers of the so-called postmodernist era, was born on May 27, 1930, in Cambridge, Maryland, to John Jacob and Georgia Simmons Barth. After finishing high school, he attended the Juilliard School of Music and then enrolled in The Johns Hopkins University in 1947, pursuing a degree in journalism. By the time he was a junior, however, because of the influence of one of his professors, he decided to become a teacher and a fiction writer instead. Barth was married to Harriette Anne Strickland in 1950 and received his bachelor's degree in creative writing the following year. By 1952, he had completed his master's degree at Johns Hopkins and had begun his doctoral work there. In 1953, he left Johns Hopkins because of lack of funds and took a teaching position in the English department at The Pennsylvania State University.

The years from 1955 to 1960 are perhaps the most important ones in John Barth's career, for during that time he published *The Floating Opera* (which was nominated for the National Book Award in 1956), *The End of the Road*, and *The Sot-Weed Factor*, and he began work on *Giles Goat-Boy*. Although Barth's first two novels are basically realistic works, they contain the seeds of the satiric element that began to dominate his writing with the publication of his second two novels. Both *The Sot-Weed Factor* and *Giles Goat-Boy* are broad, picaresque works that seem more within the tradition of the eighteenth century novels of Jonathan Swift, Laurence Stern, and Henry Fielding than the modern tradition. Yet what makes these sprawling satires distinctly modern is their self-conscious erudition and concern with the processes of fiction.

In 1967 and 1968, Barth made his alignment with the postmodernist focus on fiction as a self-reflexive art form even more explicit. First, he published a controversial essay in *The Atlantic Monthly* titled "The Literature of Exhaustion," which urged more of the kind of self-conscious experimentation being practiced by the South American writer Jorge Luis Borges. (Many misinterpreted the essay, insisting that Barth argues that fiction writers have "run out" of subjects for their work.) Second, Barth turned from the novel form to the short story, publishing *Lost in the Funhouse*, an experimental collection whose stories do not adhere to their so-called proper subject—the external world—and instead continually turn the reader's attention back to what Barth considered their real subject: the process of fiction making. The four fictional works published after *Lost in the Funhouse* are similarly focused on their own narrative structure and methods.

Barth's approach to fiction has been summarized quite pointedly in the essays that appear in his collection of occasional pieces entitled *The Friday Book*; there he asserts that the novelist is like God and God is like a novelist, for the universe itself is like a novel. This notion that the novel is not simply a view of a world but rather a world itself is a common theme of postmodernist fiction, for which Barth is now the best-known practitioner and advocate.

Barth's most admired storyteller is the heroine of *A Thousand and One Nights* (c. 1450), Scheherazade, to whom he pays homage most directly in a novella in his work *Chimera*. Yet Barth has been fascinated with mythical figures at least since 1964, when, while he was working on *Giles Goat-Boy*, he discovered such studies of myth as Joseph Campbell's *The Hero with a Thousand Faces* (1949). Since that time, Barth's fiction has been self-consciously concerned with the primal elements that make up the universe of story.

Barth insists that the prosaic in fiction is there only to be transformed into fabulation. For Barth, the artist's ostensible subject is not the main point; rather, it is only an excuse or raw material for focusing on the nature of the fiction-making process. Great literature, says Barth, is almost always, regardless of how it appears, about itself. Barth is one of the most important writers in the late twentieth century. Perhaps more than any other American writer since World War II, he has made fiction intensely conscious of itself, aware of its traditions and aware of the conventions that make it possible. If, as the main currents of modern thought suggest, reality itself is the result of fiction-making processes, then John Barth is truly a writer concerned with the essential nature of what is real.

BIBLIOGRAPHICAL REFERENCES: Good overall introductions to Barth's work include Gerhard Joseph, *John Barth*, 1970, which focuses on Barth's early fiction; David Morrell, *John Barth: An Introduction*, 1976, which contains helpful information about Barth's life and his working methods; and E. P. Walkiewicz, *John Barth*, 1986. For more specialized studies, see Jac Tharpe, *John Barth: The Comic Sublimity of Paradox*, 1974, which deals with Barth as a philosophic novelist, and Charles B. Harris, *Passionate Virtuosity: The Fiction of John Barth*, 1983, a demanding study which applies contemporary literary theory to Barth's work. The best collection of critical essays on Barth is *Critical Essays on John Barth*, 1980, edited by Joseph Waldmeir. Also valuable are discussions of Barth's work in Charles B. Harris, *Contemporary American Novelists of the Absurd*, 1971; Richard Boyd Hauck, *A Cheerful Nihilism: Confidence and the Absurd in American Humorous Fiction*, 1971; Jerome Klinkowitz, *Literary Disruptions: The Making of a Post-Contemporary American Fiction*, 1975; Frank D. McConnell, *Four Postwar American Novelists: Bellow, Mailer, Barth, and Pynchon*, 1977; Robert Scholes, *The Fabulators*, 1967; Jack O. Stark, *The Literature of Exhaustion: Borges, Nabokov, and Barth*, 1974; and Tony Tanner, *City of Words: American Fiction 1950-1970*, 1971.

Charles E. May

DONALD BARTHELME

Born: Philadelphia, Pennsylvania — *Died:* Houston, Texas
Date: April 7, 1931 — *Date:* July 23, 1989

Principal Works

SHORT FICTION: *Come Back, Dr. Caligari*, 1964; *Unspeakable Practices, Unnatural Acts*, 1968; *City Life*, 1970; *Sadness*, 1972; *Guilty Pleasures*, 1974; *Amateurs*, 1976; *Great Days*, 1979; *Sixty Stories*, 1981; *Overnight to Many Distant Cities*, 1983; *Forty Stories*, 1987.

NOVELS: *Snow White*, 1967; *The Dead Father*, 1975; *Paradise*, 1986.

Donald Barthelme is one of the most imaginative and innovative American authors of this century, and probably the most imitated short-story writer since the 1960's. He was born the oldest of five children (at least two others are also respected short-story writers). His father was a successful architect. In 1933, the family moved to Houston, which would remain one of Barthelme's part-time residences. During his two years at the University of Houston, he studied journalism; he then worked as a reporter for the *Houston Post*. After serving in the U.S. Army, Barthelme founded a literary magazine and began working at Houston's Contemporary Arts Museum, where, in 1961, he was appointed director. The next year he moved to New York and began publishing in *The New Yorker* magazine, to which he would continue to contribute regularly. The majority of his work, collected in his many short-story volumes, and even one of his two novels, *Snow White*, first appeared in *The New Yorker.*

Throughout his career, Barthelme has rejected the conventional forms of fiction: traditional narrative plot and characterization, the unities of time and space. If the novelist's task is to reflect and comment upon reality, then the novel must lack structure—since beginnings, middles, and endings are not "real." Instead, Barthelme writes fiction that at times evokes mood; frequently, he writes "metafiction," fiction that takes as its subject the very act of writing a story: Verbs and nouns take the place of plot, event, and character (*The Dead Father*). At other times, he is concerned with social themes or the dilemmas of human interaction and loneliness.

Barthelme's form is that of the verbal collage, juxtaposing the beginning, middle, or ending of a story—or a sentence—with bits of other beginnings, middles, or endings. Typically, he interrupts a narrative or dialogue with contradictory or self-reflexive material. Often, he re-creates slang or metaphor in new and outrageous terms. All these devices function to jar the reader out of his complacent expectations of human response and language. The reader must reconsider language and communication in new, more authentic terms.

Barthelme's early works are primarily concerned with social issues—modern, brainwashed society, narcotized by the media—and they portray a world of zombies spouting texts and technology in response to every emotional confrontation, as in *Come Back, Dr. Caligari*. The volumes *City Life* and *Sadness* treat, in addition, the unreliability of irony as a weapon against a spiritually sullied world. *Guilty Pleasures*, one of his most humorous books, contains numerous literary parodies, as it satirizes the tinfoil nature of contemporary America.

Barthelme has been widely praised—and imitated—because of his innovative and witty use of language, specifically the dislocations of sentences through transformations of slang, metaphor, and grammar. In fact, as Barthelme utilizes a vast array of verbal pyrotechnics—changing parts of speech, new words and spellings, puns and at times outrageous wordplay ("Jean-Paul Sartre is a Fartre")—to draw the reader's attention to impoverished human communication, he touches on larger, existential issues. In a world devoid of ultimate assurances and meanings, the only valid way of asserting one's identity and authenticity is through the authenticity of the world.

Barthelme has been criticized for not writing a body of longer, more sustained fiction. In fact, if his novels *Snow White* and *The Dead Father* were his sole publications, they would ensure him of a permanent and honored place in American letters. *Snow White* details the plight of the legendary mythic figure in the modern world, playing out the script (the fairy-tale role) to which she was born in a world of small men within the sexual, social, and moral expectations of 1960's America. *The Dead Father* focuses on the need for yet repulsiveness of authority in the form of a gigantic, dying father figure, who represents the aggregate of religious, mythic, historical, literary, and linguistic tradition. A third, less successful novel, *Paradise,* tells of a fifty-three year-old New York architect and the three girls who invade his empty apartment.

As the 1980's approached, Barthelme began, in *Great Days*, to experiment with a more poetic style that incorporated musical techniques—producing, for example, sonata-like structures (theme A, theme B, theme A) to evoke a certain mood. *Great Days* also utilizes a new dialogue form, as it explores the serious issues of time and mortality. Barthelme's characters here, interestingly, are less abstract, more human. *Overnight to Many Distant Cities* actually alternates short stories with dialogue-arias; here again one finds the Barthelme wit and the dislocations of traditional meaning in the service of eliciting an authentic response from the reader. He writes, for example, "Youth, Goethe said, is the silky apple butter on the good brown bread of possiblity."

Since the mid-1960's, the postmodern writers—including Robert Coover, William H. Gass, John Barth, and Thomas Pynchon (as well as Julio Cortázar, Italo Calvino, Robert Pinget, and Claude Simon outside the United States)—have been concerned with language and the difficulty of utilizing it as an emblem of authentic participation in an alien universe. Barthelme's work illustrates that words ultimately remain the only link with this vast and indifferent world: The creative and honest use of language is the most effective measure against isolation and loneliness.

BIBLIOGRAPHICAL REFERENCES: See *Donald Barthelme: A Comprehensive Bibliography and Annotated Secondary Checklist*, by Jerome Klinkowitz, Asa Pieratt, and Robert Murray Davis, 1977. Lois Gordon's *Donald Barthelme*, 1981, is the first book-length study of Barthelme's work, treating in depth his themes and language and discussing, in detail, each short-story collection and novel. This work was followed by Larry McCaffery's *The Metafictional Muse: The Works of Robert Coover, Donald Barthelme, and William H. Gass*, 1982, and Charles Molesworth's equally interesting *Donald Barthelme's Fiction: The Ironist Saved from Drowning*, 1982. See also Jerome Klinkowitz, *Literary Disruptions: The Making of a Post-Contemporary American Fiction*, 1975, for a superior survey of the avant-garde that also provides a fine introduction to Barthelme's inventive language and forms. Tony Tanner's *City of Words*, 1971, is a provocative survey of American fiction from 1950 to 1970, discussing Barthelme's "redemptive" rearrangements of fragments. See also the special Donald Barthelme issue of *Critique: Studies in Modern Fiction*, XVI (1975), and Charles I. Glicksberg, "Experimental Fiction: Innovation Versus Form," *Centennial Review*, XVIII (1974), 127-150, a solid survey of experimental fiction from James Joyce to Barthelme. Richard Gilman, "Donald Barthelme," *Partisan Review*, XXXIX (Summer, 1972), 382-396, presents interesting speculations on Bartheleme's imaginative yet socially pragmatic vision. Neil Schmitz, in "Donald Barthelme and the Emergence of Modern Satire," *The Minnesota Review*, I (1971), 109-118, describes how Barthelme ironically celebrates the creative/destructive consciousness in the phenomenological world. Schmitz's "What Irony Reveals," *Partisan Review*, XL (1973), 482-490, is another intelligent discussion of Barthelme's irony.

Lois Gordon

FREDERICK BARTHELME

Born: Houston, Texas
Date: October 10, 1943

PRINCIPAL WORKS

NOVELS: *War and War,* 1971; *Second Marriage*, 1984; *Tracer,* 1985; *Two Against One*, 1988.
SHORT FICTION: *Rangoon*, 1970; *Moon Deluxe*, 1983; *Chroma*, 1987.

Frederick Barthelme, like his older and more widely known brother, Donald, belongs in the forefront of the generation of post-realistic writers such as John Barth (with whom he studied at one time) and Thomas Pynchon. He was born in Houston, Texas, in 1943. His father, Donald, was an architect; his mother, Helen, was a teacher. He attended Tulane University and the University of Houston before taking a master's degree at The Johns Hopkins University in 1977. He has held jobs in several creative fields, including architecture and advertising, and at one time he intended to pursue painting as a career. His paintings have been exhibited at many galleries, including the Museum of Modern Art in New York. Since 1976 he has been associated with the University of Southern Mississippi in Hattiesburg, where he is a professor of English and directs the Center for Writers.

Barthelme's earliest work was unsuccessful commercially and critically. The stories collected in *Rangoon* were notable for their eccentricity of subject matter and their lack of conventional structure. Like his painting of the time, they drew their significance from implicit comparisons between ordinary and often radically diverse objects and situations. This effect of collage was heightened by the use of drawings and photographs. Many of the stories are characterized by a flatness of tone and imagery which reflects one of Barthelme's major themes, namely the sadness and barrenness of American life. This theme unites *Rangoon* with his first novel, *War and War,* which is a freewheeling parody of the self-conscious narrative style of writers such as Laurence Sterne. Full of allusions to philosophers and linguists, *War and War* is a static, highly intellectual showcase for Barthelme's considerable erudition. It was reviewed unfavorably in *The New York Times* and otherwise seems to have gone unnoticed.

After a period of silence, Barthelme began to publish stories more traditional in structure but still colored by the presence of what Margaret Atwood, writing in *The New York Times Book Review,* calls "seedy, greasy, plastic-coated things or lush, expensive, meretricious things," and by a cool disdain for the shallowness of American culture in general and the culture of the urban South in particular. Seventeen of these stories, including thirteen which first appeared in *The New Yorker,* were collected in *Moon Deluxe*. Stories such as the title story, "Safeway," and "Monster Deal" reveal a significant thematic development in their blurring of the roles of men and women. On balance, Barthelme's men are socially and sexually passive, if not impotent; his women are vigorous and unpredictable. The net effect of *Moon Deluxe* was of a formidable talent given over to the service of mean-spirited, if often deadly accurate, observation.

In *Second Marriage* and *Tracer,* Barthelme applied his acute vision to wider and deeper subjects. Both novels dance precariously along the jagged line between farce and pathos. In *Second Marriage*, the protagonist watches helplessly as his first wife moves in with his second and the two form a union which excludes him. In *Tracer,* the central figure becomes involved in an affair with his estranged wife's sister, whereupon the wife arrives to reclaim him. There is a strong undercurrent of feminism in the structure of the triangles in these novels in which women make the decisions. The theme of a passive male willingly or unwillingly being dominated by forceful women is again joined with sharp scrutiny of the objects, natural and man-made, which litter the desert of modern culture.

The stories in *Chroma* focus vividly on relationships which are as plain in form and as empty of substance as the indistinguishable condominiums which the characters inhabit. In the title story, for example, a wife blandly announces to her husband that she intends to stay with her boyfriend every other weekend. Barthelme's style in this volume is deadpan; some of the stories, such as "Cleo," in which a wife urges her husband to have an affair with her best friend, present ironic situations, but there is not the slightest irony in the narrative voice. The effect, finally, is of hollow comedy, often brilliantly polished, but heartless.

Two Against One, as the title implies, returns to the triangle theme of Barthelme's previous novels, but with a slight twist: The estranged husband is now faced with his wife and her male lover. The landscape is the familiar sterile urban-to-suburban one of streets and rooms without character. *Two Against One* is a novel of passage; the events center on the protagonist's fortieth birthday. Yet there is no growth, and the thick undergrowth of relationships within the triangle remains tangled and dark.

The extent of Frederick Barthelme's influence on readers is difficult to judge; his books have consistently been reviewed in major media, but he has not attained wide popularity. Perhaps the most logical extension of his talent is into the visual media, and *Tracer* has indeed been sold as a screenplay. It seems reasonable that he will be regarded as one of the most significant of the minimalist writers of the 1980's, and his laconic, understated style will be regarded as characteristic.

BIBLIOGRAPHICAL REFERENCES: Most of the critical work on Frederick Barthelme is in the form of reviews and articles. See Margaret Atwood, Review of *Moon Deluxe*, *The New York Times Book Review*, LXXXVIII (July 31, 1983), 1; Ann Hulbert, "Welcome the Wimps," *The New Republic*, CLXXXIX (October 31, 1983), 35-38; Michiko Kakutani, "Writing the Second Novel: A Symposium," *The New York Times Book Review*, XC (March 17, 1985), 1; Ron Loewinsohn, Review of *Second Marriage*, *The New York Times Book Review*, LXXXIX (September 30, 1984), 1. See also the interview with Barthelme in *Contemporary Authors*, Vol. 122, 1988, edited by Hal May and Susan Trotsky.

Robert Boyd

ROLAND BARTHES

Born: Cherbourg, France
Date: November 12, 1915

Died: Paris, France
Date: March 26, 1980

Principal Works

criticism: *Le Degré zéro de l'écriture*, 1953 (*Writing Degree Zero*, 1967); *Michelet par, lui-même*, 1954 (*Michelet*, 1986); *Mythologies*, 1957 (English translation, 1972); *Sur Racine*, 1963 (*On Racine*, 1964); *Essais critiques*, 1964 (*Critical Essays*, 1972); *La Tour Eiffel*, 1964 (*The Eiffel Tower and Other Mythologies*, 1979); *Éléments de sémiologie*, 1964 (*Elements of Semiology*, 1967); *Critique et vérité*, 1966 (*Criticism and Truth*, 1987); *Système de la mode*, 1967 (*The Fashion System*, 1983); *S/Z*, 1970 (English translation, 1974); *L'Empire des signes*, 1970 (*Empire of Signs*, 1982); *Sade, Fourier, Loyola*, 1971 (English translation, 1976); *Nouveaux essais critiques*, 1972 (*New Critical Essays*, 1980); *Le Plaisir du texte*, 1973 (*The Pleasure of the Text*, 1975); *Roland Barthes par Roland Barthes*, 1975 (*Roland Barthes by Roland Barthes*, 1977); *Fragments d'un discours amoureux*, 1977 (*A Lover's Discourse: Fragments,* 1978); *Image-Music-Text*, 1977; *Sollers écrivain*, 1979; *La Chambre claire: Note sur la photographie*, 1980 (*Camera Lucida: Reflections on Photography*, 1981); *Le Grain de la voix: Entretiens, 1962-1980,* 1981 (*The Grain of the Voice: Interviews, 1962-1980*, 1985); *A Roland Barthes Reader*, 1982; *L'Obvie et l'obtus*, 1982 (*The Responsibility of Forms*, 1985); *Le Bruissement de la langue*, 1984 (*The Rustle of Language*, 1986); *The Semiotic Challenge*, 1988.

Roland Barthes was one of the leading proponents of the new French criticism and one of the founders of structuralism. He was born in Cherbourg, France, on November 12, 1915, to the solid bourgeois family of Louis and Henriette Barthes. Louis Barthes, a naval officer, was killed in 1916, and in 1924 young Roland moved to Paris with his mother. It was in Paris that he lived most of his life and received his education. In 1939, he received a license in classical letters from the Sorbonne, and between recurring bouts of tuberculosis he taught in and around Paris while continuing his education. During the convalescence from his second attack of tuberculosis, Barthes was first published, and he began a distinguished career as a teacher, researcher, critic, and writer.

One result of Barthes's years of convalescence was that he had the time to read widely and to decide that he was more aligned to Marxist ideology than to the bourgeois ideology in which he had been reared. With this willingness to embrace leftist ideas came a willingness to question and explore many of the commonplaces of his world. It was in this frame of mind that he was introduced to modern linguistics while teaching in Alexandria, Egypt, and this introduction gave Barthes a tool with which to explore his world.

Barthes was able to acquire several scholarships after his return to France in the early 1950's. The first provided funds for him to study lexicology and the second supported his sociological study of fashion. Neither project was immediately successful, but both helped produce several of Barthes's important early works: *Writing Degree Zero, Mythologies*, and, eventually, *The Fashion System*.

Barthes was a prolific writer during the period from 1950 to 1965. He worked on projects ranging from studies of contemporary culture to essays on literary subjects. Although he published widely, including such pivotal works as the essays collected in *Critical Essays,* it was not until after the publication of his book *On Racine*, in 1963, that Barthes became a leading figure on the French intellectual scene.

In 1965, a Sorbonne professor, Raymond Picard, attacked Barthes's approach in *On Racine* and set in motion a heated debate out of which Barthes wrote *Criticism and Truth*. Because of this controversy, Barthes made a name for himself throughout the international intellectual community. In *Criticism and Truth*, Barthes concerns himself with the justification and further explanation of the structuralist agenda.

It was under the banner of structuralism, with its pretensions to a "scientific" study of literature and its emphasis on structural linguistics as the model for the human sciences, that Barthes first became known in the United States. Ironically, by the time that Barthes's structuralist works were widely available in English translation, he had already abandoned the structuralist program.

The new direction of Barthes's work was adumbrated in *S/Z*, which some critics regard as his masterpiece. *S/Z* is a line-by-line reading of *Sarrasine* (1831), an obscure novella by Honoré de Balzac. On the surface it is a structuralist work *par excellence*, formidably systematic, with each fragment of the text assigned to one or more of five narrative "codes." In reality, however, Barthes's study is an orgy of close reading, a virtuoso performance in which a gifted reader abandons himself to the pleasure of the text. The elaborate codes (which lesser readers have sought to employ, with disastrous results) are merely a pretext.

In subsequent works, Barthes largely dropped any pretense to systematizing or "scientific" criticism. He wrote prolifically throughout the 1970's, producing such brilliant, idiosyncratic books as *Roland Barthes by Roland Barthes*, a critical study of himself, and *Camera Lucida: Reflections on Photography.* He continued to work at that pace until his death on March 26, 1980, when he was struck by a laundry van while crossing a street.

It is impossible to overestimate Roland Barthes's influence on contemporary literary studies. In the decade following his death, several collections of essays and miscellaneous works were published, further suggesting the range and diversity of his interests. In his lifetime he was known as a literary theorist, one who helped to inaugurate the vogue for theory so dominant in the 1980's. Insofar as his works endure, he will be read not as a theorist but as a protean writer who sought to create new genres or hybrids of old ones, a writer who repeatedly left his would-be disciples expounding doctrines which he had discarded.

BIBLIOGRAPHICAL REFERENCES: *Roland Barthes*, by Jonathan Culler, 1983, is a lively and accessible introduction to Barthes the man and the critic. Also, see George R. Wasserman, *Roland Barthes*, 1981, for another introduction to the man and his work, and Susan Sontag, *Under the Sign of Saturn*, 1980. For an extensive Barthes bibliography, see Sanford Freedman and Carole Anne Taylor, *Roland Barthes: A Bibliographic Reader's Guide*, 1982, and "Bibliography of Roland Barthes," *Tel Quel*, XLVII (1971), 126-132. See also John Sturrock, "Roland Barthes," *The New Review*, II (1974), 13-20, for a good account of Barthes's earlier work. For application of Barthes's work, see Barbara Johnson, "The Critical Difference," *Diacritics*, VIII (1978), 2-9; Edward Jayne, "Zero-Degree Form: The Anti Dialectics of Roland Barthes," *The Minnesota Review*, Fall, 1979, 52-70; Josué V. Harari, "The Maximum Narrative: An Introduction to Barthes's Recent Criticism," *Style*, VIII (1974), 56-77; Stephen G. Nichols, "Roland Barthes," *Contemporary Literature*, X (1969), 136-146; and Yves Velan, "Barthes," *Modern French Criticism*, 1972.

Eric H. Hobson

GIORGIO BASSANI

Born: Bologna, Italy
Date: April 4, 1916

PRINCIPAL WORKS

NOVELS: *Una città di pianura*, 1940; *Gli occhiali d'oro*, 1958 (*The Gold-Rimmed Spectacles*, 1960; revised as *The Gold-Rimmed Eyeglasses*, 1975); *Il giardino dei Finzi-Contini*, 1962 (*The Garden of the Finzi-Continis*, 1965); *Dietro la porta*, 1964 (*Behind the Door*, 1972); *L'airone*, 1968 (*The Heron*, 1970).

SHORT FICTION: *Cinque storie ferraresi*, 1956 (*A Prospect of Ferrara*, 1962; best known as *Five Stories of Ferrara*); *L'odore del fieno*, 1972 (*The Smell of Hay*, 1975); *Il romanzo di Ferrara*, 1974, revised 1980.

SCREENPLAY: *The Stranger's Hands*, 1954 (with Guy Elmes and Graham Greene).

POETRY: *Storie dei poveri amante e altri versi*, 1946; *L'alba ai vetri: Poesie 1942-1950*, 1963; *In gran segreto*, 1978.

NONFICTION: *Le parole preparate e altri scritti di letteratura*, 1966; *Aldila dal cuore*, 1984.

Although Giorgio Bassani has been writing in Italy since the mid-1940's, his international reputation became established only after the publication in 1962 of the novel *The Garden of the Finzi-Continis*. The subsequent filming of the novel (directed by Vittorio di Sica) also enhanced his standing as an important novelist. Bassani was born in Bologna on April 4, 1916, but reared in Ferrara, a prosperous mercantile city about thirty miles northeast of Bologna. Bassani has focused his fiction on the city of Ferrara, specifically on its large population of Jews; he has chronicled their fate during the Fascist rule of Italy, from 1920 to 1944. Bassani's family was a prosperous middle-class Ferrarese Jewish family, and Bassani himself knows well the milieu of the Finzi-Continis, so keenly described in his novel. Educated at the University of Bologna, he studied journalism and wrote reviews and poetry in the 1930's. In 1943 he was married to Valeria Sinigallia and left the city. Up to this point his only publication had been a novel, *Una città di pianura* (a city on the plains), in 1940, published under the one-time pen name of Giacomo Marchi.

After the war Bassani took occasional work as a screenwriter and a film dubbing editor, as well as an editor for the avant-garde review *Botteghe Oscure* in Rome, from 1948 to 1960. He was also coeditor of another review, *Paragone*, from 1953 to 1955. It was in the 1950's that Bassani began issuing the short novels later collected in the 1956 book *Five Stories of Ferrara*. These tales fondly describe the citizens of Ferrara, the environs, and the sufferings of the Ferrarese, particularly the Jews of the city, under Fascism. These early stories range from the bittersweet ("Lida Mantovani") to the bitter ("A Plaque on Via Mazzini"). In all of them, however, the fate of their characters is bound with the fate of the city during the 1930's and 1940's.

With the publication of this volume, Bassani began to find substantial work as an editor with Feltrinelli, the Milan publisher, and as an instructor in the history of theater at the National Academy of Dramatic Arts in Rome. His novel *The Gold-Rimmed Eyeglasses* of 1958 placed him in the ranks of new major writers. Then in 1962 *The Garden of the Finzi-Continis* appeared, which was to become Bassani's most widely read novel.

With *Behind the Door*, Bassani continued his nostalgic look at the past in fiction. His nonwriting career rose when he assumed the post of vice president at the Italian National Radio. Since this time, however, Bassani has published only one major novel, *The Heron*, in 1968. Since then he has issued collections of stories, including *The Smell of Hay*.

Bassani appeared on the Italian literary scene as a writer quite apart from other postwar authors. Instead of producing novels about the partisans or postwar misery, Bassani chose to portray the situation of Jews under Fascism. His characters are not the stock characters of traditional Italian fiction, the peasantry or the struggling lower-class urbanites. Bassani's characters are average middle-class Ferrarese who are caught up in the whirlwind of history. Both his style and his milieu are similar in many ways to those of Henry James, whom Bassani admires. His approach is cool and descriptive, and the buildings and streets of Ferrara are prominent in his stories.

Since Bassani's output is so small, he has almost obsessively revised and reissued many of his books. He is a refined stylist, and his accurate portrayals of social classes, such as the wealthy Finzi-Contini family, mark him as a close observer of society. His focus on Jews in Ferrara is a unique view of Italian society, and his sophisticated portrayal of life under the Fascist tyranny in the 1930's and 1940's makes him a valuable observer of this nightmare period in Italy's modern history.

BIBLIOGRAPHICAL REFERENCES: H. Stuart Hughes, *Prisoners of Hope: The Silver Age of the Italian Jews 1924-1974*, 1983, covers the background and literature of Bassani's milieu. Marilyn Schneider, *Vengeance at the Victim: History and Symbol in Giorgio Bassani's Fiction*, 1986, addresses the author's canon thematically. See also "Bassani's *Il giardino dei Finzi-Contini*," in *European Patterns: Contemporary Patterns in European Writers*, 1964, edited by T. B. Harward, and "Warped Innocence," by Richard Ellmann, in *The New York Review of Books*, November 15, 1973, 23.

Philip Brantingham

H. E. BATES

Born: Rushden, Northamptonshire, England *Died:* Canterbury, England
Date: May 16, 1905 *Date:* January 29, 1974

PRINCIPAL WORKS

SHORT FICTION: *Day's End and Other Stories*, 1928; *Seven Tales and Alexander*, 1929; *The Black Boxer*, 1932; *The Woman Who Had Imagination and Other Stories*, 1934; *Cut and Come Again*, 1935; *Something Short and Sweet*, 1937; *My Uncle Silas*, 1939; *The Beauty of the Dead and Other Stories*, 1940; *The Greatest People in the World and Other Stories*, 1942; *How Sleep the Brave and Other Stories*, 1943; *The Bride Comes to Evensford and Other Tales*, 1943; *Colonel Julian and Other Stories*, 1951; *The Daffodil Sky*, 1955; *The Watercress Girl and Other Stories*, 1959; *Now Sleeps the Crimson Petal and Other Stories*, 1961; *The Wedding Party*, 1965; *The Wild Cherry Tree*, 1968.

NOVELS AND NOVELLAS: *The Two Sisters*, 1926; *Catherine Foster*, 1929; *Charlotte's Row*, 1931; *The Fallow Land*, 1932; *The Poacher*, 1935; *A House of Women*, 1936; *Spella Ho*, 1938; *Fair Stood the Wind for France*, 1944; *The Purple Plain*, 1947; *Dear Life*, 1949; *Love for Lydia*, 1952; *The Nature of Love: Three Short Novels*, 1953; *Death of a Huntsman: Four Short Novels*, 1957; *The Darling Buds of May*, 1958; *The Golden Oriole: Five Novellas*, 1962; *The Four Beauties*, 1968; *The Triple Echo*, 1970.

AUTOBIOGRAPHY: *The Vanished World: An Autobiography*, 1969; *The Blossoming World: An Autobiography*, 1971; *The World in Ripeness: An Autobiography*, 1972.

LITERARY CRITICISM: *The Modern Short Story: A Critical Survey*, 1941.

Herbert Ernest Bates was one of the most prolific British writers of the twentieth century; although he published literally dozens of novels and novellas, his reputation rests primarily on his first love: the short story.

Bates was born in the Midlands shoemaking center of Rushden, England, on May 16, 1905. Both his grandfathers had been shoemakers, and his father—a stern Methodist—owned his own shoemaking business. Yet young Bates hardly looked upon the trade with fondness, and he managed to escape the factories through education. He proved a good student, but not quite good enough to win a coveted scholarship to the public school at Wellingborough. Bates was so discouraged by this early failure that he eventually forfeited an opportunity to attend the University of Cambridge and instead began a series of odd jobs.

Bates stole time from one of these jobs—his job as a warehouseman—to write stories and poems. These early works were rejected by journal after journal until, in 1926, he finally had a novel published by Jonathan Cape. The book, *The Two Sisters*, received warm reviews but did not make him wealthy. In 1931, Bates was married to Marjorie Helen Cox and purchased a converted granary in Kent, where he lived with his wife and children until his death in 1974. To support himself and his family, he wrote more than one volume of fiction per year—in addition to reviews, essays, monographs on country life, and a column for *The Spectator*.

This massive output did not always bring critical or commercial success; indeed, for Bates the two seem almost mutually exclusive. His finest work in both the short-story and the novel form, with only a few exceptions, was written in the 1930's. Fame did not come, however, until the 1940's, when, under the pseudonym "Flying Officer X," Bates wrote two collections of stories about the military air force. (The collections were commissioned by the British Air Ministry.) Over the next decade, Bates wrote a series of commercially successful novels set in World War II—the first, *Fair Stood the Wind for France*, being the most famous and probably the best. These same novels were mostly panned by critics, who, ironically, tended to ignore much finer efforts written in the same period (such as *Dear Life*, which may well be Bates's most undervalued novel).

Bates was so embittered by the critics' attacks that more than once he threatened to stop writing novels. He did not; in fact, for the last two decades of his life his production continued unabated, and he even found two new avenues for his talents: film scripts and novellas. Bates's last major published work, the novella *The Triple Echo*, is arguably his finest piece of fiction.

Bates is best known for his mastery of the now-familiar modernist short-story devices: indirection, psychological penetration of character, and an unadorned style. Not only do his finest stories demonstrate these characteristics, but so too do such apparently atypical efforts as the often-comical Uncle Silas tales. His novels are hardly daring technically but rely instead on a rich evocation of time and place—most frequently the Midlands of the early twentieth century—and a colorful cast of characters.

Regardless of the genre, setting, or characters involved, certain themes appear repeatedly in Bates's fiction. In general, the theme is freedom versus constraint. Constraint comes in many forms, physical and spiritual: poverty, religious fanaticism, class consciousness, government bureaucracy, and soulless urban sprawl. Freedom means individuality, sexual liberation, and, always, nature.

Bates's reputation suffered after World War II. Out of economic necessity he wrote continually; from the aesthetic viewpoint, however, he wrote too much. He repeated his themes, settings, and character types until they lost their effectiveness—especially in the novel. Moreover, even in his strongest genre, the short story, it can hardly be argued that Bates grew much after his achievements in the 1930's. Still, those achievements are distinctive enough to earn for Bates a place as a major figure in modern British literature.

BIBLIOGRAPHICAL REFERENCES: *H. E. Bates*, 1983, by Dennis Vannatta, is the first book-length study of Bates's career; Vannatta provides a chronological analysis of Bates's short stories, novels, and novellas, plus a brief summary of Bates's life. In Dean R. Baldwin's critical biography *H. E. Bates: A Literary Life*, 1987, the discussion of Bates's life is far more detailed than in Vannatta's work (although the analysis of the fiction is much briefer). See also T. O. Beachcroft's *The Modest Art: A Survey of the Short Story in English*, 1968, for a discussion of Bates's use of regional materials; William Frierson's *The English Novel in Transition: 1885-1940*, 1965, for a brief discussion of Bates's literary influences; and Henry Miller's preface to *The Best of H. E. Bates*, 1963, for comment on Bates's use of nature and his treatment of women in the short stories. See also Robert Alter, "New Fiction," *New York Herald Tribune*, September 29, 1963, 18; Basil Davenport, "Epics in Miniature," *The Times Literary Supplement*, September 13, 1963, 688; Graham Greene, "Short Stories," *The Spectator*, March 16, 1934, 424; Raymond Mortimer, "Reviews: New Novels," *Nation and Athe neum*, XLIII (June 9, 1928), 332; and Colin Murry, "Without His Tutor," *Time and Tide*, May 19, 1962, 34.

Dennis Vannatta

ANN BEATTIE

Born: Washington, D.C.
Date: September 8, 1947

Principal Works

SHORT FICTION: *Distortions*, 1976; *Secrets and Surprises*, 1978; *Jacklighting*, 1981; *The Burning House*, 1982; *Where You'll Find Me*, 1986.
NOVELS: *Chilly Scenes of Winter*, 1976; *Falling in Place*, 1980; *Love Always*, 1985.
ART CRITICISM: *Alex Katz*, 1987.

Ann Beattie is perhaps the most imitated short-story writer in America and one of the writers most identified with the minimalist school of fiction. She was born to mainstream middle-class parents; her father was a Health, Education, and Welfare Department administrator, and she was reared in the nation's capital. In 1969, she earned a B.A. in English from American University and an M.A. from the University of Connecticut in 1970. She began work toward a doctorate at Connecticut but left without completing the program. She was married to and later divorced from David Gates, a musician who was once a member of the rock group Bread and afterward became a writer for *Newsweek*. Beattie taught at Harvard University and the University of Virginia. Generally regarded as literature's spokesperson for children of the 1960's, she acknowledges the role that television, rock music, and the drugs often associated with the counterculture play in her work and in the lives of her characters. She resents, however, the tendency to ignore other aspects of her work because of the critical fascination with what critic Joseph Epstein has labeled the "hippoisie."

Beattie began writing fiction while she was a student at the University of Connecticut, partly, she says, out of her boredom with graduate school. While she was still a student, her stories began to appear in small magazines such as the *Western Humanities Review* and the *Texas Quarterly.* After almost two dozen submissions, she had her first story accepted by *The New Yorker*: "A Platonic Relationship," which appeared in the April 8, 1974, issue. Since that time, she has been a regular contributor to the magazine, and most of the stories in her four collections have first appeared in its pages. Her debut in book form was almost unprecedented in modern publishing. Her first collection of stories, *Distortions*, and her first novel, *Chilly Scenes of Winter*, appeared simultaneously in 1976. Most critics, at that time and since, have preferred Beattie's stories to her novels. Although the characters and situations in *Distortions* and *Chilly Scenes of Winter* are more extreme, perhaps, than those in subsequent collections, they are typical of the themes and style associated with Beattie.

These characters are, in most cases, educated, Waspish, middle-class or upper-middle-class men, women, and children who find themselves disappointed and disillusioned despite their having achieved much of what is commonly believed to define the American Dream. They tend to be unhappy in love, in family life, and in their work, or, if not unhappy, they are merely coping, getting by, without any feeling of real satisfaction. Friendship is important to the characters and is the refuge they most often seek from the daily lives and family situations that create their conflicts. Charles, the protagonist of *Chilly Scenes of Winter*, says at one point that he knows too much to be happy, a coda of sorts for a feeling that permeates all Beattie's work: The well-educated, self-conscious generation that serve as her main characters find bliss, or the happiness of the Norman Rockwell image of family, impossible in view of their overwhelming knowledge. Thus, their struggle becomes one of balancing self-conscious knowledge of self and world with the desire for innocence and joy. In *Secrets and Surprises*, Beattie's second collection of stories, the characters tend to be a little older, and their struggles seem more mundane in some ways. *Distortions* features a dwarf who lives in a dwarf house and an extraterrestrial visitation, along with the usual relationships gone wrong and malcontents. In *Secrets and Surprises*, the characters and their lives are less overtly distorted, but the impulses and conflicts are essentially the same.

Falling in Place, Beattie's second novel, is a novel of manners, but the manners it takes as its subject are entirely contemporary. *Falling in Place* is also Beattie's most ambitious work. Its cast of characters is larger than that of the first novel, and it contains a subplot in the true, old-fashioned sense of the term. In many ways, this novel is also Beattie's most traditional work. It tells the story of two central relationships: the main plot, which deals with John Knapp's story (his love for his mistress, Nina, and the turmoil within his suburban Connecticut family), and the subplot, which chronicles the relationship of Cynthia Forrest and her lover, Peter Spangle. The events unfold during the summer of 1978, when Skylab is falling, Peter Frampton is the hot teen idol of the moment, and radio is saturated with the sounds of pop singer Blondie's hit "Heart of Glass." For the characters in this novel, the world and their lives are as fragile as the robin's egg John brings to Nina as a gift. Parents and children cannot get along; lovers cannot get along; friends cannot rescue friends from the turmoil of family and love. There are characters as distorted as any in the earlier work running around in the background of this essentially realistic world, and the solutions to the problems presented seem almost impossible to find. The story concludes, however, with a strong affirmation of love as the answer to the sense of purposelessness and ennui that has defined the world as Beattie sees it.

The Burning House and *Love Always* are more like the books that precede *Falling in Place* than they are like that novel. The characters do not solve their problems or even make the same enormous effort that the characters in *Falling in Place* make. The main character of *Love Always*, Lucy, has achieved a measure of fame since her niece Nicole, a soap-opera actress, has come to live with her aunt; it is possible that the feelings about public recognition and expectations explored in the novel are a reflection of Beattie's own feelings about her role as the writer of record for her generation. The tone in *Love Always* is more ironic and more despondent than in *Falling in Place*. *Where You'll Find Me*, like *The Burning House*, features characters who are somewhat older than those in the earlier work, and they seem more intent upon deriving meaning out of life, however bleak the possibilities for meaning may be. They want to create meaning before their chance to do so is past. They have the same awareness of life's ironies, its potential for disaster, disappointment, and stagnation as the earlier characters, but they are less concerned with noting those pitfalls than with finding ways to move beyond or around them. "Snow," a story in *Where You'll Find Me*, contains a sentence that could serve as a definition for minimalism: "Any life will seem dramatic if you omit mention of most of it." A character in another story, "Summer People," longs for a life like that in eighteenth century novels with omniscient narrators who are in control and can make readers aware of anything and everything.

Beattie is not an eighteenth century narrator with a deceptively comforting control over the world that her characters inhabit. The narrative presence in the stories in this collection and throughout her work operates on the same thin edge as the characters do, never quite willing or able to say that this is it, the truth, life, as it is and will be. Yet that presence also refuses to deny completely the possibility of moving forward with as much dignity and grace, as much quiet joy, as possible. So Beattie and her characters do not merely omit mention of detail to provide drama; they carefully select details to probe and examine for suggestions as to how they should proceed to accomplish their limited goals. Beattie's place in American letters will be assured by her careful crafting of the story form, by her important influence on the minimalist movement, and by her ability to capture time and place so vividly and astutely.

BIBLIOGRAPHICAL REFERENCES: Joseph Epstein, "Ann Beattie and the Hippoisie," *Commentary*, March, 1983, 54-58, is representative of the view of Beattie as the voice of her generation and its counterculture attitudes. See also George Garrett, "Fables and Fabliaux of Our Time," *Sewanee Review*, LV (1977), 104-110; Jane Hill, "Ann Beattie's Children as Redeemers,"

Critique: Studies in Modern Fiction, XXVII (Summer, 1986), 197-212, an essay that argues that Beattie's use of child figures in her stories and novels is evidence that her vision is not as bleak, hopeless, and untraditional as is often thought; D. Keith Mano, "Barium Enema," *National Review*, December 24, 1976, 1419-1421, an analysis typical of those who find Beattie's work too insubstantial to be satisfying as literature. There is a useful interview with Beattie in *Alive and Writing: Interviews with American Authors of the 1980s*, edited by Larry McCaffrey and Sinda Gregory, 1987.

Jane Hill

SIMONE DE BEAUVOIR

Born: Paris, France
Date: January 9, 1908

Died: Paris, France
Date: April 14, 1986

PRINCIPAL WORKS

NOVELS: *L'Invitée*, 1943 (*She Came to Stay*, 1949); *Le Sang des autres*, 1945 (*The Blood of Others*, 1948); *Tous les hommes sont mortels*, 1946 (*All Men Are Mortal*, 1955); *Les Mandarins*, 1954 (*The Mandarins*, 1956); *Les Belles Images*, 1966 (English translation, 1968).

MEMOIRS: *Mémoires d'une jeune fille rangée*, 1958 (*Memoirs of a Dutiful Daughter*, 1959); *La Force de l'âge*, 1960 (*The Prime of Life*, 1962); *La Force des choses*, 1963 (*Force of Circumstance*, 1964); *Tout compte fait*, 1972 (*All Said and Done*, 1974).

TRAVEL SKETCHES: *L'Amérique au jour le jour*, 1948 (*America Day by Day*, 1953); *La Longue Marche*, 1957 (*The Long March*, 1958).

OTHER NONFICTION: *Pour une morale de l'ambiguïté*, 1947 (*The Ethics of Ambiguity*, 1948); *Le Deuxième Sexe*, 1949 (*The Second Sex*, 1953); *Une Mort très douce*, 1964 (*A Very Easy Death*, 1966); *La Vieillesse*, 1970 (*The Coming of Age*, 1972); *La Cérémonie des adieux*, 1981 (*Adieux: A Farewell to Sartre*, 1984).

SHORT FICTION: *La Femme rompue*, 1967 (*The Woman Destroyed*, 1968); *Quand prime le spirituel*, 1979 (*When Things of the Spirit Come First: Five Early Tales*, 1982).

PLAY: *Les Bouches inutiles*, pb. 1945.

Simone de Beauvoir, one of the most provocative and controversial women of this century, was born in Paris on January 9, 1908. Her father, a lawyer and amateur actor, was extremely skeptical toward religion. De Beauvoir's mother, who submitted to her husband in most matters but proved to be dictatorial in her relationships with her two daughters, was zealously religious and insisted that her children receive a strict Catholic upbringing.

The most striking characteristic of de Beauvoir's life and work is a quest for freedom. Her childhood and adolescence, as seen in the memoirs, constantly reflect her attempts to break out of the narrow social constraints of her middle-class environment. Following a rather restrictive parochial education, de Beauvoir completed her *baccalauréat* in mathematics and philosophy and then continued her studies at the Institut Sainte-Marie, the Institut Catholique, and the Sorbonne. Although her decision to become a teacher caused considerable friction in her family, de Beauvoir began her postgraduate studies at the École Normale Supérieure and the Sorbonne. In 1929 she met Jean-Paul Sartre, with whom she formed a fruitful relationship which would span the next fifty-one years, ending only at Sartre's death in 1980. She passed her *agrégation* in philosophy in 1929, ranking second only to Sartre (who was taking the test for the second time). At age twenty-one, she was the youngest ever to pass this examination in France.

Although de Beauvoir's first completed work was repeatedly rejected by publishers, her novel *She Came to Stay* was an immediate success when it appeared in 1943. She made an unsuccessful attempt to write for the theater with *Les Bouches inutiles* (useless mouths), then returned to fiction, producing *The Blood of Others* in 1945, followed in 1946 by the much less popular *All Men Are Mortal*. Her next major work, one which catapulted her into both fame and notoriety was *The Second Sex*, which appeared in 1949. Although she did not declare her solidarity with the feminist movement until 1972, *The Second Sex* firmly established de Beauvoir as a model and inspiration for women in all parts of the world. *The Mandarins*, which proved de Beauvoir's most successful novel, was published in 1954. Building on the theoretical foundation provided by *The Second Sex*, she began writing her memoirs in an attempt to give literary expression to her experience as a woman in an often-unsympathetic world. The first volume, *Memoirs of a Dutiful Daughter*, came out in 1958, followed by *The Prime of Life* in 1960, *Force of Circumstance* in 1963, and *All Said and Done* in 1972. De Beauvoir's last major social critique, *The Coming of Age*, a study of old age which in many ways parallels the structure of *The Second Sex*, was published in 1970.

Underlying all de Beauvoir's works is the powerful concept of existential freedom and personal choice, a principle illustrated with particular force in the first two volumes of the memoirs, as de Beauvoir struggles to find herself as an individual and establish her own life. Similarly, Jean Blomart in *The Blood of Others* agonizes over his political involvement and the effect it has on those around him. The existential undertones of the works penetrate the highly complex personalities of the characters themselves, as for example Chantal's self-deception and bad faith in *When Things of the Spirit Come First*. This same inauthenticity extends to the characters in *Les Belles Images* who refuse to see the misery in the world which surrounds them.

A second major theme in de Beauvoir's work is the question of women, women's place in the world, and the complex of relationships between women and men. De Beauvoir's memoirs were written specifically to illustrate her experience as a woman, while *The Second Sex* was one of the first attempts by a woman to evaluate the female situation systematically and critically. In addition, de Beauvoir's fiction illustrates well both the fulfillment which can be gained in a relationship and the oppression and deception which can result from inauthentic relationships.

The third theme inherent in de Beauvoir's writing concerns intellectuals and their place in society and politics. The memoirs illustrate de Beauvoir's own development from a passive and isolated individual to one who is socially and politically engaged. Particularly after World World II she boldly and openly wrote against injustice, whether it be the oppression of women, the mistreatment of the aged, or the torture of Algerian nationals during their struggle for independence from France. In addition, an awareness of social conditions and an implicit challenge to personal *engagement* speak from the pages of her fictional works, both in the debate of actual political and moral questions in works such as *The Mandarins* and *The Blood of Others* and in the denouncement of social deceit in *Les Belles Images*. The extended description of nations and cultures in de Beauvoir's memoirs and travel sketches also do much to illustrate the social problems of the world, from racism and intellectual defeatism in the United States to poverty and disease in South America.

Simone de Beauvoir's position in the literary and intellectual world of the twentieth century is above all that of a woman who speaks not only for women but also others who have been deprived of their dignity. Both de Beauvoir's life and her authorship remain a provocation to her readers, as she battles illusion and self-deception and challenges each individual to be honest, to live authentically, and to join her in an ongoing struggle in the cause of humankind.

BIBLIOGRAPHICAL REFERENCES: Claude Francis and Fernande Gontier, *Simone de Beauvoir: A Life . . . A Love Story*, 1987, presents an intimate biography based on personal interviews and private correspondence; it is not always in congruence with the memoirs. For further study, see Konrad Bieber, *Simone de Beauvoir*, 1979, which offers a general biography and introduction to the author's writings, and Robert D. Cottrell, *Simone de Beauvoir*, 1975, in which the works are evaluated in the context of a biography. Also valuable are Terry Keefe, *Simone de Beauvoir: A Study of her Writings*, 1983; Axel Madsen, *The Common Journey of Simone de Beauvoir and Jean-Paul Sartre*, 1977; and Carol Ascher, *Simone de Beauvoir: A Life of Freedom*, 1981. See also Alice Schwarzer, *Simone de Beauvoir Today: Conversations, 1972-1982*, 1984; Alice Jardine, "Interviews with Simone de Beauvoir," *Signs*, V, no. 2 (1979), 224-236; Margaret A. Simons and Jessica Benjamin, "Simone de Beauvoir: An Interview," *Feminist Studies*, V, no. 2 (1979), 330-345; and John Gerassi, "Simone de Beauvoir: *The Second Sex* Twenty-five Years Later," *Society*, XIII (January/February, 1976), 79-85.

Michelle Stott

JUREK BECKER

Born: Lodz, Poland
Date: September 30, 1937

Principal Works

NOVELS: *Jakob der Lügner*, 1969 (*Jacob the Liar*, 1975); *Irreführung der Behörden*, 1973; *Der Boxer*, 1976; *Schlaflose Tage*, 1978 (*Sleepless Days*, 1979); *Aller Welt Freund*, 1982; *Bronsteins Kinder*, 1986 (*Bronstein's Children*, 1988).

SHORT FICTION: *Nach der ersten Zukunft*, 1980.

Although Jurek Becker no longer lives in East Germany (GDR), he belongs to the generation of writers who grew up in the early decades of that nation and who became increasingly critical of its system. Becker was born in Lodz, Poland, on September 30, 1937. After the Germans occupied Poland in 1939, Becker and his family were imprisoned in the Lodz ghetto. Later, Becker was transported to the concentration camps of Ravensbrück and Sachsenhausen. Only three members of his large extended family survived the ghetto and the camps. In addition to Becker and his father, one aunt managed to escape when the Germans advanced into Poland. Becker writes that he has few memories of these years, in part, he presumes, because he wants to repress them, but also because life in a camp, especially for a child who did not fully understand what was happening, was a gray and desolate period. It was a time of existing, not living, and most actions were determined by the struggle to survive.

In the summer of 1945, after his liberation from the camp, Becker was reunited with his father in the Soviet zone of Berlin, where the family had settled. Until that time, Becker had spoken Yiddish and Polish. At the age of eight, he was confronted with having to learn German. Becker attended schools in East Berlin and passed his *Abitur* (qualifying examination for university) in 1955. He served two years in the GDR army and then studied philosophy at Humboldt University in East Berlin between 1957 and 1960. After 1960, Becker devoted himself to his writing and began making a name for himself as a writer of cabaret texts and film and television scripts.

Becker's first novel, *Jacob the Liar*, was widely acclaimed and quickly translated into other languages. The work was originally written as a film script. When plans for the film failed, Becker reworked it into a novel. Becker received two prestigious prizes for the novel, the Heinrich Mann Prize of East Germany and the Charles Veillon Prize of Switzerland. (*Jacob the Liar* was eventually made into a film in East Germany.) For his second novel, *Irreführung der Behörden* (misguiding the authorities), he was awarded the literary prize of the German state of Bremen. Like his first two novels, Becker's third novel, *Der Boxer* (the boxer), was also published in both East and West Germany.

In 1976, Becker came into conflict with the government of the GDR. He was one of the original twelve prominent East German writers who signed a petition protesting the expulsion of the East German poet Wolf Biermann from the GDR. Becker resigned from the Writers' Union and was expelled from the Socialist Unity Party (the Communist Party of East Germany) on November 26, 1976, because of his refusal to withdraw his support for the petition. When Becker was invited to teach for a year at Oberlin College in the United States, he applied for an exit visa. In 1977, he was granted a passport, valid for an extended period of time. After his stay in the United States, Becker settled in West Berlin, where he continues to be a productive writer. His next works, the novel *Sleepless Days*, the story collection *Nach der ersten Zukunft* (after the first future), and the novels *Aller Welt Freund* (friend of all the world) and *Bronstein's Children*, were all published in West Germany.

Social concerns are an important aspect of Becker's writing. Although he has distanced himself from his Jewish heritage, he deals with the Holocaust in three of his novels. In *Jacob the Liar*, Becker re-creates the daily life of those imprisoned in the Lodz ghetto. He shows their courage and hope, strengthened by Jacob's lies about the approaching rescuers, as well as their terror and despair. In *Der Boxer* and *Bronstein's Children*, Becker turns to the problems faced by Jewish survivors of the camps and their children. In other works, Becker gives a critical picture of life in East Germany. In *Irreführung der Behörden* he attacks Socialist Realism, the aesthetic doctrine of the GDR, and in *Sleepless Days* he shows how a teacher prefers to become a worker rather than conform to the Party's demands. In *Aller Welt Freund*, Becker addresses such problems as world hunger, pollution, and the threat of war.

Jurek Becker has established himself as an important German-language writer, and his works have been generally positively received. He writes in a clear and concise style that often includes humor, and he portrays his characters vividly. Becker is a socially committed writer. By making readers aware of urgent social problems, he hopes that literature can contribute to progressive social change.

BIBLIOGRAPHICAL REFERENCES: A good introduction to Becker's life and early works is the section on Becker in Peter Demetz, *After the Fires: Recent Writing in the Germanies, Austria, and Switzerland*, 1986. For further study, see Heinz Wetzel et al., "Moral Issues in Jurek Becker's *Jakob der Lügner*: Contributions to a Symposium," *Seminar*, XIX, no. 4 (1983), 265-292, which provides an excellent discussion of the novel and is valuable for Becker's own views. See also Philip Manger, "Jurek Becker: *Irreführung der Behörden*," *Seminar*, XVII, no. 2 (1981), 147-163, an insightful analysis of the work as a courageous political novel, and Helen L. Cafferty, "Survival Under Fascism: Deception in Apitz's *Nackt unter Wölfen*, Becker's *Jakob der Lügner*, and Kohlhaase's 'Erfindung einer Sprache,'" *Philological Papers*, XXX (1984), 90-96, which discusses the function of Jacob's lies.

Jennifer E. Michaels

SAMUEL BECKETT

Born: Foxrock, Ireland
Date: April 13, 1906

Principal Works

PLAYS: *En attendant Godot*, pb. 1952 (*Waiting for Godot*, 1954); *Fin de partie: Suivi de Acte sans paroles*, pr., pb. 1957 (*Endgame: A Play in One Act; followed by Act Without Words: A Mime for One Player*, 1958); *All That Fall*, pr., pb. 1957, revised pr. 1968 (radio play); *Krapp's Last Tape*, pr., pb. 1958; *Embers*, pr., pb. 1959 (radio play); *Act Without Words II*, pr., pb. 1960 (one-act mime); *Happy Days*, pr., pb. 1961; *Words and Music*, 1962 (radio play); *Cascando*, 1963 (radio play); *Play*, pr., pb. 1963 (English translation, 1964); *Come and Go: Dramaticule*, pr., pb. 1965 (English translation, 1967); *Film*, pr. 1965 (screenplay); *Eh Joe*, 1966 (teleplay; *Dis Joe*, 1967); *Not I*, 1972 (teleplay); *Tryst*, 1976 (teleplay); *That Time*, pr., pb. 1976; *Footfalls*, pr., pb. 1976; *Shades*, 1977 (teleplay); *A Piece of Monologue*, pr. 1979; *Quad*, 1981 (teleplay); *Rockaby*, pr., pb. 1981; *Ohio Impromptu*, pr. 1981; *Catastrophe*, pr. 1982; *Company*, pr. 1983.

NOVELS: *Murphy*, 1938; *Molloy*, 1951 (English translation, 1955); *Malone meurt*, 1951 (*Malone Dies*, 1956); *L'Innommable*, 1953 (*The Unnamable*, 1958); *Watt*, 1953; *Comment c'est*, 1961 (*How It Is*, 1964); *Mercier et Camier*, 1970 (*Mercier and Camier*, 1974); *Le Dépeupleur*, 1971 (*The Lost Ones*, 1972); *Company*, 1980; *Mal vu mal dit*, 1981 (*Ill Seen Ill Said*, 1981); *Worstward Ho*, 1983.

SHORT FICTION: *More Pricks than Kicks*, 1934; *Nouvelles et textes pour rien*, 1955 (*Stories and Texts for Nothing*, 1967); *No's Knife: Collected Shorter Prose, 1947-1966*, 1967; *First Love and Other Shorts*, 1974; *Pour finir encore et autres foirades*, 1976 (*Fizzles*, 1976).

POETRY: *Whoroscope*, 1930; *Echo's Bones and Other Precipitates*, 1935; *Poems in English*, 1961; *Collected Poems in English and French*, 1977.

NONFICTION: *Proust*, 1931.

TRANSLATION: *An Anthology of Mexican Poetry*, 1958.

Samuel Beckett was the younger of two sons who were very close as children. The parents were loving and dutiful but demanding. Early in life, Beckett learned to restrain his emotion and to emulate the machismo of his father. Both boys, in fact, pleased their father by developing athletic interests. The family belonged to the Church of Ireland, but organized religion meant little to the future writer as a boy or later. He was sent to private schools in Dublin and, at age thirteen, to Portora Royal School, a Protestant boarding school in Enniskillen, Northern Ireland.

In 1923, Beckett entered Trinity College, Dublin, where he first exhibited his remarkable linguistic ability, achieving honors in Italian, French, and English. Upon his graduation in 1927, he taught French briefly in Campbell College, Belfast, and in 1928 accepted a fellowship at École Normale Supérieure in Paris. His literary interests brought him into the circle of the renowned Irish expatriate James Joyce, and he assisted the nearly blind writer in the preparation of the work that became *Finnegans Wake* (1939). While proud of his friendship with Joyce, he chafed at critics' tendencies to regard him as an imitator of Joyce in his lifestyle and writings, the earliest of which, chiefly poetry and criticism, date from his two years in Paris.

Although Beckett returned to Dublin to teach French at Trinity in 1930, he did not prosper there, and for the next decade he led an irregular and peripatetic existence in Ireland, England, France, and Germany, much to the dismay of his middle-class family. Slow to mature in many respects, he could neither break with his family nor accede to their pleas that he become settled, preferably in his father's business. While committed to a literary life, Beckett had considerable difficulty getting work accomplished and even more difficulty getting it accepted. He published a collection of stories, *More Pricks than Kicks*, in 1934, and a novel, *Murphy*, in 1938, but neither sold more than a few copies.

Having established Paris as his permanent residence, Beckett joined the French Resistance in 1940, barely escaping detection by the conquering Nazis and eventually fleeing to Free France with Suzanne Deschevaux-Dumesnil, to whom he was later married. Awarded a medal by the Free French government, Beckett, never much interested in politics, worked on another novel during the latter part of the war. While *Watt* was not published until 1953, it demonstrates his first mature use of the passive, uncomprehending, afflicted character so frequent in his later work, as well as his penchant for logical, linguistical, and mathematical problems and conundrums.

Back in Paris after the war, Beckett began to write in French. A trilogy of novels—*Molloy*, *Malone Dies*, and *The Unnamable*—as well as his first play, *Waiting for Godot*, resulted. Although Beckett at this point considered himself primarily a novelist, the eventual success of *Waiting for Godot* prompted him to turn increasingly to the drama and to take on increasing responsibility for the production of his plays. In *Waiting for Godot*, whose New York production in 1956 made him famous in the United States, two tramps talk paradoxically while waiting for the mysterious Godot, who never appears. Beckett called the play a tragicomedy, but critics, noting its deliberate avoidance of a realistic setting, rationality, and a sequential plot, as well as its air of anguish and impotence, began to refer to the work as an example of "the theater of the absurd." Beckett was considered the quintessential member of this absurdist movement, which also included Jean Genet, Harold Pinter, and Eugène Ionesco.

Despite the bleakness of Beckett's vision, this play and the ones that followed were rich in comic effects: slapstick humor, riddles, wordplay of various kinds. His characters do not merely look and sound humorous; they are comical in the manner of the circus clown, sad and frustrated but bravely persevering in the face of affliction. In *Endgame*, four characters, presumably the survivors of a world calamity, inhabit what appears to be a cellar room. Hamm is blind and unable to rise from his chair, Clov cannot sit down, and Nagg and Nell slowly expire in ash cans. The overriding metaphor is that of "endgame" in chess, when either the players are stalemated or one is checkmated. The deceptively simple dialogue is fertile with symbol and allusion, the play's ambiguity and irresolution suggesting modern civilization.

Although Beckett's long fiction climaxed with his trilogy, he has continued to write prose which bears resemblances to both fiction and poetry. He has also written radio plays, television plays, and a screenplay simply called *Film*. Filmed in Lower Manhattan with Buster Keaton in its principal role, *Film* achieved no commercial success but won for Beckett several international awards. After *Krapp's Last Tape* and *Happy Days*, his dramatic works grew slighter—as did his nondramatic prose, with the exception of *How It Is*. In this series of narrated fragments, the setting has become simply "mud"; the title is commonly thought to suggest "how it is" with modern human life.

Beckett's literary life has been a long one, but by his own admission he did not begin to do his best work until after World War II, when he was already middle-aged, and recognition was even longer in coming. He was fifty-three when Trinity College, which had granted him his bachelor's degree more than thirty years earlier, awarded him an honorary doctorate. In 1961, he shared the International Publishers' Prize with Jorge Luis Borges. Further international recognition came with the Nobel Prize in Literature in 1969. Since that time Beckett has continued to write but has largely eschewed the media, scholars, and the curious general public in favor of the company of old friends from the years before his fame. A shy, courteous, and modest man, Beckett has nevertheless proved to be intransigent and dictatorial in the staging of his plays.

In both his plays and his fiction, Beckett has favored the character of the down-and-outer: passive, physically (and sometimes mentally) debilitated, striving to make sense of a world without love or rationality. The reiterated line of *Happy Days*, "another happy day—so far," captures the poignant irony of his outlook as well as the humor which leavens his pessimism. The figures of Vladimir and Estragon waiting for Godot, of Malone and Hamm waiting for and enduring until death, have come to be seen as potent symbols of the human predicament in the later twentieth century. Once accustomed to his innovations, readers and audiences have responded enthusiastically to his stoic humor, the beautiful rhythms of his language, and his tough-minded refusal to accept conventional answers to profound questions.

BIBLIOGRAPHICAL REFERENCES: An exhaustive factual account of Beckett's life is Dierdre Bair, *Samuel Beckett: A Biography*, 1978. A bibliographic aid, *Samuel Beckett: His Works and His Critics*, 1970, edited by Raymond Federman and John Fletcher, covers Beckett's writings and the enormous body of Beckett criticism only through 1966. An outstanding introduction to Beckett is Hugh Kenner, *A Reader's Guide to Samuel Beckett*, 1973. Of short works summarizing Beckett's achievement, A. Alvarez, *Samuel Beckett*, 1973, is more trenchant than William York Tindall, *Samuel Beckett*, 1964. Hugh Kenner's *Samuel Beckett: A Critical Study*, 1961, which fruitfully compared Beckett to the sad-funny circus clown, remains one of the best books on his work. Others worth mentioning are Michael Robinson's sensitive study of Beckett's compassion for human beings trapped in an absurd world, *The Long Sonata of the Dead*, 1969; Ruby Cohn, *Samuel Beckett: The Comic Gamut*, 1962; Linda Ben-Zvi, Samuel Beckett, 1986; and a work which views Beckett in the tradition of introspective literature dating from Fyodor Dostoevski, Frederick J. Hoffman's *Samuel Beckett: The Language of Self*, 1962.

Many critics have concentrated on Beckett the dramatist. Eugene Webb, *The Plays of Samuel Beckett*, 1972, locates and synthesizes recurrent themes and images. Studies more interested in Beckett's plays as theatrical experiences include John Fletcher and John Spurling, *Beckett: A Study of His Plays*, 1972; Colin Duckworth, *Angels of Darkness: Dramatic Effect in Samuel Beckett with Special References to Eugène Ionesco*, 1972, which tabulates the results of an elaborate survey of audience reactions to *Waiting for Godot* and *Endgame*; and Ruby Cohn, *Just Play: Beckett's Theater*, 1980. Of works on Beckett the novelist, H. Porter Abbott, *The Fiction of Samuel Beckett: Form and Effect*, 1973, traces Beckett's development of and ultimate rejection of imitative form and notes a late transition to a kind of poetic form. Among later and more specialized accounts of Beckett's fiction are Eric Levy, *Beckett and the Voice of Species: A Study of the Prose Fiction*, 1980, and Rubin Rabinovitz, *The Development of Samuel Beckett's Fiction*, 1984. Students of Beckett's early development should consult, in addition to Bair's biography, Lawrence E. Harvey, *Samuel Beckett: Poet and Critic*, 1970, in which the focus is on the writer's poetry and criticism between 1929 and 1949. Samplings of the hundreds of articles on Beckett may be found in *Samuel Beckett: A Collection of Critical Essays*, 1965, edited by Martin Esslin; *Samuel Beckett: A Collection of Criticism*, 1975, edited by Ruby Cohn; *Critical Essays on Samuel Beckett*, 1986, edited by Patrick A. McCarthy; and *Beckett at 80/Beckett in Context*, 1986, edited by Enoch Brater.

Robert P. Ellis

BARRY BECKHAM

Born: Philadelphia, Pennsylvania
Date: March 19, 1944

PRINCIPAL WORKS

NOVELS: *My Main Mother*, 1969 (also known as *Blues in the Night*); *Runner Mack*, 1972.

BIOGRAPHY: *Double Dunk*, 1980.

EDITED TEXTS: *The Black Student's Guide to Colleges*, 1982, 1984, 1989; *The College Selection Workbook*, 1985, 1987.

Barry Earl Beckham is an innovative writer whose works capture the frustration of talented black Americans caught up in a world they cannot control. He was born in Philadelphia on March 19, 1944, the son of Clarence and Mildred Beckham. At age nine, he moved with his mother to Atlantic City, New Jersey. A successful and popular student, he was elected president of his senior class and entered Brown University in 1962, where he majored in English. In his senior year at Brown, under the direction of the novelist John Hawkes, Beckham began his first novel, *My Main Mother*, in which he draws upon his exposure to black jazz musicians in Atlantic City, his experiences with racist high school teachers, and his sense of isolation in a college class of 659 students, only eight of whom were black.

After graduation and a brief period at Columbia Law School, Beckham gained valuable experience in journalism and public relations at Chase Manhattan Bank and at Western Electric Company in New York City. *My Main Mother* received many positive reviews, and a producer quickly bought film rights. Yet the major motion picture promised on the cover of the paperback edition never materialized. Beckham returned to Brown University as a visiting lecturer in 1970 and was promoted to an assistant professorship in 1972, the same year that his second novel, *Runner Mack*, was nominated for the 1973 National Book Award.

Beckham continued to teach writing and accepted publishing contracts for a novel based on his experiences at Chase Manhattan Bank and for a biography of Earl "The Goat" Manigault, a living legend of the Harlem outdoor basketball courts. In the mid-1970's Beckham was jolted by a marital separation that ended in divorce, an event that shook his confidence and left him unable to write. Other blows followed. Without his permission, his first novel, republished in Great Britain under the new title *Blues in the Night*, came out with a lurid paperback cover; a series of ten book reviews commissioned by *The New York Times* was rejected without notice or explanation; several funding agencies rejected his grant proposals; and after he had worked for two years on the Manigault biography, his publisher rejected the whole project.

After a sabbatical from teaching and several years of depression, Beckham reaffirmed his dedication to writing in a 1978 convocation address at Brown, proclaiming the value of black writers' contributions and stressing the need for an examination of recent black culture and for writing that protrayed a "healthy, passionate relationship" between black men and women. In 1979 Beckham was promoted to associate professor and in 1980 was named director of the Graduate Writing Program at Brown, the same year that his revised biography of Earl Manigault was published under the title *Double Dunk*.

In 1982, Beckham and a group of students produced *The Black Student's Guide to Colleges*, which profiled 114 four-year colleges and evaluated their academic and social climate based on questionnaires distributed to five black students at each college. In 1984 a second edition profiling 158 colleges was produced by Beckham House Publishers, which Beckham established to produce guidance and college selection materials for black students and to promote works about the black experience. In 1987, Beckham took a leave of absence from Brown University to devote more time to his publishing business and a third edition of *The Black Student's Guide to Colleges*.

Beckham's two novels and his fictionalized biography of Earl Manigault portray talented young black men who can find no way to overcome the internal and external obstacles that prevent them from fulfilling their potential. Mitchell Mibbs, the brilliant narrator in *My Main Mother*, can only end the torment of his mother's indifference and betrayal by poisoning her. Henry Adams, the unbelievably talented baseball player in the allegorical satire *Runner Mack*, endures a macabre job interview with all the characteristics of slave auction, is taunted unmercifully by the white manager and players at his baseball tryout, and is then drafted to fight an insane Vietnam-style war set in Alaska. After joining a black revolution that fails because no one attends, he is hit and presumably killed by a Mack truck. Earl Manigault, the uneducated superstar of the outdoor basketball courts in the fictionalized biography *Double Dunk*, becomes addicted to drugs and loses his chance to escape the ghetto. In these refashionings of powerfully sad and comic experiences, Beckham does not propose any easy solutions but instead challenges readers to examine the world he has re-created.

Beckham's first novel, *My Main Mother*, which sold eighty thousand copies in paperback, received mixed reactions. Some reviewers found Mitchell Mibbs to be a very real character, while others saw him as flat and one-sided. Most, however, saw *My Main Mother* as a promise of better works to come. That promise was fulfilled in Beckham's next novel, the imaginative, surrealistic *Runner Mack*, which several reviewers have called one of the best novels by a young black writer in the 1960's and early 1970's. Out of print for several years, it was republished in 1984 by Howard University Press. Although the Earl Manigault biography has not received much critical attention, its second-person narrative style offers a unique reading experience.

BIBLIOGRAPHICAL REFERENCES: Joe Weixlmann, "Barry Beckham: A Bibliography," *College Language Association Journal*, XXV (1981), 552-528, provides a complete listing of newspaper and magazine reviews, as well as Beckham's contributions to books and periodicals and his printed remarks up to May, 1981. Barry Beckham, "Listen to the Black Graduate, You Might Learn Something," *Esquire*, LXXII (1969), 98, describes crucial college and employment experiences that shed light on his first two novels. Beckham's remarks on *My Main Mother* can be found in "First Novelists," *Library Journal*, XCIV (1969), 3473. For critical reviews of *My Main Mother*, see Peter Rowley, "The Rise and Fall of Mitchell Mibbs," *The New York Times Book Review*, November 30, 1969, 64-65; Lee A. Kearse, "American Mom," *Novel*, III (1970), 282-283; and Trudier Harris, "The Barbershop in Black Literature," *Black American Literature Forum*, XIII (1979), 112-118. Reviews and commentary on *Runner Mack* include a chapter in Phyllis Rauch Klotman, *Another Man Gone: The Black Runner in Contemporary Afro-American Literature*, 1977; Joe Weixlmann, "Out-of-Print No Longer: The Howard University Press Library of Contemporary Literature," *Black American Literature Forum*, XVIII (1984), 167-168; Joe Weixlmann, "The Dream Turned 'Daymare': Barry Beckham's *Runner Mack*," *MELUS*, VIII (1981), 93-103; Wiley Lee Umphlett, "The Black Man as Fictional Athlete: *Runner Mack*, the Sporting Myth, and the Failure of the American Dream," *Modern Fiction Studies*, XXXIII (1987), 73-83; Sanford Pinsker, "About *Runner Mack*: An Interview with Barry Beckham," *Black Images*, III (1974), 35-41.

Richard M. Shaw

BRENDAN BEHAN

Born: Dublin, Ireland
Date: February 9, 1923

Died: Dublin, Ireland
Date: March 20, 1964

PRINCIPAL WORKS

PLAYS: *Gretna Green*, pr. 1947; *The Quare Fellow*, pr. 1954; *The Big House*, pr. 1957 (radio play), pr. 1958 (staged); *An Giall*, pr. 1958; *The Hostage*, pr., pb. 1958 (translation and revision of *An Giall*); *Richard's Cork Leg*, pr. 1972 (with Alan Simpson); *The Complete Plays*, pb. 1978.

RADIO PLAYS: *A Garden Party*, pr. 1959; *Moving Out*, pr. 1952.

NONFICTION: *The Borstal Boy*, 1958; *Brendan Behan's Island: An Irish Sketchbook*, 1962; *Hold Your Hour and Have Another*, 1963; *Brendan Behan's New York*, 1964; *Confessions of an Irish Rebel*, 1965.

NOVEL: *The Scarperer*, 1964.

MISCELLANEOUS: *Poems and Stories*, 1978.

Brendan Behan emerged as a significant Irish author and playwright during the 1950's but failed to fulfill that promise in the last six years of his life. One of seven children, he was born in Dublin on February 9, 1923, the son of Stephen and Kathleen Kearney Behan. Deeply committed to Irish nationalism, Stephen Behan had been imprisoned in Kilmainhain Prison for his actions during the Irish Civil War, and Kathleen Behan was consistently outspoken in her support of Irish independence. With such a family background, Brendan's enrollments in the Fianna Éireann at the age of seven and the Irish Republican Army (IRA) at the age of fourteen are clearly understandable.

Behan's formal education was slight, consisting of six years with the School of the French Sisters of Charity and three with the Christian Brothers. Although poor, his parents enhanced this schooling by continually reading to all of their children. Behan's education was completed by his apprenticeship to the house-painting business, but his work in that trade was interrupted because of his IRA activities and subsequent imprisonment. Arrested in 1939 at the age of sixteen for carrying the makings of a homemade bomb, Behan served a three-year term in an English reform school. Then in 1942, he was arrested again for firing at policemen while they pursued three IRA officers. Sentenced to fourteen years in an Irish prison, Behan served only a portion of the time, released in 1946 under a general amnesty from the government.

Prison was to become the impetus for Behan's literary career. With the time and resources to refine his knowledge of Gaelic, Behan worked on several poems in Irish. The genius of these twelve lyric poems was recognized by their inclusion in a volume of modern Irish poetry. Prison also provided Behan with the material for his critically acclaimed autobiography *The Borstal Boy*, as well as the characters and plot for his stage play *The Quare Fellow.*

Released from imprisonment a second time, Behan painted houses, served an additional four-month sentence for falsifying his identity and reentering England to help an Irish prisoner escape, joined the Irish Press Association as a free-lance journalist (he wrote a number of distinguished columns for the *Irish Press*), and worked as a broadcaster for Ireland's national radio. During this time, Behan wrote *Moving Out* and *A Garden Party*, two short plays which aired on the radio in 1952. A third radio play, *The Big House*, was commissioned by the British Broadcasting Corporation several years later and performed in 1957. The three plays were subsequently staged at the Pike Theatre Club in 1958 in a single production.

It is with *The Quare Fellow*, *An Giall*, and *The Hostage*, however, that Behan's reputation as a dramatist lies. *The Quare Fellow* in its one-act version required considerable development; *An Giall* needed more of a translation from the Gaelic. Psychologically incapable of translating *An Giall*, Behan provided Joan Littlewood's Theatre Workshop with a script which he, Littlewood, and her cast rewrote as *The Hostage*. *The Quare Fellow* was first produced at Dublin's Pike Theatre in 1954; *An Giall* at An Damer in Dublin on June 16, 1958; and *The Hostage* in London at the Theatre Royal on October 14, 1958. Critical reaction to the plays was favorable, with *The Hostage* praised by being chosen to represent Great Britain at the 1959 *Theâtre des Nations* festival in Paris. Another stage play, *Richard's Cork Leg*, remained incomplete during Behan's life, because of his worsening alcoholism. Drinking had steadily become a problem for him from 1959 until his death five years later. Diabetic comas and alcoholic seizures put Behan into the hospital time and time again. Unable to control his alcoholism, he began tape-recording his memories for Rae Jeffs to edit. Those recordings were subsequently published as *Confessions of an Irish Rebel*, Behan's sequel to *The Borstal Boy*; *Brendan Behan's Island*, his descriptions of Ireland; and *Brendan Behan's New York*, reminiscences of poets, actors, dramatists, and fiction writers whom he had met in New York. In 1971, his last play was finished by Alan Simpson, Behan's director from the Pike Theatre. Brendan Behan died of a degenerated liver on March 20, 1964. He was survived by his infant daughter, Blanaid, and his devoted wife, Beatrice, who provided him with the stable environment in which his best writing was done.

Behan's stage productions are essentially comic. Among an unlikely mixture of characters, puns and jokes abound; music-hall songs are plentiful. The comic convention of disguise figures prominently in *The Hostage* and *Richard's Cork Leg*. All these comic touches provide a sharp counterpoint to Behan's serious plots: the hanging of a condemned man, the exchange of a British soldier's life for the execution of an Irish boy, and the hunting of a Bolshevik by the Fascists. Behan's juxtaposition of the serious and comic leads to his overall themes of the dignity of the individual, the accidental nature of life and death, and the transfiguration of the tragic by the comic. Neither obvious nor explicit, these themes pervade Behan's stage productions, lending their loosely constructed plots a certain unity.

The plot development of Behan's stage plays has often been criticized, as has his lack of in-depth characterization in *The Hostage* and *Richard's Cork Leg*. Defending his loose, at times rambling, plots and shadowy characters, some critics place Behan among the absurdists, noting that Behan, like Samuel Beckett and Eugène Ionesco, reflects characters of a formless universe in his drama. Yet critical debate never affected the public's reaction to his work. *The Quare Fellow, An Giall*, and *The Hostage* met with huge acclaim upon their performances in Dublin and London. Indeed, the man himself captivated the public. Playwright, journalist, revolutionary, Brendan Behan fascinated those he met, holding them spellbound with his talk and songs.

BIBLIOGRAPHICAL REFERENCES: Ted E. Boyle, *Brendan Behan*, 1969, and Colbert Kearney, *The Writings of Brendan Behan*, 1977, are the key critical studies of Behan's work, interweaving biographical information with critique. For further study of Behan's life and his impact on those around him, see *The World of Brendan Behan*, 1965, edited by Sean McCann, for an excellent compendium of views; Beatrice Behan, *My Life with Brendan*, 1973, for a day-by-day account of their lives from their marriage to his death; and Rae Jeffs, *Brendan Behan: Man and Showman*, 1966, concerning his tape-recorded manuscripts. See also Alan Simpson, *Beckett and Behan and a Theatre in Dublin*, 1962; "Brendan Behan: The Irish Primitive," in George Wellwarth, *The Theatre of Protest and Paradox: Developments in the Avant-Garde Drama*, 1964; Gordon Wickstrom, "The Heroic Dimension in Brendan Behan's *The Hostage*," *Educational Theatre Journal*, XXII (1970), 406-411; Raymond Porter, *Brendan Behan*, 1973; Richard Wall, "*An Giall* and *The Hostage* Compared," *Modern Drama*, XVIII (1975), 165-172; and Patrick McCarthy, "Triviality and Dramatic Achievement in Two Plays by Brendan Behan," *Modern British Literature*, III (1978), 113-121.

Jacqueline L. Gmuca

S. N. BEHRMAN

Born: Worcester, Massachusetts
Date: June 9, 1893

Died: New York, New York
Date: September 9, 1973

PRINCIPAL WORKS

PLAYS: *Bedside Manners*, pr. 1923 (with J. Kenyon Nicholson); *A Night's Work*, pr. 1924 (with Nicholson); *The Man Who Forgot*, pr. 1926 (with Owen Davis); *The Second Man*, pr., pb. 1927; *Serena Blandish: Or, The Difficulty of Getting Married*, pr. 1929; *Meteor*, pr. 1929; *Brief Moment*, pr., pb. 1931; *Biography*, pr. 1932; *Rain from Heaven*, pr., pb. 1934; *End of Summer*, pr., pb. 1936; *Amphitryon 38*, pr. 1937; *Wine of Choice*, pr., pb. 1938; *No Time for Comedy*, pr., pb. 1939; *The Talley Method*, pr., pb. 1941; *The Pirate*, pr. 1942; *Jacobowsky and the Colonel*, pr., pb. 1944; *Dunnigan's Daughter*, pr., pb. 1945; *I Know My Love*, pr., pb. 1949; *Jane*, pr., pb. 1952; *Fanny*, pr. 1954 (with Joshua Logan); *The Cold Wind and the Warm*, pr. 1958; *Lord Pengo*, pr. 1962; *But for Whom Charlie*, pr., pb. 1964.

SCREENPLAYS: *The Sea Wolf*, 1930 (with Ralph Block); *Surrender*, 1931 (with Sonya Levien); *Daddy Long-Legs*, 1931 (with Levien); *Rebecca of Sunnybrook Farm*, 1932 (with Levien); *Anna Karenina*, 1935 (with Clemence Dane and Salka Viertel); *Quo Vadis*, 1951 (with Levien and John Lee Mahin).

NOVEL: *The Burning Glass*, 1968.

MEMOIRS: *The Worcester Account*, 1954; *People in a Diary*, 1972 (also known as *Tribulations and Laughter*).

BIOGRAPHY: *Duveen*, 1952; *Portrait of Max: An Intimate Memoir of Sir Max Beerbohm*, 1960.

ESSAYS: *The Suspended Drawing Room*, 1965.

Samuel Nathaniel Behrman was one of the leading creators of American stage comedies in the 1930's. He was born June 9, 1893, in Worcester, Massachusetts, the son of Joseph and Zelda Feingold Behrman. Orthodox Jews, the Behrmans and their two oldest sons had fled persecution in Lithuania three years earlier, gradually making their way to Worcester. Joseph Behrman, a grocer, was a Talmudic scholar who taught his children Hebrew and recounted Old Testament stories as if they had occurred in his recent past. The most profound influence on young Behrman was his friend Daniel Asher, seven years his senior, who took him to his first play in 1904. The urbane Asher encouraged his friend to write and helped revise his early efforts.

After high school, Behrman toured the vaudeville circuit in a comic sketch he had written until bad health forced him to return home to attend Clark College. He was suspended for refusing to attend physical education classes and transferred to Harvard University, where he studied playwriting under George Pierce Baker. After graduating from Harvard and failing to find newspaper work, he earned a master's degree in English from Columbia University. With the advice of Asher, he turned down a teaching offer from the University of Minnesota and worked for *The New York Times* for two years, progressing from typist of classified advertisements to book reviewer while publishing several short stories.

In 1922, Behrman began collaborating on stories and plays with J. Kenyon Nicholson, and two of their plays found short-lived productions. *The Second Man* was a solo success for Behrman in 1927, but his insecurity about his continued progress as a playwright led him to begin contributing articles to *The New Yorker* in 1929, a relationship that lasted until his death. As Behrman was finally achieving his goals in 1929, he was shocked by the suicide of Asher. The impact of his mentor and his guilt over the man's death are examined in *The Worcester Account* and *The Cold Wind and the Warm*.

Like many successful playwrights of the time, Behrman began writing screenplays in 1930, primarily working with other writers on adaptations of novels. Characters in his play

Biography deride the need of artists to prostitute themselves in Hollywood, but in an essay in *The New Yorker* which appeared in 1934, Behrman defended the art of film. His film work did not distract him from writing what are considered his finest plays during the 1930's. In 1936, Behrman was married to Elza Heifetz, sister of violinist Jascha Heifetz, and their son was born the following year.

Behrman disdained such terms as "comedy of manners" and "drawing-room comedy," preferring the label "high comedy," since he used comedy as a means of seriously exploring such subjects as the role of love in marriage, the quest for success, the acquisition of wealth and power, conflicts between generations, and the threat to freedom posed by political extremes of both left and right. His plays are more concerned with the intellectual side of his characters than with the social surfaces of their lives.

Behrman's ideas are illustrated by character types who appear in his plays. One is the failed artist, a person of talent rather than genius, like the protagonist of *The Second Man*, who forsakes his true love for the comfortable life provided by associating with wealthy women. This character, a writer, cannot resist the cynical side of his nature that will not allow him to commit himself to anyone or anything. Another type is the emancipated woman, such as the heroine of *Biography*, who paints portraits of celebrities and is asked to write her memoirs, a prospect that upsets her former lovers. She resists the efforts of these ambitious, idealistic men to impose their views of the world upon her. A third type is the megalomaniac: the financiers of *Meteor* and *Dunnigan's Daughter*, the scientists of *End of Summer* and *The Talley Method*, the art dealer of *Lord Pengo*. Obsessed with power, these men attempt to dominate everyone around them. Doubts about the motives behind capitalism and science appear in many Behrman plays. The most prominent character type stands for the playwright's own liberal, humanitarian values and offsets the influence of the extremists, making a case for tolerance of the views and deficiencies of others.

Behrman's plays have been praised for their witty, sophisticated dialogue, attacked for their didacticism, lauded for their strong protagonists, and chided for offering idealized embodiments of intelligence and wit in place of believeable characters. Although Behrman's plays have been likened to those of George Bernard Shaw, W. Somerset Maugham, and Noël Coward, the most frequent comparison has been with Philip Barry, best known for *The Philadelphia Story* (pr., pb. 1939), though Behrman's characters display considerably more psychological complexity than Barry's. Unfortunately, both playwrights' works have become increasingly dated and unfashionable since the end of the 1930's.

BIBLIOGRAPHICAL REFERENCES: Kenneth T. Reed, *S. N. Behrman*, 1975, is a solid introduction to the themes of Behrman's plays. Donald Asher, *The Eminent Yachtsman and the Whorehouse Piano Player*, 1973, describes the friendship between David Asher (the author's father) and Behrman. For further study, see William R. Klink, *S. N. Behrman: The Major Plays*, 1978. See also "Drawing Room Freudians—Behrman, Osborn, Raphaelson," in W. David Sievers, *Freud on Broadway: A History of Psychoanalysis and the American Drama*, 1955; Joseph Wood Krutch, *The American Drama Since 1918: An Informal History*, 1957; Joseph Mersand, "S. N. Behrman and the American Comedy of Manners," *Player's Magazine* April, 1941, 6-8; Bruce Carpenter, "Mr. Behrman, Presenting High Comedy," *Theatre Time*, II (Winter, 1949), 17-20; and Charles Kaplan, "S. N. Behrman: The Quandary of the Comic Spirit," *College English*, XI (1950), 317-323.

Michael Adams

SAUL BELLOW

Born: Lachine, Quebec, Canada
Date: June 10, 1915

PRINCIPAL WORKS

NOVELS: *Dangling Man*, 1944; *The Victim*, 1947; *The Adventures of Augie March*, 1953; *Henderson the Rain King*, 1959; *Herzog*, 1964; *Mr. Sammler's Planet*, 1970; *Humboldt's Gift*, 1975; *The Dean's December*, 1982; *More Die of Heartbreak*, 1987.

NOVELLAS: *Seize the Day*, 1956; *A Theft*, 1989.

SHORT FICTION: *Mosby's Memoirs and Other Stories*, 1968; *Him with His Foot in His Mouth and Other Stories*, 1984.

PLAYS: *The Last Analysis*, pr. 1964; *Under the Weather*, pr. 1966 (also known as *The Bellow Plays*; includes *Out from Under, A Wen*, and *Orange Soufflé*).

TRAVEL SKETCH: *To Jerusalem and Back: A Personal Account*, 1976.

Saul Bellow, one of America's greatest novelists since World War II, was the youngest of four children of Russian-Jewish immigrants. The family moved to Chicago when Bellow was nine, and he attended public schools before going to the University of Chicago on a scholarship; he was graduated from Northwestern University in 1937. Though his father had wanted his son to be a doctor and his mother wished for him a career as a Talmudic scholar, Bellow pursued his studies in anthropology and sociology, disciplines which were to serve as a basis for his understanding of human character and the modern problems assaulting it. Additionally, his familial background in Orthodox Judaism provided a matrix from which the future writer would voice his concern for man, the noble sufferer.

By the late 1930's, Bellow was married, reading contemporary fiction, and, in a back bedroom of his Chicago apartment, was learning to write. He got a job with the Works Progress Administration (WPA) as a biographer of Midwestern writers and in 1943 served briefly in the merchant marine and then on the staff of the *Encyclopædia Britannica* as editor of the Great Books project. For a short time, he taught English at the University of Minnesota. With the publication of *Dangling Man* and *The Victim*, Bellow received a Guggenheim Fellowship, which afforded him an opportunity to live in Paris and travel about Europe. Returning to America in 1950, he spent the next ten years in New York City, scene of *Seize the Day.* He returned to Chicago and has enjoyed an association with the University of Chicago since 1962. Among his many awards are the Pulitzer Prize for *Herzog* and the culmination of his life's work, the Nobel Prize in Literature, in 1976.

Though *Dangling Man* and *The Victim* are considered apprentice works, they bear Bellow's distinguishing characteristics as a novelist: accurately realized scenes of urban and domestic life-styles and of the hero who feels alienated from his environment because of his moral insight. Recognition as a major talent came for Bellow with the publication of *The Adventures of Augie March*. A massive, sprawling novel in picaresque form, the book records in a euphorically dazzling style, reminiscent of the optimistic affirmations of Walt Whitman, the coming-of-age of its idealistic title character. It is also the host of subsidiary personalities that gives the work its special exuberance. The portrayal of the Einhorn family, for example, has a Dickensian zest that places the book in the great tradition of the nineteenth century European novel. *Seize the Day*, more economical than its predecessor, presents a more somber and confused hero in Tommy Wilhelm, who tries to maintain his dignity amid the crises of a failing marriage and career and the embittered disappointment of a domineering, unloving father. In *Henderson the Rain King*, a comic fantasy about a man who flees to Africa to find himself, Bellow creates a farcical and melodramatic world in which he satirizes the very idealism his earlier characters had upheld. The novel glistens with exuberance and an opulent skein of characters, such as King Dahfu, for example, who has read the pragmatic philosophers and who dreams of being reincarnated, after death, in the form of a lion.

With *Herzog*, Bellow produced what is generally considered his finest novel. Moses Herzog, the sensitive intellectual and student of Romanticism who writes letters to the world at large in an effort to keep his sanity and to understand his place as a moral sufferer in a world devoid of compassion, is a composite of all the heroes in Bellow's fiction. Such a hero is a man with a conscience, with a deep sense of his dignity, at conflict with a society which has become indifferent to human needs. The central dilemma for Herzog, as for all Bellow's heroes, is how to maintain self-respect and a system of values in the midst of self-effacement imposed by the social structure of postwar America. Bellow thus assumes a traditional position as a novelist. He is more concerned with the basic, unchanging values of humankind than with the psychic disorders peculiar to the modern man as reflected in much modernist fiction. As a novelist, Bellow looks back upon the "moralistic" classics of English and Russian literature, such as the works of Fyodor Dostoevski, rather than toward the aesthetically experimental psychological novels of the twentieth century.

Though his later novels, such as *Mr. Sammler's Planet* and *Humboldt's Gift*, have been criticized as being too introspectively self-indulgent, especially *The Dean's December*, Bellow remains a writer who has consistently grown with each new work. His place in American letters as a major novelist seems assured.

BIBLIOGRAPHICAL REFERENCES: Much of the best criticism of Bellow's work is contained in essays and book reviews. *Saul Bellow*, 1986, edited by Harold Bloom, is an excellent collection of some of these essays, as is *Critical Essays on Saul Bellow*, 1979, edited by Stanley Trachtenberg. Among full-length studies, one of the most readable for the general student is Keith Michael Opdahl, *Saul Bellow: An Introduction*, 1967; Robert Detweiler, *Saul Bellow, a Critical Essay*, 1967, is a brief monograph that presents Bellow as a novelist of affirmation; Jeanne Braham, *A Sort of Columbus: The American Voyages of Saul Bellow's Fiction*, 1984, examines the novels as paradigms, even allegories, of voyages of discovery in which the hero undertakes a quest to rediscover America and the self; M. Gilbert Porter, *Whence the Power? The Artistry and Humanity of Saul Bellow*, 1974, presents a close study of the Bellow hero as heir to American Transcendental philosophy as exemplified by Ralph Waldo Emerson, Henry David Thoreau, and Walt Whitman; John Jacob Clayton, *Saul Bellow: In Defense of Man*, 1979, discusses the body of Bellow's work as revealing a "psychic pattern" of oedipal conflicts and death wishes in his heroes. Malcolm Bradbury, *Saul Bellow*, 1982, concentrates on the comic aspects of Bellow's work which illuminate his humanism and its conflict with modernism. See also Judie Newman, *Saul Bellow and History*, 1984, a difficult but rewarding study which understands the novels as examinations of various theories of history.

Edward Fiorelli

ANDREY BELY
Boris Nikolayevich Bugaev

Born: Moscow, Russia
Date: October 26, 1880

Died: Moscow, Soviet Union
Date: January 8, 1934

Principal Works

NOVELS: *Serebryanny golub*, 1909-1910 (*The Silver Dove*, 1974); *Peterburg*, serial 1913-1914, book 1916, revised 1922 (*St. Petersburg*, 1959; better known as *Petersburg*); *Kotik Letayev*, 1922 (English translation, 1971); *Zapiski chudaka*, 1922; *Kreshchennyy kitaets*, 1922; *Moskovskii chudak*, 1926; *Moskva podudarom*, 1926; *Maski*, 1931.

SHORT FICTION: *Andrei Bely: Complete Short Stories*, 1979.

POETRY: *Zoloto v lazuri*, 1904; *Pepel*, 1909; *Urna*, 1909; *Khristos voskres*, 1918; *Korolevna i rytsari*, 1919; *Pervoe svidanie*, 1921 (*The First Encounter*, 1979); *Zvezda*, 1922; *Posle razluki*, 1922.

LITERARY CRITICISM: *Lug zelenyi*, 1910; *Simvolizm*, 1910; *Arabeski*, 1911; *Glossaloliya: Poema o zvuke*, 1922; *Poeziya slova*, 1922; *Ritm kak dialektika i "Medny vsadnik" issledovanie*, 1929; *Masterstvo Gogolya*, 1934; *Selected Essays of Andrey Bely*, 1985.

OTHER NONFICTION: *Dramaticheskaia simfonia*, 1902 (*The Dramatic Symphony*, 1986); *Na rubezhe dvukh stolety*, 1930; *Nachalo veka*, 1933; *Mezhdu dvukh revolyutsiy*, 1934.

Andrey Bely, a major figure in Russian symbolism at the beginning of the twentieth century, was a novelist, poet, and prolific essayist. His nonfiction writings include memoirs as well as criticism and literary theory. He was born Boris Nikolayevich Bugaev on October 26, 1880, the son of Nikolay Bugaev, a prominent professor of mathematics at Moscow University. Bely was graduated from that university in 1903 with a degree in natural sciences, but, until his literary career interfered, he fully intended to complete a second program, in philosophy. During his student years, he began to publish his "symphonies," a form now generally classified as prose but which embodies principles of musical composition.

Bely, who had avidly read the works of Arthur Schopenhauer and Friedrich Nietzsche, was also strongly influenced by the philosophy of Vladimir Solovyov, who had talked of a coming apocalyptic chaos as well as of the appearance of "Sophia," the embodiment of divine wisdom. At the start of his career Bely also began an intense and stormy friendship with fellow Symbolist poet Aleksander Blok. Between 1903 and 1910, Bely's extensive writing included numerous critical and theoretical works. Three major collections, totaling some fifteen hundred pages, appeared in 1910 and 1911, and in the course of his life he completed more than three hundred critical studies. Meanwhile he also became interested in Immanuel Kant and the neo-Kantians, whose works he read extensively. Poetry was largely the basis for his eary literary reputation; his first three collections—*Zoloto v lazuri* (gold in azure), *Pepel* (ashes), and *Urna* (the urn)—contain the verse from this period and are widely regarded as his best poetic efforts.

Bely's first novel, *The Silver Dove*, appeared only after he had become widely known as a poet, but from that point onward his major work was to be in prose. Bely conceived of *The Silver Dove* as the first part of a trilogy to be called "East or West," but as he wrote the second volume it began to grow into an independent work. The long, difficult novel *Petersburg*, now generally acknowledged to be his greatest achievement, first appeared serially in 1913-1914 and came out as a bound volume in 1916, before being drastically revised and cut for an edition that appeared in 1922. His next novel, *Kotik Letayev*, while perhaps even more imposing than *Petersburg*, has come to be well regarded by many critics.

The time that Bely spent abroad during the first half of the 1910's and again from 1921 to 1923 account for two of the most important periods in his life. In 1912 he met Rudolf Steiner and through him became deeply involved with the spiritual movement known as anthroposophy, which was to have a profound effect on much of his subsequent writing. The second period was Bely's most productive but also one of his most troubled. He became alienated from Steiner as well as from most of the Russian writers who were living in Berlin. After returning to Russia in 1923, he largely stayed out of public life, though he traveled within the Soviet Union and continued to write. Perhaps hoping to follow on the success of *Petersburg*, he completed a series of novels set in Moscow in which the stylistic experimentation is often carried to an extreme. Toward the end of his life Bely was hard at work on his memoirs; he died early in 1934, apparently from the effects of a cerebal hemorrhage suffered the previous summer.

Bely was capable of producing accomplished work in virtually any genre. His poetry, somewhat eclipsed by that of other modern poets, nevertheless contains some striking imagery and original rhythmic and graphic structures. The memoirs, though not always reliable factually, provide a lively and insightful history of both the Symbolist movement and cultural life in Russia during the early years of the century. As a critic and a thinker he was imaginative if not always systematic.

Bely's posthumous reputation owes most to his novels. Here too he is uneven; *Zapiski chudaka* (notes of an eccentric) rests uneasily on the border between fiction and autobiographical travel essay, and the Moscow novels are only intermittently successful. *Petersburg* and the highly autobiographical *Kotik Letayev*, however, enjoy a high critical reputation. *Petersburg* is set in 1905, when Russia teetered on the brink of revolution. The dark political atmosphere, the conflicts between philosophical and personal interests, the play on themes from Fyodor Dostoevski and other writers, the intricate plot centered on a time bomb in a sardine can, and the black humor that pervades much of this novel create a heady mixture that captures the chaotic mood of the period.

Bely remains a difficult artist. His wide knowledge was not always thoroughly digested, he was too anxious to write about his ideas to take the time to work them out fully, and his enthusiasm for experimenting with forms often precluded clarity. Still, he is never dull, and when most of what he attempted fell into place—as, for example, in his long autobiographical poem *The First Encounter*, written in only a few days, or in *Petersburg*—he created works that stand among the masterpieces of twentieth century literature.

BIBLIOGRAPHICAL REFERENCES: The first full-length work on Bely in English is Oleg Maslenikov, *The Frenzied Poets: Andrey Biely and the Russian Symbolists*, 1952. A survey of Bely's career is provided in Konstantin Mochulsky, *Andrei Bely: His Life and Works*, 1977. For a concise biographical account, see John Elsworth, *Andrey Bely*, 1972. An effort to explain Bely's world outlook can be found in Samuel Cioran, *The Apocalyptic Symbolism of Andrey Bely*, 1973. Two broad-ranging collections of articles are *Andrey Bely: A Critical Review*, 1978, edited by Gerald Janecek, and *Andrey Bely Centenary Papers*, 1980, edited by Boris Christa. For a collection of long studies, each devoted to a major aspect of Bely's writing, see *Andrey Bely: Spirit of Symbolism*, 1987, edited by John Malmstad.

Barry P. Scherr

JUAN BENET

Born: Madrid, Spain
Date: October 7, 1927

PRINCIPAL WORKS

NOVELS: *Volverás a Región*, 1967 (*Return to Región*, 1985); *Una meditación*, 1970 (*A Meditation*, 1982); *Un viaje de invierno*, 1972; *La otra casa de Mazón*, 1973; *En el estado*, 1977; *El aire de un crimen*, 1980; *Saúl ante Samuel*, 1980; *Herrumbrosas lanzas, I-VI*, 1983.

NOVELLAS: *Una tumba*, 1971; *Del pozo y del Numa: Un ensayo y una leyenda*, 1978; *En la penumbra*, 1983.

SHORT FICTION: *Nunca llegarás a nada*, 1961; *Cinco narraciones y dos fábulas*, 1972; *Sub rosa*, 1973; *Cuentos completos*, 1977; *Trece fábulas y media*, 1981; *Una tumba y otros relatos*, 1981.

ESSAYS: *La inspiración y el estilo*, 1965; *Puerta de tierra*, 1970; *El ángel del Señor abandona a Tobías*, 1976; *En ciernes*, 1976; *Qué fue la guerra civil?*, 1976; *La moviola de Eurípides*, 1982; *Articulos, 1962-1977*, 1983; *Sobre la incertidumbre*, 1983.

PLAYS: *Max*, pb. 1953; *Agonía confutans*, pb. 1969; *Teatro*, pb. 1970 (includes *Anastas: O, El origen de la constitución*, *Agonía confutans*, and *Un caso de conciencia*).

TRANSLATION: *A este lado del Paraiso*, 1968 (by F. Scott Fitzgerald).

Novelist and essayist Juan Benet is one of the leading figures in what has been termed the "New Wave" of Spanish literature. Benet, whose full name is Juan Benet Goitia, was born in Madrid in 1927, the son of Tomas Benet and Teresa Goitia. Benet's childhood was dramatically affected by the outbreak of the Spanish Civil War in 1936. His father was killed early in the conflict. His family left Madrid and settled for the duration of the war in San Sebastián, where Benet began his education. After the war's end, Benet returned with his family to Madrid, where he continued his studies and in 1948 enrolled in the University of Madrid's School of Civil Engineering.

Throughout his youth, Benet's older brother, Francisco, was an important shaper of the future author's literary tastes, recommending books and encouraging Benet's pursuit of a personal literary education to complement his university studies in engineering. Among those writers whose works would later have a profound influence on Benet's own were William Faulkner, Franz Kafka, Marcel Proust, Thomas Mann, and Herman Melville. As a university student, Benet moved in circles that included many of Spain's leading young writers and intellectuals, and his own literary career began in 1953, with the publication of his short play, *Max*.

Benet was graduated from the University of Madrid in 1954. He then moved to the northwest of Spain, where he remained until 1966 as a director of public works. The area of Spain in which he lived during those years would become the inspiration for Región, the mythical setting of the majority of Benet's novels. Often compared to Faulkner's Yoknapatawpha County, Región has been described as a microcosm of Spain and Spanish society at the time of the Civil War, with overtones of the decadence that would follow the war under Francisco Franco's rule.

The first of Benet's works set in Región is a collection of short stories. Published in 1961, *Nunca llegarás a nada* (you will never get anywhere) introduces Región and its inhabitants and estabishes the themes and literary style that would inform Benet's later work. The year after Benet left northern Spain for Madrid, the first of the Región novels, *Return to Región*, appeared. A difficult and enigmatic work now acclaimed as perhaps his finest book, *Return to Región* examines the legacy of the Civil War in modern Spain. Not widely read when it first appeared, the book benefited from the broad critical acclaim that greeted Benet's second Región novel, *A Meditation*, which received the Seix Barral prize in 1969.

Both novels demonstrate the complex use of language and literary allusions that have become the hallmarks of Benet's work. Like Faulkner's style, Benet's is characterized by sentences that often continue for pages, imagery rich in references to a wide range of classical and modern authors, and an obsession with the dual themes of time and memory. Benet followed *A Meditation* with *Una tumba* (a tomb), a novella cast in the mold of the ghost story, and *Un viaje de invierno* (a winter journey) and *La otra casa de Mazón* (the Mazón's other house), the third and fourth entries in the Región series.

Benet is also acclaimed for his short fiction, and in the early 1970's he published *Cinco narraciones y dos fábulas* (five narratives and two fables) and *Sub rosa*, followed in 1977 by his fifth novel, *En el estado* (in the state). A two-volume collection of stories, *Cuentos completos* (complete stories), appeared that same year, followed in 1978 by *Del pozo y del Numa: Un ensayo y una leyenda* (of the well and of Numa: an essay and a legend), which contains a novella centered on El Numa, a character from *Return to Región*.

Benet has also earned a reputation as one of Spain's foremost essayists, publishing several collections of literary and social criticism. Among the most important are *La inspiración y el estilo* (inspiration and style), *El ángel del Señor abandona a Tobías* (the angel of the Lord abandons Tobit), *La moviola de Eurípides* (Euripides' replay machine), *Qué fue la guerra civil?* (what was the civil war?), and *Articulos, 1962-1977* (articles, 1962-1977).

Sául ante Samuel (Saul before Samuel), published in 1980, continued the Región series, while *El aire de un crimen* (air of a crime) represented a departure by Benet from his usual, inaccessible style—a fact that won for its author a host of new readers. These novels have been followed in recent years by two collections of short stories, *Trece fábulas y media* (thirteen and a half fables) and *Una tumba y otros relatos* (a tomb and other tales), a novella entitled *En la penumbra* (in the shadow), and the beginning of a multivolume series, *Herrumbrosas lanzas, I-VI* (rusty lances). Also set in Región at the time of the Civil War, the novels in that series are written in the more accessible style that marks *El aire de un crimen* and seem certain to enhance Benet's reputation as one of Spain's most important literary figures.

BIBLIOGRAPHICAL REFERENCES: Many of the book-length studies of Benet's work appear only in Spanish. Among the English-language books, David K. Herzberger's *The Novelistic World of Juan Benet*, 1976, is a useful and comprehensive study that discusses the major influences on Benet's work and analyzes five of his novels. Malcolm Alan Compitello, *Ordering the Evidence: "Volverás a Región" and Civil War Fiction*, 1983, focuses on one of the author's best-known novels and places it within the context of literature about the Spanish Civil War. Vincente Cabrera, *Juan Benet*, 1983, is a comprehensive look at Benet's work by genre. *Critical Approaches to the Writings of Juan Benet*, 1984, edited by Roberto C. Monteiga, David K. Herzberger, and Malcolm Alan Compitello, offers a varied and insightful collection of essays on Benet. The book also contains a foreword by Benet and an extremely thorough bibliography, compiled by Compitello, that contains both critical works in English and those in untranslated Spanish.

Janet E. Lorenz

WALTER BENJAMIN

Born: Berlin, Germany *Died:* Port Bou, Spain
Date: July 15, 1892 *Date:* September 27, 1940

Principal Works

LITERARY CRITICISM: *Der Begriff der Kunstkritik in der deutschen Romantik*, 1919; *Goethes "Wahlverwandtschaften,"* 1922; *Der Ursprung des deutschen Trauerspiels*, 1925 (*The Origin of German Tragic Drama*, 1978); *Charles Baudelaire: Ein Lyriker im Zeitalter des Hochkapitalismus*, 1955 (*Charles Baudelaire: A Lyric Poet in the Era of High Capitalism*, 1973); *Versuche über Brecht*, 1966 (*Understanding Brecht*, 1973).

ESSAYS: *Einbahnstrasse*, 1928 (*One-Way Street and Other Writings*, 1979); *Illuminations*, 1968.

AUTOBIOGRAPHY: *Berliner Kindheit um Neunzehnhundert*, 1950; *Moskauer Tagebuch*, 1980 (*Moscow Diary*, 1986).

MISCELLANEOUS: *Gesammelte Schriften*, 1974-1985; *Reflections: Essays, Aphorisms, Autobiographical Writings*, 1978.

Walter Benjamin is a major cultural critic whose profoundly complex works reflect both a melancholic messianism and an idiosyncratic Marxism. Benjamin was little appreciated during his own life, which ended tragically in suicide; only after World War II, when Theodor Adorno, a leading member of the Frankfurt Institute of Social Research, and Gershom Scholem, distinguished scholar of the kabbalah, began publishing his works, did Benjamin's influence on modern cultural theory begin to be felt.

Born July 15, 1892, into an affluent Jewish home in the posh West End of Berlin, Benjamin's secondary education at the prestigious Friedrich-Wilhelm Gymnasium brought him under the influence of the antiauthoritarian concepts of Gustav Wyneken. He became a leader in the so-called Youth Movement but broke with the group over its enthusiastic acceptance of World War I, which Benjamin avoided by feigning sciatica. He was married to Dora Pollak in 1917, their only child Stefan being born the same year, but the couple was separated after 1924. Studying philosophy in Freiburg, Berlin, Munich, and Bern, Benjamin made contacts with Zionists and leftists, including Martin Buber and Ernst Bloch. His doctoral dissertation, *Der Begriff der Kunstkritik in der deutschen Romantik* (the concept of art criticism in German Romanticism), which examined Johann Gottlieb Fichte's metaphysics and Friedrich Schlegel's aesthetics, was published in 1919 in Bern. Rapidly rising inflation in the Weimar Republic and pressure from his parents to find suitable employment forced Benjamin to return to Germany.

Better suited by temperament to be an independent man of letters as opposed to an academic, Benjamin nevertheless sought a university career by submitting in 1925 *The Origin of German Tragic Drama* as a qualifying paper in order to teach aesthetics and literary history at the University of Frankfurt. He withdrew his application, however, when it became clear that the faculty barely understood his difficult theoretical discussion of the Baroque drama of grief. Here, as throughout his work, Benjamin sought a criticism of redemption by which the historical/material truth of a work of art would be released from the aesthetic delusion, the pretense to totality.

After giving up a chance to teach in Jerusalem, offered by his lifelong friend Gershom Scholem, Benjamin embarked on a career as a literary critic, publishing important essays on ethics, violence, and Johann Wolfgang von Goethe and translating Charles Baudelaire, Marcel Proust, and Marcel Jouhandeau. Contact with left-wing intellectuals, particularly the Latvian actress Asja Lacis, who introduced him to Bertolt Brecht, increased his interest in Marxism. Furthermore, he was much impressed by an early work of Georg Lukács, *Geschichte und Klassenbewusstsein* (1923; *History and Class Consciousness*, 1971). Benjamin visited Moscow in the winter of 1926-1927. (His work *Moscow Diary* was the direct result of that visit.) Although he declined to join the Communist Party, claiming too many "anarchist" tendencies in his personality, he was deeply interested in new currents within Soviet culture.

After the Nazi seizure of power in 1933, Benjamin began a life of exile in Paris, with extended vists to his friend Brecht in Denmark. Supporting himself in part on a stipend from the so-called Frankfurt School of critics, whose journal *Zeitschrift für Sozialforschung* (journal for social research) published a number of important articles, he developed his penetrating analysis of nineteenth century French culture and modern urban life (for example, "Paris, the Capital of the Nineteenth Century," in *Charles Baudelaire: A Lyric Poet in the Era of High Capitalism*). These interests were to have culminated in his unfinished, image-laden masterpiece, the "Passagen-Werk" (arcades project), which through the architectural arcades of nineteenth century Paris shows the sociotechnological basis of art and the fetishes of modern culture.

Throughout Benjamin's work there is an effort to brush against the grain of linguistic and symbolic illusion. Only a language free of intention could reveal truth. In *Goethe's "Wahlverwandtschaften"* (Goethe's *Elective Affinities*), he argues that the appearance of totality in the symbolic work of art, mimicking nature, should be unmasked to uncover the expressionless in human experience. Beyond the allegory of the *Trauerspiel* lies the trauma of war and plague in the seventeenth century. Every "document of civilization" is thus also a "document of barbarism." The experience (*Erfahrung*) of integrated collective memory and tradition, destroyed by the experiencing (*Erlebnis*) of the discontinuous events of modernity, leaves the storyteller without a craft. Literary criticism must recover the fragmented reality of everyday life from the dissolution of capitalistic fetishes that keep man from seeing the whole for the parts. The *flâneur*, the stroller through the Parisian arcades, embodies this alientation by being a lonely voyeur within the human crowd. The abundant luxuries in the surrounding shop windows, commodities whose exchange value shrouds their use value, obscure an understanding of the oppression required by their production. In his best-known essay, "The Work of Art in the Age of Mechanical Reproduction" (translated in *Illuminations*), Benjamin argues that technological advance provides artistic innovations that redefine the relationship between artist and audience and thereby serve to expose the contradictions of capitalism. The modern capacity to reproduce paintings destroys their "aura," the reverential attitude of the cultivated public toward authentic works of art, thus liberating culture from religious mystification and allowing it to embrace a proper political role. The social truth lying behind a standardized and unnatural life in the modern city can only be attained through "shock experiences," as in Baudelaire's assaultive use of sacred images in unholy contexts or Brecht's blunt interruption of the observer's empathy with the action onstage.

Benjamin wrote provocatively about such diverse interests as children's toys, hashish, Surrealism, and Franz Kafka. The original and unorthodox dimensions of his Marxism range from the notion that collecting antiquities, "ruins," is a means of escaping the cultural hegemony of history and that returning to a prelapsarian faith is a means of freeing revolutionary impulses. His pessimistic last essay, "Theses on the Philosophy of History," written under the shadow of the Stalin-Hitler pact of 1939, appears to despair over the possibility of meaningful political engagement. Embracing the "left melancholia" he had once criticized, abandoning faith in historical progress, Benjamin suggests that redemption from oppression could only come from a messianic interruption of time, a *Jetztzeit*, or "now-time," that allowed for the rediscovery of lost humanity. After the Nazi invasion of France, Benjamin acquired a visa to enter the United States, but with failing health, he took his own life on September 27, 1940, in Port Bou, Spain, when an official, attempting blackmail, threatened to report him and his fellow refugees to the Gestapo.

BIBLIOGRAPHICAL REFERENCES: Julian Roberts, *Walter Benjamin*, 1982, shows the Marxist continuity in Benjamin's thought, as does Susan Buck-Morss, *Walter Benjamin and the Dialectics of Seeing: A Study of the "Arcades Project,"* 1988. Gershom Scholem, *Walter Benjamin: The Story of a Friendship*, 1981, stresses his romantic messianism. Richard Wolin, *Walter Benjamin: An Aesthetic of Redemption*, 1982, argues that the "discontinuous extremes" in Benjamin's work lead ultimately to its enigmatic majesty. The importance of Benjamin to neo-Marxist and poststructuralist criticism can be seen in Terry Eagleton, *Walter Benjamin: Or, Towards a Revolutionary Criticism*, 1981. A useful collection of essays by leading Benjamin scholars and an extensive bibliography is found in *On Walter Benjamin: Critical Essays and Recollections*, 1988, edited by Gary Smith.

Bland Addison, Jr.

JOHN BERGER

Born: London, England
Date: November 5, 1926

PRINCIPAL WORKS

ART CRITICISM: *Permanent Red: Essays in Seeing*, 1960; *The Success and Failure of Picasso*, 1965; *"The Moment of Cubism" and Other Essays*, 1969; *Art and Revolution: Ernst Neizvestny and the Role of the Artist in the USSR*, 1969; *Ways of Seeing*, 1972 (with others); *About Looking*, 1980; *Another Way of Telling*, 1982 (with Jean Mohr).

NOVELS: *A Painter of Our Time*, 1958; *The Foot of Clive*, 1962; *Corker's Freedom*, 1965; *G.*, 1972.

ESSAYS: *Selected Essays and Articles: The Look of Things*, 1975; *The White Bird*, 1985 (also known as *The Sense of Sight*).

SOCIAL CRITICISM: *A Seventh Man: A Book of Images and Words About the Experience of Migrant Workers in Europe*, 1975 (with Mohr).

BIOGRAPHY: *A Fortunate Man: The Story of a Country Doctor*, 1967 (with Mohr).

SCREENPLAY: *Jonah Who Will Be 25 in the Year 2000*, 1983 (with Alain Tanner).

MISCELLANEOUS: *Pig Earth*, 1979; *And Our Faces, My Heart, Brief as Photos*, 1984; *Once in Europa*, 1987.

John Berger's achievements in the arts and criticism defy simple classification. Even the term "man of letters," which encompasses the work of literary polymaths, is inadequate, since Berger has not only written art, social, and literary criticism but also helped to produce a television series, made films, and published photographic essays. Perhaps he is best described as one of the European Left's most distinguished "men of culture and politics."

In fact, opposition to the increased specialization and division of labor which has characterized the twentieth century is one of the themes which run through Berger's varied works. With this he combines a commitment to humane art and to the political liberation and cultural recognition of those who suffer from prejudice, oppression, and powerlessness. From his youth to the present Berger has been a Marxist, but his political stance and practice have been shaped by an artistic sensibility and a sense of values which have their roots in nineteenth century art and anarcho-socialist theory.

Berger's childhood was a lonely one. His father, a director of an accounting firm, and his mother sent him to a boarding school at the age of six, and he had little to do with them thereafter. His experiences at school were not happy ones, and eventually he fled to London, where he studied painting at two art schools, before and after two years in the army during World War II. After the war he was drawn to politics, working closely with, but not joining, the Communist Party. He became interested in writing criticism and was much influenced by the historical art criticism of the Marxist Frederick Antal. For ten years he wrote criticism of contemporary art for *New Statesman*, opposing abstract expressionism and calling for a realism which would express the range and depth of human hopes. His best criticism from this period is collected in *Permanent Red*. In politics he considered himself a Communist and supported the policies of the Soviet Union until 1956, when it crushed reform movements in Eastern Europe.

In the late 1950's Berger turned from critical to creative writing, but his interests remained the same. His first novel, *A Painter of Our Time*, explores the problems of a Hungarian artist and Socialist living in exile in England. The book is typical of Berger's work in its focus on the artist's contradictions, his struggle to reconcile his desires to create serious art and to work for social transformation in his homeland. His next two novels, generally considered less successful than his first, are *The Foot of Clive*, which examines the lives of several socially typical men in a hospital ward, and *Corker's Freedom*, which describes an important day in the lives of a man who runs an employment agency and the people who come to his office. Both novels examine society and its problems, and both are influenced technically (but in different ways) by Joycean modernist experiments and by naturalism.

Berger left England permanently in 1960, and thereafter exile and alienation became increasingly important themes in his work. Ironically, between 1965 and 1972 he produced both the art criticism and the fiction which established his fame in the English-speaking world. *The Success and Failure of Picasso* and "The Moment of Cubism," related studies, place the individual artist and the movement he helped to forge in the context of the economic, political, and social history of monopolistic capitalism. Berger's Pablo Picasso is a contradictory being whose successes and failures are, given his historical situation, inevitable. These studies also contain some of Berger's best practical criticism of individual paintings. In his later study of the relatively unknown Soviet artist Ernst Neizvestny, *Art and Revolution*, Berger describes an artist living within the historical contradictions of Socialism who produced an affirmative, humanistic, and yet modernist art.

Finally, in *Ways of Seeing*, Berger and several collaborators produced (in response to Kenneth Clark's *Civilization*, 1969) a revisionist analysis of art history which became perhaps the most popular and influential television series and book about art in the decade, if not the century. In the same year (1972), Berger's novel *G.* won for him several literary awards, including the prestigious Booker Prize. *G.* is a difficult modernist historical fiction. It describes the life of an upper-class "Don Juan" as he grows to adulthood and pursues women amid the political and technological revolutions which occurred in Europe between 1880 and World War I. Berger adopts many of the experimental devices of avant-garde fiction, creating a collage of plot, social and political history, authorial asides on writing and his feelings, all in a prose which is both precise and alive to the sensual world.

At the height of his success Berger began to collaborate with the photographer Jean Mohr on books of nonfiction. One of these, *A Fortunate Man*, describes the life of a doctor in a small English town, a man whose life is fortunate because he performs hard but meaningful work for his society. The other, *A Seventh Man*, is a documentary which portrays the life of the migrant workers in Europe. During his work on this book, Berger decided to move to a village in France, to live and work among peasants. He has now published two volumes of short fiction and poetry (*Pig Earth* and *Once in Europa*) in a projected trilogy about a dying peasant culture which, he believes, embodies a way of life better adapted to the problems of the future than either the dominant capitalist or the authoritarian Socialist cultures as they now exist.

BIBLIOGRAPHICAL REFERENCES: Geoff Dyer, *Ways of Telling: The Work of John Berger*, 1986, covers Berger's canon as of 1986. See Peter Fuller, *Seeing Berger*, 1980, for a sympathetic critique of *Ways of Seeing*. For criticism and analysis of *G.*, see David Caute, "What We Might Be and What We Are," *Collisions*, 1974, 135-146; Ray Selden, "Commitment and Dialectic in Novels by Caute and Berger," *Forum for Modern Language Studies*, XI (1975). For a special issue devoted to Berger's work, see *The Minnesota Review*, Spring, 1987. See also Bruce Robbins, "Feeling Global: John Berger and Experience," *Boundary 2*, Fall, 1982/Winter, 1983, 291-308, and David James, "Cubism as Revolutionary Realism," *The Minnesota Review*, Fall, 1983, 92-109.

Michael Helfand

THOMAS BERGER

Born: Cincinnati, Ohio
Date: July 20, 1924

PRINCIPAL WORKS

NOVELS: *Crazy in Berlin*, 1958; *Rinehart in Love*, 1962; *Little Big Man*, 1964; *Killing Time*, 1967; *Vital Parts*, 1970; *Regiment of Women*, 1973; *Sneaky People*, 1975; *Who Is Teddy Villanova?*, 1977; *Arthur Rex*, 1978; *Neighbors*, 1980; *Rinehart's Women*, 1981; *The Feud*, 1983; *Nowhere*, 1985; *Being Invisible*, 1987; *The Houseguest*, 1988.

PLAY: *Other People*, pr. 1970.

Thomas Louis Berger's audience may not be a large one, but it is dedicated. There are few modern novelists as agile at manipulating the conventions of the form. He was born in Cincinnati, Ohio, in 1924, the son of Thomas Charles and Mildred (Bubbe) Berger. He served in the Army from 1943 to 1946, mainly in Germany, an experience that is reflected in *Crazy in Berlin*, the first of the four Rinehart series novels. Berger was graduated from the University of Cincinnati in 1948 and did graduate work at Columbia University. In 1950 he was married to Jeanne Redpath. He supported himself as an editor in the 1950's, working on *The New York Times Index* and *Popular Science Monthly.* In 1962 he was named a Dial Fellow for *Rinehart in Love*, and in 1965 he received the Western Heritage Award and the Richard and Hilda Rosenthal Award for *Little Big Man*. That novel was made into a successful film in 1970. Berger often published in *Esquire*, and he served as that magazine's film critic from 1972 to 1973. He has been a writer-in-residence at Kansas University, Yale University, and the University of California at Davis.

Berger's novels are often parodies of various forms of the novel. He expands on as much as he mocks conventions. The Rinehart series (*Crazy in Berlin*, *Rinehart in Love*, *Vital Parts*, and *Rinehart's Women*) forms a kind of *Bildungsroman*. There are also two coming-of-age stories with a small-town Ohio setting, *Sneaky People* and *The Feud*. Two other novels employ the tough-guy detective story conventions of Dashiell Hammett and Raymond Chandler, *Who Is Teddy Villanova?* and *Killing Time*. Then there are two dystopian novels, *Regiment of Women* and *Nowhere*. *Little Big Man* is a parody of the frontier memoir and captivity narrative, told by the lone survivor of George Armstrong Custer's Last Stand. In *Arthur Rex*, Berger reworks the material (partly in tribute to Mark Twain) by having the knights speak in modern slang and fall into sexual contretemps. The jests are good and the plotting inventive, but the jokes become attenuated after 550 pages. The method here might also be considered an inversion of the comedy of *Who Is Teddy Villanova?*, in which the tough-guy detective ornaments his talk with learned literary allusions.

Although Berger's novels seem to present a world into which the reader might step, his own comments on his work emphasize their formal design and delight in language. In one interview he said that in his novels he intended "to celebrate [a genre], to identify and applaud its glories." Politics, history, and the novelist's "reality" are far from his mind. For example, *Sneaky People* seems to take place the first week of September, 1939, but there is not one word of the momentous events of that week.

Berger is interested in how character is usually misread. The reader of Berger is usually enlightened about the truth of a character, but the character persists in his mistaken notions. Jack Crabb, who is also Little Big Man, the Cheyenne Indian, repeatedly has difficulty convincing whites that he is one of them and Indians that he is their brother. The problem is one of identity, and Berger insists that it is not an easy one. Many famous names are introduced in *Little Big Man*—Kit Carson, Wild Bill Hickok, Calamity Jane, even Walt Whitman—and each one is slightly different from the one history presents. For example, Custer is introduced by Crabb as mad with ambition, but after the Battle of Little Big Horn

Crabb's hatred turns to respect for Custer's single-minded pursuit of glory.

Berger's examination of the secrets beneath character is most obvious in *Sneaky People*, in which every character has a hidden life. Buddy Sandifer, a crass used-car salesman, thinks that his mistress, Laverne, cannot get enough of his attentions, but she would prefer to be a nun, or at least a respectable housewife. Buddy's wife, Naomi, is seen by everyone to be a feckless dreamer, when she is actually the author of steamy pornography. Ralph, their adolescent son, lives a life of private lecheries but is basically a romantic idealist. When he discovers a pistol under his father's pillow, he is sure that he is an undercover agent. At the end of the novel Naomi tells Buddy that she thinks he is limited by his faithfulness to her. Buddy is so shocked that he decides against having her killed. Each turn of the plot comes as a surprise, and along the way the reader delights in Berger's ear for the argot of the time and place.

The complications of character in Berger's novels often involve sex roles. Carlo Rinehart's wife, Genevieve, is a hard, leathery woman and a success in the business world, whereas Carlo fails in one position after another. In *Vital Parts*, he uses binoculars to watch a nubile neighbor undress. One day he is shocked to see her cavorting with a long-haired partner, who turns out to be Carlo's hippie son Blaine. In revenge he cuts off Blaine's locks while Blaine sleeps. The matter of sex roles is most radically presented in *Regiment of Women*, which takes place in the United States in the middle of the twenty-first century. Women have taken over; they wear the pants, literally, and the men wear dresses and worry about their hair. Old-fashioned conception has been replaced by artificial insemination, ex-utero nurseries, and barracks where soldiers are "milked." At first glance this might seem to be an antifeminist tract, because women have created a totalitarian state, but Berger's inversion forces the reader to translate sex role clichés in order to see present injustices.

Regiment of Women might seem to be the most topical in Berger's canon. He even sends the hero and heroine to the Maine woods as fugitives so that they can start humanity over again in the old fashion. Yet the central concern is with language. Max F. Schultz puts it this way: "Berger's many styles represent a continuing celebration of the self-regenerative powers of language. He works at the extremities of the linguistic atlas, rehabilitating coinages worn out by time, by homogenizing, and by media overuse."

BIBLIOGRAPHICAL REFERENCES: Thomas McClanahan, "Thomas Berger," in *The Dictionary of Literary Biography*, Vol. 2, 1978, edited by Jeffrey Helterman, gives a sketch of Berger's career. *Studies in American Humor*, II, nos. 1 and 2 (1983), are devoted to Berger. See also Brian W. Dippie, "Jack Crabb and the Sole Survivors of Custer's Last Stand," *Western American Literature*, IV (Fall, 1969), 189-202; Douglas Hughes, "The Schlemiel as Humanist: Thomas Berger's Carlo Reinhart," *Cithara*, XV (November, 1975), 3-21; Leo E. Oliva, "Thomas Berger's *Little Big Man* as History," *Western American Literature*, VIII (Spring/Summer, 1973), 33-54; Delbert E. Wylder, "Thomas Berger's *Little Big Man* as Literature," *Western American Literature*, III (Winter, 1969), 273-284; Brooks Landon, "The Radical Americanist," *The Nation*, CCV (August 20, 1977), 151-153; Richard Schickel, "Bitter Comedy," *Commentary*, L (July, 1970), 76, and "Interviewing Thomas Berger," *The New York Times Book Review*, LXXXV (April 6, 1980), 1; Stanley Trachtenberg, "Berger and Barth: The Comedy of Decomposition," in *Comic Relief*, 1978, edited by Sarah B. Cohen; and Frederick Turner, "Melville and Thomas Berger: The Novelist as Cultural Anthropologist," *Centennial Review*, XIII (Winter, 1969), 102-121.

John O. Lyons

ISAIAH BERLIN

Born: Riga, Latvia
Date: June 6, 1909

PRINCIPAL WORKS

PHILOSOPHY: *Historical Inevitability*, 1953; *Two Concepts of Liberty*, 1958; *Four Essays on Liberty*, 1969; *Concepts and Categories*, 1978.

HISTORY: *The Hedgehog and the Fox: An Essay on Tolstoy's View of History*, 1953; *Vico and Herder: Two Studies in the History of Ideas*, 1976; *Russian Thinkers*, 1978; *Against the Current: Essays in the History of Ideas*, 1979.

BIOGRAPHY: *Karl Marx, His Life and Environment*, 1939.

MEMOIRS: *Personal Impressions*, 1980.

CORRESPONDENCE: *Washington Despatches 1941-1945: Weekly Reports from the British Embassy*, 1981.

EDITED TEXT: *The Age of Enlightenment: The Eighteenth Century Philosophers*, 1956.

TRANSLATIONS: *First Love*, 1950 (by Ivan Turgenev); *A Month in the Country*, 1981 (by Turgenev).

In writings which have earned for him a position as one of the most remarkable political thinkers of the modern age, Isaiah Berlin has demonstrated an unusual and sweeping grasp of related disciplines, by which learning in intellectual history, moral philosophy, and literary criticism has been summoned to support an essentially liberal view of historical and social values in the twentieth century. Berlin was born on June 6, 1909, in Riga, Latvia, when that country was part of the Russian Empire; his parents were Jewish, and his father, Mendel Berlin, was a prosperous timber merchant. While early impressions of Russian life may have affected Isaiah Berlin's cultural proclivities, in 1920 his family settled in England, and after attending St. Paul's School in London, Berlin received a scholarship which allowed him to enroll at Corpus Christi College, Oxford. He was graduated with first-class honors in two subjects, and in 1932, he became a Fellow of All Souls College. He began his teaching career as a lecturer in philosophy at New College. By that time, he had already published some short articles, including music reviews; among subsequent essays were studies of induction and philosophical verification. While at this stage he did not feel impelled to produce academic writings in quantity, he found the company of other scholars and thinkers both congenial and stimulating. It would seem that the companionship of J. L. Austin, an analytical philosopher, was both diverting and rewarding; when other commitments did not impinge upon them, he and Berlin would spend hours at a time, day and night, pondering the relative merits of logical positivism, linguistic analysis, and other movements that had transformed their discipline. Other concerns were also significant to Berlin, and his full-length work *Karl Marx, His Life and Environment* set forth the philosophical sources for the ideas of the well-known socialist thinker. As an intellectual biography, many readers have regarded this study as provocative and useful, though some critics have reproached Berlin for neglecting the economic elements of Marx's theories.

Berlin spent much of World War II in the United States; in 1941, he was assigned to a branch of the British Information Service in New York, and during the four years that followed, he served as first secretary of the British embassy in Washington, D.C. He was, in effect, charged with evaluating information about political developments and America's intentions during the conflict, and he composed working drafts of the great majority of dispatches that were received in London from this office. The quality of Berlin's reports was widely recognized by members of the wartime government, including, it has been said, Winston Churchill, and indeed, in 1946, Berlin was made Commander, Order of the British Empire. Because of his background and his knowledge of Russian, Berlin was also called into service for a certain period in 1945-1946 at the British embassy in Moscow; during his travels, he met important writers such as Boris Pasternak and Anna Akhmatova. A return visit to the Soviet Union, in 1956, fortified Berlin in his convictions that literary and cultural traditions remained vital matters under the Soviet state. Upon his resumption of university work, Berlin returned to Oxford; in 1949, he became a visiting professor at Harvard University, where he lectured during subsequent terms as well. Other appointments of this sort, which he received intermittently over the years, brought him to Bryn Mawr College, the University of Chicago, Princeton University, and the City University of New York. In 1956, he married Aline de Gunzbourg. At the University of Oxford, he was appointed the Chichele Professor of Political and Social Theory in 1957, and in that year, he was knighted by the British Crown.

Many of Berlin's most influential writings originated as public lectures or as scholarly articles; rather than pursue single lines of investigation in exhaustive depth, he dealt with a series of central questions or evocative themes which in turn cast light upon various adjacent concerns. For that matter, it has been relatively rare for Berlin to undertake any inquiry within the confines of an individual discipline, and many of his most renowned efforts show a markedly eclectic approach both to philosophical and literary trends and to intellectual movements and schools of thought.

The more strictly philosophical element in Berlin's thought has been presented in works such as *Historical Inevitability*, *Two Concepts of Liberty*, and various articles, some of which have been gathered together in later compilations. As his views became more definite, it would appear that, where political theory was concerned, Berlin had grown restive with the more rigid and unyielding categories that had been applied in other areas by linguistic and analytical philosophers. The nature of history and the meaning of ethics and political justice could not, he has maintained, be grasped in the same sense that empirical truths found in the exact sciences may be understood. According to Berlin, it should be possible to reconcile postulates of determinism and historical causation with notions of human responsibility and freedom even where limits on the scope of individual action may be recognized and delimited. Thus even when its plausibility has been acknowledged some accommodation may be made with determinism without undermining concurrent beliefs in some measure of human liberty. By contrasting conceptions of freedom from coercion (that is, negative freedom) with freedom to act as the instrument of one's rational will (positive freedom), Berlin upheld the liberal tradition in Western thought by maintaining that the absence of constraints, rather than the effort to assert collective values, must be accepted in free societies. Further to complicate (though possibly also to enliven) matters, Berlin has expressed a profound skepticism about the extent to which moral principles may resolve differences among such competing principles as liberty, equality, and utility.

While in his philosophical works Berlin had rendered a distinctly positive evaluation of John Stuart Mill and his ideas, other contributions to intellectual history have dealt with thinkers as diverse as Niccolò Machiavelli, Giambattista Vico, and Johann Gottfried Herder; for such figures from earlier ages, Berlin has maintained that fundamentally pluralistic patterns of reasoning and belief may be discerned. Indeed, his interpretation of salient issues in the thought of Vico and Herder, to the effect that both of them, to a greater extent than others of their times, recognized that diversity had characterized the development of human societies, has generally been well received among intellectual historians. In a special category are Berlin's studies of Russian thought and literature. The most famous of such works almost certainly would be his essay on Leo Tolstoy's philosophy of history, which recasts the distinction between monists and pluralists as (in the telling image of the poet Archilochus) the difference between the hedgehog and the fox. This expression, which has now become almost commonplace, could on its most basic level serve, for example, to place on one side Plato and Fyodor Dostoevski and, on the other, Aristotle, William Shakespeare, and Alexander Pushkin; but this dichotomy, which would separate those with a unitary conception from those for whom multiplicity and exceptions were essential to their views, could be applied only with difficulty in some cases, and therein lay the fascination of Tolstoy's own beliefs. He professed a singlemindedness even while his inner nature pursued much more divergent approaches to the apprehension of historical reality. Other works by Berlin have presented strikingly original and artfully articulated assessments of other nineteenth century thinkers, such as Vissarion Belinsky, the literary critic, and Aleksandr Herzen, the social philosopher.

During his later years, Berlin has received many honors and awards, including honorary doctorates from universities in Great Britain, the United States, and Israel; in 1966 he became, for nine years, the president of Wolfson College, Oxford, and he was presented with the Order of Merit in 1971. The appearance of his selected writings in four volumes, which have brought together publications from many periods of his career, subsequently has done much to sustain interest in his ideas; and indeed his autobiographical sketches, which have recorded his thoughts on political figures and academic associates, in an array of essays on individuals as diverse as Franklin D. Roosevelt, Chaim Weizmann, and Aldous Huxley, have, by illuminating the qualities and characteristics of other important personages, cast light as well upon portions of his own life. In recognition of his accomplishments, he has also been honored with the Jerusalem Prize in 1980, the Erasmus Prize in 1983, and, in 1988, the Giovanni Agnelli Prize.

BIBLIOGRAPHICAL REFERENCES: Among those works of which Berlin himself took note in later editions of his works, and which deal wholly or in part with his philosophical positions, are John Passmore, "History, the Individual, and Inevitability," *The Philosophical Review*, LXVIII (1959), 93-102; Marshall Cohen, "Berlin and the Liberal Tradition," *The Philosophical Quarterly*, X (1960), 216-227; David Spitz, "The Nature and Limits of Freedom," *Dissent*, VIII (1961), 78-85; A. S. Kaufman, "Professor Berlin on 'Negative Freedom,'" *Mind*, LXXI (1962), 241-243; L. J. MacFarlane, "On Two Concepts of Liberty," *Political Studies*, XIV (1966), 77-81; and Gerald C. MacCallum, Jr., "Negative and Positive Freedom," *The Philosophical Review*, LXXVI (1967), 312-334. Other responses of noted figures to Berlin's theory of history include Pieter Geyl, "Historical Inevitability (Isaiah Berlin)," in *Debates with Historians*, 1955, 236-241, and a chapter in Morton White, *Religion, Politics and the Higher Learning*, 1959, 75-84. Articles in scholarly journals provide additional assessments, both positive and negative, of Berlin's ideas, including Kas Mazurek, "Isaiah Berlin's Philosophy of History: Structure, Method, Implications," *Philosophy and Social Criticism*, VI (1979), 391-406; Gary Frank Reed, "Berlin and the Division of Liberty," *Political Theory*, VIII (1980), 365-380; Kai Nielsen, "Formulating Egalitarianism: Animadversions on Berlin," *Philosophia*, XIII (1983), 299-316; Richard J. Arneson, "Freedom and Desire," *Canadian Journal of Philosophy*, XV (1985), 425-448; and Perez Zagorin, "Berlin on Vico," *The Philosophical Quarterly*, XXXV (1985), 290-295. For a sympathetic restatement of some important conceptions, see Roger Hausheer, "Berlin and the Emergence of Liberal Pluralism," in *European Liberty: Four Essays on the Occasion of the 25th Anniversary of the Erasmus Prize Foundation*, 1983, 49-81. *The Idea of Freedom: Essays in Honour of Isaiah Berlin*, 1979, edited by Alan Ryan, is a commemorative volume which suggests the extent to which Berlin's thought has been regarded as significant in different disciplines; among the contributors are Peter Gay, Stuart Hampshire, H. L. A. Hart, Franco Venturi, and Morton White.

J. R. Broadus

THOMAS BERNHARD

Born: Heerlen, Netherlands
Date: February 10, 1931

Died: Gmunden, Austria
Date: February 12, 1989

Principal Works

NOVELS: *Frost*, 1963; *Verstörung*, 1967 (*Gargoyles*, 1970); *Das Kalkwerk*, 1970 (*The Lime Works*, 1973); *Korrektur*, 1975 (*Correction*, 1979); *Beton*, 1982 (*Concrete*, 1984); *Der Untergeher*, 1983; *Holzfällen: Eine Erregung*, 1984 (*Woodcutters*, 1987); *Alte Meister*, 1985; *Auslöschung: Ein Zerfall*, 1986.

SHORT FICTION: *Amras*, 1964; *Prosa*, 1967; *Ungenach*, 1968; *An der Baumgrenze: Erzählungen*, 1969; *Ereignisse*, 1969; *Watten: Ein Nachlass*, 1969; *Gehen*, 1971; *Midland in Stilfs: Drei Erzählungen*, 1971; *Der Stimmen-imitator*, 1978.

POETRY: *Auf der Erde und in der Hölle*, 1957; *In hora mortis*, 1957; *Unter dem Eisen des Mondes*, 1958; *Die Irren-die Häftlinge*, 1962; *Contemporary German Poetry*, 1964 (includes selections of his poetry in English translation).

PLAYS: *Ein Fest für Boris*, pr., pb. 1970; *Der Ignorant und der Wahnsinnige*, pr., pb. 1972; *Die Jagdgesellschaft*, pr., pb. 1974; *Die Macht der Gewohnheit*, pr., pb.. 1974 (*The Force of Habit*, 1976); *Der Präsident*, pr., pb. 1975 (*The President*, 1982); *Minetti: Ein Porträt des Künstlers als alter Mann*, pr. 1976; *Die Berühmten*, pr., pb. 1976; *Immanuel Kant*, pr., pb. 1978; *Der Weltverbesserer*, pb. 1979; *Vor dem Ruhestand*, pb. 1979 (*Eve of Retirement*, 1982); *Über allen Gipfeln ist Ruh: Ein deutscher Dichterag um 1980*, pb. 1981; *Am Ziel*, pb. 1981; *Der Schein trügt*, pb. 1983; *Ritter, Dene, Voss*, pb. 1984; *Elisabeth II*, 1987; *Heldenplatz*, pb. 1988.

AUTOBIOGRAPHY: *Die Ursache: Eine Andeutung*, 1975; *Der Keller: Eine Entziehung*, 1976; *Der Atem: Eine Entscheidung*, 1978; *Die Kälte: Eine Isolation*, 1981; *Ein Kind*, 1982; *Wittgensteins Neffe: Eine Freundschaft*, 1982 (*Wittgenstein's Nephew: A Friendship*, 1988); *Gathering Evidence*, 1985 (English translation of the first five autobiographical works listed above; includes *An Indication of the Cause*, *The Cellar: An Escape*, *Breath: A Decision*, *In the Cold*, and *A Child*).

Thomas Bernhard is undoubtedly one of the most prominent Austrian writers of the latter half of the twentieth century. He was born out of wedlock in the Netherlands on February 10, 1931. His mother was the daughter of the Austrian writer Johannes Freumbichler and his father was an Austrian peasant. He spent his first years with his grandparents in Bavaria and then attended a private school in Salzburg, Austria, in 1942. Bernhard was alienated from his abusive mother but felt a close attachment to his grandfather. He eventually contracted a severe lung ailment and spent several years in a sanatorium. Bernhard had begun studying music as a child and continued this first love in 1952 after his recovery. He completed his studies in 1957 and worked for a time in Vienna and Salzburg. In 1965 he bought a farm in Ohlsdorf, Austria, and lived there until his death from heart failure on February 12, 1989. Bernhard never married.

Bernhard's literary reputation was established with his first novel, *Frost* (frost), and his first play, *Ein Fest für Boris* (a party for Boris). His tightly controlled use of language and his complex narrative style of paraphrase and quotation astounded many readers as did his pessimistic and sardonic themes. The characters in his first novel, the young medical student and the insane painter Strauch, are caught within a bleak cycle of obsessive self-reflection that alienates them from their own feelings and from those of others. It is narrated in a series of self-conscious monologues, a style that characterizes much of his narrative work. *Ein Fest für Boris* also establishes the existential themes and ironic dialogue of Bernhard's considerable dramatic writing. It deals with a party held for the crippled Boris and his legless friends, all trapped in wheelchairs and condemned to endless thoughts of suicide.

Gargoyles is similar to *Frost* with its monologues of the prince whose compulsion to think has driven him to insanity. All Bernhard's characters suffer from varying degrees of physical and mental disease. The novel *The Lime Works* continues these primarily existential themes. In this text, Konrad and his crippled wife live alone in an abandoned lime works. Konrad is obsessed with writing the ultimate intellectual treatise on the subject of hearing; he eventually goes insane and murders his wife. *Correction* deals with the genius scholar Roithammer, who constructs a house for his beloved sister; she dies shortly thereafter. He, like Konrad, is obsessed with writing a work about his childhood and commits suicide after destroying the last of the innumerable revisions he vainly attempts. Bernhard has also written a series of five autobiographical works that attempt to capture his childhood and to portray the origins of his worldview. The novel *Concrete* again deals with an alienated intellectual who seeks to write a book—this time about the composer Felix Mendelssohn—but is never quite able to get started. *Woodcutters* is a bitterly satirical and thinly veiled portrait of Viennese society; it provoked a heated controversy upon publication.

Bernhard's numerous plays echo the themes of despair, insanity, and death that inform his narrative works. In *Die Jagdgesellschaft* (the hunting party), a one-armed general is going blind and remains unaware that his beloved forest is being destroyed by an insect infestation. The play *Minetti* depicts an aging and insane actor who is asked to perform *King Lear* and, in an ongoing struggle between himself and the audience, eventually commits suicide. This theme of the integrity and obsessive character of the artist occurs in many of Bernhard's works. The stupidity of the general public is an aspect of Bernhard's often-biting criticism of Austrian, especially Viennese, society. Other Bernhard plays, such as *Die Berühmten* (the famous) and *Der Ignorant und der Wahnsinnige* (the ignorant man and the insane man), are critical of the artist's obsessive demands for technical perfection.

The comedy *Immanuel Kant* is a satirical play that attacks the thought of the well-known eighteenth century German philosopher. Bernhard's last play, *Heldenplatz* (heroes' place), also provoked bitter controversy upon its production at the 1988 Salzburg Festival. It attacks what Bernhard sees as the lingering vestiges of racism and hatred in Austrian society. It deals with a Jewish professor who had emigrated in 1938 when Adolf Hitler and the Nazis were welcomed into Vienna and who, upon his return fifty years later, commits suicide when he sees that anti-Semitic attitudes still exist within Austrian society.

The predominantly existential themes of Bernhard's writings—death, alienation, and the crippling weight of obsessive self-consciousness—make him an heir to Franz Kafka and other modernist authors of the early twentieth century. Such melancholic and morbid preoccupation with death, suicide, and disease has been, for centuries, characteristic of many writers in the Austrian tradition. Life is defined by death for Bernhard, and his writings suggest a deeply rebellious and hostile attitude toward the fact of existence. At times, especially in his vitriolic criticism of his Austrian homeland, he even appears misanthropic. The intensity and insistence of his themes and the singular and complex narrative technique of paraphrase, quotation, and repetition give Bernhard's writings a unique profile in the history of modern European literature.

BIBLIOGRAPHICAL REFERENCES: The following are important book-length collections of articles written in German: *Über Thomas Bernhard*, 1970, edited by Anneliese Botond, contains numerous articles, as does the special issue of the journal *Text und Kritik*, XLII (1974). Bernhard Sorg, *Thomas Bernhard*, 1977, and Herbert Gamper, *Thomas Bernhard*, 1977, are book-length studies that survey the author's life and works up to the mid-1970's. See also D. A. Craig, "The Novels of Thomas Bernhard: A Report," *German Life and Letters*, XXV (1972), 343-353; A. P. Dierick, "Thomas Bernhard's Austrian Neurosis: Symbol of Expedient," *Modern Austrian Literature*, XII (1979), 73-93; Hans Wolfschütz, "Thomas Bernhard: The Mask of Death," in *Modern Austrian Writing: Literature and Society After 1945*, 1980, edited by A. Best and H. Wolfschütz; Kathleen Thorpe, "The Autobiographical Works of Thomas Bernhard," *Acta Germanica*, XIII (1980), 189-200; Martin Esslin, "A Drama of Disease and

Derision: The Plays of Thomas Bernhard," *Modern Drama*, XXXIII (1981), 367-384; Francis Michael Sharp, "Literature as Self-Reflection: Thomas Bernhard and Peter Handke," *World Literature Today*, LV (Autumn, 1981), 603-607; Gitta Honegger, "Wittgenstein's Children: The Writings of Thomas Bernhard," *Theater*, XV (1983), 58-67; Gerald A. Fetz, "The Works of Thomas Bernhard: Austrian Literature?" *Modern Austrian Literature*, XVII (1984), 171-192; John Updike, "Thomas Bernhard's *Concrete*," *The New Yorker*, February 4, 1985, 97-101; and Peter Demetz, "Thomas Bernhard: The Dark Side of Life," in his book *After the Fires: Recent Writing in the Germanies, Austria, and Switzerland*, 1986.

Thomas F. Barry

WENDELL BERRY

Born: Henry County, Kentucky
Date: August 5, 1934

PRINCIPAL WORKS

POETRY: *The Broken Ground*, 1964; *Openings*, 1968; *Findings*, 1969; *Farming: A Hand Book*, 1970; *The Country of Marriage*, 1973; *An Eastward Look*, 1974; *Horses*, 1975; *To What Listens*, 1975; *Sayings and Doings*, 1975; *The Kentucky River*, 1976; *Three Memorial Poems*, 1977; *Clearing*, 1977; *A Part*, 1980; *The Wheel*, 1982; *Collected Poems, 1957-1982*, 1985; *Sabbaths*, 1987.

NOVELS: *Nathan Coulter, 1960*, revised 1985; *A Place on Earth*, 1967, revised 1983; *The Memory of Old Jack*, 1974.

SHORT FICTION: *The Wild Birds: Six Stories of the Port William Membership*, 1986.

ESSAYS: *The Long-Legged House*, 1969; *A Continuous Harmony: Essays Cultural and Agricultural*, 1972; *The Unsettling of America: Culture and Agriculture*, 1978; *Recollected Essays, 1965-1980*, 1980; *The Gift of Good Land*, 1981; *Standing by Words*, 1983; *Home Economics: Eighteen Essays*, 1985.

Wendell Erdman Berry is the outstanding nature poet of his generation. He has also established a respectable reputation as both a novelist and an essayist. Remarkably, he has managed to do all of this while running a working farm on conservationist and recyclist principles and holding a professorship at the University of Kentucky. Born into a family that had farmed in central Kentucky for five generations, Berry attended local schools before entering the nearby University of Kentucky at Lexington in 1952. Already interested in pursuing both writing and agriculture, he concentrated on literature as an academic major, acquiring his bachelor's and master's degrees at Kentucky. Attempting to focus exclusively on an academic career at the time of his marriage to Tanya Amyx in 1957, he accepted a position at New York University. That experience taught him that he could not live without farming, without maintaining the contact with the earth that he found vital. In 1959 he returned to Kentucky, joined the faculty at the university, and began working on one of the family farms.

His writing career began with the publication of the novel *Nathan Coulter* in 1960, first of the Port William series; he revised it extensively, cutting it by almost one-third, for republication in 1985. The events depicted in his first work, like those in all of Berry's work, parallel his own life. The novel tells of the maturation of the title character as he passes from the heedless selfishness of youth to accepting responsibility for taking over the family farm. Woven into the work are the stories of several other people who form the Port William community; by the end, the novel is about all of them, underscoring one of Berry's major themes: that a rural community shares a common spirit rooted in the earth, that through it each individual becomes more than himself. These characters and motifs continue in *A Place on Earth*, which makes this theme even clearer with the absence of a single central character.

In their revised forms both novels have been highly praised, some critics going so far as to call them masterpieces. Along with *The Memory of Old Jack*—which approaches the same themes from the point of view of the oldest member of the community, his memory fusing past and present instances of this common spiritual force—these works are the pinnacle of Berry's art. Unlike his poems and essays, they remain independent of ideology, of shared convictions on the part of writer and reader, for fiction, unlike other forms of writing, creates its own context; that is, fiction depends less than other forms on what might be called the truth factor, or at least the consensus factor. These novels, and the stories in *The Wild Birds*, create a successful and brilliantly integrated world of their own, one ideally suited for the illustration of Berry's abiding convictions about the necessary spiritual interaction of man and his environment.

Whereas Berry's fiction was relatively slow to gain adequate appreciation, his recognition as a poet was early and widespread. The early volumes *The Broken Ground* and *Openings* clearly announce that his business as a poet will be to celebrate farming as a symbol of the union of spirit and man in a cyclic, creative, and life-sustaining act. These themes found receptive readers in the late 1960's, when a number of factors coalesced to promote ecological awareness and the advantages of subsistence farming. Berry was quickly adopted as a poet laureate to the so-called Whole Earth movement; his poems decorated the pages of the *The Whole Earth Catalog*, especially the famous *Last Catalog*. *Farming: A Hand Book* was actually published in both hard- and softbound editions, unprecedented at the time; his contemporary essays also found prestigious publishers.

These early volumes establish Berry's major themes, identical to those of his prose and largely unchanged over a career of three decades: the sacredness of the land; man's interaction with nature as a religious ritual; and this interaction as the source of order, love, harmony, and propriety in man's social acts. These ideas form the substance, and the strength, of *Collected Poems*. Some reviewers call Berry's 1985 collection the document of a major poet, and others find it relatively easy to dismiss the collection as limited and minor. It is certainly true that he has not yet gained the public recognition of the middle-aged Robert Frost or Carl Sandburg as a "people's poet"; none of Berry's poems has passed into the common parlance, as "Stopping by Woods on a Snowy Evening" or "Chicago" has. Further, his work is no longer sought by major publishers. Still, by most measures Berry's achievement is substantial. He works in a variety of lyrical forms, disarming in their apparent simplicity yet reflecting great technical complexities. In this sense his forms are almost always the perfect vehicles for their themes, for they reflect both technical sophistication and earthy simplicity, the natural rhythms of man's interaction with the land.

Berry's essays present the detailed substantiation, the rational explication, of the themes stated imaginatively in the fiction and poetry. His later books appear under less prestigious imprints than his earlier books. Apparently his ideas are perceived as less significant (or less timely and marketable) than they were in the 1960's. Yet his arguments have the same cogency they did then, his demonstrations the same force. Pretending that megalopolises such as New York or Los Angeles can continue to function as they are functioning now is foolish, he seems to say. Berry's proposed solutions are sane and rational—and ultimately convincing. That they are no longer popular does not mean that they are wrong. Berry's work has provoked comparisons with that of Ralph Waldo Emerson and Henry David Thoreau, who were also not always popular. He deserves to be in their company, for they were as intent as he upon the preservation of the environment and the American way of life.

BIBLIOGRAPHICAL REFERENCES: Wendell Berry has not been granted extensive academic attention; most of the secondary literature as of the late 1980's consists of reviews. The most substantial account of his poetry appears in John Lang, "Close Mystery: Wendell Berry's Poetry of Incarnation," *Renascence*, XXV (Summer, 1983), 258-268. A good estimate of his work in general is Noel Perrin, "More Than One Muse," *The New York Times Book Review*, LXXXVIII (December 18, 1983), 8. Various estimates of his poetry are presented by Wyatt Prunty, "Myth, History, and Myth Again," *The Southern Review*, XX (Autumn, 1984), 958-968; Dave Smith, "Collected Poems, 1957-1982," *Poetry*, CXLVII (October, 1985), 40-42; and David Ray, "Heroic, Mock Heroic," *The New York Times Book Review*, XC (November 24, 1985), 28-29. Brian Swarm presents a solid overview in "The Restoration of Vision," *Commonweal*, CXIII (June 6, 1986), 345-346.

James Livingston

MONGO BETI
Alexandre Biyidi

Born: Akometan, Cameroon
Date: June 30, 1932

PRINCIPAL WORKS

NOVELS: *Ville cruelle*, 1954; *Le Pauvre Christ de Bomba*, 1956 (*The Poor Christ of Bomba*, 1971); *Mission terminée*, 1957 (*Mission Accomplished*, 1958; best known as *Mission to Kala*); *Le Roi miraculé: Chronique des Essazam*, 1958 (*King Lazarus*, 1960); *Remember Ruben*, 1973 (English translation, 1980); *Perpetué et l'habitude du malheur*, 1974 (*Perpetua and the Habit of Unhappiness*, 1978); *La Ruine presque cocasse d'un polichinelle: Remember Ruben deux*, 1979 (*Lament for an African Pol*, 1985); *Les Deux Mères de Guillaume Ismael Dzewatama: Futur Cammioneur*, 1982; *La Revanche de Guillaume Ismael Dzewatama*, 1984.

NONFICTION: *Main basse sur le Cameroun: Autopsie d'une décolonisation*, 1972.

Mongo Beti, one of the most important and prolific of African authors, was born in a small village close to the major town of M'Balmayo, Cameroon, on June 30, 1932. As a child, he worked on the cocoa plantations of the area and attended the Catholic missionary school in M'Balmayo. He finished his secondary studies in Yaoundé in 1951. While in Yaoundé, Beti became involved in the Cameroonian independence movement. His political commitment became even stronger at the Sorbonne, to which he received a scholarship in 1951. The stimulus of meeting other African writers and politically committed students (he joined several activist groups while in France) led to the publication of Beti's first short story, "Sans haine et sans amour" (without love or hate), a tale of the Mau Mau uprising in Kenya, in the journal *Présence Africaine* under the pseudonym of Eza Boto.

Under the same name, he published his first novel, *Ville cruelle* (cruel city), in 1954. This account of a country boy who encounters the economic injustices of the colonial system, while suffering from a rather scattered plot, reveals concerns shared by many African authors: the encounter of a traditional culture with the new dominant one, the demoralizing aspects of the colonial African city; and the progressive alienation of one who tries to live in this fragmented society.

Beti's second novel, *The Poor Christ of Bomba*, was published in 1956, under the pseudonym he was to keep, Mongo Beti (child of the Beti). This novel, dealing with the unsuccessful attempts of Father Drumont, a French missionary, to Christianize the people of Bomba, employs the irony and humor which typify Beti's later works. Seen through the eyes of Denis, a fifteen-year-old houseboy devoted to the priest, Drumont's efforts to reform the people of Bomba are shown as futile and ridiculous. The traditional society triumphs over the attempted Western overlay.

This superiority of the traditional culture is seen even more clearly in Beti's third and arguably best novel, *Mission to Kala*. Medza, a young man who has gone to the French schools and failed to get his *baccalauréat*, is sent to retrieve a woman who has gone back to her village in the bush. While there, he realizes that what he has learned in school is useless to him in that milieu: The villagers seem to know how to live with integrity, whereas Medza is now irrevocably placed between two cultures, neither of which he has mastered.

Beti's next novel, and the last one until 1973, was published in 1958. *King Lazarus* deals with the conversion of the chief of the Essazam tribe to Christianity, a change which threatens to disrupt the tribe. It is remarkable, however, that this novel does not depict the villagers favorably; they are interested in maintaining the status quo primarily out of selfish considerations, and the traditional life is seen as far less than noble.

After the publication of *King Lazarus*, Beti moved back to Cameroon, where he was jailed briefly as a result of an altercation with a Greek merchant. He left Cameroon before its independence in 1960 and returned to France to live. His fictional literary output stopped, and he concerned himself with teaching and writing political articles. Only in 1974 did he present a new novel, *Remember Ruben*, important primarily because of the relative dearth of Francophone African literature at the time. But the novel introduced a new type of character: Instead of the man lost between two cultures, the protagonist, Mor-Zamba, is one who has found the possiblity of return. This novel was closely followed by *Perpetua and the Habit of Unhappiness*. The themes are the ones that Beti developed in his later novels: the corruption of officials (now Africans), the sufferings of the innocent, and the constant search for an identity in a fragmented culture.

Uneven though some of Beti's work is, his is an important contribution to world literature. His themes are shared with other contemporary African authors, but this manner and style, marked by ironic detachment and large doses of humor (an element sometimes lacking in works that deal with serious matters), allow him to transcend what he calls "the literature of circumstance." As Thomas Melone says, Beti "has succeeded in inviting us to an impassioned debate on the destiny of man—not necessarily Cameroonian or African man, but man in general."

BIBLIOGRAPHICAL REFERENCES: Although dated, Gerald Moore, *Seven African Writers*, 1962, offers an excellent introduction to Beti's work and its importance in the tumultuous post-independence period in West Africa. A. C. Brench, *The Novelists' Inheritance in French Africa: Writers from Senegal to Cameroon*, 1967, examines the author's worldview in some depth. Eustace Palmer, *The Growth of the African Novel*, 1979, gives the most complete overview of Beti's early and middle work. See also the articles in *Choice*, October, 1976, and January, 1986; *College Language Association Journal*, March, 1976; *Journal of Black Studies*, December, 1976; *The Nation*, October 11, 1965; *New Statesman*, January 30, 1981; *The Times Literary Supplement*, May 15, 1969, and October 29, 1971; and *World Literature Today*, Winter, 1982, and Winter, 1984.

Jean-Pierre Metereau

ADOLFO BIOY CASARES

Born: Buenos Aires, Argentina
Date: September 15, 1914

PRINCIPAL WORKS

LONG FICTION: *La nueva tormenta: O, La vida multiple de Juan Ruteno*, 1935; *La invención de Morel*, 1940 (*The Invention of Morel and Other Stories from "La trama celeste,"* 1964); *Un modelo para la muerte*, 1946 (with Jorge Luis Borges); *Los que aman, odian*, 1946 (with Silvina Ocampo); *El sueño de los héroes*, 1954; *Diario de la guerra del cerdo*, 1969 (*Diary of the War of the Pig*, 1972); *Dormir al sol*, 1973; (*Asleep in the Sun*, 1978); *Plan de evasión*, 1973 (*A Plan for Escape*, 1975); *La aventura de un fotografe en La Plata*, 1985.

SHORT FICTION: *Diecisiete disparos contra lo porvenir*, 1933; *Caos*, 1934; *Luis Greve, muerto*, 1937; *Seis problemas para Isifro Parodi*, 1942 (with Borges; *Six Problems for Don Isidro Parodi*, 1981); *El perjurio de la nieve*, 1945; *Dos fantasías memorables*, 1946 (with Borges); *La trama celeste*, 1948 (in *The Invention of Morel and Other Stories from "La trama celeste,"* 1964); *Las visperas de Fausto*, 1949; *Historia prodigiosa*, 1956; *Guirnalda con amores; cuentos*, 1959; *El lado de la sombra*, 1962; *El gran serafín*, 1967; *Historias de amor*, 1972; *Historias fantásticas*, 1976; *El héroe de las mujeres*, 1978.

EDITED TEXTS: *Antología de la literatura fantástica*, 1940 (with Ocampo and Borges); *Antología poetica argentina*, 1941 (with Ocampo and Borges); *Los mejores cuentos policiales*, 1943 (with Borges); *Los mejores cuentos policiales, segunda series*, 1951 (with Borges); *Cuentos breves y extraordinarios, antología*, 1955 (with Borges; *Extraordinary Tales*, 1973); *Poesia gauchesca*, 1955 (with Borges); *Libro del cielo y del infierno*, 1960 (with Borges).

Adolfo Bioy Casares, known primarily in the United States as a longtime friend and collaborator of Jorge Luis Borges, is a novelist and short-story writer who has been credited with initiating the science-fiction genre into the Argentinian literary landscape. Bioy Casares was the son of Adolfo Bioy, a wealthy landowner, and Marta Casares. He spent his infancy both in the city and on the family ranch in the province of Buenos Aires. Very imaginative as a young boy, Bioy Casares found the night sky, pictures of the dead, and mirrors to be gateways to a marvelous reality. Both terrifying and compelling, the world of the fantastic was nurtured also by his readings. During his high school years he was particularly attracted to mathematics, but his love of writing soon triumphed.

Bioy Casares' first literary work, completed in 1928, was a fantastic thriller titled "Vanidad: O, Una aventura terrorífica" (vanity, or a terrifying adventure). At that time he was discovering nineteenth century Spanish literature, the Bible, Dante, James Joyce, and the Argentinian classics. Comic strips and popular novelettes, however, also appealed to him. Like every upper-class Argentinian, he studied at the University of Argentina Law School; yet, lacking talent in this field, he transferred to the Faculty of Philosophy and Letters but never completed his university studies. He returned to managing his father's ranch instead.

In 1932 Bioy Casares met Jorge Luis Borges. Soon a close personal friendship and lifelong collaborative effort began. Together they created the literary persona "H. Bustos Domecq" as well as an unsuccessful publishing company. During that time Bioy Casares read avidly under Borges' guidance, and aside from the literary influence of Borges himself, such writers as Franz Kafka, Robert Louis Stevenson, Joseph Conrad, Marcel Proust, and Henry James left a lasting impression on him. In 1933 he published a collection of short stories, *Diecisiete disparos contra lo porvenir* (seventeen shots at the future), under a pseudonym. This work was followed in 1935 by *La nueva tormenta* (the new storm), illustrated by the artist and writer Silvina Ocampo, to whom he was married in 1940.

Bioy Casares has consistently renounced his early writing, maintaining that his literary career began in 1940. In that year the author published one of the most widely read literary classics in Argentinian history, the work that is largely responsible for his fame: *The Invention of Morel*. The novel, awarded the Argentinian Municipal Prize in 1941, contains a surrealistic atmosphere that, as critics maintain, bears much resemblance to H. G. Wells's *The Island of Dr. Moreau* (1896). While the novel contains overtones of the gothic, it uses the vehicle of fantasy rather than the supernatural. Within the context of contemporary Argentinian literature, *The Invention of Morel* launched Argentinian science fiction, a genre in which that country has excelled in Latin America.

After publishing volumes of short stories, Bioy Casares returned to the novel in 1969 with a best-seller, *Diary of the War of the Pig*. The novel, radically different from his earlier works, focuses on Argentinian reality and the destiny of man. It is a somber work that portrays a world in which a man has no right to grow old. Yet the novel also contains the elements of hope and love. This novel was followed in 1973 by *Asleep in the Sun*, for which Bioy Casares won the much-coveted Argentinian Society of Writers' Prize. In this novel, the author returns again to the fantastic genre, the gothic, and the pseudoscientific (phrenology). Compared with the bleak irony of *Diary of the War of the Pig*, this novel is one of light humor and displays great imagination in its hallucinatory fantasies.

While some critics maintain that Bioy Casares' plots are overly ambiguous and complex, others believe that his strength lies in his complex humor. Adolfo Bioy Casares will probably best be remembered for his works of the 1940's and 1950's, works that experiment with narrative voice and discourse and that innovatively blend science fiction and fantasy. In these works the author clearly foreshadows the Latin American "new narrative" of the 1970's.

BIBLIOGRAPHICAL REFERENCES: For an interesting and informative interview with Bioy Casares, see Alicia Borinsky's "Adolfo Bioy Casares: 1975," *Modern Language Notes*, XCI (1976), 356-359. A comprehensive overview on Bioy Casares' major works can be found in D. P. Gallagher's "The Novels and Short Stories of Adolfo Bioy Casares," *Bulletin of Hispanic Studies*, CII (1975), 247-266. Suzanne J. Levine's "Parody Island: Two Novels by Bioy Casares," *Hispanic Journal*, IV (1983), 43-49, compares and contrasts *A Plan for Escape* and *The Invention of Morel*. Another article by Levine, titled "Science Versus the Library in *The Island of Dr. Moreau*, *La invención de Morel*, and *Plan de evasión*," *Latin American Literary Review*, IX (1981), 17-26, effectively traces the sources for these two novels in H. G. Wells's *The Island of Dr. Moreau*. See also Thomas C. Meehan, "The Motifs of the Homunculus and the Shrinking Man in Two Versions of a Short Story by Adolfo Bioy Casares," *Hispania*, XXVIII (1985), 79-87; Thomas C. Meehan, "Temporal Simultaneity and the Theme of Time Travel in a Fantastic Story by Adolfo Bioy Casares," *Kentucky Romance Quarterly*, XXX (1983); Thomas C. Meehan, "Temporal Themes in a Fantastic Story by Adolfo Bioy Casares," *Perspectives on Contemporary Literature*, IV (1978), 5-14; Margaret L. Snook, "The Narrator as Creator and Critic in *The Invention of Morel*," *Latin American Literary Review*, XIV (1979), 45-51.

Genevieve Slomski

EARLE BIRNEY

Born: Calgary, Canada
Date: May 13, 1904

PRINCIPAL WORKS

POETRY: *David and Other Poems*, 1942; *Now Is Time*, 1945; *The Strait of Anian: Selected Poems*, 1948; *Trial of a City and Other Verse*, 1952; *Ice Cod Bell or Stone*, 1962; *Near False Creek Mouth*, 1964; *Selected Poems 1940-1966*, 1966; *Memory No Servant*, 1968; *The Poems of Earle Birney*, 1969; *Rag and Bone Shop*, 1971; *The Bear on the Delhi Road; Selected Poems*, 1973; *What's So Big About Green?*, 1973; *The Collected Poems*, 1975; *The Rugging and the Moving Times: Poems New and Uncollected*, 1976; *Alphabeings and Other Seasyours*, 1976; *Ghost in the Wheels: Selected Poems 1920-1976*, 1977; *Fall by Fury and Other Makings*, 1978; *The Mammoth Corridors*, 1980; *Copernican Fix*, 1985.

NOVELS: *Turvey: A Military Picaresque*, 1949 (also known as *The Kootenay Highlander*, revised 1976); *Down the Long Table*, 1955.

SHORT FICTION: *Big Bird in the Bush: Selected Stories and Sketches*, 1978.

LITERARY CRITICISM: *The Creative Writer, 1966; The Cow Jumped Over the Moon: The Writing and Reading of Poetry*, 1972; *Spreading Time: Remarks on Canadian Writing and Writers I: 1926-49*, 1980.

EDITED TEXT: *Twentieth Century Canadian Poetry*, 1953.

Alfred Earle Birney is among the most important Canadian poets of his generation. He was born on May 13, 1904, in Calgary, Northwest Territories (now Alberta), Canada, a rugged region of cattle ranches and wheat farms bordered on the south and west by the Rocky Mountains. His father, Will Birney, was a farmer and later a sign-painter and decorator; his mother, Martha Robertson Birney, was Scottish, with strong musical and religious interests. Both were self-educated. Earle worked as a bank clerk, mosquito controller, paper hanger, and mountain guide before entering the University of British Columbia in 1922. He took an honors B.A. in English in 1926 and, from the University of Toronto, an M.A. in 1927. With an academic specialty in Old and Middle English, he taught at the University of California, Berkeley, and at the University of Utah before taking his Ph.D. degree (with a thesis on Geoffrey Chaucer's irony) in 1936 from the University of Toronto. Birney's verse has been marked from the beginning by a strong sense of the spoliation of beautiful natural places such as Alberta by modern civilization. His verbal ability, no doubt honed by his academic work in medieval English language and poetry, is also evident.

Beginning in 1929, Birney's experiences of the Depression drew him into the leftist political circles of Toronto, where he became known as a Trotskyite. He was active in the Communist Party and the Independent Labour Party. At this time also, a first marriage was annulled, and Birney was subsequently married to Esther Bull (they had one son and were divorced in 1977). Out of these years, personally and socially turbulent, came Birney's first published poems, which began to appear in periodicals in the late 1930's. By 1942 he had assembled his first collection, *David and Other Poems*, which won for him the Governor General's Literary Award for verse and a warm but mixed review by Northrop Frye, who praised the strong, heroic narrative of the title poem but disliked some of Birney's free-verse mannerisms. Thoroughly Canadian and even regional, Birney has always been a modernist, cosmopolitan poet.

With the coming of World War II, Birney went on active duty with the Canadian army in 1942 and served in Belgium and Holland as a major in Personnel Selection. His second volume of verse, *Now Is Time*, appeared in 1945, and his third, *The Strait of Anian*, in 1948. These collections show the influence of his wartime experience. Notable poems include "The

Road to Nijmegen," with its powerful elegiac tone and its sense of the bleak destructions of history: "the bones of tanks/ beside the stoven bridges; old men in the mist/ knifing chips from a boulevard of stumps." In 1952 came *Trial of a City and Other Verse*, in which Birney develops one of his most characteristic themes, the decay and desperate plight of urban civilization. In its long title poem, a drama mingling verse and prose, and bringing witnesses from the present and the past, the city on trial is Vancouver, and the issue is simply whether it should continue to exist. A verdict is scarcely needed: The city is seen as gripped in its own death wish, the capitalist exploitation of men and natural resources.

By the end of the 1940's Earle Birney had been firmly established as a major Canadian poet. During the 1950's he turned aside somewhat from his poetry to work on two novels, to edit an important anthology (*Twentieth Century Canadian Poetry*), and to develop as a scholar and a teacher at the University of British Columbia, where he was a professor of medieval English literature and later Chairman of the Department of Creative Writing. In his first novel, *Turvey*, Birney created a satirical extravaganza about military life which also, in its darker passages, sees war as a metaphor for all human activity. Birney's second novel, *Down the Long Table*, deals with the political milieu in Canada during the 1930's from the perspective of a radical professor whose past is being investigated by a government committee in the McCarthyite atmosphere of the early 1950's.

In the rich outpouring of Canadian verse in the later postwar period, Earle Birney's voice reached its full power. His *Ice Cod Bell or Stone* and *Near False Creek Mouth* were triumphs of a senior poet projecting a more personal tone and content; these poems used the experiences of his many and extended visits to foreign countries. An example is the longish, discursive "Cartagena de Indias" from *Near False Creek Mouth*, with its South American setting, its sympathy with the victims of centuries-long colonial exploitation, and its humor ("Where gems and indigo were sorted/ in shouting arcades/ I am deftly shortchanged"). A sense of history and a strong sense of place mix skillfully with an equally strong sense of himself as outsider in this representative poem. Birney's most important volume of this period was his *Selected Poems* of 1966, judged "the major work of Canada's major poet" by Bruce Nesbitt.

Birney was writer-in-residence at the University of Toronto and the University of Waterloo, Ontario, before retiring from academic life in 1968. Since then, as a free-lance writer and lecturer, Earle Birney has continued to publish extensively and to travel widely. His extended visits to the United States, South America, the Caribbean, Australia, Africa, and Asia have continued to influence his poetry markedly. A convenient index of Earle Birney's growing reputation is his inclusion in the influential *Norton Anthology of Modern Poetry*, in its second edition of 1988, where his long poem about Australia ("Gray Woods Exploding") and two other poems occupy a full ten pages.

BIBLIOGRAPHICAL REFERENCES: "Earle Birney," in *Contemporary Authors*, Vol. 20, 1987, edited by Linda Metzger and Deborah Straub, includes a bibliography and a critical discussion. Peter Aichinger, *Earle Birney*, 1979, is a volume in the Twayne World Authors Series, with a brief biography, criticism of major works, and a secondary bibliography; see also Peter Aichinger, "Earle Birney," in *Canadian Writers and Their Works*, 1985, edited by George Woodcock, Robert Lecker, and others, a good account with an updated biblography. Frank Davey, *Earle Birney*, 1971, and Richard Robillard, *Earle Birney*, also 1971, are good critical studies of Birney's work up to that time. *Essays on Canadian Writing*, XXI (Spring, 1981), is a special issue focusing on Birney's work in poetry, fiction, drama, and politics. See also *Earle Birney*, 1974, edited and introduced by Bruce Nesbitt, a collection of reviews and essays; A. J. M. Smith, "Earle Birney: A Unified Personality," in the same author's *Towards a View of Canadian Letters*, 1973; Peter Edwards, "Politics and Poetry: An Interview with Earle Birney," *Queen's Quarterly*, XC (1983), 122-131; and Lionel Kearns, "Birney's Bear," *Canadian Literature*, XCVII (1983), 172-175. The standard bibliography of Birney's works is

Peter Noel-Bentley, "Earle Birney: An Annotated Bibliography," in *The Annotated Bibliography of Canada's Major Authors*, Vol. 4, 1983, edited by Robert Lecker and Jack David.

James Hazen

ALGERNON BLACKWOOD

Born: Kent, England
Date: March 14, 1869

Died: London, England
Date: December 10, 1951

PRINCIPAL WORKS

SHORT FICTION: *The Empty House*, 1906; *Pan's Garden*, 1912; *Incredible Adventures*, 1914; *The Wolves of God and Other Fey Stories*, 1923 (with Wilfred Wilson); *Tongues of Fire and Other Sketches*, 1924; *The Dance of Death and Other Tales*, 1928; *Tales of the Uncanny and the Supernatural*, 1949.

NOVELS: *Jimbo*, 1909; *The Human Chord*, 1910; *The Centaur*, 1911; *Dudley and Gilderoy: A Nonsense*, 1929.

AUTOBIOGRAPHY: *Episodes Before Thirty*, 1923.

Novelist, short-story writer, and mystic, Algernon Blackwood belongs to that tradition of original writers of the supernatural that includes such luminaries as Edgar Allan Poe, M. R. James, Henry James, Sheridan Le Fanu, and W. W. Jacobs. He was born on March 14, 1869, the son of the Duchess of Manchester and a gentleman usher to Queen Victoria. Since his father was a leading speaker and writer in the Evangelical movement, Algernon was reared in a strict, Evangelical household in which such "natural impulses" as dancing, card playing, and drinking were suppressed. He was educated at a school of the Moravian Brotherhood in the Black Forest of Germany. By the age of seventeen, he had become an introspective young man who studied yoga, theosophy, and Buddhism.

Having displayed no special talent at the University of Edinburgh, Blackwood moved to Canada at the age of twenty. With some financial help from his parents, he invested in a dairy farm, but the business failed. Blackwood then bought a small hotel business in Toronto which also failed six months later. After retreating briefly to the backwoods of Ontario, Blackwood went to New York, where he found work as a third-rate reporter for the *Evening Star*. He hated his reportorial job so much that he escaped from the tedium of his work by detaching himself mentally. Blackwood began reading imaginative literature in French, German, and English in the local libraries. From these books, he derived his interest in the so-called "psychic" regions. He also found relief in the natural world, which he had begun to prefer over the world of social interaction.

In 1899, Blackwood returned to England and became involved in the dried milk business. He began writing professionally when a friend of his submitted several of his stories to a publisher without Blackwood's knowledge. These stories, which Blackwood had not intended to publish, seem to have been written as outlets for those natural desires that his Evangelical upbringing had suppressed. Not only do they reflect the pain and bitterness of his years in New York, but they also express his belief that the average person possesses extraordinary psychic powers. The publication of these stories led to his first book, *The Empty House*, a collection of ghost stories whose primary prupose is to instill fear in the reader. He considered these stories to be preparations for his more serious studies of the psychic world that were to come later.

Blackwood's first novel was an exploration into the second of his major interests: the psychology of children. *Jimbo*, which was actually written before *The Empty House*, deals with the dream of a child who has been knocked unconscious by a cow. Blackwood's next novel, *The Human Chord*, also centers on a child's fantasy world. After finishing this book, Blackwood moved to Switzerland, where he could live more cheaply.

Blackwood's third major interest, nature's relationship to man, received artistic expression in his next two novels. In 1911, Blackwood published what is considered to be his most successful novel: *The Centaur*. His conviction that all nature is filled with psychic agencies is evident in a collection of nature stories called *Pan's Garden*. The most notable of these is

"The Man Whom the Trees Loved," a hundred-page story based on the hypothesis that plants possess a humanlike consciousness. In both of these books, Blackwood drew heavily upon contemporary psychology to construct his hypothesis that human beings are themselves the source of the psychic phenomena that frighten them.

During the 1920's, Blackwood arrived at a more personal position toward the supernatural. He published several collections of short stories, such as *The Wolves of God and Other Fey Stories* and *The Dance of Death and Other Tales*. His most ambitious novel of the 1920's, *Dudley and Gilderoy*, is free of the supernatural excesses that had marred some of his earlier works. At this time, Blackwood was a member of Hermetic Order of the Golden Dawn, a society devoted to the study of magic, whose members included literary figures such as William Butler Yeats. As a result of Blackwood's investigations into the occult and mysticism, his work reflected a sincerity that set him apart from other writers of ghost stories. He was beginning to view his stories and novels as vehicles through which he could convey his views about immortality and the psychic world.

Even though Blackwood did not write much more than sketches of his travels in the last decade of his life, he became more well-known than he had ever been before. With the publication of *Tales of the Uncanny and the Supernatural*, a collection of twenty-two of his most famous stories, Blackwood finally achieved the kind of recognition that had hitherto escaped him. He gained even more recognition by reading his stories on radio and television. Ironically, Blackwood became known as the "Ghost Man," even though he had struggled for years to be known as a student of psychic phenomenon. He died in London on December 10, 1951, and his ashes were scattered at Saanen-Moser in Switzerland. Despite the success that he enjoyed at the end of his life, Blackwood felt that he had not really achieved his goals as a writer. He wanted to be taken seriously as a novelist, although it is as a short-story writer that he is remembered today. In most of his stories, he attempted to show the reader the way toward spiritual wholeness by making him aware of the psychic world.

BIBLIOGRAPHICAL REFERENCES: Derek Hudson, "A Study of Algernon Blackwood," *Essays and Studies of the English Association*, XIV, 102-114, is the best chronological study of Blackwood's life and work. For further study, see *Supernatural Fiction Writers: Fantasy and Horror*, Vol. 2, 1985, edited by E. F. Bleiler, which offers an in-depth critical analysis of several of Blackwood's representative works. See also "Elsewhere and Otherwise," *Time*, December 17, 1951, 98-100; "A. Blackwood, 82, British Novelist," *The New York Times*, December 11, 1951, 33; *Twentieth Century Authors*, 1942; edited by Stanley J. Kunitz; and J. Russell Reaver, "From Seed to Fruit: The Doubling of Psychic Landscapes in Algernon Blackwood's *The Centaur*," *Romantist*, nos. 4/5 (1980/1981), 55-58.

Alan Brown

ERNST BLOCH

Born: Ludwigshafen, Germany
Date: July 8, 1885

Died: Tübingen, West Germany
Date: August 3, 1977

PRINCIPAL WORKS

PHILOSOPHY: *Geist der Utopie*, 1918 (*Spirit of Utopia*, 1970); *Thomas Münzer als Theologe der Revolution*, 1921; *Durch die Wüste*, 1923; *Spuren*, 1930; *Erbschaft dieser Zeit*, 1935; *Das Prinzip Hoffnung*, 1954-1959 (*The Principle of Hope*, 1986); *Verfremdungen*, 1962, 1964 (partially translated as *A Philosophy of the Future*, 1970); *Atheismus im Christentum: Zur Religion des Exodus und des Reichs*, 1968 (*Atheism in Christianity: The Religion of the Exodus and the Kingdom*, 1972); *Über Karl Marx*, 1968 (*On Karl Marx*, 1971); *Subjekt-Objekt*, 1971; *Vorlesungen zur Philosophie der Renaissance*, 1972; *Zur Philosophie der Musik*, 1974; *Ästhetik des Vor-Scheins*, 1974.

The unique quality of the Marxist philosopher Ernst Bloch is his unrelenting quest to fuse theory and practice. Refusing to make a sharp distinction between philosophy on the one hand and the arts on the other, he saw his writings as political acts pointing toward a society without oppression.

Ernst Bloch, the son of Max and Berta Bloch, was born into the proletarian community of Ludwigshafen on July 8, 1885. In 1905 Bloch took up the study of philosophy and German literature at the University of Munich; he then attended the University of Würzburg, where he studied music, physics, and experimental psychology. In Berlin he became interested in sociology and was befriended by Georg Simmel, whose interests ranged from philosophy, sociology, and metaphysics to poetry. Even more important for his intellectual development was his friendship with the critic and philosopher Georg Lukács. Through Lukács Bloch was introduced to the sociologist Max Weber. In Zurich he met Walter Benjamin, an essayist and critic. Under the influence of these leading figures of intellectual life in Germany at that time he produced *Spirit of Utopia*.

During the 1920's Bloch turned toward Marxism, and his second major work, *Thomas Münzer als Theologe der Revolution* (Thomas Münzer as theologian of revolution), combined Marxist thought with religious mysticism. When the Nazi Party took power in 1933, Bloch, who was immediately blacklisted, left Germany to seek exile in Switzerland, where he completed *Erbschaft dieser Zeit* (heritage of this time), an exploration of the attraction of Fascism. He maintained that "progress" had been accompanied by a severe disorientation of the lower classes, which, in turn, created gaps in people's lives and produced a longing for the past. With his categories of synchronism and nonsynchronism, he explained the failure of modernism, which had left the masses vulnerable to the lure of Fascism.

After his expulsion from Switzerland, Bloch and his wife, Karola, spent brief periods in exile in France, Austria, and Czechoslovakia and finally settled in the United States. There, his most important work, *The Principle of Hope*, was written. As an unorthodox Marxist thinker, Bloch believed that "anticipatory illumination" provides the possibility to transform the material base through the superstructure. Art illuminates the missing qualities of contemporary life as they are experienced by the individual artist.

In 1949 Bloch received an offer to assume the chairmanship of the philosophy department at the University of Leipzig. He accepted the position under the condition that he be granted absolute freedom to teach independently from the official party line of the new Communist Party of the German Democratic Republic. In 1956, encouraged by Nikita Khrushchev's criticism of Stalinism, Bloch considered the time to be ripe for more democratic reforms within the Eastern Bloc and began to criticize the state openly. In 1957 he was prevented from lecturing and forced into retirement. He turned to lecturing in the Federal Republic of Germany, and in the summer of 1961, when the German Democratic Republic officially closed itself off from the West through the Berlin Wall, the Blochs decided not to return.

In the East he was consequently denounced as a traitor, and in West Germany he was ridiculed for having had "hope" in the Communist system and criticized for his defense of Stalin. His supporters were able to secure for him a professorship of philosophy at the University of Tübingen, where he became one of the spiritual leaders of the protest movement which dominated West German university life during the 1960's.

Although he was half blind during the last years of his life, he finished the revision for the seventeen-volume edition of his completed works. Bloch's wide-ranging interests and his expertise in several disciplines were deciding factors in his personal and political development. He remained unconventional and provocative and was not afraid to revise his own thoughts in the light of new developments.

BIBLIOGRAPHICAL REFERENCES: Wayne Hudson's *The Marxist Philosophy of Ernst Bloch*, 1982, is still the most comprehensive study of Bloch's philosophy in English. A useful bibliographical tool (ending in 1970) is provided by Thomas E. Wren, "An Ernst Bloch Bibliography for English Readers," *Philosophy Today*, XIV (Winter, 1970), 272-273. See also Jürgen Habermas, "Ernst Bloch: A Marxist Romantic," *Salmagundi*, X/XI (Fall, 1969/Winter, 1970), 311-325; Manfred Buhr, "Critique of Ernst Bloch's Philosophy of Hope," *Philosophy Today*, XIV (Winter, 1971), 259-271; and Harold H. Oliver, "Hope and Knowledge," *Cultural Hermeneutics*, II (May, 1974), 75-87.

Karin A. Wurst

ALLAN BLOOM

Born: Indianapolis, Indiana
Date: September 14, 1930

Principal Works

SOCIAL CRITICISM: *The Closing of the American Mind: How Higher Education Has Failed Democracy and Impoverished the Souls of Today's Students*, 1987.

LITERARY CRITICISM: *Shakespeare's Politics*, 1964 (with Harry V. Jaffa).

TRANSLATIONS: *Politics and the Arts: Letter to M. d'Alembert on the Theatre*, 1960 (by Jean-Jacques Rousseau); *The Republic of Plato*, 1968; *Émile: Or, On Education*, 1979 (by Rousseau).

Allan David Bloom provoked a firestorm of controversy in the United States with the publication of *The Closing of the American Mind* in 1987. His spirited critique of the effects of relativism on university students touched off continuing debate about the methods and content of higher education. Bloom was born in Indianapolis, Indiana, on September 14, 1930, the son of Allan and Malvina (née Glasner) Bloom, both social workers, both Jewish immigrants. By 1946 the family had moved to Chicago, where young Allan enrolled in a liberal arts program, with a strong emphasis on the classic texts of Western civilization, at the University of Chicago.

Earning his Ph.D. from the university in 1955, he remained as a lecturer in liberal arts until he moved to Yale University in 1962, where he taught political science for a year. In Chicago, Bloom had been profoundly influenced by the head of the university's political science department, German refugee Leo Strauss (1899-1973). Of central concern to Strauss, and thus to Bloom, was the nature of the political regime necessary to promulgate the unchanging virtues elucidated, in part, by Plato and whether such a regime was truly compatible with democratic pluralism.

Bloom's first book, a translation of a long letter on politics and the arts by Jean-Jacques Rousseau, written in 1758, was published in 1960. His second book, a collection of essays on William Shakespeare called *Shakespeare's Politics*, was written with De Paul University professor Harry V. Jaffa and published in 1964, the year Bloom received tenure at Cornell University. Another translation, this time of Plato's *Republic*, followed in 1968. Bloom emphasized that his was a literal translation so that the reader would not mistake the ancient Greek conception of virtue with the rather flaccid modern notion of "values" disinforming other, sloppier, translations.

By 1969 Cornell was swept up in a tide of student unrest, abating only (to Bloom's disgust) when the Cornell administration capitulated to a group of armed students and eliminated traditional requirements in favor of more "relevant" courses. Bloom resigned from Cornell in 1970, teaching political science for two years at the University of Toronto until he was felled by a heart attack when he was forty-one years old. He spent his recuperation time translating Rousseau's *Émile: Or, On Education*, written in 1762.

At the invitation of the Committee on Social Thought at the University of Chicago, Bloom returned to Illinois to join the faculty as a full professor in 1979. His critique of the modern American university, in a cover story for the conservative magazine *National Review* (December 10, 1982), motivated Nobel Prize-winning novelist Saul Bellow, Bloom's colleague on the committee, to encourage Bloom to expand his thoughts into a book. The result was the publication of *The Closing of the American Mind*, with an introduction by Bellow. The book rocketed to best-seller status in hardcover and later in paperback; the ten-thousand-dollar advance paid to Bloom by publisher Simon and Schuster was more than repaid. Bloom himself, a lifelong bachelor, became a millionaire.

Early reviews of the book were almost universally laudatory; a second wave of reviews questioned Bloom's interpretation of Plato and other philosophers and their influence on the American ethos. A third wave of reviews, mostly by friends of Bloom's thesis, faulted him for his adherence to the controversial views of Leo Strauss but praised him for raising public concern over the plight of higher education in the United States.

In 1988, Bloom announced the formation of a summer institute to teach the "great books" to a small group of college students. Bloom became an adjunct scholar of the American Enterprise Institute for Public Policy Research (a conservative think tank) in 1981; he also became codirector of the John M. Olin Center for Inquiry into the Theory and Practice of Democracy, which provides student fellowships at the University of Chicago and grants for visiting professors. In 1987 Bloom received the Prix Jean-Jacques Rousseau awarded by the city of Geneva, Switzerland.

BIBLIOGRAPHICAL REFERENCES: Werner J. Dannhauser, *The American Spectator*, October, 1988, 17-20, offers a summary of the most important critical reviews of *The Closing of the American Mind*. Philosopher Richard Rorty takes issue with Bloom and Strauss, and professor of government Harvey Mansfield, Jr., defends them, in *The New Republic*, CXCVIII (April 4, 1988), 28. Conservative philosopher Sidney Hook reconsiders Bloom's best-seller and finds much to disagree with in *The American Scholar*, Winter, 1989, 123-135. James Atlas, writing in *The New York Times Magazine*, January 3, 1988, 12, offers a personal portrait of Bloom and his colleagues at the University of Chicago. One of the best short introductions to the thought of Leo Strauss is by Nathan Tarcov and Thomas L. Pangle, *History of Political Philosophy*, 1987, edited by Leo Strauss and Joseph Cropsey. Bloom provides the essay on Rousseau.

Dan Barnett

HAROLD BLOOM

Born: New York, New York
Date: July 11, 1930

PRINCIPAL WORKS

LITERARY CRITICISM: *Shelley's Mythmaking*, 1959; *The Visionary Company: A Reading of English Romantic Poetry*, 1961, revised 1971; *Blake's Apocalypse: A Study in Poetic Argument*, 1963; *Yeats*, 1970; *The Ringers in the Tower: Studies in Romantic Tradition*, 1971; *The Anxiety of Influence: A Theory of Poetry*, 1973; *A Map of Misreading*, 1975; *Kabbalah and Criticism*, 1975; *Poetry and Repression: Revisionism from Blake to Stevens*, 1976; *Figures of Capable Imagination*, 1976; *Wallace Stevens: The Poems of Our Climate*, 1976; *Agon: Towards a Theory of Revisionism*, 1982; *The Breaking of the Vessels*, 1982; *Poetics of Influence*, 1986; *Ruin the Sacred Truths*, 1989.

NOVEL: *The Flight of Lucifer: A Gnostic Fantasy*, 1979.

One of the most influential literary critics of the late twentieth century, Harold Bloom has contributed to a renewed appreciation for the Romantic poets and to a clearer understanding of the relationship between writers and their predecessors. The son of William and Paula Lev Bloom, he was born in New York City on July 11, 1930. At Cornell University, where he received his B.A. in 1951, he studied under M. H. Abrams, a scholar of Romanticism, though Bloom claims that his own interest in this period antedated his college years. From Cornell, Bloom went to Yale University, receiving his Ph.D. in 1955. His dissertation on Percy Bysshe Shelley won for Bloom the John Addison Porter Prize in 1956 and became his first book, *Shelley's Mythmaking*.

Hired by Yale, he rose quickly through the academic ranks, becoming De Vane Professor of the Humanities in 1974 and more recently Sterling Professor. His work has been widely recognized: He has received a Guggenheim Fellowship (1962-1963), the Melville Cane Award (1971) for *Yeats*, the Morton Dauwen Zabel Award from the National Institute and American Academy of Arts and Letters (1981), and a MacArthur Foundation Award (1985). A prolific author of scholarly books and articles, he has written literally hundreds of introductions to various works and continues to arouse both admiration and criticism.

Even in his earliest work he broke with the conventions of the day. By the mid-1950's the New Critics (such as Cleanth Brooks and Lionel Trilling) had elevated the Metaphysical poets of the seventeenth century to the first rank of literature and relegated the Romantics to a lower position, because the latter's works seemed to lack irony. Drawing on Shelley's literary theories, Bloom sought to rehabilitate the nineteenth century writers by stressing their imaginative qualities. No longer could critics dismiss William Wordsworth and his followers as simple nature poets; Bloom, relying heavily on the writings of Martin Buber, showed that for the Romantics nature was antithetical, not sympathetic. *Shelley's Mythmaking* maintains that there is an I-Thou relationship between the imagination and its original vision, an I-It relationship between the imagination and the poetry it creates. Because the product can never match the initial inspiration, the poet is doomed to failure—and renewed effort.

Beginning in 1970 with *Yeats*, and more explicitly in *The Anxiety of Influence*, Bloom broke even more sharply with the prevailing critical orthodoxy. Writers such as M. H. Abrams and Newman Ivey White had defended the Romantics in the 1940's and 1950's; thus, Bloom's position, while dissenting from the majority, was not unique. Virtually everyone in 1970, though, maintained that the poet draws strength from the literary tradition. Following the observation of T. S. Eliot in "Tradition and the Individual Talent" (1920), received opinion agreed that "we shall often find that not only the best, but the most individual parts of [a poet's] work may be those in which the dead poets . . . assert their immortality most vigorously," that "the progress of an artist is a continual self-sacrifice, a continual extinction of personality." Abandoning Buber and rejecting Eliot, Bloom argued that each new writer, if he is "strong" (which for Bloom equals good and original) rather than "weak" (that is, derivative), seeks to assert his identity by misreading his predecessors and thus creating a space for himself in the world of literature.

The notion that the past weighs heavily on the present also appears in Walter Jackson Bate's *The Burden of the Past and the English Poet* (1970), but Bloom elaborated on the concept and developed a vocabulary of strategies to describe what he calls "misprision," or misreading. According to Bloom, there are six methods that writers use to overcome their predecessors, and to each he has given a Greek name, which makes his theory seem more esoteric than it might otherwise appear. These terms are "clinamen," swerving to avoid the predecessor; "tessera," claiming to complete what the predecessor left unfinished; "kenosis," insisting on discontinuity with the predecessor to stress one's own originality; "daemonization," finding something in the predecessor's work that the earlier writer supposedly did not know was there (as when William Blake said that John Milton was of Satan's party in *Paradise Lost* but did not know it); "askesis," rejecting the predecessor; and "apophrodes"—the return of the dead—making the modern writer the precursor rather than the follower. Elsewhere he has spoken of these devices as "crossings" and described three strategies for moving from limitation to representation, from confrontation with the predecessor to discovery and originality.

Rejecting the old humanist view that literature has meaning outside its relation to other works of literature (for example, Bloom denies that a poem is a direct response to life and insists that it always responds instead to the poems that have preceded it), he is equally unhappy with the current deconstructionist theories that regard literature as rhetoric, originating in and stumbling against linguistic constructs. For the deconstructionist, in the beginning is the metaphor (or trope). Bloom's analysis stresses the psychoanalytic rather than the linguistic, so that for him in the beginning is the maker of the metaphor, who seeks to create a place for himself in the world of letters by escaping from the tradition which traps him. Writing, Bloom believes, is an Oedipal struggle, an agon, against the past that can be embodied in an entire tradition or a particular predecessor. Each author re-creates a literary past through his own misprision and then rebels against it if he is to emerge as a strong writer.

Bloom's language, which is both violent and esoteric, has drawn criticism. So, too, has his elitist division of writers into the many who are weak—and for Bloom this category includes such revered names as T. S. Eliot—and the few who are strong. Deconstructionists object to his insistence on the primacy of the writer rather than the text; his view that the writer can never free himself from struggle strikes others as overly pessimistic, and his equating the critic with the poet because both are engaged in acts of interpretation seems hubristic to many. However bizarre or incomprehensible his theories may seem, though, his close readings of writers such as Shelley, William Butler Yeats, and Wallace Stevens (of whom he was an early champion) invariably illuminate their works, and he has helped shape the nature of the contemporary critical debate. One may dissent from his approach or conclusions, but he cannot be ignored.

BIBLIOGRAPHICAL REFERENCES: Jean-Pierre Mileur, *Literary Revisionism and the Burden of Modernity*, 1985, explores the relationship of Bloom's theories to gnosticism and history and examines his reading of the Romantics. David Fite, *Harold Bloom: The Rhetoric of Romantic Vision*, 1985, traces the development of Bloom's criticism and places him in the context of current literary theories. Jerome J. McGann, "Romanticism and the Embarrassment of Critical Tradition," *Modern Philology*, LXX (February, 1973), 243-257, discusses Bloom's often-violent language and maintains that Bloom is most effective in dealing with poets such as Wordsworth and Blake, who are in crisis. Michael Wood, "In the Literary Jungle," *The New York Review of Books*, XXII (April 17, 1975), 15-18, focuses on the Freudian element of

Bloom's criticism, especially his view of poetry as aggression. Helen Vendler, "The Poetics of Power," *The New Republic*, CLXXXVI (February 17, 1982), 31-36, examines *Agon: Towards a Theory of Revisionism*, claiming that Bloom is trying to create nothing less than a general theory of imagination. Marvin Mudrick, "Bloom, Bloom, Go Out the Room!" *Harper's*, CCLXV (August, 1982), 65-70, attacks Bloom's theories, especially those in *The Breaking of the Vessels*. Largely unsympathetic, too, is Frank Lentricchia's "Harold Bloom: The Spirit of Revenge," in *After the New Criticism*, 1980, though Lentricchia concedes Bloom's significance. Leon Wieseltier, "Summoning Up the Kabbalah," *The New York Review of Books*, XXIII (February 19, 1976), 27-31, surveys Bloom's theories as it reviews *Kabbalah and Criticism*. Robert Moynihan, "Harold Bloom," in *A Recent Imagining*, 1986, allows Bloom to present his own views on literary theory, modern critics, and Judaism. See also Peter de Bolla, *Harold Bloom: Towards Historical Rhetorics*, 1988.

Joseph Rosenblum

HEINRICH BÖLL

Born: Cologne, Germany
Date: December 21, 1917

Died: Merten, West Germany
Date: July 16, 1985

PRINCIPAL WORKS

NOVELS AND NOVELLAS: *Der Zug war pünklich*, 1949 (*The Train Was on Time*, 1956); *Wo warst du, Adam?*, 1951 (*Adam, Where Art Thou?*, 1955); *Nicht nur zur Weihnachtszeit*, 1952; *Und sagte kein einziges Wort*, 1953 (*Acquainted with the Night*, 1954); *Haus ohne Hüter*, 1954 (*Tomorrow and Yesterday*, 1957); *Das Brot der frühen Jahre*, 1955 (*The Bread of Our Early Years*, 1957); *Billard um halbzehn*, 1959 (*Billiards at Half-Past Nine*, 1961); *Ansichten eines Clowns*, 1963 (*The Clown*, 1965); *Ende einer Dienstfahrt*, 1966 (*End of a Mission*, 1967); *Gruppenbild mit Dame*, 1971 (*Group Portrait with Lady*, 1973); *Die verlorene Ehre der Katharina Blum: Oder, Wie Gewalt entstehen und wohin sie führen kann*, 1974 (*The Lost Honor of Katharina Blum: Or, How Violence Develops and Where It Can Lead*, 1975); *Fürsorgliche Belagerung*, 1979 (*The Safety Net*, 1982); *Der Vermächtnis*, 1982 (*A Soldier's Legacy*, 1985); *Frauen vor Flusslandschaft*, 1985.

SHORT FICTION: *Wanderer, kommst du nach Spa . . .* , 1950 (*Traveller, If You Come to Spa*, 1956); *Unberechenbare Gäste*, 1956; *Doktor Murkes gesammeltes Schweigen und andere Satiren*, 1958; *Entfernung von der Truppe*, 1964 (*Absent Without Leave and Other Stories*, 1965); *Eighteen Stories*, 1966; *Children Are Civilians Too*, 1970; *Die Verwundung und andere frühe Erzählungen*, 1983 (*The Casualty*, 1986); *The Stories of Heinrich Böll*, 1986.

NONFICTION: *Irisches Tagebuch*, 1957 (*Irish Journal*, 1967); *Brief an einen jungen Katholiken*, 1961; *Frankfurter Vorlesungen*, 1966; *Hierzulande*, 1967; *Aufsätze, Kritiken, Reden*, 1967; *Neue politische und literarische Schriften*, 1973; *Schwierigkeiten mit der Brüderlichkeit*, 1976; *Einmischung erwünscht*, 1977; *Missing Persons and Other Essays*, 1977; *Spuren der Zeitgenossenschaft*, 1980; *Gefahren von falschen Brüdern*, 1980; *Was soll aus dem Jungen bloss werden? Oder, Irgendwas mit Büchern*, 1981 (*What's to Become of the Boy? Or, Something to Do with Books*, 1984); *Vermintes Gelände*, 1982; *Bild, Bonn, Boenisch*, 1984.

POETRY: *Gedichte*, 1972; *Gedichte mit Collagen von Klaus Staeck*, 1980.

PLAY: *Ein Schluck Erde*, pb. 1962.

MISCELLANEOUS: *Heinrich Böll Werke*, 1977-1979.

Heinrich Theodor Böll was one of the most significant German writers of the postwar era. He was born in Cologne on December 21, 1917, to Victor and Marie Hermanns Böll, the eighth of eight children. He was educated in Catholic elementary and secondary schools.

The years of Böll's youth coincided with some of the grimmest years in modern German history—the inflated economy of the mid-1920's, the Great Depression of the early 1930's, the rise to power of the Nazis, and the early years of the Third Reich. Victor Böll lost his business in the Great Depression. The family's subsequent loss of middle-class status without clearly identifying with the working class caused an identity crisis that remained with Heinrich Böll and influenced his writing.

In 1937, Böll completed his secondary education and became an apprentice to a book dealer in Bonn. He was required to perform compulsory labor service during 1938 and 1939, after which he enrolled at the University of Cologne to study German and classical philology and literature. In 1939, he was drafted into the German army, and he served as an infantryman until taken prisoner by the Americans in 1945.

Böll returned to his native Cologne in November, 1945, together with his wife, Annemarie Cech, whom he had married in 1942. Their first son, Christoph, died shortly after birth during the harsh winter of 1945. Upon his return to Cologne, Böll began to write short stories. In an interview during the early 1960's, he admitted that he had always wanted to be a writer. He said that he wrote perhaps six novels before the war. All were either burned or lost during the war.

The first of Böll's writings, two short stories, were published in 1947, in the periodical *Karussell*. These, together with other short stories published in various periodicals and newspapers, appeared together in 1950 under the title, *Traveller, If You Come to Spa*. In 1953, Böll published his third novel, *Acquainted with the Night*, and with it he achieved financial independence.

From 1949 until his death in 1985, a steady stream of literary product flowed from his pen. Early in his career he was recognized as the most successful postwar German author. His popularity in the West was matched, and perhaps even surpassed, by his popularity in Eastern Europe and the Soviet Union. Böll criticized the materialism of postwar West German society not only in his fictional works but also in numerous essays and as a political activist. He opposed German rearmament in the 1950's, criticized the Social Democratic Party for its official abandonment of Marxist ideology in 1959, campaigned for Willy Brandt in 1969, defended the terrorist Baader-Meinhof gang in 1972, publicly left the Catholic church in 1976, and participated in a peace demonstration in Bonn in 1981. The Left hailed him as the "conscience of the nation"; the Right condemned him as a literary hack.

Recognition of Böll's literary genius came early in his career and was sustained throughout. Many international honors were bestowed upon him during his lifetime, including the Nobel Prize in Literature for 1972. He died on July 16, 1985, at his home in the Eifel Mountains near Bonn.

Böll's short stories and novels are characterized by a condemnation of militarism and war, a criticism of postwar materialism, and frequent allusions to the moral failure of Christianity and the erosion of the traditional family unit. Many critics believe that the central theme running through all Böll's writings is his belief that true Christianity is the natural foe of capitalism. In his war stories, Böll portrayed war as an absurdity, a waste of time as well as lives. His stories about postwar Germany criticize a society in which returning veterans are unable to find their niche, while former Nazis prosper from the postwar economic boom. Throughout, the institutionalized Catholic church is portrayed as hypocritical and corrupt, having capitulated to economic and political expediency at the expense of its true values.

BIBLIOGRAPHICAL REFERENCES: *A Student's Guide to Böll*, 1972, by Enid MacPherson, although dated, is still a good starting place for students. Robert C. Conrad, *Heinrich Böll*, 1981, provides a brief biographical sketch followed by an analysis of his short stories and novels. Paul Konrad Kurz gives particular attention to Böll's criticism of institutional Christianity in chapter 1 of *On Modern German Literature*, Vol. 4, 1971, translated by Mary Frances McCarthy. W. E. Yuill, "Heinrich Böll," in *Essays on Contemporary German Literature*, 1966, edited by Brian Keith-Smith, analyzes Böll's fiction with a view toward understanding him as a "Christian moralist." Wilhelm Johannes Schwartz, *Heinrich Böll, Teller of Tales: A Study of His Works and Characters*, 1969, translated by Elizabeth Henderson, and Walter Herbert Sokel, "Perspective and Dualism in the Novels of Böll," in *The Contemporary Novel in German: A Symposium*, 1967, edited by Robert R. Heitner, both stress the theme of alienation in Böll's work. *Postwar German Literature: A Critical Introduction*, 1970, by Peter Demetz, and *Heinrich Böll: Withdrawal and Re-Emergence*, 1973, by James Henderson Reid, assess Böll's place with respect to his contemporaries and the German narrative tradition. See also *Heinrich Böll on His Death: Selected Obituaries and the Last Interview*, 1985, translated by Patricia Crampton, and Erhard Friedrichsmeyer, *The Major Works of Heinrich Böll: A Critical Commentary*, 1974.

Paul R. Waibel

ROBERT BOLT

Born: Sale, England
Date: August 15, 1924

PRINCIPAL WORKS

PLAYS: *A Man for All Seasons*, pr. 1954 (radio play), pr. 1960 (staged); *The Last of the Wine*, pr. 1955 (radio play), pr. 1956 (staged); *The Critic and the Heart*, pr. 1957; *Flowering Cherry*, pr. 1957; *The Tiger and the Horse*, pr. 1960; *Gentle Jack*, pr. 1963; *The Thwarting of Baron Bolligrew*, pr. 1965; *Brother and Sister*, pr. 1967; *Vivat! Vivat Regina!*, pr. 1970; *State of Revolution*, pr., pb. 1977.

SCREENPLAYS: *Lawrence of Arabia*, 1962; *A Man for All Seasons*, 1966; *Doctor Zhivago*, 1966; *Ryan's Daughter*, 1970; *Lady Caroline Lamb*, 1972; *The Bounty*, 1984; *The Mission*, 1986.

Robert Oxton Bolt is an intelligent craftsman and a traditional playwright who relies on history for his subject matter. His fame rests as much on his highly successful screenplays as on his stage plays. He was born in Sale, Manchester, the son of a shopkeeper. He was educated there, and in 1940 he began a career as an insurance agent. While still in his teens, he joined the Communist Party, an affiliation he later rejected, deciding that it had "nothing to do with democracy or freedom." In 1943, he began his studies in economics at Manchester University. From 1943 to 1946 he served in the Royal Air Force, stationed in South Africa and the Gold Coast. After World War II, he returned to Manchester University, receiving a degree in history in 1949. After earning a teaching certificate at University College, Exeter, he taught in Devon and Millfield. During his teaching career, he began writing plays for children and also a variety of radio plays for the British Broadcasting Corporation.

The Critic and the Heart was his first play for the stage, and it followed the plot and structure of W. Somerset Maugham's play *The Circle* (1921). *Flowering Cherry*, a domestic drama, was Bolt's first success. His protagonist, a dissatisfied insurance salesman, is, according to Bolt, a "man who substitutes violent words for action." The play, which is reminiscent of the work of Anton Chekhov, is conventionally naturalistic. *The Tiger and the Horse* has as its protagonist a university don who is committed to a philosophy of withdrawal. His neglect drives his wife mad, and only when he can involve himself in her care can he engage himself in opposing the hydrogen bomb, a cause that Bolt supported during the 1950's. Bolt summarized these plays as "fourth wall drama with puzzling, uncomfortable, and pretentious overtones."

A Man for All Seasons is Bolt's most popular and his best-known work. Bolt depicts Sir Thomas More as a thoroughly engaging and moral man who is thrust into an untenable situation by the quest for power of Henry VIII and Cardinal Wolsey and Thomas Cromwell. The actions of the main characters are commented upon by the Common Man, a Brechtian narrator who slips in and out of the action, directly addressing the audience. It is a very theatrical piece, making full use of the flexibility of nonnaturalistic staging.

His next play, *Gentle Jack*, was not very successful. It is a play of ideas, through which Bolt attempted to work out an analogy between pagan folklore and the immorality of capitalism. In *Vivat! Vivat Regina!*, Bolt continued his historical adaptations as he dramatized the conflict between Elizabeth I and Mary, Queen of Scots. In *State of Revolution*, he explored the frictions between Vladimir Ilich Lenin and Joseph Stalin, to some extent idealizing the aspirations of the Bolsheviks and underscoring the compromises forced upon them.

During the 1960's and early 1970's, Bolt became an accomplished screenwriter, completing such projects as *Dr. Zhivago* and *Ryan's Daughter*, as well as the adaptation of *A Man for All Seasons*. These works were essentially romantic in conception and epic in scope, relying heavily on visuals for effect. Some have suggested that Bolt's success in Hollywood was not too surprising, since he is, in spite of his liberal political views, a traditionalist in his values, conceptions, and directions. He won Academy Awards for *Lawrence of Arabia*, *Doctor Zhivago*, and *A Man for All Seasons*.

All Bolt's work demonstrates a preoccupation with the question of selfhood and identity. The predicament of his protagonists is how to assert that sense of self in a world where violence and unrest are set against the individual and his or her social conscience. Bolt's successes have largely been in the area of historical drama, where he can incorporate devices of effective staging from any age, using them as a means to an end and never as an end in themselves. Bolt has said that his intention in writing plays is "not to give a history lesson, but to create an effective, entertaining, and truthful evening in the theatre." Most would agree with critic Niloufer Harben, who says that "Bolt is basically a conventional playwright putting over history in a popular way."

BIBLIOGRAPHICAL REFERENCES: Because Bolt is basically a traditional playwright, major critics have not been drawn to him, and few have dealt with him substantially. The only full-length work devoted to him is Ronald Hayman's very sketchy *Robert Bolt*, 1969, which covers only the early work. See also "Five Dramas of Selfhood," in *The New Theatre of Europe*, edited by Robert W. Corrigan, 1962; J. C. Trewin, "Two Morality Playwrights: Robert Bolt and John Whiting," in *Experimental Drama*, edited by William A. Armstrong, 1963; Anselm Atkins, "Robert Bolt: Self, Shadow, and the Theater of Recognition," *Modern Drama*, X (1967), 182-188; William Free, "Robert Bolt and the Marxist View of History," *Mosaic*, XIV (Winter, 1981), 51-59; Benedict Nightingale, *A Reader's Guide to Fifty Modern British Plays*, 1982, 370-378; and "Three Plays of the 1960's," in Niloufer Harben, *Twentieth Century English History Plays: From Shaw to Bond*, 1987.

Lori Hall Burghardt

MARÍA LUISA BOMBAL

Born: Viña del Mar, Chile
Date: June 8, 1910

Died: Santiago, Chile
Date: May 6, 1980

Principal Works

NOVELS: *La última niebla*, 1934 (*The Final Mist*, 1982; previously revised and translated as *The House of Mist*); *La amortajada*, 1938 (revised and translated as *The Shrouded Woman*, 1948).

SHORT FICTION: *New Islands and Other Stories*, 1982.

María Luisa Bombal is one of the best-known Chilean fiction writers. She was born in Viña del Mar, Chile, on June 8, 1910. Her father died when she was nine years old, and at the age of twelve she traveled to Paris with her mother and sisters. She received most of her formal education in France, receiving a degree in French literature from the Sorbonne. These years in France had a profound effect on Bombal's literary development: She was exposed to the work of many avant-garde artists; she attended lectures by Paul Valéry, studied violin with Jacques Thibaud, and was a member of Fortunat Strowsky's literary workshop, where she won her first prize as an author for a story written in French. She also continued to read and write in Spanish, a language to which she referred as a secret love, a natural impulse to be cultivated in private. Among the books she would later speak of as important to her development were Johann Wolfgang von Goethe's *Die Leiden des jungen Werthers* (1774; *The Sorrows of Young Werther*, 1779), Ricardo Güiraldes' *Don Segundo Sombra* (1926), and the novels of Selma Lagerlöf. She would later be profoundly moved by her readings of Virginia Woolf's fiction and essays.

When one of her uncles discovered that she was acting at L'Atelier, a theater workshop directed by Charles Dullin, María Luisa Bombal was abruptly sent back to Chile in 1931. She moved to Buenos Aires two years later, accompanying her longtime friend Pablo Neruda and his wife. She became a part of the group of illustrious writers gathered around Victoria Ocampo and her magazine, *Sur*, and much of her fiction first appeared in the pages of this publication. She became friends with other writers such as Federico García Lorca, Alfonsina Storni, Conrado Nalé Roxlo, and Jorge Luis Borges. In 1934, Bombal wrote her first novel, *The Final Mist*, while she shared a kitchen table with the poet Pablo Neruda, who was working on *Residencia en la tierra* (1933, 1939, 1947; *Residence on Earth and Other Poems*, 1946, 1973). Both these books were landmarks in Latin American literature at the time of their publication. *The Final Mist*, published in 1934, incorporated techniques of French avant-garde writing in order to depict Latin American reality in a new way. The book startled and excited its readers with its new possibilities of perception and description. *The Final Mist* is a narrator's account of her life within a sterile marriage and the dreams, hopes, and fantasies that make her survival possible. In the novel, there is no clear dividing line between concrete facts and fantastic imaginings. Reality is a mysterious mixture of factual events, dreams, and fantasies. Subjectivity and objectivity cannot be defined separately, and the fusion is both lyrical and ambiguous. At first, the novel seems to be an account of the narrator's escape from an oppressively loveless marriage into a romantic love affair, but later in the novel, it seems more likely that she has invented her lover, that she has imposed a dreamworld upon an otherwise unbearable existence. The uncertainty is never resolved but becomes part of a misty, dreamlike, even supernatural landscape, a shadowy drama of light and dark, ice and fire, life and death. The novel is both the story of a frustrated woman and a depiction of the new dimension she creates for herself.

A second novel, *La amortajada* (the shrouded woman), was published in 1938. Another mysterious realm is explored, as the narrator, who has just died, moves back through her memories of life and forward into a new dimension of death. Past and present are juxtaposed, the factual and the imaginary, the concrete and the supernatural. As in *The Final Mist*, a new reality is created out of the complex fusion of the feminine and the fantastic. Both *The Final Mist* and *La amortajada* portray woman's role in society as a powerless one; men make the important life choices, and women must cope with them as best they can, by drawing on their immensely creative, intuitive imaginations and on their sense of physical fusion with the universe. The rational logic of men limits them to a factual plane, whereas women are in touch with primordial depths of emotional coherence which cannot be defined in rational, scientific terms.

In 1939, Bombal made a short visit to the United States, where she met William Faulkner, Sherwood Anderson, and Erskine Caldwell. That same year, *Sur* published "New Islands" and "The Tree," Bombal's most acclaimed and most anthologized story. "The Tree" tells the story of Brigida's life, recalled by her as she listens to a concert. She reflects upon the emptiness and sadness of her experiences and becomes conscious of her increasing ability to comprehend and define her own identity. In flashbacks, she traces the gradual failure of her marriage and her dependence upon the symbolic tree of the title, which mitigates harsh reality and facilitates fantasy. When the tree is cut down, Brigida must face her real self and her circumstances.

In Buenos Aires, Bombal was married to the Argentine painter Jorge Larcos, from whom she was separated two years later. She later married Count Fal de Saint-Phalle, an international banker, with whom she lived for thirty years in the United States, not returning to Chile until after his death in 1970. They had one daughter, Brigitte, who became a professor of mathematics.

In 1946, *Sur* published "The Story of María Griselda" and Bombal rewrote her first novel into a much longer English version published under the title *The House of Mist* in 1947. She and her husband also rewrote and extended her second novel in an English version, and *The Shrouded Woman* was published in the United States in 1948. The novels did not meet with great critical success in the English editions, but they have continued to be highly acclaimed in their spare and lyrical Spanish originals.

For years, María Luisa Bombal said that she was working on a novel, "El Canciller," which she had written originally in English in 1954 as "The Foreign Minister" but not published. She also spoke of writing poetry, stories, filmscripts, and another novel, "Embrujo y el Señor de Mayo" (enchantment and Mr. de Mayo), about an earthquake in Chile. A children's story, "La Maja y el ruiseñor" (La Maja and the nightingale), was published in 1960. In 1977 Bombal was awarded the prize of the Academia Chilena de la Lengua, and in 1979 she won the Joaquin Edwards Bello Regional Literature Prize. She was ill for many years and died in a hospital in Santiago on May 6, 1980. A collection of her short stories in English translation, published in 1982 under the title *New Islands and Other Stories* includes the translation of the Spanish original of *La última niebla*. Since her death, Bombal has been one of the most discussed and critically analyzed of the contemporary Latin American writers, and it is appropriate that one of the major Chilean literary prizes today has been named the María Luisa Bombal Award.

BIBLIOGRAPHICAL REFERENCES: For criticism on Bombal in English, see the appropriate chapter in Ian M. Adams, *Three Authors of Alienation*, 1975; Thomas O. Bente, "María Luisa Bombal's Heroines: Poetic Neuroses and Artistic Symbolism," *Hispanófila*, XXVIII (1984), 103-113; Margaret V. Campbell, "The Vaporous World of María Luisa Bombal," *Hispania* XLIV (September, 1961), 415-419; Andrew P. Debicki, "Structure, Imagery, and Experience in María Luisa Bombal's "The Tree," *Studies in Short Fiction*, VIII (1971), 123-129; Linda Gould Levine, "María Luisa Bombal from a Feminist Perspective," *Revista/Review Interamericana*, IV (1974), 148-161; Esther W. Nelson, "The Space of Longing: *La última niebla*," *The American Hispanist*, III (1977), 7-11; Mercedes Valdivielso, "Social Denunciation in the Language of 'The Tree' by María Luisa Bombal," *Latin American Literary Review*, IX

(1976), 70-76; and Lorna Valeria Williams, "*The Shrouded Woman*: Marriage and Its Constraints in the Fiction of María Luisa Bombal," *Latin American Literary Review*, X (1982), 21-30.

Mary G. Berg

EDWARD BOND

Born: Hollaway, North London, England
Date: July 18, 1934

PRINCIPAL WORKS

PLAYS: *The Pope's Wedding*, pr. 1962; *Saved*, pr. 1965; *Early Morning*, pr., pb. 1968; *Narrow Road to the Deep North*, pr., pb. 1968; *Black Mass*, pr. 1970; *Lear*, pr. 1971; *Passion*, pr., pb. 1971; *Bingo: Scenes of Money and Death*, pr. 1973; *The Sea*, pr., pb. 1973; *The Fool*, pr. 1975; *A-A-America!*, pr., pb. 1976; *Stone*, pr., pb. 1976; *We Come to the River*, pr., pb. 1976; *The Bundle: Or, New Narrow Road to the Deep North*, pr., pb. 1978; *The Woman*, pr. 1978; *The Worlds*, pr. 1979; *The Cat*, pr. 1980; *Restoration*, pr., pb. 1981; *Summer*, pr., pb. 1982; *Derek*, pb. 1983; *Red, Black, and Ignorant*, pb. 1985; *The War Plays*, pb. 1985; *Human Cannon*, pb. 1985.

Edward Bond, one of the most controversial figures in twentieth century drama, is a political activist with carefully articulated social and theatrical theories. One of four children, Bond was the son of working-class laborers. During World War II, he was evacuated to Cornwall. Upon his return to London, he attended a secondary school until he was fifteen, when he was asked to leave. Bond credits this event, and his entire background, with "the making" of his political consciousness. In 1948, he was deeply affected by a production of William Shakespeare's *Macbeth* (1606). As a result of this experience, he knew that he had to write for the theater.

After leaving school, Bond worked at odd jobs until he was drafted in 1953. Being in the military served as a catalyst for writing seriously, and when he returned to civilian life two years later, Bond found a favorable climate for new writers. The English Stage Company, located at the Royal Court, was formed in 1956 as a writers' theater. Bond's first play, *The Pope's Wedding*, was performed there in December, 1962.

Bond gained both notoriety and acclaim with *Saved* in 1965. On stage, a baby is stoned to death by working-class youths who are totally disenfranchised and numbed by the society in which they live. The play was banned for its violence and earthy language. Bond insisted that these qualities were integral to depicting the lives of these individuals. His view that "people are not born violent" but become so as a result of a capitalistic, technological society forms the underlying premise for his entire canon.

The techniques that Bond developed for exploring his ideas are varied and reveal an extensive knowledge of such writers as Shakespeare, Bertolt Brecht, and Karl Marx. In Bond's later plays, he attempted to render his Socialist vision less obliquely and to establish his exploration of social problems more clearly in the present. In *The Worlds*, strikers and terrorists are pitted against Trench, a cynical, corrupt capitalist. The main problem centers on the uses of violence: Can violence ever be condoned? Bond suggests that the end can justify the means. *Red, Black, and Ignorant* is a blunt attack on the barbarism of a civilization which enforces its values by threats of nuclear annihilation.

In his plays, Bond has constantly turned to crucial periods in history to examine the social, ethical, and political roots of present situations in order to alter them. As he developed his dramatic skills and political philosophy, he moved from depicting the problems of society, as in *Saved*, to demonstrating how these problems can be solved, as in *The Worlds*.

Bond demands much of the theater; he sees it as a medium of communication which can and should reach the people, severing itself from its clearly patrician roots in the process. The difficulty facing Bond is that England has neither a Marxist culture nor a popular dramatic medium capable of conveying these sophisticated social and political ideas. Bond's solution, according to critic David Hirst, is the manipulation of particular dramatic genres which are representative of the ideas of their time: for example, the comedy of manners

(*Restoration*) and the fifth century Greek tragedy (*The Woman*). These dramatic strategies allow Bond to express the complexity of his ideas.

Bond is clearly one of the leading writers of political theater. He has stressed throughout his career the need "to make the analysis of politics part of the aesthetic experience." His plays have been acclaimed by many critics, yet they have not had a similar reception among the very people for whom they were intended. His literariness makes his works inaccessible to the working class, and his indirection does not penetrate the economic security of the paying audience.

BIBLIOGRAPHICAL REFERENCES: Richard Scharine, *The Plays of Edward Bond*, 1976, is a sympathetic study of the plays up to *The Sea*. Simon Trussler's *Edward Bond*, 1976, is a very short but detailed study of Bond's work up to *Bingo*. One of the best studies is Tony Coult's *The Plays of Edward Bond*, 1977. Malcolm Hay and Philip Roberts' *Edward Bond: A Companion to the Plays*, 1985 (rev. ed.), and *Bond: A Study of His Plays*, 1980, are excellent sources to examine the evolution and stage production of the plays. David Hirst in *Edward Bond*, 1985, explores Bond's dramatic strategies through *The Worlds*. *Bond on File*, compiled by Philip Roberts, 1985, is a very useful collection of brief plot summaries, Bond's commentaries, and the critical reaction to the plays. Lou Lappin in *The Art and Politics of Edward Bond*, 1987, explores the central role of the artist figure in selected plays. See also "Edward Bond," in *The Second Wave: British Drama for the Seventies*, by John Russell Taylor, 1971, 77-93; Arthur Arnold, "Lines of Development in Bond's Plays," *Theatre Quarterly*, V, no. 2 (1972), 15-19; Philip Roberts, "The Search for Epic Drama: Edward Bond's Recent Work," *Modern Drama*, XXIII (December, 1981), 458-478; Frances Rudemacher, "Violence and the Comic in the Plays of Edward Bond," *Modern Drama*, XXIII (September, 1980), 258-268; Katherine Worth, "Bond's *Restoration*," *Modern Drama* XXIV (December, 1981), 479-493; Jenny Spencer, "Edward Bond's Dramatic Strategies," in *Contemporary English Drama*, edited by C. W. E. Bigsby, 1981, 123-137; Robert L. Tener, "Edward Bond's Dialectic: Irony and Dramatic Metaphors," *Modern Drama*, XXV (September, 1982), 423-434; and Terry Eagleton, "Nature and Violence: The Prefaces of Edward Bond," *Critical Quarterly*, XXVI (Spring/Summer, 1984), 127-135.

Lori Hall Burghardt

DIETRICH BONHOEFFER

Born: Breslau, Germany
Date: February 4, 1906

Died: Flossenberg, Germany
Date: April 9, 1945

PRINCIPAL WORKS

THEOLOGY: *Sanctorum Communio*, 1930 (*The Communion of Saints*, 1963); *Akt und Sein*, 1931 (*Act and Being*, 1950); *Nachfolge*, 1937 (*The Cost of Discipleship*, 1948); *Gemeinsames Leben*, 1939 (*Life Together*, 1954); *Ethik*, 1949 (*Ethics*, 1955); *Widerstand und Ergebung: Aufzeichnungen aus der Haft*, 1951, revised 1964, 1970 (*Prisoners for God: Letters and Papers from Prison*, 1953; revised as *Letters and Papers from Prison*, 1967, 1971).

Dietrich Bonhoeffer is one of the most influential Protestant theologians of the twentieth century. Born in Breslau, Germany, the sixth in a line of eight children, he was reared in Berlin in an academic atmosphere. His father, a distinguished professor of psychiatry and neurology, taught at the University of Berlin. Bonhoeffer naturally gravitated toward a university career, but unlike his father he was more interested in theology than in the natural sciences. Influenced by the historical theologians Karl Holl, Adolf von Harnack, and Rheinhold Seeberg, and deeply affected by the writings of Karl Barth, Bonhoeffer attempted to combine a theological and sociological understanding of the Church in his doctoral dissertation, entitled *The Communion of Saints*. He was granted a Ph.D. in 1930; during the same year he also studied in New York at the Union Theological Seminary with Reinhold Niebuhr.

In 1931, Bonhoeffer returned to Germany and accepted an appointment at the University of Berlin as a lecturer in systematic theology. Not long afterward he published *Act and Being*, a work in which he argued that Christianity is reducible to neither a philosophy of transcendence (*Akt*) nor a philosophy of being (*Sein*); also, it could not be explained without reference to philosophical concerns. Thus, according to Bonhoeffer, philosophical attempts to account for the meaning of Christian revelation are not exhaustive; yet all Protestant and Catholic theologies have nevertheless been influenced by transcendental metaphysics and ontology, and theories of being and of knowledge. Bonhoeffer's point, and what characterizes all of his subsequent writings, is that it is not possible to make meaningful statements about God apart from the notion of revelation in Jesus Christ. In fact, to understand Christian revelation one must always examine the concrete and historical aspect of revelation in Christ as opposed to any philosophical explication.

Bonhoeffer resisted the persecution of the Jews and the Nazification of the Church from the time Adolf Hitler first seized power in 1933. Frustrated and sorely disappointed by the passivity and lack of resistance among all the churches in Germany at that time, he accepted a pastorate for Germans in London from 1933 to 1935. Yet when the Confessing Church (formed by Christians who actively resisted Nazi domination) established its own seminary in Finkenwald, he returned to Germany and served as its director. He continued to prepare young men for ordination clandestinely until 1940, even though the state authorities had closed the school in 1937. It was here that Bonhoeffer wrote *Life Together*, a book on the practices of private confession, prayer, and common discipline which he hoped would serve as a spiritual renewal for the secular world, and *The Cost of Discipleship*, a polemic directed against the doctrine of what he termed "cheap grace" promulgated by Protestant churches at the time; an unlimited offer of forgiveness was, to Bonhoeffer, merely a cover for moral laxity. Bonhoeffer first became widely known through these writings.

After repeated conflicts with the Gestapo, Bonhoeffer considered taking refuge in the United States under the sponsorship of Reinhold Niebuhr at Union Theological Seminary. Yet, having spent four weeks at the seminary, he returned to Germany, convinced that he would have no effect on the Christian revival of his country if he did not directly share the tribulations of other Germans during the war. Back in Germany, and despite the restrictions placed on his activities, Bonhoeffer became an active force in the resistance movement while he worked for the Department of Military Intelligence (which, in fact, was a center for those who opposed Hitler). He traveled to Sweden in May of 1942 to convey to the British government a conspiracy to remove Hitler and propose a negotiated peace; to his chagrin, the Allies' policy of unconditional surrender stymied this plan. On April 5, 1943, Bonhoeffer was arrested on the charge of suspicion and imprisoned. When the attempted assassination of Hitler on July 20, 1944, failed, Bonhoeffer was directly linked to the conspiracy and hanged with five thousand others on April 9, 1945, at Flossenberg.

From 1939 to 1943, Bonhoeffer had begun writing a manuscript on Christian ethics that he regarded as the culmination of his lifework; however, the work was never completely finished and survives only in fragmentary form. Published posthumously in 1949, *Ethics* is Bonhoeffer's most concerted and systematic attempt to reject a philosophically based moral framework. In it he rejects the notion that theological ethics moves from general abstract ethical principles to specific Christian precepts, and he proposes a view which calls for a unitive and concrete ethical framework based on revelatory events in the life of Jesus Christ.

The letters and papers Bonhoeffer wrote in prison during the last two years of his life have become the most influential of all of his work. *Letters and Papers from Prison*, as it is best known, contains a memorable interpretation of modern history. According to Bonhoeffer, the "god of explanation" belongs to man's spiritual adolescence and is gradually disappearing from history. By this he means that man no longer has to rely upon or adopt a particular metaphysical perspective, or specific view of God's transcendence, in order to call himself a Christian. Rather, man must live with Christ in a modern, nonreligious world—in short, to live *for* others—and the Church must affirm his maturity to do so in an exclusively secular context. Losing his sense of otherworldliness and his concentration on personal salvation will therefore liberate man and allow him to focus on aspects of life in this world. It was Bonhoeffer's belief in such a "religionless Christianity" that enabled him to write about imitating Jesus, "the man for others," and sharing "in God's sufferings in the world." On a personal level, this belief justified his own participation in the conspiracy against Hitler and assured his place as a martyr for Christianity.

The heroism Bonhoeffer displayed at the end of his life has called much attention to his personal character, but that has not overshadowed the interest he has garnered over the years as a theologian. Bonhoeffer has been earnestly studied by large numbers of students not only for his radical critique of the contemporary church and the secular environment in which Christianity currently exists but also for his interpretation of twentieth century theology and its emphasis on what he considered to be the insignificant aspects of religious life. His ideas are still influencing movements in church reform and ministry, especially in the efforts of theologians to propose a secular Christianity, or secular meaning of the Gospel, and in the formulation of a theology of hope. Unfortunately, Bonhoeffer's own formulation of these ideas is not complete, and he was prevented from making any sustained impact on the field of theology in his lifetime by the Nazi regime.

BIBLIOGRAPHICAL REFERENCES: *Dietrich Bonhoeffer: Man of Vision, Man of Courage*, 1967, by Eberhard Bethge, is the definitive biography by Bonhoeffer's friend and executor of his estate. For a detailed analysis of Bonhoeffer's Christology, see John A. Phillips, *The Forms of Christ in the World*, 1967; for further study on this topic, see *The Place of Bonhoeffer*, 1962, edited by Martin E. Marty. *The Theology of Dietrich Bonhoeffer*, 1960, by J. D. Godsey, is still one of the best studies of the relation between his theology and his secular involvement; Ernest Feil, *The Theology of Dietrich Bonhoeffer*, 1985, is another good study on the same subject. *World Come of Age*, 1967, edited by Ronald Gregory Smith, is an admirable collection of essays by leading theologians on various aspects of Bonhoeffer's thought. *I Knew Dietrich Bonhoeffer*, 1966, edited by Wolf-Dieter Zimmermann and Ronald Gregory Smith, is an interesting collection of personal impressions by those who knew Bonhoeffer. An elucidation of how Bonhoeffer's involvement in the Confessing Church can help shed light on the political problems in South Africa is by John W. De Gruchy, *Bonhoeffer and South Africa*, 1984. James A. Burtness provides an examination of Bonhoeffer's ethics and its implications for the contemporary Christian in *Shaping the Future*, 1985.

Thomas Derdak

ARNA BONTEMPS

Born: Alexandria, Louisiana
Date: October 13, 1902

Died: Nashville, Tennessee
Date: June 4, 1973

PRINCIPAL WORKS

NOVELS: *God Sends Sunday*, 1931; *Black Thunder*, 1936; *Drums at Dusk*, 1939.

ANTHOLOGIES: *The Poetry of the Negro*, 1949, revised 1971 (with Langston Hughes); *The Book of Negro Folklore*, 1958 (with Hughes); *American Negro Poetry*, 1963; *Great Slave Narratives*, 1969; *The Harlem Renaissance Remembered*, 1972.

CHILDREN'S LITERATURE: *Popo and Fifina: Children of Haiti*, 1932 (with Hughes); *You Can't Pet a Possum*, 1934; *Sad-Faced Boy*, 1937; *The Fast Sooner Hound*, 1943 (with Jack Conroy); *We Have Tomorrow*, 1945; *Slappy Hooper*, 1946 (with Conroy); *The Story of the Negro*, 1948; *Sam Patch*, 1951 (with Conroy); *Chariot in the Sky*, 1951; *The Story of George Washington Carver*, 1954; *Lonesome Boy*, 1955; *Frederick Douglass: Slave, Fighter, Freeman*, 1959; *Famous Negro Athletes*, 1964; *Hold Fast to Dreams*, 1969; *Young Booker*, 1972.

SHORT FICTION: *The Old South*, 1973.

HISTORY: *They Seek a City*, 1945 (with Conroy; revised as *Anyplace But Here*, 1966); *One Hundred Years of Negro Freedom*, 1961.

BIOGRAPHY: *Father of the Blues*, 1941 (with W. C. Handy); *Free at Last: The Life of Frederick Douglass*, 1971.

POETRY: *Personals*, 1963.

PLAY: *St. Louis Woman*, pb. 1946 (with Countée Cullen).

CORRESPONDENCE: *Arna Bontemps-Langston Hughes Letters: 1925-1967*, 1980.

Arna Wendell Bontemps began his literary career writing poetry, yet his fame as one of the twentieth century's most prolific and versatile black writers rests on his association with the Harlem Renaissance, on one widely anthologized short story, on his children's books, and on his novel *Black Thunder.* Born in Alexandria, Louisiana, on October 13, 1902, the son of musician, brickmason, and lay minister Paul Bontemps and teacher Marie Pembroke, he grew up in Los Angeles, California, attending boarding school and earning his B.A. from Pacific Union College (1923) and his M.A. from the University of Chicago (1943). After his mother died when he was twelve, Bontemps lived with his grandmother and her younger brother. His father's inclination toward fundamentalist Christianity and his disinterest in African-American folk heritage contrasted with his granduncle's affinity for drink, gambling, music, and spontaneity. Bontemps ultimately sided with his granduncle and chose African folk expression, even though his father's persistent influence left him ambivalent.

In the 1920's, Bontemps left his Los Angeles post-office job for New York City, where he quickly achieved poetic success. In 1926, he married schoolteacher Alberta Johnson. He acquainted himself with the major figures of the Harlem Renaissance and began a correspondence and collaboration with Langston Hughes. His Harlem period culminated in the early years of the Great Depression, not with poetry but with prose. His first novel, *God Sends Sunday,* described the exciting life of a black jockey in the 1880's. The children's book he wrote with Hughes (*Popo and Fifina: Children of Haiti*) met an acknowledged need for juvenilia with black characters.

Bontemps moved to Alabama in 1931 to teach. There, he was influenced by the trial of the Scottsboro Boys. He wrote several stories, some unpublished until 1973. The best one, "A Summer Tragedy," portrays two old sharecroppers who have lost everything. Their dignified joint suicide relieves them from the real tragedy: the plight of the old and poor in an uncaring society. Bontemps left Alabama to return to California to write what has come to be regarded as his single best work, *Black Thunder,* a romanticized historical account of the Gabriel Prosser slave rebellion near Richmond, Virginia, in 1800.

By 1938 Bontemps had moved to Chicago; shortly afterward, he received his first Rosenwald Fellowship, which allowed him to travel and to enroll in the University of Chicago's graduate school. His third and final novel, *Drums at Dusk*, failed critically. He worked for the Illinois Writers Project and began a writing partnership with Jack Conroy that lasted into the 1950's. During the 1940's, Bontemps became a librarian at Fisk University, where he stayed until his death, except for stints at Yale University and the University of Illinois, Chicago Circle. He and Countée Cullen adapted *God Sends Sunday* as the play *St. Louis Woman*, which was then further adapted into a successful Broadway musical in 1946. In the 1950's and 1960's, Bontemps developed biographical juvenilia concentrating on the black experience.

Always shining through Bontemps' works is an unapologetic view of black history and black people at their worst and their best. His biographies of Frederick Douglass, Booker T. Washington, and George Washington Carver affirmed his early recognition that he could neither shed his "Negroness" nor break with the past. Neither was possible; both were unthinkable.

BIBLIOGRAPHICAL REFERENCES: Arthur P. Davis, *From the Dark Tower: Afro-American Writers, 1900-1960*, 1974, provides a helpful discussion of Bontemps' poetry and novels, although Robert E. Fleming, *James Weldon Johnson and Arna Wendell Bontemps: A Reference Guide*, 1978, eclipses Davis for thoroughness. David Littlejohn's interpretations in *Black on White: A Critical Survey of Writing by American Negroes*, 1961, and Robert Bone's judgment of Bontemps as a transitional figure in *The Negro Novel in America*, 1965 (rev. ed.) and in *Down Home: A History of Afro-American Short Fiction from Its Beginnings to the End of the Harlem Renaissance*, 1974, are both contested by Sterling Brown's description of Bontemps as a "giant" in "Arna Bontemps: Co-Worker, Comrade," *Black World*, XXII (September, 1974). Discussions of the significance of myth and folklore appear in Jane Campbell, *Mythic Black Fiction: The Transformation of History*, 1986, and in Bernard Bell, *The Afro-American Novel and Its Tradition*, 1987. The suicide in "A Summer Tragedy" is discussed in Stephen Bennet and William Nichols, "Violence in Afro-American Fiction: An Hypothesis," *Modern Fiction Studies*, XVII (Summer, 1971). See also *Black World*, XX (September, 1971), an issue dedicated to Bontemps; Houston Baker, Jr., "Arna Bontemps: A Memoir," *Black World*, XXII (September, 1973), 4-9; and "Arna Bontemps," in *Interviews with Black Writers*, 1973, edited by John O'Brien.

Joseph A. Alvarez

JORGE LUIS BORGES

Born: Buenos Aires, Argentina *Died:* Geneva, Switzerland
Date: August 24, 1899 *Date:* June 14, 1986

Principal Works

NOVEL: *Un modelo para la muerte*, 1946 (with Adolfo Bioy Casares).

SHORT FICTION: *Historia universal de la infamia*, 1935 (*A Universal History of Infamy*, 1972); *El jardín de senderos que se bifurcan*, 1941; *Seis problemas para don Isidro Parodi*, 1942 (with Bioy Casares; *Six Problems for Don Isidro Parodi*, 1981); *Ficciones, 1935-1944*, 1944 (English translation, 1962); *Dos fantasías memorables*, 1946 (with Bioy Casares); *El Aleph*, 1949, 1952 (translated in *The Aleph and Other Stories, 1933-1969*, 1970); *La muerte y la brújula*, 1951; *La hermana de Eloísa*, 1955 (with Luisa Mercedes Levinson); *Cuentos*, 1958; *Crónicas de H. Bustos Domecq*, 1967 (with Bioy Casares; *Chronicles of Bustos Domecq*, 1976); *El informe de Brodie*, 1970 (*Doctor Brodie's Report*, 1971); *El matrero*, 1970; *El congreso*, 1971 (*The Congress*, 1974); *El libro de arena*, 1975 (*The Book of Sand*, 1977); *Narraciones*, 1980.

SCREENPLAYS: *Los orilleros y El paraíso de los creyentes*, 1955 (with Bioy Casares); *Les Autres*, 1974 (with Bioy Casares and Hugo Santiago).

POETRY: *Fervor de Buenos Aires*, 1923, 1969; *Lunda de enfrente*, 1925; *Cuaderno San Martín*, 1929; *Poemas, 1923-1943*, 1943; *Poemas, 1923-1953*, 1954; *Obra poética, 1923-1958*, 1958; *El hacedor*, 1960 (*Dreamtigers*, 1964); *Obra poética, 1923-1964*, 1964; *Seis poemas escandinavos*, 1966; *Siete poemas*, 1967; *El otro, el mismo*, 1969; *Elogio de la sombra*, 1969 (*In Praise of Darkness*, 1974); *El oro de los tigres*, 1972 (translated in *The Gold of Tigers: Selected Later Poems*, 1977); *Selected Poems, 1923-1967*, 1972; *La rosa profunda*, 1975 (translated in *The Gold of Tigers*); *La moneda de hierro*, 1976; *Historia de la noche*, 1977; *La cifra*, 1981; *Los conjurados*, 1986.

NONFICTION: *Inquisiciones*, 1925; *El tamaño de mi esperanza*, 1926; *El idioma de los argentinos*, 1928; *Evaristo Carriego*, 1930 (English translation, 1984); *Figari*, 1930; *Discusión*, 1932; *Las Kennigar*, 1933; *Historia de la eternidad*, 1936; *Nueva refutación del tiempo*, 1947; *Aspectos de la literatura gauchesca*, 1950; *Antiguas literaturas germánicas*, 1951 (with Delia Ingenieros; revised as *Literaturas germánicas medievales*, 1966, with María Esther Vázquez); *Otras inquisiciones*, 1952 (*Other Inquisitions*, 1964); *El "Martin Fierro*," 1953 (with Margarita Guerrero); *Leopoldo Lugones*, 1955 (with Betina Edelberg); *Manual de zoología fantástica*, 1957 (with Guerrero; *The Imaginary Zoo*, 1969, revised as *El libro de los seres imaginarios*, 1967, *The Book of Imaginary Beings*, 1969); *La poesía gauchesca*, 1960; *Introducción a la literatura inglesa*, 1964 (with Vázquez); *Introducción a la literatura norteamericana*, 1967 (with Esther Zemborain de Torres; *An Introduction to American Literature*, 1971); *Prólogos*, 1975; *Qué es el budismo?*, 1976 (with Alicia Jurado); *Cosmogonías*, 1976; *Libro de sueños*, 1976; *Siete noches*, 1980 (*Seven Nights*, 1984); *Nueve ensayos dantescos*, 1982.

MISCELLANEOUS: *Obras completas*, 1953-1967; *Antología personal*, 1961 (*A Personal Anthology*, 1967); *Labyrinths: Selected Stories and Other Writings*, 1962, 1964; *Nueva antología personal*, 1968; *Adrogue*, 1977; *Obras completas en colaboración*, 1979 (with others); *Borges: A Reader*, 1981; *Atlas*, 1984 (with María Kodama; English translation, 1985).

Jorge Luis Borges, South America's most famous writer of short fiction, was born on August 24, 1899, in Buenos Aires, Argentina, the son of Jorge Guillermo Borges, a lawyer and psychology teacher, and Leonor Acevedo de Borges, a descendant of old Argentine and Uruguayan families. An extremely intelligent child who spent much of his childhood indoors, Borges has named his father's library as the most important influence on his career. Based on his reading in that library, he began writing at the early age of six, imitating classical Spanish authors such as Miguel de Cervantes and others.

Borges attended school in Switzerland during World War I. While there he became strongly influenced by his reading of the French Symbolist poets as well as such English prose writers as G. K. Chesterton and Thomas Carlyle. After the war, he spent two years in Spain, where he became the disciple of Rafael Casinos-Asséns, leader of the so-called Ultraist movement in poetry. It was at this time that he also began writing poetry himself.

Borges published his first book of stories, *A Universal History of Infamy*, in 1935; however, his most important stories did not appear until 1941, when they were published under the title *El jardín de senderos que se bifurcan* (the garden of the forking paths). When his third collection of stories, *Ficciones*, was published in 1944, he was awarded a literary prize by the Argentine Society of Writers. Because of increasing blindness, he was forced to stop reading and writing in the late 1950's; however, his mother became his secretary, and he continued to work by dictating to her.

In 1961, Borges was awarded a major European literary prize in conjunction with Samuel Beckett. As a result of this recognition, his international reputation began to grow rapidly; he was invited to the United States to give several lectures. Soon after, translations of his books began to appear, and he received a number of honorary doctorates and literary prizes from universities and professional societies. Borges died in Geneva, Switzerland, on June 14, 1986.

Jorge Luis Borges might well be called a writer's writer, for the subject of his stories is more often the nature of writing itself than actual events in the world. By the same token, Borges should be seen as a metaphysical writer, for his stories most often focus on the fantastic metaphysical paradoxes which ensnare those who think. Because of Borges' overriding interest in aesthetic and metaphysical reality, his stories often resemble fables or essays.

One of his best-known stories, "Pierre Menard, Author of the Quixote," deals with a French writer who decides to write the *Don Quixote*, in spite of the fact that it has already been written by Cervantes. Borges then compares the two versions and finds them identical; however, he argues that the second version is richer, more ambitious, and in many ways more subtle than Cervantes' original. In another well-known story, "Funes the Memorious," Borges presents a character who is unable to forget details of his experience, no matter how small.

If the situations of these two men seem alien to ordinary human experience, it is because Borges is interested in the extraordinary nature of metaphysical rather than physical reality. The fact that Pierre Menard can rewrite *Don Quixote* from the original, yet create a more complex and subtle work, can be attributed to the notion that one reads a present work with all previous works inscribed within it. The fact that Funes is condemned to remember every single detail of his experience means that he can never tell stories because he is unable to abstract from his experience.

Borges maintains that human reality is the result of language and game, as well as the result of the projection of the mind itself. "Tlön, Uqbar, Orbis Tertius" explores the intellectual productions of an imaginary planet; "The Library of Babel" deals with a library that is infinite in its circular and cyclical structure; "The Lottery in Babylon" deals with a lottery which transforms all reality itself into chance.

Borges' most common technique is to take previously established genres such as the science-fiction story, the detective story, or the philosophical essay, and parody those forms by pushing them to absurd extremes. Thus, most of Borges' fictions are puzzling, frustrating, sometimes shocking, often humorous, but they are always profoundly thought-provoking.

BIBLIOGRAPHICAL REFERENCES: The first two important English-language books on Borges appeared in 1969: Carter Wheelock's study of archetypal symbols, entitled simply *The Mythmaker: A Study of Myth and Symbol in the Short Stories of J. L. Borges*, and Ronald Christ's well-received study of Borges' allusions to other authors, entitled *The Narrow Act: Borges' Art & Illusion*. A general introduction entitled simply *Jorge Luis Borges* by Martin S.

Stabb appeared in 1970 in the Twayne World Authors series, and another introduction, by George R. McMurray, also entitled *Jorge Luis Borges*, appeared in 1980 in Ungar's Modern Literature Monographs. Although each of the critical studies cited above includes some biographical information, for a more detailed biography, see Emir Rodríguez Monegal, *Jorge Luis Borges: A Literary Biography*, 1978. See also *Critical Essays on Jorge Luis Borges*, 1987, edited by Jaime Alazraki, and Fernando Sorrentino, *Seven Conversations with Jorge Luis Borges*, 1982.

Charles E. May

TADEUSZ BOROWSKI

Born: Żytomierz, Poland
Date: November 12, 1922

Died: Warsaw, Poland
Date: July 3, 1951

Principal Works

SHORT FICTION: *Pożegnanie z Marią*, 1948; *Kamienny świat*, 1948; *This Way for the Gas, Ladies and Gentlemen, and Other Stories*, 1967.

POETRY: *Gdziekolwiek ziemia*, 1942; *Arkusz poetycki*, 1944; *Imiona nurtu*, 1945; *Poszukiwania*, 1945; *Poezje*, 1974.

NONFICTION: *Byliśmy w Oświęcimiu*, 1946 (with Janusz Nel-Siedlecki and Krystyn Olszewski).

MISCELLANEOUS: *Utwory zebrane*, 1954.

Tadeusz Borowski is best known as a chronicler of the Holocaust. Both his fiction and his poetry attest the searing experiences of the concentration camps and the general horror of life under the heel of Fascism. Arrested at age twenty, he came of age under terrifying conditions, witnessing starvation, brutality, suffering, and death at an age when he should have been completing his studies and beginning his career and family.

Borowski was born in Żytomierz in the Polish Ukraine on November 12, 1922. Both his parents were forced into exile for political reasons during his childhood. From the age of eight until their release, Borowski was cared for by an aunt. Following his mother's return in 1934, the family lived in poverty in Warsaw. Growing up amid the turmoil of prewar Europe, Borowski understood the absurdity of the human condition. During the German Occupation Borowski had to attend underground classes to finish high school. The day of his final examinations, he witnessed the roundup of deportees in Warsaw, which he was to describe later in "Graduation on Market Street."

Before his arrest on February 25, 1943, Borowski worked as a night watchman and stockboy while continuing his education through underground classes. He studied Polish language and literature and became active in a group of young poet-conspirators, publishing a mimeographed volume of poems in 1942, *Gdziekolwiek ziemia* (wherever the earth). When his fiancée, Maria Rundo, a colleague, was arrested by the Nazis, Borowski went in search of her and was taken prisoner at the same friend's apartment where she had been captured. *Arkusz poetycki* (a folio of verse), a collection of six love poems, was published in 1944 and circulated by friends while Borowski and Rundo were at Auschwitz.

Borowski was imprisoned at Auschwitz until 1944. As the Allies advanced, he was moved with other inmates to camps in Germany. On May 1, 1945, Dachau was liberated by the Allies; Borowski, transferred to a camp for displaced persons, was finally freed in September. Unable to be reunited with Rundo, who was in Sweden, Borowski continued to write poetry and collaborated with two other released prisoners on a book called *Byliśmy w Oświęcimiu* (we were in Auschwitz), published in Munich in 1946. A book of verse, *Imiona nurtu* (names in the stream), came out in 1945.

Despite the Communist takeover, Borowski persuaded Rundo to return to Poland with him. They were married, and in 1947 and 1948 Borowski published two collections of short stories on his concentration camp and postwar experiences: *Pożegnanie z Marią* (farewell to Maria) and *Kamienny świat* (world of stone). Turning his attention to journalism, Borowski accepted a post in the Press Section at the Polish Military Mission in Berlin in 1949.

Returning to Poland a year later, he devoted himself to Socialist activism. On July 3, 1951, a few days after his daughter was born, he committed suicide by breathing gas. Although his suicide has not been explained, it has been suggested that the concentration camp experience finally overwhelmed him. Also, he was apparently suffering from guilt over an affair, he had been recently disillusioned when an old friend was tortured by Polish Security, and he felt trapped in a propaganda job which was wasting his talents. It is possible, however, that someone else turned on the gas, making Borowski a victim of political assassination. In any case, Borowski's death, at age twenty-eight, was a tragic loss.

If one quality distinguishes Borowski's work, it is his insistence on confronting evil and telling the whole truth about it. His stories of the concentration camps are marked by a cool, matter-of-fact narration; the storyteller's lack of passion is astonishing, given the horror of the events depicted. The stories suggest that a sensitive person must abandon emotion in order to survive such experiences.

Although Borowski was a common prisoner and acted with courage, he tells his stories through a narrator who is in a position to benefit by others' sufferings and who becomes dehumanized as ordinary feelings and values are pushed out by the camp mentality. Watching the Kapo distribute second helpings of soup in "A Day at Harmenz," he repeats an unwritten rule of the camp: "The sick, the weaklings, the emaciated, have no right to an extra bowl of water with nettles. Food must not be wasted on people who are about to go to the gas chamber." Readers are shocked at this reversal of humane values, but the prisoner has become hardened by what he has seen.

Borowski's poetry deals with love and intimacy, separation, fear, loss, and nature's tender indifference to human suffering. One poem describes the deportees' view of blooming apple trees, fields and cottages, clouds and birds: "It's a quiet land, I said—again my old mistake." Another expresses the longing of the displaced person for the beloved: "Maybe we'll meet—and know joy? . . . Listen: Read this poem,/ if somewhere/ you're living."

Borowski's place in world literature is growing as more of his writing becomes available to non-Polish readers through translation. The work best known to English readers is *This Way for the Gas, Ladies and Gentlemen, and Other Stories*. In Poland, Borowski is more highly regarded for his poetry than for his fiction, but in both genres his work is marked by vivid imagery, emotional precision, and understated narration of unthinkable realities. His work is valuable not only as a record and reminder of the Holocaust but also as a unique contribution to the art of written expression.

BIBLIOGRAPHICAL REFERENCES: The 1976 edition of *This Way for the Gas, Ladies and Gentlemen* contains Jan Kott's biographical introduction. A chapter on Borowski's life and work, "Tadeusz Borowski's Story," appears in Edward L. Dusza, *Poets of Warsaw Aflame*, 1977. Critical commentaries may be found in *Modern Slavic Literatures*, II (1976); Wiktor Woroszylski, "The Prosecutor Within," *Polish Perspectives*, III (1960), 27-30; A. Alvarez, "The Literature of the Holocaust," *Commentary*, XXXVIII (1964), 65-69; Jan Walc, "When the Earth Is No Longer a Dream and Cannot Be Dreamed Through to the End," *The Polish Review*, XXXII (1987), 181-194; and Andrzej Wirth, "A Discovery of Tragedy (The Incomplete Account of Tadeusz Borowski)," *The Polish Review*, XII (1967), 43-52. Five translated poems appear with explanatory comments in Addison Bross, "Five Poems by Tadeusz Borowski," *The Polish Review*, XXVIII (1983), 43-49. See also Czesław Miłosz, "Beta, the Disappointed Lover," in *The Captive Mind*, 1981.

Marian Price

ELIZABETH BOWEN

Born: Dublin, Ireland
Date: June 7, 1899

Died: London, England
Date: February 22, 1973

Principal Works

SHORT FICTION: *Encounters*, 1923; *Ann Lee's and Other Stories*, 1928; *Joining Charles*, 1929; *The Cat Jumps and Other Stories*, 1934; *Look at All Those Roses*, 1941; *The Demon Lover*, 1945; *The Early Stories*, 1951; *Stories by Elizabeth Bowen*, 1959; *A Day in the Dark and Other Stories*, 1965; *Elizabeth Bowen's Irish Stories*, 1978; *The Collected Stories of Elizabeth Bowen*, 1981.

NOVELS: *The Hotel*, 1927; *The Last September*, 1929; *Friends and Relations*, 1931; *To the North*, 1932; *The House in Paris*, 1935; *The Death of the Heart*, 1938; *The Heat of the Day*, 1949; *A World of Love*, 1955; *The Little Girls*, 1964; *Eva Trout*, 1968.

PLAY: *Castle Anna*, pr. 1948 (with John Perry).

AUTOBIOGRAPHY: *Seven Winters*, 1942; *Pictures and Conversations*, 1975.

LITERARY STUDY: *English Novelists*, 1946.

ESSAYS: *Collected Impressions*, 1950; *Afterthought: Pieces About Writing*, 1962; *The Mulberry Tree: Writings of Elizabeth Bowen*, 1986.

TRAVEL SKETCH: *A Time in Rome*, 1960.

OTHER NONFICTION: *Bowen's Court*, 1942; *The Shelbourne: A Center of Dublin Life for More Than a Century*, 1951; *The Good Tiger*, 1965.

Elizabeth Dorothea Cole Bowen, born in Dublin, Ireland, on June 7, 1899, the only child of a landed Protestant attorney, Henry Charles Cole Bowen, and his wife, Florence Colley Bowen, was a distinguished Anglo-Irish writer. Her introverted and shy parents responded to their only child with emotional vagueness and hired nurses and governesses to supervise her schedule. Though stories were read to her, she was not permitted to learn to read before she was seven years old, for fear it would stress her mind. During these early years, which Bowen articulates in her first autobiography, *Seven Winters*, she spent the winter months of each year in Dublin and the rest of the year at Bowen's Court, the eighteenth century estate deeded to her ancestor Colonel Bowen, a professional soldier who was a lieutenant colonel in Oliver Cromwell's army in 1653.

Throughout her life, Bowen was not only reticent about discussing personal experiences but elusive when asked overt questions. Much of her childhood was buried within her, until she began to write. This emotional diffidence resulted from the traumas which occurred between her seventh and thirteenth years. Her father had a mental breakdown when she was seven years old, and her mother died of cancer when Bowen was thirteen. After her father's hospitalization, the doctor recommended that Bowen and her mother leave Ireland and go to England to live. There they settled near her mother's cousins on the Kent coast. After the death of her mother, Bowen became afflicted with a significant but well-controlled stammer. One word that she could never say without stammering was "mother." After her mother's death, Bowen attended Downe House, a girls' boarding school in Kent, and during the first year, insisted upon wearing a black armband. She loved Downe House and remained in school from 1914 to 1917, leaving to go to art school in London.

The early and painful tragedies of Bowen's life are adroitly circumvented in her essays, short stories, and novels. Though Bowen planned a career in art, she soon decided she lacked enough talent and turned to writing short stories. "Breakfast," the first story that she completed, is the opening story of her first publication, *Encounters*. Though a major theme in Bowen's writing centers on the perceptions of and by children—for example, *The Death of the Heart* and *The Little Girls*—these attitudes are always transformed from the personal to the universal. In fact, the personal grounds her fiction. Like her own personality, her characters are extremely perceptive, very human, and full of fun, conversation, wit, sarcasm, and laughter. They are never moody, introspective, or gloomy—they like to attend parties and picnics. Bowen loved to travel and talk, and *A Time in Rome* and *The Shelbourne* reflect her unusual verbal ability to paint scenes of places and regions.

Bowen's painterly perceptions dominate her style and descriptive passages in her fiction through her narrators and characters, who are astutely observant of rooms, landscapes, and social mores. Her recurrent preoccupation appears throughout her canon to be a sense of place, an interest in a child's perception, and her insistence upon middle-class manners and behaviors. Early attitudes or social behavior and place permeate her consciousness and writings. Having an income large enough to support these values provided Bowen with ingenuity and determination, for Bowen's Court, which she inherited in 1930, after her father's death, cost a great deal to maintain. The proceeds of her writings were poured into that house. For years, she was a regular reviewer for *The Observer*, *The Spectator*, *Horizon*, and *New Statesman*. Bowen married Alan Charles Cameron in 1923, who then managed her publishing affairs.

Critics proclaimed Bowen's writing reached maturity with the publication of the highly acclaimed novel *The House in Paris*. Thereafter and through World War II, Bowen carefully ordered her life to include writing, publishing, speaking, and reviewing. During World War II, while living in London, besides being an air-raid warden and having her house in Regent's park bombed a number of times, she worked on or completed some of her most important stories, for example, "The Demon Lover," "Ivy Gripped the Steps," and the novels *The Heat of the Day* and *A World of Love*. Thereafter, Bowen traveled for the British Council, spoke and wrote for the British Broadcasting Corporation (BBC), and continued to write until her death. Her posthumously published *Pictures and Conversations* includes autobiography and chapters of a novel. Though her writings have gone in and out of print and have been published in numerous foreign languages, including Japanese and Serbo-Croatian, there has been at least one complete reprinting of all of her novels. Bowen's writing, from 1923 to 1973, reflects with consummate skill and perception an exploration of middle-class society in Ireland, England, France, Italy, and the United States. She reveals the contradictions, problems, and complexities of society with a rich intensity, verbally painted with extraordinary deftness.

BIBLIOGRAPHICAL REFERENCES: *Elizabeth Bowen*, 1981, edited by J'nan Morse Sellery and William O. Harris, includes a descriptive and enumerative bibliography of Bowen's writings (books and pamphlets, contributions to books, pamphlets, and periodicals, translations, manuscripts, radio and television productions and appearances) and a checklist of writings about her. See also "Elizabeth Bowen: A Check List," *Bulletin of the New York Public Library*, LXXIV (April, 1970), 219-274. Two critical biographies, Victoria Glendinning, *Elizabeth Bowen: A Biography*, 1978, and Hermione Lee, *Elizabeth Bowen: An Estimation*, 1981, are valuable for integrating her life and writings. For biographical interest, see also Charles Ritchie, *The Siren Years: Undiplomatic Diaries 1937-1945*, 1974; May Sarton, "Elizabeth Bowen," in *A World of Light: Portraits and Celebrations*, 1970. Additionally, a prefatory essay by Hermione Lee in *The Mulberry Tree: Writings of Elizabeth Bowen*, 1986, provides a discourse on Bowen's essays, reviews, prefaces, letters, broadcasts, and autobiographies. For important earlier critical commentary, see also A. E. Austin, *Elizabeth Bowen*, 1971; Harriet Blodgett, *Patterns of Reality: Elizabeth Bowen's Novels*, 1975; Jocelyn Brooke, *Elizabeth Bowen*, 1952; James Hall, *The Lunatic Giant in the Drawing Room: The British and American Novel Since 1930*, 1968; Jane Rule, "Elizabeth Bowen 1899-1973," in *Lesbian Images*, 1975; and for one of the first critical commentaries on Bowen's fiction, see William Heath, *Elizabeth Bowen: An Introduction to Her Novels*, 1961.

J'nan Morse Sellery

JANE BOWLES

Born: New York, New York *Died:* Málaga, Spain
Date: February 22, 1917 *Date:* May 4, 1973

PRINCIPAL WORKS

NOVEL: *Two Serious Ladies*, 1943.
PLAY: *In the Summer House*, pr., pb. 1954.
SHORT FICTION: *Plain Pleasures*, 1966; *The Collected Works of Jane Bowles*, 1966; *Feminine Wiles*, 1976; *My Sister's Hand in Mine*, 1978.

Jane Bowles, author of a novel, short stories, and one full-length play, has, despite her limited opus, been proclaimed by such writers as Tennessee Williams as a major American writer of prose fiction. Born Jane Auer in New York City in 1917, she was the daughter of Clair Stajer, who had been trained as a teacher, and Sidney Major Auer, who died when his daughter was thirteen. Following her father's death, the daughter was cared for by her affectionate, possessive, and ambitious mother. Problems between mothers and daughters surface throughout Bowles's work. In *In the Summer House*, for example, Gertrude Eastman imagines that her daughter is "plotting something." After one semester at public school, Mrs. Auer enrolled her daughter at Stoneleigh, an exclusive girl's school. Less than six months later, Jane fell from a horse, breaking her leg. Because of continuing medical problems, she was sent to a clinic in Leysin, Switzerland, where she was educated for the next two years by a private tutor. On the journey back to the United States, while reading *Voyage au bout de la nuit* (1932), Bowles met its author, Louis-Ferdinand Céline. Upon her return to America, she announced, "I am a writer, and I want to write."

Between 1914 and 1937, Bowles lived with her mother in New York City, where she briefly attended acting school before writing "Le Phaéton hypocrite" in French, all copies of which have been lost. In 1937, she met Paul Bowles, composer and author, whom she married in 1938. After a stay in Central America and Paris, the Bowleses returned to New York City and, subsequently, lived in a farmhouse on Staten Island, the model for Miss Goerling's house in *Two Serious Ladies*. After traveling in Mexico, they shared a brownstone in Brooklyn Heights with such well-known figures as W. H. Auden, Benjamin Britten, and Gypsy Rose Lee. From 1947 until 1967, when she entered a hospital in Málaga, Spain, Bowles spent most of her time in Tangier, Morocco. During that twenty-year period, however, she rarely wrote about Morocco or the life around her.

In *Two Serious Ladies*, Bowles introduces the themes of sin, loneliness, and salvation—motifs which inform much of her subsequent work. Written in three parts, the novel shifts between the worlds of New York and Panama. Like Bowles herself, the characters in *Two Serious Ladies* are rootless and peripatetic; they seek a home but also fear the constraints that such ordered existences impose. A "nest," for example, may turn out to be a brothel. Following "A Guatemalan Idyll" in 1941, "A Day in the Open" in 1945, and "Plain Pleasures" in 1946, Bowles published "Camp Cataract" in 1949, often considered to be her most successful short story. The story utilizes Bowles's essential plot: One woman seeks to escape from the traditional pattern of her life while another woman advocates restraint, prudence, and dependency. Themes of alienation and dependency dominate Bowles's only full-length drama, *In the Summer House*. Much like Laura in Tennessee Williams' *The Glass Menagerie* (pr. 1944), the main character, Molly, occupies a dreamworld buttressed by her strong-willed and manipulative mother. Like many of Bowles's characters, Molly cannot communicate with those around her. In such a charged mother-daughter relationship, love becomes destructive as the young Molly murders an outgoing young girl her own age whom she considers a rival for her mother's affection.

The main characters in Bowles's fiction are usually women who feel isolated and guilt-ridden in a world stripped of myth. Bowles's fictional terrain is that of a nightmare where fear and loneliness are givens. The only respite from such anxiety is a retreat to prelapsarian childhood, or to eccentricity and madness. It is difficult to characterize Bowles's style; however, terms such as Kafkaesque and surrealistic seem appropriate. Unlike such contemporaries as William Faulkner, Flannery O'Connor, and Carson McCullers, Bowles's art is neither rooted in a sense of place nor set in a specific social milieu. Relatively little has been written about Bowles's work, perhaps because of the notion, shared by Bowles herself, that she belonged to a European rather than American tradition. As a result of her fall from a horse and ensuing medical complications, a formative segment of Bowles's education took place in Europe. She felt that her limp marked her as different even to the most casual observer. Moreover, growing up, Bowles was curiously distanced from her Jewish background. She attempted to write while living in Morocco, a cultural milieu thoroughly different from what she had experienced. Despite the publication of *The Collected Works* in 1966 and an expanded collection, *My Sister's Hand in Mine*, in 1978, Bowles continues to be viewed as something of an underground writer. Nevertheless, she has commanded a loyal coterie of admirers including John Ashbery, Kenneth Koch, and James Purdy.

BIBLIOGRAPHICAL REFERENCES: Millicent Dillon, *A Little Original Sin: The Life and Work of Jane Bowles*, 1981, provides a complete account of Bowles's life and work. Another useful study is Paul Bowles's autobiography, *Without Stopping*, 1972, which sheds light on the marriage of the two authors, their life in Morocco, and Jane Bowles's writer's block. See also *World Authors, 1950-1970*, 1975, edited by John Wakeman; James Kraft, "Jane Bowles as Serious Lady," *Novel: A Forum on Fiction*, I/II (1967/1969), 273-277; Millicent Dillon, "The Three Exiles of Jane Bowles," *Confrontation*, 1984, 72-74; Robert Lougy, "The World and Art of Jane Bowles (1917-1973)," *College English Association Critic*, XLIX (1986/1987), 157-173. Other helpful articles include *The New York Times Book Review*, May 9, 1943, and January 29, 1967; *The New York Review of Books*, December, 1966; and *Saturday Review*, January 14, 1967.

Suzann Bick

PAUL BOWLES

Born: Jamaica, New York
Date: December 30, 1910

PRINCIPAL WORKS

NOVELS: *The Sheltering Sky*, 1929; *Let It Come Down*, 1952; *The Spider's House*, 1955; *Up Above the World*, 1966; *Points in Time*, 1982.

SHORT FICTION: *A Little Stone: Stories*, 1950; *The Delicate Prey and Other Stories*, 1950; *The Hours After Noon: Short Stories*, 1959; *A Hundred Camels in the Courtyard*, 1962; *The Time of Friendship: A Volume of Short Stories*, 1967; *Pages from Cold Point and Other Stories*, 1968; *Three Tales*, 1975; *Collected Stories*, 1979; *Midnight Mass*, 1981.

AUTOBIOGRAPHY: *Without Stopping: An Autobiography*, 1972.

POETRY: *Scenes*, 1968; *The Thicket of Spring: Poems, 1926-1969*, 1972; *Next to Nothing*, 1976; *Next to Nothing: Collected Poems, 1926-1977*, 1981.

NONFICTION: *Their Heads Are Green and Their Hands Are Blue*, 1963.

TRANSLATION: *No Exit*, 1946 (by Jean-Paul Sartre).

Paul Bowles was gifted in so many areas that his dentist father and schoolteacher mother feared that their only child would find no real direction. They had little cause to worry. By age sixteen, their son had composed music and published his first poem in the trendy literary magazine *transition*.

Finishing secondary school at midterm in 1928, Bowles enrolled in New York's School of Design and Liberal Arts, waiting out the months before admission to the University of Virginia in September, 1928. By March of 1929, he had bolted to Paris on a six-month adventure. Out of money, he rushed back to New York, living on earnings as a book store clerk. He spent every spare moment writing his first, unpublished, novel, "Without Stopping," a work which provided the title for his autobiography in 1972. Another semester in Charlottesville, Virginia, convinced him that he knew better ways to learn than the university could offer.

Bowles returned to New York to study music with composer Aaron Copland, who, recognizing Bowles's unique musical ability, urged him to study in Paris with Nadia Boulanger, a suggestion Bowles embraced eagerly. In 1931, Bowles met Gertrude Stein and Alice B. Toklas in Paris. Both encouraged him in his writing, and Toklas recommended that Bowles, who preferred summer over winter, try living in Morocco, which afforded a yearlong mild climate. Bowles followed this suggestion. After he and Copland spent part of the summer with Stein and Toklas in the South of France, they settled into life in Tangier. There Bowles remained. He first devoted himself to music, but in 1937, after meeting his future wife, novelist Jane Bowles, he turned to writing full-time.

Bowles found writing more satisfying than composing music because of the precision language permits. He found that the strangeness of Arab culture and the clash between it and modern Western culture provided him with a context for expressing his ingrained nihilism, which was substantially heightened by his exposure to writers such as Albert Camus, André Gide, and Jean-Paul Sartre. Bowles's translation of Sartre's *Huis-clos* (pr. 1944; *No Exit*, 1946) is the standard English version of the play. Bowles's childhood exposure to the short stories of Edgar Allan Poe also influenced his writing.

Bowles's first and second novels, *The Sheltering Sky* and *Let It Come Down*, remain his best-known works. *The Sheltering Sky* is the engrossing tale of Kit and Port Moresby, New Yorkers who, with their friend Tunner, tackle North Africa. They venture into the Sahara, whose barrenness mirrors the barrenness of their lives. They are, according to Bowles, travelers, not merely tourists. The Moresbys have traveled for the twelve years of their peripatetic marriage, now threatened by adulterous affairs. They send Tunner off with two other Americans, Mrs. Lyle and her son Eric, who are having an incestuous affair, and try to save their marriage. Port, however, neglecting to have his typhoid immunization, contracts the disease. Kit leaves his bedside to go into town and meet Tunner, on his return. She is locked out of the fort in which they have been staying, and, during that night, Port dies. Kit joins the caravan of an Arab band, becoming involved with two of the Arab men. Wifely objections to her presence eventually force Kit, now on the brink of insanity, back to Oran, where she wanders into the Casbah, presumably never to return. The thesis of this metaphoric, nihilistic novel is that nothing exists beyond the sheltering sky referred to in its title. The here exists, the now exists, neither of them meaningful. They are, however, all that people have; beyond them lies an abyss.

In his other novels, Bowles is directly concerned with how and whether the two worlds he knows best can ever understand each other, if one can ever have meaning for the other. The answer his characters suggest is that there is little meaning even in their own worlds; to look for meaning in alien worlds is unrealistic. *Let It Come Down*, set in Tangier, focuses on a bank clerk, Nelson Dyar from New York, who has come to Tangier seeking adventure. He kills an Arab by accident and is exposed to the whole treachery of Tangier's exotic society. The novel is absurdist in the way Camus' writing often was and emphasizes, as do most of Bowles's short stories and his two other novels, the question of bridging opposing cultures.

In 1960, Bowles began collecting and translating Moghrebi literature, both oral and written. He translates it into English in an attempt to preserve the native literature of his adopted home. Because of his self-banishment from the United States and from mainstream literary circles, Bowles has not gained the recognition that the quality of his work demands. He has, however, had a persistent following of sophisticated readers, and he is beginning to be recognized as one of the most profound writers of modern literature.

BIBLIOGRAPHICAL REFERENCES: Harvey Breit's early interview, "Talk with Paul Bowles," *The New York Times Book Review*, March 9, 1952, 19, remains a valuable early resource, as do John W. Aldridge's observations in his chapter on Bowles in *After the Lost Generation: A Critical Study of the Writers of Two Wars*, 1951, revised 1958, which focuses on *The Sheltering Sky*. Christopher Sawyer-Lauçanno, *An Invisible Spectator*, 1989, is a thoroughly researched biography which relies on interviews with Bowles's closest associates; it also includes an interview with Bowles himself. Johannes Willem Bertens' *The Fiction of Paul Bowles: The Soul Is the Weariest Part of the Body*, 1979, offers substantive information but does not develop the interconnections between Bowles's writing and that of other existential writers. Lawrence D. Stewart's *Paul Bowles: The Illumination of North Africa*, 1974, is a careful, well-documented monograph. *Twentieth Century Literature*, XXXIII (Fall/Winter, 1986), is devoted completely to Bowles. See also Joseph Voelker's "Fish Traps and Purloined Letters: The Anthropology of Paul Bowles," *Critique*, XXVII (Fall, 1985), and Linda W. Wagner's "Paul Bowles and the Characterization of Women," *Critique*, XXVII (Fall, 1985), a feminist appraisal of Bowles. Sanford Pinsker's article "Post-War Civilization and Its Existential Discontents: Paul Bowles's *The Sheltering Sky*," in the same issue of *Critique*, is also worthwhile.

R. Baird Shuman

KAY BOYLE

Born: St. Paul, Minnesota
Date: February 19, 1903

Principal Works

SHORT FICTION: *Short Stories*, 1929; *Wedding Day and Other Stories*, 1930; *First Lover and Other Stories*, 1933; *The White Horses of Vienna and Other Stories*, 1936; *The Crazy Hunter and Other Stories*, 1940; *Thirty Stories*, 1948; *The Smoking Mountain: Stories of Postwar Germany*, 1951; *Nothing Ever Breaks Except the Heart*, 1966; *Fifty Stories*, 1980; *Life Being the Best and Other Stories*, 1988.

NOVELS AND NOVELLAS: *Plagued by the Nightingale*, 1931; *Year Before Last*, 1932; *Gentlemen, I Address You Privately*, 1933; *My Next Bride*, 1934; *Death of a Man*, 1936; *Monday Night*, 1938; *Primer for Combat*, 1942; *Avalanche*, 1943; *A Frenchman Must Die*, 1946; *1939: A Novel*, 1948; *His Human Majesty*, 1949; *The Seagull on the Step*, 1955; *Three Short Novels*, 1958; *Generation Without Farewell*, 1960; *The Underground Woman*, 1975.

POETRY: *A Glad Day*, 1938; *American Citizen Naturalized in Leadville, Colorado: A Poem*, 1944; *Collected Poems*, 1962; *Testament for My Students and Other Poems*, 1970; *This Is Not a Letter and Other Poems*, 1985.

ESSAYS: *The Long Walk at San Francisco State and Other Essays*, 1970; *Words That Must Somehow Be Said: The Selected Essays of Kay Boyle, 1927-1983*, 1985.

CHILDREN'S LITERATURE: *The Youngest Camel*, 1939; *The Youngest Camel Reconsidered and Rewritten*, 1959; *Pinky, the Cat Who Liked to Sleep*, 1966; *Pinky in Persia*, 1968.

For more than half a century Kay Boyle has fused personal experience and social commitment in finely wrought fiction, poetry, and essays. The daughter of Howard Peterson Boyle and Katherine Evans Boyle, she was born in St. Paul, Minnesota, on February 19, 1903. Her grandfather, Jesse Peyton Boyle, who founded West Publishing Company, producer of legal texts, provided the family with enough money to travel extensively, so Boyle spent her childhood in a variety of places, including Philadelphia, Atlantic City, Europe, and Cincinnati. Jesse Peyton Boyle also gave his granddaughter a model for stubborn, conservative characters in her fiction, as her mother served as the prototype for her forward-looking, compassionate figures.

Because of the family's frequent moves, Boyle received little formal education, though she did study architecture for two years at the Ohio Mechanics Institute (1917-1919). Encouraged by her mother, she went to New York in 1922, where her sister, Joan, was working for *Vogue*. Boyle briefly served on the staff of this magazine before moving to the more congenial *Broom*, a literary journal. She also began publishing: "Monody to the Sound of Zithers" appeared in *Poetry* in 1922, and *Broom* published "Morning" in its issue for January, 1923.

On June 24, 1922, she was married to Robert Brault, an engineer, and the following year the couple went to France to spend the summer with Brault's parents. Boyle was to remain in Europe for eighteen years, living in Paris, the South of France, England, and Austria. She was divorced and remarried. Boyle began to write about her experiences while rearing half a dozen children. During this period she won two O. Henry awards, for "White Horses of Vienna" in 1935 and for "Defeat" in 1941, and she received a Guggenheim fellowship in 1934. Back in the United States, she was married to her third husband, Joseph von Franckenstein, an Austrian who served with the Austrian army during World War II and later with the American occupation in Germany. Boyle returned to Europe in 1946 as a correspondent for *The New Yorker*, but in 1953 she lost this position after she was accused of harboring Communist sympathies, a charge that also cost her husband his job with the government.

Following von Franckenstein's death in 1963, Boyle moved to San Francisco, where she joined the faculty of San Francisco State University (retired 1979) and helped establish a chapter of Amnesty International. Her writings have earned for her membership in the National Institute of Arts and Letters, and the American Academy of Arts and Letters. She also received a second Guggenheim Fellowship (1961); fellowships from Wesleyan University, the Radcliffe Institute for Independent Study, and the National Endowment for the Arts (1980); and honorary doctorates from Columbia University, the University of Chicago, Skidmore College, and Southern Illinois University. Active politically as well as literarily, she was jailed in 1968 after a sit-in at the Oakland Induction Center to protest the Vietnam War.

Boyle's political concerns have informed her writing since the 1940's. Having witnessed the rise of Nazism, she devoted much of her fiction during and immediately following World War II to the conflict between totalitarianism and the democracies. "Defeat" criticizes French complacency toward the German Occupation. "War in Paris" satirizes a Mrs. Hodges, whose sole concern with Fascist militarism is its effect on her cat, and "Battle of the Sequins" shows Americans squabbling over blouses while Europe burns. On the back cover of *Primer for Combat* she urged readers to buy war bonds to promote "the survival of that freedom, honor, and human dignity which can be lost if" people fail to act. In *The Underground Woman* and *Testament for My Students and Other Poems* she has addressed more recent issues, such as the Vietnam War and civil rights.

Her own experiences have served as the basis of much of her work. *The Underground Woman* draws on her anti-Vietnam War activities, the hero of *Primer for Combat* bears many similarities to her third husband, and *My Next Bride* is based on the six months she spent at Neuilly, France, where Raymond Duncan had established a commune. At its best, though, her writing transcends the personal to examine the universal need for love and the difficulty of finding it. Occasionally her characters succeed. In "Astronomer's Wife" the heroine finds happiness with a plumber, and in *Year Before Last* Hannah and Eve, both in love with Martin, reach an uneasy truce. More often Boyle shows love betrayed. In *Gentlemen, I Address You Privately*, Munday, a former priest, helps Ayton, an escaped seaman, hide from the authorities. In return, Ayton sells Munday's beloved piano and flees with three lesbians, leaving behind not only Munday but also Leonie, who sheltered him and who is carrying his child. "Wedding Day" portrays a mother's indifference to her daughter's sadness over her impending marriage and the inability of the girl's brother to help despite his love for his sister.

Sandra Whipple Spanier has observed that Boyle's reputation would be higher had she produced a different kind of literature. Instead of writing about politics in the 1930's, she chose the less fashionable subject of personal relationships. Later, when she did turn to public issues, she often sacrificed characterization and plot to moral. An unflattering review by Edmund Wilson, who condemned *Avalanche*, her one popular success, also hurt, and the need to produce stories for money led to works that were not always carefully crafted. Yet her eye for detail, her ear for dialogue, and her concern for love and social justice justify the early praise she received and well deserve the renewed interest in her work.

BIBLIOGRAPHICAL REFERENCES: Roberta Sharp, "A Bibliography of Works by and About Kay Boyle," *Bulletin of Bibliography*, XXXV (October, 1978), 180-189, provides a good list of primary and secondary sources. Sandra Whipple Spanier, *Kay Boyle: Artist and Activist*, 1986, the first book-length study of the author, also includes a useful bibliography. Richard C. Carpenter, "Kay Boyle: The Figure in the Carpet," *Critique: Studies in Modern Fiction*, VII (Winter, 1964/1965), 65-78, focuses on *The Crazy Hunter and Other Stories* to show how Boyle treats the theme of love. Carpenter has also published another study of the author, "Kay Boyle," *English Journal*, XLII (November, 1953), 425-430. Harry T. Moore, "Kay Boyle's Fiction," *The Kenyon Review*, XXII (Spring, 1960), 323-326, a review of *Generation Without Farewell*, surveys Boyle's writings to 1960 and praises her skill. Richard Howard, "Poetry Chronicle," *Poetry*, CII (July, 1963), 250-259, reviewing her *Collected Poems*, is less flattering but admires her mixture of poetic prose and prosaic poetry. Other useful pieces on

Boyle include Sandra Whipple Spanier's introduction to *Life Being the Best and Other Stories*, 1988; Evelyn Harter, "Kay Boyle: Experimenter," *Bookman*, LXXV (1932), 249-253; Harry T. Moore, "Kay Boyle's Fiction," in *The Age of the Modern and Other Essays*, 1971; Katherine Anne Porter, "Kay Boyle: Example to the Young," in *The Critic as Artist: Essays on Books, 1920-1970*, 1972, edited by G. H. Harrison; David Margo, "Kay Boyle," in *Women Writers of the West Coast: Speaking of Their Lives and Careers*, 1983, edited by Marilyn Yalom; and David R. Mesher, "Kay Boyle: An Eightieth Birthday Interview," *The Malahat Review*, LXV (July, 1983), 82-95.

Joseph Rosenblum

T. CORAGHESSAN BOYLE

Born: Peekskill, New York
Date: 1948

PRINCIPAL WORKS

NOVELS: *Water Music*, 1981; *Budding Prospects: A Pastoral*, 1984; *World's End*, 1987.
SHORT FICTION: *The Descent of Man*, 1979; *Greasy Lake and Other Stories*, 1985.

T. Coraghessan Boyle combines an affection for the surreal with a sure sense of comic voice and timing to produce fiction that is often bizarre but entertaining. He was born in Peekskill, New York, in 1948. He holds master of fine arts and doctorate degrees from the University of Iowa and teaches English at the University of Southern California. He has won a Pushcart Prize (1977), the St. Lawrence Prize (1980), and the Aga Kahn Prize (1981). Along with contemporaries such as Max Apple, he is a leader in the reaction against minimalist fiction. His characters, sometimes based on caricatures of figures from popular culture, may be unusual in appearance or behavior but manage to think and talk as human beings. On balance, his work presents a humorous if not always optimistic view of modern times and of American culture.

Boyle's first collection, *The Descent of Man*, begins with an epigraph from Tarzan: "Ungowa." The animal energy of that human utterance is an apt prelude to stories which examine, among other things, what it means to be human. In the title story, a researcher finds herself in love with a brilliant chimpanzee who translates abstract philosophical works such as Charles Darwin's *The Descent of Man* (1871) into the symbol language called Yerkish. The sureness of Boyle's ear for comedy is apparent in the opening paragraph of "We Are Norsemen," a story about Vikings that shows that even those who rape and plunder may have their times of depression. The often-subtle differences between masculine and feminine are the subject in "A Women's Restaurant," in which the protagonist is led by his obsession with feminine behavior to renounce his own sex. There is much graphic violence in the stories in *The Descent of Man*, but it is handled with wit and ironic intelligence, so that it generally enlightens rather than frightens.

Water Music is a long, picaresque novel that manages to be many things at once. On the first level, it is a strong, fast-paced account of the Scottish explorer Mungo Park and his hairbreadth escapes from torture and death in Africa. It is also the story of Ned Rise, a small-time London thief who seeks to elevate himself. *Water Music* is told, as often as not, in a jazzy twentieth century American slang that mocks solemn nineteenth century sentimentalism. The presence of an intrusive narrator who is always ready to point out ironies or make jokes at the expense of the characters and capable of inserting chapter titles such as "Oh, Mama, Can This Really Be the End?" is reminiscent of eighteenth century satires.

Budding Prospects is both a novel and a kind of handbook for the growing of marijuana—or rather a cautionary account of how not to grow it. At the same time, it is a wry commentary on the passing of the hippie generation and the introduction of business tactics into the distribution of controlled substances. Vogelgesang (German for "birdsong"), an ephemeral confidence man, hires a team of ambitious former hippies to raise a crop of marijuana; the enterprise is doomed from the beginning, but Felix, the narrator, survives the experience with his dignity and sense of humor intact. The conflict between marijuana growers and society, exemplified by the cop Jerpbak, is as melodramatic as Jerpbak's mirrored sunglasses. There is both comic relief and philosophical content in this novel, and the effect is to make *Budding Prospects* seem less than serious fiction.

In the stories contained in *Greasy Lake and Other Stories*, Boyle recaptures the strangeness of his earliest work but adds a seasoned, patient acceptance of the weaknesses of human nature that was missing in stories such as "The Descent of Man." The title story, with its epigraph from rock singer Bruce Springsteen, relates a night out for some young suburban males who "wheeled our parents' whining station wagons out on the street [and] left a patch of rubber half a block long." The rest of their adventure is an equally strange interplay of the romantic and the real, with the ultimate reality of death coinciding with the destruction of the station wagon. The implicit satire on the shallowness of rock culture is carried over into "All Shook Up," in which a bad Elvis Presley impersonator flashes across the paths of a couple with troubles of their own. Other stories in the collection deal with themes such as surrogate motherhood ("Caviar") and pie-in-the-sky politics ("The New Moon Party") with varying degrees of surrealism. The most effective piece in the collection is a somber reminiscence of the final days of Robert Johnson, a blues guitarist of the 1930's.

In *World's End*, Boyle creates another sprawling novel with multiple layers and strands of plot and a large, often bizarre, cast of characters. In the largest sense, the novel is about the Hudson River landscape and the character of its citizens; it spans more than three hundred years of history and an equally wide range of socioeconomic classes. Its twin poles are the Peekskill Riots of 1949, in which a group of neo-Nazis assaulted Jews and blacks, and the events surrounding the establishment of Dutch family dynasties in the seventeenth century. The Van Brunt family begins life in America as indentured servants to the wealthy Van Warts, and the descendants of the two families are intertwined in the twentieth century events. Many of the story's incidental details, and something of the character of the protagonist, Walter Van Brunt, are autobiographical, based on Boyle's adolescence in Peekskill (called "Peterskill" in the novel). *World's End* is an effective combination of history and comedy that reinforces Boyle's significant place in contemporary fiction.

BIBLIOGRAPHICAL REFERENCES: For a personal profile of Boyle, see Paul Ciotti, "The Doctor Is In," *Los Angeles Times Magazine*, II (August 3, 1986), 16-21. Reviews of his novels and collections of stories may be found in *The New York Times Book Review* (December 27, 1981; June 6, 1982; July 1, 1984; June 9, 1985; July 21, 1985; and September 27, 1987); in *The Washington Post Book World* (February 7, 1982, and June 23, 1985); and in *The Times Literary Supplement* (June 20, 1980; February 26, 1982; September 14, 1985; and January 31, 1986). There is a brief but useful interview with Boyle in *Publishers Weekly*, CCXXXII (October 9, 1987), 71-72.

Robert Boyd

MALCOLM BRADBURY

Born: Sheffield, England
Date: September 7, 1932

PRINCIPAL WORKS

NOVELS: *Eating People Is Wrong*, 1959; *Stepping Westward*, 1965; *The History Man*, 1975; *Rates of Exchange*, 1983.

NOVELLAS: *Cuts: A Very Short Novel*, 1987; *Mesonge: Structuralism's Hidden Hero*, 1987 (also known as *My Quest for Mesonge*).

PLAY: *The After Dinner Game*, pb. 1982.

CRITICISM: *What Is a Novel?*, 1973; *The Novel Today*, 1977; *Saul Bellow*, 1982; *The Modern American Novel*, 1983; *No, Not Bloomsbury*, 1987; *The Modern World: Ten Great Writers*, 1988.

EDITED TEXTS: *Modernism: 1890-1930*, 1978 (with James McFarlane); *An Introduction to American Studies*, 1981 (with Howard Temperley).

MISCELLANEOUS: *Unsent Letters: Irreverent Notes from a Literary Life*, 1988.

Malcolm Bradbury is among the handful of contemporary British fiction writers who have managed to extend the range of the English novel by simultaneously working within and against the liberal-realist tradition that has dominated British writing in the nineteenth and twentieth centuries. Equally important, his career encapsulates the shift which has occurred in postwar British fiction from a more or less provincial realism to a decidedly international postmodernism.

Bradbury was born on September 7, 1932, in Sheffield, England. Attending college during the 1950's, he was among the many middle- and lower-middle class students to benefit from the expansion of England's university system immediately after World War II. His first novel, *Eating People Is Wrong*, draws extensively on Bradbury's student days at three "redbrick" universities (Leicester, London, and Manchester) and evidences an obvious but by no means slavish debt to Kingsley Amis' first novel, also set in a redbrick university, *Lucky Jim* (1954), which began the assault on social and academic privilege and pretense. Both novels are satirical. They belong to the English comic novel tradition and, more specifically, to the subgenre of the "campus novel." What especially distinguishes Bradbury's novel is a depth of moral concern which derives from the liberal-humanist tradition that Bradbury both endorses and questions. This doubleness of vision and intent becomes much more evident in his second novel, *Stepping Westward*. Here, Bradbury, drawing on his own experiences at American universities in the mid- and late 1950's, focuses on the plight of a young, iconoclastic English novelist as he acts out his part of visiting writer-in-residence in the American cultural and academic wilderness. Reversing the direction of the Jamesian international novel, Bradbury juxtaposes not only two nations and societies but also, more important, two very different kinds of liberalism and two very different narrative styles. The result is a work in which each is tested but no one emerges entirely victorious or entirely unscathed by Bradbury's satire and skepticism. He probes a number of cultural, political, moral, and literary issues without attempting to impose any definitive solutions. As novelist and as moralist, he seeks to provoke rather than propound.

Just as his work as a novelist cannot be separated from his belief in liberal humanism, neither can it be separated from his work as literary critic. Even as a critic in the tradition of Matthew Arnold and F. R. Leavis, Bradbury has demonstrated a deep and ever-increasing interest in the contemporary literary theories which have largely supplanted the liberal-humanist tradition. Awareness of and attraction to contemporary theory has not, however, prevented Bradbury from stubbornly maintaining his faith in character (the literary representation of the liberal-humanist individual) and his belief that literature in general and the novel in particular exists every bit as much in a social and historical context as it does as an intextual space, or event. In the face of the postmodern challenge to individual (bourgeois) authorship and merely "readable" (consumable) texts, Bradbury insists upon his own authorial existence and authority, but in an increasingly self-conscious way which pays deference to the very forces Bradbury would like to defeat.

Thus, Bradbury does not nostalgically and anachronistically indulge himself and his reader by writing conventional novels of social and moral concern, but neither are his novels examples of postmodern play. *The History Man* is at once a critique of the sociological perspective that has displaced both the individual self and narrative art and a pyrotechnically postmodern text in which Bradbury makes use of a variety of innovative techniques in an effort to discover how much, or how little, of the liberal-humanist tradition remains viable following the onslaught of dehumanization in all of its forms: political, social, academic, and aesthetic. The conflicts in Bradbury's fiction between old England and new England (*Eating People Is Wrong*) and between England and America (*Stepping Westward*) have escalated in *The History Man* to the point that the individual is in danger of disappearing altogether in a world, as in a fiction, in which style has replaced substance and technical mastery has replaced moral concern.

Bradbury's moral and narrative interests lead as if inevitably to the densely stylized prose of *The History Man* and to the parodic, Thomas Pynchon-like richness of *Rates of Exchange*. The main character of this latter novel, another of Bradbury's inept and befuddled academics, finds himself displaced by a multiplicity of political, narrative, and linguistic systems. Yet the fact that he is displaced paradoxically ensures his presence in Bradbury's novel of comic despair and postmodern permutations. Clownish, inconsequential, and virtually insignificant, Professor Petworth survives not as hero or even as protagonist but as the poststructuralist "trace" of the liberal-humanist self. Bradbury refuses to relinquish that self, even as he acknowledges the growing odds against its continued existence in a world in which it and the novel grow ever more marginal. As a writer of short stories, a parodist, a satirist, a writer of radio and television plays, and above all a critic and novelist, Malcolm Bradbury has consistently sought to explore both the possibilities as well as the limitations of the liberal-humanist aesthetic. He has sought to adopt the techniques and assumptions of postmodernism and poststructuralism to extend the boundaries of that aesthetic, about whose survival he has grown increasingly determined and increasingly skeptical.

BIBLIOGRAPHICAL REFERENCES: The most comprehensive study is Robert A. Morace's *The Dialogical Novels of Malcolm Bradbury and David Lodge*, 1987, which discusses Bradbury's work (the novels in particular) from the perspective of Mikhail Bakhtin's theory of dialogism. Patricia Waugh's discussion of Bradbury as an innovator in her *Metafiction*, 1984, is especially useful. Peter Widdowson's "The Anti-History Men: Malcolm Bradbury and David Lodge," *Critical Quarterly*, XXVI (1984), 5-32, views Bradbury in a quite different light, as a closet conservative who uses certain innovative techniques to mask a reactionary bourgeois aesthetic. For less tendentious discussions of individual novels, see Martin Green's "Transatlantic Communications: Malcolm Bradbury's *Stepping Westward*," in *Old Lines, New Forces*, 1976, edited by Robert K. Morris; Richard Todd's "Malcolm Bradbury's *The History Man*: The Novelist as Reluctant Impresario," *Dutch Quarterly Review of Anglo-American Letters*, XI (1981), 162-182; and Robert S. Burton's "A Plurality of Voices: Malcolm Bradbury's *Rates of Exchange*," *Critique: Studies in Modern Fiction*, XXVIII (1987), 101-106. Indispensable interviews have appeared in John Haffenden, *Novelists in Interview*, 1985; Heide Ziegler and Christopher Bigsby, *The Radical Imagination and the Liberal Tradition*, 1982; and *Dutch Quarterly Review of Anglo-American Letters*, XI (1982), 183-196.

Robert A. Morace

RAY BRADBURY

Born: Waukegan, Illinois
Date: August 22, 1920

PRINCIPAL WORKS

SHORT FICTION: *Dark Carnival*, 1947; *The Martian Chronicles*, 1950; *The Illustrated Man*, 1951; *The Golden Apples of the Sun*, 1953; *The October Country*, 1955; *A Medicine for Melancholy*, 1959; *The Machineries of Joy*, 1964; *I Sing the Body Electric!*, 1969; *The Stories of Ray Bradbury*, 1980; *The Toynbee Convector*, 1988.

NOVELS: *Fahrenheit 451*, 1953; *Dandelion Wine*, 1957; *Something Wicked This Way Comes*, 1962; *Death Is a Lonely Business*, 1985.

PLAYS: *The Anthem Sprinters and Other Antics*, pb. 1963; *The World of Ray Bradbury: Three Fables of the Future*, pr. 1964; *The Day It Rained Forever*, pb. 1966; *The Pedestrian*, pb. 1966; *The Wonderful Ice Cream Suit and Other Plays*, pb. 1972; *Pillar of Fire and Other Plays for Today, Tomorrow, and Beyond Tomorrow*, pb. 1975.

SCREENPLAYS: *It Came from Outer Space*, 1952 (with David Schwartz); *Moby Dick*, 1956 (with John Huston); *Icarus Montgolfier Wright*, 1961 (with George C. Johnson); *The Picasso Summer*, 1967 (with Edwin Boyd).

POETRY: *Old Ahab's Friend, and Friend to Noah, Speaks His Piece: A Celebration*, 1971; *When Elephants Last in the Dooryard Bloomed: Celebrations for Almost Any Day in the Year*, 1973; *Where Robot Mice and Robot Men Run Round in Robot Towns: New Poems, Both Light and Dark*, 1977; *The Haunted Computer and the Android Pope*, 1981.

ANTHOLOGIES: *Timeless Stories for Today and Tomorrow*, 1952; *The Circus of Dr. Lao and Other Improbable Stories*, 1956.

Ray Douglas Bradbury used his elegiac short stories, often in the genres of fantasy and science fiction, to comment on the beguiling power of the imagination and the dehumanizing pressures of technocracies. He once said that he would have liked to have been born on Halloween. He was forced to settle for the real date of August 22, 1920, in Waukegan, Illinois. His father, Leonard Spaulding Bradbury, was a lineman with the Waukegan Bureau of Power and Light; his mother, Esther Marie (Moberg) Bradbury, had emigrated as a child from Sweden. Bradbury grew up with an older brother, who later appeared in fictionalized form in his stories.

The most important event of his childhood occurred when he was twelve years old. A carnival had come to town for the Labor Day weekend, and he attended the performance of a magician, Mr. Electrico, who sat in an electric chair, causing sparks to jump between his teeth and every white hair on his head to stand erect. Bradbury and the magician became friends, and their walks and talks along the Lake Michigan shore behind the carnival so energized his imagination that, a few weeks after this encounter, he began to write stories for at least four hours a day, a practice that soon became habitual.

In 1932 his family moved to Arizona, where they had previously spent some time in the mid-1920's, largely because of his father's need to find work. In 1934, the family left both Arizona and Waukegan behind and settled in Los Angeles, which became Ray Bradbury's permanent home. He attended Los Angeles High School, becoming involved with theatricals and journalism. He also went to film theaters several times a week, wrote a thousand words a day, and joined the Science Fiction Society, where he met such professional writers as Henry Kuttner and Robert A. Heinlein. After he was graduated from high school in 1938, Bradbury worked for several months in a theater group sponsored by the actress Laraine Day and for several years as a newsboy in downtown Los Angeles. He took these jobs for subsistence while he dedicated most of his energy to writing. His early efforts owed much to Burroughs, but as he grew older he began studying such writers as Thomas Wolfe and Ernest Hemingway. His own style became a blend of these influences: the clean colloquial rhythms of Hemingway and the rich poetic metaphors of Wolfe.

Bradbury's poor eyesight prevented him from serving in the army during World War II, so he was free to launch his writing career. In the early 1940's, he submitted stories to such pulp magazines as *Weird Tales* and *Amazing Stories*. His first published story, "Pendulum," a collaborative effort, appeared in 1941, and his first independent sale, "The Piper," appeared in *Thrilling Wonder Stories* in February, 1943. As a young writer, he received stimulus by going to Los Angeles libraries, taking books from shelves, and reading randomly until story ideas came tumbling into his mind. In 1945, he sold "The Big Black and White Game" to the prestigious *American Mercury*, and it was later republished in *The Best American Short Stories of 1946*. His stories soon began to appear regularly in such magazines as *Collier's*, *The Saturday Evening Post*, *The New Yorker*, *Harper's Magazine*, and *Mademoiselle*. Since these magazines paid well, he was able to marry Marguerite Susan McClure, a former English teacher at the University of California in Los Angeles (UCLA), a union that eventually produced four daughters.

Dark Carnival, his first book, resulted from the encouragement of August Derleth, a publisher of fantasy literature. This compilation of his early horror stories also included poetic portrayals of the lonely and the anguished. In his second book, he abandoned the grotesque for Mars. He had been writing what on the surface seemed to be science-fiction stories but what in reality were explorations of humanity in challenging settings. Because publishers wanted a Mars novel rather than a collection of Mars stories, Bradbury added narrative transitions to twenty-six of his stories and produced *The Martian Chronicles*, which established his reputation as a sophisticated stylist with a distinctive imagination. *The Martian Chronicles*, considered by many Bradbury's best book, is a lyrical account of Earth's colonization of Mars from 1999 to 2026. During the first two decades after publication, it sold more than three million copies, even though space science was revealing that Bradbury's Mars of canals, water, and a breathable atmosphere was possible only in fiction.

Bradbury's best-known collection, *The Illustrated Man*, also dates from this period; several of the stories in that volume explore the threats posed by technology to human values. During the time that Bradbury worked on *The Illustrated Man*, he published a story, "The Fireman," in *Galaxy Science Fiction*, that he thought he could expand into a novel. A fire chief informed him that book paper first burns at 451 degrees Fahrenheit, and this fact gave him the title. He wrote the novel in twenty days on a pay-typewriter in the basement of the library at the University of California in Los Angeles. *Fahrenheit 451*, which deals with a book-burning fireman in a future society, is only secondarily concerned with totalitarianism, technology, and censorship. At its core, this novel is rooted in Bradbury's deep love for libraries and books. Like *The Martian Chronicles*, *Fahrenheit 451* is basically optimistic, for Montag, the book burner, ends up with other nonconformists memorizing the classic books that helped to create and nurture human civilization.

In the mid-1950's, Bradbury traveled to Europe in connection with a screenplay of *Moby Dick* that he wrote with John Huston. When *Moby Dick* appeared, several film critics appreciated Bradbury's work more than Huston's. Upon his return to the United States, Bradbury began writing television scripts for such shows as *Alfred Hitchcock Presents*, *Suspense*, and *The Twilight Zone*.

During the late 1950's and early 1960's, Bradbury's stories and novels centered directly on his Midwestern childhood, without being camouflaged by a science fiction or fantasy setting. *Dandelion Wine* is a nostalgic account of small-town life in the 1920's, told through a delicate mixture of pleasant childhood memories and the unpleasant fears of loneliness and death. In *Something Wicked This Way Comes*, Bradbury's favorite book, a father tries to save his son from the evil forces of a mysterious traveling carnival.

After *Something Wicked This Way Comes*, Bradbury's output of fiction decreased, and he turned to such forms as plays, poems, and essays. He had been fascinated by the theater since childhood, and in the 1960's and 1970's, he devoted much of his time to adapting several of his stories into plays for his Pandemonium Theatre Company. Although most of his work has been produced in California, a few of his plays have appeared Off-Broadway, including *The World of Ray Bradbury—Three Fables of the Future*. He also began to write humorous poetry in the 1970's. His plays and poems were not welcomed by most critics, who advised him that his talent was in short fiction. Despite this cool critical reception, Bradbury continued in the 1980's to diversify his activities—by helping make *Fahrenheit 451* into an opera and *Dandelion Wine* into a musical, by helping plan Spaceship Earth for Walt Disney World in Florida, and by helping design a twenty-first century city near Tokyo.

Bradbury's later work has not achieved the stature of his early work. Critics quickly recognized the importance of his first story collections in popularizing science fiction and lowering the barriers that isolated it from traditional literary forms. Unlike many writers for the pulps, Bradbury was a careful craftsman sensitively attuned to the subtleties of language. He has been called America's official science-fiction writer, the world's greatest living science-fiction writer, the Norman Rockwell of science fiction, and the Walt Disney of science fiction, although a strong case can be made that Bradbury is not really a science-fiction writer at all: Isaac Asimov has shown that Bradbury's stories about Mars are saturated with scientific incongruities and that they depict not possible futures but moral lessons for the present. In fact, Bradbury is essentially a short-story writer and a romantic. Most of his books are short-story compilations, his novels are stitched-together short stories, and his plays are adapted short stories. His romanticism surfaces in the themes he often explores: the conflict between human vitality and machine control, between the creative individual and the conforming group, between the innocence of childhood and the corruption of adulthood, between the shadow and the light in every human soul.

BIBLIOGRAPHICAL REFERENCES: For an extensive bibliography of Ray Bradbury, see William F. Nolan, *The Ray Bradbury Companion: A Life and Career History, Photolog, and Comprehensive Checklist of Writings with Facsimiles from Ray Bradbury's Unpublished and Uncollected Work in All Media*, 1975. There is also a good bibliography in *Ray Bradbury*, 1980, edited by Martin Henry Greenberg and Joseph D. Olander, an anthology of criticism by experts who seek to defend Bradbury against the charges that he is an opponent of science and technology and a sentimentalist about childhood. Other book-length studies of Bradbury include Benjamin P. Indick, *The Drama of Ray Bradbury*, 1977, and George Edgar Slusser, *The Bradbury Chronicles*, 1977. Critical articles on Bradbury's work are numerous. Some representative contributions are the following: Lee Ash, "WLB Biography: Ray Bradbury," *Wilson Library Bulletin*, XXIX (November, 1964), 268; Marvin E. Mengeling, "Ray Bradbury's *Dandelion Wine*: Themes, Sources and Styles," *English Journal*, October, 1971, 877-887; Steven Dimeo, "Man and Apollo: A Look at Religion in the Science Fantasies of Ray Bradbury," *Journal of Popular Culture*, Spring, 1972, 970-978; Anita T. Sullivan, "Ray Bradbury and Fantasy," *English Journal*, December, 1972, 1309-1314; "Two Views: Willis E. McNelly, 'I. Ray Bradbury—Past, Present, and Future,' A. James Stupple, 'II. The Past, The Future, and Ray Bradbury,' " in *Voices for the Future: Essays on Major Science Fiction Writers, Volume 1*, 1976, edited by Thomas D. Clareson; Wayne L. Johnson, "The Invasion Stories of Ray Bradbury," in *Critical Encounters: Writers and Themes in Science Fiction*, 1978, edited by Dick Riley; Noël M. Valis, "*The Martian Chronicles* and Jorge Luis Borges," *Extrapolation*, XX (Spring, 1979), 50-59; William F. Toupence, "Some Aspects of Surrealism in the Work of Ray Bradbury," *Extrapolation*, XXV (Fall, 1984), 228-238.

Robert J. Paradowski

IGNÁCIO DE LOYOLA BRANDÃO

Born: Araraquara, Brazil
Date: July 31, 1936

PRINCIPAL WORKS

NOVELS: *Bebel que a cidade comeu*, 1968; *Zero*, 1974 (English translation, 1975); *Dentes ao sol*, 1977; *Não verás país nenhum: Memorial descritivo*, 1981 (*And Still the Earth: An Archival Narration*, 1985); *O beijo não vem da boca*, 1985; *O ganhador*, 1987.

SHORT FICTION: *Depois do sol*, 1965; *Cadeiras proibidas*, 1976. *Pega ele, silêncio*, 1976.

TRAVEL SKETCH: *Cuba del Fidel, viagem à ilha proibida*, 1978.

Ignácio de Loyola Brandão is most noted for his socially conscious fiction of resistance during the years of authoritarian military rule in Brazil, 1964 to 1985. He was born in a small city in the state of São Paulo, where he wrote film reviews as a teenager; cinematic technique is evident in his narrative work. At twenty, he moved to the cosmopolitan city of São Paulo, where he worked for numerous newspapers and magazines. As a journalist he covered students' movements, workers' organizations, and living conditions in the slums. These concerns appear with some frequency in his fiction, which is marked by journalistic language and documentary approaches.

Because of the climate of fear and repression of the early 1970's, Brandão's controversial book *Zero* was rejected by several publishers. It first appeared in Italy, in a prestigious series of contemporary Latin American fiction in translation. After the book's success in Europe, a Brazilian publisher risked releasing the original, which was an immediate sensation and won a significant national book award in 1975. Military authorities banned it, but a campaign led by intellectuals and publishers resulted in a new authorization. At the end of the decade, *Zero* again appeared on best-seller lists in Brazil. After that time, Brandão produced several new titles and saw his work translated into English, Spanish, French, and German.

Brandão's personal definition of literature foregrounds "the defense of human dignity and the denouncement of oppressive systems." He regards his imaginary constructs as "portraits of our time" that should "make people aware of the reality in which they live." He is not concerned with traditional notions of artistic value or the "literary level" of language. His view of modern society is conveyed formally, through slang and the disarticulation of temporal and presentational structures. Brandão's fiction probes the life of the city, lending significance to unheroic individuals who represent the masses inhabiting the modern metropolis. The stories of *Depois do sol* (after the sun) examine debasement, material misery, and associated emotions. Similarly, Brandão's first novel dramatizes human tragicomedies in São Paulo, with considerable reference to the mass media.

Zero depicts life in a large city in a mythical "America-Latindia" and constitutes an allegory of underdevelopment and repression in Latin American nations. In this exacerbated portrait of urban agony, physical and psychological violence abounds. Historically, the most sensitive aspect is its portrayal of the persecution (including torture) of the political opposition. Cruelty and macabre cynicism are also seen in the savage pursuit of money. The squalor of the masses is contrasted with the frolicking of the country-club set. In the novel, an anonymous common man, clearly emblematic of the collectivity, gains consciousness of his situation and becomes a revolutionary in search of freedom.

While Brandão's concerned position is nothing new in Latin American literature, his formal reinforcement of fundamental views is innovative. *Zero* draws on multiple genres and levels: crude reporting, television news, advertising, soap opera, film, theater, satire, and farce. Brandão dismantles the linearity of realism, reflecting social chaos and agitation in a narrative collage that utilizes footnotes, a newspaper layout, comic balloons for quotes, graphs, drawings, and other unusual effects.

The novel *Dentes ao sol* (teeth to the sun), while not as important a work as *Zero*, further shows Brandão's strategy of conscious fragmentation in the construction of a worldview. In contrast, *And Still the Earth* is linear in concept, somewhat like *feuilleton* or soap opera. This work of quasi science fiction focuses on a Brazil of the future where manipulation of technology is of paramount importance. Dehumanization and social control come into play in different lights. There are echoes of George Orwell's Big Brother authority figure from *Nineteen Eighty-Four* (1949), but the nation's colonial condition and destiny are viewed through environmental destruction. The original Portuguese title parodies a patriotic and idyllic poem of the late nineteenth century that promised Brazilian youth a nation of unparalleled beauty and potential. Here, Brandão portrays a fictional future with no country at all. This abiding concern with national conditions and the implementation of innovative but appropriate narrative means to convey such preoccupations are what distinguish Brandão in late twentieth century Brazilian literature.

BIBLIOGRAPHICAL REFERENCES: English-language commentary on this author is very limited. For contextualization in the urban tradition, see Elizabeth Lowe, *The City in Brazilian Literature*, 1982. See also Emir Rodriguez Monegal, "Fiction Under the Censor's Eye," *World Literature Today*, LIII (Winter, 1979), pp. 19-22; and Kenneth Krabbenhoft, "Ignácio de Loyola Brandão and the Fiction of Cognitive Estrangement," *Luso Brazilian Review*, XXIV (1987), pp. 35-46.

Charles A. Perrone

RICHARD BRAUTIGAN

Born: Tacoma, Washington
Date: January 30, 1935

Died: Bolinas, California
Date: September, 1984

PRINCIPAL WORKS

NOVELS: *A Confederate General from Big Sur*, 1964; *Trout Fishing in America*, 1967; *In Watermelon Sugar*, 1968; *The Abortion: An Historical Romance, 1966*, 1971; *The Hawkline Monster: A Gothic Western*, 1974; *Willard and His Bowling Trophies: A Perverse Mystery*, 1974; *Sombrero Fallout: A Japanese Novel*, 1976; *Dreaming of Babylon: A Private Eye Novel, 1942*, 1977; *The Tokyo-Montana Express*, 1980; *So the Wind Won't Blow It All Away*, 1982.

SHORT FICTION: *Revenge of the Lawn: Stories, 1962-1970*, 1971.

POETRY: *The Galilee Hitch-Hiker*, 1958; *Lay the Marble Tea*, 1959; *The Octopus Frontier*, 1960; *All Watched Over by Machines of Loving Grace*, 1967; *Please Plant This Book*, 1968; *The Pill Versus the Springhill Mining Disaster*, 1968; *Rommel Drives on Deep into Egypt*, 1970; *Loading Mercury with a Pitchfork*, 1976; *June 30th, June 30th*, 1978.

Richard Gary Brautigan is identified as a link between the Beat Generation of the 1950's and the counterculture movement of the 1960's. He was born on January 30, 1935, in Tacoma, Washington. His father, Bernard Brautigan, abandoned his mother, Lula Mary Keho Brautigan, while she was pregnant with Richard. Lula Brautigan remarried at least three times, and when Richard was nine years old, his mother abandoned him and his younger sister Barbara for a short period. Brautigan began writing as a teenager, sometimes staying up all night to work on his poetry. He left home at the age of eighteen, and moved to San Francisco, where he befriended writers such as Lawrence Ferlinghetti, Allen Ginsberg, Michael McClure, Robert Duncan, and Philip Whalen, with whom he shared an apartment for a while.

In 1957, a selection of Brautigan's poems appeared with poems by three other young writers in *Four New Poets*, produced by Inferno Press, a small San Francisco publisher. In the following year, White Rabbit Press published Brautigan's first volume of poetry, *The Galilee Hitch-Hiker*. The booklet contains nine poems narrated by a gentle speaker who describes imaginative encounters with the French Symbolist poet Charles Baudelaire.

Always a swift and prolific writer, Brautigan sometimes wrote as many as ten poems a day during this period. Another small San Francisco publisher, Carp Press, issued Brautigan's next two volumes of poetry, *Lay the Marble Tea*, in 1959, and *The Octopus Frontier*, in 1960. These first three books show Brautigan to be a poet of synesthesia and humor. His strength lay in his ability to fuse disparate images through striking similes.

Brautigan's first published novel was actually the second he wrote: *A Confederate General from Big Sur*. The story, told by Jesse, a naïve student of theology, is about the life of Lee Mellon, a resident of Big Sur who believes he is a general in the Confederate army. The book is a satire on the hippie life-style of the 1960's. Although written before *A Confederate General from Big Sur*, *Trout Fishing in America* was Brautigan's second published novel. It is widely regarded as the most important of his works. *Trout Fishing in America* is the fragmented story of a man in search of the perfect trout stream, symbolic of the American frontier dream. What the narrator finds instead are scenes of industrial violence and environmental perversion. In one chapter, for example, used trout streams are for sale for six dollars per foot in a place called the Cleveland Wrecking Yard. Yet just as the speaker's imagination has created the negative vision of the wrecking yard, he is capable of magically transcending it: He sees trout in the stacked lengths of stream, and he puts his hand in the water, noting that it is cold and feels good.

Trout Fishing in America established Brautigan as one of the most recognizable voices of the 1960's. College students throughout America identified with the book's style and themes. In the late 1960's Brautigan suddenly rose from anonymity and poverty to fame and fortune.

In Watermelon Sugar, Brautigan's third novel, is narrated by a young man who lives in a commune called "iDEATH," a part of the larger community of Watermelon Sugar, population 375. The story takes place in the distant future; for the residents of Watermelon Sugar, ancient history is represented by the Forgotten Works, a place filled with "high piles" of undecipherable and useless artifacts.

In the 1970's, Brautigan turned to writing parodies of standard popular genres. *The Abortion* appeared in 1971, followed by both *The Hawkline Monster* and *Willard and His Bowling Trophies* in 1974, *Sombrero Fallout* in 1976, and *Dreaming of Babylon* in 1977. In his last two novels, *The Tokyo-Montana Express* and *So the Wind Won't Blow It All Away*, Brautigan returned to the comic, anecdotal style and eccentric characters that had garnered him so much interest in *Trout Fishing in America*. Reviews of these last two novels were mixed, however, with several critics noting that Brautigan's unique style, which had seemed so fresh in the 1960's, had lost its appeal by the 1980's.

At the age of forty-nine, Richard Brautigan shot himself. The suicide probably occurred sometime in late September, 1984, but the actual date of his death cannot be determined, as his badly decomposed body was not discovered until October 25, 1984.

Brautigan's style is light, rapid, and conversational. In *Trout Fishing in America* and his other early novels, Brautigan might be criticized for being merely sentimental over the loss of the once-pristine American frontier, if it were not for the humorous tone of his narrator's protean imagination. Although sometimes tedious, his liberal repetition of key words and phrases emphasizes the ironic innocence of characters surrounded by images of violence, death, betrayal, and emptiness. Shy, lonesome, and impassioned, they are not hardened by the loss of the American pastoral myth. Most often they passively accept their fate.

The enormous, though short-lived, popularity of Brautigan's work during the American counterculture revolution may have worked against his long-term reputation, signaling to some critics that Brautigan's work was only the product of its time. Yet, while American critical interest in Brautigan's work began to lag in the 1970's, European, and especially French, critics discovered textural complexities that Americans did not perceive until the 1980's, when critics Edward Halsey Foster and Marc Chenetier noted, for very different reasons, that Brautigan deserved new study. One of the most unconventional writers of an unconventional era, Brautigan cannot easily be defined.

BIBLIOGRAPHICAL REFERENCES: *Richard Brautigan*, 1983, by Edward Halsey Foster, provides the best critical overview of Brautigan's work. Marc Chenetier's *Richard Brautigan*, 1983, presents the argument that Brautigan deserves to be reconsidered, particularly as he attempts to redefine narrative and genre. Terence Malley's *Richard Brautigan*, 1972, though somewhat dated in style, is of interest. For further study, see Jay Boyer, *Richard Brautigan*, 1987; Josephine Henden, *Vulnerable People*, 1978, which studies the sociopolitical stances of Brautigan's characters; Jack Hicks, *In the Singer's Temple*, 1981; Bruce Cook, *The Beat Generation*, 1970; and Manfred Putz, *The Story of Identity: American Fiction of the Sixties*, 1979. The following articles may also be of interest: Neil Schmitz, "Richard Brautigan and the Modern Pastoral," *Modern Fiction Studies*, Spring, 1973, 109-125; Arlen J. Hansen, "The Celebration of Solipsism: A New Trend in American Fiction," *Modern Fiction Studies*, Spring, 1973, 5-15; Brad Hayden, "Echoes of *Walden* in *Trout Fishing in America*," *Thoreau Society Quarterly*, VII (July, 1976), 21-25; Robert Kern, "Williams, Brautigan, and the Poetics of Primitivism," *Chicago Review*, XXVII (Summer, 1975), 47-57; Brooke Horvath, "Richard Brautigan's Search for Control over Death," *American Literature*, LVII (1985), 434-455; and Lawrence Wright, "The Life and Death of Richard Brautigan," *Rolling Stone*, XI (April, 1985), 29.

Bill Hoagland

BERTOLT BRECHT

Born: Augsburg, Germany
Date: February 10, 1898

Died: East Berlin, East Germany
Date: August 14, 1956

PRINCIPAL WORKS

PLAYS: *Baal*, wr. 1918, pb. 1922 (English translation, 1963); *Trommeln in der Nacht*, wr. 1919-1920, pr., pb. 1922 (*Drums in the Night*, 1961); *Die Hochzeit*, wr. 1919, pr. 1926 (also known as *Die Keinbürgerhochzeit*; *The Wedding*, 1970); *Im Dickicht der Städte*, pr. 1923 (*In the Jungle of Cities*, 1961); *Mann ist Mann*, pr. 1926 (*A Man's a Man*, 1961); *Die Dreigroschenoper*, pr. 1928 (*The Threepenny Opera*, 1949); *Aufstieg und Fall der Stadt Mahagonny*, pb. 1929 (*Rise and Fall of the City of Mahagonny*, 1957); *Happy End*, pb. 1929; *Der Jasager*, pr. 1930 (*He Who Said Yes*, 1946); *Die Massnahme*, pr. 1930 (*The Measures Taken*, 1960); *Die heilige Johanna der Schlachthöfe*, pb. 1931 (*St. Joan of the Stockyards*, 1956); *Der Neinsager*, pb. 1931 (*He Who Said No*, 1946); *Die Mutter*, pr., pb. 1932 (*The Mother*, 1965); *Furcht und Elend des dritten Reiches*, pr. 1938 (*The Private Life of the Master Race*, 1944); *Leben des Galilei*, wr. 1938-1939, pr. 1943, revised 1945-1947 and 1955-1956 (*The Life of Galileo*, 1947); *Der gute Mensch von Sezuan*, wr. 1938-1940, pr. 1943 (*The Good Woman of Setzuan*, 1948); *Mutter Courage und ihre Kinder*, pr. 1941 (*Mother Courage and Her Children*, 1941); *Herr Puntila und sein Knecht, Matti*, wr. 1940, pr. 1948 (*Mr. Puntila and His Hired Man, Matti*, 1976); *Der aufhaltsame Aufstieg des Arturo Ui*, wr. 1941, pb. 1957 (*The Irresistible Rise of Arturo Ui*, 1972); *Die Gesichte der Simone Machard*, wr. 1941-1943, pb. 1956 (with Lion Feuchtwanger; *The Visions of Simone Machard*, 1961); *Schweyk im zweiten Weltkrieg*, wr. 1941-1943, pb. 1957 (*Schweyk in the Second World War*, 1975); *Der kaukasische Kreidekreis*, wr. 1944-1945, pr. 1948 (*The Caucasian Chalk Circle*, 1948); *Die Tage der Commune*, wr. 1948-1949, pr. 1956 (*The Days of the Commune*, 1971); *Der Hofmeister*, pr. 1950 (*The Tutor*, 1972); *Der Prozess der Jeanne d'Arc zu Rouen, 1431*, pr. 1952 (*The Trial of Jeanne d'Arc at Rouen, 1431*, 1972); *Don Juan*, pr. 1953 (English translation, 1972); *Pauken und Trompeten*, pb. 1956 (*Trumpets and Drums*, 1972).

NOVELS: *Der Dreigroschenroman*, 1934 (*The Threepenny Novel*, 1937, 1956); *Die Geschäfte des Herrn Julius Caesar*, 1956.

POETRY: *Hauspostille*, 1927, 1951 (*Manual of Piety*, 1966); *Lieder, Gedichte, Chöre*, 1934 (*Songs, Poems, Choruses*, 1976); *Svendborger Gedichte*, 1939 (*Svendborg Poems*, 1976); *Selected Poems*, 1947; *Hundert Gedichte*, 1951 (*A Hundred Poems*, 1976); *Gedichte und Leider*, 1956 (*Poems and Songs*, 1976); *Gedichte*, 1960-1965; *Bertolt Brecht: Poems, 1913-1956*, 1976.

SCREENPLAYS: *Kühle Wampe*, 1932 (English translation, 1933); *Hangmen Also Die*, 1943; *Das Lied der Ströme*, 1954; *Herr Puntila und sein Knecht, Matti*, 1955.

SHORT FICTION: *Geschichten von Herrn Keuner*, 1930, 1958; *Kalendergeschichten*, 1948 (*Tales from the Calendar*, 1961); *Prosa*, 1965-1967.

NONFICTION: *Kleines Organon für das Theater*, 1948 (*A Little Organum for the Theatre*, 1951); *Brecht on Theatre*, 1964; *Schriften zum Theater*, 1964-1967.

AUTOBIOGRAPHY: *Autobiographische Aufzeichnungen, 1920-1954*, 1975 (partially translated as *Diaries, 1920-1922*, 1979).

The reigning genius of modern theater internationally is Bertolt Brecht, born Eugen Berthold Brecht in the Bavarian city of Augsburg on February 10, 1898. Brecht came from bourgeois origins. His father began as a clerk in a paper mill and rose through the ranks to become its manager. Brecht completed his secondary education in Augsburg's *Realgymnasium* in 1917, after being threatened with dismissal the preceding year because he had written a pacifist essay, which was not to be countenanced in a Germany at war. Brecht's pacifist sentiments, which resulted in his being awarded the International Stalin Peace Prize in 1954, remained strong through his lifetime and are at the thematic center of much of his writing.

Entering the University of Munich upon completing his secondary education, Brecht was a student for a year in its medical faculty. Then he was conscripted, and during his military service he was a corpsman in a military hospital in Augsburg. His conscription marked the end of his formal education. After he left the military, he supported himself in Munich as a free-lance writer. He often wrote theatrical reviews, thereby gaining a broad exposure to theater during the postwar years.

In 1924, two years after he was married to his first wife, Marianne Zoff, from whom he was divorced in 1927, Brecht was in Berlin at the Deutsches Theater, where he worked with Max Reinhardt for two years. In 1926, however, Brecht began to study Marxist economics, which was to change the course of his life significantly. Convinced at an early age that theater's role in society is essentially educational and didactic, Brecht began to show substantial influence from Erwin Piscator's political theater in his dramatic theory, particularly in such early political pieces as *A Man's a Man* and *The Threepenny Opera*, the first of his plays to use songs to stop rather than advance the action.

As Brecht's work became increasingly political, the Nazis were seizing power in Germany, from which Brecht and his wife, Helene Weigel, to whom he was married in 1929, ultimately had to flee after the police in January, 1933, broke up a performance of *The Measures Taken* in Erfurt. They settled temporarily in Denmark. Less than three months after the Brechts left Germany, the Nazis publicly burned Brecht's works. In 1935, they revoked his German citizenship.

Brecht and his family stayed in Denmark until 1939. Then, apprehensive about being so close to Germany, they moved to Sweden, later to Finland, and finally, in 1941, to the United States. They lived for six years in Santa Monica, California, where Brecht worked intermittently with film studios, although only one of his screenplays, *Hangmen Also Die*, was produced. In 1947, one day after the House Committee on Un-American Activities officially declared he was not pro-Communist, Brecht left the United States for Zurich.

Brecht is best known for his new theories of theater that center on a concept of epic theater best explained in *A Little Organum for the Theatre* and in the notes to *Rise and Fall of the City of Mahagonny.* This approach to theater—and to directing, in which Brecht was fully engaged—is quite opposite to Konstantin Stanislavsky's theory of method acting. Brecht's was consciously and calculatedly a theater of alienation in the sense that Brecht did not want to involve audiences in the action of his plays, did not want them to identify so much with his plays' characters that they would miss the plays' social and political impact. In his anti-dramatic works, actors are witnesses to events rather than participants in events.

According to Brecht, it is ultimately the social and political impression plays make upon audiences that marks their success or failure as vehicles capable of changing society. Although Brecht's theater is a theater of ideas, he writes specifically for common people, not for intellectual or academic audiences. He hopes that his plays will be performed not only in theaters but also in schools, union halls, factories—wherever workers gather. His fundamental aim is to deliver an abstract philosophy in a container—a play—designed to entertain as it instructs, as is evidenced in plays such as *The Life of Galileo* and in *The Caucasian Chalk Circle*.

Brecht returned to Germany in 1948, this time to East Berlin, where he became the artistic manager of the Deutsches Theater, where he had begun his career. The next year, he and his wife established the Berliner Ensemble. He spent his final years preparing materials for his new theater and directing many of the plays performed in it. When he died of a coronary thrombosis on August 14, 1956, Brecht's wife, one of the best interpreters of his work, took his place in the Berliner Ensemble.

BIBLIOGRAPHICAL REFERENCES: There is an enormous secondary literature on Brecht, who has captured the interest of scholars as much as any playwright since William Shakespeare. Among the most accessible books to focus on his career are Michael Morley's *Brecht: A Study*, 1977, and Willy Haas's *Bert Brecht*, 1970, each of which presents a brief overview that will serve as a reasonable starting point for readers not ready to approach more specialized Brecht scholarship. In a class generally with these books is John Fuegi's *Bertolt Brecht: Chaos According to Plan*, 1987, which is slightly more specialized than the first two but is accessible to general readers, as is Fuegi's earlier *The Essential Brecht*, 1972. Those interested in Brecht's political philosophy as it is applied to drama will profit from reading Keith A. Dickson's *Towards Utopia: A Study of Brecht*, 1978, which captures succinctly the philosophical and political spirit of what Brecht tried to accomplish in both his writing and his directing. Focusing more closely on Brecht as a director with a political agenda is Darko Suvin's *To Brecht and Beyond: Soundings in Modern Dramaturgy*, 1984. Among the many Brecht bibliographies available, Reinhold Grimm's *Bertolt Brecht*, first published in 1961, is useful because it is periodically updated. Among the many biographical studies, Ronald Hayman's *Brecht*, 1983, is the most accessible survey of Brecht's life and career. While valuable for factual information, Hayman's book is unreliable in its critical judgments. Also worth consulting is James F. Lyons' *Bertolt Brecht in America*, 1980, which not only documents Brecht's American sojourn but also traces the development of his international reputation as a playwright.

R. Baird Shuman

HOWARD BRENTON

Born: Portsmouth, England
Date: December 13, 1942

PRINCIPAL WORKS

PLAYS: *Ladder of Fools*, pr. 1967; *Gargantua*, pr. 1969; *Gum and Goo*, pr. 1969; *Revenge*, pr. 1969; *Heads*, pr. 1969; *The Education of Skinny Spew*, pr. 1969; *Christie in Love*, pr. 1969; *Wesley*, pr. 1970; *Cheek*, pr. 1970; *Fruit*, pr. 1970; *Scott of the Antarctic: What God Didn't See*, pr. 1971; *Lay By*, pr. 1971 (with Brian Clark, Trevor Griffiths, David Hare, Steven Poliakoff, Hugh Stoddart, and Snoo Wilson); *Hitler Dances*, pr. 1972; *How Beautiful with Badges*, pr. 1972; *Measure for Measure*, pr. 1972; *England's Ireland*, pr. 1972 (with David Elgar, Tony Bicât, Clark, Francis Fuchs, Hare, and Wilson); *A Fart for Europe*, pr. 1973 (with Elgar); *Mug*, pr. 1973; *Magnificence*, pr., pb. 1973; *Brassneck*, pr. 1973 (with Hare); *The Churchill Play: As It Will Be Performed in the Winter of 1984 by the Internees of Churchill Camp Somewhere in England*, pr., pb. 1974; *The Saliva Milkshake*, pr. 1975; *Weapons of Happiness*, pr., pb. 1976; *Government Property*, pr. 1976; *Epsom Downs*, pr., pb. 1977; *Deeds*, pr. 1978 (with Griffiths, Ken Campbell, and Hare); *Sore Throats*, pr., pb. 1979; *A Short Sharp Shock!*, pr. 1980 (with Tony Howard); *The Romans in Britain*, pr. 1980; *Thirteenth Night*, pr., pb. 1981; *The Genius*, pr., pb. 1983; *Sleeping Policemen*, pr. 1983 (with Tunde Ikoli); *Bloody Poetry*, pr. 1984; *Pravda: A Fleet Street Comedy*, pr., pb. 1985 (with Hare).

SCREENPLAY: *Skin Flicker*, 1973.

TELEPLAYS: *Lushly*, 1971; *The Saliva Milkshake*, 1975; *The Paradise Run*, 1976.

POETRY: *Notes from a Psychotic Journal and Other Poems*, 1969; *Sore Throats and Sonnets of Love and Opposition*, 1979.

TRANSLATIONS: *The Life of Galileo*, 1981 (by Bertolt Brecht); *Danton's Death*, 1981 (by Georg Büchner).

Howard Brenton writes plays of political and social satire that have been successful on the middle-class stages of London's legitimate theater. The son of a policeman who later became a Methodist minister, Brenton began writing plays at the age of nine, and his early works from the 1970's concern children whose violence imitates that of the adult world in which they belong. During this period in his career, Brenton developed the large, cartoonlike quality of his characters, his vision of an Orwellian society in decay, and the images of sexual perversity that are his trademarks.

In 1969, Brenton found himself the sole audience member at a performance by the newly established fringe company, Portable Theatre, so the show was canceled and everyone went out for a drink. Brenton's meeting there with David Hare resulted immediately in a commission to write a play, *Christie in Love*, and eventually grew into a collaborative relationship that produced many plays, the most successful being *Pravda*.

The plays Brenton wrote during his years with the Portable Theatre are highly experimental and provocative and were designed for small spaces and limited budgets. In plays such as *Christie in Love*, Brenton presents evil characters (in this case, a notorious British murderer of young women) as more sympathetic than the hypocritical keepers of the society's morality who pursue them. Brenton demythologizes the creations of human sentimentality in works such as *Wesley*, *Scott of the Antarctic*, and, later, *The Churchill Play*, in which historical heroes are shown in a less favorable light than that in which history paints them. Consistently rejecting psychological realism, Brenton creates characters to represent attitudes and ideas, particularly those of particular classes and political viewpoints, but he always presents his most evil and hypocritical subjects with a level of humanity and sympathy that prevents them from becoming stereotypes. This trait may stem from the influence of Bertolt Brecht, who focused on the hypocritical evil of so-called pillars of society and on the humanity of the poor and the criminal.

When the Portable Theatre disbanded in 1972, mainly because of financial problems caused by the fact that most fringe theaters would not book the controversial *England's Ireland*, a piece dealing with British army violence in Northern Ireland, Brenton began writing plays for larger, middle-class theaters. Not only was the content of the plays problematic for the mainstream theaters but also the techniques Brenton brought from the Portable Theatre, which relied on minimal sets and costumes but maximum effect through grim depictions of violence, caused friction between the playwright and the public.

Through Brenton's command of his art, and the public's willingness to be challenged, however, Brenton became one of the leading figures of British postwar theater, and certainly the most successful of the political postwar playwrights. Two of Brenton's most well-regarded works are *The Churchill Play* and *Pravda*. The former was written on the occasion of the centenary of Winston Churchill's birth, but it is in no sense an homage to the celebrated war leader. The play takes place in an imaginary future in which all dissenters from the established political line are detained in concentration camps. In *The Churchill Play*, a play performed by the inmates of one of the camps criticizes the necessity for the strict law and order Churchill espoused. *Pravda* concerns the rise to eminence of a sleazy South African businessman interested in the newspaper business. At first, the snobbish British Fleet Street elite shun his advances, but later the elite greedily agree to his wishes, despite his lack of decorum, reactionary politics, and use of violence. The leading role of Lambert Le Roux is a powerful characterization: it was played by Anthony Hopkins for the play's original performance.

All Brenton's plays challenge complacency, whether from the upper classes or from revolutionary terrorists. All preconceived notions, stereotypes, and comfortable beliefs are scrutinized in these plays designed to implicate the audience in the misdeeds of the corrupters and the corrupted. Brenton is a political playwright of the highest caliber who resists the easy path of propaganda, relying instead on his ability to create strong characters and use thought-provoking conflict to ignite the conscience of his audience.

BIBLIOGRAPHICAL REFERENCES: The most inclusive analysis of Brenton's styles is a chapter entitled "Cartoon Nightmares," in David Ian Rabey, *British and Irish Political Drama in the Twentieth Century: Implicating the Audience*, 1986. A good reading of *The Churchill Play* and earlier works can be found in the chapter "Howard Brenton: Portable Theatre and the Fringe," in John Bull, *New British Political Dramatists*, 1983, which also contains an interesting political chronology of Great Britain from 1968 to 1983 that helps provide a context for Brenton's work. A clear general view can be found in the chapter "Howard Brenton," in Oleg Kerensky, *The New British Drama: Fourteen Playwrights Since Osborne and Pinter*, 1979. See also Ben Cameron, "Howard Brenton: The Privilege of Revolt," *Theater*, XII (1981), 28-33.

Joanne Butcher

BREYTEN BREYTENBACH

Born: Bonnievale, Cape Province, South Africa
Date: September 16, 1939

PRINCIPAL WORKS

POETRY: *Die ysterkoei moet sweet*, 1964; *Die huis van die dowe*, 1967; *Kouevuur*, 1969; *Lotus*, 1970; *Oorblyfsels. Uit die pelgrim se verse na 'n tydelike*, 1970; *Skryt. Om 'n sinkende skip blou te verg*, 1972 (*Sinking Ship Blues*, 1977); *Met ander woorde. Vrugte van die droomvan stilte*, 1973; *Het huis van de dove*, 1976 (includes *Die ysterkoei moet sweet*, *Die huis van die dowe*, and *Kouevuur*); *Met andere woorden*, 1976 (includes *Lotus*, *Oorblyfsels*, *Skryt*, and *Met ander woorde*); *Voetskrif*, 1976; *Blomskrif*, 1977; *In Africa Even the Flies Are Happy: Selected Poems, 1964-1977*, 1978; *And Death as White as Words: An Anthology of the Poetry of Breyten Breytenbach*, 1978; *('YK')*, 1983; *Buffalo Bill: Panem et circenses*, 1984.

NONFICTION: "Vulture Culture: The Alienation of White South Africa," in *Apartheid*, 1971; *'n Seisoen in die paradys*, 1976 (*A Season in Paradise*, 1980); *The True Confessions of an Albino Terrorist*, 1983; *End Papers: Essays, Letters, Articles of Faith, Workbook Notes*, 1986; *Judas Eye: Self-Portrait, Deathwatch*, 1988.

NOVEL: *Mouroir: Mirrornotes of a Novel*, 1984; *Memory of Snow and Dust*, 1989.

SHORT FICTION: *Katastrofes*, 1964; *Om te vlieg 'n Opstel in vyf ledemate en 'n Ode*, 1971; *Miernes*, 1980.

Breyten Breytenbach, one of South Africa's foremost Afrikaner critics of apartheid and the country's most experimental poet, essayist, and novelist, was born in Bonnievale, in Cape Province. The son of Oubaas Breytenbach, a laborer, farmer, and miner, and his wife Ounooi, Breytenbach came of age in Wellington, eventually studying painting at the Michael's School of Art in Cape Town and attending the University of Cape Town. While a student, he began writing experimental poetry in his native Afrikaans. In 1959, he left South Africa by freighter for Europe; working in a factory in England and, later, as a cook on a private yacht off the southern coast of France as well as at other temporary jobs, he settled in Paris in 1961. While continuing to paint and to write poems and short stories, he met and married in that same year a Vietnamese woman, Ngo Thi Hoang Lien Yolande Bubi. For the next ten years, Breytenbach's paintings appeared in European exhibitions at Paris, Amsterdam, Rotterdam, Brussels, and in the United States, in Minneapolis. His simultaneous recognition as a poet and writer came rapidly; he won the Afrikaans Press prize in 1964 for his poems in *Die ysterkoei moet sweet* (the iron cow must sweat) and for his stories in *Katastrofes* (catastrophes). Influenced by his polylingual access to other literatures, Breytenbach's poetry of this period evoked the political subversion of such poets as Osip Mandelstam, François Villon, and Federico García Lorca; the rich pathos of love such as that found in Pablo Neruda and George Seferis; and the visual imagery of the fantastic such as seen in the French Symbolists, especially Arthur Rimbaud, and in the forerunners of Surrealism, notably Isidore Ducasse (also known as the Comte de Lautréamont).

Attempting to return to South Africa, Breytenbach was repeatedly denied a visa, based on the government's objection to his Asian wife (racially mixed marriages were illegal). His avant-garde poetry, mingling autobiographical revulsion at apartheid policies and reverence for the beauty of the South African landscape and its peoples, continued to garner praise—even in South Africa. His next three books of poems—*Die huis van die dowe* (the house of the deaf), *Kouevuur* (gangrene; literally, cold fire), and *Lotus*—were all awarded the South African Central News Agency prize in their respective years of publication. Only Breytenbach had claimed the prestigious award three times. As his international reputation began to grow through translations into Dutch and German, he published *Oorblyfsels. Uit die pelgrim se verse na 'n tydelike* (remnants from the pilgrim's verses after [or toward] a temporary),

Skryt. Om 'n sinkende skip blou te verg (cry/write: to paint a sinking ship blue) and *Met ander woorde. Vrugte van die droomvan stilte* (in other words: fruits of the dreams of stillness). These books of poems showed an increasingly fractured syntax, a propensity for neologism, and a dispassionate introspection. Tempering subdued Buddhist meditation with the deprivations of exile, Breytenbach's wordplay bridged the gulf between his readers' distant knowledge of political suffering and the direct, physical experience of those actually suffering. Images of imprisonment, despair, starvation, torture, and death disoriented readers by substituting mixed metaphors, wit, and humor, and abruptly juxtaposed tones in near parodies of documentary reportage. The realities of South African apartheid, he suggested, were beyond direct communication in any language.

In 1973, the Breytenbachs were permitted a three-month visa to visit South Africa. At a conference of Afrikaans writers in Cape Town, he exhorted those present to attack apartheid for its self-isolating, self-destructive consequences to all South Africans. *A Season in Paradise* recounted this journey both in his interior integration of childhood, youth, and exile and in the awe for the beautiful but varied landscape. The nightmarish mythologies of bigotry and brutality pervaded the linguistic constructions, drawing on biblical allusions, children's rhymes, folk sayings, and compound words to create a text in which the psychological symbols of heaven and hell were reversed. The literal journey became, in effect, a celebration of death in order to clear the way for new life in South Africa. Two years after Breytenbach's return to Paris, he entered South Africa again but in disguise on a false passport. Arrested three months later in November, 1975, under the Terrorist Act, he admitted an attempt to form a white wing of the African National Congress, Okhela (Zulu for "spark"), which espoused the armed, revolutionary overthrow of the apartheid government. Sentenced to nine years in prison, he was to serve seven years before his release. While in prison, the poems in *Voetskrif* (footscript) were smuggled out and published. Even during his two years of solitary confinement, however, Breytenbach continued to win European literary prizes and have his paintings exhibited in major cites. *Blomskrif* (flower writing), containing new and selected poems, was his last poetry to be published in South Africa while he remained in prison. Ironically, with the publication of two collections of poems in English, *And Death as White as Words* and *In Africa Even the Flies Are Happy*, Breytenbach's international audience grew significantly, despite his having been utterly isolated from the world.

After Breytenbach's release in 1983, he vowed to stop writing in Afrikaans, preferring instead to dictate and then rework his texts in English. Blurring the genres of autobiography, fiction, poetry, and essay, his subsequent writings, save for two collections of poems, were to demonstrate, often with intermingled poems, the search not only for new language, but also for a renewed commitment to the destruction of apartheid. In *The True Confessions of an Albino Terrorist*, at the end of which he appended the Okhela manifesto he had written, he examined realistically the penal system, recalling his experiences in vivid details while arguing implicitly that political oppression is grounded in the degradation of an individual's body. In *Mouroir*, he portrays imagistically the consequences of imprisonment upon his own psyche in surrealistic prose that is marked by abrupt entries and disappearances of characters, by scenes of confusion and desolation, and by minute attention to the details of torture and hangings.

Breytenbach's exploration of the paradoxes of South African life, amplified by his innovative techniques, have earned him universal attention, if not praise. Consistently moving from the quiet center of Buddhist meditation (particularly Zen), his intent has been to embrace the tensions between love and terror, life and death, tenderness and brutality, Africa and Europe, and creation and decay. His South African critics have sometimes found him too ambitious, too radical, too romantic, too blasphemous, and too difficult; many critics, however, including André Brink (one of South Africa's leading Afrikaner novelists), have concluded that both his passionate antiapartheid commitment and his complex aesthetics will endure. As long as apartheid remains in South Africa, Breytenbach's work will continue to draw new readers who seek personal and political analyses beyond the pat reprimand. As apartheid oppression dwindles and disappears, readers will discover a postmodern poet whose political convictions could not be contained within mere formal nor even modern aesthetics.

BIBLIOGRAPHICAL REFERENCES: André Brink's introduction to Breytenbach's *A Season in Paradise*, 1980, translated by Rike Vaughn (Persea Books), provides a useful overview of Breytenbach's development. On his poetry, see Desmond Graham, "The Evidence of Poetry," *Stand*, XX (1979), 75-80; P. P. van der Merwe, "Breyten Breytenbach and the Poet Revolutionary," *Theoria*, LVI (1981), 51-72, which also contains biographical information; Terrence Des Pres, "Rimbaud's Nephew," *Parnassus*, XI (1983/1984), 83-102; and Gerald Moore, "The Martian Descends," *Ariel*, XVI, (1985), 3-12. For a biographical approach to Breytenbach's prison writings, see Sheila Roberts, "Breyten Breytenbach's Prison Literature," *The Centennial Review*, XXX (1986), 304-313; and J. U. Jacobs, "Breyten Breytenbach and the South African Prison Book," *Theoria*, LXVIII (1986), 95-105. A suggestive introduction to Breytenbach's pyrotechnic aesthetics may be found in Nadine Gordimer, "New Notes from Underground," *The Atlantic*, CCLIV (1984), 114-116.

Michael Loudon

ANDRÉ BRINK

Born: Vrede, Orange Free State, South Africa
Date: May 29, 1935

Principal Works

NOVELS: *Lobola vir die lewe*, 1962; Die ambassadeur, 1963 (*The Ambassador*, 1964; best known as *File on a Diplomat*); *Miskien nooit: 'n Somerspel*, 1967; *Kennis van die aand*, 1973 (*Looking on Darkness*, 1974); *'n Omblik in die wind*, 1975 (*An Instant in the Wind*, 1976); *Gerugte van reën*, 1978 (*Rumours of Rain*, 1978); *'n Droë wit seison*, 1979 (*A Dry White Season*, 1979); *Houd-den-bek*, 1982 (*A Chain of Voices*, 1982); *Die muur die pes*, 1984 (*The Wall of the Plague*, 1984).

SHORT FICTION: *Die meul teen die hang*, 1958; *Rooi*, 1965 (with others); *Oom Kootjie Emmer*, 1973; *'n Emmertjie wyn: 'n versameling dopstories*, 1981; *Oom Kootjie Emmer en die nuwe bediling: 'n stinkstorie* 1983; *Loopdoppies: Nog dopstories*, 1984.

NONFICTION: *Mapmakers: Writing in a State of Siege*, 1983 (best known as *Writing in a State of Siege*).

André Brink is the first Afrikaans writer to have achieved an international reputation. Because of his competence in English, he can undertake his own translations. Brink recoils from the common bigotry that marks South Africa and speaks against racism in a voice of persuasive commitment. He finds it "a very simple, if very disgusting fact" that "essentially more than ninety percent of Afrikaans writers are more or less pro-establishment, pro-system, pro-government." For such views he was one of the first Afrikaans writers to suffer the censorship and bannings regularly imposed upon English-language authors. Yet he has deliberately avoided martyrdom or exile, preferring to exist in his country as an academic while making his concerns and protests entirely apparent in his novels. This situation has caused him to comment on the intolerable existence of the Afrikaans writer, an existence which is "by the very nature of his position, a cultural schizophrene."

After obtaining master's degrees in both English and Afrikaans at Potchefstroom University, Brink spent two years in Paris. The political, literary, and intellectual freedom there astounded him and allowed him to work on an innovative novel, *Lobola vir die lewe* (pledge for life). Although mild by international standards, it horrified the Calvinists for its mention of sex, and so began the national condemnation of Brink's work.

His concern to modernize both Afrikaans and the Afrikaner motivated his involvement in the launching of the magazine *Sestiger* ("Sixty-ite"). The magazine was directed less against the political restrictions of the society than against its constraints on artistic liberty. Both the topics and the language of its articles seemed radical for the time. Brink editorialized that an artist must be "a spiritual saboteur." Because that kind of proclamation in the context of South Africa was unusual, if not dangerous, it was surprising that the journal survived even two harassed years. Its demise in 1965, contrived by an angered establishment, did not terminate the association, and the more innovative Afrikaans writers continued to be grouped as the "sestigers." Later, this term became a sort of national swearword.

Brink was a prodigious worker. Jake Cope calculates that by the age of thirty Brink had written twenty-five books of all kinds—including travelogues, plays, and numerous translations into Afrikaans of popular literature. At this time Brink produced his first clearly political novel deriving from the "July raids" upon subversives by the police. Some of Brink's friends were brought to trial on charges of sabotage. The book was refused publication, and during 1968 and 1969 Brink again retreated to Paris. He decided that he must return, however, incensed by the realization that "no Afrikaans writer has yet tried to offer a serious political challenge to the system." His view of his countrymen was both scornful and specific: "One can hardly expect any truly great writing from . . . Afrikaner word-mongers who are . . . pro-apartheid." In a revised form, *Looking on Darkness* was published in 1973. It describes the forbidden relationship between a "coloured" man and a white British woman and exposed its inevitable criminal consequence, the cruel brutality of the security police. *Looking on Darkness* became the first Afrikaans novel to be banned by the predominantly Afrikaner censorship board.

Brink's next work, *An Instant in the Wind*, has a historical setting in the Cape some two hundred years ago. It was not banned. Perhaps historical distance helped temper the provocative material. Even here the tale threatens Afrikaner morality, telling of the relationship between a white woman, lost in the veld, and a runaway mulatto slave. They fall in love and blissfully reenact the Garden of Eden. Leaving that idyllic state, they return to Cape Town, where the social conventions are reinstated and the woman accepts her racial status and betrays her slave lover, who is tortured to death.

Rumours of Rain has a different construction, a complex interior monologue by its main character, Martin Mynhardt, who, by greedy ambition, raises himself from rural poverty to power and wealth. He considers and finally condemns an alternative pattern of life which his friend pursues, rejecting the Afrikaner establishment so vehemently and totally that it becomes necessary that he turn Communist and join the underground guerrilla movement. In betraying his friend, Mynhardt displays the consequences of the degraded values by which he has lived and thus propounds a moral dilemma to readers.

A Dry White Season was written during the national agitation over the death in captivity of the black consciousness leader Steve Biko. Although there is no deliberate use of this event, the plot tells of the political and moral awakening of Ben, a very ordinary Afrikaner teacher. Gordon Ngubeni, a decent black cleaner at Ben's school, so vigorously tries to investigate how his son died while in prison that he is himself arrested. His own death in detention is explained as suicide. A magistrate says that the security police are not to blame. Provoked by the injustice of this decision, Ben breaks from all the casual assumptions of his regular life and commits himself to exposing the cruelties which the system tolerates. His determination destroys him. His family and friends turn against him. Thugs smash his windows, damage his car, and send letter bombs, and the police turn a blind eye to these harassments. His life shattered, Ben is mysteriously killed by a hit-and-run motorist. The importance of this book is the accusation it implicitly brings against the ordinary, decent Afrikaner who manages to avoid confronting the system that his indifference permits.

In Brink's *The Wall of the Plague*, the setting is Europe, but the preoccupations remain the same. A black Cape Town woman with a white lover, hoping to escape the racism that has oppressed her, travels to France to research a film on the Black Death, the great plague of the fourteenth century (the analogy with South Africa is patent). Meeting Mandla, a black activist, she is forced to reexamine her experience. She falls in love with him, finding in his angry passion a fervor, both emotional and political, which she had never known with her white friends. When he is killed, perhaps by South African agents, she realizes, though the ending remains somewhat vague, that she cannot escape the obligations of her background and the commitments it requires of her. The conclusion moves beyond the ideal of racial equality into the awareness that only those who have suffered the humiliations of color will be able to counter the politics of apartheid.

Brink has already published a significant body of work. Each of his books examines the misery and humiliation of his country and his people. In presenting the despair and dilemmas of honorable people of humane conscience such as himself, he exposes the terrifying tragedy of South African history and its violent future consequences.

BIBLIOGRAPHICAL REFERENCES: There is little secondary material on Brink available. One useful article is Allan Findley, "André Brink and the Challenge from Within South Africa," in *The Proceedings from the Second Nordic Conference for English Studies*, 1984, edited by

Haken Ringbom and Matti Rissanen. Reviews of *A Chain of Voices* include Jane Kramer, *The New York Review of Books*, XXIX (December 2, 1982), 8; Julian Moynahan, *The New York Times Book Review*, LXXXVI (June 13, 1982), 1; and Roger Owen, *The Times Literary Supplement*, May 14, 1982, 536. For background information on South African literature, see *From South Africa*, 1988, edited by David Bunn and Jane Taylor; Jack Cope, *The Adversary Within*, 1982; G. E. Gorman, *The South African Novel in English Since 1950*, 1978; and Stephen Gray, *South African Literature*, 1979.

John F. Povey

VERA BRITTAIN

Born: Newcastle, England
Date: 1893

Died: London, England
Date: March 29, 1970

PRINCIPAL WORKS

AUTOBIOGRAPHY: *Testament of Youth*, 1933; *Testament of Friendship*, 1940; *Testament of Experience*, 1957; *Chronicle of Youth*, 1981; *Chronicle of Friendship*, 1986.

SOCIAL CRITICISM: *Women's Work in Modern Britain*, 1928; *Halcyon: Or, The Future of Monogamy*, 1929; *Thrice a Stranger*, 1938; *England's Hour*, 1941; *On Becoming a Writer*, 1947; *Search After Sunrise*: *A Traveller's Story*, 1951; *Lady into Woman: A History of Women from Victoria to Elizabeth II*, 1953; *The Women at Oxford*, 1960; *Radclyffe Hall: A Case of Obscenity?*, 1968.

NOVELS: *The Dark Tide*, 1923; *Not Without Honour*, 1924; *Honourable Estate*, 1936; *Account Rendered*, 1945; *Born 1925: A Novel of Youth*, 1948.

BIOGRAPHY: *Valiant Pilgrim: The Story of John Bunyan and Puritan England*, 1950; *Envoy Extraordinary: A Study of Vijaya Lakshmi Pandit and Her Contribution to Modern India*, 1965.

POETRY: *Verses of a VAD*, 1918; *Poems of the War and After*, 1934.

CORRESPONDENCE: *Wartime Letters to Peace Lovers*, 1940; *Humiliation with Honour*, 1942.

Vera Mary Brittain is known principally for her moving account of her experiences as a nurse in World War I, *Testament of Youth*, and for her later pacifist and feminist writings. She was born in 1893 in Newcastle, England, to a wealthy industrialist, Thomas Brittain, and his wife, Edith Bervon Brittain. Her only brother, Edward, to whom she was especially devoted, was born two years later. An affluent, secure childhood was partially marred by her father's attacks of melancholia and the lack of intellectual stimulation for bright young girls so common to Edwardian England. Determined to break out of the stuffy mold which had been set for her, Brittain won an exhibition to Somerville College, Oxford, in 1914. She spent only a year there before becoming a VAD (volunteer nurse) in London and France, following the example of her brother and her fiancé, Roland Leighton, who had joined the British army and had been sent to the front after the outbreak of World War I. Her fiancé's death in 1915, her brother's in 1918, and those of several close friends throughout the war left Vera Brittain a changed woman when she returned to Oxford in 1919 to take her degree in 1921.

As an older student who had been virtually shell-shocked by the deaths of loved ones, Brittain differed greatly from the average callow eighteen-year-old and thus was naturally drawn to Winifred Holtby, who had also nursed during the war. After taking their degrees, Brittain and Holtby moved to London to become writers. Brittain's first novels, *The Dark Tide* and *Not Without Honour*, are journeyman attempts to learn her craft and find a proper voice. Holtby, who was more successful with the novel form than was Brittain, is best remembered for *South Riding* (1936). Brittain married the political economist George Catlin in 1925 and had two children, one of whom, Shirley Williams, became a prominent member of Parliament in the 1970's and 1980's.

In 1929 Vera Brittain began the work for which she is best known, *Testament of Youth*, which was published in 1933 to immediate acclaim and is an account of her life from 1910 to 1925. *Testament of Youth* is the only memoir of World War I from a female perspective and ranks with Robert Graves's *Goodbye to All That* (1929) and Siegfried Sassoon's memoirs as the most telling accounts of the illusions of prewar England and of the gradual disillusionment of a generation of young men. In addition, *Testament of Youth* shows the growth of a bright young woman from a cosseted background into a profoundly sad but strong adult. Brittain had attempted unsuccessfully to put her war experiences into novel form but learned from *Testament of Youth* that nonfiction writing was her forte. The poignancy and immediacy of *Testament of Youth* are bolstered by the fact that the work is based on her own copious journals from the period and contains war poetry written by Brittain, Roland Leighton, and Rupert Brooke.

Throughout the rest of her life Brittain was a prolific writer of both books and nonfiction articles for periodicals such as *The Times Literary Supplement* and *Time and Tide*; yet in 1936 she published her most successful novel, *Honourable Estate*, which contains both the feminist and pacifist themes for which she was famous. One character, Janet Rutherston, a would-be activist for women's rights, is crushed by her insensitive clergyman husband, while another, Ruth Alleyndene, who is much like Brittain herself, attends the University of Oxford, becomes a nurse in World War I, has an affair with a soldier who is killed, and later marries Janet Rutherston's son, who has learned feminism from his mother.

The gathering storm of World War II in the 1930's led Brittain and her husband into the role of speakers for the pacifist cause; Brittain was considered an effective public speaker. During the war she edited a pacifist newsletter and published *Wartime Letters to Peace Lovers* and *Humiliation with Honour*, a rationale for her war views which takes the form of letters to her fifteen-year-old son, John, who had been evacuated to the United States with his sister for safety from the London blitz. The war years also saw the publication of *Testament of Friendship*, Brittain's tribute to her friend Winifred Holtby, who had died in 1936; *Testament of Experience* rounds out her trilogy of autobiographical testaments.

During the postwar years Brittain returned to feminist themes in *Lady into Woman*, which traces the evolution of modern women begun in her earlier *Women's Work in Modern Britain*. She also wrote a biography of Vijaya Lakshmi Pandit (the sister of the Indian leader Jawaharlal Nehru), *Envoy Extraordinary*, and *Radclyffe Hall: A Case of Obscenity*, an explication of her defense of the lesbian writer Radclyffe Hall during the latter's trial for obscenity in the 1920's.

Vera Brittain died on March 29, 1970, in London. Her work underwent a renaissance in the 1980's after Masterpiece Theatre produced an excellent television series based on *Testament of Youth* and both feminists and pacifists rediscovered her writings. Brittain is best remembered for her autobiographical books and for her works of social criticism rather than for her novels and poetry. *Testament of Youth*, especially, brilliantly captures the pity of World War I through the acute sensibility of a brilliant and empathetic young woman. Brittain was at her best when her pen reflected the hand that held it.

BIBLIOGRAPHICAL REFERENCES: Hilary Bailey, *Vera Brittain*, 1987, is a good general study of Brittain's life and writings. Some useful short studies include ones by Yvonne A. Bennett, "Vera Brittain: Feminism, Pacifism, and the Problem of Class, 1900-1953," *Atlantis*, XII (1987), 18-23; Jean Pickering, "On the Battlefield: Vera Brittain's *Testament of Youth*," *Women's Studies*, XIII (1986), 75-85; and Muriel Mellown, "Reflections on Feminism and Pacifism in the Novels of Vera Brittain," *Tulsa Studies in Women's Literature*, II (1983), 214-228.

Isabel B. Stanley

HERMANN BROCH

Born: Vienna, Austria
Date: November 1, 1886

Died: New Haven, Connecticut
Date: May 30, 1951

Principal Works

NOVELS: *Die Schlafwandler*, 1931-1932 (*The Sleepwalkers*, 1932); *Die unbekannte Grösse*, 1933 (*The Unknown Quantity*, 1935); *Der Tod des Vergil*, 1945 (*The Death of Virgil*, 1945); *Die Schuldlosen*, 1950 (*The Guiltless*, 1974); *Der Versucher*, 1953 (also known as *Demeter* and *Bergroman*; *The Spell*, 1986).

SHORT FICTION: *Short Stories*, 1966.

ESSAYS: "James Joyce und die Gegenwart," 1936 ("James Joyce and the Present Age," 1949); *Hofmannsthal und seine Zeit*, 1964 (*Hugo von Hofmannsthal and His Time: The European Imagination, 1860-1920*, 1984); *Zur Universitätsreform*, 1969; *Gedanken zur Politik*, 1970; *Menschenrecht und Demokratie*, 1971.

PLAY: *Die Entsühnung*, pb. 1933 (also as . . . *Denn sie wissen nicht, was sie tun*; *The Atonement*, 1972).

CORRESPONDENCE: *Hermann Broch-Daniel Brody: Briefwechsel, 1930-1951*, 1970; *Briefe über Deutschland, 1945-1949*, 1986.

MISCELLANEOUS: *Gesammelte Werke in zehn Bänden*, 1952-1961; *Kommentierte Werkausgabe in dreizehn Bänden*, 1974-1981.

Although Hermann Broch is not one of the best-known writers of the twentieth century, artists and scholars consider him to be among the great modern writers, such as James Joyce, André Gide, Franz Kafka, and Thomas Mann.

He was born on November 1, 1886, in Vienna, Austria. His father, Joseph Broch, was a wealthy textile merchant and owner of a spinning mill. Broch's mother, Johanna Schnabel, came from one of Vienna's distinguished and wealthy families. As was customary in those days, it was determined that as the oldest son, Broch was to take over the family textile company. Consequently, he attended a modern secondary school, where he studied the natural sciences and French before advancing to the Vienna Institute for Weaving Technology. His period of apprenticeship was served in textile mills in Germany, England, and Bohemia, as well as in the United States—specifically, Atlanta, Memphis, and New Orleans. He entered the family business in 1908.

During the next year, he became a reserve officer in the Austrian army and attained the rank of lieutenant. At this time, he converted from the Jewish faith to Catholicism for social reasons. Also in 1909, he married Franziska ("Fanny") von Rothermann; they were divorced in 1922. His only child, Hermann Friedrich Broch de Rothermann, was born in 1910.

Working as an unpaid director of the family spinning mill in Teesdorf, a tiny village in Lower Austria, was most disagreeable to Broch. In his nightly solitary hours Broch commenced his studies of philosophy and mathematics, which eventually led him to enroll at the University of Vienna. Now that he was in the capital again, he frequented the Viennese literary and artistic cafés, where he met writers such as Karl Kraus, Robert Musil, and Franz Werfel, and the painters Albert Paris Gütersloh and Georg Krista. He read the works of psychologist Otto Weininger and began a systematic study of the philosophers Arthur Schopenhauer and Immanuel Kant.

To his interest in philosophy and literature Broch added a third lifelong concern, namely, politics. During and after World War I he devoted considerable energy to promoting welfare programs and reforms, an activity in which he was engaged until his death. These activities gradually led Broch in 1927 to sell the textile plant and devote himself completely to his studies and writings.

Broch's first major literary work was the trilogy *The Sleepwalkers*. In this "polyhistorical novel," Broch presents a panoramic view of political, social, economic, and philosophical development in Germany in three parts representing three different times: 1888 ("The Romantic"), 1903 ("The Anarchist"), and 1918 ("The Realist"). The first volume of this trilogy, which illustrates the decline of German bourgeois society, presents a Prussian world of fossilized conventions and an empty concept of honor symbolized by the uniform of the imperial guardsman Joachim von Pasenow. Pasenow's entire life is determined by the obligation to maintain "the family honor." From this semifeudal, aristocratic society of the first book the scene shifts in the second volume to a Rhenish metropolis, where the insignificant bookkeeper August Esch fights for advancement to chief accountant, using blackmail and bribery. The trilogy ends with the triumph of Huguenau, a totally amoral and unscrupulous army deserter who does away with von Pasenow and Esch. Thus Broch illustrates the total disintegration of any system of social and moral values. In the epilogue, however, Broch develops a counterpart to this total decay with a vision of a new homogeneous and coherent world of man.

Broch's most important literary work is *The Death of Virgil*. He started writing this novel in Austria in 1937, continued it while a political prisoner in a German concentration camp in 1938, and completed it, only after many other activities had interrupted his work, in the United States in 1945. The greatness of Broch's novel is frequently attributed to the mode in which it is written. It is actually a single, extended inner monologue in which Virgil's thoughts and visions are systematically elevated from the depth of presentiment to a consciously articulated word. *The Death of Virgil* has often been compared with James Joyce's *Ulysses* (1922); among other things, the works share techniques of experimental writing.

During the last decade of his life Broch devoted considerable time and energy to the study of mass psychology and mass psychological occurrences. This philosophical investigation had already begun, however, in his fictional writings, as 1935 and 1936 manuscripts of his "mountain novel" can attest. One year before his death, Broch returned to the work on this novel, a fictionalized investigation of the problem of a "mass response to Hitler, of everyday hysteria, and mass-consumption barbarism." When he died on May 30, 1951, in New Haven, Connecticut, Broch had completed less than half of the third version of the manuscript. The novel *Der Versucher* (The tempter), an adaptation of different chapters of the three versions of the manuscript, is indeed the third great novel in Broch's oeuvre. (The English translation, *The Spell*, is based on the first version of the manuscript.)

Although *The Sleepwalkers* and *The Spell* may be more accessible to the reader than *The Death of Virgil*, all Broch's works—fictional and philosophical—are highly intricate examinations of the "universal totality of the human condition."

BIBLIOGRAPHICAL REFERENCES: Useful general introductions to Broch include Ernestine Schlant, *Hermann Broch*, 1978; Malcolm R. Simpson, *The Novels of Hermann Broch*, 1977; and Theodore Ziolkowski, *Hermann Broch*, 1964. For Broch studies on a multiplicity of topics, see the special issue of *Modern Austrian Literature*, 1980, edited by Donald Dariau, and *Hermann Broch: Literature, Philosophy, Politics*, 1988, edited by Stephen D. Dowden. For studies on specific aspects of Broch's work, see Dorrit Cohn, *The Sleepwalkers: Elucidations of Hermann Broch's Trilogy*, 1966; David Horrocks, "The Novel as History: Hermann Broch's 'Die Schlafwandler,'" in *Weimar Germany, Writers and Politics*, 1982; Hermann Weigand, "Broch's Death of Virgil," in *Publication of the Modern Language Association*, 1947; John J. White, "Hermann Broch," in *Mythology in the Modern Novel*, 1971; and Joseph P. Strelka, "Hermann Broch," in *Major Figures of Modern Austrian Literature*, 1988, edited by Donald G. Dariau.

Thomas H. Falk

HAROLD BRODKEY

Born: Alton, Illinois
Date: 1930

PRINCIPAL WORKS

SHORT FICTION: *First Love and Other Sorrows*, 1957; *Stories in an Almost Classical Mode*, 1988.

NONFICTION: *Avedon: Photographs, 1947-1977*, 1978 (with Richard Avedon).

Harold Brodkey is so reclusive that most of what is known about his life comes to readers through his stories. Even his exact birth date is a closely guarded secret, although it is known that he was born in 1930. The few facts known about his life suggest that he is the son of Joseph and Doris Brodkey and of another set of adoptive parents, none of whom was much interested in literature. Brodkey's natural father is thought to have been unable to read or write. His natural mother could speak six languages. Brodkey spent his formative years in St. Louis. He then entered Harvard University, from which he was eventually graduated. In 1980, he married novelist Ellen Schwamm. They would have one daughter, Emily, and make their home in New York City's Upper East Side.

Although he has published relatively little, Brodkey is generally regarded by thoughtful and perceptive readers as one of the most meticulous craftsmen at work in literature today. It is known that he is at work on a huge, Proustian novel, "A Party of Animals," based on his life from birth to the end of college. Portions of this novel—under contract since 1961 to Farrar, Straus & Giroux—have appeared in *The New Yorker*, *New American Review*, and *Esquire*. The book is purported to exceed two thousand pages in typescript, and it is estimated that Brodkey minimally takes each page through fifteen revisions, some pages through dozens more.

First Love and Other Sorrows earned for Brodkey the enthusiastic praise of John Cheever, Mark Schorer, Frank O'Connor, and other well-known readers. Critics were particularly impressed by Brodkey's ability to structure syntax, commenting often on the intricacy of his punctuation and of its function in creating sentences whose parts interlock with a startling symmetry. Brodkey does not seek in his writing to depict so much as to create experience.

To analyze Brodkey's sentences is a remarkable experience. Many of them exceed one hundred words. The best of them are structured like Gothic cathedrals: Words dash down the nave to the transept. Flying buttresses of clauses and phrases support their superb equilibrium; the mortar, intricately and indivisibly a part of the total structure, is the conscious, labored punctuation that Brodkey uses as no other writers have.

Brodkey's punctuation is never incidental to his words; in Brodkey, it is a fundamental part of the total structure he erects, and this structure is always a syntactic structure at which he has arrived consciously. The colon is among his favorite marks of punctuation. He uses it, as one critic has observed, tyrannically.

Brodkey's most frequently cited story is "Sentimental Education," an autobiographical piece that depicts the growing together of two young people, college classmates, who with each other discover the wonders of their bodies, finally losing their virginity to each other. The sexual imagery is clear yet tasteful and restrained. Brodkey is intricate in his presentation of detail, clinically, objectively recounting all of his own most vivid memories from every conceivable point of view.

Most of his stories, like this one, reveal Brodkey struggling to discover Brodkey. It has taken him nearly thirty years to dredge up the first twenty years of his own life. Just as Eugene O'Neill retreated into his work space between 1939 and 1941 to confront the pain of his life as he wrote *Long Day's Journey into Night* (pr., pb. 1956), Brodkey has devoted himself to understanding himself, to sorting out all that is Brodkey, all that has gone into framing this curiously complicated creature into the being he is.

Brodkey is an intensely private person not because he wants to project a persona, but rather because he is working full-time to discover the mysteries—not some, but all, of the mysteries—of his own existence. He shares these mysteries with readers only when he is ready, never until he is satisfied that what he presents is valid, honest, accurate. The absolutism of Brodkey's intellectual integrity causes him to be misunderstood, but his concern is more with art than with public image.

The first four stories of his *First Love and Other Sorrows* deal with adolescence and have been widely acclaimed as the best stories in the volume. His protagonist, a universal figure used metaphorically, is nameless. His sensitivity yields him insufferable pain but also enables him to achieve unique insights. Unhappy with his life, his surroundings in St. Louis, he pins his hopes on his intellect, on the sheer power of his brains. Yet that will not erase his childhood; rather, it may possibly assure the childhoods of his offspring.

Many of the eighteen stories in *Stories in an Almost Classical Mode* deal with childlike perceptions of life. Some of these stories are the length of novellas. This tightly packed six-hundred-page book achieves a magnificence of language and interwoven structure that makes one eager for Brodkey's forthcoming novel.

On the surface, Brodkey is an intensely subjective writer. His work is undeniably autobiographical. In his short fiction, he examines the entire span of his life microscopically, almost minute by minute, and the examination is so calculatedly detached, disinterested, unbiased that it becomes an objective presentation of subjectivity. His invention, notable in his singular punctuation, is verbal as well. Brodkey uses hyphens profusely to generate adjectivals ten or twelve words long. His narratives, which examine the past in order to understand all time and the inner self, establish new modes of seeing and saying.

BIBLIOGRAPHICAL REFERENCES: No full biography of Harold Brodkey details his life and work. Indeed, information about him is relatively scarce, much of it confined to reviews of his one book of stories. The most feeling and revealing presentation is D. Keith Mano's "Harold Brodkey: The First Rave," *Esquire*, January, 1977, which is now dated. Anatole Broyard's "A Critic's Adventure," *The New York Times Book Review*, April 26, 1981, supplements Mano's consideration but, at one page, hardly provides enough information to satisfy the curious student of Brodkey. William Goyen's critique of *First Love and Other Sorrows*, *The New York Times Book Review*, January 12, 1958, provides a few illuminating biographical details, as does Mary Shiras' review in *Commonweal* (February 7, 1958), which applauds Brodkey's work but expresses reservations about the narrowness of his scope. Among the reviews of *Stories in an Almost Classical Mode*, Frank Kermode's in *The New York Times Book Review*, September 18, 1988, is detailed and sensitive.

R. Baird Shuman

JOSEPH BRODSKY

Born: Leningrad, Soviet Union
Date: May 24, 1940

Principal Works

POETRY: *Stikhotvoreniya i poemy*, 1965; *Elegy to John Donne, and Other Poems*, 1967; *Ostanovka v pustyne: Stikhotvoreniya i poemy*, 1970; *Debut*, 1973; *Selected Poems*, 1973; *Konets prekrasnoi epokhi: Stikhotvoreniya 1964-1971*, 1977; *Chast rechi: Stikhotvoreniya 1972-1976*, 1977; *V Anglii*, 1977; *Verses on the Winter Campaign 1980*, 1980; *A Part of Speech*, 1980; *Rimskie elegii*, 1982; *Novye stansy k Avguste: Stichi k M. B., 1962-1982*, 1983; *Uraniia: Novaya kniga stikhov*, 1987; *To Urania*, 1988.
NONFICTION: *Less Than One: Selected Essays*, 1986.
PLAY: *Mramor*, pb. 1984 (*Marbles*, 1985).

Born in Leningrad on May 24, 1940, Joseph Brodsky experienced the horrors of life at a very early age, for he was one of the few survivors of the nine-hundred-day Siege of Leningrad (1941-1944). Throughout his childhood he endured the hardships not only of postwar Russia but also of being Jewish in an anti-Semitic society. After dropping out of school at the age of fifteen, he worked at a variety of jobs while educating himself in Russian and comparative literature, the history of religion, philosophy, and foreign languages. Polish was among the first languages he learned, and in Polish he first read the works of Franz Kafka and William Faulkner. Brodsky began writing poetry in 1958 and soon found a place for himself in the literary circles of Leningrad. There he became a very close friend of the Russian poet Anna Akhmatova, who declared him to be "the most gifted poet of his generation."

If he was the most gifted, however, he quickly became one of the most oppressed. Throughout the early 1960's the authorities denounced his poetry as pornographic and anti-Soviet. When Soviet officials refused to publish his poems, he began reciting them on street corners in his liturgical style and distributing his own copies of them. In January of 1964 he was arrested on charges of social parasitism and sentenced to five years of hard labor in the Arkhangelsk region. While serving his sentence, he took up a study of English and American poets and was particularly drawn to the works of Robert Frost. Thanks to pressure exerted on the Soviet authorities by intellectuals at home and abroad, Brodsky was released from the labor camp in November, 1965, after serving twenty months of his sentence. He returned to Leningrad and continued writing and translating poetry in his native city until June, 1972, when he was "invited" to leave the Soviet Union. After leaving his homeland, Brodsky went to the United States, where he held academic positions at the University of Michigan, Queens College in New York, Ohio State University, Mount Holyoke College, and Columbia University.

Anna Akhmatova and Robert Frost were not the only modern poets to leave their mark on Brodsky; among his other favorites are Osip Mandelstam, W. H. Auden, and Czesław Miłosz. Beginning with his first collection, *Stikhotvoreniya i poemy* (poems and narrative verse), Brodsky pursued the traditional forms of the short lyric and the longer poem. His poetry reflects not only a consciousness of classical motifs involving figures from Western myth and religion but also an awareness of his debt to those great poets who lived before him. Examples of that awareness may be found in his "Elegy to John Donne" and "Verses on the Death of T. S. Eliot," which appears in the volume *Ostanovka v pustyne* (a halt in the wilderness). Experimenting with meter, free verse, and rhyme schemes, Brodsky explores the themes of love, art, language, death—all the dimensions of human life—often making use of irony, humor, and puns but always with a serious end.

After his exile in 1972, Brodsky's poetry took on a particular concern for the theme of exile, or separation, in all of its aspects: the separation of one person from another, of the poet from his native tongue, of words from their meanings. Torn from a familiar existence, the individual must acquire what Brodsky calls "the art of estrangement" and forge his own existence through his own consciousness; such is the general issue addressed in his collection of essays *Less Than One*. As a poet in exile, Brodsky became a poet *of* exile, a role especially reflected in *Konets prekrasnoi epokhi* (the end of a beautiful epoch) and his next two collections. For Brodsky, silence is the place of exile, and his task is to fetch the poetic word from silence, not only to declare but also to overcome the condition of exile. Like the death that accentuates life, silence calls forth the poet's word, which may bridge the gap between what has been torn asunder. While the poet here announces the nature of human exile, he also turns his reader's gaze toward that sky which spans the exile and the kingdom, revealing that "within" and "above" are synonyms.

The world's acknowledgment of the importance of Brodsky's place in the history of literature came on October 22, 1987, when he was awarded the Nobel Prize in Literature. Although he is a Russian poet divorced from his Russian public, his testimony on life has captured the attention of audiences worldwide. As W. H. Auden once described him, Brodsky is a poet who has "an unusual capacity to envision material objects as sacramental signs, messengers from the unseen." His readers continue to receive his message in a vision of what is hale, whole, and holy in life.

BIBLIOGRAPHICAL REFERENCES: Although, given his stature as a poet, the secondary resources in English on Brodsky are relatively sparse, they are rapidly growing in number. Highly informative overviews of Brodsky's life and work may be found in the revised edition of *Russian Literature Since the Revolution* by Edward J. Brown, 1982, and in Peter France, *Poets of Modern Russia*, 1983. A general discussion of Brodsky's poetry also appears in Sidney Monas, "Words Devouring Things: The Poetry of Joseph Brodsky," *World Literature Today*, LVII (1983), 214-218. The collection of poetry that has received the most attention from scholars is *Ostanovka v pustyne*. Insightful articles on this volume include Alexander Zholkovsky, "Writing in the Wilderness: On Brodskij and a Sonnet," *Slavic and East European Journal*, XXX (Fall, 1986), 404-419; R. D. Sylvester, "The Poem as Scapegoat: An Introduction to Joseph Brodsky's Halt in the Wilderness," in a special Russian issue of *Texas Studies in Literature and Language*, XVII (1975), 303-325; and Carl R. Proffer, "A Stop in the Madhouse: Brodsky's *Gorbunov and Gorchakov*," *Russian Literature Triquarterly*, I (1971), 342-351. For a thoughtful examination of Brodsky's *Chast rechi*, see John Bayley, "Sophisticated Razzmatazz," *Parnassus*, IX (Spring/Summer, 1981), 83-90.

David Patterson

ANITA BROOKNER

Born: London, England
Date: July 16, 1938

PRINCIPAL WORKS

NOVELS: *The Debut*, 1981 (also known as *A Start in Life*); *Providence*, 1982; *Look at Me*, 1983; *Hotel du Lac*, 1984; *Family and Friends*, 1985; *The Misalliance*, 1986; *A Friend from England*, 1987; *Latecomers*, 1988.

CRITICISM: *The Genius of the Future: Studies in French Art Criticism*, 1971.

BIOGRAPHY: *Watteau*, 1968; *Greuze: The Rise and Fall of an Eighteenth-Century Phenomenon*, 1972; *Jacques-Louis David*, 1980.

TRANSLATIONS: *Utrillo*, 1960 (by Waldemar George); *The Fauves*, 1962 (by Jean Paul Crespelle).

Anita Brookner, the only child of Newsom and Maude Schiska Brookner, was born in London, England, on July 16, 1938. She attended James Allen's Girls' School; received a B.A. from King's College, University of London; and completed a Ph.D. in art history from Courtauld Institute of Art in London. She began her teaching career as a visiting lecturer at the University of Reading in Reading, England, where she taught from 1959 to 1964. In 1964 she became a lecturer at the Courtauld Institute, where from 1977 to 1987 she was a reader in art history with the rank of professor. She was Slade Professor at the University of Cambridge from 1967 to 1968, the first woman ever to hold the position. In 1984, Brookner won the Booker Prize for her novel *Hotel du Lac*. In 1988 she gave up teaching to concentrate on her writing career.

Brookner's writing initially grew out of her academic career. Her field of expertise is late eighteenth and early nineteenth century French painting, and her first book was *Watteau*, a brief introductory study of the French painter. She followed this book with a volume of six essays of comparative criticism titled *The Genius of the Future*; the essays examined the personalities and accomplishments of Denis Diderot, Stendhal, Charles Baudelaire, Émile Zola, the brothers Goncourt, and Joris-Karl Huysmans. This volume was a product of Brookner's Slade lectures at Cambridge. She followed this work with *Greuze: The Rise and Fall of an Eighteenth Century Phenomenon*. She presented Jean-Baptiste Greuze as a painter who attempted to reestablish nostalgia as a part of the abstract intellectual milieu of the mid-eighteenth century art world. Following her study of Greuze was *Jacques-Louis David*, appearing in 1980. Brookner's portrait of David is one of an artist whose life and work embodied and reflected much of the fundamental thought, belief, and behavior of the eighteenth century.

During a long summer vacation, Brookner wrote her first novel, *The Debut*, published in 1981. Brookner's own awareness of the impact of art on life and her involvement in the academic world are reflected in this novel. The main character, Dr. Ruth Weiss, is a professor of literature at a London university. Like Brookner, Ruth grew up reading English novels, especially Charles Dickens, in which patience and virtue were ultimately rewarded; yet the stifling life she lived under the eye of her strong-willed mother leads her to study Honoré de Balzac. Through a scholarship she escapes to Paris to read Balzac and live her own life. Her adventure is cut short when she is called back to London to tend to her aging parents.

Brookner continued her examination of the thinking single woman in *Providence* and *Look at Me*. Her fourth novel, *Hotel du Lac*, is also about a lonely, literate, well-to-do woman. Edith Hope, the heroine, is a successful writer of romantic fiction, and the book turns on the contrast between the lives of the characters in her fiction and her own life. *Hotel du Lac* is about loneliness, but, in spite of its subject, there is wit and humor in this novel. Edith is disappointed in love and seems unable to fit the conventional mold; yet unlike Brookner's earlier heroines, Edith comes to accept this situation and finds value in what she does have.

Brookner followed *Hotel du Lac* with *Family and Friends*, a novel in which her cast of characters is expanded to include all the members of the London-based Dorn family: Sofka, a Jewish-European matriarch, and her three children. In a departure from the 1980's settings of previous novels, *Family and Friends* begins in the 1930's. In this novel Brookner also expands her examination of love, exploring not only romantic relationships but also the love between parents and children, sisters and brothers. Her examination of the Dorn family reveals the breakdown of traditional social codes which allowed family life to operate smoothly.

The Misalliance, Brookner's sixth novel, returns to the 1980's and the exploration of one woman's attempts to come to terms with loneliness. Middle-aged Blanche Vernon is separated from her husband of twenty years, who has left her for a younger woman. Blanche is attractive, intelligent, and financially well-off, but the departure of her husband has left her without a defined social position. With no activity to occupy her, Blanche involves herself in the lives of others, particularly those of an irresponsible young woman and her small daughter, in whom Blanche senses a loneliness similar to her own. A surprising turn at the end of *The Misalliance* leaves the reader wondering what life holds for Blanche Vernon.

Brookner's seventh novel, *A Friend from England*, appeared in 1987. Rachel, the emancipated heroine and narrator of the novel, has protected herself from emotional pain by refusing to allow others to become intimate with her. She makes friends with the Livingstones, a thoroughly conventional and innocent family who cannot fully understand Rachel's stripped-down, modern life. Rachel's own lack of understanding becomes clear when, in an attempt to protect the Livingstones, she learns the depth of their innocence. Despite all of her worldliness, this encounter leaves Rachel feeling ignorant and incomplete.

In *Latecomers*, Brookner broadens her scope by making her main characters male. Both men came to England from Germany before World War II: Hartmann from Munich and Fibrich from Berlin. A sense of displacement, seen before in *Providence*, pervades this book. Fibrich returns to Berlin for a visit in an attempt to overcome his sense of loss.

BIBLIOGRAPHICAL REFERENCES: For excerpts of reviews, see *Contemporary Literary Criticism*, Vol. 32, 1985, and Vol. 34, 1985. For complete reviews, individual sources must be consulted. Ann Gottlieb reviewed *The Debut* in *The New York Times Book Review*, March 29, 1981, 14-15. A review of *Providence* by Frances Taliaferro appeared in *Harper's Magazine*, CCLXVIII (1984), 75-76. Several excellent reviews of *Hotel du Lac* are widely available: John Gross, *The New York Times*, January 22, 1985, C17; Adam Mars-Jones, "Women Beware Women," *The New York Review of Books*, XXXII (January, 1985), 17-19; and Anne Tyler, "A Solitary Life Is Still Worth Living," *The New York Times Book Review*, February 3, 1985, 1. *The Misalliance* was reviewed by Fernanda Eberstadt in *The New York Times Book Review*, March 29, 1987. Deborah Singmaster reviewed *A Friend from England* in *The Times Literary Supplement*, August 21, 1987. Two interviews with Brookner reveal not only connections between her life and her books but also techniques she employs when writing: Shusha Guppy, "The Art of Fiction XCVIII," *The Paris Review*, XXIX (1987), 147-169, and Amanda Smith, *Publishers Weekly*, September 6, 1985, 67-68.

Bonnie C. Plummer

GWENDOLYN BROOKS

Born: Topeka, Kansas
Date: June 7, 1917

PRINCIPAL WORKS

POETRY: *A Street in Bronzeville*, 1945; *Annie Allen*, 1949; *Bronzeville Boys and Girls*, 1956; *The Bean Eaters*, 1960; *Selected Poems*, 1963; *In the Mecca*, 1968; *Riot*, 1969; *Family Pictures*, 1970; *Aloneness*, 1971; *Beckonings*, 1975; *Primer for Blacks*, 1980; *To Disembark*, 1981.

NOVEL: *Maud Martha*, 1953.

AUTOBIOGRAPHY: *Report from Part One*, 1972.

MISCELLANEOUS: *The World of Gwendolyn Brooks*, 1971.

Gwendolyn Brooks was born on June 7, 1917, in Topeka, Kansas. Shortly after her birth, her family moved to Chicago, where she was reared and where she has since made her home. During the 1930's, Brooks received her associate degree in literature and arts from Wilson Junior College and served as publicity director for the National Association for the Advancement of Colored People (NAACP) Youth Council in Chicago. She married in 1939 and gave birth to two children. She was later divorced.

A major voice in contemporary American poetry, Brooks published her first book of poetry, *A Street in Bronzeville*, in 1945. It introduces themes that would occupy Brooks for two decades, the first half of her career: the search for dignity and happiness in a society which denies both to many people, the twin oppressions of racism and poverty, life in the American family, and the trauma of world war.

Her early poetry is characterized by a uniform narrative stance. A sensitive observer tells verse stories about ordinary people, many of whom are ghetto dwellers entrapped by social, economic, and racial forces they can neither control nor understand. Brooks catalogs the many ways her characters seek security and hope: through religion, through integration of the races, and through careless and profligate living. Pursued to excess, these misdirected forays, these escapes, have one thing in common—they fail. These activities are used to mask frightful uncertainty and insecurity. Yet they actually extend and intensify the cycle of hopelessness.

Taken together, Brooks's poems about ordinary people produce a vivid and complex picture of America's poor, with poverty both sign and symbol of racism and injustice. The poor are uneducated (or undereducated), victimized by racism and crime, trapped by society and their own inadequacies. The poet-narrator's attitude toward them is one of wistful sympathy; she herself is a part of the life she describes.

One of Brooks's main contentions at this point in her career was that political and social freedom for black people would tear down the walls between the races, that such freedom would bring relief from demeaning poverty and ignorance. It must be added, however, that in the most pessimistic moments in her early poetry she suggests that freedom for black people is impossible in American society. Recognition and honors crowned Brooks's early career. She was the first black woman to receive the Pulitzer Prize in poetry, and she was appointed Poet Laureate of Illinois on Carl Sandburg's death.

Beginning in 1968, the direction of Brooks's work changed. In her poetry, essays, and speeches, Brooks launched what she called the "new music," the poetry of black mystique and the black revolution. She explained her new role: "I want to write poetry that will appeal to many, many blacks, not just blacks who go to college but also those who have their customary habitat in taverns and the street. . . . Anything I write is going to issue from a concern with and interest in blackness and its progress." Brooks turned away from the careful portraiture of her early work to pursue a more emotional and personal type of polemic poetry. She would continue to experiment with new poetic forms and new attitudes to express her commitment to the cause of black unity in the United States.

In 1981, Brooks published a book of poems, *To Disembark*, composed of versions of several previously published poems. The poems serve as a continuing call for blacks to disengage from all that represents the oppressive life of white America. Brooks suggests in "Riot," as well as in other poems, that this disengagement may require violent disturbance and anarchy. The bitter, militant tone of the book caused one critic to label it a "distressing celebration of violence." In 1985, Brooks was appointed Poetry Consultant for the Library of Congress.

BIBLIOGRAPHICAL REFERENCES: The most thorough study of Brooks's poetry is D. H. Melhem, *Gwendolyn Brooks, Poetry and the Heroic Voice*, 1987. A collection of critical essays about Brooks and her work is found in *A Life Distilled: Gwendolyn Brooks, Her Poetry and Fiction*, 1987, edited by Maria K. Mootry and Gary Smith. The most helpful collection of Brooks's ideas about her work is found in an interview with Brooks by George Stavros, *Contemporary Literature*, II (1970), 1-20. Other important studies are Arthur P. Davis, "Gwendolyn Brooks: Poet of the Unheroic," *College Language Association Journal*, VII (1963), 114-125; William H. Hansell, "The Role of Violence in Recent Poems of Gwendolyn Brooks," *Studies in Black Literature*, V (1974), 21-27; and Patricia H. Lattin and Vernon E. Lattin, "Dual Vision in Gwendolyn Brooks's *Maud Martha*," *Critique: Studies in Modern Fiction*, XXV (1984), 180-188.

Charles M. Israel

RITA MAE BROWN

Born: Hanover, Pennsylvania
Date: November 28, 1944

PRINCIPAL WORKS

NOVELS: *Rubyfruit Jungle*, 1973; *In Her Day*, 1976; *Six of One*, 1978; *Southern Discomfort*, 1982; *Sudden Death*, 1983; *High Hearts*, 1986; *Bingo*, 1988.

NONFICTION: *A Plain Brown Rapper*, 1976; *Starting from Scratch: A Different Kind of Writer's Manual*, 1988.

POETRY: *The Hand That Cradles the Rock*, 1971; *Songs to a Handsome Woman*, 1973.

SCREENPLAY: *The Slumber Party Massacre*, 1982.

TELEPLAY: *I Love Liberty*, 1982.

TRANSLATION: *Hrotsvitra: Six Medieval Latin Plays*, 1971.

Since the publication of her autobiographical first novel, *Rubyfruit Jungle*, Rita Mae Brown has been an important literary force within the feminist and gay rights movements. She was born on November 28, 1944, in Hanover, Pennsylvania. She was adopted by Ralph Brown and his wife, Julia Buckingham. She attended the University of Florida and received a B.A. degree from New York University in 1968. That same year, she earned a cinematography certificate from the New York School of Visual Arts. From 1969 to 1970, she was employed by Sterling Publishing of New York City as a photography editor. From 1970 to 1971, she lectured in sociology at Federal City College in Washington, D.C. She was a fellow of the Institute for Policy Studies in Washington, D.C., from 1971 to 1973, receiving her Ph.D. there in 1973. She has been a visiting member of the faculty in feminist studies at Goddard College in Plainfield, Vermont, since 1973. She is also a member of the board of directors of Sagaris, a feminist school.

Although Brown had published two books previously, *Rubyfruit Jungle* was the work which first attracted widespread attention. The novel's debut was inauspicious. After *Rubyfruit Jungle* was rejected by the major publishing houses, it was brought out by Daughters, Inc., a small company specializing in feminist works. The novel sold a surprising seventy thousand copies, thus encouraging a large firm, Bantam Books, to acquire publication rights in 1977. Another 300,000 copies were printed, and sales eventually exceeded one million.

Rubyfruit Jungle is a picaresque novel whose protagonist, Molly Bolt, has been likened to Huckleberry Finn. Molly is also bright, lusty, and lesbian. While some view the novel as a lesbian "statement," others argue that it is, rather, the familiar apprenticeship story of a spirited American who is also a lesbian. Most homosexual fiction features characters who are tragic victims, Brown says, whereas her work is funny and compels the reader to laugh. Her third novel, *Six of One*, is set in a town on the Pennsylvania-Maryland border over a period of some seventy years. The events of the novel are viewed through the eyes of several earthy, sassy townswomen, probably modeled on members of Brown's own family. The town is part Southern, and Brown's treatment of Southern culture and attitudes in this novel, and later in *Southern Discomfort*, has caused some readers to think of her as a Southern writer. (Brown rejects all labels vehemently.) *Southern Discomfort* ranges farther south, in fact. It is set in Montgomery, Alabama, and treats an interracial and intergenerational love affair, and the scandal which it causes.

Sudden Death is set in the world of professional women's tennis. Some have viewed it as a *roman à clef* based upon the great champion Martina Navratilova. Brown says that her real motivation for writing the novel was a promise exacted from her by a dying friend. Judy Lacy, a sportswriter, had intended to write a novel using professional tennis as a background. In 1980, she was dying of a brain tumor and realized that she would never write the book. Brown reluctantly promised to write the book instead, and *Sudden Death* is the result.

Since the early 1980's, Brown has devoted much of her energies to screenwriting, an activity which she characterizes as totally unlike novel writing. Her work in this field has been widely diverse. She worked on the script for Norman Lear's 1982 television special, *I Love Liberty.* She also wrote the screenplay for *The Slumber Party Massacre*.

Rita Mae Brown is consistently praised for the vitality, wit, and audacity of her fiction. In reaching a wide audience, she has apparently overcome what she considers the very real prejudices against the work of lesbian writers. She is extremely versatile and has written in every genre except the drama and the epic poem. A play, she says, is definitely in her future.

BIBLIOGRAPHICAL REFERENCES: See Bertha Harris, review of *Rubyfruit Jungle*, *The Village Voice*, April 4, 1974, 36; Jane Rule, "Four Decades of Fiction," in *Lesbian Images*, 1975; Joan Larkin, "In Short: *In Her Day*," *Ms.*, V (April, 1977), 44; Terry Curtis Fox, "Up from Cultdom and Down Again," *The Village Voice*, XXII (September 12, 1977), 41; John Fludas, "Books in Brief: *Six of One*," *Saturday Review*, V (September 30, 1978), 52; Liz Mednick, "How to Beat a Dead Horse Senseless," *New York Arts Journal*, XII (November/December, 1978), 25-26; Shelly Temchin Henze, "Rita Mae Brown, All-American," *New Boston Review*, IV/V (April/May, 1979), 17-18; and Susan Kennedy, "Catching Up: *Six of One*," *The Times Literary Supplement*, December 7, 1979, 104. See also Annie Gottlieb, "Passion and Punishment," *The New York Times Book Review*, March 21, 1982, 10; Charlotte M. Meyer, review of *Southern Discomfort*, *The American Book Review*, (January/February, 1983), 22; Elisabeth Jakab, "Tennis and Diplomacy," *The New York Times Book Review*, June 19, 1983, 12; Gary Davenport, "The Fugitive Hero in New Southern Fiction," *The Sewanee Review*, XCI (Summer, 1983), 439-445; Marcelle Thiébaux, review of *Sudden Death*, *Best Sellers*, XLIII (July, 1983), 120; Leslie Fishbein, "*Rubyfruit Jungle*: Lesbianism, Feminism, and Narcissism," *International Journal of Women's Studies*, VII (March/April, 1984), 155-159; and Florence King, "Rita Mae Brown's Tomboy Scarlett O'Hara," *The Washington Post Book World*, May 4, 1986, 3.

Patrick Adcock

ERNEST BUCKLER

Born: Dalhousie West, Nova Scotia
Date: July 19, 1908

Died: Bridgetown, Nova Scotia
Date: March 4, 1984

PRINCIPAL WORKS

FICTION: *The Mountain and the Valley*, 1952; *The Cruelest Month*, 1963; *The Rebellion of Young David and Other Stories*, 1975.

NONFICTION: *Oxbells and Fireflies: A Memoir*, 1968; *Nova Scotia: Window on the Sea*, 1973 (with Hans Weber).

MISCELLANEOUS: *Whirligig: Selected Prose and Verse*, 1977.

Ernest Buckler wrote poetic prose about Nova Scotia, particularly of life in its Annapolis Valley. He spent some seventy years there and lived elsewhere for only a few years in his twenties. Having taken his B.A. degree in mathematics at Dalhousie University in Halifax, Nova Scotia, he took an M.A. degree in philosophy at the University of Toronto. He then worked in Toronto for the Manufacturers Life Insurance Company before returning to the Annapolis Valley in 1936, at age twenty-eight. Buckler spent the remainder of his life on a farm near Bridgetown, Nova Scotia, except for his last few years, which he passed in a rest home in Bridgetown. From his small room there he could look out on a mountain looming as significantly as the one in his first and best-known book. He described himself as a farmer who wrote, not as a writer who farmed.

Nevertheless, from the later 1930's he was writing short stories, poems, and articles which were published in *Esquire* and such Canadian periodicals as *The Atlantic Advocate*, *Saturday Night*, and *Maclean's*, as well as radio scripts for the Canadian Broadcasting Corporation. Some of these short stories prefigure characters and episodes in his novel *The Mountain and the Valley*, which he said took him six years to write. This *Bildungsroman* shows the maturing of David Canaan, the sensitive observer amid a farming family, whose members also have deep feelings but do not or cannot articulate them. Significant turning points in David's development and in his relations with his parents, brother, twin sister, and friends are presented in the novel's six main sections. Buckler's capacity for combining realistic detail with symbolic import, expressed in rich imagery and luxuriant language, is the outstanding feature of Buckler's prose. The prologue and epilogue frame the last day of David's life, when he finally ascends the mountain and dies while experiencing a vision of the writer's power to express the unity of life.

Buckler's second novel, *The Cruelest Month*, concerns a group of people who assemble in a rural retreat, where they engage in a series of long discussions of self-revelation and self-analysis. These discussions lead to various changes in the characters, further stimulated by the cathartic effect of a threatening forest fire. The novel is self-consciously literary, from the echo of the opening line of T. S. Eliot's *The Waste Land* (1922) in its title to the names of the protagonist, Paul Creed, and the retreat, Endlaw, which anagrammatically invokes Walden. (Buckler continues to engage in such wordplay in *Whirligig*.)

His next book, *Oxbells and Fireflies*, consists of vignettes about country life, drawing largely on his own experience of a way of life that had passed or was passing. Anecdotal and affectionate, these memoirs make pleasant reading. *Nova Scotia: Window on the Sea* treats the same material, but it is complemented by many fine photographs by Hans Weber. A collection of Buckler's short stories, including "Penny in the Dust," the very moving story of a father and son, was edited by Robert D. Chambers and published under the title *The Rebellion of Young David and Other Stories*. Some of these stories have affinities with episodes in Buckler's novels. The whimsical and witty side of Buckler is seen in full in *Whirligig*, a collection of satires, humorous sketches, and light verse. In it, Buckler has Ophelia asking Ann Landers how to deal with her problems with Hamlet; eavesdropping on rural telephone lines and bawdy epigrams are also discussed.

Not surprisingly from one with professional training in philosophy, Buckler is keenly aware of the problem of subjectivity in perception. In David's transfiguring experience as he climbs the mountain in the last chapter of *The Mountain and the Valley*, he realizes that his "inside was nothing but one great white naked eye of self-consciousness, with only its own looking to look at." As he looked at the frozen landscape, however, "it was as if the outline of the frozen landscape *became* his consciousness: that inside and outside were not two things, but one." This recognition leads Buckler constantly to describe phenomena as realistically as possible and to present them metaphorically, in a quest to express a unity which can be apprehended only for a moment. At its best, his richly imaginative prose conveys a sense of what such unity might be.

BIBLIOGRAPHICAL REFERENCES: Selected reviews and early criticism of Buckler's work are included in *Ernest Buckler*, 1972, edited by Gregory M. Cook. Alan R. Young, *Ernest Buckler*, 1976, is an introductory study. Buckler's work is carefully considered in Robert D. Chambers, *Sinclair Ross and Ernest Buckler*, 1978. See also John Orange, "Ernest Buckler: An Annotated Bibliography," in *Annotated Bibliography of Canada's Major Authors*, Vol. 3, 1981, edited by Robert Lecker and Jack David.

Christopher M. Armitage

WILLIAM F. BUCKLEY, JR.

Born: New York, New York
Date: November 24, 1925

PRINCIPAL WORKS

NONFICTION: *God and Man at Yale*, 1951; *McCarthy and His Enemies*, 1954 (with L. Brent Bozell); *Up from Liberalism*, 1959; *Rumbles Left and Right*, 1963; *The Unmaking of a Mayor*, 1966; *The Jeweler's Eye*, 1968; *The Governor Listeth*, 1971; *Inveighing We Will Go*, 1972; *Four Reforms: A Guide for the Seventies*, 1973; *Execution Eve and Other Contemporary Ballads*, 1975. *A Hymnal: The Controversial Arts*, 1978; *Right Reason*, 1985.

MYSTERY AND DETECTIVE FICTION: *Saving the Queen*, 1976; *Stained Glass*, 1978; *Who's on First*, 1981; *Marco Polo, If You Can*, 1982; *The Story of Henri Tod*, 1984; *See You Later, Alligator*, 1985; *High Jinx*, 1986; *Mongoose, R.I.P.*, 1987.

AUTOBIOGRAPHY: *Cruising Speed: A Documentary*, 1971; *Airborne: A Sentimental Journey*, 1976; *Atlantic High*, 1982; *Overdrive: A Personal Documentary*, 1983; *Racing Through Paradise*, 1987.

CHILDREN'S LITERATURE: *The Temptation of Wilfred Malachey*, 1985.

EDITED TEXT: *Did You Ever See a Dream Walking? Conservative Thought in the Twentieth Century*, 1987.

William Francis Buckley, Jr., is the founder, leader, and most famous exponent of modern American conservatism. He was born in New York City on November 24, 1925, the sixth child of wealthy oilman and entrepreneur Will Buckley and his wife, Aloise. The father of ten children, Will Buckley was a man of strong political opinions and intense religious faith, and his son grew up in an atmosphere of unwavering commitment to laissez-faire capitalism and the Roman Catholic church—and hostility toward Communism. These beliefs have remained the core of William F. Buckley's personal and public philosophy.

Buckley received his early education at home from private tutors, at St. John's Beaumont, a Catholic boarding school in England, and at a small private academy near Sharon, Connecticut. In September, 1946, after two years in the United States Army (where he became a second lieutenant), Buckley entered Yale University. Though he soon established a reputation as a champion debater, his greatest ambition was to become editor of the *Yale Daily News*, the elite and highly influential campus newspaper. Upon attaining this position in his junior year, Buckley sparked controversy by using the paper's editorial pages to attack the prevailing liberal ideology of the faculty and administration. Yet he remained personally popular and shortly before graduation, in 1950, was named Undergraduate of the Year.

Buckley had been so disturbed by what he viewed as the antireligious climate at Yale that, almost immediately after graduating, he began to write his first book, *God and Man at Yale*, published in 1951. In it, he charged that Yale had abandoned the philosophy of its founders, based upon the acceptance of Christianity and free enterprise, and had developed in its place a relativistic orthodoxy which encouraged Atheism and Socialism. To Buckley's great surprise, the book was an instant best-seller and raised storms of angry debate. He was soon deluged with offers for speaking engagements. Having to articulate his views in public helped him to forge them into a coherent new approach to politics and philosophy, one that rejected traditional definitions of "conservatism" as simply defending the status quo. Buckley's new conservatism was aggressively individualistic, rebellious, and antisecularist.

After a short stint working for the *American Mercury*, a moribund conservative magazine, Buckley became involved in the public debate about Senator Joseph McCarthy, who had become notorious by publicly accusing the State Department of employing large numbers of Communists and Communist sympathizers. When McCarthy could not substantiate his charges, he was discredited, and "McCarthyism" came to mean unfounded character assassination. Buckley, who admired McCarthy, collaborated with L. Brent Bozell, his former Yale debating partner, to write *McCarthy and His Enemies*. Though critical of some of McCarthy's methods, the book strongly defended the need to root out of the American government those who supported, either intentionally or inadvertently, Communist efforts to subvert American interests.

At the urging of friends and colleagues, Buckley decided, in 1955, to create a new magazine, the *National Review*, which has been the main journal of conservative opinion since its first issue appeared in April, 1956. As its editor, Buckley has used the *National Review* to lead and shape the American conservative movement by giving a platform to such major political theorists as James Burnham and Russell T. Kirk, as well as to younger talents such as Joan Didion and Garry Wills.

Most of the *National Review*'s loyal readers, which include former President Ronald Reagan, however, are attracted by the sparkling wit and incisive analytical writing of Buckley himself. Many of his editorials, lectures, and newspaper columns (which are carried by more than one hundred dailies across the country) have been collected in several books: *Rumbles Left and Right*, *The Governor Listeth*, *A Hymnal: The Controversial Arts*, and others. All these works are characterized by Buckley's sharp debating style, strong command of logic, witty and often-ironic humor, and eloquence in defense of his conservative ideals.

Buckly has also made lasting contributions to political philosophy in such works as *Up from Liberalism*, which exposes weaknesses in liberal ideology; *Did You Ever See a Dream Walking?*, a compendium of conservative theory edited and introduced by Buckley; and *Four Reforms*, which addresses the specific areas of welfare, taxation, education, and crime.

Much of Buckley's power to influence others, however, has derived from his status as a celebrity. In 1965, he ran a semiserious campaign as a candidate for mayor in New York City on a platform of tough crime prevention and welfare reform. Though he never really expected to win, Buckley was surprised at his popularity among average voters, and he received 13.4 percent of the vote in a three-way race. His account of the campaign, *The Unmaking of a Mayor* is one of his most entertaining books.

In 1966, Buckley began broadcasting a syndicated weekly television talk show, *Firing Line*, which has featured a wide variety of famous guests in conversations and debates. Buckley's unusual conversational style, peppered with sesquipedalian terms and Latinisms, strange rhythms and odd pauses, all wrapped in an immense smile and a highly engaging manner, have made the show popular with audiences of all political opinions.

Buckley has also written several popular autobiographical works employing a day-by-day, diary-like style to create an intimate, dramatically personal record of events. In *Cruising Speed*, he documents one week in his life as editor of the *National Review*. His expertise as a transoceanic sailor is reflected in *Airborne: A Sentimental Journey*. In 1983, he published a book of reflections, *Overdrive*.

Buckley's wide-ranging interests have also been reflected in his fictional works, several of which have become best-sellers. His espionage novels, inspired by a nine-month tour of duty with the Central Intelligence Agency in 1950-1951, are not only extremely entertaining but also provide a vehicle for the expression of Buckley's view of the history of Soviet-American relations in the Cold War era. Among these works, his first, *Saving the Queen*, is generally considered to be the best. Buckley has even written a children's story, *The Temptation of Wilfred Malachey*. He remains the clearest, most eloquent, and certainly the best-known spokesman for the conservative vision of America.

BIBLIOGRAPHICAL REFERENCES: The first book-length biography of Buckley is John B. Judis, *William F. Buckley, Jr.: Patron Saint of the Conservatives*, 1987, which is extremely hostile to its subject and portrays conservatism virtually as a psychological aberration. Though strong on biographical detail, the book analyzes Buckley's ideas superficially. A much more serious, though equally hostile, examination of Buckley's thought is David Burner and Thomas R.

West, "William F. Buckley, Jr., and *National Review*," in *Column Right: Conservative Journalists in the Service of Nationalism*, 1988. The remarkably close personal and professional relationships among members of the Buckley family are discussed in Charles L. Markmann, *The Buckleys: A Family Examined*, 1973. In Whittaker Chambers, *Odyssey of a Friend: Whittaker Chambers' Letters to William F. Buckley, Jr., 1954-1961*, 1969, the poignant and sensitive correspondence of a former Communist agent reveals much about the development of Buckley's personal and political ideals. David Franke has compiled *Quotations from Chairman Bill*, 1970, a collection of Buckley witticisms. As a celebrity, Buckley has often been the subject of short articles in many popular magazines, but most of these are of little lasting interest. Perhaps the most revealing was a lengthy interview with Buckley which appeared in *Playboy*, May, 1970, 75.

Thomas C. Schunk

FREDERICK BUECHNER

Born: New York, New York
Date: July 11, 1926

PRINCIPAL WORKS

NOVELS: *A Long Day's Dying*, 1950; *The Season's Difference*, 1952; *The Return of Ansel Gibbs*, 1958; *The Final Beast*, 1965; *The Entrance to Porlock*, 1970; *Lion Country*, 1971; *Open Heart*, 1972; *Love Feast*, 1974; *Treasure Hunt*, 1977; *The Book of Bebb*, 1979; *Godric*, 1980; *Brendan*, 1987.

THEOLOGY: *The Magnificent Defeat*, 1966; *The Hungering Dark*, 1969; *The Alphabet of Grace*, 1970; *Wishful Thinking: A Theological ABC*, 1973; *The Faces of Jesus*, 1974; *Telling the Truth: The Gospel as Tragedy, Comedy, and Fairy Tale*, 1977; *Peculiar Treasures*, 1979; *A Room Called Remember*, 1984; *Whistling in the Dark*, 1988.

AUTOBIOGRAPHY: *The Sacred Journey*, 1982; *Now and Then*, 1983.

Frederick Buechner (pronounced "Beek-ner") was born in New York City on July 11, 1926, one of two sons of Carl Frederick and Katherine Buechner. The family moved many times during his childhood and became even more unsettled after Buechner's father committed suicide. Buechner was ten years old at the time, and the impact of his father's death was to make of him a rather bookish, brooding, even clinical observer of human life and its folly—as evidenced in the rarefied and intellectualized characterizations in his early modernist novels. In his later fiction Buechner renders compassionate descriptions of the tension between faith and doubt in troubled twentieth century lives. Buechner eventually completed his secondary education at the exclusive Lawrenceville School in New Jersey in 1943. After three years in the military, he completed his B.A. in English at Princeton University. It was during his senior year at Princeton that Buechner conceived and wrote his first novel, *A Long Day's Dying*. He returned to the Lawrenceville School to teach directly after graduation, occasionally conducting writing seminars in New York City.

When *A Long Day's Dying* appeared in 1950 it was highly praised by most critics, who focused on its labored, "Jamesian" narrative voice and its sophisticated treatment of the fragmented relationships on a college campus in postwar America. One critic, however, characterized it ruefully as "writing for a teacher," implying that it was constructed to fit within the dominant critical mode of the time, the so-called New Criticism, which prized such qualities as ambiguity and ambivalence. With the publication of his second novel, *The Season's Difference*, Buechner seemed destined to take his place among those despairing voices within American fiction (William Styron, Norman Mailer, Truman Capote) who looked bleakly heavenward, discovering only an empty sky bereft of divine comfort or direction. Buechner soon decided to seek a life as a full-time writer and moved to New York in 1953. There his conversion to Christianity and his subsequent seminary education altered his course irrevocably.

Upon hearing a moving sermon by the eminent preacher George Buttrick, Buechner experienced a deeply felt commitment to Jesus Christ and then attended Union Theological Seminary from 1954 to 1958. After his ordination as a Presbyterian minister in 1958, Buechner served as school chaplain and chairman of the department of religion at Phillips Exeter Academy until 1967. During this time he produced two novels whose characters clearly reflect a new humanness and humor uncharacteristic of the somber, tortured protagonists of his two earlier novels. Both *The Return of Ansel Gibbs* and *The Final Beast* focus on the exigencies of modern life, marking Christian faith as a daily affirmation, not a once-for-all declaration, his characters charged with fighting off the temptation of "cheap grace." After leaving Exeter in 1967, Buechner became a full-time writer and lecturer, living with his wife, Judith, and his family in Vermont.

Two collections of sermons, *The Magnificent Defeat* and *The Hungering Dark*, had been published in the late 1960's, consisting of addresses Buechner had composed for chapel devotions at Exeter and guest sermons at local congregations. Five theological works followed in the 1970's, highlighted by his compelling volume, published in 1977, *Telling the Truth*, a reinterpretation of the life of Christ from a storyteller's point of view that illuminates Buechner's own narrative strategies.

In this period the prolific Buechner also completed five novels: *The Entrance to Porlock*, a retelling of the Oz stories as modern myth, and the celebrated Bebb tetralogy (*Lion Counry, Open Heart*, *Love Feast*, and *Treasure Hunt*—later published as one volume, *The Book of Bebb*). This bawdy chronicle of the rogue preacher Leo Bebb and his spiritually reticent son-in-law, Antonio Parr, both satirizes and celebrates the improbable joy and disreputable shenanigans of those who profess belief in the gospel of Christ.

In the decade of the 1980's, Buechner turned toward introspection and to history, authoring two terse autobiographical volumes and two historical novels focusing on obscure Christian saints of the Middle Ages. *The Sacred Journey*, Buechner's first volume of autobiography, details key events of his childhood and adolescence and recalls the formative influences he encountered during his undergraduate years at Princeton. It concludes with Buechner's recounting of the composition and unexpected critical acclaim of his first two novels and his eventual, and seemingly coincidental, conversion to Christianity. *Now and Then*, published a year later, completes his autobiographical reflections, beginning with his seminary days in New York City and moving on to an account of Buechner's unlikely development of three different vocations after his graduation and ordination: chaplain/teacher, religious novelist, and popular theologian. *Godric* and *Brendan*, feigned biographies of two prominent, ancient believers, represent a new narrative focus for him, as Buechner successfully re-created and then meshed the language and culture of older times and themes reflective of the challenges of contemporary Christians in the West.

The primary audience for Buechner's work comprises two groups of readers: those for whom his Christian experience is both instructive and illuminating of their own faith and those who, with little regard for his religious conviction, admire his effortless prose and skillful depiction of the tensions and anxieties of modern life. Buechner has often said that his books are too religious for secular readers and too secular for religious readers. The truth is, throughout the winding path of his literary career, Buechner has had a consistently enthusiastic, though sometimes modest, readership among both kinds of readers. As memoirist, theologian, or storyteller, Buechner refuses to explain away the tensions of faith or paint a simplistic picture of the spiritual dimensions of life. He believes that even the most crushing defeats can be overcome by the irresistible grace of God, a force that operates both with and without human assistance. It is not the logician's syllogism but the narrative of the graceful storyteller which sheds lights on this profound discovery. Few religious writers contemporary with Buechner are his equal in communicating the meaning of Christianity in a time when the Christian vocabulary and worldview are considered defunct and impotent. He is thus rightly ranked with Flannery O'Connor and Walker Percy as one of the preeminent Christian fiction writers of the late twentieth century.

BIBLIOGRAPHICAL REFERENCES: In the absence of a definitive, full-length, biocritical assessment of Buechner, two volumes may be recommended that offer preliminary critical judgments of his theological and novelistic achievements. The more comprehensive of these is Marjorie McCoy, *Frederick Buechner*, 1988, which helpfully integrates Buechner's theology with both his early and his later novels. Marie-Hélène Davies, *Laughter in a Genevan Gown: The Works of Frederick Buechner, 1970-1980*, 1985, as the title indicates, focuses almost exclusively on Buechner's most prolific decade. An early critical work places Buechner in perspective amid the waning of modernism, John Aldridge, *After the Lost Generation*, 1951. See also Amos Wilder, *Theology and Modern Literature*, 1958; Ihab Hassan, *Radical Inno-*

cense: The Contemporary American Novel, 1961; and Nathan A. Scott, *The Broken Center*, 1966. Two Buechner interviews are particularly illuminating: Kenneth Gibble, "Listening to My Life: An Interview with Frederick Buechner," *The Christian Century*, November 16, 1983, 1042-1044, and "Frederick Buechner: Novelist to 'Cultured Despisers,'" *Christianity Today*, XXV (May 29, 1981), 44. Also valuable is Buechner's essay "Faith and Fiction," in *Spiritual Quests: The Art and Craft of Religious Writing*, 1988, edited by William Zinsser.

Bruce L. Edwards

MIKHAIL BULGAKOV

Born: Kiev, Russia
Date: May 15, 1891

Died: Moscow, Soviet Union
Date: March 10, 1940

PRINCIPAL WORKS

NOVELS: *Belaya gvardiya*, 1927, 1929 (*The White Guard*, 1971); *Teatralny i roman*, 1965 (*Black Snow: A Theatrical Novel*, 1967); *Master i Margarita*, 1966-1967 (*The Master and Margarita*, 1967).

PLAYS: *Dni Turbinykh*, pr. 1926 (*Days of the Turbins*, 1934); *Bagrovy ostrov*, pr. 1928 (*The Crimson Island*, 1972); *Kabala svyatosh*, pr. 1936 (*A Cabal of Hypocrites*, 1972; also known as *Molière*); *Beg*, pr. 1957 (*Flight*, 1969).

SHORT FICTION: *Diavoliada*, 1925 (*Diaboliad and Other Stories*, 1972); *Sobache serdtse*, 1968 (*The Heart of a Dog*, 1968).

BIOGRAPHY: *Zhizn gospodina de Molyera*, 1962 (*The Life of Monsieur de Molière*, 1970).

Mikhail Afanasyevich Bulgakov is one of the most revered and widely read twentieth century Russian authors. He was born in the Ukrainian capital Kiev on May 15, 1891, into a highly educated family that was devoted to Russia's religious and cultural heritage. After initial tutoring at home, supervised by his father, a professor of theology, Bulgakov attended the best local high school and subsequently completed medical studies at the University of Kiev. He was graduated at the height of World War I and immediately served in field hospitals. The revolution of 1917 and postwar upheavals in the Ukraine caused Bulgakov, now married, to establish residence in Moscow. There he followed in the footsteps of Anton Chekhov by giving up medicine in favor of literature.

Bulgakov had a sharp eye for the incongruities attending the violent postrevolutionary social changes, and he developed a flair for satirizing them in feuilletons. His sarcastic impressions, however, soon collided with an ever stricter Communist censorship. Because of his subsequent continuous clashes with censors, Bulgakov's career of publishing and play production follows no neat chronological pattern. Some works, such as his vicious attack on the folly of social experiments, *The Heart of a Dog*, were published only posthumously. A similar fate befell his most important work, *The Master and Margarita*. Of his first novel, *The White Guard*, detailing the defeat of antirevolutionary forces, two sections appeared serialized in 1925. The rest was prohibited, and this became a pattern for many other works. *The White Guard* appeared first in its complete form in Paris; it did not appear in the Soviet Union until 1966.

Other works by Bulgakov, having been issued incompletely in one form, were sometimes reworked and offered to the censors under different titles. Thus *The White Guard* reemerged as the play *Days of the Turbins* and, notwithstanding numerous attacks on it, enjoyed a lengthy run. Bulgakov's other dramatic ventures fared less well. *Flight*, written in 1927, was banned in 1928 because it gave a positive portrayal of counterrevolutionary figures. The experimental *The Crimson Island*, depicting an island revolt in comic terms, had a brief run before castigation by Joseph Stalin forced its removal in early 1929. In the same year *A Cabal of Hypocrites*, based on Molière's life, was rejected; it reappeared briefly in 1936 as *Molière*. It was allowed seven performances before negative reviews in *Pravda* necessitated its closing.

Bulgakov's early literary recognition rests primarily on shorter satiric prose pieces, collected in *Diaboliad and Other Stories*. Through delicate political maneuvering, these parodies escaped crucial censorial cuts and fully displayed Bulgakov's talent for deft, sarcastic phrasing. By 1930, however, he realized that he could not preserve his authorial integrity under the prevailing conditions. He requested and received permission from Stalin to stage other writers' officially approved, often-trite propagandist productions. When that task became too disagreeable, he assisted the Bolshoi Theater in fashioning operatic librettos into politically acceptable works. These accommodations to the requirements of the regime brought him a relatively secure and comfortable life-style while simultaneously permitting him to write as he pleased in private in the hope of more liberal times to come. Also during this period, Bulgakov divorced a second wife and married a third, the great love of his life, Yelena Shilovsky, who not only became his secretary and editor when nephrosclerosis struck him in 1939 but also faithfully preserved all unpublished manuscripts and solicited Western help in securing their full publication. Bulgakov died on March 10, 1940, and was accorded an official funeral by the Soviet government.

One of the manuscripts unpublished at Bulgakov's death, *The Master and Margarita*, became his ticket to posthumous fame. Without this novel, Bulgakov would have been but one of many suppressed Soviet writers. As it is, Bulgakov used the last ten years of his life to create secretly what many consider a masterpiece and term the most important Russian novel of the twentieth century. Its very publication history contributed to its reputation. During the relatively relaxed censorship period following Stalin's death, the Soviet Union allowed a censored version to appear serialized in 1966-1967; that generated immediate intense reader interest. The 1969 printing of the full text in West Germany, obtained through the efforts of Bulgakov's widow and followed by translation into many languages, brought Bulgakov to Western attention. Widespread acclaim motivated a definitive Soviet version for internal consumption in 1973. Since then, Bulgakov has been fully rehabilitated and recognized as a major author.

The Master and Margarita encompasses many satirical views of Soviet life under Stalin that were censored in Bulgakov's earlier pieces. It also serves as a good example of his experimental style and gives insight into his philosophical preoccupations. Critics are in disagreement about the definitive meaning of his ideas, which are presented in inscrutable, often conflicting and fantastic terms. The political exposés are carried out by Satan and his retinue rather than by avenging angels. Bulgakov periodically interrupts his panorama of Stalinist intrigue with chapters depicting a very unbiblical Jesus in a style stripped of all hagiographical language. These Jerusalem sections are the product of Bulgakov's "Master," a persecuted writer consigned to a comfortable Hell by a benevolent devil for obscure reasons. The other title figure, Margarita, possessing symbolic traces of the Virgin Mary, a witch and the author's wife, forsakes heaven to share the Master's fate.

Many readers and analysts, especially Russians, discern deeply hidden metaphysical implications in the narrative, and numerous books and essays attempt to offer explanation. Most agree that Bulgakov attempts to juxtapose Roman injustice at the time of Christ to Soviet oppression. A part of the critical literature less generously views the work as disjointed and overloaded with poorly integrated biographical material. Bulgakov did write many versions of the novel, frequently putting it aside for long periods in order to begin other pieces left unfinished, among them *Black Snow*, and he died without having completed the final revision of *The Master and Margarita*. Yet even Bulgakov's partial detractors find the book strikingly original and spellbinding. There is universal agreement that the spiritual plane is elevated above the material, though in a bizarre fashion. Fascination with the novel led to widespread interest in and publication of all Bulgakov's output. Material scattered throughout Soviet archives permitted scholars to gain a comprehensive view of his achievements. While much of value for the Slavic specialist evolved from these collections, the overriding interest in Bulgakov is attributable to his mysterious *The Master and Margarita*, which continues to captivate audiences worldwide.

BIBLIOGRAPHICAL REFERENCES: The most comprehensive treatment of Bulgakov's life and work is by Ellendea Proffer, *Bulgakov*, 1984. For a more concise but also fairly complete literary biography, see Nadine Natov, *Mikhail Bulgakov*, 1985. Samples of Bulgakov's prose and dramatic output, as well as critical articles, are found in the special Bulgakov edition of *Russian Literature Triquarterly*, Carl and Ellendea Proffer, eds., no. 15, 1978. An excellent sampling of diverging critical opinions covering a wide range of Bulgakov's work is available in the special Bulgakov issue of *Canadian-American Slavic Studies*, Nadine Natov, ed., XV, nos. 2/3, 1981. For a thorough critical biography, see A. Colin Wright, *Mikhail Bulgakov: Life and Interpretation*, 1978. Andrew Barratt, *Between Two Worlds: A Critical Introduction to "The Master and Margarita,"* 1987, puts forth an imaginative approach to understanding Bulgakov's most important work. The following provide shorter, more general analyses of Bulgakov's significance or explanations of specific themes: Ewa Thompson, "The Artistic World of Michail Bulgakov," *Russian Literature*, no. 5 (1973), 54-64; Lewis Bagby, "Eternal Themes in Mixail Bulgakov's *The Master and Margarita*," *The International Fiction Review*, I (1974), 27-31; Elizabeth Beaujour, "The Use of Witches in Fedin and Bulgakov," *Slavic Review*, XXXIII (1974), 695-707; Pierre Hart, "*The Master and Margarita* as Creative Process," *Modern Fiction Studies*, XIX (1973), 169-178; Ellendea Proffer, "On *The Master and Margarita*," in *Major Soviet Writers*, Edward J. Brown, ed. (1973), 388-411; Gleb Struve, "The Re-emergence of Mikhail Bulgakov," *Russian Review*, XXVII (1968), 338-343; and Diana Burgin, "Bulgakov's Early Tragedy of the Scientist-Creator: An Interpretation of *The Heart of a Dog*," *Slavic and East European Journal*, XXII, no. 4 (1978), 494-508.

Margot K. Frank

ED BULLINS

Born: Philadelphia, Pennsylvania
Date: July 2, 1935

Principal Works

PLAYS: *Dialect Determinism: Or, The Rally*, pr. 1964; *Clara's Ole Man*, pr. 1965; *How Do You Do?*, pr. 1965; *The Theme Is Blackness*, pr. 1966; *The Electronic Nigger*, pr. 1968; *Goin' a Buffalo*, pr. 1968; *In the Wine Time*, pr. 1968; *The Gentleman Caller*, pb. 1968; *We Righteous Bombers*, pr. 1969; *In New England Winter*, pb. 1969; *A Ritual to Raise the Dead and Foretell the Future*, pr. 1970; *The Duplex*, pr. 1970; *The Fabulous Miss Marie*, pr. 1971; *Ya Gonna Let Me Take You Out Tonight, Baby?*, pr. 1972; *The Taking of Miss Janie*, pr. 1975; *The Mystery of Phyllis Wheatley*, pr. 1976; *I Am Lucy Terry*, 1976; *Jo Anne!*, pr. 1976; *Home Boy*, pr. 1976; *Daddy*, pr. 1977; *Sepia Star: Or, Chocolate Comes to the Cotton Club*, pr. 1977; *Michael*, pr. 1978; *Leavings*, 1980.

NOVEL: *The Reluctant Rapist*, 1973.

POETRY: *To Raise the Dead and Foretell the Future*, 1971.

MISCELLANEOUS: *The Hungered One: Early Writings*, 1971.

Ed Bullins is one of the outstanding black dramatists in the United States. He was born on July 2, 1935, in a ghetto in Philadelphia, Pennsylvania. As a child, he was an excellent student at a white grade school. With his transfer to an inner-city junior high school, he joined a gang and became a "street nigger," as he termed it. He dropped out of high school and joined the U.S. Navy in 1952, staying for three years. He moved to California in 1958 and, after receiving a general equivalency diploma, went to Los Angeles City College part-time in 1961. His move to San Francisco a few years later was the catalyst for both his black activist period and his playwriting, which were inextricably connected.

Between 1965 and 1967, when Bullins left San Francisco, he wrote a dozen short plays in two major styles: black revolutionary plays and plays of black contemporary life. *Dialect Determinism* is an example of the former in its emphasis on raising the black consciousness. *Clara's Ole Man* is a naturalistic slice of ghetto life. In all these plays, Bullins generates the conflict through those blacks who have accepted the white view of success and denied their origins and culture in the process.

During these years, Bullins and Malcolm X founded Black House, a cultural and political institution associated with the Black Panther Party. He left the party in 1967, after Eldridge Cleaver had decided to join with white radicals. In 1968, after Bullins was brought to New York as playwright-in-residence at the New Lafayette Theater, a trio of his plays, entitled *The Electronic Nigger* (which included *Clara's Ole Man*), was produced. He was awarded the Vernon Rice Award, which resulted in his selection as guest editor of a black theater issue of *Drama Review* in the summer of 1968.

An important aspect of Bullins' career at the New Lafayette was his work on a proposed group of twenty plays, which he called "the Twentieth Century Cycle." The plays were to depict the lives of several young men growing up on a ghetto street in the 1950's and 1960's. He produced the first play, *In the Wine Time*, in 1968; it features a favorite Bullins device, also found in *Clara's Ole Man*: an extended bout of wine-drinking ending in verbal and physical violence. The New Lafayette continued to produce Bullins' plays until it closed for lack of funds in 1973.

Bullins' greatest critical success was the 1975 production of *The Taking of Miss Janie*, which received both the Obie Award and the Drama Critics Circle Award for the Best American Play. It is a long one-act play which depicts a past and a possible repeat rape of a white woman by a black man. Using a prologue, epilogue, and flashback, Bullins describes the relationship of the couple—the anger of Monty and the resignation of Janie—as a means of exploring black-white relationships in the United States. The play is powerful, violent, and personal as well as social. The theatrical experimentation contributes to the overall impact.

In 1976, Bullins premiered four productions, received another Guggenheim grant for playwriting, and began supervising the New York Shakespeare Festival's playwriting workshop. Three of these plays deal with historical black women who have taken on mythic qualities: Phyllis Wheatley, Lucy Terry, and Joan Little. *Home Boy* is fifth in the Twentieth Century Cycle and reveals Bullins' increasing preoccupation with music.

In Bullins' later work, he focuses less on black-white issues and more on the everyday situations of black life. According to Leslie Sanders, "The world Bullins depicts pursues self-understanding on its own terms, in its own language, and by its own standards." In *Daddy*, the sixth play of the cycle, the musician-father figure tries to come to some understanding with the wife and children he left behind years earlier. He comes to realize that manhood is defined through the family and not through sexual conquests, a theme which runs through many of Bullins' plays. After 1977, new plays by Bullins appeared less frequently on New York stages.

From his revolutionary origins, Ed Bullins has matured into a black dramatist of power and vision. He explores the inner as well as the outer forces that keep black people from realizing their potential and their freedom. He is an exceptional craftsman who creates tough, vivid characters and who has an excellent ear for the language of the ghetto. He has an understanding and acceptance of these characters, many of whom are based on biographical elements in his life. Because Bullins is so prolific, his work is predictably uneven. Yet at his best, in such plays as *Clara's Ole Man* and *The Taking of Miss Janie*, he is a writer of penetrating and unflinching honesty.

BIBLIOGRAPHICAL REFERENCES: For an excellent overview and analysis of Bullins' works, see Leslie Sanders, "'Like Niggers': Ed Bullins' Theater of Reality," in *The Development of Black Theater in America*, 1988. See also Jervis Anderson, "Profiles: Dramatist," *The New Yorker*, June 16, 1973, 40-79; Robert L. Tener, "Pandora's Box: A Study of Ed Bullins' Dramas, *College Language Association Journal*, XIX (1976), 533- 544; Warren R. True, "Ed Bullins, Anton Chekhov, and the 'Drama of Mood,'" *College Language Association Journal*, XX (1977), 521-532; W. D. E. Andrews, "Theater of Black Reality: The Blues Drama of Ed Bullins," *Southwest Review*, LXVI (1979), 78-90; Samuel J. Bernstein, "*The Taking of Miss Janie*," in *The Strands Entwined: A New Direction in American Drama*, 1980; Peter Bruck, "Ed Bullins: The Quest and Failure of an Ethnic Community Theatre," in *Essays in Contemporary American Drama*, edited by Hedwig Bock and Albert Wertheim, 1981; Ruby Cohn, *New American Dramatists: 1960-1980*, 1982; Myles Raymond Hurd, "Bullins' *The Gentleman Caller*: Sources and Satire," *Notes on Contemporary Literature*, XIV (1984), 11-12; Nicholas Canaday, "Toward Creation of a Collective Form: The Plays of Ed Bullins," *Studies in American Drama, 1945-Present*, I (1986), 33-47; and Leslie Sanders, "*Dialect Determinism*: Ed Bullins' Critique of the Rhetoric of the Black Power Movement," in *Belief Versus Theory in Black American Literary Criticism*, 1986, edited by Joe Weixlmann and Chester Fontenot.

Lori Hall Burghardt

ANTHONY BURGESS

Born: Manchester, England
Date: February 25, 1917

PRINCIPAL WORKS

NOVELS: *Time for a Tiger*, 1956; *The Enemy in the Blanket*, 1958; *Beds in the East*, 1959; *The Doctor Is Sick*, 1960; *The Right to an Answer*, 1960; *Devil of a State*, 1961; *One Hand Clapping*, 1961; *The Worm and the Ring*, 1961; *A Clockwork Orange*, 1962; *Inside Mr. Enderby*, 1963; *Nothing Like the Sun*, 1964; *A Vision of Battlements*, 1965; *The Long Day Wanes*, 1965 (includes *Time for a Tiger*, *The Enemy in the Blanket*, and *Beds in the East*); *Tremor of Intent*, 1966; *Enderby*, 1968; *MF*, 1971; *Napoleon Symphony*, 1974; *The Clockwork Testament: Or, Enderby's End*, 1974; *Beard's Roman Woman*, 1976; *1985*, 1978; *Man of Nazareth*, 1979; *Earthly Powers*, 1980; *The End of the World News*, 1983; *Enderby's Dark Lady*, 1984; *The Kingdom of the Wicked*, 1985; *The Pianoplayers*, 1986; *Any Old Iron*, 1989.

NONFICTION: *Re Joyce*, 1965 (also known as *Here Comes Everybody: An Introduction to James Joyce for the Ordinary Reader*); *Shakespeare*, 1970; *Joysprick: An Introduction to the Language of James Joyce*, 1972; *Hemingway and His World*, 1978; *This Man and Music*, 1983; *Flame into Being: The Life and Work of D. H. Lawrence*, 1985; *Homage to Qwert Yuiop*, 1986.

AUTOBIOGRAPHY: *Little Wilson and Big God*, 1987.

Anthony Burgess is one of the most prolific and by many accounts one of the most important British novelists of the later twentieth century. There is no question of his productivity: In a publishing career of some thirty years he has seen more than sixty books into print, including novels, criticism, essays, translations, plays, screenplays, short stories, children's books, and poems. Under the name John Wilson he has also gained wide respect as a composer of music. This prodigality of production has ironically worked to his disadvantage, some critics and reviewers finding it hard to associate great quality with great quantity. Yet the entertainment quotient of his fiction is unequaled, as is his control of the technical bases of narrative writing. Furthermore, his themes are characteristically deep, sweeping, and significant.

Educated in local schools and at the University of Manchester, Burgess did not start out to be a writer. From Manchester he obtained a degree in musical composition in 1940, though he did also develop an avid interest in English language and literature. Upon graduation he joined the army, serving during World War II first as a musician and then in intelligence in Gibraltar. Discharged in 1946, he held a number of jobs over the next seven years, including playing jazz piano and teaching in a grammar school. In 1954 he went to Malaya as an education commissioner in the British Colonial Service, and there he began writing. He assembled materials for his early trilogy, *The Long Day Wanes*. In these three novels Burgess uses the experiences of a young British teacher to illustrate the decline of British imperial prestige and the conflicts between European values and local traditions and practices.

One event in Malaya confirmed Burgess in his decision to write professionally. In 1959, following a lengthy illness, colonial physicians detected a brain tumor, remanding him to England for specialist treatment. There, he was told he had one year to live. Deciding that he wanted to produce as much as he could in the time he had left, he began to write furiously. He finished five novels that year, and he left the hospital cured. He has hardly slowed that furious pace since.

Those five novels, all published astonishingly within a twenty-month period, marked the advent of a serious voice and an eye for piercing satiric detail. All relatively short, they resemble the early novels of Evelyn Waugh more than anything else, rivaling Waugh in ease of characterization, sprightly dialogue, stylistic control, and appreciation of the absurd in modern life. Like early Waugh, they also combine skillful entertainment with serious implicit themes. Though all hold up well, *The Right to an Answer* and *Devil of a State* remain particularly attractive, and *The Worm and the Ring* anticipates the technical triumphs to come. Following these novels Burgess began experimenting with the various kinds of fiction, producing parodies of futurist fantasy, science fiction, travel fiction, portrait-of-the-artist fiction, historical fiction, romantic fiction, and espionage fiction. The resulting group of novels established his critical reputation.

Burgess is best known for one of these experimental novels, *A Clockwork Orange*, which, though impressive, is hardly more distinguished or brilliant than his other works. Still, it combines topical problems with linguistic bravura, centering on juvenile gangs that speak an invented jargon called "Nadsat," made up of elements of crude Russian and Cockney slang. Alex, the protagonist, revels in senseless violence, for which he is arrested and sentenced to forced behavior modification. Burgess raises questions about the ethics of such compulsory reformation. When made into a film in 1971 by Stanley Kubrick, the novel secured Burgess' fame.

The novels that followed are equally impressive in different ways. *Inside Mr. Enderby* introduces a character Burgess develops in subsequent novels. Enderby, an aging poet of reclusive habits and venerable English eccentricities, is forced into direct contact with the harsh realities of modern life; his reactions constitute a hilarious critique of Western civilization. The books also analyze the plight of the artist in society. During this period Burgess also published a number of works of criticism, especially of the work of James Joyce.

The filming of *A Clockwork Orange* in 1971 introduced Burgess to Hollywood as a screenwriter; subsequent publicity brought invitations to serve as writer-in-residence at many American and British universities. These experiences soon began to influence his fiction, which simultaneously became broader, more expansive, and more complex. The first of these novels is *MF*; in it Burgess fuses his themes of the modern denigration of art and the artist, cultural incest, and racial consciousness as an enemy of cultural evolution. He demonstrates here, as he will again, his belief that the United States is running the risk of losing real freedom by closing itself off from external influences and by abandoning a sense of values. *Napoleon Symphony* is Burgess' most ambitious formal work, an attempt to construct a novel about the later life of Napoleon Bonaparte on the formal basis of the melodic structure of Ludwig van Beethoven's *Eroica* symphony (1804). The themes are those of *Enderby* and *MF*, but the formal experimentation is stunningly original. Of the same period is his imaginative biography, *Shakespeare*, arguably the best single work on the playwright.

In the 1980's, Burgess both built upon and extended his previous work, alternating between relatively slight, often-delicate entertainments and weighty and expansive novels. *Earthly Powers* is a monumental undertaking; it traces the intertwined lives of two men—one an aging homosexual novelist, the other a Catholic monsignor who eventually becomes a pope. The scope of this novel allows Burgess to develop his philosophical and theological themes in depth. *The End of the World News* is lighter and more facile; in it Burgess plays dazzling verbal and formal games. Varied and intriguing, Burgess' canon is undoubtedly one of the most impressive of twentieth century British literary figures.

BIBLIOGRAPHICAL REFERENCES: The best detailed study of work published in the first twenty years of Burgess' career is Geoffrey Aggeler, *Anthony Burgess: The Artist as Novelist*, 1979. Samuel Cook's *Anthony Burgess*, 1981, is less detailed but contains good material on his themes and technical innovations. Bernard Bergonyi includes an interesting chapter on Burgess in *The Situation of the Novel*, 1970. Robert K. Morris discusses the thematic consistency of Burgess' novels in *Consolations of Ambiguity: An Essay on the Novels of Anthony Burgess*, 1972. Two later studies include newer material and cover more of Burgess' writing: Robert

Martin Adams, *After Joyce: Studies in Fiction After "Ulysses,"* 1977, and Richard Matheros, *The Clockwork Universe of Anthony Burgess*, 1978.

James Livingston

KENNETH BURKE

Born: Pittsburgh, Pennsylvania
Date: May 5, 1897

PRINCIPAL WORKS

PHILOSOPHY: *Permanence and Change: An Anatomy of Purpose*, 1935; *A Grammar of Motives*, 1945; *A Rhetoric of Motives*, 1950; *The Rhetoric of Religion: Studies in Logology*, 1961; *Perspectives by Incongruity*, 1964; *Terms for Order*, 1964; *Language as Symbolic Action: Essays in Life, Literature, and Method*, 1966; *Dramatism and Development*, 1972.

LITERARY CRITICISM: *Counter-Statement*, 1931; *Attitudes Toward History*, 1937; *The Philosophy of Literary Form: Studies in Symbolic Action*, 1941.

POETRY: *Book of Moments: Poems 1915-1954*, 1955; *Collected Poems, 1915-1967*, 1968.

FICTION: *The White Oxen and Other Stories*, 1924; *Towards a Better Life, Being a Series of Epistles, or Declamations*, 1932; *The Complete White Oxen: Collected Short Fiction of Kenneth Burke*, 1968.

CORRESPONDENCE: *The Selected Correspondence of Kenneth Burke and Malcolm Cowley*, 1988.

Kenneth Duva Burke puzzles anyone hoping to classify him within a narrow genre of American letters. His long career covers a range of subjects: social philosophy, music, poetry, literary criticism, fiction, and economics. Yet his most important contributions have been to the study of rhetoric. Burke sees rhetoric as an integral part of everyday life and demonstrates his theories by drawing upon numerous bits of culture gleaned from a lifetime of inquiry and self-education. His work results in a breadth of ideas that makes him one of the most fascinating figures in twentieth century philosophy.

He was born in Pittsburgh on May 5, 1897, to working-class parents and shared his childhood with his lifelong friend Malcolm Cowley. He attended Peabody High School in Pittsburgh. A semester at Ohio State University preceded a year at Columbia University, where Burke finally left academe and pursued his ambition to write. In New York, Burke joined a group of young American writers based in bohemian Greenwich Village, including Malcolm Cowley, Edna St. Vincent Millay, Hart Crane, Allen Tate, and E. E. Cummings. In 1919, he married Lillian Batterham and soon was supporting a family of three daughters through assorted writing and editing assignments.

In 1921, Burke joined the staff of *The Dial*, a literary magazine, where he worked as editor, music critic, and occasional contributor. In 1924, he published his first book, a collection of short stories entitled *The White Oxen and Other Stories*. He began submitting to other publications as well, including *The Nation* and *The New Republic*, and in 1929 received the Dial Award for outstanding contribution to American letters. After a brief stint researching for several government agencies, Burke published in 1931 his first book of literary criticism, *Counter-Statement*, in which he responds to literature as a piece of rhetoric that reveals the author's self. Despite his early publishing success, Burke's personal life disintegrated during these years as he fell in love with his wife's sister, Elizabeth Batterham. He divorced Lillian and in 1933 married Elizabeth. The couple had two sons. The emotional turmoil of those years resulted in his novel, *Towards a Better Life, Being a Series of Epistles, or Declamations*, published in 1932.

Like many writers during the 1930's, Burke felt some attraction to the ideals of Communism, although he never formally joined the Communist Party. His 1935 book, *Permanence and Change: An Anatomy of Purpose*, reflected the influence of Communist doctrine, particularly in its application to poetry. That year Burke took part in the first Writers' Congress, a Party-sponsored gathering of important American literary figures, and accepted a position on the Executive Committee of the League of American Writers. He participated in the second Writers' Congress in 1937, but by the third meeting, in 1939, political actions such as Stalinist purges and Soviet cooperation with Nazi attacks in Europe had extinguished his enthusiasm for Communism.

In 1937, Burke joined the New School of Social Research in New York as a lecturer in criticism, the start of a long teaching career. From 1943 to 1961, he taught at Bennington College in Vermont, where he received an honorary doctorate degree in 1966. Burke spent most of his career as a visiting professor at various institutions, including Harvard University, the University of Chicago, and Princeton University. He has distinguished himself not only as an instructor but also as a prolific theorist and writer. *The Philosophy of Literary Form*, published in 1941, collects critical essays and reviews written during the 1930's. His major contributions to the modern study of rhetoric—*A Grammar of Motives*, *A Rhetoric of Motives*, *The Rhetoric of Religion*, and *Language as Symbolic Action*—demonstrate the breadth of his scholarship and his interest in the role of symbolism in everyday rhetoric. In 1981 Burke received the National Medal for Literature, an award honoring living American writers for their achievements in American letters.

Burke's impact on rhetorical study stems from his theory of dramatism, explored in *A Grammar of Motives*. Defining a human being as a symbol-user who seeks to move others to action, he uses the image of stage drama to explain a rhetor's motives. Dramatism centers on five key terms that constitute the "pentad." The "act" describes what took place, while the "scene" depicts the background, the setting for the act. The "agent" is the person or kind of person who performs the act, the "agency" explains the means or instruments used by the agent, and the "purpose" represents the end of those means. When the critic employs these terms to describe a rhetorical act, he examines the ratio, or relationship, between the different elements in the pentad, to discover motive. While Burke originally intended the pentad to be confined within the boundaries of a particular rhetorical exchange such as a speech, many rhetoricians have extended its concepts to the study of the entire rhetorical situation, where the speech itself is the act and the other terms of the pentad frame the context for that act.

Burke's importance as a theorist remains a subject of debate. Many supporters acknowledge the scope of his study and his approach to fundamental rhetorical and philosophical questions as evidence of the most powerful mind of this century. For Burke enthusiasts, the breadth of his work offers continual challenge and opportunity for new applications. Yet Burke's detractors, particularly philosophers, criticize him on the basis of that same broadness. They fault Burke's theories with inconsistency and vagueness and credit his range to an eagerness to exhibit his self-taught education. Problems of style, language, and terminology all fuel a controversy over Burke's merits. His theories are difficult and challenging to even the most practiced reader of rhetorical theory. In spite of the debate over his place in rhetorical tradition, however, Kenneth Burke's volumes of commentary on the twentieth century establish him as a substantial figure in contemporary letters.

BIBLIOGRAPHICAL REFERENCES: Greig E. Henderson, *Kenneth Burke: Literature and Language as Symbolic Action*, 1988, suggests that Burke's dramatism can serve to mediate among the sharply divergent approaches that dominate contemporary literary theory. *Critical Responses to Kenneth Burke: 1924-1966*, 1969, edited by William Rueckert, offers a wide range of criticism and detailed bibliographies. Although dated, the book is valuable in placing Burke within a critical tradition. *Kenneth Burke and the Drama of Human Relations*, 1963, also by Rueckert, offers an excellent explanation of dramatism and outlines Burke's major concepts. Students of speech and rhetoric will find particular value in Marie Hochmuth Nicols, "Kenneth Burke and the 'New Rhetoric,'" *Quarterly Journal of Speech*, XXXVIII (April, 1952), 96-113. Biographical information, though incomplete, can be found in Armin Paul Frank, *Kenneth Burke*, 1969. More recent biographical sketches include John Woodcock, "An Inter-view with Kenneth Burke," *The Sewanee Review*, LXXXV (October-December, 1977), 704-718; Ben Yagoda, "Kenneth Burke," *Horizon*, XXIII (June, 1980), 66-69; and Carlin

Romano, "A Critic Who Has His Critics: Pro and Con," *Philadelphia Inquirer*, March 6, 1984, D1. See also Malcolm Cowley, *Exile's Return: A Literary Odyssey of the 1920's*, 1951; Daniel Aaron, *Writers on the Left: Episodes in American Literary Communism*, 1961; Matthew Josephson, *Life Among the Surrealists: A Memoir*, 1962; and "Thirty Years Later: Memories of the First American Writers' Congress" *The American Scholar*, XXXV (Summer, 1966), 495-516.

Carolyn S. Terry

WILLIAM S. BURROUGHS

Born: St. Louis, Missouri
Date: February 5, 1914

PRINCIPAL WORKS

NOVELS: *Junkie*, 1953 (better known as *Junky*); *The Naked Lunch*, 1959 (better known as *Naked Lunch*); *The Soft Machine*, 1961; *The Ticket That Exploded*, 1962; *Nova Express*, 1964; *The Wild Boys: A Book of the Dead*, 1971; *Port of Saints*, 1973; *Cities of the Red Night*, 1981; *The Place of Dead Roads*, 1983; *The Burroughs File*, 1984; *Queer*, 1985; *The Western Lands*, 1987.

CORRESPONDENCE: *The Yage Letters*, 1963 (with Allen Ginsberg); *Letters to Allen Ginsberg: 1953-1957*, 1983.

OTHER NONFICTION: *APO-33 Bulletin: A Metabolic Regulator*, 1966; *The Job: Interviews with William S. Burroughs*, 1970 (with Daniel Odier); *Electronic Revolution 1970-71*, 1971.

MISCELLANEOUS: *The Exterminator*, 1960 (with Brion Gysin); *Minutes to Go*, 1960 (with Sinclair Beiles, Gregory Corso, and Gysin); *Time*, 1965; *White Subway*, 1965; *The Dead Star*, 1969; *Apomorphine*, 1969; *The Last Words of Dutch Schultz*, 1970; *Exterminator!*, 1973; *The Book of Breeething*, 1974; *Oeuvre Croisee*, 1976 (with Gysin; also known as *The Third Man*); *Blade Runner: A Movie*, 1979; *Interzone*, 1989.

After the death of Jack Kerouac in 1969, William S. Burroughs assumed the undisputed title as the United States' foremost avant-garde novelist. His parents, Mortimer Burroughs, the son of the inventor of the adding machine, and Laura Lee, daughter of John D. Rockefeller's press agent, fell heir to only a small fraction of the Burroughs Company fortune, so their second son, named for his inventor grandfather, was born into the upper middle class rather than the upper class. Burroughs was educated at private schools in St. Louis and New Mexico and was graduated from Harvard University in 1936. He tried medical school in Germany, then graduate study in archaeology, before moving to New York and finding his way into the bohemian life.

Burroughs rejected the bourgeois life-style of his parents. He sought out the city's underworld and became familiar with the ways of drug users, petty thieves, and pimps and prostitutes. He began to express his sexual preference for men. Near the end of World War II, in the neighborhood around Columbia University, Burroughs made the acquaintance of Allen Ginsberg and Jack Kerouac, who would become with him the core of the group of writers known as the Beats. It was during this same period that Burroughs began a lifelong dalliance with heroin addiction. He supplemented a small monthly income from his family by pushing drugs and committing petty crimes.

The influences on Burroughs' writing are clear, though extremely varied. His interest in hard-boiled detective fiction dates from his adolescence. The form of the vaudeville routine, the utopian vision of Alfred Korzybski, Reichian psychology, Oswald Spengler's view of civilization, and Mayan cosmology came later. *Junky* was Burroughs' first novel. It was published under the pseudonym William Lee out of consideration for his parents. Printed by Ace Books in a back-to-back edition with another book about drug addiction, *Junky* went virtually unnoticed. Like *Junky*, *Queer*, written in 1952 but not published until 1985, chronicles the adventures of its hero in the underworld of drug addicts, criminals, and homosexuals in a deadpan tone that belies its sense of humor.

It is, however, upon his third novel that Burroughs' reputation as the most innovative, extreme, and bizarre postwar American novelist rests. *Naked Lunch* was published first in France in 1959, and after a series of legal battles over attempts to ban it, Grove Press brought it out in the United States in 1966. The book presents a surrealistic version of the addict's life, including some of the same details presented realistically in *Junky*, but it adds to this presentation a mixture of science fiction, explicit sadomasochism, and Burroughsian "routines" (based on vaudeville comedy) to create the most unusual texture of any recent American novel.

After *Naked Lunch*, under the influence of the Canadian painter Brion Gysin, Burroughs began to employ Gysin's "cut-up" method of writing. A text is literally cut with scissors in some instances and rearranged. With a method based on cut-up but with the same themes of homosexuality and drug addiction, and an increasingly nightmarish vision of the authority of society, Burroughs produced a trilogy: *The Soft Machine*, *The Ticket That Exploded*, and *Nova Express*.

In the 1970's Burroughs abandoned the cut-up method to return to his previous tough, realistic style. *The Wild Boys* and *Port of Saints* recount the adventures of a group of homosexual warrior packs that spread over Earth, practicing their own tribal customs and speaking their own languages. During this same decade, Burroughs also began to write in the form of the film script, producing *The Last Words of Dutch Schultz* and *Blade Runner*.

Burroughs began his fourth decade as a writer by publishing the only other novel of his to receive critical acclaim comparable to that accorded *Naked Lunch*. *Cities of the Red Night* involves the parallel adventures of a band of homosexual pirates and a private detective named Clem Snide. One of the cities alluded to in the title is plagued by a sexual virus that seems to have anticipated the acquired immunodefiency syndrome (AIDS) epidemic. The second novel in Burroughs' second trilogy, *The Place of Dead Roads*, features a homosexual gunslinger named Kim Carsons, modeled after Burroughs himself. The trilogy concludes with *The Western Lands*, in which the protagonist, Joe the Dead, tries to use his knowledge of evolutionary biology to avoid death.

Many reviewers, literary critics, and scholars find the work of William Burroughs either disgusting or unreadable. That fact, however, has not prevented him from establishing a cult of readers both in the United States and in Europe. His special appeal among younger readers indicates that his vision impresses those with a stake in the future. There is no question that Burroughs treats subjects that most authors—and readers—prefer to ignore. He has also treated his life as something of an experiment. Add to this his forthright homosexuality and libertinism, and the literary results seem almost bound to produce scandal. Burroughs' situation is complicated by the circumstance that America has seldom had, and never appreciated, a literary avant-garde. That explains why Burroughs is still better appreciated in France than in his own country. Nevertheless, no one in the United States doubts that he is a serious writer; he is simply difficult to categorize.

BIBLIOGRAPHICAL REFERENCES: Ted Morgan's critical biography, *Literary Outlaw: The Life and Times of William S. Burroughs*, 1988, is a detailed, sympathetic portrait by a longtime friend of Burroughs. *With William Burroughs: A Report from the Bunker*, 1981, by Victor Bockris, details the novelist's life with his secretary James Grauerholz in their basement apartment in Greenwich Village in the late 1970's. In *The Job*, 1970, Daniel Odier presents a long interview in which Burroughs expounds on many of his pet theories, literary and nonliterary, including his use of the cut-up method of composition. For bibliographical information, see Michael B. Goodman, *William S. Burroughs: An Annotated Bibliography of His Works and Criticism*, 1975, and Joe Maynard and Barry Miles, *William S. Burroughs: A Bibliography, 1953-1973*, 1978. Robin Lydenberg's *Word Cultures: Radical Theory and Practice in William S. Burroughs' Fiction*, 1987, is a scholarly analysis that draws on contemporary literary theory. In contrast, Jennie Skerl's *William S. Burroughs*, 1985, a volume in Twayne's United States Authors series, is an introductory study, with a biographical sketch and an overview of Burroughs' career. See also Eric Mottram, *William Burroughs*, 1971.

James T. Jones

MICHEL BUTOR

Born: Mons-en-Baroeul, Lille, France
Date: September 14, 1926

Principal Works

NOVELS: *Passage de Milan*, 1954; *L'Emploi du temps*, 1956 (*Passing Time*, 1960); *La Modification*, 1957 (*Second Thoughts*, 1958; better known as *A Change of Heart*); *Degrés*, 1960 (*Degrees*, 1961); *6,810,000 Litres d'eau par seconde: Étude stéréophonique*, 1965 (*Niagara: A Stereophonic Novel*, 1969).

PLAYS: *Réseau aérien: Texte radiophonique*, 1962 (radio play); *Votre Faust: Fantaisie variable genre Opéra*, pb. 1962 (with Henri Pousseur).

POETRY: *Illustrations I-IV*, 1964-1976; *La Rose des vents: 32 Rhumbs pour Charles Fourier*, 1970; *Dialogue avec 33 variations de Ludwig van Beethoven sur une valse de Diabelli*, 1971; *Travaux d'approche*, 1972; *Matière de rêves*, 1975; *Second sous-sol: Matière de rêves 2*, 1976; *Envois*, 1980; *Explorations*, 1981; *Exprès*, 1983; *Chantier*, 1985.

LITERARY CRITICISM: *Répertoire I-V: Études et conférences*, 1960-1982 (partially translated in *Inventory*, 1968); *Essais sur les modernes*, 1964; *Essais sur "les essais,"* 1968; *Essais sur le roman*, 1969; *Résistances*, 1983 (with Michel Launay).

OTHER NONFICTION: *Le Génie du lieu*, 1958 (*The Spirit of Mediterranean Places*, 1986); *Histoire extraordinaire: Essai sur un rêve de Baudelaire*, 1961 (*Histoire Extraordinaire: Essay on a Dream of Baudelaire*, 1969); *Les Mots dans la peinture*, 1969; *Où: Le Génie du lieu 2*, 1971; *Intervalle*, 1973; *Boomerang: Le Génie du lieu 3*, 1978 (*Letters from the Antipodes*, 1981).

MISCELLANEOUS: *Mobile: Étude pour une représentation des États-Unis*, 1962 (*Mobile: Study for a Representation of the United States*, 1963); *Description de San Marco*, 1963; *Portrait de l'artiste en jeune singe: Capriccio*, 1967; *Matière de rêves*, 1975; *Explorations*, 1981.

Michel Butor is the most popular of the loosely defined group of postwar avant-garde French novelist-theoreticians practicing the New Novel. He was born in a suburb of the northern French industrial city of Lille on September 14, 1926, the fourth of seven children; his father, Émile, was a railway inspector. The family moved to Paris when Michel Butor was three, settling in a busy commercial street in a middle-class district on the eastern fringe of the Latin Quarter, close to the universities and literary cafés. Butor's later public persona has been said to mix bourgeois respectability and bohemianism in something of the same way as the place in which he was reared (he has also rebelled spectacularly against his family's devout Catholicism). He attended the parochial school and the Lycée Louis-le-Grand during the depressing years of the German Occupation. The stagnation of French intellectual life at this time affected the teaching in schools, and Butor turned to intense private study of Franz Kafka, Marcel Proust, James Joyce, and William Faulkner, all influences on his later work. He also began moving in intellectual, especially philosophical, circles and began writing poetry in the mode of André Breton and the Surrealists.

In 1944, Butor entered the University of Paris, earning the equivalents of a master's degree and a teaching diploma but twice failing the national competitive exams for the doctoral-level *agrégation en philosophie*, apparently because of his inability to confine himself to the required reading. His life took a decisive turn in 1950, when he took a teaching post in Egypt's Nile Valley. There, he wrote his first (virtually unnoticed) novel, stored memories for his travel writing, and set the pattern for his subsequent life as what he has called a "traveling salesman of French culture."

Butor has an extreme sensitivity to the spirit of different places; his wide-ranging travels have allowed him to explore world history from the perspectives of different cultures. His time as a lecturer in the northern English city of Manchester, 1951 to 1953, is intensely evoked in his second novel, *Passing Time*. His time as visiting professor at Middlebury College and Bryn Mawr College, 1959 to 1960, produced his attempt, in the prose-rhapsody *Mobile: Study for a Representation of the United States*, to capture the clash of color, sound, and light that is America. Teaching engagements in Buffalo and New Mexico led also to *Niagara* in 1965 and *Où: Le Génie du lieu 2* (where/or: the spirit of the place, 2) in 1971. He has traveled also in the Far East, Australia, and Europe (particularly Greece). He met his wife, Marie-Jo, during a trip to Geneva in 1956; they have four children. After 1972, the family was based in Nice.

True literary notoriety arrived with Butor's third novel, *A Change of Heart*, which won for him one of France's highest literary awards, the Prix Renaudot, in 1957. This great success made Butor a public figure. He has been a reader for the prestigious publishing house of Gallimard since 1958, has been awarded doctorates in both philosophy and literature, and in 1975 became professor of modern French literature and language at the University of Geneva. Among other honors, he has also been awarded the French Order of Merit. Yet none of this has taken away from the radicalism of his work and his position: On May 21, 1968, he and about ten other writers staged a polite "invasion" of the headquarters of the moribund French Society of Writers; he is a founder-member of the new Writers' Union.

Butor's creative work since his last "true" novel, the 1960 novel-about-a-novel, *Degrees*, has consistently provoked controversy. He has shifted decisively toward mixed-media and collaborative work, and toward textual collages and "open" form, seeking to undermine the notions of textual authority and linear narration, to cast doubt on familiar theories of genre and form, and to represent more truly the world-in-flux. Since it is only through stories that one apprehends reality, Butor believes, those stories must not perpetuate the falsities of outmoded forms.

BIBLIOGRAPHICAL REFERENCES: Michael Spencer, *Michel Butor*, 1974, is a thoroughly readable and useful survey, short on critical jargon. Mary Lydon's *Perpetuum Mobile: A Study of the Novels and Aesthetics of Michel Butor*, 1980, is a wider-ranging and more reflective study. Jennifer Waelti-Walter's adoption, in *Michel Butor: A Study of His View of the World and a Panorama of His Work, 1954-1974*, 1977, of Butor's own plan for organizing and discussing his work makes for freshness and critical insight; the book also has valuable illustrations. In *The Narratives of Michel Butor: The Writer as Janus*, 1978, Dean McWilliams rather too single-mindedly develops the idea of a "monomyth" at the heart of Butor's work. See also John Sturrock's *The French New Novel*, 1969: His long introductory overview is as valuable as his chapter on Butor. In *Representation in Contemporary French Fiction*, 1986, Dina Sherzer focuses on *Mobile* as a "polyvalent" text, a "multidimensional montage." Vivian Mercier, in his chapter on Butor in *The New Novel: From Queneau to Pinget*, 1966, focuses on "the schema and the myth." Henri Peyre, *French Novelists of Today*, 1967, is somewhat old-fashioned but nevertheless precise, thorough, and useful for its historical perspective.

Joss Marsh

GUILLERMO CABRERA INFANTE

Born: Gibara, Cuba
Date: April 22, 1929

PRINCIPAL WORKS

NOVELS: *Tres tristes tigres*, 1967 (*Three Trapped Tigers*, 1971); *La habana para infante difunto*, 1979 (*Infante's Inferno*, 1984).

SHORT FICTION: *Así en la paz como en la guerra*, 1960; *Vista del amanecer en el trópico*, 1974 (*A View of Dawn in the Tropics*, 1979); *Exorcismos de esti(l)o*, 1976.

SCREENPLAYS: *Wonderwall*, 1968; *The Vanishing Point*, 1970; *Under the Volcano*, 1972.

NONFICTION: *Un oficio del siglo XX*, 1963; *O*, 1975; *O/G: Cabrera Infante*, 1975; *Arcadia todas las noches*, 1978; *Holy Smoke*, 1986.

Guillermo Cabrera Infante, a writer whose satiric, imaginative prose has been compared with that of Lewis Carroll, James Joyce, Jonathan Swift, and Laurence Stern, is considered to be one of Latin America's most original and influential writers. Born in Gibara, a small city on the northern coast of Cuba's Oriente Province, Cabrera Infante was the second child and first son of Guillermo Cabrera Lopez, a journalist, and Zoila Infante. Because his parents were founders of the Communist Party in Cuba, Guillermo Cabrera Infante was reared in a volatile environment, surrounded by those whose mission in life was to overthrow the existing order.

After teaching himself to read (at the age of four) by deciphering *Dick Tracy* and *Tarzan* comic books, Cabrera Infante was sent to a Quaker school. When he was twelve, the entire family emigrated to Havana. Although extremely poor, he managed to attend high school and study at the school of journalism, simultaneously working at various odd jobs. Receiving his bachelor's degree in 1948, Cabrera Infante subsequently studied medicine at Havana University in 1949, and again from 1950 to 1954. In 1952, he was imprisoned and later fined for publishing a short story containing English obscenities. Then he began writing a screenplay (in 1953) under the pseudonym Guillermo Cain in *Carteles* magazine, of which he became fiction editor in 1957. He married for the first time in 1953 and had two daughters, Ana and Carola. Following his divorce in 1961, he married a young actress named Miriam Gómez.

After the revolution, in 1959, Cabrera Infante briefly held several official posts as cultural attaché; he was sent to Brussels by the Cuban government. It was during this period that the author felt temporarily but officially exiled; thereafter he came to regard his exile as permanent. He founded *Lunes*, a cultural journal and literary supplement of *Revolución* (the pro-Castro newspaper which he helped to edit), and he edited this journal until it was banned by the government in 1961. Becoming increasingly disillusioned after Castro's rise to power, Cabrera Infante became completely alienated with the suppression of *Lunes* in 1961.

In 1960, Cabrera Infante published his first book, *Así en la paz como en la guerra* (in peace as in war), a collection of short stories which, taken together, construct a coherent portrait of Cuban middle-class life during the 1950's. The author's candor, his use of colloquial speech, and the delicate balance between humor and tragedy all foreshadow the style and tone of his masterpiece, *Three Trapped Tigers*.

It was *Three Trapped Tigers*, the novel for which he is best known, which established Cabrera Infante as one of the most original and witty novelists to have emerged in Latin America. Plotless in the accepted sense, the work develops from a carefully structured pastiche of monologues, some spoken and some written in letter form, rendered in the vernacular of Havana of the late 1950's. The long and ambitious novel (referred to as a five-hundred-page joke by Cabrera Infante—packed with puns, anagrams, tongue twisters, number games, and typographical errors) functions on several levels. It constructs an intimate and nostalgic diary of the late-night adventures and discussions of a group of friends and of their efforts at solidarity and political action. It also is an indictment of a society in demise, a grotesque parody of European and North American civilization. It even contains parodies of seven prominent Cuban writers, each of whom describes with self-conscious artistry the death of Leon Trotsky.

In 1963, Cabrera Infante published *Un oficio del Siglo XX* (a twentieth century job), a collection of film reviews. The next year he was promoted to chargé d'affaires in Belgium and his novel *Three Trapped Tigers* won the prestigious Spanish prize Joan Petit-Biblioteca Breve in 1964; however, it was this early and much more overtly political version of the novel which won the prize; the novel was rewritten in its present form when Cabrera Infante became convinced of the incompatibility of literature and politics.

In 1965, the author traveled to Havana to attend his mother's funeral. As the result of some political machinations, however, he was detained in Cuba for four months before being allowed to leave the country, this time permanently and without any official position. His novel was banned in Spain, where he lived from 1965 to 1966, and was not published until 1967. After becoming a naturalized British citizen, he went to Hollywood, where a screenplay of his was made into a successful film, entitled *Vanishing Point*. He was awarded a Guggenheim Fellowship for creative writing in 1971 and in 1972.

While writing the film script for *Under the Volcano*, an adaptation of Malcolm Lowry's novel, Cabrera Infante suffered a severe nervous breakdown. The author's self-prescribed remedy was to write several books almost concurrently: *A View of Dawn in the Tropics*, a work which attempts to destroy the myth of Cuban history by creating histories containing the historical passages as capsules of language; *O*, a collection of articles and essays; and *Exorcismos de esti(l)o* (exorcising style), published in Spain; the first book was again banned in Spain in 1974, 1975, and 1976. *Infante's Inferno*, the first erotic novel to be written in Spanish, was published in 1979. The work consists of a series of amorous adventures ranging from the autoerotic through various premarital and extramarital experiences.

Although Cabrera Infante remains in disfavor in his native Cuba, where all of his books are banned, he is said to have much influence on modern Cuban writers. While some critics maintain that Cabrera Infante is a linguistic exhibitionist, they nevertheless acknowledge the author's wit and talent. They further maintain that Cabrera Infante's neologisms and other modernist techniques offer a critique of decadence while seeming to indulge in it. Other critics assert, on the other hand, that his imaginative linguistics, his abandonment of traditional literary forms, and his loosely structured narratives are his triumph, his personal political statement on behalf of individual freedom and his major contribution to Latin American literature. The author himself hoped that his contribution to the modern Latin American novel would be "the shaky foundations of a future movement to disrespectfulness."

BIBLIOGRAPHICAL REFERENCES: John S. Brushwood, *The Spanish American Novel: A Twentieth Century Survey*, 1975, contains a brief section devoted to Cabrera Infante's work, concentrating specifically on *Three Trapped Tigers*; the work also includes extensive notes and a bibliography. Seymour Denton, in *Prose Fiction of the Cuban Revolution*, 1984, examines the unique and worldwide impact of the revolution on Cuban literature; Cabrera Infante is among the authors discussed. Doris Meyer, editor of *Lives on the Line: The Testimony of Contemporary Latin American Authors*, 1988, provides an overview of Cabrera Infante's life and offers an English translation of one of his short stories. See also Isabel Alvarez-Borland, "Readers, Writers, and Interpreters in Cabrera Infante's Texts," *World Literature Today*, IV (1987), 553-558; Juan Goytisolo, "A Cervantean Reading of *Three Trapped Tigers*," *Review of Contemporary Fiction*, II (1984), 20-34; Ivar Ivask, "Focus on Guillermo Cabrera Infante," *World Literature Today*, IV (1987), 535-538; and Alfred J. MacAdam, "Seeing Double: Cabrera Infante and Cain," *World Literature Today*, IV (1987), 543-548.

Genevieve Slomski

ERSKINE CALDWELL

Born: White Oak, Georgia
Date: December 17, 1903

Died: Paradise Valley, Arizona
Date: April 11, 1987

PRINCIPAL WORKS

NOVELS: *The Bastard*, 1929; *Poor Fool*, 1930; *Tobacco Road*, 1932; *God's Little Acre*, 1933; *Journeyman*, 1935; *Trouble in July*, 1940; *All Night Long: A Novel of Guerrilla Warfare in Russia*, 1942; *Tragic Ground*, 1944; *A House in the Uplands*, 1946; *The Sure Hand of God*, 1947; *This Very Earth*, 1948; *Place Called Estherville*, 1949; *Episode in Palmetto*, 1950; *A Swell-Looking Girl*, 1951; *A Lamp for Nightfall*, 1952; *Love and Money*, 1954; *Gretta*, 1955; *Claudelle Inglish*, 1958; *Jenny by Nature*, 1961; *Close to Home*, 1962; *The Last Night of Summer*, 1963; *Miss Mamma Aimee*, 1967; *Summertime Island*, 1968; *The Weather Shelter*, 1969; *The Earnshaw Neighborhood*, 1972; *Annette*, 1974.

SHORT FICTION: *American Earth*, 1931; *Mama's Little Girl*, 1932; *Message for Genevieve*, 1933; *We Are the Living: Brief Stories*, 1933; *Kneel to the Rising Sun and Other Stories*, 1935; *Southways: Stories*, 1938; *Jackpot: The Short Stories of Erskine Caldwell*, 1940; *Georgia Boy*, 1943; *Stories by Erskine Caldwell: 24 Representative Stories*, 1944; *The Caldwell Caravan: Novels and Stories*, 1946; *Jackpot: Collected Short Stories*, 1950; *The Courting of Susie Brown*, 1952; *Complete Stories*, 1953; *Gulf Coast Stories*, 1956; *Certain Women*, 1957; *When You Think of Me*, 1959; *Men and Women: 22 Stories*, 1961.

NONFICTION: *Tenant Farmer*, 1935; *Some American People*, 1935; *You Have Seen Their Faces*, 1937 (with Margaret Bourke-White); *North of the Danube*, 1939 (with Bourke-White); *Say! Is This the U.S.A.?*, 1941 (with Bourke-White); *All-Out on the Road to Smolensk*, 1942 (with Bourke-White; also known as *Moscow Under Fire: A Wartime Diary, 1941*); *Russia at War*, 1942 (with Bourke-White); *The Humorous Side of Erskine Caldwell*, 1951; *Around About America*, 1964; *In Search of Bisco*, 1965; *In the Shadow of the Steeple*, 1967; *Deep South-Memory and Observation*, 1968; *Writing in America*, 1968; *Afternoons in Mid-America*, 1976 (with Virginia Fletcher Caldwell).

AUTOBIOGRAPHY: *Call It Experience: The Years of Learning How to Write*, 1951; *With All My Might*, 1987.

Erskine Preston Caldwell, a prolific and popular writer of novels about the American South and of photojournalistic travelogues, has eluded easy definition. Styled variously as a humorist, social critic, and writer in the "Southern Renaissance" tradition, he has also been vilified as a pornographer and pulp novelist. Caldwell simply regarded himself as a writer, a storyteller about the worlds he observed in America and elsewhere. Based on the enormous, and continued, sales of his best-known works, *Tobacco Road* and *God's Little Acre*, his principal reputation continues to rest on his depictions of poverty and sensuality in the rural American South. Indeed, many stereotypes and metaphors about poor Southern whites draw on Caldwell's works.

Caldwell was born on December 17, 1903, "in a three-room manse" in Coweta County, Georgia, the only child of the Reverend Ira Sylvester Caldwell, a preacher in the Associate Reformed Presbyterian church, whose travels as a troubleshooting minister for the denomination kept the Caldwell family on the move from one rural church to another. Young Caldwell's interest in writing developed early. In 1917 he drafted his first piece of fiction, "A Boy's Own Story of City Life," about Beale Street in Memphis, Tennessee. While attending high school in Wrens, Georgia, in 1919 and 1920, he began to write and do other chores for the local *Jefferson Reporter.* He became a baseball "string" correspondent for several Augusta, Macon, and Atlanta dailies. Few of his stories were published, but he continued to write for newspapers until 1926. The journalistic experienced proved valuable, for, by Caldwell's own account, it taught him to write quickly and efficiently in a manner capable of reaching a wide audience, a practice that both shaped Caldwell's style and drove him to prolific production. Journalism fascinated Caldwell throughout his life, and his most successful nonfiction bears the stamp of Caldwell the journalist.

In 1920 Caldwell entered Erskine College, his father's alma mater, but he withdrew after three semesters. The ever curious and peripatetic Caldwell spent his weekends traveling around the South Carolina countryside. In the spring of 1922, while traveling to New Orleans, he was jailed for nine days in Bogalusa, Louisiana, ostensibly for failing to pay his rent but in fact because he was suspected of being a labor organizer for the Industrial Workers of the World. Caldwell frequently recalled that, even more than his earlier travels with his father among tenant farmers, the injustice and powerlessness he felt in the Bogalusa jail awakened his social conscience. Caldwell left Erskine to attend the University of Virginia in 1923. Caldwell neither read much nor studied hard; he later confessed that throughout his life he rarely read others' work and never sampled more than one work by any one author. As a novelist, Caldwell wrote from instinct rather than from learning. At Virginia the passion to write seized Caldwell. He ran with a small group of self-proclaimed writers-to-be, dashed off poems and ephemera for the *Virginia Reel*, and placed similar items in several national humor magazines. The Southern Renaissance, with its emphasis on "real people as subjects," had reached Virginia during Caldwell's brief stay (he was never graduated) and, in his own words, inspired him "to write about the people I knew as they really lived, moved, and talked."

Caldwell eloped with Helen Lannigan, with whom he eventually had three children. The Caldwells moved to Mt. Vernon, Maine, in the mid-1920's. In 1929 the Heron Press published a small edition of Caldwell's short novel *The Bastard*, a book remarkable only for the local furor it caused when it was banned in Portland. His second novelette, *Poor Fool*, was published in 1930, with a similar response. Thus Caldwell had entered into clashes with censors that would nag his work thoughout his career.

In 1932 Caldwell published *Tobacco Road*, which he had written after a brief return to backcountry Georgia. The year 1933 saw the publication of Caldwell's second Southern novel, *God's Little Acre*. The book sold well. It also thrust Caldwell into prominence when the New York Society for the Suppression of Vice brought charges against the book. Although he was exonerated in a famous judicial decision, Caldwell never shook the public's perception of his work as mild pornography. This reputation at least boosted sales; so, too, did Jack Kirkland's stage adaptation of *Tobacco Road*, which opened on Broadway in 1933 and ran for more than seven years. Indeed, it was Caldwell's vision of "tobacco road" that lodged in the public mind. His two Southern novels sold more than seven million copies by the 1950's, and along with the long-running play, brought Caldwell the fortune that escaped his fictional characters.

In 1935 he met Margaret Bourke-White, the *Life* photographer, whom he would marry in 1939 and with whom he collaborated on the famous photo-essay volume *You Have Seen Their Faces*, about sharecropping and Southern poverty. Caldwell and Bourke-White produced other books together as well. Caldwell's criticism of American capitalism, his affinity with Russia, and his part in making the propaganda film *Mission to Moscow* (1943) led some critics to tar him as a Communist—a charge Caldwell always denied. Caldwell divorced Bourke-White in 1942. Two more marriages would follow.

Caldwell's literary reputation declined in proportion to his prolific output and robust sales through special paperback contracts. His final novel, *Annette*, was published in 1974. Caldwell's travel books fared better than his fiction. His *Afternoons in Mid-America*, completed in collaboration with his fourth wife, Virginia Fletcher Caldwell, recalled an invigorated Caldwell style. While in chemotherapy for lung cancer, Caldwell completed his autobiography *With All My Might*, which was published one month before his death.

Caldwell never accepted the critics' tag as a novelist of the "grotesque"; rather, he considered himself a Southern writer. As his principal literary legacies, Caldwell bequeathed to American literature enduring images of bleak Southern landscapes and "poor white" characters marked by lassitude and libido; a flat writing style; the primacy of storytelling as the role of the novelist, whom Caldwell regarded as a recorder more than a creator of characters' actions and thoughts; and an insistence on imagination as the soul of the creative process.

BIBLIOGRAPHICAL REFERENCES: The best collection of Caldwell criticism is Scott MacDonald's *Critical Essays on Erskine Caldwell*, 1951, which reprints most of the important reviews and essays from the 1930's through the 1970's and includes MacDonald's own spirited defense of Caldwell. Robert Cantwell wrote *The Humorous Side of Erskine Caldwell*, published in 1951, but the first full treatment of Caldwell is James Korges's pamphlet *Erskine Caldwell*, 1969. See also Sylvia Jenkins Cook, *From Tobacco Road to Route 66: The Poor White in Fiction*, 1976; Hartmut Heuermann, *Erskine Caldwell's Short Stories*, 1974; and *Conversations with Erskine Caldwell*, 1988, edited by Edwin T. Arnold.

Randall M. Miller

HORTENSE CALISHER

Born: New York, New York
Date: December 20, 1911

PRINCIPAL WORKS

NOVELS: *False Entry*, 1961; *Textures of Life*, 1963; *Journal from Ellipsia*, 1965; *The New Yorkers*, 1969; *Queenie*, 1971; *Standard Dreaming*, 1972; *Eagle Eye*, 1973; *On Keeping Women*, 1977; *Mysteries of Motion*, 1983; *The Bobby-Soxer*, 1986.

NOVELLAS: *"The Railway Police" and "The Last Trolley Ride,"* 1966; *Saratoga, Hot*, 1985.

SHORT FICTION: *In the Absence of Angels*, 1951; *Tale for the Mirror*, 1962; *Extreme Magic*, 1964; *The Collected Stories of Hortense Calisher*, 1975.

NONFICTION: *What Novels Are*, 1969.

AUTOBIOGRAPHY: *Herself*, 1972; *Kissing Cousins*, 1988.

EDITED TEXT: *The Best American Short Stories*, 1981 (with Shannon Ravenel).

Hortense Calisher's background is urbane secular-Jewish, with an often-emphasized splash of the Southern—her father was from Richmond. (Both Calisher's father and her father's father were married and started families late, as do many of her fictional males.) Born and educated in New York City (her B.A. is from Barnard College, where she studied literature and philosophy), she has lived there or nearby for most of her life. After graduation from college, she worked as a sales clerk, as a model, and for some years as a social worker. In 1935 she was married to Heaton Bennett Heffelfinger, an engineer by whom she had a son and a daughter and from whom she was divorced in 1958. In 1959 she was married to Curtis Harnack, also a writer, who, like her first husband, was a Gentile. In her autobiographical collection *Herself*, which includes thoughts on writing, on values, and on her contemporaries, she said that she always preferred Christian boys. Also in *Herself*, Calisher obliquely mentions her children, referring once or twice to emotional problems her daughter had when reaching maturity but otherwise saying little about matters domestic. She does indicate that she spent much time traveling for the United States Information Agency in the 1950's; on a trip to the Far East she noted that Japanese writers had maintained that their own literature differed from Western literature in that they had no sense of original sin. If that is so, there is a definite Oriental quality to Calisher's fiction.

Calisher was awarded a Guggenheim Fellowship in 1952 and 1953 and has received many other awards, both literary and academic. She has written that she does not care for academic life. Nor does she believe much in creative writing classes, she has been on the faculties of Barnard College, Sarah Lawrence College, Brandeis University, Columbia University, Bennington College, Washington University, and Brown University.

Although she wrote poetry in the 1930's, Calisher has published none of it. She saw her first story, "A Box of Ginger," in print in *The New Yorker* in 1948. Her best-known and anthologized story, "In Greenwich There Are Many Gravelled Walks," is another early effort, and in it much is encapsulated that appears with variations in other short fiction pieces—and in her novels. In this early piece, Peter, a young man who has driven his hysterical and sometimes nymphomaniacal mother to a sanatorium, decides to visit the apartment of an older friend, a homosexual, which Peter is not. The middle-aged man is another recurring type, a remittance man whose family pays him to keep his distance; the fellow is in the process of leaving his lover for another, who is in the room when Peter visits. The daughter of the fickle homosexual arrives—he was married once upon a time—and while conversation continues in the front room, the rejected lover jumps to his death, the replacement makes himself scarce, and the young heterosexuals get acquainted. All of this occurs in a very few pages. As Calisher has said, "A story is an apocalypse, served in a very small cup."

Calisher's characters are sophisticated, and they often seem to resemble the characters in

Henry James's works. They are intellectuals, certainly, but people whose approach to life is primarily aesthetic. Indeed, she often has been compared to James and to Marcel Proust, though in *Herself* she notes that she read these authors only after she was established. Thus it is more likely that she has not learned from them, per se; she is simply one of their sort. In short, her stories are ones similar to many that appear in *The New Yorker,* whose editors for a long time enjoyed first-refusal rights on what she wrote.

Most often, sexuality is the metaphor Calisher uses to explore the convolutions and unpredictable twists of the human psyche. Her characters have hidden curiosities that are revealed at least in part; these revelations hint at more mysteries yet unexplored, and not necessarily sexual ones. While her characters generally experience some defeat and feelings of hopelessness, Calisher's stories champion self-awareness and the principles of love. She has, especially, been praised for her insight into women's lives, but her work could not be labeled "feminist." Indeed, it is much broader, compassionately probing the psychology of human motivations.

BIBLIOGRAPHICAL REFERENCES: Calisher's books have been reviewed singly in the best journals and by the best reviewers, but little criticism has been directed toward the corpus as a whole. See Emily Hahn, "In Appreciation of Hortense Calisher," *Wisconsin Studies in Contemporary Literature*, VI (Summer, 1965), 243-249, and David K. Kirby, "The Princess and the Frog: The Modern American Short Story as Fairy Tale," *The Minnesota Review,* IV (Spring, 1973), 145-149. For an extensive, informative review, see *The Paris Review,* XXIX (Winter, 1987), 156-187. See also Jean W. Ross, *Contemporary Authors*, Vol. 22, 1988, edited by Deborah A. Straub, and Carolyn Mataleae, "Hortense Calisher," *Dictionary of Literary Biography,* Vol. 2, edited by Jeffrey Helterman.

J. H. Bowden

MORLEY CALLAGHAN

Born: Toronto, Ontario, Canada
Date: February 22, 1903

PRINCIPAL WORKS

NOVELS: *Strange Fugitive*, 1928; *It's Never Over*, 1930; *A Broken Journey*, 1932; *Such Is My Beloved*, 1934; *They Shall Inherit the Earth*, 1935; *More Joy in Heaven*, 1937; *The Loved and the Lost*, 1951; *The Many Coloured Coat*, 1960; *A Passion in Rome*, 1961; *A Fine and Private Place*, 1975; *Close to the Sun Again*, 1977; *A Time for Judas*, 1983; *Our Lady of the Snows*, 1985; *A Wild Old Man on the Road*, 1988.

SHORT FICTION: *A Native Argosy*, 1929; *No Man's Meat*, 1931; *Now That April's Here and Other Stories*, 1936; *The Varsity Story*, 1948; *Morley Callaghan's Stories*, 1959; *No Man's Meat and The Enchanted Pimp*, 1978; *The Lost and Found Stories of Morley Callaghan*, 1985.

CHILDREN'S LITERATURE: *Luke Baldwin's Vow*, 1948.

MEMOIRS: *That Summer in Paris: Memories of Tangled Friendships with Hemingway, Fitzgerald, and Some Others*, 1963.

PLAYS: *Turn Home Again*, pr. 1940 (also known as *Going Home*); *To Tell the Truth*, pr. 1949; *Season of the Witch*, pb. 1976.

Edward Morley Callaghan's writing career, which began in the 1920's, spans more than six decades. He is one of Canada's foremost novelists. Born in Toronto, on February 22, 1903, to an Irish Catholic family, he attended Withrow Public School and Riverdale Collegiate, then proceeded to St. Michael's College, University of Toronto, where he earned a B.A. in general arts in 1925 and subsequently enrolled in Osgoode Hall Law School. While he was an undergraduate, he took a part-time position as a reporter with the Toronto *Daily Star*. In 1923, while working there, he met Ernest Hemingway, who read some of Callaghan's stories and urged the fledgling writer to keep writing.

Callaghan published his first short story, "A Girl with Ambition," in *This Quarter*, a Parisian magazine, in 1962. This story was one that Hemingway had commended. In that year, he visited New York briefly and met several literary figures, including Ford Madox Ford, Katherine Anne Porter, and William Carlos Williams. By the time he was graduated from law school in 1928, he had established himself as a writer: He had published several short stories in American and European magazines, had a story ("A Country Passion") selected for inclusion in an anthology edited by J. Edward O'Brien, and had his first novel, *Strange Fugitive*, published by Charles Scribner's Sons. Set in the days of Prohibition, this novel introduced a theme that was to recur in Callaghan's novels: the alienation of the social outcast. The following year, he published a collection of short stories, *A Native Argosy*, and with his wife, Loretto Florence Dee, traveled to Paris, where they spent the summer in the company of Hemingway and F. Scott Fitzgerald. His experiences with these writers are recorded in *That Summer in Paris*.

In 1930, after residing for about eight months in a farmhouse in Pennsylvania and a hotel in New York City, he returned to take up permanent residence in Toronto and began publishing a book a year until 1937. His most notable novels of this period are *Such Is My Beloved* and *More Joy in Heaven*. During the next decade, a period Callaghan saw as "the dark period" of his life, he produced very little. He turned his attention to writing reviews and articles on current events and to adapting *They Shall Inherit the Earth* as a play, *Turn Home Again*. He wrote another play, *To Tell the Truth*, a novel for juvenile readers, *Luke Baldwin's Vow*, and *The Varsity Story*, a fictionalized history of the traditions of the University of Toronto.

In 1951, he returned to serious fiction with a novel that is considered to be among his best, *The Loved and the Lost*, which won that year's Governor General's Literary Award for fiction. Nine years later, he published *A Passion in Rome*, his only novel with a non-Canadian setting, on which he had begun working after spending a few weeks in Rome on a journalistic assignment at the time of Pope Pius XII's death in 1958. After another dry period of more than a decade, Callaghan published in 1975, at the age of seventy-two, *A Fine and Private Place*, which initiated another creative phase that has since continued unabated. The three other novels that followed have been well received and clearly show (particularly *Close to the Sun Again*) that his creative ability has not waned and that he is a major talent in Canadian literature.

Throughout his writing career, Callaghan has published numerous short stories in European and North American magazines, many of which have been collected in *The Native Argosy*, *Now That April's Here*, *Morley Callaghan's Stories*, and *The Lost and Found Stories of Morley Callaghan*. Some critics consider his stories to be an even more impressive achievement than his novels. In both novels and stories, Callaghan examines the moral and spiritual issues involved in the struggles of individuals, invariably outcasts on the fringe of society, to accommodate themselves to a society that perversely expects them to conform to its dubious standards. Up against a world that lacks common humanity, they are subjected to poverty, loss, fear, and betrayal.

Critics have complained, however, that Callaghan's novels tend to stereotype women, depicting them as either saints or wantons, as is evident in the early *The Loved and the Lost* and the later *A Time for Judas*. Callaghan's protagonists, like Hemingway's, tend to explore their private emotions and feelings in public places, and his prose is spare, compact, and lucid. Though he creates graphic scenes and brilliant character portraits, his settings and characters recurringly have symbolic and allegorical functions.

In 1965, Edmund Wilson identified Callaghan as "perhaps the most unjustly neglected novelist in the English-speaking world." Though critics, when Wilson spoke, had not recognized Callaghan's worth, this is not true today. Callaghan's early works continue to attract readers and scholars, and his later novels have been widely and favorably reviewed. A few critics have charged him with being too fond of the melodramatic, of not capturing the complexity of the issues he discusses, and of depicting clichéd, sentimental characters and situations, but Callaghan's works cannot be dismissed summarily as melodramatic, sentimental, or banal.

BIBLIOGRAPHICAL REFERENCES: George Woodcock, "Lost Eurydice: The Novels of Morley Callaghan," *Canadian Literature*, XXI (1964), 21-35; Edmund Wilson, *O Canada: An American's Notes on Canadian Culture*, 1965, 9-31; and Desmond Pacey, "Fiction 1920-1940," in *The Literary History of Canada*, 1965, edited by C. F. Klinck, are three of the earliest critical evaluations of Callaghan's novels. For further study, see Brandon Conron, *Morley Callaghan*, 1966, which provides a sound introduction to Callaghan's novels and stories. Two shorter introductory studies are Victor Hoar, *Morley Callaghan*, 1969, and Patricia Morley, *Morley Callaghan*, 1978. Fraser Sutherland, *The Style of Innocence: A Study of Hemingway and Callaghan*, 1972, examines the parallels in Callaghan's and Hemingway's fiction. *The Callaghan Symposium*, 1981, edited by David Staines, has several fine reevaluations and a comprehensive bibliography of Callaghan's work to 1979. Another useful collection of critical essays is Brandon Conron, *Morley Callaghan*, 1975. Callaghan has an extended interview with Donald Cameron in "There Are Gurus in the Woodwork," in his *Conversations with Canadian Novelists*, 1973. See also Hugo McPherson, "The Two Worlds of Morley Callaghan," *Queen's Quarterly*, LXIV (1957), 350-365; Frank Watt, "Morley Callaghan as Thinker," *Dalhousie Review*, LVIII (1973), 19-25; John Orange, "Callaghan and the Critics," *Journal of Canadian Fiction*, XV (1975); D. M. Korte, "The Christian Dimension of Morley Callaghan's *The Many Coloured Coat*," *English Quarterly*, VIII (1975), 11-15; John Kendle, "Spiritual Tiredness and Dryness of the Imagination: Social Criticism in the Novels of Morley Callaghan," *Journal of Canadian Fiction*, XVI (1976), 115-130; D. J. Dooley, "The Leopard and the Church: The Ambiguities of Morley Callaghan," in his *Moral Vision in the*

Canadian Novel, 1979; Robin Matthews, "Callaghan, Joyce, and the Doctrine of Infallibility," *Studies in Canadian Literature*, VI (1981), 286-293.

Victor J. Ramraj

ITALO CALVINO

Born: Santiago de las Vegas, Cuba
Date: October 15, 1923

Died: Siena, Italy
Date: September 19, 1985

PRINCIPAL WORKS

NOVELS: *Il sentiero dei nidi di ragno*, 1947, 1957, 1965 (*The Path to the Nest of Spiders*, 1956); *Il visconte dimezzato*, 1952 (*The Cloven Viscount*, 1962); *Il barone rampante*, 1957 (*The Baron in the Trees*, 1959); *Il cavaliere inesistente*, 1959 (*The Non-Existent Knight*, 1962); *I nostri atenati*, 1960 (*Our Ancestors*, 1980), includes *The Cloven Viscount*, *The Non-Existent Knight*, and *The Baron in the Trees*; *La città invisibili*, 1972 (*Invisible Cities*, 1974); *Se una notte d'inverno un viaggiatore*, 1979 (*If on a Winter's Night a Traveler*, 1981); *Palomar*, 1983 (*Mr. Palomar*, 1985).

SHORT FICTION: *Ultimo viene il corvo*, 1949 (*Adam, One Afternoon, and Other Stories*, 1957); *L'entrata in guerra*, 1954; *La giornata d'uno scrutatore*, 1963 (*The Watcher and Other Stories*, 1971); *Le cosmicomiche*, 1965 (*Cosmicomics*, 1968); *Ti con zero*, 1967 (*T Zero*, 1969); *Gli amore difficili*, 1970 (*Difficult Loves*, 1984); *Sotto il sole giaguaro*, 1986 (*Under the Jaguar Sun*, 1988).

EDITED TEXTS: *La letteratura americana e altri saggi*, 1951; *Fiabe italiane: Raccolte della traizione popolare durante gli ultimi cento anni e transcritte in lingua dai vari dialetti*, 1956 (*Italian Folktales*, 1975); *Cesare Pavese: Lettere, 1926-1950*, 1966.

Italo Calvino, Italian novelist, short-story writer, and critic, has been called one of the world's best fabulists—for the fables he wrote as well as for those he edited. Calvino was born in Cuba, where his father, Mario Calvino, a botanist, was on an agronomy mission. His mother, Eva Mameli, was also a botanist. Although his parents were not able to interest him in a scientific career, Calvino's intense feeling for nature and his passion for precise description are undoubtedly as much scientific as poetic; in his later years he came to view the problems of science, literature, and philosophy as inextricably intertwined.

In 1940, as a compulsory member of the Young Fascists, Calvino took part in the Italian occupation of the French Riviera. Three years later, at the age of nineteen, he joined the Italian Resistance and from 1943 to 1945 fought the Germans in the Ligurian Mountains. At the end of the war he settled in Turin, becoming a student of literature at the University of Turin. He was graduated from the university in 1947, having completed a thesis on Joseph Conrad.

Soon thereafter Calvino became an editor for the Einaudi publishing company, and he befriended the writers Elio Vittorini and Cesare Pavese. Between 1959 and 1966 he also co-edited with Vittorini a journal that elicited debate on the role of the intellectual in modern society. He contributed to other leftist publications as well. Calvino was married to Chichita Singer, a translator, in 1964 and had one daughter, Giovanna.

The troubled yet intense years of the anti-Fascist movement and the aftermath of World War II were the backdrop to Calvino's beginnings as a writer. The leading writers of postwar Italy, who had been prevented from writing about the world around them by government censorship, later began to draw upon their oppressive environment for their fiction; together they formed the neorealist literary movement (which reproduced real situations using traditional methods). Calvino, however, was soon to abandon its tenets and expand the possibilities of his fiction, using the traditional fable form to write nontraditional fiction.

Conceived in the height of neorealism was his first novel, *The Path to the Nest of Spiders*. This work immediately gained for its author critical praise from, among others, Pavese. Calvino chose to view the Resistance through the eyes of a streetwise boy from the Genoa slums who often uses obscene language. The boy manages to retain his innocence and sense of wonder throughout his adventures with a rough group of partisans. Using the boy as the narrator, Calvino is able to give an accurate, irreverent, and simultaneously fantastic, portrayal of historical events he had witnessed. Yet the boy is endowed with charm and freshness, qualities that remained characteristic of Calvino's heroes, especially in his many short stories and novels, despite the serious or tragic subject matter of these works.

Calvino's penchant for transforming reality into fable is perhaps best expressed in three "fantastic novels" he collected in a trilogy titled *Our Ancestors*. The protagonists of these three novels are "our ancestors" because they precede the reader's time metaphorically and chronologically; they are the fantastic projections of the good and evil halves of every man—the fictional representations of human idiosyncrasies, fears, and alienations. Yet they are also the source of enlightenment and courage. Chivalric epics, philosophical tales, adventure novels, and folktales are freely used by Calvino in these ingenious novels.

Calvino is fascinated with the act of narrating and the nature of writing itself. *Cosmicomics* and *T Zero* are short pieces narrated by a "character" called "Qfwfq"; these stories ostensibly treat such scientific topics as the distance of the Moon from Earth, the origin of birds, and the disappearance of dinosaurs. In fact, however, each piece, though it explores distant times and places, is predominantly the author's reflection on his written creation, a tale telling itself, a "metafiction."

This reflection is continued by Calvino in *Invisible Cities* and is concluded in the novel *If on a Winter's Night a Traveler*, about a reader who can never finish the novels that he has begun reading. *If on a Winter's Night a Traveler* uses a frame device that includes ten different beginnings of unfinished novels-within-the-novel, each parodying in a different way the writing of a novel and each presenting different problems of contemporary life.

Calvino's ability to fuse and juxtapose fantasy and reality led critics such as John Updike and John Gardner to laud Calvino and compare him with two other master storytellers noted for using the same technique in their fiction: Jorge Luis Borges and Gabriel García Márquez. Calvino's unique contribution as a writer is that he, perhaps better than anyone else of his generation, observed and captured the spirit of the times in which he lived and transformed his philosophical, sociological, and moral observations into unclassifiable but unique literary inventions. His writing exhibits an unshakable faith in the power of reason and fantasy to understand, and therefore to overcome, the caprice of history.

BIBLIOGRAPHICAL REFERENCES: *The Writer as Fablemaker: The Literary Adventure of Italo Calvino*, 1976, by Sara Maria Adler, is one of the best studies of Calvino in English. JoAnn Cannon, in *Italo Calvino: Writer and Critic*, 1981, gives a brief overview of Calvino's works in the light of his theory of literature. Albert H. Carter's *Italo Calvino: Metamorphosis of Fantasy*, 1987, also very effectively traces Calvino's use of the fantastic in his major works. I. T. Olken, in *With Pleated Eye and Garnet Wing*, 1984, discusses Calvino's literary influences in an attempt to portray him as both eclectic and antiparochial. John Robert Woodhouse's *Italo Calvino: A Reappraisal and an Appreciation of the Trilogy*, 1968, argues that Calvino's trilogy has been misunderstood; Woodhouse successfully defends the trilogy as a complex and truly imaginative work.

Genevieve Slomski

JOSEPH CAMPBELL

Born: New York, New York
Date: March 26, 1904

Died: Honolulu, Hawaii
Date: October 30, 1987

PRINCIPAL WORKS

NONFICTION: *Where the Two Came to Their Father*, 1943 (with Maud Oakes and Jeff King); *A Skeleton Key to "Finnegans Wake,"* 1944 (with Henry Morton Robinson); *The Hero with a Thousand Faces*, 1949; *The Masks of God, Volume I: Primitive Mythology*, 1959; *The Masks of God, Volume II: Oriental Mythology*, 1962; *The Masks of God, Volume III: Occidental Mythology*, 1964; *The Masks of God, Volume IV: Creative Mythology*, 1968; *The Flight of the Wild Gander: Explorations in the Mythological Dimension*, 1969; *Myths to Live By*, 1972; *The Mythic Image*, 1975 (with M. J. Abadie); *Tarot Revelations*, 1980 (with Richard Roberts); *The Historical Atlas of World Mythology: Volume I, The Way of the Animal Powers*, 1984; *The Inner Reaches of Outer Space*, 1986; *The Historical Atlas of World Mythology, Volume II: The Way of Seeded Earth*, 1988; *The Power of Myth*, 1988 (with Bill Moyers).

EDITED TEXTS: *Myths and Symbols in Indian Art and Civilization*, 1946 (by Heinrich Zimmer); *The King and the Corpse; Tales of the Soul's Conquest of Evil*, 1948 (by Zimmer); *Philosophies of India*, 1951 (by Zimmer); *The Portable Arabian Nights*, 1952; *Papers from the Eranos Yearbooks, Six Volumes: Spirit and Nature*, 1954; *Mysteries*, 1955; *The Art of Indian Asia*, 1955 (by Zimmer); *Man and Time*, 1957; *Spiritual Disciplines*, 1960; *Man and Transformation*, 1964; *Mystic Vision*, 1969; *Myths, Dreams, and Religion*, 1970; *The Portable Jung*, 1972; *My Life and Lives: The Story of a Tibetan Incarnation*, 1977 (by Rato K. Losang).

A scholar, teacher, and writer, Joseph Campbell translated his lifelong interest in mythology into books and lectures that brought a cohesive overview to the world's stories and legends. Born in New York in 1904, Campbell was the son of Charles William and Josephine (Lynch) Campbell. As a boy, Campbell became fascinated by American Indian culture after a visit to the American Museum of Natural History and a performance of Buffalo Bill's Wild West Show. His interest in Indian folklore was broadened during his college years by his readings in Eastern religion and philosophy. His study would lead him to the belief that there was in fact one world mythology that manifested itself in various ways from culture to culture.

While attending Columbia University, Campbell captained the college track team as a successful half-mile runner and played the saxophone in a local jazz band. He received a graduate fellowship from the university in 1927 and went to France to begin doctoral research in the field of Arthurian romances. In Paris, he encountered for the first time the works of James Joyce and Thomas Mann, the paintings of Pablo Picasso, and the writings of psychoanalyst Carl Jung, and he returned to Columbia in 1929 determined to expand his field of research to include new ideas concerning the interrelationship of art, dreams, and myths. When the university rejected his plan, he left the doctoral program and spent the next five years living on his savings in Woodstock, New York, where he read for ten to twelve hours a day. In 1934, he accepted an invitation to teach at Sarah Lawrence College, where he would remain for the next thirty-eight years as a member of the faculty.

In 1938, Campbell married his former pupil, Jean Erdman, a dancer with the Martha Graham Company. During the years that followed, he continued his teaching and coauthored two books, *Where the Two Came to Their Father*, with Maud Oakes and Jeff King, and *A Skeleton Key to "Finnegans Wake,"* with Henry Morton Robinson. He also edited several volumes of Heinrich Zimmer's writings on Indian culture and religion.

In the mid-1940's, Campbell began work on the book which would establish him as one of the world's leading authorities on mythology: *The Hero with a Thousand Faces*. Published in 1949, the book remains a seminal work in the field of interpreting and understanding myths and legends, providing its readers with a unifying view of mythology as a manifestation of the deepest needs of the human psyche. Myth, Campbell says, "is the secret opening through which the inexhaustible energies of the cosmos pour into human cultural manifestation." Drawing on Carl Jung's work on dreams and archetypes, Campbell finds recurring images and themes throughout the world's many cultural mythologies and posits that the stories themselves act as guideposts along the path to the realization that, in Campbell's words, "the essence of oneself and the essence of the world: these two are one."

Campbell continued his exploration of myths and their meaning in a four-volume work titled *The Masks of God*, which outlines four classifications of mythology: primitive, Oriental, Occidental, and creative. The title is a reference to Campbell's description of mythical images as symbols which provide mankind with a means of contemplating the transcendent (that which ultimately defies description or analysis), and the books examine the forms these symbols have taken in various eras and cultures. He also served as editor on six volumes of the Eranos Yearbooks, published between 1954 and 1969, and began a career as a speaker, appearing at seminars and in lecture halls around the world. Several of these lectures, delivered at The Great Hall of the Cooper Union Forum in New York between 1958 and 1971, were published in book form in 1972 under the title *Myths to Live By.*

The year 1972 also marks Campbell's retirement from teaching. He began devoting himself entirely to his writing and speaking engagements after that time. Campbell served as the editor of *The Portable Jung* and explored the meaning of recurring images in the great world religions in *The Mythic Image*. In the early 1980's, Campbell began *The Historical Atlas of World Mythology.* In *The Way of the Animal Powers* and *The Way of the Seeded Earth*, the two volumes he had completed by the time of his death, Campbell charts the evolution of mythology throughout early human history. Space exploration and the possibilities for knowledge unlocked by growing scientific understanding of the workings of the universe led him to write *The Inner Reaches of Outer Space*, in which he suggests that contemplation of the cosmos can lead to a fuller understanding of the subtleties of one's own inner spiritual life.

In 1988, several months after Campbell's death from cancer, a six-hour series titled *Joseph Campbell and the Power of Myth* appeared on American public television. Recorded over the last two years of Campbell's life, the program consists of edited conversations between Campbell and journalist Bill Moyers. The series sparked widespread interest in Campbell's work, and both *The Hero with a Thousand Faces* and a book based on the program soon appeared on *The New York Times* best-seller list. The key to the series' success—and to the influence Campbell's work has had on audiences outside academia—is his ability to communicate ideas of substance and complexity with great clarity. His writings have inspired novelists, choreographers, and filmmakers, including director George Lucas, whose "Star Wars" films were shaped by *The Hero with a Thousand Faces*. Campbell's work continues to provide his readers with an intelligent and insightful means of utilizing the message of mythology in their own lives.

BIBLIOGRAPHICAL REFERENCES: Useful journal articles on Campbell include Donald Newlove, "The Professor with a Thousand Faces," *Esquire*, LXXXVIII (September, 1977), 99, a profile of Campbell, and Michael Ventura's "Homage to Joseph Campbell," *L.A. Weekly*, November 13, 1987, 29, a tribute to Campbell which appeared shortly after his death. Also of interest is K. C. Cole, "Master of the Myth," *Newsweek*, November 14, 1988, 60. "Earthrise: The Dawning of a New Spiritual Awareness" is a lengthy interview with Campbell that appeared in *The New York Times Magazine*, April 15, 1979, and "Myths in Our Lives," *The Utne Reader*, September/October, 1988, 92, features an excerpt from Bill Moyers' many hours of conversations with Campbell. See also *Joseph Campbell and the Power of Myth*, a six-part videotape series available from the Corporation for Public Broadcasting.

Janet E. Lorenz

ALBERT CAMUS

Born: Mondovi, Algeria
Date: November 7, 1913

Died: Near Villeblevin, France
Date: January 4, 1960

PRINCIPAL WORKS

NOVELS: *L'Étranger*, 1942 (*The Stranger*, 1946); *La Peste*, 1947 (*The Plague*, 1948); *La Chute*, 1956 (*The Fall*, 1957); *La Mort heureuse*, 1971 (*A Happy Death*, 1972).

SHORT FICTION: *L'Exil et le royaume*, 1957 (*Exile and the Kingdom*, 1958).

PLAYS: *Caligula*, pb. 1944 (English translation, 1948); *Le Malentendu*, pr., pb. 1944 (*The Misunderstanding*, 1948); *L'État de siège*, pr., pb. 1948 (*State of Siege*, 1958); *Les Justes*, pr. 1949 (*The Just Assassins*, 1958).

NONFICTION: *L'Envers et l'endroit*, 1937; *Noces*, 1938; *Le Mythe de Sisyphe*, 1942 (*The Myth of Sisyphus*, 1955); *L'Homme révolté*, 1951 (*The Rebel*, 1956); *L'Été*, 1954; *Carnets: Mai 1935-fevrier 1942*, 1962 (*Notebooks*, 1963); *Carnets: Janvier 1942-mars 1951*, 1964 (*Notebooks*, 1963); *Lyrical and Critical Essays*, 1968.

Albert Camus, an Algerian-born French writer of novels, short stories, dramas, essays, and journalism, is one of the most significant literary figures of the twentieth century. He recoiled from the dogmas of totalitarianism and organized religion that dictated man's behavior, from existentialism's despairing emphasis on human anxiety and forlornness, and from nihilism's insistence that how human beings behaved did not matter. Instead, he achieved a literature of exigent moral questioning which clung to a Hellenistic faith in individualism, seeking a formula through which a person could live in dignity and decency within a godless, irrational, "absurd" universe.

Camus was reared in poverty when his father died of war wounds ten months after the boy's birth and his illiterate mother was forced to earn a meager living as a cleaning woman. Encouraged by a remarkable teacher in grade school, he won a scholarship to an Algerian *lycée*, where he studied philosophy and read widely but also played soccer and swam. In 1930, he had the first of what were to be many attacks of tuberculosis. In 1934, he made a disastrous, one-year marriage and also joined the Communist Party, only to leave it three years later.

During the mid-to-late 1930's, Camus began to keep his lifelong notebooks; he also wrote journalistic essays, founded a theatrical company, and wrote his first novel, *A Happy Death* (though it was not published until 1972), a trial run for *The Stranger*. Rejected for military service because of his tuberculosis in 1939, he married Algerian-born Francine Faure in December, 1940. Possessed by a Don Juanesque need to conquer women, he had numerous affairs, as well as a liaison with the actress Maria Casarès that lasted intermittently from 1944 until his death in 1960.

In 1942, Camus left Algeria for Paris, working there as a journalist and publisher's editor; in 1943, he became editor of the resistance newspaper, *Combat*. In 1942, Camus also published what were to prove his two most influential texts: *The Stranger* and *The Myth of Sisyphus*. Together with his play *Caligula*, these works develop, narrate, and dramatize his core concept of absurdism. For Camus, the absurd is the void between man's need for a universe that is coherent, lucid, and rational, and the reality of the universe as largely incoherent, meaningless, and irrational.

In *The Myth of Sisyphus*, Camus argues that man should renounce any nostalgia for a divinely ordered world and should instead adopt an ethic of heroic hedonism, of passionately lucid living. Accordingly, the protagonist of *The Stranger*, Meursault, recognizes the world's conventions and codes as arbitrary and senseless, comes to realize that he has loved life intensely for its physical pleasures, and greets his death by execution exultantly. In *Caligula*, the Roman emperor seeks to educate his subjects for an absurd world by torturing and killing a large number of them, finally inciting the Patricians to rebel against his monstrous rule and murder him.

The next cycle of Camus' works, centering on the absurd, is best represented by his long essay *The Rebel* and his novel *The Plague*. In *The Rebel*, Camus rejects both the metaphysical attempts to abolish an absurd universe incarnate in religion and the political attempts to cancel absurdism exemplified by totalitarian political regimes. In *The Plague*, he presents a variety of human responses to the plague's toll of undeserved suffering and unjust death.

Camus' career in the 1950's was characterized by extreme tensions. His friendship with the philosopher Jean-Paul Sartre ended in sharp public dispute because Sartre condoned Stalinism while Camus vehemently condemned it. With Algeria's Muslims demanding that the land of his birth become a nation independent of France, Camus found himself unwilling either to support or to oppose their uprising. His notebooks show that his thoughts during this decade were dominated by depressed moods. He developed a years-long writer's block which was only partially thawed by the composition of what was to be his last complete novel, *The Fall*.

The Fall is an ironic, deceptive book in which the first-person narrator, Jean-Baptiste Clamence, tells his life story to an unnamed, silent auditor who may well be humankind. Overcome by guilt from not aiding a suicidal woman, Clamence seeks to expiate his failure by attempting to baptize his listeners into a tyranny of universal sin and shame. For Camus, such a judgment amounts to a false clemency, since he regarded guilt as accidental, relative, and individual, while personal freedom and dignity were to him man's most cherished values.

In 1957, Camus was awarded the Nobel Prize, at age forty-four its second youngest recipient. He began work on what he announced would be his first long novel, "Le Premier Homme" (the first man). He had written about one hundred pages of it when on January 4, 1960, the sports car in which he rode as a passenger smashed into two trees, killing him instantly. Since his death, Camus' reputation has fluctuated, with the Anglo-American world continuing to admire his work while the younger generation of Frenchmen has almost ignored it. His stature as a courageously committed humanistic writer, impatient with mysticism and skeptical regarding all ideological claims, however, should survive the ebb and flow of popular sentiment.

BIBLIOGRAPHICAL REFERENCES: One of the most extensive bibliographies in English is Robert F. Roeming, *Camus: A Bibliography*, 1968. Two good biographies that have appeared are Herbert R. Lottman, *Albert Camus: A Biography*, 1979, a 753-page tome that is weighty in both senses of the word, and Patrick McCarthy, *Camus*, 1982, which is half the length of Lottman's biography, and far more judgmental. One of the best critical studies is Germaine Brée, *Camus*, 1964 (rev. ed.). Brée was a friend of Camus and was granted access to much unpublished material. Her work's one flaw is perhaps an overly sympathetic stance. Brée has also edited *Camus: A Collection of Critical Essays*, 1962, which includes Sartre's eulogy, as well as nineteen other contributions by such distinguished writers as Rachel Bespaloff and Nicola Chiaromonte. John Cruickshank, *Albert Camus and the Literature of Revolt*, 1960, is a well-balanced study with discerning analyses of *The Rebel* and *The Fall*. An interpretation highly charged with modern critical theory is Brian J. Fitch, *The Narcissistic Text: A Reading of Camus' Fiction*, 1982. A unique response to Camus is Robert J. Champigny, *A Pagan Hero: An Interpretation of Meursault in Camus' "The Stranger,"* 1969. Champigny, a French philosopher and poet, places himself within Camus' text to concentrate on the character of Meursault, ignoring all other aspects of *The Stranger*. This incisive and often profound essay is one that the specialized reader will find illuminating.

Gerhard Brand

ELIAS CANETTI

Born: Rutschuk, Bulgaria
Date: July 25, 1905

Principal Works

NOVEL: *Die Blendung*, 1935 (*Auto-da-Fé*, 1946; also known as *The Tower of Babel*).

PLAYS: *Hochzeit*, pb. 1932 (*The Wedding*, 1984); *Komödie der Eitelkeit*, pb. 1950 (*Comedy of Vanity*, 1983); *Die Befristeten*, pb. 1956 (*The Numbered*, 1964; also known as *Life-Terms*).

NONFICTION: *Fritz Wotruba*, 1955 (English translation, 1955); *Masse und Macht*, 1960 (*Crowds and Power*, 1962); *Aufzeichnungen 1942-1948*, 1965; *Die Stimmen von Marrakesch: Aufzeichnungen nach einer Reise*, 1967 (*The Voices of Marrakesh: A Record of a Visit*, 1978); *Der andere Prozess: Kafkas Briefe an Felice*, 1969 (*Kafka's Other Trial*, 1974); *Alle vergeudete Verehrungen: Aufzeichnungen 1949-1960*, 1970; *Die gespaltene Zukunft*, 1972; *Macht und Überleben*, 1972; *Die Provinz des Menschen: Aufzeichnungen 1942-1972*, 1973 (*The Human Province*, 1978); *Das Gewissen der Worte*, 1975 (*The Conscience of Words*, 1979); *Der Beruf des Dichters*, 1976; *Das Geheimherz der Uhr: Aufzeichnungen 1973-1985*, 1987.

AUTOBIOGRAPHY: *Die gerettete Zunge: Geschichte einer Jugend*, 1977 (*The Tongue Set Free: Remembrance of a European Childhood*, 1979); *Die Fackel im Ohr: Lebensgeschichte 1921-1931*, 1980 (*The Torch in My Ear*, 1982); *Das Augenspiel: Lebensgeschichte 1931-1937*, 1985 (*The Play of the Eyes*, 1986).

MISCELLANEOUS: *Der Ohrenzeuge: Fünfzig Charaktere*, 1974 (*Earwitness: Fifty Characters*, 1979).

When Elias Canetti was awarded the Nobel Prize in Literature in 1981, he was recognized as a preserver and transmitter of classical German culture in an age when the individual is threatened by the powerful brutality of the masses. Canetti was born on July 25, 1905, in Rutschuk, Bulgaria. His father, Jacques Canetti, belonged to a merchant family of Sephardic Jews who had settled in Turkey several centuries before moving to Bulgaria. His mother, Mathilde Artitti, also belonged to one of the old and distinguished Sephardic families. The parents had met while studying in Vienna and spoke German—almost as a secret language—when they were together. The common language of the Jewish community was Ladino, an old form of Spanish, and Canetti also heard and understood Hebrew and Bulgarian, as well as perhaps a dozen languages and dialects at this early stage of life.

When Canetti was six years old the family moved to England, where he added English and French to the list of languages he knew. Following the sudden death of his father, his mother decided to move to the Continent, where they lived in Vienna, Zurich, and Frankfurt, and Canetti learned and mastered German, the language he has used for all of his writings. Upon completion of secondary school in 1924 Canetti attended the University of Vienna. Although he completed his study of chemistry with a doctorate in 1929 to satisfy the wishes of his family, he never worked professionally as a chemist.

In 1930-1931 he wrote his major novel *Auto-da-Fé*, which did not appear in print, however, until a suitable publisher was found in 1935. Two sources had a great influence on Canetti's work, not only in writing this novel but also on his work in general: the great Austrian poet and satirist Karl Kraus and the events surrounding the burning of the Palace of Justice in Vienna on July 15, 1927. In his Nobel lecture Canetti noted that the writer and critic Karl Kraus taught him "to hear imperturbably the sounds of Vienna" and to be forever opposed to war.

The personal experience of participating in the crowd on the day the Palace of Justice was burned by an angry and unorganized group had a profound and lasting impact on Elias Canetti. He happened to meet a man who would later serve as a prototype for the protagonist of his novel, Peter Kien. This man was lamenting the burning of the paper files in the building rather than realizing and lamenting the killing of almost one hundred people. The man, like Kien, demonstrated a life devoid of human compassion and a life devoted to the unreality of a totally bureaucratic world. For Canetti, however, the experience led to a lifetime study of the nature and power the crowd can have on the actions of the individual.

Crowds and Power was published almost thirty years after Canetti had completed the novel. Its impetus harks back not only to the 1927 experiences but also to Canetti's observations made on the rise of Adolf Hitler and National Socialism in Germany and, after the 1938 annexation, in Austria. He and his wife, Venetia, were among the last Jews to leave Vienna for Paris, moving the following year to London. There, for the next twenty years, Canetti conducted this monumental study of the origin, constitution, and behavior of crowds from primeval to modern times. *Crowds and Power* ranks as one of the premier studies of that topic.

As a companion to his major works conducted in London exile, Canetti began writing aphorisms. Selections from 1942 to 1985 have been published in *The Human Province* and *Das Geheimherz der Uhr* (the secret heart of the clock). While some of the aphorisms relate to specific readings Canetti was engaged in at various times, most are reflections on specific issues he studied, such as the Jews and their fate, myths of various cultures, crowds and power, wars and revolutions, and languages. During this period Canetti also wrote a series of essays on Karl Kraus, Confucious, Hermann Broch, Stendhal, Aristophanes, Leo Tolstoy, and Hitler, among others.

In recent years Canetti's three plays, *The Wedding*, *Comedy of Vanity*, and *Life-Terms*, have been well received in the United States as well as in Europe in theaters staging more daring and experimental dramas. In these absurd dramas, Canetti has created "acoustic masks," in which he suggests that individuals have acoustic characteristics unique unto themselves. This same notion is, among other things, articulated in Canetti's travel diary *The Voices of Marrakesh* and in his autobiographical writings: *The Tongue Set Free*, *The Torch in My Ear*, and *The Play of the Eyes*. The autobiography, additionally, serves as a highly perceptive history of the earlier decades of this century. Canetti has created the "acoustic masks" of former times and different places in his very elegant style of writing.

Since receiving the Nobel Prize, Canetti has continued to be cited for his extraordinary and revolutionary work. He never was, nor will he ever be, a popular, best-selling author. Fellow artists and writers, as well as scholars, have recognized him as a profound thinker and, in the words of Iris Murdoch, as "one of our great imaginers and solitary men of genius." Canetti set out to "grab this century by the throat" and will continue to do so in the next. What he said about Franz Kafka is equally applicable to his own work: "One turns good when reading him, but without being proud of it."

BIBLIOGRAPHICAL REFERENCES: See Dagmar Barnouw, "Elias Canetti: Poet and Intellectual," in *Major Figures of Contemporary Austrian Literature*, 1987, edited by Donald G. Daviau, undoubtedly one of the most knowledgeable pieces of criticism on *Crowds and Power* and a fine introduction to Canetti. *Essays in Honor of Elias Canetti*, 1985, edited by Michael Hulse, consists of nine essays examining Canetti's work as a whole and ten investigating specific aspects of his writings. *Modern Austrian Literature*, XVI, nos. 3/4 (1983), is a special double issue devoted entirely to Canetti scholarship. Ingo Seidler, "Who Is Elias Canetti?" in *Cross Currents: A Yearbook of Central European Culture*, 1982, edited by Latislav Matejka and B. A. Stolz, is an informative introduction to Canetti's life and work, with a translation of some forty aphorisms. See also Susan Sontag, "Mind as Passion," in *Under the Sign of Saturn*, 1980; Sontag examines the two major books, *Auto-da-Fé* and *Crowds and Power*, in great detail, positioning them at the core of Canetti's writings.

Thomas H. Falk

TRUMAN CAPOTE

Born: New Orleans, Louisiana
Date: September 30, 1924

Died: Bel Air, California
Date: August 25, 1984

PRINCIPAL WORKS

NOVELS AND NOVELLAS: *Other Voices, Other Rooms*, 1948; *The Grass Harp*, 1951; *A Christmas Memory*, 1966; *The Thanksgiving Visitor*, 1969; *Answered Prayers: The Unfinished Novel*, 1986.

SHORT FICTION: *A Tree of Night and Other Stories*, 1949; *Breakfast at Tiffany's: A Short Novel and Three Stories*, 1958.

PLAYS: *The Grass Harp*, pb. 1952; *The House of Flowers*, pb. 1968 (with Harold Arlen).

NONFICTION: *The Muses Are Heard*, 1956; *In Cold Blood: A True Account of a Multiple Murder and Its Consequences*, 1966.

TRAVEL SKETCH: *Local Color*, 1950.

MISCELLANEOUS: *Observations*, 1959 (with Richard Avedon); *The Selected Writings of Truman Capote*, 1963; *Trilogy: An Experiment in Multimedia*, 1969 (with Eleanor Perry and Frank Perry); *The Dogs Bark: Public People and Private Places*, 1973; *Music for Chameleons*, 1980.

For almost forty years, Truman Capote was in the news. He first attracted public interest as a precocious wunderkind of fiction. Later he became known not only for his short stories and novels but also for his nonfiction. His literary reputation was almost equaled by his reputation as a jet-setter. He was a drawing card for interview shows and newspaper features. Any story or article of his, even in his declining years, became a featured work in popular magazines.

Born in New Orleans, September 30, 1924, to Lillie Mae Faulk (later changed to Nina) and Arch Persons, he was named Truman Streckfus Persons. After his parents' divorce and his mother's remarriage, Truman took the surname of his adoptive stepfather and became known only as Truman Capote. He had an unhappy and lonely childhood, which became the subject of much of his work. His sense of abandonment and betrayal remained with him throughout his life.

Capote achieved success at a very young age with the publication of *Other Voices*, *Other Rooms* and *A Tree of Night and Other Stories*. Yet some critics objected to or disliked the dark, gothic, psychological strain of the fiction. Some were repelled by the homosexual themes, but other critics praised the style and innovativeness of the work. Two later works of fiction found more favor. *The Grass Harp* and *A Christmas Memory* are tender, poetic, and often-humorous stories, but the theme of the lost child is central in these pieces. A favorite story of most Capote readers is *Breakfast at Tiffany's*, with its unforgettable heroine, Holly Golightly, who dreamed of but failed to find a life of security.

Capote's nonfiction pieces, later published as books, have an enduring quality. Various essays, portraits, and commentaries may be found in Capote collections. The best of these writings depicts the talented but also the narcissistic, sometimes shallow, often-lonely men and women whom the public and the media transform into twentieth century gods. Capote captures, in his imagistic prose, the materialistic, frenetic world of wealth and fame about which he was ambivalent: He was critical of it but eager to be part of it.

The high point of Capote's career was reached with *In Cold Blood*, a new form that he called a "nonfiction novel," part journalism, part creative story. Yet after the publication of that work, it became clear that the man was at odds with the artist. Capote published a series of short stories which were to be part of a projected novel called *Answered Prayers*. It is the story of the sexual peccadilloes of socialites, artists, dancers, editors, photographers, and film celebrities. Soon after he began the novel, Capote became an isolated, defensive man. At the time of his death, in 1984, that work was incomplete, but it was published posthumously in 1986 as *Answered Prayers: The Unfinished Novel*. Capote's last published work in his lifetime, *Music for Chameleons*, demonstrates that Capote still had, on occasion, a painter's eye and a musician's ear.

BIBLIOGRAPHICAL REFERENCES: Gerald Clarke, *Capote: A Biography*, 1988, is the only complete biography of Capote, beginning with various relatives before his birth and ending with his death. For a close examination of Capote's early years, see John Malcolm Brinnin, "The Picture of Little T. C. in a Prospect," in *Sextet: T. S. Eliot and Truman Capote and Others*, 1981, and *Truman Capote: Dear Heart, Old Buddy*, 1986. Changes in Capote's personality described by Brinnin are listed in journalistic detail by Donald Windham in *Lost Friendships: A Memoir of Truman Capote, Tennessee Williams, and Others*, 1987. Jack Dunphy, *Dear Genius: A Memoir of My Life with Truman Capote*, 1987, is part novel, part reminiscence. Helen S. Garson, *Truman Capote*, 1980, is a combination of biography and critical analysis, and William Nance, *The Worlds of Truman Capote*, 1970, is the first lengthy study of Capote's work, ending with *In Cold Blood*. See also a useful interpretation of Capote's dark stories in Paul Levine, "Truman Capote: The Revelation of the Broken Image," *The Virginia Quarterly Review*, XXXIV (1958), 600-617. For an analysis of Capote's major themes, see Helen S. Garson, "Truman Capote," in *Fifty Southern Writers After 1900*, 1987, edited by Joseph Flora and Robert Bain. Among the bibliographies and checklists of Capote's work, the most comprehensive is Robert J. Stanton's *Truman Capote: A Primary and Secondary Bibliography*, 1980. Lawrence Grobel's *Conversations with Capote*, 1985, records discussions held during a brief period toward the end of Capote's life. Thomas Inge, *Interviews*, 1987, includes every important interview Capote gave.

Helen S. Garson

ALEJO CARPENTIER

Born: Havana, Cuba
Date: December 26, 1904

Died: Paris, France
Date: April 24, 1980

PRINCIPAL WORKS

NOVELS: *¡Ecué-Yamba-O! Historia Afro-Cubana*, 1933; *El reino de este mundo*, 1949 (*The Kingdom of This World*, 1957); *Los pasos perdidos*, 1953 (*The Lost Steps*, 1956); *El acoso*, 1956 (*Manhunt*, 1959); *El siglo de las luces*, 1962 (*Explosion in the Cathedral*, 1963); *El derecho de asilo*, 1972; *El recurso del método*, 1974 (*Reasons of State*, 1976); *Concierto barroco*, 1974 (*Concert Baroque*, 1976); *La consagración de la primavera*, 1978; *El arpa y la sombra*, 1979.

SHORT FICTION: *Guerra del tiempo*, 1958 (*War of Time*, 1970).

ESSAYS: *La música en Cuba*, 1946; *Tientos y diferencias*, 1964; *Afirmación literaria latinoamericana*, 1978; *La novela latinoamericana en vísperas del nuevo siglo y otros ensayos*, 1981.

Alejo Valmont Carpentier is a seminal figure in the development of twentieth century Latin American literature. A perennial nominee for the Nobel Prize in Literature, Carpentier ranks with Miguel Ángel Asturias and Jorge Luis Borges as one of the major influences on the emergence and international recognition of the Latin American novelist in the second half of the twentieth century. Carpentier was born in Havana, Cuba, on December 26, 1904, the son of Jorge Julian Carpentier, a French architect, and Lina Valmont, a Russian language teacher. His parents had emigrated from France to Cuba two years earlier. They were convinced that Cuba, independent as a result of the Spanish-American War, was a place to create a future away from the world-weariness of the European continent. Both were fluent in Spanish; both were amateur musicians. Consequently, young Alejo was reared to be completely bilingual and with a knowledge and passion for music which permeated every aspect of his later intellectual and artistic life.

Asthmatic as a child, Carpentier spent his early school years divided equally between Havana and the rural outskirts of the city, where early direct contact with African elements of Cuban society was to have a lasting influence on his understanding of his country's (and the Caribbean's) rich and complex cultural identity. His first attempts at writing date from 1916. Throughout his teens, until his registration as a student of architecture at the University of Havana in 1922, he produced stories imitative of his (and his father's) favorite French and Spanish authors: Alexander Dumas, *père*, Honoré de Balzac, Anatole France, Pío Baroja, Benito Pérez Galdós, and Vicente Blasco Ibáñez.

Forced into full-time employment by the breakup of his parents' marriage, Carpentier left the university after one year of study to begin a career in journalism. Following a brief trip to Paris, where he absorbed many of the new artistic developments of postwar Europe (represented by the works of James Joyce, Pablo Picasso, and Igor Stravinsky), he returned to Havana and enthusiastically embraced avant-garde cultural groups and supported movements of social and political protest. In 1926, after a trip to Mexico and a meeting with the revolutionary painter Diego Rivera, Carpentier signed a manifesto denouncing the regime of the Cuban dictator, Gerardo Machado (1925 to 1933). The following year, he was imprisoned for political activities. In prison, he wrote the draft of his first novel, *¡Ecué-Yamba-O!* (Lord, praised by thou!), a historically important narrative (thematically and stylistically) in the development of the Afro-Cuban movement of the 1930's. A unique synthesis of armchair anthropology, social criticism, and formal experimentalism, the novel's final version was not completed and published until 1933 in Madrid. Fearing for his safety, Carpentier went into exile upon his release from prison in 1927, spending the next eleven years (from 1928 to 1939) in France. There he wrote, developing his craft and increasing his knowledge of new tendencies in the arts, particularly music and literature; he also met many of the leading poets and painters of surrealism, exploring their theories and techniques while reading, he later said, "everything I could about America, from the letters of Columbus to the writers of the eighteenth century" in order to discover the "contexts" and the "essences" of Latin America.

From 1939, the year of his return to Cuba, to 1945, Carpentier's creative energy was divided equally between music research, writing, and traveling. In 1946, he moved to Caracas, Venezuela, and the fruits of this earlier period began to appear: in 1946, *La música en Cuba* (Cuban music), the first attempt at a systematic, historical survey of Cuban music from its colonial origins through the twentieth century (a study to which all of Carpentier's subsequent writings are, to some degree, indebted); in 1949, *The Kingdom of This World*, a novel of the Haitian Revolution inspired by a visit to that tiny Caribbean country in 1943; and in 1953, his most universally acclaimed (and most autobiographical and personal) novel, *The Lost Steps*. In the preface to *The Kingdom of This World*, Carpentier wrote that the trip to Haiti which had inspired the novel also revealed to him the fantastic nature of the Caribbean and the South American continent and of their history: "What is the whole history of America but a chronicle of the marvellous-real?" In *The Lost Steps*, the alienated writer-composer protagonist undertakes a journey from North America to a South American jungle in search of indigenous, primitive musical instruments. He discovers, however, that magical dimension Carpentier called *lo real-maravilloso*: "the marvellous reality" of South America, where different stages of the human past and different levels of man's cultural evolution coexist in a natural, telluric grandeur which resists description from outside by an old or inherited cultural perspective. In *The Lost Steps*, the most persistent and characteristic thematic concerns and stylistic devices of Carpentier's later works can be found: music, architecture, mythology, and the circular nature of time, to name a few.

In 1956, Carpentier published *Manhunt*, a short novel which, like *The Lost Steps*, reveals his fascination with the music of Ludwig van Beethoven. *War of Time*, an important collection of stories exploring the ambiguous and complex nature of temporal experience, was published in 1958, and in 1959, the year of the Cuban Revolution, Carpentier returned to Cuba with the almost completed manuscript of his second most acclaimed novel, *Explosion in the Cathedral*. Published in 1962, the year Carpentier was appointed director of the Cuban National Publishing House, *Explosion in the Cathedral* is an intriguing, complex attempt to dramatize the impact of the French Revolution on the entire Caribbean and to reveal how, more often than not, the painful and costly process of abrupt social transformation brings about in the end feelings of frustration and disillusionment. In 1966, Carpentier was removed from his directorship and appointed as Cuban cultural attché in Paris. From 1966 to 1980, he continued to produce essays and novels in which his principal social and artistic concerns were explored. Critics, at times, attacked his work for being too "essayistic," for having too little psychological development of characters, for the ornate and complex style of his language (Carpentier called it "baroque"), and for his political allegiance to the Fidel Castro regime. Despite hostile assessments from both the political Right and the political Left, however, international recognition of his importance continued to grow during this period. In 1975, he was awarded an honorary doctorate by the University of Havana and the Alfonso Reyes Prize for Literature by the Mexican government. In 1976, he was elected an Honorary Fellow of the University of Kansas, and in 1978, he received Spain's highest literary award, the Miguel de Cervantes Prize, from King Juan Carlos in Madrid.

Carpentier's work now enjoys universal praise. His importance to thematic expansion and technical innovation in the Latin American narrative has been acknowledged by world-famous novelists such as Argentina's Julio Cortázar, Mexico's Carlos Fuentes, and Colombia's Nobel laureate, Gabriel García Márquez. His position as a major novelist of the twentieth century is assured and is reflected in the constantly increasing number of translations of his works.

BIBLIOGRAPHICAL REFERENCES: Roberto Gonzalez-Echeverria and Klaus Muller-Bergh, *Alejo Carpentier: Bibliographical Guide*, 1983, is a most important bibliographical source of primary and secondary works. For further study, see Roberto Gonzalez-Echeverria, *Alejo Carpentier: The Pilgrim at Home*, 1977, the first book-length study of Carpentier in English by an extremely astute critic; Lloyd King, *Alejo Carpentier, Caribbean Writer*, 1977, a perceptive, stimulating, and well-informed short study; Frank Janney, *Alejo Carpentier and His Early Works*, 1981, a discussion of the early style; and Donald Shaw, *Alejo Carpentier*, 1985, an introductory, chronological overview of all Carpentier's work. A lengthy interview, including discussions of Carpentier's major works up to *Explosion in the Cathedral*, is Luis Harss and Barbara Dohmann, "Alejo Carpentier: Or, The Eternal Return," in *Into the Mainstream: Conversations with Latin American Writers*, 1967. Both Richard Young, *Carpentier: "El reino de este mundo": A Critical Guide*, 1983, and Verity Smith, *Carpentier: "Los pasos perdidos," A Critical Guide*, 1983, are brief but incisive approaches to these important works. See also Frances Wyers Weber, "*El acoso*: Alejo Carpentier's War on Time," *Publications of the Modern Language Association of America*, LXXVIII (1963), 440-448; David William Foster, "The Everyman Theme in Alejo Carpentier's 'El Camino de Santiago,'" *Symposium*, XVIII (1964), 229-240; Steven Bell, "Carpentier's *El reino de este mundo* in a New Light: Towards a Theory of the Fantastic," *Journal of Spanish Studies: Twentieth Century*, VIII (1980), 29-43; Terry Peavler, "The Source for the Archetype in *Los pasos perdidos*," *Romance Notes*, XV (1974), 58-87; Helmy Giacoman, *Homenaje a Alejo Carpentier*, 1970; Roland E. Bush, "*Art of the Fugue:* Musical Presence in Alejo Carpentier's *Los pasos perdidos*," *Revista de Música Latino Americana/Latin American Music Review*, VI (Fall/Winter, 1985), 129-151.

Roland E. Bush

RAYMOND CARVER

Born: Clatskanie, Oregon
Date: May 25, 1938

Died: Port Angeles, Washington
Date: August 2, 1988

PRINCIPAL WORKS

SHORT FICTION: *Put Yourself in My Shoes*, 1974; *Will You Please Be Quiet, Please?*, 1976; *Furious Seasons and Other Stories*, 1977; *What We Talk About When We Talk Above Love*, 1981; *The Pheasant*, 1982; *Cathedral*, 1983; *If It Please You*, 1984; *The Stories of Raymond Carver*, 1985; *Where I'm Calling From*, 1988.

POETRY: *Near Klamath*, 1968; *Winter Insomnia*, 1970; *At Night the Salmon Move*, 1976; *Two Poems*, 1982; *This Water*, 1985; *Where Water Comes Together with Other Water*, 1985; *Ultramarine*, 1986.

NONFICTION: *Fires: Essays, Poems, Stories*, 1983.

In his relatively short career as a professional author, Raymond Carver established a critical reputation as the most powerful and innovative short-story writer of his generation. He was born on May 25, 1938, in a small town in northwestern Oregon; however, before he started school his family moved to Yakima, Washington, where his father worked as a logger. Carver once declared that the most important, although in many ways the most negative, influence on his early hopes to become a writer was the fact that he married and became a father before he was twenty. The need to support his family made the work he really wanted to do practically impossible.

Carver moved his wife and two children to California in 1958, where he enrolled at Chico State College, a small school in the California State College system. There, he enrolled in a creative writing class taught by John Gardner, who was soon to make a name for himself as a writer; Gardner encouraged Carver in his own writing efforts. Carver transferred to Humboldt State University, a northern coastal school, where he received his degree in 1963.

Although Carver was busy writing during the 1960's and publishing his poetry and fiction in various small magazines, his big break did not come until 1970, when he was honored with a National Endowment for the Arts Discovery Award for Poetry. With the money he received, he could spend time revising many of the stories which appeared in his first important book, *Will You Please Be Quiet, Please?* Although Carver was soon publishing in reputable journals and gaining recognition, he was also plagued with the disease of alcoholism. In 1977, when *Will You Please Be Quiet, Please?* was nominated for the National Book Award, he was hospitalized several times. Yet Carver said that June 2, 1977, was the date he would stop drinking forever; it was a decision that had a significant effect on his writing style and career.

Carver's professional career began to blossom in the late 1970's and 1980's: he received a Guggenheim Fellowship in 1979, published a highly praised collection of stories entitled *What We Talk About When We Talk About Love* in 1981, and published another significant collection, *Cathedral*, in 1983. Moreover, his personal life improved significantly. Following his divorce from his first wife in the late 1970's, Carver met and began living with the writer Tess Gallagher. In 1987, after he had put together yet another collection of both old and new stories, Carver, a heavy smoker, was diagnosed as having lung cancer. He died in Port Angeles, Washington, on August 2, 1988.

Raymond Carver's first two collections of short stories shocked readers with their violence and puzzled them with their laconic Chekhovian style. *Will You Please Be Quiet, Please?* contains twenty-two stories which provide stark images of lives lived in quiet desperation. In many of the stories in this collection the characters are thrown out of their everyday routine and caught in situations where they feel helpless and estranged.

Whereas the stories in Carver's first important collection are relatively drained of imagery and recall the style of Ernest Hemingway, the stories in his second major collection, *What We*

Talk About When We Talk About Love, are even more radically spare in their language; indeed, they are so minimal that they seem mere dehumanized patterns with no life in them at all. Whatever theme they may have is embodied in the bare outlines of sometimes shocking, sometimes trivial events and in the spare and reticent dialogue of the characters who seem utterly unable to articulate the nature of their isolation. The most basic theme of Carver's stories is the tenuous union between men and women and the mysterious separations that always seem imminent.

The stories that appear in two of Carver's later collections, *Cathedral* and *Where I'm Calling From*, are more hopeful than the earlier stories, perhaps because they were mainly written after Carver had been cured of alcoholism and had met Tess Gallagher. They are also more voluble and detailed, exhibiting an increasing willingness on the part of Carver to discuss, explain, and explore the emotions and situations that give rise to the stories. Instead of separation, Carver's later stories move toward union or reunion.

Raymond Carver is, in the opinion of many critics, the most important figure in the renaissance of interest in short fiction sparked in American literature in the 1980's. He belongs in a line of modern short-story writers that begins with Anton Chekhov and progresses through such masters of the form as Sherwood Anderson, Eudora Welty, Katherine Anne Porter, Ernest Hemingway, and Bernard Malamud. On the basis of a small output of stories, Carver will remain a significant figure in the history of modern American literature.

BIBLIOGRAPHICAL REFERENCES: Authur M. Saltzman, *Understanding Raymond Carver*, 1988, is the first book-length study of Carver's work; Saltzman's book is an introductory guide intended for the student and the nonacademic reader. See also William Stull's "Raymond Carver," *Dictionary of Literary Biography Yearbook*, 1984, and Charles May's "Raymond Carver," in *Critical Survey of Short Fiction*, 1987. Also helpful is an interview with Carver conducted by Mona Simpson, "The Art of Fiction," *The Paris Review*, XXV (1983), 192-221. The two most helpful critical essays are David Boxer and Cassandra Phillips, "*Will You Please Be Quiet, Please?* Voyeurism, Dissociation, and the Art of Raymond Carver," *The Iowa Review*, X (1979), 75-90, and William L. Stull, "Beyond Hopelessville: Another Side of Raymond Carver," *Philological Quarterly*, LXIV (1985), 1-15.

Charles E. May

JOYCE CARY

Born: Londonderry, Ireland
Date: December 7, 1888

Died: Oxford, England
Date: March 29, 1957

Principal Works

NOVELS: *Aissa Saved*, 1932; *An American Visitor*, 1933; *The African Witch*, 1936; *Castle Corner*, 1938; *Mister Johnson*, 1939; *Charley Is My Darling*, 1940; *A House of Children*, 1941; *Herself Surprised*, 1941; *To Be a Pilgrim*, 1942; *The Horse's Mouth*, 1944; *The Moonlight*, 1946; *A Fearful Joy*, 1949; *Prisoner of Grace*, 1952; *Except the Lord*, 1953; *Not Honour More*, 1955; *The Captive and the Free*, 1959; *Cock Jarvis*, 1974.

SHORT FICTION: *Spring Song and Other Stories*, 1960.

POETRY: *Verses by Arthur Cary*, 1908; *Marching Soldier*, 1945; *Drunken Sailor*, 1947.

NONFICTION: *Power in Men*, 1939; *The Case for African Freedom*, 1941; *The Process of Real Freedom*, 1943; *Britain and West Africa*, 1946; *Art and Reality*, 1958; *Selected Essays*, 1976.

AUTOBIOGRAPHY: *Memoir of the Bobotes*, 1960.

Arthur Joyce Lunel Cary successfully mated modern fiction's playful experimentation with form and language to the traditional novel's firm reliance upon plot and character. Shortly after Cary's birth in Ireland, his father, Arthur Cary, moved the family to England. Cary was reared knowing three worlds: London, where his family lived, Devon, where the family holidayed; and Ireland, where he vacationed with grandparents. These contrasting worlds taught him to see the world through varied perspectives. When he was ten, his mother Charlotte died, and when he was fifteen, his stepmother Dora also died. Cary attended boarding school at Hurstleigh and Clifton, but he was an unremarkable student. For four years, Cary dreamed of becoming a painter. On a trip to France in 1904, he discovered Impressionism and moved to Paris in 1906 as an art student. A year later, he went to Edinburgh but by 1908 decided that canvas was not his medium. The experiences of these years came to fruition in Cary's first fictional trilogy about the artist Gulley Jimson, whose bohemian life and visual imagination infuse the novel with unpredictable emotion and vivid metaphors.

Cary entered the University of Oxford in 1909 to study law and barely took his degree in 1912. Without prospects for a profession, Cary went to the Balkans, where war had broken out. After his return to England a year later, he found a position in the colonial service and went to Nigeria in 1914. There he fought against the German East African army for four years and assisted in postwar reconstruction. At various times, he served as a policeman, tax collector, and engineer. Like other colonial administrators-turned-artists (Rudyard Kipling and George Orwell, for example) whose imaginations were shaped in England's empire, Cary learned to see the world with non-British eyes. These years provided Cary with the situations, characters, and themes of four early novels describing the sometimes comic, often tragic interaction of Western imperialism and African tribalism.

In 1920, Cary returned to England. With his wife Gertrude Ogilvie, whom he had married in 1916 while on leave, Cary settled in Oxford. He lived in the same house for thirty-seven years: There he wrote prodigiously, fathered five children, and nursed his wife through a fatal illness. Cary supported himself by penning predictable but lively short stories for popular magazines. Once he had achieved some financial security, he turned to serious fiction. His first novel after Africa, *Aissa Saved*, was neither a monetary nor a critical success, but with each succeeding book he gained a reputation as a competent practitioner of the panoramic novel about social conflict. Cary switched his focus from Africa to Ireland, publishing *Castle Corner* in 1938 as the first volume of a projected trilogy. Sensing that the traditional storytelling mode could not express the complicated reality he wished to communicate, Cary abandoned the project and his narrative method. *Mister Johnson* marks a watershed in Cary's development as a novelist. The novel, set in Africa, is told from a unique point of view: a third-person narration cast in the present tense. It recounts how a black civil servant (Johnson) and a white district officer (Rudbeck) pool their imaginations and energies to build a road. Cary's unexpected narrative method introduces the reader into the unfamiliar experience of an African European shared vision. Though the book ends tragically with Johnson's death at Rudbeck's hands, Cary discovered how to delineate character through narrative innovation: not character as in external appearances but character as a unique set of perceptions. Unlike some modernists, however, Cary used narrative innovation as a tool to explore character, not as an end in itself.

By 1941, Cary was well reputed enough to earn the James Tait Black Memorial Prize for the best British novel of the year. Yet he was just on the verge of his greatest accomplishment, a trilogy of first-person novels about the world of painting. Each novel records the losses and loves of three intertwined lives. *Herself Surprised* is Sara Monday's narrative of her romances with the artist Gulley Jimson and the art critic Tom Wilcher. *To Be a Pilgrim* is Wilcher's account of his life spent in the acquisition of paintings. *The Horse's Mouth* is Jimson's story of his quest to paint a masterpiece. Each novel is told in a distinctive voice, its sentences, syntax, and similes the inimitable utterances of a unique speaker. Though not arranged chronologically, the novels rework the same episodes and reinterpret the conflicting emotions of three people whose fates interweave like tapestry threads of different colors. From afar, the threads form one picture, up close, they reveal myriad variations. Given its composition during the dark years of World War II, this trilogy is a remarkable celebration of the human spirit. Though none of the protagonists lives "happily ever after" in the popular novel tradition, they survive their experiences as infinitely rich, infinitely complex, and infinitely joyous beings.

In the final decade of his life, Cary was considered a foresighted writer. Because of his novels about Africa, he was, during and after World War II, an authoritative commentator on its future. Because of his trilogy about art, Cary commanded respect as a philosopher of aesthetics. His observations on politics and art expressed hope to a war-weary world. His last three novels form a trilogy that studies the political tensions which led up to World War II. It seems to conclude that human salvation lies with individuals, not ideologies. His last writings, composed during the illness that took his life, discuss how art imitates, transcends, and transforms reality.

At the beginning of the twentieth century, writers and readers alike speculated that the novel was dead. Two centuries of imaginative effort seemed exhausted. The fiction that most people read followed familiar formulas for plot, character, and theme. Fiction produced by rebellious experimenters (such as James Joyce) seemed too convoluted, too self-consciously different, to reach a wide readership. Cary demonstrated that the conventional taste for an interesting story about interesting characters in a contemporary setting could be met—and enhanced—through new narrative methods. With William Faulkner, Virginia Woolf, and many others, Cary showed by mid-century that the novel was not dead. Appropriately, his only novel to make the Book-of-the-Month Club list was his best, *The Horse's Mouth*.

BIBLIOGRAPHICAL REFERENCES: The reader who needs a brief overview of Cary's life and works should start with Walter E. Allen, *Joyce Cary*, 1963, no. 41 in the British Council's Writers and Their Works series of monographs. R. W. Noble, *Joyce Cary*, 1973, is a more substantial study of Cary's personal philosophy as it grew from his experiences and is expressed in the novels. A full, authoritative work is Malcolm Foster, *Joyce Cary: A Biography*, 1968, comprehensive, thoroughly documented, and eminently readable. See also two important interviews: "The Novelist at Work: A Conversation Between Joyce Cary and Lord David Cecil," *Adam International Review*, XVIII (November/December, 1950), and "An Interview with Joyce Cary," in *Writers at Work: The Paris Review Interviews*, 1958, edited by Malcolm Cowley. An affectionate recollection by Enid Starkie, "Joyce Cary: A Portrait," in *Essays by*

Divers Hands, 1963, recalls their literary and personal friendship. Two general studies surveying Cary's works are Andrew Wright, *Joyce Cary: A Preface to His Novels*, 1958, and Kinley E. Roby, *Joyce Cary*, 1974, in the Twayne series. Three works study Cary's concept of freedom but come to different conclusions: Robert Bloom, *The Indeterminate World: A Study of the Novels of Joyce Cary*, 1962, and Charles G. Hoffman, *Joyce Cary: The Comedy of Freedom*, 1964, read the novels as philosophic commentaries on a variety of human experiences, but Barbara Fish, *Joyce Cary: The Writer and His Theme*, 1980, interprets the novels as links in one spiritual autobiography. More specialized studies are Molly Mahood, *Joyce Cary's Africa*, 1965, and Hazard Adams, *Joyce Cary's Trilogies: Pursuit of the Particular Real*, 1983. *Modern Fiction Studies*, IX (Autumn, 1963), devotes the entire issue to essays on Cary.

Robert M. Otten

CARLOS CASTANEDA

Born: Cajamarca, Peru
Date: December 25, 1925

Principal Works

ANTHROPOLOGY: *The Teachings of Don Juan: A Yaqui Way of Knowledge*, 1968; *A Separate Reality: Further Conversations with Don Juan*, 1971; *Journey to Ixtlan: The Lessons of Don Juan*, 1972; *Tales of Power*, 1974; *The Second Ring of Power*, 1977; *The Eagle's Gift*, 1981; *The Fire from Within*, 1984; *The Power of Silence*, 1987.

Carlos César Arana Castaneda is an anthropologist who writes like a novelist. Despite having many detractors, his work experienced a great vogue for nearly a decade, and by 1975 more than four million copies of his books were in print. Even his biography is disputed. He claims to have been born in São Paulo, Brazil, on December 25, 1935. Some reference works accept this place of birth but give December 25, 1931, as the date. He claims that he was born into a prominent Italian family of another name, the son of a mother who died when he was a child and a father who was a professor of literature. According to his story, he legally took the name Castaneda in 1959. Yet United States immigration records indicate that he was born at Cajamarca, Peru, on December 25, 1925, the son of César Arana Burungaray, a goldsmith, and Susan Castaneda Nova. According to these records, he was using the name Castaneda as early as 1951. When confronted with these discrepancies, Castaneda dismissed them as inconsequential.

Castaneda was graduated from the Colegio Nacional de Nuestra Señora de Guadalupe and later studied painting and sculpture at the National School of Fine Arts in Lima. In 1951, he emigrated to Los Angeles, California. He initially studied psychology at Los Angeles City College between 1955 and 1959. In the latter year, he became a student at the University of California at Los Angeles (UCLA), where he received a B.A. in anthropology in 1962. He was to study intermittently at UCLA for the next nine years, earning an M.A. in 1964 and Ph.D. in 1970. While a student, Castaneda spent five years in Mexico, apprenticed to a Yaqui sorcerer. It was the account of this apprenticeship that would bring him literary celebrity and much money.

Castaneda's field of graduate study was ethnomethodology, and as early as 1960 he had set out to study the Indians' use of medicinal herbs in the southwestern United States. In the summer of that year, he met Don Juan Matus, an aged member of the Yaqui tribe, a man reputed to have extraordinary powers. First in Arizona and later in Sonora, Mexico, Don Juan initiated Castaneda into the ritual use of peyote and other hallucinogens. By the autumn of 1965, Castaneda had almost come to regard the visionary states shared with the old Indian as an alternate reality, a reality totally at odds with the rationalistic Western tradition. Castaneda turned the notes he had taken during his apprenticeship into a master's thesis. Then, in June, 1968, the University of California Press published the work under the title *The Teachings of Don Juan: A Yaqui Way of Knowledge*. The modest run of two thousand copies excited great interest. The book was reissued as a paperback and immediately became a best-seller. It was taken up by the antiestablishment counterculture, which viewed Don Juan as a folk hero and Castaneda as his amanuensis.

Also in 1968, Castaneda returned to Mexico to show Don Juan the book in which he was the central character. There, Castaneda had more experiences which defied his scientific rationalism. The result was *A Separate Reality: Further Conversations with Don Juan*. Other books followed in rapid succession: *Journey to Ixtlan*, an account of nonpsychedelic-related exercises practiced during the author's apprenticeship, and *Tales of Power*, which recounts further and even more extravagant experiences with Don Juan, now joined by another sorcerer, Don Genaro. Castaneda's doctoral dissertation was essentially the text of *Journey to*

Ixtlan. *The Second Ring of Power* tells of Castaneda's encounter with Don Juan's women disciples and was received with mixed reviews.

Castaneda's subject matter and personality have made him a controversial figure. Despite his defenders within the academic community, when Castaneda received his Ph.D. in anthropology, the more staid members of the profession reacted as if the University of California had granted a doctorate in magic. After becoming famous, he gave interviews in which his date and place of birth, his parents' names, and the entire history of his childhood conflict with the official record. Even the date of his Ph.D. ranges from 1970 to 1973 in contemporary works of reference. Some critics have implied that, given the fact that no one except Castaneda has actually seen Don Juan, the books may be largely works of imagination. Others respond that, since Castaneda is essentially a gifted novelist, the literal truth of the accounts is not a crucial factor. He attempted to teach at the University of California at Irvine but discovered that he was too much of a celebrity to lecture effectively there. He has since led a rather reclusive life. Nevertheless, as F. Scott Fitzgerald became the spokesman for the Jazz Age, Carlos Castaneda caught the spirit (or one major part of the spirit) of the turbulent 1960's and 1970's: a radical questioning of the values of American life, even of the American perception of reality.

BIBLIOGRAPHICAL REFERENCES: The provocative and controversial nature of Castaneda's work is reflected in the titles of the following books. See Richard DeMille, *Castaneda's Journey: The Power and the Allegory*, 1976. The same author edited and contributed to *The Don Juan Papers: Further Castaneda Controversies*, 1980. See also N. Drury, *Don Juan, Mescalito, and Modern Magic: The Mythology of Inner Space*, 1978; Sam Holroyd, *PSI and the Consciousness Explcsion*, 1977; and D. C. Noel, *Carlos Castaneda*, 1975. Noel also edited *Seeing Castaneda: Reactions to the "Don Juan" Writings of Carlos Castaneda*, 1976. See David Silverman, *Reading Castaneda: A Prologue to the Social Sciences*, 1975. A number of articles originally appearing in periodicals are collected in books listed above. Castaneda's work is also examined in these articles: Dudley Young, "The Magic of Peyote," *The New York Times Book Review*, September 29, 1968, 30; Richard Gott, "Mushrooms," *New Statesman*, January 14, 1972, 51-52; "Don Juan and the Sorcerer's Apprentice," *Time*, March 5, 1973, 36-45; William Kennedy, "Fact or Fiction," *The New Republic*, November 16, 1974, 28-30; Douglas McFerran, "The Castaneda Plot," *America*, February 26, 1977, 162-164; and Sam Keen, "Don Juan's Power Trip," *Psychology Today*, December, 1977, 40.

Patrick Adcock

WILLA CATHER

Born: Gore, Virginia
Date: December 7, 1873

Died: New York, New York
Date: April 24, 1947

PRINCIPAL WORKS

NOVELS: *Alexander's Bridge*, 1912; *O Pioneers!*, 1913; *The Song of the Lark*, 1915; *My Ántonia*, 1918; *One of Ours*, 1922; *A Lost Lady*, 1923; *The Professor's House*, 1925; *My Mortal Enemy*, 1926; *Death Comes for the Archbishop*, 1927; *Shadows on the Rock*, 1931; *Lucy Gayheart*, 1935; *Sapphira and the Slave Girl*, 1940.

SHORT FICTION: *The Troll Garden*, 1905; *Youth and the Bright Medusa*, 1920; *Obscure Destinies*, 1932; *The Old Beauty and Others*, 1948; *Willa Cather's Collected Short Fiction, 1882-1912*, 1970; *Uncle Valentine and Other Stories*, 1973.

POETRY: *April Twilights*, 1903.

ESSAYS: *Not Under Forty*, 1936; *Willa Cather on Writing*, 1949.

CRITICISM: *The Kingdom of Art*, 1966.

JOURNALISM: *Willa Cather in Europe*, 1956; *The World and the Parish*, 1970.

MISCELLANEOUS: *Writings from Willa Cather's Campus Years*, 1950.

Willa Cather stands as one of the major novelists and interpreters of the American pioneer experience. She was born on Willow Shade Farm in Gore, Virginia, on December 7, 1873, the oldest child of Charles and Mary Virginia (Boak) Cather. When she was nine, her father decided to homestead with his relatives on the divide between the Little Blue and Republican rivers, northwest of Red Cloud, Nebraska. Cather later remembered her first impressions of the cold, flat, naked prairie, stretching on to the horizon. After a year of homesteading, Charles Cather moved his family back into Red Cloud and opened a farm mortgage office.

Cather was a precocious and unconventional child, excelling at school, absorbing the culture of immigrant families, and seeking out adult company. After high school in 1890, she entered the University of Nebraska in Lincoln. There she showed the first evidence of her literary talents. She wrote for the two campus literary magazines and worked as a theater critic for the *Nebraska State Journal*.

Upon graduation in 1895, Cather accepted an editorial position with the *Home Monthly* in Pittsburgh. There she became close friends with Isabelle McClung, daughter of a wealthy judge, and moved in with the McClungs in 1900. Cather and Isabelle McClung traveled together to Europe in the summer of 1903. While living in Pittsburgh, Cather taught English at Allegheny High School and published two early works, *April Twilights* and *The Troll Garden*. In 1906, S. S. McClure discovered one of Cather's stories and invited her to join his magazine staff in New York. Cather gained valuable experience as an editor for *McClure's*, publishing many of her early stories there. On a research trip to Boston, she met Sarah Orne Jewett, who advised her to devote herself to writing and to try a novel if her artistic gifts were ever to mature. Cather took this advice and completed her first novel, *Alexander's Bridge*, the same year that she left *McClure's*. From that point onward, she would be a full-time writer.

In 1912, an invitation from her brother took Cather to Arizona, where she saw the cliff dwellings near Flagstaff. This discovery would later be reflected in *The Song of the Lark*. The trip west also put Willa back in touch with her Nebraska roots and inspired her to begin her second novel, *O Pioneers!*. *My Ántonia* was published soon after, in 1918. Cather's remarkable heroines in these novels—Alexandra Bergson, Thea Kronborg, and Ántonia Shimerda—celebrate the pioneer virtues of idealism, generosity, vision, and vitality. They resist the greed and materialism that Cather believed were stifling American life. In the character of the opera singer Thea Kronborg, Cather also celebrates the artist who transcends her provincial roots and develops her artistic gifts. The other protagonists, Alexandra Bergson and Ántonia Shimerda, draw their strength from the land itself and triumph over the limitations of their circumstances.

World War I and its aftermath marked a period of disillusionment for Willa Cather. She believed that postwar America was gripped by a new commerical spirit that was inimical to the spirit. The hero of *One of Ours*, Claude Wheeler, is a young, idealistic American who volunteers for service in France and loses his life in the war. Marian Forrester, in *A Lost Lady*, is a brilliant, attractive woman who is financially compromised by the unscrupulous Ivy Peters after her husband's death. Godfrey St. Peters, in *The Professor's House*, is a disillusioned middle-aged professor, oppressed by his greedy family and sustained only by the memory of his former student Tom Outland, who died in the war. The income from Outland's invention becomes a source of dissension within St. Peters' family and leads to Godfrey's attempted suicide.

Cather found respite from this pervasive materialism in two forces: the discovery of one's "true" self through a suitable vocation, something that involved an idealistic dedication to a worthwhile cause, and the recovery of one's past, or cultural roots. Father Jean Latour, the French Jesuit priest in *Death Comes for the Archbishop*, finds his mission in reforming the corrupt church in the Southwest. Cather's fascination with older cultures continued with *Shadows on the Rock*, a historical novel set in seventeenth century Quebec which celebrates the richness and stability of the French culture transplanted to the New World.

Willa Cather has taken her place as one of the major twentieth century American novelists. Her fictional works show the benefits of her early drama criticism, especially in her critical ideal of the novel, *démeublé*, a narrative stripped to its essentials. Though her most memorable characters were her female protagonists, she sometimes employed a male narrator and she was adept in depicting the male sensibility. Her greatest strengths lay in the lyrical intensity of her pastoral novels, her celebration of the pioneer spirit, and her recognition of how the cultural heritage of Europe has enriched the American experience.

BIBLIOGRAPHICAL REFERENCES: Bernice Slote's survey of Willa Cather scholarship in *Sixteen Modern American Authors*, 1973, edited by Jackson R. Bryer, has been updated by James Woodress for the 1987 edition. Joan Crane has published *Willa Cather: A Bibliography*, 1982. James Woodress' *Willa Cather: A Literary Life*, 1987, the definitive literary biography, builds on his earlier *Willa Cather: Her Life and Art*, 1970. Other recent critical biographies include Sharon O'Brien, *Willa Cather: The Emerging Voice*, 1987; Phyllis C. Robinson, *Willa: The Life of Willa Cather*, 1983; and Philip Gerber, *Willa Cather*, 1975. See also Dorothy Van Ghent, *Willa Cather*, 1964, and Elizabeth S. Sergeant, *Willa Cather: A Memoir*, 1953. Critical studies of Cather's work include Susan Rosowski, *The Voyage Perilous: Willa Cather's Romanticism*, 1986; Marilyn Arnold, *Willa Cather's Short Fiction*, 1984; *Critical Essays on Willa Cather*, 1984, edited by John J. Murphy; David Stouck, *Willa Cather's Imagination*, 1975; *The Art of Willa Cather*, 1973, edited by Bernice Slote and Virginia Faulkner; *Willa Cather and Her Critics*, 1967, edited by James Schroeter; Edward A. Bloom and Lillian D. Bloom, *Willa Cather's Gift of Sympathy*, 1962; David Daiches, *Willa Cather: A Critical Introduction*, 1951; and Mildred Bennett, *The World of Willa Cather*, 1951.

Andrew J. Angyal

LOUIS-FERDINAND CÉLINE
Louis-Ferdinand Destouches

Born: Courbevoie, France
Date: May 27, 1894

Died: Meudon, France
Date: July 1, 1961

PRINCIPAL WORKS

NOVELS: *Voyage au bout de la nuit*, 1932 (*Journey to the End of the Night*, 1934); *Mort à crédit*, 1936 (*Death on the Installment Plan*, 1938); *Guignol's band I*, 1944 (English translation, 1954); *Féerie pour une autre fois, I*, 1952; *Féerie pour une autre fois, II: Normance*, 1954; *Entretiens avec le professeur Y*, 1955 (*Conversations with Professor Y*, 1986); *D'un château l'autre*, 1957 (*Castle to Castle*, 1968); *Nord*, 1960 (*North*, 1972); *Le Pont de Londres: Guignol's band, II*, 1964; *Rigodon*, 1969 (*Rigadoon*, 1974).
ESSAYS: *Mea culpa, suivi de La vie et l'œuvre de Semmelweis*, 1936 (*Mea Culpa, with The Life and Work of Semmelweiss*, 1937).

One of the most controversial figures of twentieth century literature, Louis-Ferdinand Céline was born Louis-Ferdinand Destouches in Courbevoie on May 27, 1894. His father, Ferdinand-Auguste, worked for an insurance company; his mother, Marguerite-Louise-Céline, was a dealer in lace. Soon after his birth, the Destouches family moved to the Passage Choiseul in Paris, close to his mother's small shop. Louis-Ferdinand attended public schools until 1904, when his parents sent him to Diepholz, Germany, in the hope that he would learn a second language and thereby improve his prospects for a business career; the following year he attended an English boarding school.

After returning to France, Céline prepared his *baccalauréat*, passing the first part of his examination in 1912. Later that year, one of many disputes with his parents led to his three-year enlistment in a cavalry unit. His right arm and shoulder were wounded in Ypres on October 25, 1914; he won commendations for his conduct under fire (evidence shows that, despite claims to the affirmative, Celine was never trepanned). The following year he underwent a period of convalescence in London, where he pursued numerous dancers and actresses.

From 1916 to 1917, Céline worked as an agent for a French lumber company in the Cameroons. He spent the next three years working for the Rockefeller Foundation in Brittany, delivering lectures on the prevention of tuberculosis and completing his second *baccalauréat* in July, 1919. He married Edith Follet; in 1920 their daughter Colette was born.

Two years after receiving his medical degree in 1923, Céline completed work on his doctoral thesis, "La Vie et l'œuvre de Philippe-Ignace Semmelweis," which earned for him a bronze medal from the University of Paris. This study of a doctor driven insane when the medical establishment refused to adopt his pioneering antiseptic procedures is an early example of Céline's preoccupation with pettiness and persecution.

Although his future as a conventional medical practitioner looked extremely promising, Destouches soon abandoned his family and practice at the Place de Lices and began work as a doctor for the League of Nations. From 1925 to 1927, he served in Switzerland, England, the Cameroons, and North America. Returning to Paris in 1928, he began working as a doctor by day and writing by night. Céline, who claimed that he began writing to raise money he could not earn as a doctor of the poor, began work in a public clinic in 1931.

The publication of *Journey to the End of the Night* in 1932 brought immediate fame to the pseudonymous Céline. Following the exploits of the anarchist Ferdinand Bardamu, this first of Céline's great autobiographical fantasies nearly won the coveted Goncourt Prize but instead received the less prestigious Renaudot Prize. In 1936, his second masterpiece, *Death on the Installment Plan*, recounted in flashback the misadventures of the incorrigible boy Ferdinand.

As World War II approached, Céline became a cultural pariah, because of his authorship of an appalling series of Fascist and anti-Semitic pamphlets. Although the fact that the pseudonym "Céline" stood for a nihilistic, paranoid persona does not excuse his inflammatory writing during the Nazi reign of terror, it should also be recognized that throughout his literary life the fiercely misanthropic writer showered invective on every sort of human target, including supporters of the Nazis.

In 1939, Céline attempted to enlist in the French army but was rejected because of poor health. During most of the war he worked as a doctor in Paris, visiting hospitals in Berlin in 1942. The following year he married the ballet dancer Lucette Almanzor (fascinated by classical dance, Céline wrote ballets throughout his career). In 1944, Céline and Lucette fled from France to Germany, eventually moving to Denmark in 1945. Accused by his home country of collaboration, he was imprisoned in Copenhagen from December, 1945, to February, 1947, during which time he was attacked in essays by French literati such as Jean-Paul Sartre. Although Céline was tried in absentia and found guilty by French courts in 1950, he received amnesty the following year. A minor resurgence of public interest preceded his death and secret burial in 1961.

Céline's writings offer a sweeping, farcical, bracingly uncompromising vision of humanity at its most pathetic and unpromising. As exemplified in his two most admired works, *Journey to the End of the Night* and *Death on the Installment Plan*, Céline's prose is notable for its unusual imagery and audacious language. His easily recognizable style, characterized by terse verbal ejaculations separated (or joined) by three dots, is widely credited with revolutionizing French literature with its wild, slang-filled vocabulary. His imagery is provocative, sometimes hallucinatory, and replete with exaggeration.

The bulk of Céline's works have been relatively neglected by scholars and translators, partly because they have been considered inferior but also because of the stigma that arose in the wake of his activities during the Nazi period. Nevertheless, his work has received increasing attention among writers and critics. Henry Miller and Kurt Vonnegut, Jr., are among the devotees who have expressed their admiration for this troubling literary innovator.

BIBLIOGRAPHICAL REFERENCES: *Céline and His Critics*, 1986, edited and translated by Stanford L. Luce, is a collection of French essays pertaining to various facets of Céline's life. J. H. Matthews, *The Inner Dream: Céline as Novelist*, 1978, is an extended treatment of the writer by a perceptive scholar of Surrealism and other modern French movements; Patrick McCarthy's *Céline: A Critical Biography*, 1975, approached its subject from a conventional biographical perspective. Milton Hindus, *The Crippled Giant*, 1960, is a major work by one of Céline's major correspondents. David O'Connell, *Louis-Ferdinand Céline*, 1976, and David Hayman, *Louis-Ferdinand Céline*, 1965, briefly summarize the author's life and work. Erika Ostrovsky's *Céline and His Vision*, 1967, and *Voyeur Voyant: A Portrait of Louis-Ferdinand Céline*, 1971, are flattering studies by a Céline enthusiast. Major authors who have written about Céline include Clifton Fadiman, "Misanthrope, Twentieth Century Style," *The New Yorker*, August 27, 1938, 56-58; George Steiner, "Cry Havoc," *London Mercury*, August 30, 1934, 106-115; John Updike, "The Strange Case of Dr. Destouches and M. Céline," *The New Yorker*, LII (September 13, 1976), 154-161; and Kurt Vonnegut, Jr., "A Nazi Sympathizer Defended at Some Cost," in *Palm Sunday*, 1981.

David Marc Fischer

BLAISE CENDRARS
Frédéric Louis Sauser

Born: La Chaux-de-Fonds, Switzerland
Date: September 1, 1887

Died: Paris, France
Date: January 21, 1961

Principal Works

NOVELS: *L'Or: La Merveilleuse Histoire du général Johann August Suter*, 1925 (*Sutter's Gold*, 1926); *Moravagine*, 1926 (English translation, 1968); *La Plan de l'aiguille*, 1927 (*Antarctic Fugue*, 1948); *Les Confessions de Dan Yack*, 1928; *Emmène-moi au bout du monde*, 1956 (*To the End of the World*, 1967).

POETRY: *Les Pâques à New York*, 1912 (*Easter in New York*, 1966); *La Prose du Transsibérien et de la petite Jehanne de France*, 1913 (*The Trans-Siberian Express*, 1964); *Le Panama: Ou, Les Aventures de mes sept oncles*, 1918 (*Panama: Or, The Adventures of My Seven Uncles*, 1931); *Dix-neuf Poèmes élastiques*, 1919; *Feuilles de route*, 1924, 1927; *Poésies complètes*, 1944; *Complete Postcards from the Americas*, 1976.

AUTOBIOGRAPHY: *L'Homme foudroyé*, 1945 (*The Astonished Man*, 1970); *La Main coupée*, 1946 (*Lice*, 1973); *Bourlinguer*, 1948 (*Planus*, 1972); *Le Lotissement du ciel*, 1949.

Although he later claimed that he was born in Paris, at the celebrated hotel on rue Saint-Jacques, Blaise Cendrars was, in fact, born in La Chaux-de-Fonds, Switzerland, in 1887, the son of a restless, peripatetic Swiss clock merchant. Truth and fancy, fact and myth, are inextricably blended in the narratives of his life, as in his poetry and fiction. "One of the greatest liars of all time," this worldwide adventurer, this "Marco Polo of the twentieth century," this "Homer of the Trans-Siberian," never lost sight of the fact that art is the lie which tells the truth.

Before he was out of his teens, Frédéric Louis Sauser had spent several years in St. Petersburg, in the ferment of prerevolutionary Russia. By 1911, he was in New York and had chosen the name Blaise Cendrars. His pseudonym suggests a major motif of his life and work: *cendres* (ashes), *ars* (art), and "Blaise," which he identified as a transmutation of *braise* (embers), with homophonic suggestion of "blaze," declare his lifelong insistence that "to write is to burn alive." Before World War I, after the publication of *Easter in New York*, he was established as a central figure in the Paris avant-garde. The lyrical incantatory quality of his innovative poetry left its mark on such writers as Guillaume Apollinaire, as well as the Dadaists, the Surrealists, and the cubists. *The Trans-Siberian Express*, for example, was printed in multicolored type on folded two-meter sheets with illustrations by Sonia Delaunay. With 150 copies printed, Cendrars announced, in a typical gesture, that his poem soared as high as the Eiffel Tower. Yet for all of his involvement with the various schools and "isms" of modernist art, Cendrars insisted that he stood apart from all movements.

True to his philosophy of immersion in experience and, as a foreigner, true to France, Cendrars enlisted in the Foreign Legion; in the fall of 1915 he was wounded by shell fire, and his right arm was amputated. Shattered by the war, physically and spiritually, Cendrars in his work increasingly recorded an apocalyptic sense of an age of disintegration. Such works as *Moravagine* address the chaos, the violence, the irrational, schizoid, and destructive forces at work in the modern world. After the war, Cendrars, still traveling, indulged his "world hunger" in such works as *Panama*, where he celebrated the European Express train as "the finest church in the world." Indicative of the scope of Cendrars' influence is the fact that *Panama* was translated and illustrated by John Dos Passos, who paid tribute in his foreword to the "creative tidal wave" of Cendrars' poetry.

Four novels published in the 1920's constitute his major achievement in fiction. *Sutter's Gold*, in terse prose and straightfoward narrative, tells the incredible but true story of John Augustus Sutter, the Swiss immigrant who lived the American Dream. One of the richest men in the world, he had already realized the agrarian-based dream of plenitude in the Garden of the New World when gold was discovered in his land, and he was utterly ruined by the mobs which devastated his California empire. A compelling tragic parable, it is one of the masterpieces of the American experience. If Sutter is one of the powerful creators inhabiting Cendrars' universe, the title character of his next novel, *Moravagine* (whose name means "death-to-the-vagina"), is one of the dark destroyers, a mad, sadistic, anarchic figure who quests nihilistic extinction throughout a chaotic world. Dan Yack, protagonist of the next two novels, alternates between a life of action and contemplative retreat, between pursuit of and flight from love. While the Dan Yack story may have been intended as a resolution of the tensions implicit in the first two novels—the polarity of making and unmaking, doing and being undone—these novels are not as successful as the first two.

Throughout the 1920's and 1930's, Cendrars continued his travels, turning increasingly to journalism, and, with the coming of World War II, he served as a war correspondent. His world shattered by yet another war, in which he again suffered personal tragedy (the death of his younger son), Cendrars renounced literature and embraced silence. He lived quietly in Aix-en-Provence, studying the Bible, the saints, and the mystics until he again exploded onto the literary scene with what may be his most remarkable work of all: the autobiographical tetralogy which begins with *The Astonished Man* and concludes with the ecstatic levitations of *Le Lotissement du ciel* (the settlement of the sky). These extraordinary works, at once autobiographical, mythical, and mystical, expand the possibilities of autobiographical narrative.

In the 1950's Cendrars returned to live in Paris, where he became a public figure, making radio broadcasts and receiving literary and cultural awards. He continued to write, working on unfinished novels such as the great love story of Mary Magdalene. He retained his power to shock, as in the novel *To the End of the World*, a slashing exposé of decadence. His imagination fertile and his pen active to the end, Cendrars died in Paris in 1961, having realized, perhaps, all of his dreams except his long-declared intention to book passage on the first journey to the moon. His literary achievement rich and diverse, his influence pervasive, he left behind a major body of poetry, substantial work in fiction and other genres, and a compelling personal legend. Cendrars evokes the modern cosmopolitan spirit as richly as any other twentieth century writer.

BIBLIOGRAPHICAL REFERENCES: Walter Albert, in "Blaise Cendrars: A Temporal Perspective," *Texas Studies in Literature and Language*, IV (1962), 321-329, and in his introduction to *Selected Writings of Blaise Cendrars*, 1966, suggests that Cendrars lacked discipline and form and thus his work never achieved its rich potential. Jay Bochner, on the other hand, in his *Blaise Cendrars: Discovery and Re-creation*, 1978, provides a more thoroughgoing and balanced assessment of Cendrars' complete work. Monique Chefdor, in the extensive introduction to Cendrars' *Complete Postcards from the Americas*, 1976, gives a useful and detailed overview of the life and work. For further study, see Jean Rousselot, *Blaise Cendrars*, 1955. See also Mary Ann Caws, "Blasie Cendrars: A Cinema of Poetry," in *The Inner Theatre of Recent French Poetry*, 1972; John Dos Passos, "Homer of the Transsiberian," in *Orient Express*, 1927; and Henry Miller, *The Books in My Life*, 1952.

H. R. Stoneback

AIMÉ CÉSAIRE

Born: Basse-Pointe, Martinique
Date: June 25, 1913

Principal Works

POETRY: *Cahier d'un retour au pays natal*, 1939, 1947, 1956 (*Memorandum on My Martinique*, 1947; best known as *Return to My Native Land*, 1968); *Les Armes miraculeuses*, 1946 (*Miraculous Weapons*, 1983); *Soleil cou coupé*, 1948 (*Beheaded Sun*, 1983); *Corps perdu*, 1950 (*Disembodied*, 1983); *Ferrements*, 1960 (*Shackles*, 1983); *Cadastre*, 1961 (*Cadastre: Poems*, 1973); *Moi, Laminaire*, 1982; *Aimé Césaire: The Collected Poetry*, 1983.

PLAYS: *Et les chiens se taisaient*, pb. 1956; *La Tragédie du Roi Christophe*, pb. 1963 (*The Tragedy of King Christophe*, 1964); *Une Saison au Congo*, pb. 1966 (*A Season in the Congo*, 1968); *Une Tempête, d'après "La Tempête" de Shakespeare: Adaptation pour un théâtre negre*, pr., pb. 1969 (*The Tempest*, 1974).

ESSAYS: *Discours sur le colonialisme*, 1950 (*Discourse on Colonialism*, 1972).

MISCELLANEOUS: *Œuvres complètes*, 1976.

Aimé Fernand Césaire, once regarded as the most prominent poet of the Caribbean world, was a cofounder (with Léopold Senghor and Léon Damas) of the influential *négritude* movement, which sought to restore the cultural identity and dignity of colonized Africans in the 1950's. The second of six children, Aimé Césaire was the son of Fernand Césaire, who held a minor bureaucratic post as a tax inspector, and Marie Hermine, a dressmaker. While his family's standard of living was close to that of the rural poor, the level of education of both his father and his paternal grandfather, as well as his father's status as a functionary, set them apart from most black families in Martinique. Eugénie, widow of Aimé Césaire's grandfather, Fernand Césaire, assumed the role of first teacher to the Césaire children; under her tutelage, Aimé learned to read and write by the age of four, two years before he entered primary school. While primary education was free, secondary education necessitated considerable financial sacrifice. Nevertheless, Césaire's family moved to Fort-de-France in order to provide their children with a secondary education. Learning the French language and its culture (in addition to learning the first language of all Martinicans—Creole) was the paramount social goal for black children born into families attempting to achieve middle-class status. The family's conscious effort to inculcate French cultural norms made it easier for the Césaire children to acclimate themselves to the somewhat alien surroundings of the Lycée Victor Schoelcher in Fort-de-France. Yet as a writer and poet, Césaire would be faced much later with the painful task of cutting those ties to the French language and culture that he had developed in the process of assimilation.

At the urging of one of his teachers, Césaire went on to attend the Lycée Louis-le-Grand to prepare him for entrance into the École Normale Supérieure in Paris, where he met two African students who were to have an important personal influence on his black identity: Ousmane Socé and Léopold Senghor, both from Senegal. (Senghor was to become the first president of the independent republic of Senegal and Socé his first ambassador to the United States.) Senghor joined Césaire and Léon Damas in 1934 in a collective venture intended to bring together on the common ground of blackness the students from Africa and the West Indies. In 1947, Césaire joined the foremost black intellectuals and writers in French, as well as such white supporters as Jean-Paul Sartre, Albert Camus, and André Gide, in founding the literary and cultural journal *Présence africaine*, initially devoted to endorsing *négritude*, then to supporting the literature and thought of the black world in general.

It was Césaire who coined the neologism *négritude* in his call for a resurrection of black values and a war against cultural assimilation in an article written for the student newspaper, *L'Étudiant noir.* Yet Césaire was to lead a life of endless contradictions: He argued against cultural assimilation, for example, while preparing for the entrance examinations to the École Normale Supérieure. After the exams in 1935, he spent the summer in Martinique, where he began writing what was later to become *Return to My Native Land*. In 1939, when Césaire returned to Martinique for the longest uninterrupted stay of his adult life, the values that would nourish his literary and political activity for the next decade were firmly established.

On July 10, 1937, Césaire was married to Suzanne Roussy, a Martinican student whom he had met while working at the *L'Étudiant noir.* The first of their several children was born in 1938. (The marriage eventually ended after a long separation, and Césaire never remarried.) Unlike most writers of his generation in Europe, Aimé Césaire spent the war years at home, primarily writing. He was also elected mayor of Fort-de-France and deputy from central Martinique on the Communist ticket. Thus, the Surrealist poet committed to black identity soon found himself representing a colonial branch of a Stalinist political party—another contradiction. (Césaire's break with the Party came in 1956, and in 1958 he led the independent Socialist Martinican Progressive Party.) From 1941 to 1945, Césaire edited the literary magazine *Tropiques*. The poems written during that period were published as *Miraculous Weapons*, a collection highly praised by the Surrealist poet André Breton. Yet Césaire's Surrealist practice as a poet reached its peak in 1948, with the publication of *Beheaded Sun*. While *Shackles* is a more mature work, it affirms the crisis in Césaire's vision of a unified neo-African civilization. Between 1960 and 1982, Césaire published no further collections of poetry, and while his final collection, published in 1982, was favorably received, most of its themes and techniques were more fully and convincingly treated in *Shackles*.

After 1960, Césaire launched a second career as a playwright, collaborating with the French director Jean-Marie Serreau. Together they produced one very significant play, *The Tragedy of King Christophe*, and *The Tempest*, a very original adaptation of the well-known play by Shakespeare. *A Season in the Congo* has been less well received, in part on political grounds, in part because the author may have been too emotionally involved with his subject, the political murder of Patrice Lumumba. These plays, as well as the earlier *Et les chiens se taisaient* (and the dogs hold their noise), are viewed as tragedies about decolonization.

Césaire's activity as a major poet spans two decades, from the late 1930's to the late 1950's. His poetic as well as his political contribution consists of an abrupt and violent departure from the dominant French tradition in search of his African past; a replacing of European cultural norms by a syncretic mythology; a dramatization of the hopeful historical period of independence; and a reflective, elegiac rendering of the gap between aspiration and fulfillment in politics.

BIBLIOGRAPHICAL REFERENCES: James A. Arnold, *Modernism and Négritude: The Poetry and Poetics of Aimé Césaire*, 1981, is a detailed study of Césaire's life and work in the context of the cutural and literary movements of the period. Susan Frutkin's work, *Aimé Césaire: Black Between Worlds*, 1973, describes Césaire's conflict between being French and being Martinican. Ronnie Leah Scharfman's *Engagement and the Language of the Subject in the Poetry of Aimé Césaire*, 1987, is an excellent, although brief, study of the treatment of language, *négritude*, and women in Césaire's poetry. See also Thomas Hale, "Structural Dynamics in a Third World Classic: Aimé Césaire's *Cahier d'un retour au pays natal*," *Yale French Studies*, LIII (1976), 163-174; Hilary Okam, "Aspects of Imagery and Symbolism in the Poetry of Aimé Césaire," *Yale French Studies*, LIII (1976), 175-196; Ronnie Scharfman, "Repetition and Absence: The Discourse of Deracination in Aimé Césaire's *Nocturne d'un nostalgie*," *The French Review*, LVI (1983), 572-578; Émile Snyder, "Aimé Césaire: The Reclaiming of the Land," in *Exile and Tradition: Studies in African and Caribbean Literature*, 1976, edited by Rowland Smith; and Émile Snyder, "A Reading of Aimé Césaire's *Return to My Native Land*," *L'Esprit créateur*, X (1970), 197-212.

Genevieve Slomski

RAYMOND CHANDLER

Born: Chicago, Illinois
Date: July 23, 1888

Died: La Jolla, California
Date: March 26, 1959

Principal Works

MYSTERY AND DETECTIVE NOVELS: *The Big Sleep*, 1939; *Farewell, My Lovely*, 1940; *The High Window*, 1942; *The Lady in the Lake*, 1943; *The Little Sister*, 1949 (also known as *Marlowe*); *The Long Goodbye*, 1953; *Playback*, 1958.

MYSTERY AND DETECTIVE STORIES: *Five Murderers*, 1944; *Five Sinister Characters*, 1945; *Finger Man and Other Stories*, 1946; *Red Wind*, 1946; *The Simple Art of Murder*, 1950; *Killer in the Rain*, 1964; *The Smell of Fear*, 1965; *The Midnight Raymond Chandler*, 1971.

CORRESPONDENCE: *Selected Letters of Raymond Chandler*, 1981.

Raymond Chandler was one of the most significant writers of detective fiction in the United States. Like Dashiell Hammett, Chandler took the murder story out of the English drawing room and put it back on the mean streets, where violence and mayhem generally took place. He was born in Chicago on July 23, 1888, the son of Maurice Benjamin Chandler, an engineer from Philadelphia, and Florence Thornton, from Waterford, Ireland. His father worked for various railroads, and the family lived a peripatetic existence. His parents were divorced (his father was an alcoholic), and Chandler and his mother moved to London, living with her family. In 1900 he entered Dulwich College, one of the better English public schools. After leaving Dulwich, he sought a literary career, composing poetry and writing reviews, but met with only marginal success. In 1913, shortly before World War I, he returned to the United States and settled in Los Angeles, the city he was to make famous through his creation, Philip Marlowe.

In 1917 Chandler joined the Canadian army and fought on the Western Front. After the war he returned to Southern California, and, although he still wanted to pursue a literary career, for economic reasons he became a businessman. Rootless in the most rootless of cities, he was married to Cissy Pascal, eighteen years his senior. During the 1920's Chandler was a successful oil executive, but by the early 1930's his life was in turmoil. He began drinking heavily, and in 1932, in the depths of the Great Depression, he was fired. He again turned to literature.

At the age of forty-five literary success seemed unlikely. Yet, drawn to pulp magazines, particularly *Black Mask*, and to the works of Dashiell Hammett, Chandler began to write. "Blackmailers Don't Shoot" was published in December, 1933, and during the next six years Chandler wrote approximately twenty short stories, many appearing in *Black Mask*. Never making much money during those years, Chandler explored the genre of the detective story and found his own voice. He experimented with various creations for his lead character and finally settled upon Philip Marlowe, a private detective. Chandler also discovered that, for him, a first-person narrator worked best. His short story years were his apprenticeship. Emphasizing blackmail and kidnapping, with money and sex as motives, and with violence, actual and potential, always in the background, Chandler's stories were in the mainstream of hard-boiled detective fiction of the 1930's.

Chandler was more of a literary stylist than many of his pulp magazine contemporaries. His English education had perhaps inculcated in him a greater awareness of the craft of writing, and his experience as an outsider—first in England and then in the United States—may have given him a sensitivity for language and its uses. Influenced by Hammett and Ernest Hemingway, Chandler attempted to improve the reputation of a lightly regarded field of literature. Using metaphor and simile in dazzling ways, Chandler's stories had a unique tone and voice. He has often been imitated but never equaled. Philip Marlowe became Chandler's knight-errant. In his essay "The Simple Art of Murder," published in 1944,

Chandler described his detective. Marlowe is "a man of honor—by instinct . . .without thought of it, and certainly without saying it." Still, Marlowe was no saint, and over time he evolved, although the code he followed remained recognizable, hard-boiled but sentimental.

Chandler's first novel, *The Big Sleep*, was published in 1939. His decision to write longer works was partially economic—novels potentially paid better. Chandler also believed that his style and approach demanded a wider stage. His composing technique in his early novels was to use his previously produced short stories. He cannibalized their plots and stitched them together, forming a whole. Many criticized his plotting abilities (there were often loose ends), but for him the portrayal of a particular milieu was paramount. The evolving environment of Southern California, the power and corruption of wealth, the lives of those caught up in the labyrinth were the subjects of his novels.

Hollywood beckoned, and Chandler developed a love-hate relationship with the film industry. *The Big Sleep* (1946), starring Humphrey Bogart, became a film classic, and Chandler became a screenwriter himself. In his novel *The Little Sister*, he wrote about the corrupting influence of Hollywood's greed upon traditional American values. In 1953, as his wife lay dying, Chandler finished *The Long Goodbye*. Featuring Marlowe, the novel was Chandler's most ambitious attempt to stretch the possibilities of the detective genre. Longer than his early novels, *The Long Goodbye* is more the story of personal alienation and the fragility of friendships and family relations than a typical hard-boiled detective story. In *The Long Goodbye* Chandler hints of the familial difficulties later portrayed by Ross Macdonald. His last novel, *Playback*, published in 1958, was a minor coda. By then, with his wife dead, Chandler was drinking heavily and had attempted suicide. He died in 1959.

Chandler chose to write in a field which has, like science fiction, always been suspect, and although W. H. Auden argued that Chandler should be judged simply as a writer, it is as the creator of Philip Marlowe, private detective, that he will be remembered.

BIBLIOGRAPHICAL REFERENCES: The standard biography is by Frank MacShane, *The Life of Raymond Chandler*, 1976. An important early biography is by Philip Durham, *Down These Mean Streets a Man Must Go*, 1963. *Raymond Chandler Speaking*, 1962, edited by Dorothy Gardiner and Katherine Sorely Walker, is of considerable value. William Marling, *Raymond Chandler*, 1986, is both a brief biographical summary and a literary analysis of Chandler's work. Miriam Gross, in *The World of Raymond Chandler*, 1977, has brought together a collection of reflections on Chandler by such figures as Julian Symons, John Houseman, Clive James, Natasha Spender, and Jacques Barzun. Other studies include Jerry Speir, *Raymond Chandler*, 1981; Edward Margolies, *Which Way Did He Go? The Private Eye in Dashiell Hammett, Raymond Chandler, Chester Himes, and Ross Macdonald*, 1982; Peter Wolfe, *Something More than Night: The Case of Raymond Chandler*, 1985; and Keith Newlin, *Hard-boiled Burlesque: Raymond Chandler's Comic Style*, 1984.

Eugene S. Larson

BRUCE CHATWIN

Born: Sheffield, England
Date: May 13, 1940

Died: Nice, France
Date: January 17, 1989

Principal Works

TRAVEL SKETCH: *In Patagonia*, 1977.

NOVELS: *The Viceroy of Ouidah*, 1980; *On the Black Hill*, 1982; *The Songlines*, 1987; *Utz*, 1988.

In the twelve years prior to his death, Bruce Chatwin produced five books of superlative quality. In the process he invented a new form of the novel somewhere between travel literature, pure fiction, and the novel of ideas. He was born to a middle-class family in the Midlands at Sheffield. His father, Charles Leslie Chatwin, was a lawyer who served in the navy during the war. His mother was Margharita Turnell Chatwin. Chatwin was sent to a very good boys' school, Marlborough, and at the age of eighteen he was working as a porter at Sotheby's, the international art dealer. By chance he identified a Pablo Picasso gouache as a counterfeit, despite the fact that he had no formal training as an expert; on the strength of his talent for assessing paintings, he became a working member of the staff, specializing in the Impressionists, as well as dealing with art from the South Seas and Africa. By his early twenties he was a senior official at Sotheby's, and it was there that he met his wife, Elizabeth Chandler.

He left Sotheby's after an illness, advised by his physician to do some traveling. He went to Africa and studied archaeology at Edinburgh University for a short time. On the strength of some photographs he had taken in the desert, he was offered a job as an art consultant with the London *Sunday Times*. He worked there until 1975, often traveling to develop material for the paper, but in that year he decided that he wanted to go to Patagonia to write a book about that remote section of southern South America. *In Patagonia* was an enormous success, in part because it was quite unlike any normal travel literature. Everything Chatwin had done up to that time had been somewhat unusual, and his first book was consistent with that pattern: It was a kind of anti-travel book. Some critics disliked the work, but in the main the book was praised for its refusal to stick to the facts and its curious collection of local tall tales and eccentric history. He called the unusual mix of history, myth, autobiography, anthropology, and occasional fiction a "search."

Chatwin's next work took the idea of fusing fiction and fact a step further. Working on a book about the slave trade in Dahomey, Chatwin threw up fact for fiction by imagining the life of a slave trader who became so important to the local chiefs that he became a figure of political power in the old port of Ouidah, founding a dynasty which lasted into the twentieth century. While the resulting work, *The Viceroy of Ouidah*, is partly based on fact, the actual historical facts are hardly important to the grand, grotesque world of extravagant eccentricity which some critics believed was too enthusiastically inclined to rich description of sometimes comic, often colorfully vulgar and violent action. The work proved, however, that Chatwin was clearly an authentic and very original talent who could not be classified as a mere travel writer.

Chatwin's next book, *On the Black Hill*, could be seen as a drawing back from eccentric distances; set in the hills on the Welsh-English border, it revealed not only that Chatwin was enormously clever and blessed with a daring imagination (as the first two books had suggested) but also that he could write with considerable feeling. The tale of two Welsh twins living out their interdependent lives in the natural richness, and sometime social and physical squalor, of farm life had all the energy of the earlier books, but Chatwin's preternatural gift for telling seemingly unconnected stories and the fecundity of his descriptive talent came together in a novel that is tonally reminiscent of Thomas Hardy. Chatwin did not stay home for long, however; in *On the Black Hill*, the suggestion was made that men were meant to be wanderers, and Chatwin himself continued to wander through the world. The result was *The Songlines*, a peculiar study of aboriginal life in Australia told from an unnerving point of view which is partly autobiographical (the narrator is called Bruce) but again a charming mishmash of anthropology, anecdote, history, and fiction, held together by the philosophic quest for the answer to the question of whether, in settling down, man has offended God, who meant him always to wander.

Interestingly perverse in all of his work, Chatwin chose in his last novel, *Utz*, which was nominated for but did not win the Booker Prize, to explore the life of Utz, a rich man settled, almost to the point of claustral retreat, with his priceless collection of Meissen porcelain. Utz, the last of a line of Czech aristocrats, is surrounded by the collectivist state in Prague, jealously determined to take the figurines into nationalist ownership upon his death. Fastidiously detailed in its handling of the porcelain as art, the novel reminds the reader of Chatwin's early career at Sotheby's, but it goes further in ways which link it with his prior novels in its exploration of the obsessive search for value, for what makes life worth living.

"What might have been" is a legitimate speculation; Chatwin seems to have been on his way to making an important place for himself as one of the twentieth century's improvisational manipulators of the novel. Shortly after the publication of *Utz*, and following a long illness which had confined him to a wheelchair, Chatwin died at the age of forty-eight. He left five elegant, minor masterpieces: tiny, perfect works of art.

BIBLIOGRAPHICAL REFERENCES: There is a valuable interview with Chatwin in *Granta*, XXI (Spring, 1987), 21-37. On *In Patagonia*, see Sybille Bedford, *The New York Review of Books*, November 9, 1978, 45, and Alastair Reid, *The New Yorker*, LIV (October 9, 1978), 186. On *The Viceroy of Ouidah*, see John Thompson, *The New York Times Book Review*, December 4, 1980, 7; Ronald Nevans, *The Saturday Review of Literature*, November, 1980, 80; and John Hemming, *The Times Literary Supplement*, December 5, 1980, 1380. On *The Songlines*, see David Malouf, *The Times Literary Supplement*, September 4, 1987, 948; Phoebe-Lou Adams, *The Atlantic*, November, 1987, 122; and David Rieff, *The New Republic*, November 30, 1987, 36. On *Utz*, see Peter Conrad, *Observer*, September 25, 1988, 43. See also Patrick Leigh Fermor, *The Spectator*, February 18, 1989, 19; Redmond O'Hanlon, *Observer*, January 22, 1989; Kim Heron, "A Love-Hate Affair with Art," *The New York Times Book Review*, XCIV (January 15, 1989), 3; and Michele Field, *Publishers Weekly*, CCXXXII (August 7, 1987), 430.

Charles Pullen

JOHN CHEEVER

Born: Quincy, Massachusetts
Date: May 27, 1912

Died: Ossining, New York
Date: June 18, 1982

PRINCIPAL WORKS

SHORT FICTION: *The Way Some People Live*, 1943; *The Enormous Radio and Other Stories*, 1953; *The Housebreaker of Shady Hill and Other Stories*, 1958; *Some People, Places, and Things That Will Not Appear in My Next Novel*, 1961; *The Brigadier and the Golf Widow*, 1964; *The World of Apples*, 1974; *The Collected Stories of John Cheever*, 1978.

NOVELS: *The Wapshot Chronicle*, 1957; *The Wapshot Scandal*, 1964; *Bullet Park*, 1969; *Falconer*, 1977; *Oh What a Paradise It Seems*, 1982.

CORRESPONDENCE: *The Letters of John Cheever*, 1988.

Disparaged or neglected during much of his career, John Cheever eventually achieved a degree of literary recognition and respect, both as a novelist and as a writer of short stories, rivaled only by his friend Saul Bellow. Cheever was born in Quincy, Massachusetts, on May 27, 1912. The breakdown of his parents' marriage, coupled with his father's loss of self-esteem and his mother's growing independence, had a profound effect on the young Cheever. His expulsion from Thayer Academy in 1929 put an end to his formal education but started him on his way toward a literary career when *The New Republic* published his story "Expelled" the following year. Although Cheever served his literary apprenticeship during the Depression years, his writing, then and later, remained almost entirely free of the political themes that characterized the writing of many of his contemporaries.

Fiction, Cheever liked to say, is the most exalted form of human communication, as indeed it is in his best works. He was equally insistent that it is not "crypto-autobiography." Here, however, Cheever was being less than honest, for while his stories and novels do not record his life per se, they do reflect the author's own obsessive doubts and desires, which he struggled so hard to keep from public view and which in the fiction he tended to treat in comic fashion (thus defusing its potential explosiveness). The surface of that fiction, like the gentlemanly pose Cheever liked to adopt when dealing with interviewers, formed a genial mask behind which lay the terrors of Cheever's world. The simple, highly readable surface of his seemingly realistic prose first lulls the reader into complacent acceptance and then suddenly slips to reveal the presence of a depth of fantasy and fear. His realistic depiction of his largely affluent, generally suburban characters is deceptive insofar as it masks the spiritual longings which they find so difficult to fulfill or even acknowledge in the modern age. Cheever treats his modern pilgrims with a mixture of comic affirmation and ironic skepticism as they and their author make their way toward the spiritual light. The characters share with Cheever the desire to "leech self-pity" out of their emotional spectrums, to overcome their dependency on alcohol and drugs, and to celebrate the world that lies before them, "like a stupendous dream."

Yet the affirmations do not come easily. Against the desire for transcendence and spiritual wholeness, Cheever posits the discontinuity of his characters' world, or, rather, the discontinuity of their relationship to that world and the similar discontinuity of the narratives in which he places them. Their affluence and social status prove precarious, and their lives are beset by a host of financial, psychological, and spiritual uncertainties. Driving around their well-kept communities or commuting to work, they suffer attacks of "otherness." Even in their jobs, communities, and homes they feel like "spiritual nomads" wandering the Westchester hills in search of some lost wholeness of being. Not surprising, many of them suffer the pangs of nostalgia, the most dread of all the ills in Cheever's fiction, for nostalgia turns one away from the world and the transcendent vision it embodies to a morbid fascination with one's past and one's self. The connection between self and world is neither linear nor logical; consequently, Cheever's fictions, both long and short, follow no clearly causal line of plot development but instead make abundant use of narrative parallelism, intuitive leaps, and strange correspondences. It is a fiction less of logic than of magic—oddly so, given that Cheever has so often been read as a writer of conventional realist fiction.

The stories in Cheever's first book, *The Way Some People Live*, were realistic (written in imitation of Ernest Hemingway). *The Enormous Radio and Other Stories* evidences a groping toward a more personal style and vision, one in which the metamorphosis of the real into the fantastic, the factual into the psychological, has begun to play a decisive role, along with an inchoate interest in narrative form. In 1957 he published his first novel, *The Wapshot Chronicle*, which his more convention-minded reviewers denigrated as a mere collection of stories badly spliced together. The following year he published a third collection, *The Housebreaker of Shady Hill and Other Stories*, which had all the unity of a novel. More novels and more collections appeared before the appearance of "Cheever's triumph," the novel *Falconer*, in 1977, which, despite the shift in setting from suburb to prison, still deals with the typically Cheeveresque theme of confinement, both emotional and spiritual.

The success of *Falconer* led to the publication of the retrospective collection, *The Collected Stories of John Cheever* and the long-overdue recognition of Cheever as a major American writer. Just as important, *The Collected Stories of John Cheever* changed the way in which American reviewers and critics viewed the short-story form: no longer as inferior to the novel, but as its equal. Cheever's career had especially suffered as a result of the supposed disparity. That he was a writer of stories, and worse, of stories which were published in *The New Yorker*, was, critics felt, a crippling limitation. Furthermore, that he should appear to be an apologist from the American middle class in an age of social activism and a realist in an age of innovation sealed his doom. Only toward the end of his career did the critics begin to reexamine Cheever's fiction and their own assumptions about it. Having overcome the narrowness of critical fashion and having exorcised his own personal demons, Cheever enjoyed a brief period of triumph before his death. He died of cancer on June 18, 1982, shortly after completing a truncated version of the "bulky novel" he had planned, *Oh What a Paradise It Seems*, a typically Cheeveresque combination of irony and affirmation.

BIBLIOGRAPHICAL REFERENCES: Resources for the study of Cheever and his work are especially good. There are five useful bibliographies: Francis J. Bosha's *John Cheever: A Reference Guide*, 1981 (the annotated listing of reviews is especially noteworthy); Dennis Coates's checklist in *Bulletin of Bibliography*, XXXVI (1979), 1-13, and another by Coates, a supplement, in *Critical Essays on John Cheever*, 1983, edited by R. G. Collins; Deno Trakas' "John Cheever: An Annotated Secondary Bibliography (1943-1978)," *Resources for American Literary Study*," IX (1979), 181-199; and Robert A. Morace's bibliographical essay in *Contemporary Authors*, 1986, edited by James Martine, which discusses all available resources. Scott Donaldson's *John Cheever: A Biography*, 1988, is thorough and dependable—far more so than the interesting memoir *Home Before Dark*, 1984, written by Susan Cheever, the author's daughter. Donaldson has also edited *Conversations with John Cheever*, 1987. Samuel Coale's *John Cheever*, 1977, and Lynne Waldeland's *John Cheever*, 1979, are both introductory in nature. George Hunt's *John Cheever: The Hobgoblin Company of Love*, 1983, is longer and less limited in scope. *Critical Essays*, 1982, edited by R. G. Collins, reprints some of the most important reviews, interviews, and criticism, as well as a handful of new pieces, including Coale's "Cheever and Hawthorne: The American Romancer's Art," one of the finest Cheever essays yet to appear. Collins' two Cheever essays, "Fugutive Time," *Studies in American Fiction*, XII (1984), 175-188, and "From Subject to Object and Back Again," *Twentieth Century Literature*, XXVIII (1982), 1-13, are particularly insightful. James O'Hara's two essays on *The Wapshot Chronicle* (one critical, the other textual) deserve special mention: *Critique*, XXII (1980), 20-30, and *Massachusetts Studies in English*, VII (1980), 20-25. See also the essays on *Falconer* by Glen M. Johnson, in *Studies in American Fiction*, IX

(1981), and Robert A. Morace's lengthy "From Parallels to Paradise: The Lyric Vision of John Cheever," *Twentieth Century Literature* XXXV (1989), which analyzes Cheever's aesthetic in terms of his vision and thereby provides a useful corrective to those who regard Cheever as a writer of conventional fiction and as a master storyteller but a failed novelist.

Robert A. Morace

FRANK CHIN

Born: Berkeley, California
Date: February 25, 1940

PRINCIPAL WORKS

PLAYS: *The Chickencoop Chinaman*, pr. 1972; *The Year of the Dragon*, pr. 1974.
SHORT FICTION: *The Chinaman Pacific and Frisco R. R. Co.*, 1987.
ANTHOLOGY: *Aiiieeeee!: An Anthology of Asian-American Writers*, 1975 (with others).

Best known for his drama, Frank Chew Chin, Jr., belongs to the vanguard of the Asian American writers who began to publish in the 1960's and 1970's. Appearing on the literary scene in the wake of the Civil Rights movement and the black arts movements, Asian-American writers of Chin's generation differed from most of their Asian American predecessors in that they depicted characters, situations, and sentiments that exploded the majority of white stereotypes of Asian Americans. Chin's generation sought to establish a more realistic, less sentimentalized image of Asian Americans, with their strengths and weaknesses unvarnished, their joys and sorrows revealed, and their humanity unmitigated.

Born on February 25, 1940, in Berkeley, California, Frank Chin grew up in the Chinatowns of Oakland and San Francisco. He was graduated from the University of California at Berkeley, winning several prizes for fiction writing. In 1961, he earned a fellowship to the writers' workshop at the University of Iowa. After Iowa, Chin worked for the Southern Pacific Railroad; he was the first Chinese American brakeman on the rails laid by his forefathers. Chin left the railroad company to be a writer-producer for KING-TV in Seattle, airing several shows on the Public Broadcasting Service (PBS) and *Sesame Street*. Chin left Seattle to teach Asian American studies at San Francisco State University and the University of California at Davis. With a group of scholars, he organized the Combined Asian American Resources Project (CARP), which collected materials now housed in the Bancroft Library of the University of California at Berkeley. CARP has since been responsible for the publication of key Asian American texts by the University of Washington Press. In 1972, Chin founded the Asian American Theater Workshop in San Francisco with the support of the American Conservatory Theater (where he has been a writer-in-residence).

Chin's earliest recognition came in the form of awards for his oft-anthologized short stories, many gathered in *The Chinaman Pacific and Frisco R. R. Co.* Several of Chin's stories are set in Chinatown, San Francisco, and are dominated by themes of decay, death, and the lack of communication between Chinatown and Anglo society as well as between the different generations of Chinatown dwellers.

Chin has published numerous essays, mostly literary or social commentaries (sometimes verging on diatribes) that seek to clarify Asian American history and dispel the stereotypes of Asian Americans that Chin perceives white society to have created. These stereotypes, Chin maintains, have been fueled by love and hate. The odious are the stereotypes of the Yellow Peril or the sinister (but ultimately impotent) evil imperators, such as Fu Manchu; such stereotypes lie behind the United States, anti-Asian exclusionary immigration laws, and anti-Japanese internment camps. Equally insidious are the stereotypes of love from which white society has created the myth of Asian Americans as a model minority, a myth used to palliate white guilt vis-à-vis African Americans and whose effect pits Asian Americans against other ethnic minorities. According to Chin, the white-controlled publishing establishment has helped to perpetuate such myths by printing works that depict Asian Americans in stereotyped ways. Chin's discursive rhetoric is always inventive and vigorous but may strike some ears as shrill. While his critique of stereotypes is generally justified, some readers object to his confining definition of "Asian Americans" as only those Asians born in the United States.

Chin's plays *The Chickencoop Chinaman* and *The Year of the Dragon* illustrate well his ideas about ethnic minorities. Chin is the first Chinese American playwright to have had serious drama produced on the New York stage and on national television. In resisting stereotypes, in defining a truer-to-life (if abrasive) identity for Asian Americans, Chin has sometimes been described as the John Osborne, the angry young man, of his generation of Chinese Americans. Painful truths told with exuberant verbal pyrotechnics are trademarks of Chin's theater, and the characteristic gamut of his language ranges from black ghetto dialect to hipster talk to authentic Chinatown Cantonese (not the imaginary Hollywood cant of Charlie Chan).

The Chickencoop Chinaman treats the theme of identity through dispelling stereotypes, demythologizing, and disillusion. It is experimental in technique, with an almost cinematic use of montage, flashbacks in time, symbolic stage sets, and surrealistic, dreamlike sequences. Each of the play's two acts has a scene in Limbo (a surreal transitional time-space located between realistic time-spaces), a sequence recollecting a past obsession with a mythic figure (the miracle-working Helen Keller in act 1, the popular culture hero Lone Ranger in act 2), and scenes set in the realistic location of 1960's Pittsburgh, where the problem of the Chinese American protagonist's identity is resolved. The protagonist must struggle to locate his identity somewhere between the image of the virile African American boxer-athlete and that of the emasculated, timid chicken of a Chinaman.

The Chickencoop Chinaman perplexed most Anglo reviewers when it was staged. Chin's second play, *The Year of the Dragon*, is more conventionally structured and was accorded a national audience via a television production by Public Broadcasting Service's PBS Theatre in America. *The Year of the Dragon* also treats the theme of identity but focuses more sharply on questions of worth: the worth of an individual to loved ones (family) and of a minority ethnic group to its majority society. These questions are fleshed out in the exposition of the psychological conflicts and confrontations in a well-established family of San Francisco's Chinatown. Again, it is stereotypes—familial and societal—that chiefly obscure individual worth and ethnic identity.

Frank Chin's literary career has significantly enriched and defined the field of Asian American literature. His well-crafted short fiction, his abrasive essays, and above all his daring and verbally exuberant drama have brought the richly unique and deeply human complexities of Asian American life to the attention of the American public. Evenhandedly, he has criticized the falsifying myths and stereotypes of self and ethnicity held by both Asians and whites. Frank Chin is an important pioneer among the Asian Americans who wrote about a slice of American ethnic life with a distinctively Asian American voice.

BIBLIOGRAPHICAL REFERENCES: For a thoroughgoing general commentary on Chin's literary achievement and stature, see "Chinatown Cowboys and Warrior Women," in *Asian American Literature: An Introduction to the Writings and Their Social Context*, 1982, by Elaine Kim. Dorothy Ritsuko McDonald has written a valuable introduction to *"The Chickencoop Chinaman" and "The Year of the Dragon": Two Plays*, 1981. Eight reviews are conveniently reproduced in "The Chickencoop Chinaman," *New York Theatre Critics' Reviews*, XXXIII, no. 15 (September 25, 1972), 237-240. A brief but balanced review of *The Year of the Dragon* was written by Clive Barnes in *The New York Times*, June 3, 1974, 39.

C. L. Chua

NOAM CHOMSKY

Born: Philadelphia, Pennsylvania
Date: December 7, 1928

PRINCIPAL WORKS

LINGUISTICS: *Syntactic Structures*, 1957; *Current Issues in Linguistic Theory*, 1964; *Aspects of the Theory of Syntax*, 1965; *Topics in the Theory of Generative Grammar*, 1966; *Cartesian Linguistics*, 1966; *Language and Mind*, 1967; *Studies on Semantics in Generative Grammar*, 1972; *The Logical Structure of Linguistic Theory*, 1975; *Reflections on Language*, 1975; *Language and Responsibility*, 1979; *Rules and Representations*, 1980; *Lectures on Government and Binding*, 1981; *Knowledge of Language: Its Nature, Origin, and Use*, 1985.

POLITICS: *American Power and the New Mandarins*, 1969; *At War with Asia: Essays on Indochina*, 1970; *For Reasons of State*, 1973; *Peace in the Middle East? Reflections on Justice and Nationhood*, 1974; *After the Cataclysm: Postwar Indochina and the Reconstruction of Imperial Ideology*, 1979 (with Edward S. Herman); *The Washington Connection and Third World Fascism*, 1979 (with Herman); *Towards a New Cold War: Essays on the Current Crisis and How We Got There*, 1982; *The Fateful Triangle: The United States, Israel, and the Palestinians*, 1983; *Turning the Tide: U.S. Intervention in Central America and the Struggle for Peace*, 1985; *Pirates and Emperors: International Terrorism in the Real World*, 1986; *The Chomsky Reader*, 1987; *The Culture of Terrorism*, 1987; *Manufacturing Consent: The Political Economy of the Mass Media*, 1988 (with Herman).

Noam Chomsky achieved fame both as a pioneer in the field of linguistics and as a political dissenter. He was born on December 7, 1928, in Philadelphia, the son of William Chomsky, a Russian Jewish immigrant who taught Hebrew, and his wife, Elsie (Simonofsky) Chomsky. During his studies for a doctorate, Chomsky engaged in the theoretical work that produced a new type of linguistics: generative transformational grammar. Soon after receiving a Ph.D. in linguistics from the University of Pennsylvania in 1955, he became assistant professor of modern languages and linguistics at Massachusetts Institute of Technology (MIT). When his groundbreaking *Syntactic Structures* was published in 1957, Noam Chomsky's unorthodox linguistic theories had only a few supporters in the academic world. He gained a wider reputation in 1959 by publishing a blistering review of *Verbal Behavior* (1957), a work by the behaviorist psychologist B. F. Skinner. By 1965, when Chomsky's second major theoretical work, *Aspects of the Theory of Syntax*, appeared, his theories had won acceptance in universities throughout the United States.

From the mid-1960's onward, Chomsky was known as the most articulate opponent of the Vietnam War in academic circles. In 1969 his essays on the Vietnam War and on American liberal intellectuals' alleged responsibility for that war, written for various magazines since 1966, were published in *American Power and the New Mandarins*. Later, two other collections of essays on the war appeared, *At War with Asia* and *For Reasons of State*; the latter also included an attack on behaviorist psychology and two essays expounding Chomsky's political ideal of libertarian socialism.

With the end of the Vietnam War, Chomsky's type of political analysis went out of fashion for a while. In the 1980's his popularity was revived somewhat by widespread anxiety about the growing United States involvement in Central America. In *The Fateful Triangle*, Chomsky accuses the United States of encouraging what he regards as Israeli intransigence toward the Palestinian Arabs; in *Turning the Tide*, he attacks American policy toward Nicaragua and El Salvador; and in *Manufacturing Consent*, he criticizes as biased American press and television coverage of United States foreign policy. By the end of 1988, Chomsky was still writing and speaking about American foreign policy and was still teaching courses in linguistics at MIT.

Prior to Chomsky, linguistics accepted behaviorist psychology's explanation of how human beings learn language. Behaviorists, who saw no substantial difference between animal learning and human learning, contended that human beings learn language the way they learn anything else, by response to environmental stimulus and by habit. Chomsky argues that the speed with which children learn their native language and their ability to create new sentences that they have not heard before cast doubt on any stimulus-response theory of language learning. Instead, Chomsky contends, children have innate genetic equipment, shared with none of the lower animals, allowing them to grasp the grammar of their native tongue.

Chomsky insists that linguistics go beyond the mere description of previously undescribed languages. Its goals, he argues, ought to be those of making explicit that set of rules, or generative grammar, by which the native speaker of a language produces all grammatical sentences and only grammatical sentences; of stating such rules with mathematical precision; and of discovering the universal grammar, or set of rules governing speech production in all languages. In a generative grammar, Chomsky contends, the sounds and words of a sentence, the surface structure, are generated from the deep structure, those underlying grammatical relationships most important to meaning, through transformational operations. Chomsky uses this deep-structure/surface-structure dichotomy to explain such previously unexplained phenomena as sentence ambiguity.

In his politics as in his linguistics, Chomsky is an iconoclast. Although sometimes critical of Soviet actions, Chomsky rejects the Cold War dichotomy between a righteous United States and an evil Soviet Union in favor of a dichotomy between bullying big powers and righteous small countries. He sees American intervention in both Vietnam in the 1960's and Central America in the 1980's as an act of aggression by a big power against smaller countries; he regards such intervention as immoral in principle and as a reflection of deep-rooted imperialistic tendencies. The real goal of American foreign policy makers, according to Chomsky, is not to promote democracy but to secure for American corporate interests the markets and resources of the Third World.

Chomsky thinks that Americans, like Russians, can be blinkered by ideology. In the 1960's, he saw the influence of behaviorism behind liberal intellectuals' support for, and involvement in the making of, America's Vietnam policy. In the 1980's, he argued that an unthinking acceptance of the dogma of the United States' inevitably beneficent role in the world keeps journalists from sufficiently criticizing the actions of either their own government or the governments of such U.S. allies as El Salvador and Israel.

During the Vietnam War, critics accused Chomsky of making too sweeping an indictment of his fellow intellectuals, of resorting too often to vituperation rather than rational argument, of underestimating the dangers to American security, and of applying simplistic moralism to a complex moral dilemma. Chomsky's polemics of the 1980's aroused similar complaints. Yet despite the opposition that it provoked, Chomsky's relentless hammering undoubtedly did much to make American public opinion, by the end of the 1980's, profoundly skeptical about the benefits of United States military intervention abroad.

Although Chomsky's political views have been considered dogmatic by some, his linguistic theory is no inflexible dogma. Criticized by other scholars, it has been modified by Chomsky himself. The deep-structure/surface-structure dichotomy, for example, was first stated explicitly in 1965; his sharp distinction between the grammaticality and the meaningfulness of a sentence was erased in 1965, only to be reasserted five years later. Sociolinguists fault Chomsky for ignoring the societal context of language use, philosophers have questioned his notion of an innate human faculty for learning language, and some of his own disciples have at times disagreed with their master.

Yet however much Chomsky's linguistic theories have been disputed, it is indisputable that Chomsky is one of the major thinkers of the twentieth century, a man read as much for the questions he raised as for the answers he tried to give. His theories revived the old debate among philosophers about the existence of the mind. By discrediting behaviorism, Chomsky forced rethinking among psychologists as well, stimulating research on speech perception and childhood language acquisition.

BIBLIOGRAPHICAL REFERENCES: Daniel Yergin, "The Chomskyan Revolution," *The New York Times Magazine*, December 3, 1972, 42, provides a good intellectual biography of Chomsky the linguist. "John Is Easy to Please," in Ved Mehta, *John Is Easy to Please: Encounters with the Written and the Spoken Word*, 1971, paints a vivid word picture of the scholarly controversy aroused by Chomsky's theories. Other good surveys include Justin Leiber, *Noam Chomsky: A Philosophical Overview*, 1975, and Fred D'Agostino, *Chomsky's System of Ideas*, 1986. "The Chomskyan Revolution," in Frederick J. Newmeyer, *The Politics of Linguistics*, 1986, gives a good account of the spread of Chomskyanism in American academe in the 1960's and the emergence of rival schools of thought later. For a good brief account of Chomsky's political activity in the 1960's, see "Noam Chomsky," in *Current Biography*, 1970, 80-83. Two works place Chomsky's views on the war within a wider context: Sandy Vogelgesang, *The Long Dark Night of the Soul: The American Intellectual Left and the Vietnam War*, 1974, and "The War in Vietnam: The Perspective of the Intellectual," in Charles Kadushin, *The American Intellectual Elite*, 1974. For an example of Vietnam-era criticism of Chomsky's politics, see Dennis Wrong, "Chomsky: Of Thinking and Moralizing," *Dissent*, XVII (January/February, 1970), 75-81; for a critique from the 1980's, see Alan Tonelson, "Institutional Structure Blues," *The New York Times Book Review*, April 13, 1986, 28. For details on Chomsky's political activity in the 1980's, the reader may consult Paul Barker, "Noam Chomsky's Two Worlds," *New Society*, LVI (April 2, 1981), 7-10, and Brian Morton, "Chomsky Then and Now," *The Nation*, CCXLVI (May 7, 1988), 646-652.

Paul D. Mageli

KATE CHOPIN

Born: St. Louis, Missouri
Date: February 8, 1851

Died: St. Louis, Missouri
Date: August 22, 1904

PRINCIPAL WORKS

SHORT FICTION: *Bayou Folk*, 1894; *A Night in Arcadie*, 1897.
NOVELS: *At Fault*, 1890; *The Awakening*, 1899.
MISCELLANEOUS: *The Complete Works of Kate Chopin*, 1969.

Katherine O'Flaherty Chopin may well be the most important American female realist writer of the late nineteenth century, and in *The Awakening* she produced a masterpiece worthy of comparison with Gustave Flaubert's *Madame Bovary* (1857; English translation, 1886). The daughter of the rich Irish immigrant Thomas O'Flaherty and his second wife, Eliza Feris, a descendant of an old Creole family, Katherine O'Flaherty was born in St. Louis Missouri, on February 8, 1851. When she was four years old, her father died in a railway accident; the event affected her deeply, and the account of a similar catastrophe plays a central role in "The Story of an Hour" (1894).

Four generations of women lived in the O'Flaherty household when Kate was young. Especially influential was her great-grandmother Victoria Verdon Charleville, who taught her music and French; Chopin learned to speak and play flawlessly. Madame Charleville also told her great-granddaughter many stories about old St. Louis without moralizing her tales. From her, Chopin learned to present her accounts without attempting to condemn characters or draw conclusions for her audience.

After receiving her degree from the St. Louis Academy of the Sacred Heart in 1868, she married Oscar Chopin, a prosperous New Orleans businessman who was tolerant of his wife's unconventional habits, such as smoking and going about unescorted. Together the couple had six children.

In 1879, following financial reverses, the family moved to Cloutierville, Natchitoches Parish, Louisiana, the setting of many of Chopin's best stories. Oscar Chopin died of swamp fever in Janury, 1883; Kate Chopin successfully managed the family business for a year before returning to her mother's house in St. Louis. Her mother's death the next year depressed her. To help her cope with her grief, her obstetrician, Dr. Frederick Kolbenheyer, urged her to try her hand at creative writing.

Her first publication appeared in 1888, and the first volume of *America*, a magazine published in Chicago, carried Chopin's poem "If It Might Be" in its January 10, 1889, issue. Over the next decade she wrote some one hundred short stories and three novels (one of these she destroyed) that introduced readers to a new region of the United States and that broke new ground in the exploration of the female psyche. The harsh reviews of *The Awakening*, a novel widely regarded at the time as immoral, shocked and depressed her. Between 1900 and her death in 1904 she wrote little and published only three pieces, two of them in the children's magazine *Youth's Companion*.

Although *The Awakening* is her boldest as well as her best work, Chopin was never a conventional writer. Even her first attempt at long fiction, *At Fault*, breaks with tradition. It was only the sixth American novel to treat divorce and the first to recognize that in some cases dissolving a marriage is the best course to follow. Early short stories also anticipate the central concern of *The Awakening*, Edna Pontellier's quest for fulfillment. "Euphrasie," written in 1888, presents a traditional woman who lets others, namely men, decide her fate. Paula Von Stoltz in "Wiser than a God" (1889) rejects marriage for a career, and the heroine in "A Point at Issue" (1889) agrees to wed only because she believes that she can remain independent within marriage. Chopin neither praises nor condemns any of these women; she merely records their lives to suggest the possibilities available.

In the larger canvas of the novel, Chopin can more fully explore Edna Pontellier's mind, again without judging her extramarital affair or her suicide. Edna sees various role models: the happily married, unadventurous Adèle Ratignolle; the independent pianist Madame Reisz; the sensual Alcée Arobin, who becomes Edna's lover for a time; and the enigmatic Robert Lebrun, with whom she might have a fulfilling relationship if only they did not abandon each other at crucial moments. At the end of the work Edna emerges into full consciousness to assert her liberty by embracing death.

Accurately recording the speech, habitat, and customs of Creoles, Acadians, blacks, and Indians of the bayou country of Louisiana, Kate Chopin presented a previously unexplored literary landscape. Unlike the local colorists with whom she has been linked, she did not, however, indulge in nostalgia or sentimentality, and her settings remain exactly that, never assuming the primacy they have in much of the period's regional writing. Even more revolutionary are her explorations of the mental landscapes of her heroines and her appreciation of the power of sexual passion at a time when even male American authors generally shunned this subject. "The Storm," written in 1898, likens an adulterous liaison to a cyclone, fierce but natural and potentially renewing. Recognizing the tale's advanced views, Chopin did not attempt to publish it during her lifetime, and it appeared in print only in 1969. Such daring plunged her into obscurity for almost half a century following her death, but it has at last guaranteed for her a secure place in American letters.

BIBLIOGRAPHICAL REFERENCES: Per Seyersted has written the definitive biography, *Kate Chopin: A Critical Biography*, 1969. He also edited *The Complete Works of Kate Chopin*, which contains most of her writing. This two-volume work is supplemented by *A Kate Chopin Miscellany*, 1979, edited by Seyersted and Emily Toth. Included in this volume is a translation of Cyrille Arnavon's pioneering study, which appeared as the preface to his 1953 French edition of *The Awakening*. An earlier anecdotal biography by Daniel S. Rankin, *Kate Chopin and Her Creole Stories*, 1932, contains some material not in Seyersted's account; Rankin also reprints eleven stories and some other pieces by Chopin. Kenneth Eble's laudatory "A Forgotten Novel: Kate Chopin's *The Awakening*," *Western Humanities Review*, X (1956), 261-269, initiated a revival of interest in Chopin's work in the United States. Other useful articles on this novel include Donald A. Ringe, "Romantic Imagery in Kate Chopin's *The Awakening*," *American Literature*, XLIII (1973), 580-588; Cynthia Wolff, "Thanatos and Eros: Kate Chopin's *The Awakening*," *American Quarterly*, XXV (1973), 449-471; Ruth Sullivan and Steward Smith, "Narrative Stance in Kate Chopin's *The Awakening*," *Studies in American Fiction*, I (1973), 62-75. George Spangler, "Kate Chopin's *The Awakening*: A Partial Dissent," *Novel: A Forum on Fiction*, III (1970), 249-255, challenged the general view of the ending as successful in that work. Among more general studies of the fiction are Joan Zlotnick, "A Woman's Will: Kate Chopin's Selfhood, Wifehood, and Motherhood," *Markham Review*, III (1968), 1-5; Peggy Skaggs, *Kate Chopin*, 1985; Elizabeth McMahan, "Nature's Decay: Kate Chopin's Presentation of Women and Marriage in Her Short Fiction," *Turn-of-the-Century Women*, II (1985), 32-35; and Joyce C. Dyer, "Epiphanies Through Nature in the Stories of Kate Chopin," *University of Dayton Review*, XVI (1983/1984), 75-81.

Joseph Rosenblum

AGATHA CHRISTIE

Born: Torquay, Devon, England
Date: September 15, 1890

Died: Wallingford, England
Date: January 12, 1976

Principal Works

MYSTERY AND DETECTIVE NOVELS: *The Mysterious Affair at Styles*, 1920; *The Secret Adversary*, 1922; *The Murder on the Links*, 1923; *The Man in the Brown Suit*, 1924; *The Secret of Chimneys*, 1925; *The Murder of Roger Ackroyd*, 1926; *The Big Four*, 1927; *The Mystery of the Blue Train*, 1928; *The Seven Dials Murder*, 1929; *The Murder at the Vicarage*, 1930; *The Sittaford Mystery*, 1931 (also as *The Murder at Hazelmoor*); *The Floating Admiral*, 1932 (with others); *Peril at End House*, 1932; *Lord Edgware Dies*, 1933 (also as *Thirteen at Dinner*); *Murder on the Orient Express*, 1934 (also as *Murder on the Calais Coach*); *Three Act Tragedy*, 1934 (also as *Murder in Three Acts*); *Death in the Clouds*, 1935 (also as *Death in the Air*); *Why Didn't They Ask Evans?*, 1935 (also as *The Boomerang Clue*); *The A.B.C. Murders*, 1936 (also as *The Alphabet Murders*); *Cards on the Table*, 1936; *Murder in Mesopotamia*, 1936; *Death on the Nile*, 1937; *Dumb Witness*, 1937 (also as *Poirot Loses a Client*); *Appointment with Death*, 1938; *Hercule Poirot's Christmas*, 1938 (also as *Murder for Christmas*); *Murder Is Easy*, 1939 (also as *Easy to Kill*); *Ten Little Niggers*, 1939 (also as *And Then There Were None* and *Ten Little Indians*); *One, Two, Buckle My Shoe*, 1940 (also as *The Patriotic Murders*); *Sad Cypress*, 1940; *Evil Under the Sun*, 1941; *N or M?*, 1941; *The Body in the Library*, 1942; *The Moving Finger*, 1942; *Five Little Pigs*, 1942 (also as *Murder in Retrospect*); *Death Comes as the End*, 1944; *Towards Zero*, 1944; *Sparkling Cyanide*, 1945 (also as *Remembered Death*); *The Hollow*, 1946 (also as *Murder After Hours*); *Taken at the Flood*, 1948 (also as *There Is a Tide . . .*); *Crooked House*, 1949; *A Murder Is Announced*, 1950; *They Came to Baghdad*, 1951; *They Do It with Mirrors*, 1952 (also as *Murder with Mirrors*); *Mrs. McGinty's Dead*, 1952; *After the Funeral*, 1953 (also as *Funerals Are Fatal*); *A Pocket Full of Rye*, 1953; *Destination Unknown*, 1954 (also as *So Many Steps to Death*); *Hickory, Dickory, Dock*, 1955 (also as *Hickory, Dickory, Death*); *Dead Man's Folly*, 1956; *4:50 from Paddington*, 1957 (also as *What Mrs. McGillicuddy Saw!*); *Ordeal by Innocence*, 1959; *Cat Among the Pigeons*, 1960; *The Pale Horse*, 1961; *The Mirror Crack'd from Side to Side*, 1963 (also as *The Mirror Crack'd*); *The Clocks*, 1964; *A Caribbean Mystery*, 1965; *At Bertram's Hotel*, 1965; *Third Girl*, 1966; *Endless Night*, 1967; *By the Pricking of My Thumbs*, 1968; *Hallowe'en Party*, 1969; *Passenger to Frankfurt*, 1970; *Nemesis*, 1971; *Elephants Can Remember*, 1972; *Postern of Fate*, 1973; *Curtain: Hercule Poirot's Last Case*, 1975; *Sleeping Murder*, 1976.

MYSTERY AND DETECTIVE STORIES: *Poirot Investigates*, 1925; *Partners in Crime*, 1929; *The Thirteen Problems*, 1932; *Parker Pyne Investigates*, 1934 (also as *Mr. Parker Pyne, Detective*); *Murder in the Mews and Other Stories*, 1937 (also as *Dead Man's Mirror and Other Stories*); *Poirot on Holiday*, 1943; *Poirot Lends a Hand*, 1946; *The Labours of Hercules*, 1947; *The Witness for the Prosecution and Other Stories*, 1948; *The Mousetrap and Other Stories*, 1949 (also as *Three Blind Mice and Other Stories*); *Double Sin and Other Stories*, 1961; *Thirteen Clues for Miss Marple*, 1966; *Poirot's Early Cases*, 1974; *Miss Marple's Final Cases and Others*, 1979.

ROMANCES: *Giants' Bread*, 1930; *Unfinished Portrait*, 1934; *Absent in the Spring*, 1944; *The Rose and the Yew Tree*, 1948; *A Daughter's A Daughter*, 1952; *The Burden*, 1956.

PLAYS: *Black Coffee*, pr. 1930; *Ten Little Niggers*, pr. 1943 (also as *Ten Little Indians*); *The Mousetrap*, pr. 1952; *Witness for the Prosecution*, pr. 1953; *Spider's Web*, pr. 1954; *Verdict*, pr. 1958; *The Unexpected Guest*, pr. 1958; *Rule of Three: Afternoon at the Seaside, The Patient, The Rats*, pb. 1963; *Akhnaton*, pb. 1973 (also as *Akhnaton and Nefertiti*).

POETRY: *The Road of Dreams*, 1925; *Poems*, 1973.

TRAVEL: *Come, Tell Me How You Live*, 1946, revised 1976.

AUTOBIOGRAPHY: *An Autobiography*, 1977.

The acknowledged "Queen of Crime," Agatha Christie remains perhaps the world's best-known and most popular mystery writer. Born Agatha Mary Clarissa Miller, Christie was the child of an English mother, Clarissa Boehmer Miller, and an American father, Frederick Alvah Miller. After her father's death, Christie was educated at home by her mother, who encouraged her talents as a storyteller. She later studied piano and voice in Paris. Hers was a typically upper-middle-class British upbringing; the environment in which she was reared would form the basis for nearly all of her later novels.

In 1914, she married Colonel Archibald Christie, with whom she had a daughter, Rosalind. During her husband's service in World War I, Christie worked in a Red Cross hospital in Torquay, where she began writing her first novel, *The Mysterious Affair at Styles*. Completed toward the end of the war, the book was rejected by several publishers before it finally appeared in print in 1920. *The Mysterious Affair at Styles* introduces Christie's famous Belgian detective, Hercule Poirot, a small, eccentric man with a waxed moustache and an unshakable belief in the deductive powers of his "little grey cells." During the course of Christie's long and prolific career, Poirot would appear in dozens of her novels, including *The Murder of Roger Ackroyd* and *Murder on the Orient Express*, which became a popular film. He remains surpassed in fame as a fictional sleuth only by Sherlock Holmes.

It was *The Murder of Roger Ackroyd*, published in 1926, that firmly established Christie's reputation as a mystery writer. Its surprising and controversial conclusion won for her an international following and demonstrated what would become the hallmark of her style: a talent for devising fiendishly clever plots that lead her readers away from the true solution while still presenting them with all the relevant clues to the killer's identity. The year 1926 also marked what would remain the most mysterious episode in Christie's own life: her still-unexplained ten-day disappearance. After vanishing from her home one day in December, she became the object of a widely publicized search and was eventually found at a hotel in Harrowgate, registered under the name of her husband's lover. Doctors ruled that Christie had been suffering from temporary amnesia, and she refused until her death to discuss the episode, omitting it entirely from her autobiography fifty years later. In 1928, she and Archibald Christie were divorced, although she retained his name professionally throughout her life.

Two years later, Christie married archaeologist Max Mallowan and wrote her tenth book, *The Murder at the Vicarage*, which introduced Miss Jane Marple to her reading public. An elderly, white-haired spinster, Miss Marple relies on intuition and an uncanny understanding of human nature to solve her cases, hiding a shrewd intelligence behind woolly scarves and her ever-present knitting needles. Christie's sleuths have also included Superintendent Battle of Scotland Yard, the retired government statistician, Mr. Parker Pyne, and Tuppence and Tommy Beresford, a wealthy crime-solving couple, but only Miss Marple has shown herself to be a worthy rival to Poirot in the public's affections. Among the best of the Miss Marple mysteries are *The Body in the Library*, *A Murder Is Announced*, *4:50 from Paddington* (better known as *What Mrs. McGillacuddy Saw!*), and *The Mirror Crack'd from Side to Side*.

In 1930 Christie also wrote the first of six romantic novels under the name Mary Westmacott, but the books never approached the popularity of her mysteries. It was during this period that she began accompanying her husband regularly on his digs throughout the Middle East. The region, as well as Christie's growing knowledge of archaeology, inspired several of her mysteries, including *Murder in Mesopotamia* and *Death on the Nile*. As Agatha Christie Mallowan, she also wrote a travel book describing her experiences entitled *Come, Tell Me How You Live*. In 1939, Christie published one of her best-known books, *Ten Little Niggers* (known in the United States as *And Then There Were None* or *Ten Little Indians*), in which ten people stranded on an island estate are murdered one by one. The book became a popular stage play in 1943, adapted by Christie herself. During World War II, Christie worked in the dispensary of a London hospital but continued to write steadily. Indeed, throughout her career, she would produce an average of one book a year, in addition to numerous plays and some thirty collections of short stories. Each book took approximately six weeks to complete, and she maintained in interviews that her best ideas came to her in the bathtub.

In 1952, Christie wrote *The Mousetrap*, a play that would go on to become London's longest-running production. She followed it with *Witness for the Prosecution*, for which she received the New York Drama Critics Circle Award in 1955, and *Spider's Web*. Some of Christie's critics complained that her later books were sluggish and less imaginative than her earlier efforts. In 1975, the year before her death, the last of the Hercule Poirot mysteries was published. *Curtain* had been written many years earlier and set aside until Christie was certain that her writing career was nearing its close. The book contains not only Poirot's final case, but his death as well; a fact which led *The New York Times* to run a front-page obituary notice, the first time in the newspaper's history that a fictional character had been so honored. The final Miss Marple mystery, also written earlier in her creator's career, appeared in 1976, shortly after Christie's death at the age of eighty-five.

Agatha Christie's work enjoys a worldwide following, and her books have been published in more than one hundred languages. Her mastery of the techniques of the mystery plot has had an extensive influence on those writers who have followed her into the genre, and the simplicity of her books—there is very little description, and her characters are often two-dimensional—is the result of a writing style in which everything is centered on a strong, intricately constructed story line. Christie has been criticized for focusing her stories on a narrow segment of society and for her ordinary use of language, but her brilliant plotting and ability to disguise clues even as she reveals them have been praised. In a way that is true of perhaps no other writer, her name remains synonymous with the murder mystery.

BIBLIOGRAPHICAL REFERENCES: Janet Morgan, *Agatha Christie: A Biography*, 1984, is a well-researched and informative examination of Christie's life. Derrick Murdoch, *The Agatha Christie Mystery*, 1976, is less thorough but still of interest. Robert Barnard, *A Talent to Deceive: An Appreciation of Agatha Christie*, 1980, offers a fascinating analysis of Christie's work by a fellow mystery author, while *Agatha Christie: First Lady of Crime*, 1977, edited by H. R. F. Keating, contains a collection of essays on Christie whose authors include Julian Symons, Edmund Crispin, and Emma Lathen. See also G. C. Ramsey, *Agatha Christie: Mistress of Mystery*, 1967; Frank Behre, *Studies in Agatha Christie's Writings*, 1967; Russell H. Fitzgibbon, *The Agatha Christie Companion*, 1980; and Randall Toye, *Agatha Christie Who's Who*, 1980.

Janet E. Lorenz

JOHN PEPPER CLARK

Born: Kiagbodo, Nigeria
Date: April 6, 1935

PRINCIPAL WORKS

PLAYS: *Song of a Goat*, pr., pb. 1961; *The Masquerade*, pb. 1964; *The Raft*, pb. 1964, revised 1978; *Three Plays*, pb. 1964; *Ozidi*, pb. 1966; *The Boat*, pr. 1981.

POETRY: *A Reed in the Tide: A Selection of Poems*, 1965; *Casualities: Poems, 1966-68*, 1970; *A Decade of Tongues*, 1981.

NONFICTION: *America, Their America*, 1964; *The Example of Shakespeare: Critical Essays on African Literature*, 1970.

John Pepper Clark has played an important role in the development of Nigerian literature in English through his association with the important art journal *Black Orpheus*. He took an honors degree in English at Ibadan University, where he established a student poetry magazine called *The Horn*. After graduation, he became a journalist on the *Lagos Daily Express*. He undertook research in the Ibadan University Institute for African Studies and was finally appointed a professor of English at the University of Lagos. The decade from 1960 to 1970 saw his most important publications.

As a dramatist, Clark draws upon local African themes but lends them a greater dramatic impact by incorporating elements of British and Greek classical drama. *Song of a Goat* (the title clearly refers to the Greek origin of tragedy, "goat song") depicts the sexual tension which develops when a virile younger brother seduces his frustrated sister-in-law and fathers a child for his impotent elder brother. The complication of the plot derives from African tradition, which, holding childbearing as a necessity, requires that a family member should take the place of the husband to fill the barren womb. Unhappily, the couple does not proceed in formal duty but falls madly and lustfully in love. They enflame the husband's jealousy to the point where he kills his own brother to his personal anguish and social shame. The elevated diction of its blank verse lines adds to the extraordinary power of this widely performed play. *The Masquerade* continues the plot, as the inevitable public curse that follows from the wicked deed works itself out in the manner of Oedipus' redemption.

In production, Clark's plays have a powerful impact, but there has been African criticism that Clark has borrowed too freely from international sources and so has diluted what should be essentially African subjects. It may have been this recurrent complaint that caused him to write *Ozidi*, a less theatrically effective but a far more "African" play derived from a traditional ritual enacted in his birthplace. He later recorded this ritual in a documentary film.

As a poet, Clark is primarily a lyricist whose lines record his own inheritance with sensitive affection. "Night Rain," with its childhood memory of awaking to the sound of rain falling on the roof thatch, and the gentle family recollection of "For Granny," shows an unexpectedly tender side of a public personality which has sometimes seemed abrasive. No book exhibits this more clearly than his petulent complaints about the United States which arose from a period on a journalist fellowship at Princeton University. To be fair, there were false expectations on both sides, but in the resulting book, *America, Their America*, Clark's reactions are reported in styles ranging from sardonic wit to brutal vehemence. His reactions to the racism he claims to have encountered are delivered with genuine passion. His more general grievances are likely to rouse resentment in many American readers.

Although he was born in the separatist eastern region, during the Biafran War Clark supported the federal side. For that he received open condemnation from his friends. Yet his decision was more humane than political, and the terrible human consequences revived his poetry. His war poems, collected in *Casualties*, become a poignant and despairing response to the cruelties of war suffered on both sides. The collection takes his poetry into a more solemn and profound vein. The death of his friend Christopher Okigbo was a crushing spiritual blow.

After the peace, when Clark took up his academic position, he turned from creative writing to criticism. *The Example of Shakespeare* brings together a number of seminal articles that had been published in journals such as *Transition* and *African Forum*. "The Legacy of Caliban" extends the African opinion that Prospero should be perceived as a colonialist exploiter of the native inhabitants.

In 1980, Clark gave up his professorial post and retired to his home village of Kiagbodo. Working from that base, he has continued to concern himself with traditional drama and the establishing of a repertory theater in Lagos. Clark's importance stems in part from the fact that his energy and personality provided encouragement and opportunities for the many younger writers who have established a major national literature. At the same time his work reveals explicitly the constant inner struggle of the African author, who must somehow manage to express his African experience and identity in a language which is simultaneously internationally expressive and personally alien.

BIBLIOGRAPHICAL REFERENCES: For an overview of Clark's life and work, see Robert Wren, *J. P. Clark*, 1984. Useful articles on Clark's drama include William Conner, "Diribi's Incest," *World Literatures Written in English*, XVIII, no. 2 (1979), 278-286, and John Ferguson, "Nigerian Drama Written in English," *Modern Drama*, XI (May, 1968), 10-26. See also R. N. Egudu, "The Poetry and Drama of J. P. Clark," in *Introduction to Nigerian Literature*, 1971, edited by B. King; Paul Obeakaran, "John Pepper Clark and Stephen Crane," *Research in African Literatures*, XIII (Spring, 1982), 53-59; and John Povey, "Two Hands a Man Has," *African Literature Today*, I (1968), 36-47. *Perspectives on African Literature*, 1971, edited by Christopher Heywood, and *Theatre in Africa*, 1978, edited by O. Ogunba, provide good background for the beginning student of Clark.

John F. Povey

WALTER VAN TILBURG CLARK

Born: East Orland, Maine
Date: August 3, 1909

Died: Reno, Nevada
Date: November 10, 1971

PRINCIPAL WORKS

NOVELS: *The Ox-Bow Incident*, 1940; *The City of Trembling Leaves*, 1945; *The Track of the Cat*, 1949; *Tim Hazard*, 1951.

SHORT FICTION: *The Watchful Gods and Other Stories*, 1950.

POETRY: *Ten Women in Gale's House and Shorter Poems*, 1932.

NONFICTION: *The Journals of Alfred Doten, 1849-1903*, 1973.

Walter Van Tilburg Clark stands at the head of a small group of writers who in the first half of the twentieth century elevated fiction about the American West from formula to literature. In 1917, Clark's father moved the family from Maine to Reno, Nevada, where he had been appointed president of the University of Nevada. Young Clark grew to love the life of the Old West. In 1927, Clark entered the University of Nevada, where he earned a B.A. and an M.A. in English. While there, he spent much of his time writing (mostly poetry) and studying ancient literature, philosophy, and contemporary poetry, particularly that of Robinson Jeffers, whom he imitated in his own verse. He earned a second M.A. in English at the University of Vermont. In the early 1930's, Clark married Barbara Morse, and a year later they moved to Cazenovia, New York, where Clark was to begin five years of teaching at the local high school. He wrote intensively, despite heavy teaching and coaching duties, and published in a national magazine for the first time. It was also during this period that Clark began writing fiction in earnest.

According to Clark, *The Ox-Bow Incident*, his best-known novel, had started as a parody of formulaic fiction about cowboys, "horse operas," but with Nazism a growing horror in Europe and war looming, the story became a fable of Fascism, dramatically exploring the themes of justice and demagoguery. The story opens in the fictional Bridger's Wells, a sleepy town near the Sierra Nevada. News comes that cattle rustlers have killed a local cowboy. Angry debate ensues, and a natural leader organizes a vigilante posse; even those who doubt the legality or morality of this action go with the group. They set off as a late snowfall turns the landscape into a vision of harsh contrasts, with black cliffs and white ground. Nature itself seems to oppose the expedition. The posse eventually hangs three suspicious-looking men; returning to town, however, the group discovers that no crime has been committed at all, and each vigilante must face the fact that he has given in to the mob's impulse to follow any strong leader and thus, is party to murder.

In 1945, *The City of Trembling Leaves* was published. It is the story of Timothy Hazard, a would-be composer in Reno. Structured like a symphony in its recombinations of themes, the novel reveals the artist's troubled quest for a vocation. Among these themes are misbegotten young love, mature love, the dissolution of a family, and, as in all Clark's novels, the monitory influence of the wilderness on human dilemmas.

After 1950, Clark published little, although he continued to write steadily. Critics refer to his "silent period" and suggest as its cause the increasing demands of teaching at the University of Nevada and other institutions, his method of revising by completely rewriting, and the massive project of editing a frontier journalist's diaries. For all that, Clark probably failed to publish for the very reasons that his early works were successful. He scrupulously searched for truth in life. As Clark wrote in a letter to his son, Robert, writing was to him a means of discovering what to feel and believe about life. That discovery seems to have become increasingly difficult as Clark saw life in the West change rapidly following World War II.

Clark's main theme was civilization, and the West was his raw material, as fellow Westerner Wallace Stegner has written. Clark sometimes philosophizes at length, but his talents for suspense and description still make his fiction among the most gripping by regional writers. When he died in Reno in 1971, despite two decades without a major publication of fiction, he was held in the highest esteem for having rescued Westerners from being portrayed as gunslingers and for having illustrated their ambivalent role in the development of the American character.

BIBLIOGRAPHICAL REFERENCES: *Walter Van Tilburg Clark: Critiques*, edited by Charlton Laird, 1983, presents a varied introduction to Clark's life and works in essays by friends and admirers; although the quality of the critiques varies, most contain useful analyses of his major themes. Also see Max Westbrook, *Walter Van Tilburg Clark*, 1969, for a detailed study of archetypal patterns in Clark's fiction that applies the psychology of Carl Gustav Jung and the anthropological theories of Mircea Eliade. For insightful comments on Clark's contribution to the literature of the West, see John R. Milton, *The Novel of the American West*, 1980, 195-229. For a partly unsympathetic view of Clark's regionalism, see Edmund Wilson, "White Peaks and Limpid Lakes: A Novel about Nevada," *The New Yorker*, XXI, May 26, 1945, 75-77. See also Kenneth Andersen, "Character Portrayal in *The Ox-Bow Incident*," *Western American Literature*, IV (1970), 287-298; Donald E. Houghton, "The Failure of Speech in *The Ox-Bow Incident*," *English Journal*, LIX (1970), 1245-1251; L. L. Lee, "Walter Van Tilburg Clark's Ambiguous American Dream," *College English*, XXVI (February, 1965), 382-387; and Max Westbrook, "The Indian in the Mirror: Clark's *The Track of the Cat*," *Western American Literature*, XX (1985), 19-33.

Roger Smith

ARTHUR C. CLARKE

Born: Minehead, England
Date: December 16, 1917

PRINCIPAL WORKS

NONFICTION: *Interplanetary Flight*, 1950; *The Exploration of Space*, 1951; *The Exploration of the Moon*, 1954; *Going into Space*, 1954; *The Coast of Coral*, 1956; *The Making of a Moon*, 1957; *The Reefs of Taprobane*, 1957; *Voice Across the Sea*, 1958; *The Challenge of the Spaceship*, 1959; *The Challenge of the Sea*, 1960; *The First Five Fathoms*, 1960; *Indian Ocean Adventure*, 1961 (with Mike Wilson); *Profiles of the Future*, 1962; *Man and Space*, 1964 (with others); *Indian Ocean Treasure*, 1964 (with Wilson); *The Treasure of the Great Reef*, 1964; *Voices from the Sky*, 1965; *The Promise of Space*, 1968; *First on the Moon*, 1970 (with others); *Into Space*, 1971 (with Robert Silverberg); *Report on Planet Three*, 1972; *Beyond Jupiter*, 1972 (with Chesley Bonestall); *The View from Serendip*, 1977; *1984: Spring, A Choice of Futures*, 1984; *Arthur C. Clarke's July 20, 2019: Life in the 21st Century*, 1986.

SCIENCE FICTION: *Prelude to Space*, 1951; *The Sands of Mars*, 1951; *Islands in the Sky*, 1952; *Childhood's End*, 1953; *Expedition to Earth*, 1953; *Earthlight*, 1955; *Reach for Tomorrow*, 1956; *The City and the Stars*, 1956; *Tales from the White Hart*, 1957; *The Deep Range*, 1957; *The Other Side of the Sky*, 1958; *Across the Sea of Stars*, 1959; *A Fall of Moondust*, 1961; *From the Ocean, from the Stars*, 1962; *Tales of Ten Worlds*, 1962; *Dolphin Island*, 1963; *Glide Path*, 1963; *Prelude to Mars*, 1965; *The Nine Billion Names of God*, 1967; *"The Lion of Comarre," and "Against the Fall of Night,"* 1968; *2001: A Space Odyssey*, 1968 (with Stanley Kubrick); *Of Time and Stars: The Worlds of Arthur C. Clarke*, 1972; *The Lost Worlds of 2001*, 1972; *The Wind from the Sun*, 1972; *The Best of Arthur C. Clarke*, 1973; *Rendezvous with Rama*, 1973; *Imperial Earth*, 1976; *The Fountains of Paradise*, 1978; *2010: Odyssey Two*, 1982; *The Sentinel: Masterworks of Science Fiction and Fantasy*, 1983; *The Songs of Distant Earth*, 1986; *2061: Odyssey Three*, 1987; *Cradle*, 1988 (with Gentry Lee).

Arthur Charles Clarke is a commercially successful and very highly respected contemporary science-fiction writer. Born on December 16, 1917, in Minehead, a coastal town in Somersetshire, England, he was the oldest of the four children of Charles Wright and Norah (Willis) Clarke. Clarke's father was a post office engineer and farmer. "My youth," Clarke recalls, "was spent alternating between the seaside and my parents' small farm." Having developed an early interest in science (from reading about dinosaurs), Clarke built a telescope at the age of thirteen and mapped the Moon with it. From 1928 to 1936 he attended Huish's Grammer School, Taunton, and wrote for the school's literary magazine.

Since poverty prevented his attending college, Clarke worked for the British Civil Service as an auditor from 1936 to 1941. During this time he joined the British Interplanetary Society, becoming its chairman. During World War II Clarke served as a radar instructor in the Royal Air Force, rising to the rank of flight lieutenant. While in the military he wrote several articles on electronics and sold his first science-fiction stories. In an article published in *Wireless World* (October, 1945), Clarke predicted the development of communications satellites. A veterans' grant enabled him to attend King's College, the University of London, where he received his bachelor's degree (with first-class honors) in physics and math in 1948. From 1949 to 1951, Clarke was an assistant editor at *Science Abstracts*, a publication of the Institution of Electric Engineers, London. In 1951 Clarke became a full-time writer.

"My literary interests," Clarke has noted, "are divided equally between fiction and nonfiction." His first success was an introduction to astronautics, *Interplanetary Flight*, followed by related works, *The Exploration of Space* and *The Exploration of the Moon*. Clarke won esteem as a science writer. Critic Ray Gibbons praised "Clarke's ability to reduce complex subjects to simple language and his steadfast avoidance of fantasy as a substitute for factual narration."

Clarke concurrently wrote science fiction. His *Prelude to Space* was hailed as "a compelling realistic novel of interplanetary flight." Other works came quickly: *The Sands of Mars*, *Islands in the Sky*, "Against the Fall of Night," and "The Lion of Comarre." A milestone was *Childhood's End*, for it placed Clarke in the mainstream of Anglo-American science-fiction writers. Basil Davenport of *The New York Times* added Clarke's name to those of "Olaf Stapleton, C. S. Lewis, and H. G. Wells, "the very small group of writers who have used science fiction as the vehicle of philosophical ideas—not merely ideas about the nature of future society, but ideas about the End of Man." In 1952 Clarke received the International Fantasy Award for his work.

Long interested in underwater exploration and photography, Clarke began, with Mike Wilson, to swim off the Great Barrier Reef of Australia and the coasts of Sri Lanka. These experiences inspired works set in the sea, including *The Challenge of the Sea*, *The First Five Fathoms*, and, with Mike Wilson, *Indian Ocean Adventure* and *Indian Ocean Treasure*—as well as such novels as *Dolphin Island* and *Cradle*.

Clarke's collaboration with Stanley Kubrick on the film and novel *2001: A Space Odyssey* was another turning point. Clarke emerged as both a scientist and a storyteller. Clifton Fadiman's prediction was fulfilled: "Clarke is no mere dreamer. If he roves space, it is with a slide rule in hand." Two more novels, *2010: Odyssey Two* and *2061: Odyssey Three*, explored the evolutionary impact of human life in space. Encounters with extraterrestrials were discussed, a theme developed in *Rendezvous with Rama*, winning for Clarke a second Nebula Award and the Hugo Award. Life in space inspired *Imperial Earth* (composed for the American Bicentennial), *The Fountains of Paradise* (which envisioned a vast elevator to the heavens), and *The Songs of Distant Earth* (an epic of human pilgrims fleeing a dying Earth).

Clarke is also a futurist, as evidenced in *Profiles of the Future* and other works. He contends that "anything that is theoretically possible will be achieved in practice, no matter what the technical difficulties, if it is desired greatly enough." Open-ended in his hopes for humankind, "Clarke's Law" states, "When a distinguished but elderly scientist states that something is possible, he is almost certainly right. When he states that something is impossible, he is very probably wrong."

For years Clarke was a popular lecturer in the United Kingdom and the United States. By the mid-1950's he took up residence in Colombo, Sri Lanka, a decision reinforced by his divorce in 1964 from Marilyn Mayfield. (The couple had been married in 1953.) In 1979 Clarke became Chancellor of Moratuwa University. "Baldish" and "bespectacled," he is fond of diving, photography, and table tennis. A world-class writer, Clarke's reputation is secure. Godfrey Smith, writing in *The New York Times*, said, "He writes clear prose which draws its solidity and confidence from his formal scientific training but it is occasionally laced with passages of something like poetry."

BIBLIOGRAPHICAL REFERENCES: Fine full-length studies of Clarke and his writing are John Hollow, *Against the Night, the Stars: The Science Fiction of Arthur C. Clarke*, 1983; Eric S. Rabkin, *Arthur C. Clarke*, 1980 (rev. ed); George Edgar Slusser, *The Space Odysseys of Arthur C. Clarke*, 1977; and *Arthur C. Clarke*, 1977, edited by Joseph D. Olander and Martin Harry Greenberg. Two specialized articles on Clarke are Alexander Nedelkovich, "The Stellar Parallels: Robert Silverberg, Larry Niven, and Arthur C. Clarke," *Extrapolation*, XXI (1980), 348-360, and Sam M. Lehman-Wilzig, "Science Fiction as Futurist Prediction: Alternative Visions of Heinlein and Clarke," *The Literary Review*, XX (1976), 133-151. For essays dealing with particular Clarke novels, see Tom Moylan, "Ideological Contradictions in Clarke's *The City and the Stars*," *Science Fiction Studies*, IV (1977), 150-157, and Daniel J. Leary, "The Ends of Childhood: Eschatology in Shaw and Clarke," *The Shaw Review*, XVI (1973), 67-68. See also Luch Menger, "The Appeal of *Childhood's End*," *Critical Encoun-*

ters: Writers and Themes in Science Fiction, 1978, edited by Dick Riley. Among the more helpful studies of *2001* are David Boyd, "Mode and Meaning in *2001*," *Journal of Popular Film*, VI (1978), 202-215; Alan Brody, "*2001* and the Paradox of the Fortunate Fall," *Hartford Studies in Literature*, I (1969), 7-19; Victor A. Doyno, "*2001*^{2}: Years and Shapes," *Hartford Studies in Literature*, I (1969), 131-132; David G. Hoch, "Mythic Patterns in *2001: A Space Odyssey*," *Journal of Popular Culture*, IV (1971), 961-965; Norman N. Holland, "*2001*: A Psychosocial Explication," *Hartford Studies in Literature*, I (1969), 20-25; John Hollow, "*2001* in Perspective: The Fiction of Arthur C. Clarke," *Southwest Review*, LXI (1976), 113-128, Max Kozloff, "*2001*," *Film Culture*, XLVIII (1970), 53-56; Terry Otten, "The Fallen and Evolving Worlds of *2001*," *Mosaic*, XIII (Spring/Summer, 1980), 41-50; and Robert Rogers, "The Psychology of the 'Double' in *2001*," *Hartford Studies in Literature*, I (1969), 34-36.

C. George Fry

JEAN COCTEAU

Born: Maisons-Lafitte, France
Date: July 5, 1889

Died: Milly-la-Forêt, France
Date: October 11, 1963

PRINCIPAL WORKS

POETRY: *La Lampe d'Aladin*, 1909; *Le Prince frivole*, 1910; *La Danse de Sophocle*, 1912; *Le Cap de Bonne-Espérance*, 1919; *Poésies (1917-1920)*, 1920; *Escales*, 1920; *Vocabulaire*, 1922; *Plain-Chant*, 1923; *Poésie (1916-1923)*, 1924; *Cri écrit*, 1925; *Prière mutilée*, 1925; *L'Ange Heurtebise*, 1925; *Opéra*, 1927; *Morceaux choisis*, 1932; *Mythologie*, 1934; *Allégories*, 1941; *Poèmes*, 1945; *La Crucifixion*, 1946; *Anthologie poétique*, 1951; *Clair-obscur*, 1954; *Gondole des morts*, 1959; *Cérémonial espagnol du phénix*, 1961; *Le Requiem*, 1962.

PLAYS: *Antigone*, pr. 1922 (English translation, 1961); *Orphée*, pr. 1926 (*Orpheus*, 1933); *Oedipus-Rex*, pr. 1927 (English translation, 1961); *La Voix humaine*, pr., pb. 1930 (*The Human Voice*, 1951); *La Machine infernale*, pr., pb. 1934 (*The Infernal Machine*, 1936); *L'École des veuves*, pr., pb. 1936; *Les Chevaliers de la table ronde*, pr., pb. 1937 (*The Knights of the Round Table*, 1955); *Les Parents terribles*, pr., pb. 1938 (*Intimate Relations*, 1952); *Les Monstres sacrés*, pr., pb. 1940 (*The Holy Terrors*, 1953); *La Machine à écrire*, pr., pb. 1941 (*The Typewriter*, 1948); *Renaud et Armide*, pr., pb. 1943; *L'Aigle à deux têtes*, pr., pb. 1946 (*The Eagle Has Two Heads*, 1946); *Bacchus*, pr. 1951 (English translation, 1955); *Théâtre complet*, 1957; *Five Plays*, 1961; *L'Impromptu du Palais-Royal*, pr., pb. 1962; *The Infernal Machine and Other Plays*, 1964.

NOVELS: *Le Potomak*, 1919; *Le Grand Écart*, 1923 (*The Grand Écart*, 1925); *Thomas l'imposteur*, 1923 (*Thomas the Impostor*, 1925); *Le Livre blanc*, 1928 (*The White Paper*, 1957); *Les Enfants terribles*, 1929 (*Enfants Terrible*, 1930; also known as *Children of the Game*); *Le Fantôme de Marseille*, 1933; *La Fin du Potomak*, 1939.

NONFICTION: *Le Coq et l'Arlequin*, 1918 (*Cock and Harlequin*, 1921); *Le Secret professionnel*, 1922; *Lettre à Jacques Maritain*, 1926 (*Art and Faith*, 1948); *Le Rappel à l'ordre*, 1926 (*A Call to Order*, 1926); *Opium: Journal d'une désintoxication*, 1930 (*Opium: Diary of a Cure*, 1932); *Essai de la critique indirecte*, 1932 (*The Lais Mystery: An Essay of Indirect Criticism*, 1936); *Portraits-souvenir, 1900-1914*, 1935 (*Paris Album*, 1956); *La Belle et la bête: Journal d'un film*, 1946 (*Beauty and the Beast: Journal of a Film*, 1950); *La Difficulté d'être*, 1947 (*The Difficulty of Being*, 1966); *The Journals of Jean Cocteau*, 1956; *Poésie critique*, 1960.

SCREENPLAYS: *Le Sang d'un poète*, 1930 (*The Blood of a Poet*, 1932); *Le Baron fantôme*, 1943; *L'Éternel retour*, 1943 (*The Eternal Return*, 1948); *La Belle et la bête*, 1946 (*Beauty and the Beast*, 1947); *L'Aigle à deux têtes*, 1946; *Ruy Blas*, 1947; *Les Parents terribles*, 1948 (*Intimate Relations*, 1952); *Les Enfants terribles*, 1950; *Orphée*, 1950 (*Orpheus*, 1950); *Le Testament d'Orphée*, 1959 (*The Testament of Orpheus*, 1968); *Thomas l'Imposteur*, 1965.

An artist possessed of many extraordinary talents, Jean Cocteau astonished the world for more than five decades with the originality of his poems, novels, plays, films, paintings, drawings, and critical articles. Prolific, brilliant, and charming, Cocteau earned the admiration and friendship of intellectuals and artists from many fields: The painter Pablo Picasso, the composer Igor Stravinsky, the writer André Gide, and the filmmaker Luis Buñuel were counted among his friends. Born near Paris on July 5, 1889, into a wealthy bourgeois family, the young Cocteau enjoyed all the advantages of his situation. The theater enchanted him, as well as music halls and the circus; he hated the Lycée Condorcet, which he attended from 1900 to 1902, finding the classrooms gloomy and the teachers uninspiring. He began writing at an early age and read his first poems aloud at the Théâtre Fémina on April 4, 1908; soon after, he founded a literary magazine with several friends.

As a mature young man, Cocteau became interested in all the new movements which flourished around him in Paris: Surrealism, Dada, cubism, and the promise of cinema. A keen interest in music prompted him to cultivate a relationship with the composer Eric Satie, who was surrounded by numerous fledgling composers. These musicians, along with several others, eventually formed a group known as Les Six, for whom Cocteau was the unofficial spokesman; they explored new melodic and harmonic possibilities of music and opened new vistas to contemporary composition. Cocteau supported their efforts through his critical writings, particularly *Cock and Harlequin*. Contact with members of the Ballets Russes who were visiting Paris inspired Cocteau to create scenarios for the numerous ballets.

Cocteau's concern with language and poetic imagery became apparent with the publication of his first novel, *Le Potomak*, in 1919, along with the publication of many volumes of poetry before and after that novel. His interest in spoken theater was manifested in 1927, and 1928, when *Antigone* and *Orpheus* were published. Reaching beyond traditional techniques, Cocteau cultivated a form of writing which blended symbolism with evocative narration, stressing irony and the beauty found in the commonplace. Some years later, his description of the snowball fight in *Children of the Game* distilled the essence of adolescent psychology through the creation of almost mythic characters who defy conventions with movements of ferocious poetry, scorning the adults around them. Dargelos, a character probably based on Cocteau's friend Raymond Radiguet, hurls a hard snowball which wounds his friend Paul; the two boys represent disillusioned and introverted adolescents, tragic in their pursuit of liberation from a life of dogma and bourgeois morality.

Perhaps most brilliant as a filmmaker, Cocteau wrote and directed four full-length feature films and participated in the production of several others. The combination of literary genius, visual inspiration, and symbolic conception places these works among the masterpieces of world cinema. *The Blood of a Poet* shows the portrait of a creative person trapped in a world of violent events which have no bearing on his inner life. In *Beauty and the Beast* truth is revealed under the mask of a fairy tale; dream is mingled with reality as Cocteau stamps the tale with his own temperament and vision. This film is not merely a diversion for the public; it is an expression of Cocteau's insights into the nature of friendship and love. In *Orpheus* and *The Testament of Orpheus*, Cocteau synthesizes the themes of many of his earlier works, traversing the frontier which separates life from death. The thoughts of the poet triumph over reality, establishing the supremacy of creativity and imagination over worldly matters. The aesthetic problem of the origin of artistic inspiration is posed, but it is solved only by death: The source of genius remains inpenetrable and mysterious.

Cocteau's perceptions are generally expressed in brief statements and aphorisms which do not explain his art; he sought to avoid the traps of words through simple and bare language, enhanced by the skill of a magician. He considered all forms of art to be varieties of poetry which depict, innocently but seriously, the memories of the artist who is a revealer, an unveiler, of objects seen in a new light, without preconceptions. A singular sincerity, an almost religious need to stand naked before the public, governed his expression; once achieved, lucidity would control the evocative description of past and present. Books function as faithful mirrors of things seen: Those of Cocteau revel in enigmas of life and morality which cannot be solved but which form a persistent part of existence.

BIBLIOGRAPHICAL REFERENCES: *Cocteau: A Biography*, 1970, by Francis Steegmuller, is the fullest critical biography available in English; Frederick Brown, *An Impersonation of Angels*, 1968, also casts light on Cocteau's life and artistic development. Bettina L. Knapp's study *Jean Cocteau*, 1970, provides an excellent overview of his work, as does Wallace Fowlie's *Jean Cocteau: The History of a Poet's Age*, 1966, and Margaret Crosland's *Jean Cocteau*, 1955. Cocteau's theater works are studied by Neal Oxenhandler in *Scandal and Parade*, 1957, and the films are analyzed in depth by René Gilson in *Jean Cocteau: An Investigation into His Films and Philosophy*, 1969, and Arthur B. Evans in *Jean Cocteau and His Films of Orphic Identity*, 1977. See also Lydia Crowson, *The Esthetic of Jean Cocteau*, 1978; Arthur K.

Peters, *Jean Cocteau and André Gide: An Abrasive Friendship*, 1973; and Elizabeth Sprigge and Jean-Jacques Kihm, *Jean Cocteau: The Man and the Mirror*, 1968.

Raymond M. Archer

J. M. COETZEE

Born: Cape Town, South Africa
Date: February 9, 1940

Principal Works

NOVELS: *Dusklands*, 1974; *In the Heart of the Country*, 1977; *Waiting for the Barbarians*, 1980; *Life and Times of Michael K*, 1983; *Foe*, 1986.

LITERARY CRITICISM: *White Writing: On the Culture of Letters in South Africa*, 1988.

A critically acclaimed novelist, critic, and opponent of apartheid, John Michael Coetzee is one of the leading contemporary authors of South African literature. An Afrikaner who writes in English, he was born in Cape Town on February 9, 1940, and spent his childhood on an isolated farm in the stony semidesert of the Karroo. He was educated at the University of Cape Town and spent some time in London, England, as a computer programmer before earning his Ph.D. at the University of Texas, Austin, in 1969 on a Fulbright exchange program. While studying Anglo-Saxon and linguistics, Coetzee began reading colonial accounts of the exploration of South West Africa. Among these histories of the Hottentots, he found an account written by a remote eighteenth century ancestor, Jacobus Coetzee, which was to give rise to his first novel, *Dusklands*.

After teaching at the State University of New York at Buffalo for two years, Coetzee returned to South Africa in 1971 to take a teaching position at the University of Cape Town. He brought with him the half-finished manuscript of *Dusklands*, which he finished and published in 1974. As he published scholarly essays on linguistics, modern European literature, and South African literature, Coetzee also began to establish his reputation as a novelist. His second novel, *In the Heart of the Country*, won for him the premier South African literary award in 1980, the Central News Agency (CNA) Award. Coetzee won his second CNA Award with *Waiting for the Barbarians*, and in 1982, his novels began reaching a broader audience by being regularly published outside South Africa. He has won numerous literary prizes, including the Booker Prize in 1983 for *Life and Times of Michael K*, the Prix Fémina Étranger in 1985, and the Jerusalem Prize for the Freedom of the Individual in Society in 1987.

Coetzee's novels are often described as metaphysical, allegorical, or postmodern. Avoiding the realistic novel of character or social commentary, Coetzee nevertheless is concerned in his writing with the dynamics of oppression and injustice. *Waiting for the Barbarians*, for example, is set in a frontier town of a civilization known only as the "Empire," which is apparently being threatened by nomadic, dark-skinned tribes called the "Barbarians." The novel focuses on the town's civil magistrate, who initially acquiesces in the military's imprisonment and torture of the Barbarians, until a crisis of conscience prompts him to reject the Empire's viewpoint. The parallels with the South African situation are obvious. While *Waiting for the Barbarians* is set in an indefinite time and place, *Life and Times of Michael K* takes place in a futuristic South Africa torn by civil war. This lyrical novel follows the attempts of the slow and inarticulate Michael K to escape the senseless bureaucracy of the city for the pastoral peace and freedom of the country.

Oppression within the context of colonialism appears in almost all Coetzee's novels. *Dusklands* juxtaposes the American intervention in Vietnam to the exploration of South Africa by the Dutch in the eighteenth century. *In the Heart of the Country* examines the power struggles between a domineering Afrikaner father, his lonely and half-crazed spinster daughter, and the blacks who work for them on an isolated farm in South Africa. *Foe* retells the untold story of *Robinson Crusoe* (1719), revealing that Crusoe actually died on the voyage back to England and that his story was told to Daniel Defoe by the woman who lived with him on the island. In this account, Friday is not Defoe's intelligent savage who quickly learns to appreciate the benefits of Western civilization. Rather, he is a dumb-mute, rendered speechless and unable to tell his story by the mysterious loss of his tongue.

In all of his works, Coetzee considers the nature of oppression and its effects on both the oppressor and the oppressed. He is especially concerned with those marginalized groups who are often treated as "others": blacks and women. His fiction also is cognizant of how language and writing participate in oppression. His critical study of South African literature, *White Writing*, examines the European myths through which South African writers have seen the land, themselves, and others. Coetzee's novels demonstrate an increasing concern to allow the oppressed to speak, even as he struggles to speak for them without becoming an oppressor himself. These thematic concerns are also reflected in Coetzee's postmodern style, which includes narrative ambiguities and repetitions, lyrical and nonlinear prose, allegorical characters, and surreal landscapes. Although he rejects such comparisons, his work is often seen as similar to that of Samuel Beckett and Franz Kafka.

While Coetzee is frequently applauded for the powerful social and political implications of his works, a few critics remain unsatisfied with his lack of realism and apolitical narrative stance. On the one hand, Coetzee's use of allegory allows his novels to make universal statements about violence and injustice. Yet some readers believe that Coetzee's work is too metaphysical and lacks the specificity needed to comment on the social and material problems of South Africa. In general, though, Coetzee's work is highly respected for its moral insights, its protest against injustice, and its skillful use of postmodern techniques.

BIBLIOGRAPHICAL REFERENCES: Analysis of J. M. Coetzee's work remains limited in the United States. A popular introduction to Coetzee's work can be found in Michael Scrogin, "Apocalypse and Beyond: The Novels of J. M. Coetzee," in *The Christian Century*, May 18, 1988, 503-505. Other general studies are those of Robert M. Post, "Oppression in the Fiction of J. M. Coetzee," *Critique: Studies in Modern Fiction*, XXVII (1986), 67-77, and Stephen Watson, "Colonialism and the Novels of J. M. Coetzee," *Research in African Literature*, XVII (1986), 370-392. For essays that examine Coetzee in the context of other South African writers such as Nadine Gordimer and Athol Fugard, see Andre Brink, "Writing Against Big Brother: Notes on Apocalyptic Fiction in South Africa," *World Literature Today*, LVIII (1984), 189-194; Richard G. Martin, "Narrative, History, Ideology: A Study of *Waiting for the Barbarians* and 'Burger's Daughter,' " *Ariel*, XVII (1986), 3-21; Rowland Smith, "The Seventies and After: The Inner View in White, English-Language Fiction," in Malvern Van Wyk Smith and Don Maclennan, eds., *Olive Schreiner and After: Essays on Southern African Literature in Honor of Guy Butler*, 1983; and Michael Vaughan, "Literature and Politics: Currents in South African Writing in the Seventies," *Journal of Southern African Studies*, IX (1982), 118-138. Of the individual novels, *Waiting for the Barbarians* has generated the most critical interest. Representative essays include Debra A. Castillo, "The Composition of the Self in Coetzee's *Waiting for the Barbarians*," *Critique: Studies in Modern Fiction*, XXVII (1986), 78-90; Susan V. Gallagher, "Torture and the Novel: J. M. Coetzee's *Waiting for the Barbarians*," *Contemporary Literature*, XXIX (1988), 277-285; and Dick Penner, "Sight, Blindness and Double-Thought in J. M. Coetzee's *Waiting for the Barbarians*," *World Literature Written in English*, XXVI (1986), 34-45.

Susan VanZanten Gallagher

ROBERT COLES

Born: Boston, Massachusetts
Date: October 12, 1929

Principal Works

SOCIAL STUDIES: *Children of Crisis, I: A Study of Courage and Fear*, 1967; *The Image Is You*, 1969; *Still Hungry in America*, 1969; *Uprooted Children: The Early Lives of Migrant Farmers*, 1970; *Migrants, Sharecroppers, Mountaineers: Volume II of Children of Crisis*, 1971; *The South Goes North: Volume III of Children of Crisis*, 1971; *Eskimos, Chicanos, Indians: Volume IV of Children of Crisis*, 1978; *Privileged Ones: The Well-Off and Rich in America: Volume V of Children of Crisis*, 1978; *Women of Crisis, I: Lives of Struggle and Hope*, 1978 (with Jane Coles); *Women of Crisis, II: Lives of Work and Dreams*, 1980 (with Coles); *The Moral Life of Children*, 1986; *The Political Life of Children*, 1986.

BIOGRAPHY: *Erik Erikson: The Growth of His Work*, 1970; *Dorothy Day: A Radical Devotion*, 1987; *Simone Weil: A Modern Pilgrimage*, 1987.

LITERARY CRITICISM: *Irony in the Mind's Life: Essays on Novels by James Agess, Elizabeth Bowen, and George Eliot*, 1974; *William Carlos Williams: The Knack of Survival in America*, 1975; *Walker Percy: An American Search*, 1978; *Flannery O'Connor's South*, 1980; *That Red Wheelbarrow: Selected Literary Essays*, 1988; *The Call of Stories: Teaching and the Moral Imagination*, 1989.

ESSAYS: *Farewell to the South*, 1972; *The Mind's Fate: Ways of Seeing Psychiatry and Psychoanalysis*, 1975; *Harvard Diary: Reflections on the Sacred and the Secular*, 1988; *Times of Surrender: Selected Essays*, 1988.

Robert Martin Coles is a leading authority on the lives of the socially and economically deprived, especially children; he has also produced a substantial body of literary criticism and biography, directed not at fellow academics but at the general reader. He was born in Boston on October 12, 1929, to Philip Winston and Sandra Young Coles. Coles himself is from a well-to-do family. His father was a politically conservative engineer who was trained at the Massachusetts Institute of Technology. His mother was a deeply religious woman who both praised his accomplishments and warned against pride and self-centeredness. Coles's excellent education and training began in the prestigious Boston Latin School and then at Harvard University, where he was a Phi Beta Kappa English major in 1950. He took his M.D. degree in 1952 at Columbia University College of Physicians and Surgeons. Coles also enrolled in courses at Union Theological Seminary during this period. Between 1955 and 1958, he continued his medical studies at the University of Chicago and in Boston hospitals. Following his stint in the military, he continued his training with residences and fellowships in psychiatry.

It was during the period of his service in the Air Force that Coles's career took a decisive turn. He was stationed in Biloxi, Mississippi, as chief of neuropsychiatric services at Keesler Hospital and saw the early efforts at integration in the Deep South. This experience, about which he has written often, made an indelible impression on him. When his service was over, he established a practice in Vinings, Georgia, where he regularly called on black families and white families caught in the throes of integration. Coles decided to concentrate his professional work on studying the "children of crisis." He also became an active member of the civil rights movement. He spent eight years collecting data and published the first volume of *Children of Crisis* in 1967.

The method he created for this and subsequent studies is called "social psychiatry," which employs techniques for oral history, psychology, and anthropology. He frequently gains an understanding of children's inner world by studying their drawings, examples of which are included in the text of *Children of Crisis*. The focus of Coles's work has been on the strength, dignity, and resiliency of children and dispossessed families. This approach has led many scholars and political leaders to praise him for showing the human side—the hopes, frustrations, convictions, and prejudices of the poor and dispossessed in the United States and abroad.

In 1969, Coles published *Still Hungry in America*, a book that helped to get the American government's food stamp program established. In 1971, he published two more volumes of his study of children, *Migrants, Sharecroppers, Mountaineers* and *The South Goes North*. *Eskimos, Chicanos, Indians* and *Privileged Ones* both appeared in 1978. In that year, he also launched (with his wife Jane) a new two-volume study, *Women of Crisis*.

Coles has carried his studies abroad to examine how nationalism and political loyalty are taught to children in the strife-torn areas of Ireland and South Africa. Two volumes appeared in 1986: *The Moral Life of Children* and *The Political Life of Children*.

Coles's work has received widespread attention from scholars, political leaders, and the public. Scholars generally credit him with developing an important new approach to the study of the influence of social conditions upon the dispossessed. Political leaders have used him and his work in expert testimony on the social ills that need to be addressed, and the general public has found that his studies reveal the human side of those on the fringe of society.

Coles is best known for his pioneering work in social psychiatry, yet he has also maintained what might be called a second career teaching and writing about literature. For many years at Harvard University, Coles has taught literature to graduate students in medicine, law, business, theology, and education as well as general undergraduates; his courses, which emphasize the enduring value of literature as a guide to life, are among the most popular at the university. Coles's studies of writers such as William Carlos Williams, Walker Percy, and Flannery O'Connor are extensions of his teaching. His book *The Call of Stories*, published in 1989, makes a compelling case for the importance of teaching literature, drawing heavily on the responses of students over the years.

BIBLIOGRAPHICAL REFERENCES: For an interview with Coles, see Judy Boppell Peace, "What Are We Doing to Our Children?" *The Other Side*, XV (May, 1979), 14-22. There is a useful biographical essay in *The New York Times Biographical Service*, IX (1978), 3. There are also reviews of his books in popular and scholarly journals. For *Children of Crisis*, Vol. I, see *Harvard Educational Review*, XXXVIII (1968), 373; *Still Hungry in America*, *The New York Times Book Review*, April 13, 1969, 24; *Women of Crisis*, Vol. I, *The Christian Science Monitor*, August 14, 1978, 23; Vol. II, *The New York Times Book Review*, July 6, 1980, 10; *The Moral Life of Children* and *The Political Life of Children*, *The New York Times Book Review*, January 19, 1981. See also "Robert Coles Reconsidered: A Critique of the Portrayal of Blacks as Culturally Deprived," *Journal of Negro Education*, L, no. 4 (1981), 381-388; "Contributions to Psychohistory: Individual Experience in Historiography and Psychoanalysis, Significance of Erik Erikson and Robert Coles," *Psychological Reports*, XLVI, no. 2 (1980), 591-612.

Stephen A. McKnight

COLETTE
Sidonie-Gabrielle Colette

Born: Saint-Sauveur-en-Puisaye, France *Died:* Paris, France
Date: January 28, 1873 *Date:* August 3, 1954

Principal Works

LONG FICTION: *Claudine à l'école*, 1900 (*Claudine at School*, 1956); *Claudine à Paris*, 1901 (*Claudine in Paris*, 1958); *Claudine en ménage*, 1902 (*The Indulgent Husband*, 1935; also known as *Claudine Married*); *Claudine s'en va*, 1903 (*The Innocent Wife*, 1934; also known as *Claudine and Annie*); *La Retraite sentimentale*, 1907 (*Retreat from Love*, 1974); *L'Ingénue Libertine*, 1909 (*The Gentle Libertine*, 1931; also known as *The Innocent Libertine*); *La Vagabonde*, 1911 (*The Vagabond*, 1955); *L'Entrave*, 1913 (*Recaptured*, 1932; best known as *The Shackle*); *Mitsou: Ou, Comment l'esprit vient aux filles*, 1919 (*Mitsou: Or, How Girls Grow Wise*, 1930); *Chéri*, 1920 (English translation, 1929); *Le Blé en herbe*, 1923 (*The Ripening Corn*, 1931; also known as *The Ripening Seed*, 1955); *La Fin de Chéri*, 1926 (*The Last of Chéri*, 1932); *La Naissance du jour*, 1928 (*A Lesson in Love*, 1932; also known as *Break of Day*); *La Seconde*, 1929 (The Other One, 1931); *La Chatte*, 1933 (*The Cat*, 1936); *Duo*, 1934 (*Duo*, 1935; also known as *The Married Lover*); *Julie de Carneilhan*, 1941 (English translation, 1952); *Gigi*, 1944 (English translation, 1952).

SHORT FICTION: *Chambre d'hôtel*, 1940 (*Chance Acquaintances*, 1955); *Le Képi*, 1943; *The Tender Shoot and Other Stories*, 1959.

NONFICTION: *Dialogues de bêtes*, 1904 (*Creatures Great and Small*, 1957); *L'Envers du music-hall*, 1913 (*Music-Hall Sidelights*, 1957); *La Maison de Claudine*, 1922 (*My Mother's House*, 1953) *Ces Plaisirs*, 1932 (better known as *Le Pur et l'impur*, 1941; *The Pure and the Impure*, 1967); *Mes apprentissages*, 1936 (*My Apprenticeships*, 1957); *Journal à rebours*, 1941, and *De ma fenêtre*, 1942 (translated together as *Looking Backwards*, 1975); *L'Étoile vesper*, 1946 (*The Evening Star*, 1973); *Le Fanal bleu*, 1949 (*The Blue Lantern*, 1963); *Places*, 1970.

CORRESPONDENCE: *Letters from Colette*, 1980.

MISCELLANEOUS: *Œuvres complètes de Colette*, 1948-1950; *The Works*, 1951-1964; *7 by Colette*, 1955.

Sidonie-Gabrielle Colette, one of the most famous French women writers of her era, was born on January 28, 1873, in the Burgundian village of Saint-Sauveur. Colette and her brother, Léo (born 1868), were reared in a provincial country house full of books and animals, surrounded by a magnificent garden. Sido, Colette's mother and the principal influence on her life, had a vast knowledge of plants and animals. In this atmosphere Colette developed an uncanny ability to commune with nature and communicate with animals, qualities she always associated both with innocence and with her mother's home in Saint-Sauveur.

In 1890 the family moved to Châtillon-Coligny. There Colette met Henri Gauthier-Villars, or Willy, a bohemian publicist and raconteur whom she married in May, 1893. Some scholars believe that Colette's life and writing were dominated by a struggle between forces embodied by Sido, who represented innocence, and forces embodied by Willy, who represented experience.

In 1900 her first novel was published as *Claudine at School* under her husband's pen name, Willy. Soon thereafter, Willy began the practice of locking Colette in her room for four hours each day with an assigned number of pages to write. In 1904 she published *Creatures Great and Small*, her first book written under the name "Colette Willy," a byline she would use until 1923. The book, composed of dialogues between her cat and her dog, was the first of several works based on animal themes.

Although Colette loved Willy, she believed that he had betrayed their love in every way. Their problems, depicted by Colette in *My Apprenticeships*, resulted in the couple's separation in 1906 and ended in divorce in 1910. In 1906, Colette began performing in music halls to earn a living. A fictionalized chronicle of those years can be found in *The Vagabond*, *The Shackle*, and *Mitsou*.

Colette's sexual preference was for men, but during her years on the vaudeville circuit she formed a romantic liaison with the Marquise de Belboeuf (better known as Missy), a mainstay of the Parisian lesbian demimonde. In 1910 she met the future statesman Henri de Jouvenal. She married him in 1912, the same year her beloved Sido died. Her daughter was born in 1913. When World War I broke out in Europe in 1914, Colette did volunteer work as a night nurse. She later was awarded membership in the Legion of Honor for her wartime activities.

During the 1920's Colette published some of her best literary works. These included *My Mother's House*, *Chéri*, and *The Last of Chéri*. In the mid-1920's, after her divorce from Jouvenal, she met Maurice Goudeket, a pearl broker, to whom she was married in 1935. Although debilitating arthritis confined her to bed in 1942, during World War II she wrote two volumes of nonfiction, translated together as *Looking Backwards*. Her last work of fiction, *Gigi*, appeared in 1944; her last major book, *The Blue Lantern*, was published in 1949. Colette died quietly on August 3, 1954. She was the first Frenchwoman to be given a state funeral with full honors.

All Colette's novels and many of her short stories are devoted to an analysis of the relationship between the sexes. She believed that the needs of men and women were both different and incompatible. Thus, she maintained, no real communication between the sexes is possible, and true love and independence are, particularly for women, mutually exclusive. While in many of her novels it is the female whose independence is forfeited, in *Duo*, a late novel, the struggle between the sexes results in the man's death.

A theme closely connected with sexual combat is Colette's conviction that women rather than men are centered, connected to nature, and have a "taste for survival"—that is, a capacity to adapt to reality, absorb life's shocks, and carry on with their lives. Therefore all Colette's female protagonists live in the present. Lea in *The Last of Chéri* and Camille in *The Cat*, for example, face the collapse of their lives and adjust to the future. Chéri and Alain, however, attempt to recapture a lost past and enter a "kingdom of adult childhood" whose idyllic nature was modeled on Colette's life in Sido's home at Saint-Sauveur.

Nearly all Colette's novels are short, feature crisp dialogue, and are written in standard form. Indeed, Chéri is often lauded as a model neoclassical novel. Colette seldom experimented with structure or technique in fiction. She believed that the way to express abstract ideas such as truth or beauty was not through mawkish prose but through precise descriptions of physical details filtered through sensation, impression, and memory.

BIBLIOGRAPHICAL REFERENCES: For critical studies of Colette, see Elaine Marks, "Colette," in *A Critical Bibliography of French Literature*, edited by Douglas Alden and Richard Brooks, Vol. 6, 1980. There are dozens of literary biographies of Colette available in English. Many scholars consider Michele Sarde, *Colette Free and Fettered*, 1980, to be the standard work in the field. Also very useful are Allan Massie, *Colette*, 1986; Nicole Ward Jouve, *Colette*, 1987; Genevieve Dormann, *Colette: A Passion for Life*, 1985; Margaret Crosland, *Colette: The Difficulty of Loving*, 1973; Elaine Marks, *Colette*, 1960; and Joan Hinde Stewart, *Colette*, 1983. Also interesting are the memoirs of Colette's third husband, Maurice Goudeket, *Close to Colette*, 1972. Robert Cottrell, *Colette*, 1974, provides an excellent analysis of her major novels. Ilene Olken, *Colette: Aspects of Imagery*, 1959, offers the reader valuable analyses of Colette's literary techniques.

Nancy E. Rupprecht

JOHN COLLIER

Born: London, England
Date: May 3, 1901

Died: Pacific Palisades, California
Date: April 6, 1980

PRINCIPAL WORKS

SHORT FICTION: *Epistle to a Friend*, 1931; *No Traveller Returns*, 1931; *Green Thoughts*, 1932; *The Devil and All*, 1934; *Variations on a Theme*, 1935; *Presenting Moonshine*, 1941; *The Touch of Nutmeg and More Unlikely Stories*, 1943; *Fancies and Goodnights*, 1951; *Pictures in the Fire*, 1958.

NOVELS: *His Monkey Wife: Or, Married to a Chimp*, 1930; *Full Circle: A Tale*, 1933 (also known as *Tom's A-Cold: A Tale*); *Defy the Foul Fiend: Or, The Misadventures of the Heart*, 1934.

SCREENPLAYS: *The African Queen*, 1951 (with others); *Milton's Paradise Lost: Screenplay for Cinema of the Mind*, 1973.

NONFICTION: *Just the Other Day: An Informal History of Britain Since the War*, 1932 (with Ian Lang).

MISCELLANEOUS: *The John Collier Reader*, 1972.

John Collier rightfully belongs to the first rank of minor writers of short fiction in the twentieth century. He was born in London, England, on May 3, 1901, into a family of accomplished professionals. The son of John George Collier, the writer was educated privately. Collier never attended a university or earned a degree, although learned readers of his fiction will discern allusions to William Shakespeare, and Dante in his work and would never suspect his lack of formal education. His early inclination was toward poetry, and indeed he wrote and published poems while still in his early twenties. A truly cosmopolitan writer leading a cosmopolitan life, Collier lived for lengthy periods in London, France, California, New York, and Virginia.

Collier's fiction is consistently recognizable for its bent toward the supernatural, its obsession with fantasy, and its surprise endings. Reviewers have most often compared his works to those of Edgar Allan Poe and O. Henry; beyond that, comparisons can scarcely be made with any genuine authenticity. Collier probes the ironic and humorous, the macabre and diabolical. He uses contrivance and satire, and he often fictionalizes murder stories. His reason for writing is always to make a point toward defining human nature and existence, and the ghosts, angels, demons, jinn, and alchemists who people his work serve only as means toward this end.

Collier stopped writing poetry around the time he turned thirty. He then focused his attention primarily on fiction, and, indeed, during the 1930's he published three novels and a significant portion of his short stories. Of these works, his first novel, *His Monkey Wife*, published in 1930, proved his most important contribution to literature. The story is that of one Mr. Fatigay, a harmless, nondescript teacher of English in Africa, who falls in love with and eventually marries a precocious chimp named Emily; he does so after ending his long engagement to Amy, the 1930's version of the Victorian lady. The novel is full of witticisms of the day. Its success and survival, however, depended greatly upon the shock effect wrought by two sentences from the concluding chapter: "Behind every great man there may indeed be a woman, and beneath every performing flea a hot plate, but beside the only happy man I know of—there is a chimp," and "The candle, guttering beside the bed, was strangled in the grasp of a prehensile foot, and darkness received, like a ripple in velvet, the final happy sigh." The first of these needs no explanation; the "happy sigh" of the second quotation, the last sentence of the novel, refers to the copulation between man and monkey, between husband and wife. Clearly, it is easy to understand why Collier has been so often accused of misogyny: He is guilty of it.

The other two novels evidence the same disregard for women. *Full Circle* was written as a futuristic novel set in England in 1995, a time when mankind, after some war, is reduced to a primitive existence in which fur-clad men bind together in tribes and steal women, literally by brute force, from neighboring, rival tribes; the captured women are then traded and bartered, acquired and cast off, in the most savage ways. Moreover, women as objects do not enjoy any more respect than livestock owned by the men. The same antifeminism surfaces again in Collier's third and last novel, *Defy the Foul Fiend*. Readers would be at fault, however, to dismiss Collier's novels as a 1930's expression of woman-hating; in all three works, men are revealed as enshrouded in their faults, blunders, stupidity, and wickedness just as women are covered in their silliness, weakness, phoniness, and post-Victorian hypocrisy; women are exposed as deserving objects of contempt, but men fare no better.

Of the several dozen short stories which Collier wrote during a period of four decades (most of which have been collected in *The John Collier Reader*), few are directly concerned with the relation between men and women as expressed in the novels. His best story is "The Chaser," an exquisitely contrived piece in which a young man in love visits an alchemist's shop to buy a love potion; the druggist informs the young man about another product he carries: a "cleaning fluid," or "spot remover," which is odorless, tasteless, colorless, and "imperceptible to any known method of autopsy." This chaser, the reader learns slowly, will be the expensive product the young customer will surely and eventually return to purchase if he is foolish enough to buy the one-dollar love potion. In another popular and oft-reprinted story, "De Mortuis . . . ," a medical doctor new to a small town in New York, having moved there after marrying a native daughter, is thought by male acquaintances to have murdered his wife when they find him digging in the basement. These male friends then reveal the previous sexual indiscretions of the wife and they contrive to help the doctor hide the murder since they deem it justifiable. At the end, it is learned that the woman is not yet dead, but the reader knows that she soon will be.

Collier's domain is indeed the short story. To summarize these two typical examples is to understate his craftsmanship. The author's works thrive because of his ability to create imaginative and farfetched plots, to turn phrases, to capture dialogue exactingly, and to involve the reader in the world of fantasy and the supernatural. All these qualities served him well in his work, usually as a collaborator, on Hollywood screenplays. The most successful of these scripts was *The African Queen*. He also wrote *Milton's Paradise Lost: Screenplay for Cinema of the Mind*, which has not been produced. It is clear that Collier's fame will survive for his short stories.

BIBLIOGRAPHICAL REFERENCES: Collier's work has received little serious critical attention in the form of scholarly articles or book-length studies. Yet many of the reviews of his work are most useful. Josiah Titzwell, in a review published in *Booklist*, May, 1931, has provided the best comments about the use of humor in *His Monkey Wife*. *Full Circle* is discussed in a review published in *Books*, May 7, 1933. W. R. Benet discusses the wit of *Defy the Foul Fiend* in a review published in *The Saturday Review of Literature*, August 4, 1934. *The Touch of Nutmeg and More Unlikely Stories* is reviewed by Marjorie Farber in *The New York Times*, January 23, 1944 (she compares Collier's stories to those of Saki). The collection *Fancies and Goodnights* is discussed by Basil Davenport in *The Saturday Review of Literature*, December 22, 1951. John Updike commented on *Milton's Paradise Lost: Screenplay for Cinema of the Mind* in a review published in *The New Yorker*, August 20, 1973, 84-86.

Carl Singleton

PADRAIC COLUM

Born: Collumbkille, Longford, Ireland
Date: December 8, 1881

Died: Enfield, Connecticut
Date: January 11, 1972

PRINCIPAL WORKS

PLAYS: *Broken Soil*, pb. 1903; *The Land*, pr., pb. 1905; *The Fiddler's House*, pr., pb. 1907; *Thomas Muskerry*, pr., pb. 1910; *Balloon*, pb. 1929; *Moytura: A Play for Dancers*, pr., pb. 1963; *The Challengers*, pr. 1966 (includes *Monasterboice, Glendalough*, and *Cloughoughter*); *Carricknabauna*, pr. 1967 (also known as *The Road Round Ireland*).

POETRY: *Wild Earth and Other Poems*, 1907; *Flower Pieces: New Poems*, 1938; *The Collected Poems of Padraic Colum*, 1953; *Irish Elegies*, 1958; *The Poet's Circuits: Collected Poems of Ireland*, 1960; *Images of Departure*, 1969.

CHILDREN'S LITERATURE: *The King of Ireland's Son*, 1916; *The Adventures of Odysseus*, 1918; *Legends of Hawaii*, 1937; *The Frenzied Prince: Being Heroic Stories of Ancient Ireland*, 1943; *A Treasury of Irish Folklore*, 1954.

NOVELS: *Castle Conquer*, 1923; *The Flying Swans*, 1957.

SHORT FICTION: *Selected Short Stories of Padraic Colum*, 1985.

BIOGRAPHY: *Our Friend James Joyce*, 1958 (with Mary Colum); *Ourselves Along: The Story of Arthur Griffith and the Origin of the Irish Free State*, 1959.

During his seventy years as a writer, Padraic Colum composed creative works in such diverse areas as theater, lyric poetry, children's literature, short and long fiction, and biography. Before his emigration to the United States in 1914, he played a key role in the Irish Literary Revival. While in the United States, he became a very gifted teller of folktales for children and continued to refine his skill as a lyric poet. He completed his most admired book of poetry, *Images of Departure*, in 1969 at the age of eighty-seven. He enriched the cultural life of both his native Ireland and his adopted country, the United States.

Unlike almost all the important Irish writers of his generation (including James Joyce, William Butler Yeats, Lady Augusta Gregory, and John Millington Synge), Padraic Colum was not from a well-to-do or even a middle-class family. His was a family of peasants. During his childhood, he knew intimately the suffering and the hopes of Irish farmers. In his literary works, Colum describes eloquently and persuasively the basic dignity and the universality of common people not only in Ireland but in many other countries as well.

Padraic Colum was born on December 8, 1881, in Collumbkille, in the county of Longford, Ireland. He was the eldest of the eight children born to Patrick and Susan Collumb. His father was in charge of the workhouse in which Padraic Colum was born. Unfortunately, his father was an alcoholic and failed to support his family properly. In 1890, his family moved close to Dublin, and only then could Colum begin his formal education, which would last only eight years. Colum overcame this inadequate schooling. In many ways he was a self-educated man. In 1901, he joined the Gaelic League and began to pursue his lifelong interest in Irish culture and folklore. In the same year, he started using the name Padraic Colum instead of his given name, Patrick Collumb. "Padraic" is the Gaelic form for "Patrick," and Saint Colum was a famous Irish saint and poet. Colum soon met James Joyce, who recognized his skill as a writer. James Joyce and Padraic Colum would remain close friends until Joyce's death in 1941.

The first decade of the twentieth century was an extraordinarily productive period in Colum's literary career. In 1903, he became one of the founding members of Dublin's Abbey Theatre. Between 1903 and 1910, he wrote three important plays: *Broken Soil* (revised in 1907 and renamed *The Fiddler's House*), *The Land*, and *Thomas Muskerry*. These powerful plays, which, as Colum himself admitted, were strongly influenced by the dramatic realism of

Henrik Ibsen, portrayed common Irish people in an unsentimental manner. The witty dialogues in *The Land* and *The Fiddler's House* were greatly admired by Dublin theatergoers, who appreciated Colum's ironic commentaries on contemporary social problems in Ireland. *Thomas Muskerry*, however, provoked intense public discussion in Ireland because it portrayed the cruel exploitation of the title character by members of his own family. Thomas Muskerry himself is the only sympathetic character in this play. While dramatically effective, *Thomas Muskerry* does present a fairly bleak view of the world. A modern scholar, Sanford Sternlicht, has compared *Thomas Muskerry* to William Shakespeare's *King Lear* (pr. c. 1605-1606). Muskerry, like King Lear, comes to understand his profound dignity only after much undeserved suffering. After his dramatic masterpiece *Thomas Muskerry*, Colum rarely wrote for the stage. In the early 1960's, however, he did write five fascinating one-act Nō plays on Irish themes.

It was also during the first decade of the twentieth century that Padraic Colum began to write lyric poetry. His 1907 *Wild Earth and Other Poems* established his reputation as the major Irish Catholic poet of his generation. In such finely crafted poems as "The Plougher," "A Drover," and "An Old Woman of the Roads," Colum avoided facile sentimentality and conveyed to his readers his belief that a search for meaning and happiness can coexist with a tragic vision of the world. The twenty-five poems in *Wild Earth and Other Poems* present very eloquently the true dignity of Irish peasants, whose apparently simple and yet emotionally complex lives point to the difficulty of facing such complex realities as death, the loss of love, religious faith, and poverty. In composing the poems in this collection, Colum took recognizable situations and character types from Irish popular culture and developed them with an eloquence and psychological complexity never before attained in Irish poetry.

In 1909, Padraic Colum met Mary Maguire, a graduate of University College, Dublin. Three years later they married, and they emigrated to the United States together. Like her husband, Mary Colum was a writer. The couple often taught literature courses together at Columbia University. Her major literary work was her 1947 autobiography, *Life and the Dream*. Between 1914 and his wife's death in 1957, Padraic Colum wrote some twenty-five books for children, numerous short stories, and two novels: *Castle Conquer* and *The Flying Swans*. *The Flying Swans*, his most creative work of fiction, is a *Bildungsroman* which describes the aesthetic and moral development of an Irish writer named Ulick O'Reheill. Similarities between *The Flying Swans* and Joyce's *A Portrait of the Artist as a Young Man* (1916) and *Ulysses* (1922) have been noted by many critics. Although Joyce's influence on his friend and biographer Padraic Colum is undeniable, *The Flying Swans* is still an original novel which, unfortunately, has never received the critical attention it deserves.

Between the publication in 1916 of *The King of Ireland's Son* and his 1954 anthology *A Treasury of Irish Folklore*, Padraic Colum was famous above all for his refined retelling of folktales for children. He used all of his skill as a writer in order to encourage creativity in children and to transmit the essential values of popular culture and legends to young readers. Colum never limited himself to Irish legends. His folktales were set in such diverse cultures as ancient Greece, medieval Scandinavia, the Middle East, and Hawaii. Colum's children's books continue to bring pleasure to new generations of young readers.

Despite the apparent diversity in his contribution to lyric poetry, drama, fiction, and children's literature, there is a definite unity in Padraic Colum's works. He consistently expressed in very refined verse and prose the universal values in mythology, folklore, and popular culture. His writings made generations of readers more sensitive to the beauty in daily life. His contemporaries in Ireland and the United States recognized his importance as a writer. Both Irish and American universities granted him honorary doctorates, and he received medals from both the Poetry Society of America and the Academy of Irish Letters. Although critics have generally praised his creativity as a poet and playwright, his two novels and numerous works of children's literature have not attracted much scholarly attention.

BIBLIOGRAPHICAL REFERENCES: Zack Bowen, *Padraic Colum: A Biographical-Critical Introduction*, 1970, is an excellent general work based largely on interviews granted by Padraic Colum in the 1960's. Sanford Sternlicht, *Padraic Colum*, 1985, is the most comprehensive study of Colum's literary career. The January, 1973, issue of *The Journal of Irish Literature*, which deals solely with Padraic Colum, contains many informative essays on his life and works. See also Lionel Trilling, "Mr. Colum's Greeks," *The Griffin*, 1956, 4-15; Alan Denson, "Padraic Colum: An Appreciation with a Checklist of His Publications," *The Dublin Magazine*, VI, no. 1 (1967), 50-67; Richard J. Loftus, *Nationalism in Modern Anglo-Irish Poetry*, 1964; and Richard Fallis, *The Irish Renaissance*, 1977.

Edmund J. Campion

EVAN S. CONNELL, JR.

Born: Kansas City, Missouri
Date: August 17, 1924

Principal Works

SHORT FICTION: *The Anatomy Lesson and Other Stories*, 1957; *At the Crossroads*, 1965; *St. Augustine's Pigeon*, 1980.

NOVELS: *Mrs. Bridge*, 1959; *The Patriot*, 1960; *The Diary of a Rapist*, 1966; *Mr. Bridge*, 1969; *The Connoisseur*, 1974; *Double Honeymoon*, 1976.

POETRY: *Notes from a Bottle Found on the Beach at Carmel*, 1963; *Points for a Compass Rose*, 1973.

HISTORY: *A Long Desire*, 1979; *The White Lantern*, 1980; *Son of the Morning Star*, 1984.

Evan Shelby Connell, Jr., is one of the more versatile and wide-ranging figures in twentieth century American letters. Novelist, short-story writer, poet, and historian, he moves in his interests from the modern world to the vanished societies of antiquity. Born in Kansas City, Missouri, on August 17, 1924, Connell interrupted his education at Dartmouth College to become a Naval pilot during World War II. With the end of the war, he utilized the GI Bill to obtain his B.A. from the University of Kansas. After further study at Stanford, Columbia, and San Francisco State universities, Connell chose to make his career in the literary field. While he did serve from 1959 to 1965 as an editor of *Contact*, a small literary magazine, his dominant concern was to create his own work. The public, however, largely ignored him for many years, and to help support himself while writing, he had to read meters, pass out handbills, deliver packages, and work in an unemployment office.

In his fiction, Connell depicts the loneliness and frustration of middle-class Americans struggling through lives devoid of meaning. While his short stories are pervaded by this theme, it is his novels that most sharply delineate his sense of the emptiness of contemporary existence. Beginning with India Bridge of *Mrs. Bridge*, a repressed, mentally abused suburban housewife whose domineering husband has left her without a shred of self-esteem, Connell's novels create a gallery of disconnected, desolate characters. *Mrs. Bridge* is perhaps the work that most represents Connell's concerns, although *Mr. Bridge*, an in-depth portrayal of Indian Bridge's spouse, Walter, a self-righteous, narrow, joyless workaholic, and *Double Honeymoon*, the story of Karl Muhlback, a bored businessman and recent widower who stumbles into an obsessive, tragic affair with an unstable younger woman, are also graphic expressions of his views.

Even as Evan Connell has traversed his bleak modern landscape, he has looked back into the past, first as a poet, then as a historian. It is an exciting, colorful past. Connell is fascinated by the fabled cultures and exotic personalities of yesteryear. In 1963, Connell published a book-length poem, *Notes from a Bottle Found on the Beach at Carmel*, using constantly shifting voices from different epochs to present the multiplicity of myths, superstitions, and religious beliefs humans have used to make sense of the world and their place in it. A similarly composed epic poem, *Points for a Compass Rose*, documents man's lust for blood and war through the ages. In *A Long Desire* and *The White Lantern*, Connell moves to straight narrative history. Both books consist of essays dealing with legend, historic mysteries, and especially the exploits of individuals in quest of glory, gold, knowledge, and the penetration of the unknown: conquistadors, wandering Vikings, polar explorers, alchemists, and savants. There is some didacticism in these works. Connell seems to believe that human beings can be enriched by an understanding of the seamless nature of history and that much can be learned from the triumphs and mistakes of the past. Except for *Points for a Compass Rose*, which draws numerous parallels between the United States in Vietnam and earlier destructive aggressors, Connell does not insist on lessons. He appears more caught up in the romantic allure of his subjects.

Connell's interest in picturesque history has grown dominant in his work. With the exception of a few short stories, his writings since 1979 have moved in this direction. *Son of the Morning Star*, published in 1984, deals with the violent, myth-laden Indian wars on the Plains. In the process, it tackles two of the most enduring questions in American popular history: what Indian fighter George Custer was really like and what actually happened at the Battle of the Little Bighorn. Connell never fully solves either mystery, but he does provide one of the most complete, evenhanded, and readable accounts yet of Custer's exploits and the campaigns against the Sioux.

Since the publication of *Mrs. Bridge*, which has been hailed for its depiction of a woman caught in the trap of domesticity, Evan Connell has enjoyed a moderately significant critical following. *Mr. Bridge* added to his reputation, and *Points for a Compass Rose* was nominated for a National Book Award. Few book buyers, though, paid any attention to his work until *Son of the Morning Star*, which caught the public's attention. It became a best-seller, was quickly issued in paperback, and was even marketed in cassette tapes. The National Book Critics Circle voted it among the finest nonfiction volumes of the year, and *Time* magazine named it one of the ten best books of 1984. The Custer book's success also resulted in the reprinting of almost all Connell's previous works.

BIBLIOGRAPHICAL REFERENCES: Except for an early study, Gus Blaisdell, "After Ground Zero: The Writings of Evan S. Connell, Jr.," *New Mexico Quarterly*, XXXV (Summer, 1966), 181-207, Connell has attracted little scholarly interest. Newspapers, periodicals, and reference works are the major sources for insight into Connell and his writings. *The New York Times* has done the best job of tracking Connell's career. Two important essays built upon interviews are Lawrence M. Bensky, "Meet Evan Connell, Friend of Mr. and Mrs. Bridge," April 20, 1969, and Samuel Freedman's article on Connell, February 13, 1985, C19. *The New York Times* has also published helpful reviews on Connell: Herbert Mitgang, "Prose Candles for Mankind," review of *Points for a Compass Rose*, June 30, 1973, 31; Anatole Broyard, "An Unsuitable Risk," review of *Double Honeymoon*, May 23, 1976; and Paul Zweig, "Attic Trove," review of *The White Lantern*, July 20, 1980.

Clarke L. Wilhelm

MARC CONNELLY

Born: McKeesport, Pennsylvania
Date: December 13, 1890

Died: New York, New York
Date: December 21, 1980

PRINCIPAL WORKS

PLAYS: *Dulcy*, pr., pb. 1921 (with George S. Kaufman); *To the Ladies*, pr. 1922 (with Kaufman); *Merton of the Movies*, pr. 1922 (with Kaufman); *Helen of Troy*, pr. 1923 (with Kaufman); *Beggar on Horseback*, pr. 1924 (with Kaufman); *Be Yourself*, pr. 1924 (with Kaufman); *The Wisdom Tooth*, pr., pb. 1926; *The Wild Man of Borneo*, pr. 1927 (with Herman J. Mankiewicz); *The Green Pastures: A Fable*, pb. 1929; *The Farmer Takes a Wife*, pr., pb. 1934 (with Frank B. Elser); *Everywhere I Roam*, pr. 1938 (with Arnold Sundgaard); *The Flowers of Virtue*, pr. 1942; *A Story for Strangers*, pr. 1948; *Hunter's Moon*, pr. 1958; *The Portable Yenberry*, pr. 1962.

NOVEL: *A Souvenir from Qam*, 1964.

AUTOBIOGRAPHY: *Voices Offstage: A Book of Memoirs*, 1968.

SCREENPLAYS: *Whispers*, 1920; *Exit Smiling*, 1926; *The Suitor*, 1928 (short); *The Bridegroom*, 1929; *The Uncle*, 1929; *The Green Pastures*, 1936; *Captains Courageous*, 1937 (with others); *I Married a Witch*, 1942; *Crowded Paradise*, 1956.

RADIO PLAY: *The Mole on Lincoln's Cheek*, 1941.

Playwright, director, journalist, teacher, author, and actor, Marcus Cook Connelly is best known as George S. Kaufman's first collaborator and as the author of the popular religious drama *The Green Pastures*. His father, Patrick Connelly, was an actor and became the proprietor of the White Hotel in McKeesport, where Marc first learned about acting while watching the most famous actors and actresses of the time practice in front of a mirror. When Connelly was seven, his parents took him to Pittsburgh for his first visit to the professional theater, and he was so mesmerized that he believed that he was in church. This initial impression led him to his lifelong conviction that the theater is a place where the spirit is nourished. Convinced that he had found his true calling, Connelly began writing and producing numerous plays on the second floor of his father's hotel at the age of eleven. After moving to Pittsburgh, Connelly began to write short, humorous pieces for a local newspaper, the *Pittsburgh Press*. After a year, he was hired by the *Gazette Times* as humor columnist, news reporter, and assistant drama critic. It was during this period that Connelly began writing plays, skits, and lyrics for musicals.

In 1920, when Connelly was fired from his job as press agent for a musical comedy, he started his collaborations with George S. Kaufman, who was the drama critic of *The New York Times*. Between 1920 and 1924, Connelly and Kaufman wrote several plays and musical comedies together, at least four of which are of permanent interest to the theater. All of their plays attack the elevation of fashionable art over classical art. While they worked together, Connelly and Kaufman were also members of the Round Table of the Algonquin Hotel, and the influence of the other writers who belonged to this informal lunch group can be easily detected in their many collaborations. Their first play, *Dulcy*, was based on a fatuous character created by the columnist F. P. Adams and was used as a vehicle for Lynn Fontanne.

After the termination of his partnership with Kaufman, Connelly joined the ranks of established writers such as Alexander Woollcott and Edna Ferber who contributed to Harold Ross's fledgling magazine *The New Yorker* with essays, skits, satires, and travel articles. One of Connelly's short stories, "Coroner's Inquest," won for him an O. Henry Award in 1930. To the extent that all the works produced during this time are concerned with the man isolated from society, they can be viewed as preparation for his greatest work: *The Green Pastures*.

While *The Green Pastures* (based on Roark Bradford's *Ol' Man Adam an' His Chillun*) is ostensibly another one of Connelly's "hopeful" plays, it stands apart from his previous works because of the scale of its vision. In this play, Connelly links the struggles of the Jews with those of the blacks, thereby promising black audiences that they too could become active in their own cause. The play went on to establish various long-run records and to win for Connelly the Pulitzer Prize, thereby reflecting an awakening social conscience in the United States. In 1935, Warner Bros. purchased the film rights and hired Connelly to direct, stage, and cast the film, making him the highest paid writer in Hollywood at the time. Revived in 1951, *The Green Pastures* enjoyed only a short run and was severely criticized by prominent black writers for its portrayal of the American black.

For most of the 1930's and the early 1940's, Connelly made his home in Hollywood, where he wrote the screenplays for such films as *Captains Courageous* and *I Married a Witch*. Although some critics rank these screenplays among the greatest produced by Hollywood at the time, none of the works belonging to this period approaches *The Green Pastures*.

Connelly returned to Broadway in 1942 with *The Flowers of Virtue*, but when it failed, he ceased to write for the stage for the duration of the war. In fact, he did not have a single successful play produced or published after World War II. He became a professor of playwriting at Yale University from 1947 to 1952 and was elected president of the National Institute of Arts and Letters in 1953. In 1964, Connelly wrote his first novel, *A Souvenir from Qam*, a romantic comedy laced with Algonquin humor; it received favorable reviews. After writing this novel, he seemed to have been content to spend the rest of his life as an elder statesman of letters, devoting his time to traveling, acting, and writing his autobiography, *Voices Offstage*. He died in 1980.

Connelly's reputation as a playwright rests primarily on *The Green Pastures*, which is one of the most important plays in American drama. Admittedly, he has written other fine plays, such as *Beggar on Horseback* and *The Wisdom Tooth*, but they are considered to be minor forms. Most of his other "good" plays are of historical interest primarily for the insights they provide into the 1920's and the 1930's. Even though he did not revolutionize the theater and inspire scores of imitators, Connelly has been an important influence. The social satires that he wrote with George S. Kaufman introduced a new kind of comedy to theater, comedy evident in such plays as Neil Simon's *The Odd Couple* (pr. 1965).

The intent in all Connelly's plays was not so much to expound a philosophical view of life as it was to turn the theater into what he called a "benign drug" that allowed people to forget about their troubles for a while. Thus, his plays offend modern sensibilities and appear to be hopelessly unrealistic because of their championship of the "born loser" and their affirmation of the emergence of humanistic qualities in all people, even under the most unbearable conditions. Yet in his refusal to lecture morality to his audience, he allied himself with ancient Greek dramatists, who preferred to provide their audiences with the tools with which to examine their lives.

BIBLIOGRAPHICAL REFERENCES: Paul T. Nolan, *Marc Connelly*, 1969, does not cover the last twelve years of his life but is, nevertheless, the best critical biography available. For a glimpse into Connelly's years with the Algonquin Round Table, see Margaret Case Harriman, *The Vicious Circle: The Story of the Algonquin Round Table*, 1951; Franklin P. Adams, *The Diary of Our Own Samuel Pepys*, 1935; Alexander Woollcott, *The Enchanted Aisles*, 1924. See also Tom Cripps's introduction to *The Green Pastures*, 1979, and Nick Aaron Ford, "How Genuine Is *The Green Pastures*?" *Phylon*, Spring, 1960, 67-70.

Alan Brown

CYRIL CONNOLLY

Born: Coventry, England
Date: September 10, 1903

Died: London, England
Date: November 26, 1974

Principal Works

NOVEL: *The Rock Pool*, 1936.
ESSAYS: *Enemies of Promise*, 1938; *The Condemned Playground*, 1945.
MISCELLANEOUS: *The Unquiet Grave: A Word Cycle*, 1944.

Cyril Vernon Connolly is perhaps best known as England's "Golden Boy" of literature, who never fulfilled his early promise to be the finest writer of his generation. Instead, he led a life of indolence, self-pity, and indulgence in high living and social fecklessness. He was born in Coventry, England, the son of Matthew Connolly, a professional soldier, and Muriel Vernon Connolly, who was descended from a distinguished Anglo-Irish family. He began his education at a good school, St. Cyprian's, where Eric Blair (later to be known as George Orwell) was a schoolmate. His formal education was to be an important influence on his life, and his next school, Eton College, the finest and most socially important school in England, was to fix upon him a reputation for literary promise. He became part of the social elite of Eton, a member of the eminent inner circle "Pop," even though his family was not particularly prominent and he was not much of an athlete. He was, however, widely admired as the liveliest intellect in the school, and much was expected of him.

Connolly went to Balliol College, Oxford, and continued to flourish there as one of the brightest undergraduates, but his reputation was blighted when he took only a third-class degree, to the surprise of everyone. His career in the real world began rather unprepossessingly, first as a child's tutor and then as a personal secretary to the American man of letters Lloyd Logan Pearsall Smith. By the late 1920's he was working regularly as a journalist in London, and he began to build a reputation as a reviewer for the *New Statesman*. In 1930, he was married to an American, Jean Bakewell; she had a modest private income, and they lived on that and his earnings as a free-lance writer, settling for a time in the South of France.

In 1936, Connolly's novel, *The Rock Pool*, a clever satire about Britons living in an artists' colony on the Riviera, was published. It showed promise, but no more promise than the work of his contemporaries Evelyn Waugh, Anthony Powell, and Graham Greene, all of whom were schoolmates of Connolly at one time or another. His second book, *Enemies of Promise*, was to gain a wider reception as one of the best and most perceptive attacks upon the English public school system, but again it was not the great book that was to put him at the front of his generation of writers.

Connolly continued to work as a journalist in London, and in 1939 he founded *Horizon*, which was to become the finest literary magazine of the 1940's and certainly one of the best British journals of the twentieth century. He edited it until its termination in 1949, and it would have been, for a lesser man, sufficient proof of a distinguished literary career. Yet Connolly was as much convinced of his capacity for greater things as anyone else was; nevertheless, he never seemed able to settle down to the hard labor of writing a great novel. His personal life was chaotic (he was married three times), and his indulgence in the pleasures of literary celebrity (too much entertainment, too much good food and drink) seemed to get in the way of his writing.

His greatest success was with a book, *The Unquiet Grave*, which first appeared in *Horizon*, supposedly written by someone called Palinurus. It was to become something of a cult classic, an intriguing mix of fiction, autobiography, and occasional essay. In it, he took on the character of a sophisticated man contemplating the failure of his life within the context of a charming, wide-ranging medley of quotations from the classical to modern authors. The book features a stunning display of French allusions passed off with effortless elegance and a range of emotion beginning in despair, swinging into tender reminiscence of past pleasures, and ending in an operatic gesture of worldly-wise resignation. If he could not write the great novel, he at least proved that he ought to have been able to write it, given the range of learning and magnanimous wisdom that *The Unquiet Grave* displays.

Connolly was never to write anything more substantial or anything more popular. In his later years, he contented himself with journalism, and he was, until his death from heart trouble in 1974, the chief book critic for the London *Sunday Times*. He is acknowledged as one of the finest essayists of his time, but often with the qualification that he ought to have done more with his gifts. He has become a very minor figure in English letters in the late twentieth century and his reputation is likely to fade even further as time passes. Nevertheless, two works remain important. *Enemies of Promise* is still considered one of the finest studies of a peculiar British phenomenon, the great public school, and *The Unquiet Grave* has become a minor classic, a twentieth century addition to the world of humane, elegant thought, in which style, now somewhat out of fashion, is as important as content.

BIBLIOGRAPHICAL REFERENCES: Michael Shelden, *Friends of Promise: Cyril Connolly and the World of "Horizon,"* 1989, is a biographical study of Connolly and his circle. D. J. Enright, *Conspirators and Poets*, 1966, includes a succinct assessment of Connolly's career. Samuel Hynes, *The Auden Generation: Literature and Politics in England in the 1930's*, 1972, a general study of the British writers of the period, puts Connolly clearly in the intellectual context so essential to understanding his work. Stephen Spender's *The Thirties and After*, 1978, is also helpful in that regard, as is Valentine Cunningham's *British Writers of the Thirties*, 1988. Graham Greene's collection of essays on the public schools, *The Old School*, helps to explain *Enemies of Promise*. The Greene collection, published in 1984, contains essays on the subject by several of Connolly's contemporaries. Evelyn Waugh's *The Diaries of Evelyn Waugh*, 1976, and *Evelyn Waugh: A Biography*, by Christopher Sykes, 1975, are helpful in understanding the peculiar closed society of the upper-middle-class English schoolboy which was carried into university and then into their later careers. In the same vein, Anthony Powell's four-volume autobiography, *To Keep the Ball Rolling*, 1976-1982, offers insights into Connolly's life and work. Kingsley Martin, *New Statesman Profiles*, 1958, sketches Connolly's journalistic career.

Charles Pullen

JOSEPH CONRAD

Born: Near Berdyczew, Poland
Date: December 3, 1857

Died: Bishopsbourne, England
Date: August 3, 1924

PRINCIPAL WORKS

NOVELS: *Almayer's Folly*, 1895; *Lord Jim*, 1900; *Nostromo*, 1904; *The Secret Agent*, 1907; *Under Western Eyes*, 1910; *Chance*, 1913; *Victory*, 1915; *The Shadow-Line*, 1917; *The Arrow of Gold*, 1919; *The Rescue*, 1920; *The Rover*, 1923; *Suspense*, 1925.

SHORT FICTION: *An Outcast of the Islands*, 1896; *The Nigger of the "Narcissus,"* 1897; *Heart of Darkness*, 1902; *Youth: A Narrative and Two Other Stories*, 1902; *Typhoon and Other Stories*, 1902.

AUTOBIOGRAPHY: *The Mirror of the Sea*, 1906; *A Personal Record*, 1912; *Notes on Life and Letters*, 1921.

CORRESPONDENCE: *The Collected Letters of Joseph Conrad: Volume I, 1861-1897*, 1983; *The Collected Letters of Joseph Conrad: Volume II, 1898-1902*, 1986; *The Collected Letters of Joseph Conrad: Volume III, 1903-1907*, 1988.

Born Jósef Teodor Konrad Korzeniowski, the son of a Polish nobleman, writer, and militant nationalist, this great English novelist adopted the name of Joseph Conrad after many years of adventure at sea. He settled in England and became a naturalized British subject in 1886, only eight years after he had learned to speak and write English. Considered to be one of the supreme stylists in English, his third language (he had mastered French earlier), Conrad revealed in his letters that writing was an enormous struggle for him and a calling he worked at strenuously and with all of his heart. He left Poland in 1874, attracted to the life of the sea but also downhearted about the fate of his native land, which had been burdened by Russian dominance for so long. Much of Conrad's fiction, particularly his political trilogy, *Nostromo*, *The Secret Agent*, and *Under Western Eyes*, reflects his fatalistic view of history and his skepticism about the possibilities of progress in human affairs.

No consideration of Conrad's genius can leave out a discussion of *Heart of Darkness*, a brooding, agonizing, and penetrating exploration of the human heart. Narrated by Marlow, who appears in some of Conrad's other great work as his fictional alter ego, *Heart of Darkness* questions whether human beings have really learned how to govern themselves, to civilize the raw, primordial conflicts that threaten the very concept of humanity. Set in the context of an imperial world—Conrad begins with passages on Rome's conquering of Britain—in which European powers have invaded Africa, *Heart of Darkness* becomes Marlow's quest to find Kurtz, a European who has become a kind of god to the natives but who ends his life exclaiming of "the horror" that has attended his domination of these people, of the human sacrifices that are the result of his rule.

Conrad lived in the heyday of the British Empire, in a time when it was still possible to presume that England would rule its farflung colonies forever. Conrad admired the humanity of the British but implied that their seeming superiority was as illusory as that of any empire. *Lord Jim*, for example, concentrates on a sailor's heroic image of himself and his tormented conscience once he fails the first test of the hero: the opportunity to stay with his sinking ship and save lives. Jim's shame at jumping ship is admirable in the sense that he calls himself to account, but it is also unrealistic. His remorse is an index of his romantic view of himself and of the individual's power over his own impulses.

In *Nostromo*, one of Conrad's most impressive novels, he creates a South American country, Costaguana, shaken by revolution and corrupted by European investors. The country becomes a metaphor for history, in which changes of regime are received as signs of progress but are actually emblematic of a repetitive pattern that is futile. Conrad's bitter experience in Poland led him to distrust all solutions that were merely political or economic. His later novels such as *The Secret Agent* and *Under Western Eyes* are prescient studies of twentieth century political violence and revolutions.

With his Polish background, Conrad brought a sophistication into English fiction and a worldview that it sorely lacked. That he succeeded so well is a tribute not only to the soundness of his ideas but also to his fictional technique. Many of his novels are experimental and innovative. He uses multiple narrators and bold shifts in time and perspective to create a very dense and complex sense of history. At the same time, he never loses sight of the humanity of his characters. There is much humor in novels such as *The Secret Agent*, and the feel for the rhythms of the sea in his early short fiction shows the pleasure he took in life. For all of his philosophy, Conrad remains a sensory writer. He has created a fictional world to which generations of readers have reacted in a visceral way.

BIBLIOGRAPHICAL REFERENCES: There is a vast critical literature on Conrad that began to be produced shortly after his death. Perhaps the most important early criticism and biographies to consult are Gérard Jean-Aubry, *Joseph Conrad: Life and Letters*, 1927, and Jessie Conrad, *Joseph Conrad and His Circle*, 1935. *Conrad: A Collection of Critical Essays*, edited by Marvin Mudrick, 1966, provides a sound if brief introduction to Conrad's career as well as including several important studies of his work. The Norton Critical Edition of *Heart of Darkness*, edited by Robert Kimbrough, 1963, contains an excellent annotated bibliography. Any thorough study of Conrad's writing would have to include these classic studies: John Dozier Gordon, *Joseph Conrad: The Making of a Novelist*, 1940; F. R. Leavis, *The Great Tradition: George Eliot, Henry James, Joseph Conrad*, 1948; Douglas Hewitt, *Conrad: A Reassessment*, 1952; Paul Wiley, *Conrad's Measure of Man*, 1954; Thomas Moser, *Joseph Conrad: Achievement and Decline*, 1957; Robert F. Haugh, *Joseph Conrad: Discovery in Design*, 1957; Albert J. Guerard, *Conrad the Novelist*, 1958; and Leo Gurko, *Joseph Conrad: Giant in Exile*, 1962. Two specialized studies on Conrad's background and politics are also worth consulting: Gustav Morf, *The Polish Heritage of Joseph Conrad*, 1930; Eloise K. Hay, *The Political Novels of Joseph Conrad*, 1963. Conrad has been well served in several distinguished biographies: Jocelyn Baines, *Joseph Conrad: A Critial Biography*, 1960; Frederick R. Karl, *Joseph Conrad: The Three Lives*, 1979; and Zdzisław Najder, *Joseph Conrad: A Chronicle*, 1983. Najder's work is of special importance, for he is a Polish scholar particularly well versed in the early sources of Conrad's life and art.

Carl Rollyson

ROBERT COOVER

Born: Charles City, Iowa
Date: February 4, 1932

Principal Works

NOVELS: *The Origin of the Brunists*, 1965; *The Universal Baseball Association, Inc. J. Henry Waugh, Prop.*, 1968; *The Public Burning*, 1977; *Gerald's Party*, 1986.

SHORT FICTION: *Pricksongs and Descants*, 1969; *The Water Pourer*, 1972; *Hair o' the Chine*, 1979; *After Lazarus*, 1980; *A Political Fable*, 1980; *Charlie in the House of Rue*, 1980; *The Convention*, 1981; *Spanking the Maid*, 1981; *In Bed One Night and Other Brief Encounters*, 1983; *A Night at the Movies: Or, You Must Remember This*, 1987; *Whatever Happened to Gloomy Gus of the Chicago Bears*, 1987.

PLAY: *A Theological Position*, pb. 1972.

Robert Coover has written in a variety of literary forms—short fiction, plays, filmscripts, novellas, and a handful of review-essays on writers for whom he has a special affinity (Samuel Beckett and Gabriel García Márquez in particular). It is through the novel, however, that he has achieved his greatest renown. A major figure in twentieth century American literature, he has demonstrated no interest whatsoever in the celebrity and mass appeal that in the West are often equated with literary success. On the other hand it is from the same mass culture that Coover has drawn the subjects of his fiction: baseball, Cold War paranoia, apocalyptic religion, Charles Chaplin, Richard Nixon, and Dr. Seuss's Cat in the Hat, for example.

Coover was born on February 4, 1932, in the small mining town of Charles City, Iowa, where his father managed the local newspaper. After college, a tour of duty in the Navy, and marriage, Coover began teaching (at Bard College and other colleges) while devoting as much time as possible to his writing. Unlike the majority of "academic" writers, Coover has spent most of his career away from the universities, at least until the early 1980's, when he joined the faculty of Brown University. Encouraged to expand and elaborate on the mining materials in his early story "Blackdamp" (1961), Coover produced the work that established his importance as a young as well as daring—and, to some reviewers, iconoclastic—writer, *The Origin of the Brunists*, winner of the 1966 William Faulkner Award.

The thematic and technical preoccupations of Coover's entire career can be found in this first novel. Coover is in many ways a moralist determined to show man the error of his ways. He positions man not at the center of the world but rather at the center of the fictions man constructs in order to explain that world and make it amenable to human habitation and man's inflated sense of his own self-importance. Longing for stasis and immortality, his characters persist in believing in such used-up forms and ideas as realism, reason, progress, religion—in short, all the metaphors they have come to accept as reality. This acceptance prevents them from taking responsibility for their own existence not as the begotten and beloved of God but as the begetter of the fictive beliefs by which they live. Coover's narrative method stands as the antithesis of his characters' static obsessiveness. Rather than be imprisoned by fiction, Coover exploits fiction's metaphoric possibilities so as to make it increasingly difficult for the reader to do to these fictions what Coover's characters do to theirs: confuse them with reality.

This dual tendency—to exploit the metaphoric possibilities and to widen the gap between meaningless reality and exhaustively meaningful fiction—is one that becomes heightened over the course of Coover's career. Coover moves from a quasi realism in *The Origin of the Brunists* and a thin separation between myth and reality in *The Universal Baseball Association* to a doubling of narrative voices and overrich historical texture in *The Public Burning* and a full exploitation of narrative's permutational possibilities in *Spanking the Maid* and

Gerald's Party. By exploiting his characters' confusion over the ways in which fiction and fictive beliefs come to overwhelm and supplant protean, meaningless reality, Coover undermines fiction's authority and the suspension of disbelief it demands. In this way he liberates the reader not from fiction, or from fiction-making, which he sees as a basic human need, but rather from the stranglehold of any one fiction or fictive system. In effect what Coover does is to privilege the making of fiction, the imaginative process itself, over the fictions that it produces: process over product, the maker over the consumer.

Not surprisingly, Coover has been linked to those writers (John Barth, Donald Barthelme, William H. Gass, and others) who have been termed "metafictionists." Metafiction is experimental, self-reflexive, and highly self-conscious. Instead of mimetically representing a reality whose existence is taken for granted, metafiction examines its own existence, its own status as fiction and, by extension, as metaphor for all those fictions which the metafictionists believe man has unwisely allowed to rule his life. Yet unlike certain metafictionists, Coover seems as concerned with preserving narrative interest as he is with disrupting it, and more concerned than most metafictionists with the moral consequences of man's unwillingness to take responsibility for his own mythmaking. The means Coover employs to express this concern is comedy, particularly that of cartoons and silent films: the sudden transformations of the one and the slapstick, pratfalls, and Chaplinesque befuddlement of the other.

The metafictional dimension of Coover's writing is most overtly present in the collection entitled *Pricksongs and Descants* and perhaps most brilliantly if more obliquely employed in *The Universal Baseball Association*. The various strains of Coover's narrative style are most fully realized in his ambitious and densely woven novel *The Public Burning*, subtitled "a historical romance." The difficulties Coover faced in getting the manuscript of this novel published, the hostility of certain influential as well as literal-minded reviewers, and subsequent legal challenges left Coover less than happy with the literary marketplace in the United States. His later works have evidenced a certain distaste for the general reader. Either they have been published in small editions by even smaller alternative publishing houses (such as *In Bed One Night and Other Brief Encounters* and *Charlie in the House of Rue*) or they read less like novels than as assaults on the reader's patience and sensibilities (such as *Spanking the Maid* and *Gerald's Party*). Even so, they continue to evidence Coover's interest in formal innovation and moral concern, however oblique or inverted that concern may appear.

BIBLIOGRAPHICAL REFERENCES: The most illuminating overview of Coover's art appears in Larry McCaffery's *The Metafictional Muse: The Works of Robert Coover, Donald Barthelme, and William H. Gass*, 1982. More comprehensive but less rigorously argued is Lois Gordon's *Robert Coover: The Universal Fictionmaking Process*, 1983. Richard Andersen's *Robert Coover*, 1981, is a standard literary biography. The brief discussions in Robert Scholes's *Fabulation and Metafiction*, 1979, and David Lodge's *The Modes of Modern Writing: Metaphor, Metonymy, and the Typology of Modern Literature*, 1977, are especially illuminating. The most important interviews appear in *First Person*, 1973, edited by Frank Gado; *The Radical Imagination and the Liberal Tradition*, 1982, edited by Heide Ziegler and Christopher Bigsby; and *Anything Can Happen*, 1983, edited by Tom LeClair and Larry McCaffery. See also Jackson I. Cope, "Robert Coover's Fictions," *The Iowa Review*, II (Fall, 1971), 94-110; Neil Schmitz, "Robert Coover and the Hazards of Metafiction," *Novel*, VII (Spring, 1974), 210-219; Frank W. Shelton, "Humor and Balance in Coover's *The Universal Baseball Association, Inc.*," *Critique: Studies in Modern Fiction*, XVII (1974), 78-90; Margaret Heckard, "Robert Coover, Metafiction, and Freedom," *Twentieth Century Literature: A Scholarly and Critical Journal*, XXII (May, 1976), 210-227; Arlen J. Hansen, "The Dice of God: Einstein, Heisenberg, and Robert Coover," *Novel*, X (Fall, 1976), 49-58; Neil Berman, "Coover's *The Universal Baseball Association*: Play as Personalized Myth," *Modern Fiction Studies*, XXIV (Summer, 1978), 209-222; Kathryn Hume, "Robert Coover's Fiction: The Naked and the Mythic," *Novel*, XII (Spring, 1979), 127-148; Tom LeClair, "Robert Coover, The Public

Burning, and the Art of Excess," *Critique*, XXIII (Spring, 1982), 5-28; Robert A. Morace, "Robert Coover, the Imaginative Self, and the Tyrant Other," *Papers on Language and Literature*, XXI (Spring, 1985), 192-209; and J. Allensworth, "Robert Coover: A Bibliographic Chronicle of Primary Materials," *Bulletin of Bibliography*, XLI (June, 1984), 61-63.

Robert A. Morace

JULIO CORTÁZAR

Born: Brussels, Belgium
Date: August 26, 1914

Died: Paris, France
Date: February 12, 1984

Principal Works

NOVELS: *Los premios*, 1960 (*The Winners*, 1965); *Rayuela*, 1963 (*Hopscotch*, 1966); *62: Modelo para armar*, 1968 (*62: A Model Kit*, 1972); *Libro de Manuel*, 1973 (*A Manual for Manuel*, 1978).

SHORT FICTION: *Bestiario*, 1951; *Final del juego*, 1956 (*End of the Game and Other Stories*, 1963; also known as *Blow-Up and Other Stories*); *Las armas secretas*, 1958; *Todos los fuegos el fuego*, 1966 (*All Fires the Fire and Other Stories*, 1973); *Octaedro*, 1974; *Alguien que anda por ahí y otros relatos*, 1977 (*A Change of Light and Other Stories*, 1980); *Queremos tanto a Glenda y otros relatos*, 1981 (*We Love Glenda So Much and Other Stories*, 1983); *Deshoras*, 1983.

POETRY: *Presencia*, 1938; *Los reyes*, 1949; *Pameos y meopas*, 1971; *Salvo el crepúsculo*, 1984.

NONFICTION: *Buenos Aires Buenos Aires*, 1968 (English translation, 1968); *Viaje alrededor de una mesa*, 1970; *Literatura en la revolución y revolución en la literatura*, 1976 (with Mario Vargas Llosa and Oscar Collazos); *Prosa del observatoria*, 1972 (with Antonio Galvez); *Paris: The Essence of Image*, 1981; *Los autonautas de la cosmopista*, 1983; *Nicaragua tan violentamente dulce*, 1984.

MISCELLANEOUS: *Historias de cronopios y famas*, 1962 (*Cronopios and Famas*, 1969); *La vuelta al día en ochenta mundos*, 1968; *Último round*, 1969; *Fantomas contra los vampiros internacionales: Una utopía realizable*, 1975; *Un tal Lucas*, 1979 (*A Certain Lucas*, 1984).

Julio Cortázar, unquestionably one of the pivotal figures in Latin American literature, is a master of the short story. In addition, his novel *Hopscotch* is widely considered to be one of the first great Spanish American novels. Born in Brussels on August 26, 1914, the son of Julio José and María Descotte de Cortázar, Cortázar learned French along with his native Spanish. This French-Argentine duality forms one of the leitmotifs of his work. His father abandoned the family soon after its return to Argentina in 1920, and Julio was reared by his mother and aunt. Earning degrees in primary and secondary education, with a concentration in literature, he first taught high school in several small towns and in Mendoza. He then taught French literature at the University of Cuyo, but his agitation against the Peronist regime earned his arrest and caused his subsequent resignation from the university. During his teaching years, he wrote steadily but, dissatisfied with the quality of his work, refused to publish anything—except, in 1938, hidden under the pseudonym Julio Denis, the collection of poems *Presencia* (presence) and in 1949, under his own name, the long philosophic-dramatic poem *Los reyes* (the kings) and a few magazine stories. In fact, it was Jorge Luis Borges, with whose work Cortázar's has often been compared, who published his compatriot's first story, "House Taken Over," in *Los Anales de Buenos Aires*.

Oppressed by the political and literary atmosphere of his native land, Cortázar, awarded a scholarship by the French government to study in Paris, seized this chance of escape and left Argentina in 1951 to settle permanently in Paris, where he earned his living working as a free-lance translator and for the United Nations Educational, Scientific, and Cultural Organization (UNESCO). In 1953, Cortázar married Aurora Bernárdez, also a free-lance translator and also Argentinian. The year 1951 marked the official start of Cortázar's literary career with the publication of *Bestiario* (bestiary), his first collection of short stories. *Bestiario* contains Cortázar's trademark signature, the gradual intrusion of a mysterious subversive element into the lives of ordinary people. Rarely is this force seen as an instrument of good, or at least liberating change, but rather as an obsessive harbinger of destruction and death.

(Julio Cortázar is the Spanish translator of the collected works of Edgar Allan Poe.)

Cortázar's next volume of short stories, *End of the Game and Other Stories*, contains some of his most famous prose. Stories such as "Axolotl" and "The Night Face Up" have become classics of the genre, and "Devil's Drool" introduced Cortázar to an international audience with Michelangelo Antonioni's cinematic version *Blow-Up* (1966), although the film bears little relation to the story. By 1960, Cortázar was widely known as a craftsman of intricate, beautifully written short stories, especially with cunning, sleight-of-hand endings, but the publication in that year of *The Winners* marked a drastic change in his artistic vision. The purely aesthetic gives way to the metaphysical, and the characteristic preoccupations of his work begin to emerge clearly. Variously interpreted as allegory, social satire, or thinly camouflaged political criticism, *The Winners* recounts the ill-fated voyage of a group of passengers who have received tickets for a mysterious cruise as a state lottery prize.

Hopscotch is Cortázar's masterpiece. An immediate success, it won for the Argentinian international acclaim, helped by the prizewinning English translation of Gregory Rabassa. *Hopscotch* demands active reader participation. According to the "Table of Instructions" at the beginning, there are at least two ways to read the novel, and the reader has to choose which path to follow through the book—a path that is never-ending, since the last two chapters refer endlessly to earlier ones. The main narrative of *Hopscotch* deals with the Argentinian Horacio Oliveira's endeavor to shatter the mundane world of supposed reality and rationality and find the secret harmony underlying all things. Artistically, by means of its disjoined structure, the originality of its language, its black humor, often aimed directly inward, and, above all, its self-conscious awareness of itself as artistic creation, *Hopscotch* represents a manifesto against all closed literary structures and credos.

After *Hopscotch*, Cortázar continued with his literary experimentation. *62: A Model Kit* is a demonstration of the literary theories put forth by the writer Morelli in the concluding paragraphs of *Hopscotch*. There is no basic structure, no unifying sense of time, space, character, or plot. The reader literally has to piece together the disparate components of the work to create a comprehensible whole. Much of Cortázar's later work can best be called "collage." *A Manual for Manuel* combines fiction and history, the thriller with true statistics and articles concerning political torture and oppression. Cortázar had often been criticized for his seeming indifference to the social and political realities of his native land, a charge he vehemently refuted. Nevertheless, toward the end of his life, his writing began to manifest overt political implications. He donated the royalties of *A Manual for Manuel* to the families of political prisoners and became a supporter of the Cuban and Nicaraguan governments. Nicaragua awarded him the Rubén Darío Order of Cultural Independence.

Cortázar's last collagelike work, *A Certain Lucas*, describes an expatriate Argentine writer living in Paris struggling humorously with the passage of time and growing illness. Cortázar himself, gravely ill with leukemia, spent much of his last months in and out of hospitals before dying of a heart attack on February 12, 1984.

Cortázar was gifted with a sense of whimsy. He used humor to awaken the reader from passivity and reveal opportunities of wider significance. He once said, "I've always thought that humor is one of the most serious things there are." This humor, along with all of his innovative techniques and linguistic fireworks, is enlisted in aid of one cause, the shattering of all artificial, conventional barriers that hinder the search for self-realization. Cortázar's characters are expatriates, exiled not only physically from their native land but from their inner selves as well. Along with Jorge Luis Borges and Gabriel García Márquez, Cortázar's importance as a major figure in the emergence of Latin American literature is not debated. His originality, inventiveness, and daring use of language have been recognized and acclaimed. Yet it is this same language which has earned for him the most criticism. His harshest critics have insisted that the surface is dazzling but hides the fact that there is nothing profound underneath. Others accuse him of pomposity, elitism, and self-indulgent erudition. Some scold him for playing too many games in his works. This charge of lack of purpose or seriousness has been most severe among his fellow Latin Americans, who have derided his "abandonment" of his country and have ridiculed his image as Frenchified and artificially cosmopolitan. Cortázar himself answered the last criticism by insisting that it was time for Latin Americans to see themselves as citizens of the world and stop making cultural isolation a virtue. The political content of his later work and his interest in social concerns also helped to silence these critics. Cortázar purposely used devices such as endless literary illusions to irritate the reader and force him to contemplate the work: He did not wish his books to be an easy read.

BIBLIOGRAPHICAL REFERENCES: For Cortázar's novels, see Evelyn Picon Garfield, *Julio Cortázar*, 1980; Steven Brody, *The Novels of Julio Cortázar*, 1976; Robert Brody, *Julio Cortázar: "Rayuela,"* 1976; and David W. Foster, *Currents in the Contemporary Argentine Novel*, 1975. Two of the best collections of essays on Cortázar's work are *The Fiction of Julio Cortázar: The Final Island*, 1978, edited by Jaime Alazraki and Ivar Ivask, and Manual Durán, *La vuelta a Cortázar en nueve ensayos*, 1968. Well-known interviews with Cortázar can be found in Luis Larss and Barbara Dahmann, *Into the Mainstream*, 1966; Evelyn Picon Garfield, *Cortázar por Cortázar*, 1978; and Rita Guilbert, *Seven Voices*, 1973. For general discussion of Cortázar and his place in contemporary Latin American fiction, see John S. Brushwood, *The Spanish-American Novel*, 1975; *The Latin American Short Story*, 1983, edited by Margaret Sayers Peden; Kessel Schwartz, *A New History of Spanish-American Fiction*, 1972, which probably contains the best bibliography of Cortázar's earlier work; and especially, José Donoso, *The Boom in Spanish American Literature: A Personal History*, 1977, translated by Gregory Kolmakos. See also Keith Cohen, "Cortázar and the Apparatus of Writing," *Contemporary Literature*, XXV (1984), 15-27; Amaryll B. Chanady, "Julio Cortázar's Fiction: The Unfinished Quest," *Antigonish Review*, LVII (1984), 45-83; and Carlos Fuentes, "Julio Cortázar 1914-1918: The Simón Bolívar of the Novel," *The New York Times Book Review*, LXXXIX (March 4, 1984).

Charlene Suscavage

NOËL COWARD

Born: Teddington, England
Date: December 16, 1899

Died: Port Royal, Jamaica
Date: March 26, 1973

Principal Works

PLAYS: *I'll Leave It to You*, pr. 1919; *The Better Half*, pr. 1922; *The Young Idea*, pr. 1922; *London Calling*, pr. 1923; *Fallen Angels*, pb. 1924; *The Rat Trap*, pb. 1924; *The Vortex*, pr. 1924; *Easy Virtue*, pr. 1925; *Hay Fever*, pr., pb. 1925; *On with the Dance*, pr. 1925; *The Queen Was in the Parlour*, pr., pb. 1926; *This Was a Man*, pr., pb. 1926; *Home Chat*, pr., pb. 1927; *The Marquise*, pr., pb. 1927; *This Year of Grace!*, pr. 1928, pb. 1929; *Bitter Sweet*, pr., pb. 1929; *Private Lives*, pr., pb. 1930; *Some Other Private Lives*, pr. 1930; *Cavalcade*, pr. 1931; *Words and Music*, pr. 1932; *Design for Living*, pr., pb. 1933; *Conversation Piece*, pr., pb. 1934; *Point Valaine*, pr., pb. 1935; *Tonight at 8:30*, pb. 1935 (includes *We Were Dancing*, pr. 1935; *The Astonished Heart*, pr. 1935; *Red Peppers*, pr. 1935; *Hands Across the Sea*, pr. 1935; *Fumed Oak*, pr. 1935; *Shadow Play*, pr. 1935; *Family Album*, pr. 1935; *Ways and Means*, pr. 1936; and *Still Life*, pr. 1936); *Operette*, pr., pb. 1938; *Set to Music*, pr. 1939; *Blithe Spirit*, pr., pb. 1941; *Present Laughter*, pr. 1942; *This Happy Breed*, pr. 1942; *Sigh No More*, pr. 1945; *Pacific 1860*, pr. 1946; *Peace in Our Time*, pr., pb. 1947; *Ace of Clubs*, pr. 1950; *Island Fling*, pr. 1951; *Relative Values*, pr. 1951; *Quadrille*, pr., pb. 1952; *After the Ball*, pr. 1954; *Nude with Violin*, pr. 1956; *South Sea Bubble*, pr., pb. 1956; *Look After Lulu*, pr., pb. 1959; *Waiting in the Wings*, pr., pb. 1960; *High Spirits*, pr. 1961; *Sail Away*, pr. 1961; *The Girl Who Came to Supper*, pr. 1963; *Suite in Three Keys: Come into the Garden Maude*, *Shadows of the Evening*, *A Song at Twilight*, pr., pb. 1966; *Cowardy Custard*, pr. 1972; (also known as *Cowardy Custard: The World of Noël Coward*); *Oh! Coward*, pr. 1972 (also known as *Oh Coward! A Musical Comedy Revue*).

NOVEL: *Pomp and Circumstance*, 1960.

SHORT FICTION: *Terribly Intimate Portraits*, 1922; *Chelsea Buns*, 1925; *Spangled Unicorn*, 1932; *To Step Aside*, 1939; *Star Quality: Six Stories*, 1951; *The Collected Short Stories*, 1962; *Pretty Polly Barlow and Other Stories*, 1964; *Bon Voyage and Other Stories*, 1967.

POETRY: *Not Yet the Dodo*, 1967.

NONFICTION: *Present Indicative*, 1937; *Australia Visited*, 1941; *Middle East Diary*, 1944; *Future Indefinite*, 1954.

SCREENPLAYS: *Bitter Sweet*, 1933; *In Which We Serve*, 1942; *This Happy Breed*, 1944; *Blithe Spirit*, 1946; *Brief Encounter*, 1946; *The Astonished Heart*, 1949.

TELEPLAY: *Post Mortem*, 1931.

MISCELLANEOUS: *The Lyrics of Noël Coward*, 1965.

In the two decades between World War I and World War II, Noël Pierce Coward set the style for smart, sophisticated comedies of upper-class manners. He was the son of Violet Veitch and Arthur Sabin Coward, an employee of a musical publisher in London. Both his parents were musical (they had met in a church choir) but were never sufficiently talented to make their living at it. When Coward was six, the family moved to Sutton in Surrey, where the father became a traveling salesman for a piano company, and, three years later, they moved again, this time to London. There, to supplement the family income, his mother took in paying guests and also launched her son's theatrical career in 1911 by helping arrange his first professional appearance as Prince Mussel in the children's play *The Goldfish*. Other roles followed, including Slighty in *Peter Pan*, and soon Coward was accepted as one of the West End's foremost juvenile talents. In 1918, he was called up for the military but served less than a year, being discharged for medical reasons before the Armistice was signed with Germany in November. That same year he had written his first play, *The Rat Trap*, which was not produced until 1926.

His real theatrical debut as playwright occurred with the light comedy *I'll Leave It to You*, performed in 1919. It ran in London for only thirty-seven performances, although the critic of *The Daily Mail* found it promising. This favorable review was stimulus enough for Coward, who threw himself into writing and acting, giving the London stage at least one or two, sometimes five, of his plays or musicals per year for the next twenty seasons.

His play *The Vortex*, performed in 1924, firmly established his fame. In the production he created the lead part of Nicky Lancaster. The London success prompted him to take the play to New York, where he duplicated his triumph. This amoral, sophisticated satire, which involved the young hero coming home from Paris to find his mother having an affair with the lover of his former girlfriend, was viewed with a certain repulsive attraction, no doubt adding to its popularity. Making absurd situations believable was Coward's speciality. Even while admitting the repugnance of the characters, critics acknowledged Coward's skill as a writer, his ability to create interest and tension.

Coward immediately became the darling of the international set, whose members adored his irreverence and daring, his ability to write witty dialogue for characters who did not have to worry about next month's rent. For this ability, he has often been called superficial and sometimes dismissed for being all tinsel and fluff. Coward, however, was a keen observer of the class system in his own country, a system which he satirized mercilessly. His goal, as he once confessed, was always to write good plays with good parts. He concentrated on entertainment and left the social implications to others. His realm was the stage, and he could portray nostalgia, poignancy, and melancholy as well as merriment and insouciance. Of his plays, his favorite was *Blithe Spirit*, a farce about spiritualism. This comedy had an astonishing first run: 1,997 performances. This was a record for its time—and remains a standard for theatrical group revivals.

One of Coward's talent, which he may have acquired from his parents, was his ability to write songs. He composed more than one hundred, inserting them into his plays and revues. Many have remained popular favorites: "I'll See You Again," "Some Day I'll Find You," "Mad Dogs and Englishmen," "Mad About the Boy," "I'll Follow My Secret Heart," "The Stately Homes of England," and "Don't Let's Be Beastly to the Germans." His lyrics display his consummate mastery of rhyme and phrasing, showing he was always on the alert for the unexpected. He could also be liltingly sentimental.

Coward often regretted that his more popular image of the brittle and superficial bon vivant obscured his worth as a serious writer. Someday, he quipped, "when Jesus has definitely got me for a sunbeam, my works may be adequately assessed." Coward was in a way the victim of his own hard work and professionalism: He made it seem so easy that people were convinced that it really was.

BIBLIOGRAPHICAL REFERENCES: Useful secondary sources on Coward include Patrick Braybrooke, *The Amazing Mr. Noël Coward*, 1933, which as its title suggests is unabashedly idolatrous; Leslie Cole, *The Life of Noël Coward*, 1976; Robert Greacen, *The Art of Noël Coward*, 1953, a long general essay on the playwright's work; Robert F. Kiernan, *Noël Coward*, 1986, an interestingly written summary of Coward's life and creative genius, especially good in the section on his verse; and Milton Levin, *Noël Coward*, 1968, one of the best summaries of Coward's life and works, with perceptive comments about his major plays. Raymond Mander and Jo Mitchenson, *Theatrical Companion to Coward: A Pictorial Record of the First Performances of the Theatrical Works of Noël Coward*, 1957, with an introduction by Terence Rattigan, is a basic source, complete with casts' and critics' comments about the productions. Sheridan Morley, *A Talent to Amuse: A Biography of Noël Coward*, 1969, is a competent treatment of his life. See also James Agate, "The Ingenium of Noël Coward," in *My Theatre Talks*, 1971; John Mason Brown, "English Laughter—Past and Present," *The Saturday Review of Literature*, November, 1946, 24-28; J. C. Furnas, "The Art of Noël Coward," *Fortnightly Review*, December, 1933, 709-716; John Raymond, "Play, Orchestra,

Play," *New Statesman*, October, 1958, 563-564; John Whiting, "Coward Cruising," *The London Magazine*, August, 1962, 64-66; and the biographies in *Current Biography*, 1941, 179-180, and 1962, 89-91.

Wm. Laird Kleine-Ahlbrandt

MALCOLM COWLEY

Born: Near Belsano, Pennsylvania
Date: August 24, 1898

Died: New Milford, Connecticut
Date: March 27, 1989

PRINCIPAL WORKS

LITERARY CRITICISM: *Exile's Return: A Literary Odyssey of the 1920's*, 1934, 1951; *The Literary Situation*, 1954; *Think Back on Us: A Contemporary Chronicle of the 1930's*, 1967; *A Many-Windowed House: Collected Essays on American Writers and American Writing*, 1970; *The Lesson of the Masters*, 1971; *A Second Flowering: Works and Days of the Lost Generation*, 1973; *The Flower and the Leaf: A Contemporary Record of American Writing Since 1941*, 1985.

POETRY: *Blue Juniata*, 1929; *The Dry Season*, 1941; *Blue Juniata: Collected Poems*, 1968.

NONFICTION: *Writers at Work: The "Paris Review" Interviews*, 1958; *Black Cargoes: A History of the Atlantic Slave Trade, 1518-1865*, 1962 (with Daniel Pratt Mannix); *And I Worked the Writer's Trade*, 1978.

MEMOIRS: *The Dream of the Golden Mountains: Remembering the 1930's*, 1980; *The View from Eighty*, 1980.

CORRESPONDENCE: *The Faulkner-Cowley File: Letters and Memories, 1944-1962*, 1966; *The Selected Correspondence of Kenneth Burke and Malcolm Cowley, 1915-1981*, 1988.

ANTHOLOGIES: *The Portable Hemingway*, 1944; *The Portable Faulkner*, 1946; *The Portable Hawthorne*, 1948; *The Complete Poetry and Prose of Walt Whitman*, 1948; *The Stories of F. Scott Fitzgerald*, 1951; *Great Tales of the Deep South*, 1955; *The Lessons of the Masters: An Anthology of the Novel from Cervantes to Hemingway*, 1971 (with Howard E. Hugo).

Malcolm Cowley is best known as the contemporary chronicler of the generation of American writers, mostly male, who matured during World War I and achieved fame during the 1920's and 1930's. Cowley was born near Belsano, Pennsylvania, a village south of Pittsburgh, on August 24, 1898, the son of a physician, William Cowley, and his wife, Josephine. He attended school in Pittsburgh and developed a lifelong friendship with writer and critic Kenneth Burke when they attended the same high school in that city.

In 1915, Cowley entered Harvard University and stayed there until 1917, when he went to France to serve in the American Ambulance Service but actually drove a munitions truck. He returned to the United States and attended Harvard University for the spring term of 1918 but again left to enter the Army until the Armistice. At that time, Cowley moved to Greenwich Village, where he tried to support himself by writing book reviews for a penny a word. He married Marguerite Bairds, and they both returned to Cambridge, Massachusetts. He was graduated from Harvard Phi Beta Kappa in the winter of 1920.

Between 1921 and 1923, Cowley received an American Field Service Fellowship that allowed him to study for a year at the University of Montpellier and to live a second year at Giverny, fifty miles south of Paris, where he was able to meet both American and English expatriate writers and French artists he called "the Dada crowd" (later "the Surrealist crowd"). He also earned extra money from editorial work for, and contributions to, American and French magazines, especially *Secession* and *Broom*.

Cowley returned to the United States in the summer of 1923 and worked for *Sweet's Architectural Catalogue*, but he soon gave that up to do free-lance writing and translations from the French. He was also working on semiautobiographical poetry which traced his mental and emotional development. This poetry, published in 1929 as *Blue Juniata*, was well received critically and launched Cowley on his career as a man of letters.

Only a week before the stock market crash of 1929, Edmund Wilson chose Cowley as his replacement as literary editor of *The New Republic*, a position Cowley held for almost twenty years. This job decisively affected his career: It shifted his focus from poetry to prose and defined the style and length of his essays, which first appeared in the journal (but have since been collected in *Think Back on Us*, *A Many-Windowed House*, and *The Flower and the Leaf*). It also gave him a perspective on writing as a craft as well as an art, and on publishing as a trade. Cowley's personal life changed dramatically as well. In 1932, he was divorced from his first wife and married Muriel Maurer, with whom he had one child. They purchased a small farm in Sherman, Connecticut, where they settled permanently. There, Cowley was able to pursue and write about the avocations he liked best: gardening, fishing, and hunting.

During the early years of the Depression, Cowley became a political radical who supported a variety of leftist causes and adopted a Marxist perspective, which shaped his first and most famous extended work of criticism, *Exile's Return*. In this work, Cowley comments on writers of his own generation who rebelled against American society first through exile and art and later by returning to their own country and committing their art to the tasks of social reconstruction. In the revised edition, Cowley modifies this interpretation somewhat and adds a chapter on important writers he had not previously covered. Nevertheless, it remains the most important and most characteristic of Cowley's books because it introduces his abiding interests in literary generations and in the historical study of the relation of art and artists to society. When it was first published in 1934, the book received praise from youthful but unimportant critics and damnation from older, established ones. As a result of this criticism, Cowley did not write another critical study for twenty years.

Cowley has, however, left a record of his life in the 1930's in his memoir *The Dream of the Golden Mountains*. Aside from his work for *The New Republic*, Cowley was one of many intellectuals and artists who actively supported Socialist and anti-Fascist causes. Like many intellectuals, by the end of that decade Cowley had become disillusioned with politics and had withdrawn into his literary work. Unfortunately, leftist connections caused Cowley trouble in later years, including an attack by the Dies Committee which forced his resignation from a government job with the Office of Facts and Figures in 1942.

In the 1940's Cowley renewed his interest in writers of his own generation. His introduction to *The Portable Faulkner* rescued the work of a future Nobel Prize winner from obscurity by explaining and praising the totality of his literary project. A later work, *The Faulkner-Cowley File*, collects the correspondence of these two men and includes the letters Cowley used to write the introduction. After Cowley gave up his position at *The New Yorker*, he became an editor for Viking Press. He was also a visiting lecturer in various colleges and universities. In these positions he was able to encourage and help talented young writers such as Jack Kerouac and Ken Kesey. It was not until after the Korean War that Cowley wrote another book-length study, *The Literary Situation*, about the post-World War II generation of writers.

After he turned seventy, Cowley reached his peak of literary productivity. He returned to his own literary generation, to Ernest Hemingway, F. Scott Fitzgerald, and William Faulkner in *A Second Flowering* and to minor figures such as Conrad Aiken and S. Foster Damon in *And I Worked the Writer's Trade*. Later still, he published two volumes of memoirs, *The Dream of the Golden Mountains* and *The View from Eighty*, a delightfully written discussion about the life of an active octogenarian. Cowley's earliest ambition was to be a man of letters, a person who could write well in several forms. Although he is best known for his literary criticism, there is no doubt that he made significant contributions to all the forms he has attempted. Cowley died of a heart attack in March, 1989.

BIBLIOGRAPHICAL REFERENCES: For further information about Cowley, see a collection of interviews conducted with the writer, *Conversations with Malcolm Cowley*, 1986, edited by Thomas Daniel Young. See also *Malcolm Cowley: A Checklist of His Writings, 1915-1973*, 1975, edited by Diane U. Eisenberg; James Michael Kempf, *The Early Career of Malcolm Cowley: A Humanist Among Moderns*, 1985; Kenneth Schuyler Lynn, "Malcolm Cowley Forgets," in *The Air-Line to Seattle: Studies in Literary and Historical Writings About*

America, 1983; and Daniel Aaron, *Writers on the Left*, 1961. Cowley's own memoirs are among the best sources for an understanding of his place in literary history.

Michael Helfand

JAMES GOULD COZZENS

Born: Chicago, Illinois | *Died:* Stuart, Florida
Date: August 19, 1903 | *Date:* August 9, 1978

Principal Works

NOVELS: *Confusion*, 1924; *Michael Scarlett*, 1925; *Cock Pit*, 1928; *The Son of Perdition*, 1929; *S.S. San Pedro*, 1931; *The Last Adam*, 1933 (also known as *A Cure of Flesh*); *Castaway*, 1934; *Men and Brethren*, 1936; *Ask Me Tomorrow*, 1940; *The Just and the Unjust*, 1942; *Guard of Honor*, 1948; *By Love Possessed*, 1957; *Morning, Noon, and Night*, 1968.

SHORT FICTION: *Children and Others*, 1964.

MISCELLANEOUS: *Just Representations*, 1978.

The carefully crafted novels of James Gould Cozzens marked a course for twentieth century American fiction against which the novels of his contemporaries continue to be judged. Cozzens was born in Chicago, Illinois, August 19, 1903, the only child of Henry William and Bertha Wood Cozzens; he spent his childhood on Staten Island, New York, and later at the Kent School in Connecticut. His first published work (at age seventeen) was an article in the *Atlantic Monthly* on preparatory school student government. He entered Harvard University in 1922 and there was encouraged in his writing by the poet Robert Hillyer, an instructor in English. While a freshman he wrote his first novel, *Confusion*, concerning the effect of excessive cultivation on a beautiful French girl. It was published in 1924, when he was twenty-one years old. Unable to cope with his situation as an undergraduate celebrity, he rusticated himself to Nova Scotia, where he wrote his second novel, *Michael Scarlett*, a historical novel about William Shakespeare's England, and then went to Cuba, where he tutored the children of the American operators of a Cuban sugar plantation. This experience provided the background for two other novels, *Cock Pit*, and *The Son of Perdition*. All four of these youthful novels Cozzens later dismissed as inferior work. In December, 1927, he was married to Sylvia Bernice Baumgarten, a successful literary agent.

With *S.S. San Pedro*, Cozzens began to give evidence of his mature manner. A short novel based on accounts of the sinking of the British steamer *Vestris* in 1928, *S.S. San Pedro* was a selection of the Book-of-the-Month Club, and thus brought Cozzens a wider readership. In his next novel, *The Last Adam*, also a Book-of-the-Month Club choice, Cozzens established the direction which most of his later novels were to take. Published in England as *A Cure of Flesh* and made into a film with Will Rogers, it is set in a small Connecticut town. The chief character, a physician, is forced to confront the conflict between the tight, restrictive code of the town and his own professional and moral imperatives. Such a fictional situation enabled Cozzens to describe with particular detail the technical circumstances of a professional as he interacts with a variety of people in a circumscribed society. The prose is clear, careful, and unobtrusive, and the interrelationships of the characters are skillfully drawn. These characteristics were continued in *Men and Brethren* (the profession studied is now that of the clergy, particularly the liberal Episcopalian clergy) and in *The Just and the Unjust*. The latter, which treats the ethical and legal aspects of a murder trial, was a highly acclaimed best-seller which brought Cozzens into prominence as a leading American novelist. The short novel *Castaway*, appeared in 1934. In this fantasy, a man finds himself alone in a large department store after some imaginary disaster has destroyed a major city. Despite his sudden access to every material resource he might have once desired, he finds himself unable to cope with his isolation and the limitations of his inner resources. This novelette represents Cozzens' only excursion into the experiments with fictional forms and techniques which other writers of the time were essaying.

Cozzens was almost unique among important writers of his generation in not developing new fictional forms, in not adopting the themes of alienation and rebellion of the Lost

Generation, and in not being swept up into the social and political causes and controversies of the Depression years. In 1933 he had moved with his wife to a farm near Lambertville, New Jersey, where he scrupulously avoided contacts with the press, with writers' organizations, and with political manifestos. When he sought modern models he found them in Aldous Huxley, John Galsworthy, and Somerset Maugham; he worked in a tradition of the social novel identified with Jane Austen, George Eliot, Henry James, and Edith Wharton.

During World War II, Cozzens served as an Air Force officer, writing training manuals, technical articles, and speeches. His intimate knowledge of military command decisions provided the material for *Guard of Honor*, a novel focused on the racial tensions in a Southern air base. It won for him the Pulitzer Prize in fiction for 1949.

With the publication of *By Love Possessed* in 1957, Cozzens' career reached a turning point. This novel, although his most ambitious, with the manipulation of multiple layers of action in a restricted time frame and an opulent style, repeated his now-familiar themes of the conflicts of reason and passion, duty and expediency, authority and liberty. In various editions, several million copies were sold, and it was awarded the Howells Medal by the American Academy of Arts and Letters in 1960. Nevertheless, some critics who saw in the book a mirror of the aesthetic and social conservatism of the 1950's praised or attacked the book and its reception as representative of the times. Cozzens collected his generally undistinguished short stories in 1964, and in 1968 published his thirteenth and last novel, *Morning, Noon, and Night*, in which the chief character offers comments on writing which are close to Cozzens' own views. Until his death in 1978, he remained in seclusion.

Cozzens' career was marked by early minor successes; by steady development as a literary craftsman of intelligent, complex novels read enthusiastically by a small group of devoted readers; and finally by the writing of a very popular novel which brought to him a wide readership and prominent critical attention. In his best works (*The Last Adam*, *The Just and the Unjust*, *Guard of Honor*, and *By Love Possessed*), he demonstrates the continued viability of the kind of novel which analyzed middle-class society dispassionately, without a program for its reform. His novels revealed no innovations in fictional technique, he eschewed both the sensational and the sentimental, and he was aggressively contemptuous of literary fashions. Nevertheless, his best novels stand as major accomplishments of twentieth century fiction.

BIBLIOGRAPHICAL REFERENCES: For many years the only source of biographical information about Cozzens was the inaccurate unsigned interview in *Time*, LXX (September 2, 1957), 72-74; Matthew J. Bruccoli, *James Gould Cozzens: A Life Apart*, 1983, is now the standard biography. Book-length studies of the novels began with Frederick Bracher, *The Novels of James Gould Cozzens*, 1959, still the best and most detailed treatment. Other studies are Harry J. Mooney, Jr., *James Gould Cozzens*, 1963; Desmond E. S. Maxwell, *Cozzens*, 1964; and Granville Hicks, *James Gould Cozzens*, 1966. Pierre Michel, *James Gould Cozzens*, 1974, includes comment on the last novel and the short stories. The most complete listing of periodical criticism is to be found in Pierre Michel, *James Gould Cozzens: An Annotated Checklist*, 1971. The entire issue of *Critique: Studies in Modern Fiction*, I (1958), was devoted to Cozzens. A useful collection of essays in appreciation of Cozzens' work from 1949 to 1978 is *James Gould Cozzens: New Acquist of True Experience*, 1970, edited by Matthew J. Bruccoli. Favorable views of Cozzens' achievement can be found in John W. Ward, "James Gould Cozzens and the Condition of Modern Man," *The American Scholar*, XXVII (1957/1958), 92-99, and Robert E. Scholes, "The Commitment of James Gould Cozzens," *Arizona Quarterly*, XVI (1960), 129-144. Two essays sharply critical of Cozzens' achievement are Irving Howe, "James Gould Cozzens: Novelist of the Republic," *The New Republic*, CXXXVIII (1958), 15-19, and Dwight Macdonald, "By Cozzens Possessed," *Commentary*, XXV (1958), 36-47.

William L. Phillips

MICHAEL CRICHTON

Born: Chicago, Illinois
Date: October 23, 1942

PRINCIPAL WORKS

NOVELS: *A Case of Need*, 1968; *The Andromeda Strain*, 1969; *The Terminal Man*, 1972; *The Great Train Robbery*, 1975; *Eaters of the Dead*, 1976; *Congo*, 1980; *Sphere*, 1987.

NONFICTION: *Five Patients: The Hospital Explained*, 1970; *Jasper Johns*, 1977; *Travels*, 1988.

SCREENPLAYS: *Westworld*, 1973; *Coma*, 1978; *The Great Train Robbery*, 1979; *Looker*, 1981.

John Michael Crichton, son of Zula (Miller) Crichton and John Henderson, onetime president of the American Association of Advertising Agencies, grew up in Roslyn, Long Island. He is the oldest of four children, including two sisters and a brother, Douglas, with whom he has collaborated under the joint pseudonym Michael Douglas. Frequently described as an overachiever, Crichton sold his first writing at age fourteen. He intended to major in writing in college, but instead he studied anthropology at Harvard University, from which he was graduated summa cum laude with an A.B. in 1964, adding the M.D. degree in 1969. By the time that he had completed medical school at age twenty-six, Crichton had written six mystery novels, five potboilers, and a more promising work entitled *A Case of Need*, which earned for him the Edgar Allan Poe Award of the Mystery Writers of America. The novel features a doctor who performs abortions; he is arrested for the murder of a teenager who dies as the result of an operation that he did not perform.

Because Crichton no longer intended to practice medicine after graduation and because his dean was aware of his growing fame as a writer, (*The Andromeda Strain* had been accepted for publication), he was allowed to alter his last year of studies at Massachusetts General Hospital and research the book *Five Patients: The Hospital Explained*. In *Five Patients*, Crichton not only documents cases but also offers a convincing analysis of both the training of physicians and the quality of health care available in the United States.

Meanwhile, *The Andromeda Strain* launched his career as a best-selling novelist. Capitalizing on peak interest in high technology and the space race, the plot tells of four scientists in a Nevada desert laboratory located below the ground; they have five days to save the world from an alien bacterial strain brought to Earth when an unmanned U.S. research satellite unexpectedly returns. A formula effort written in the style of Crichton's hero, Alfred Hitchcock, *The Andromeda Strain* was condemned by critics because of its forgettable characters and lack of passion but was well received by the general public because of its swift plot and facile writing.

The Terminal Man utilized up-to-date medical knowledge about stereotaxic procedures and brought Crichton further popular attention. Thirty-four-year-old Harold Benson suffers from psychomotor epilepsy and consequently becomes the first human being to have a computer implanted in his brain. Again, Crichton uses a time-lapse crisis to build the climax. Like *The Andromeda Strain*, this book quickly received a film offer, inevitably inviting comparison to the James Bond novels, and praise for its verisimilitude and scorn for what some critics called cheap entertainment.

Now Crichton was in limbo: "I had graduated from Harvard, taught at Cambridge, climbed the Great Pyramid, earned a medical degree, married and divorced, . . . published two best-selling novels, and . . . made a movie." *The Great Train Robbery*, set in London in 1855, was Crichton's next effort. Based on the heist of valuable gold bullion worth twelve thousand pounds and intended for British troops in the Crimea, this popular entertainment was made into a film in 1979, with the author serving as director. One critic complained of the novel's "little essays and digressions." Another called it a *ballet mécanique*. Still, Crichton succeeded as a popular storyteller.

He continued with the device of using purported historical evidence, like William Shakespeare, Jonathan Swift, and others before him, in *Eaters of the Dead*, his tribute to Beowulf and King Rothgar's Meade Hall. The plot centers on a document attributed to Ibn Fadlan, a tenth century Turkish emissary to Russia who chronicled his abduction by Norsemen and his subsequent aid in their defeat of cannibals who ate the fallen warriors. Literary scholars praised Crichton's work, while popular critics argued against its density and pedantry.

Crichton's impressionistic biographical tribute *Jasper Johns* makes connections between himself, the modern American artist, and admirers who want to understand Johns's creative process. Conversational in tone and illustrated with sixty color plates, the material was praised as "perfectly suited to its subject."

In *Congo*, a group of four—including a communicative gorilla named Amy—sets out to acquire a cache of industrial diamonds located at a ruined city in the interior of Africa. Aided by a satellite computer hookup to their Texas base, their quest ultimately brings them up against a rare troop of gorillas trained to guard the site. Despite unfavorable comparisons to the work of Walt Disney and George Lucas, Crichton's novel climbed the best-seller list.

Sphere focuses on Norman Johnson, professor of psychology who, along with several other specialists representing various fields, is called to a crash site in the Pacific Ocean where a huge spaceship has fallen from the sky. The group must assess the threat imposed. With a nod to Jules Verne and a bow to *The Andromeda Strain*, *Sphere* is an example of slick formula writing. Crichton appears trapped in repeated patterns.

In *Travels*, Crichton captivatingly reprises the journeys he has made—inward and outward—to increase his knowledge and locate background material for his novels. The memoir recalls his medical school years (1965-1969), and his many excursions to foreign lands (1971-1986), providing deep insights into both the man and the writer.

BIBLIOGRAPHICAL REFERENCES: See Jean W. Ross's interview with Crichton in *Contemporary Authors, New Revision Series*, XIII, 1984, edited by Linda Metzger; Robert L. Sims, "Michael Crichton," in *Dictionary of Literary Biography*, 1982, edited by Karen L. Rood, Jean W. Ross and Richard Ziegfeld; John Lear, "Is There a Lunar Microbe Stranger Than Science Fiction?" *Saturday Review*, LII (June 28, 1969), 29. For reviews of specific works, see Webster Schott, review of *The Andromeda Strain*, *The New York Times Book Review*, LXXIV (June 8, 1969), 4; L. E. Sissman, review of *The Great Train Robbery*, *The New Yorker*, LI (August 4, 1975), 89; and Robin McKinley, review of *Sphere*, *The New York Times Book Review*, XCII (July 12, 1987), 18.

Clifton L. Warren

MART CROWLEY

Born: Vicksburg, Mississippi
Date: August 21, 1935

Principal Works

PLAYS: *The Boys in the Band*, pr., pb. 1968; *Remote Asylum*, pr. 1970; *A Breeze from the Gulf*, pr. 1973.

SCREENPLAYS: *Fade In*, 1967; *The Boys in the Band*, 1970.

TELEPLAY: *Bluegrass*, 1988.

Martino Crowley, shortened to Mart Crowley, was the only child of devout, conservative, Catholic parents who sent him to a Roman Catholic high school in Vicksburg and urged him to attend the University of Notre Dame. Crowley balked and went to Los Angeles, drawn there by his early fascination with films and film stars. Soon his father, a transplanted Midwesterner of Irish ancestry, compromised and allowed Crowley to attend the Catholic University of America in Washington, D.C. Two years of that atmosphere, however, was all that the starstruck Crowley could take, and he fled from Catholic University to the University of California at Los Angeles to study art, hoping to prepare himself to become a designer of film sets. He soon returned to Catholic University, where he developed a close association with classmate James Rado, one of the writers of the rock musical *Hair* (which ran in New York in 1968). Crowley worked in summer stock theater in Vermont during his summers at Catholic University.

Upon graduation in 1957, Crowley's interest in drama drew him to California to write scripts and work with production companies. From 1964 to 1966, he worked as private secretary for Natalie Wood, whom he had met when they worked together on William Inge's *Splendor in the Grass* (1961).

Discouraged when his filmscript of Dorothy Baker's novel *Cassandra at the Wedding* (1962) was not produced, Crowley left California in 1966 and spent a year in Rome. By 1967, Crowley's fortunes were improving; Paramount Pictures filmed his screenplay *Fade In*. The studio's failure to release the film, however, led Crowley to begin psychoanalysis to help him deal with his ensuing depression and anxiety. Through this psychoanalysis, he reached his decision to write an overtly homosexual play about gays celebrating the birthday of one of their friends.

The basic idea for *The Boys in the Band* had occurred to Crowley eight years earlier, and he had occasionally returned to it, but psychoanalysis provided him with the self-knowledge he needed to bring such a play to fruition. The actual writing proceeded quickly once Crowley reached his decision to write the play; he completed the script in five weeks during the summer of 1967. Crowley's agent, although enthusiastic about his writing, doubted that any producer would touch a play as overtly homosexual as this one. The script, nevertheless, reached Robert Barr, who decided to produce it.

Casting the play presented problems because established actors would not risk stereotyping themselves by taking roles in a play about homosexuals. When the play opened at the Vandam Theater in January, 1968, therefore, it was cast with virtual unknowns. By April of the same year, *The Boys in the Band* had moved to an Off-Broadway theater where, save for a sprinkling of homophobic reviews, it was well received.

The action is set in the New York apartment of a gay man, Michael, host of a birthday party for a gay friend, Harold, who arrives late. Meanwhile, amidst queenly banter and dancing, Michael's former college roommate, Alan, who has left his wife, arrives and precipitates much of the play's action, which includes a telephone game not unlike the "get-the-guest" ploy Edward Albee uses in *Who's Afraid of Virginia Woolf?* (1962).

The importance of *The Boys in the Band*, which ran for more than a thousand performances on Broadway, is that it is the first play in American theater to deal head-on with an exclusively homosexual situation. Tennessee Williams created homosexual characters, such as Brick in *Cat on a Hot Tin Roof* (1955) and Sebastian in *Suddenly Last Summer* (1958); William Inge included in his later plays some overtly gay characters, such as Vince in *Natural Affection* (1963) and Pinky in *Where's Daddy?* (1966). These characters, however, were aberrations. In *The Boys in the Band*, it is Alan, the only straight character in the play, who is aberrant. The play reached a broad audience on Broadway and a still broader one when, in 1970, it was released as a film using Crowley's screenplay.

Later the same year, Crowley's next play, *Remote Asylum*, was produced in Los Angeles at the Ahmanson Theatre and evoked no favorable comment. Set in Acapulco, it presents a hodgepodge of unlikely sycophants to a has-been female film star. The characters strike out at one another in ways that recall the bickering of Albee's characters in *Who's Afraid of Virginia Woolf?*, but the play does not have Albee's strong central premise to justify its sustained shouting, contention, and bitchiness. *Remote Asylum*, understandably, did not reach Broadway.

With *A Breeze from the Gulf* in 1973, Crowley was moving in more productive directions. This highly autobiographical play about an only child between ages seventeen and twenty-five and his parents—the smothering mother addicted to drugs, the indulgent father to alcohol—offers moments of tremendous psychological insight, although much of the time it talks and psychoanalyzes itself to death. The play suggests a considerable talent not totally in control of its medium. With *The Boys in the Band*, Crowley cut through the thicket that blocked the way to frank dramatic presentations of the homosexual life-style, and for this pioneering effort he is best remembered.

BIBLIOGRAPHICAL REFERENCES: A strong assessment of Crowley's work is James W. Carlsen's "Images of the Gay Male in Contemporary Drama," in *Gayspeak: Gay Male and Lesbian Communication*, edited by James W. Chesebro, 1981. Georges-Michel Sarotte, *Like a Brother, Like a Lover: Male Homosexuality in the American Novel and Theater from Herman Melville to James Baldwin*, translated by Richard Miller, 1978, also provides interesting comments on Crowley as a pioneer in gay drama. Judy Klemesrud considers the casting problems for *The Boys in the Band* in "You Don't Have to Be One to Play One," *The New York Times*, CXVIII (September 29, 1968), 1, 3. Stuart W. Little and Arthur Cantor comment on Crowley's early work in *The Playmakers*, 1970.

R. Baird Shuman

COUNTÉE CULLEN

Born: New York, New York
Date: May 30, 1903

Died: New York, New York
Date: January 9, 1946

PRINCIPAL WORKS

POETRY: *Color*, 1925; *The Ballad of the Brown Girl*; *An Old Ballad Retold*, 1927; *Copper Sun*, 1927; *The Black Christ and Other Poems*, 1929; *The Medea and Some Poems*, 1935; *On These I Stand: An Anthology of the Best Poems of Countée Cullen*, 1947.

PLAYS: *Medea*, pr. 1935; *One Way to Heaven*, pb. 1936; *St. Louis Woman*, pr. 1946; *The Third Fourth of July*, pb. 1946.

NOVEL: *One Way to Heaven*, 1932.

CHILDREN'S LITERATURE: *The Lost Zoo (A Rhyme for the Young, but Not Too Young)*, 1940; *My Lives and How I Lost Them*, 1942.

Countée Cullen was the poet laureate of the Harlem Renaissance. Born in New York City, Cullen was reared in the parsonage of Salem Methodist Episcopal Church in the middle of Harlem, where his father, the Reverend Frederick Cullen, was the pastor and an influential personality in the social, political, and cultural life of New York City. After his graduation from DeWitt Clinton High School in New York, Cullen entered New York University, from which he was graduated in 1923 with a bachelor's degree and a Phi Beta Kappa key. In the fall of that year he entered Harvard University and studied for a master's degree in English with the renowned educator and author George Lyman Kittredge. For most of the rest of his life, Cullen lived in New York City.

Harlem during the 1920's was a vital cultural center. There, community theater groups, weekly newspapers with a national circulation, and "racial uplift" associations flourished. Journals such as *The Crisis*, the house organ of the National Association for the Advancement of Colored People (NAACP), showcased the work of young writers whose names soon became household words among black, and some white, Americans.

Cullen benefited from the "New Negro" movement and from the preferred position his excellent education gave him. His developing talent as a poet justified the interest in his work. When he was in high school, Cullen had won a citywide poetry contest with his poem "I Have a Rendezvous with Life." His first poem published in *The Crisis* also appeared while he was in high school. His first poem to be published in a white publication was "To a Black Boy" in *Bookman*. By the time he had been awarded his bachelor's degree, Cullen had published poems in *Century*, *Harper's Magazine*, *The American Mercury*, *The Nation*, *Poetry Magazine*, *Vanity Fair*, and *Palms*. In 1925, his senior year at New York University, Cullen was awarded first prize in the Intercollegiate Poetry Contest sponsored by the Poetry Society of America, as well as the John Reed Memorial Prize offered by *Poetry Magazine*. Also that year, *Color*, Cullen's first book of poems, was published. His second book of poems, *Copper Sun*, appeared in 1927. By this time he had seen individual poems appear in most of the American literary magazines.

No black American author had been so widely published previously. Walter F. White, assistant executive secretary of the NAACP, was particularly helpful in introducing Cullen to the power structure in American publishing. During this time, the apex of his productive years and the period in which he and his literary works were most popular, Cullen also edited a special issue of *Palms* and became assistant editor of *Opportunity*. On April 10, 1928, Cullen and Nina Yolande DuBois, popular Baltimore schoolteacher and daughter of the scholarly editor of *The Crisis*, were married in the principal social event of the season before some three thousand guests at Salem Methodist Episcopal Church.

Cullen was most productive as a poet, although he did publish one novel for adults and adapted his translation of Euripides' *Medea* (431 B.C.) for the stage. He also wrote a version of his novel *One Way to Heaven* for theatrical production. He worked with the Black author Arna Bontemps on an adaptation of Bontemps' novel *God Sends Sunday* (1931) under the title *St. Louis Woman*. His first children's novel, *The Lost Zoo*, was published in 1940; the second one, *My Lives and How I Lost Them*, appeared in 1942. For the last fifteen years of his life, Cullen taught English and French at Frederick Douglas Junior High School in New York City. He worked diligently on what would become *St. Louis Woman* and had hoped to complete a final anthology of poems. He was unable to complete either of these projects, having been incapacitated by bouts with high blood pressure that had plagued him for several years. He died on January 9, 1946. Thousands of people attended his funeral at Salem Methodist Episcopal Church. His father, who had resigned from the pastorate of the church, died the following May in New York City.

Although he wrote and published literally scores of poems, Cullen employed a fairly small number of themes consistently in his writing. As had been a part of an aesthetic used by black Americans in folk and conscious art for many years, Cullen paralleled the sufferings of the ancient Hebrews with that of black Americans. One of his earliest published poems, "Christ Recrucified," enunciates these sufferings in a fine sonnet that was never reprinted in any of the collections of poems that Cullen published. It is a stinging attack on persecution of black Americans in the American South that begins, "The South is crucifying Christ again/ By all the laws of ancient role and rule." The subject of the poem combines religion with social protest, as was characteristic of Cullen's poetry. Indeed, Cullen's most serious poetry carried on an argument with God for making blacks bear the suffering and injustice brought about by racial discrimination. Like fellow poets and preachers of the era, Cullen also utilized often the theme of "Ethiopianism," which attributed beauty and strength and dignity to black Americans by virtue of their lineage from Mother Africa. His long poem "Heritage" begins with the rhetorical question "What is Africa to me?" and rejects the practices of American culture as restrictions upon the more natural exercises of the mind, body, and spirit that one would find among the so-called heathen of Africa. In many other works as well, Cullen affirmed the guiding principle of the Harlem Renaissance—that "black is beautiful," as a later generation would declare.

BIBLIOGRAPHICAL REFERENCES: Darwin T. Turner, *In a Minor Chord: Three Afro-American Writers and Their Search for Identity*, 1971, contains a trenchant analysis of the poet's major works and themes. Turner uses some of Cullen's principles of criticism for black American authors to show that in most of his works the poet does not follow his own advice. Jean Wagner, *Black Poets of the United States*, 1973, contains analyses of the works of most of the best-known black poets; Wagner also provides detailed biographical narratives. Clearly, he holds a bias against Cullen and criticizes him more stringently than does Turner. Nevertheless, the work is helpful for understanding Cullen's work and the milieu in which it was produced. Arthur P. Davis, *From the Dark Tower: Afro-American Writers, 1900 to 1960*, 1974, is far less analytical than the Turner or Wagner books. The discussion does delineate the recurring themes of Cullen's poetry and his one adult novel. The most comprehensive bibliography is Margaret Perry, *A Bio-Bibliography of Countée Cullen, 1903-1946*, 1971. Alain Locke, ed., *Four Negro Poets*, 1927, is an anthology of works by Cullen, Jean Toomer, Claude McKay, and Langston Hughes, with critical commentary by Locke. Inasmuch as Locke knew all the authors personally, this work is particularly useful, though dated. Also valuable is Edward E. Walrond, *Walter White and the Harlem Renaissance*, 1978, for a detailed account of how officers of the NAACP fostered the careers of young black writers during the 1920's. Arthur P. Davis, "The Alien and Exile Theme in Countée Cullen's Racial Poems," *Phylon*, XIV (Fourth Quarter, 1953), 390-400, helps one to understand a major psychological aspect of Cullen's aesthetic. See also Charlotte E. Taussig, "The New Negro as Revealed in Cullen's Poetry," *Opportunity*, V (April, 1927), 111; Bertram L. Woodruff, "The Poetic Philosophy of

Countée Cullen," *Phylon*, I (Third Quarter, 1940), 213-223; and Walter C. Daniel, "Countée Cullen as Literary Critic," *College Language Association Journal*, XIV (March, 1971), 281-290.

Walter C. Daniel

EUCLIDES DA CUNHA

Born: Cantagalo, Brazil *Died:* Rio de Janeiro, Brazil
Date: January 20, 1866 *Date:* September 15, 1909

PRINCIPAL WORKS

NOVEL: *Os sertões*, 1902 (*Rebellion in the Backlands*, 1944).
ESSAYS: *Contrastes e confrontos*, 1906; *À margem da história*, 1909.
AUTOBIOGRAPHY: *Canudos (Diário de uma expedição)*, 1939.

Euclides da Cunha is considered one of the greatest Brazilian writers and one of the outstanding stylists in the Portuguese language. Born in 1866 in the municipality of Cantagalo, Euclides da Cunha lost his mother when he was barely three years old and spent a considerable part of his early life with relatives in Rio de Janeiro and Bahia. His formative years are marked by three major influences, which were to leave a lasting imprint on his life and career. From his father, a poet and lover of books, young Cunha learned to appreciate literature in general and poetry in particular. At Colégio Aquino in Rio de Janeiro, where he completed his secondary education, he was introduced to the abolitionist, republican, and positivist ideas that constitute the essence of his thought. Finally, at the Polytechnic School and at the War College he received a solid scientific training. An act of insubordination against the imperial minister of war, inspired by strong republican beliefs, led to Cunha's dismissal from the War College in 1888, but he was reinstated after the proclamation of the republic one year later and was graduated with a degree in mathematics and sciences in 1891.

After serving as a military field engineer for five years, Cunha resigned from the army to pursue careers as a public works engineer in São Paulo and as a journalist for *O Estado de São Paulo*. It was as a correspondent for this newspaper that Cunha had the experience that would form the basis for his masterpiece, *Rebellion in the Backlands*. In 1897 he traveled to the backlands of Bahia to cover the suppression by the army of a yearlong uprising in the village of Canudos led by Antônio Conselheiro, a charismatic mystic whose apocalyptic message of a better and more just time attracted thousands of the dispossessed poor to the area. Although religious fanaticism has always been a relatively common response to the impoverished conditions in the Brazilian northeast, the rebellion at Canudos stirred a national hysteria because it was perceived as a threat to the young republic. Refusing to pay taxes and calling the government of the republic "the law of the hound," the rebels were in turn accused of plotting the return of the monarchy. An ardent republican, Cunha at first supported the government's efforts to crush the rebellion but, as he witnessed the backlanders' heroic resistance, he developed a growing sympathy for them. In *Rebellion in the Backlands*, Cunha denounces the events at Canudos as a national crime caused by a complete lack of understanding of the reality in the backlands and the rebels' true motives. Despite Cunha's initial difficulty in finding a publisher, the book became an overwhelming success and led to the author's election to the Brazilian Historical and Geographic Institute and to the Brazilian Academy of Letters in 1903.

Cunha spent the last seven years of his life in a variety of public posts, including those of surveyor of frontiers and professor of philosophy. In 1906 he published *Contrastes e confrontos* (contrasts and comparisons), a collection of essays dealing with historical, political, and ethnological topics. Appointed to the chair of logic at Colégio Pedro II, a distinguished public institution in Rio de Janeiro, Cunha delivered his inaugural lecture on July 21, 1909, less than a month before he was assassinated on September 15 by the lover of his estranged wife. His second collection of essays, *À margem da história* (on the margin of history) was published posthumously in late 1909.

Rebellion in the Backlands is unquestionably Cunha's most important and original work. The first two parts ("The Land," a geographic treatise on the region, and "Man," a study of the ethnic origins of the backlanders, the psychology of Conselheiro, and the social organization of the village) give Cunha the opportunity to display his solid grounding in a variety of fields, including geology, botany, and ethnology. The third part, "The Battle," an account of the bloody conflict viewed as determined by the ecological, ethnic, and biological conditions described in the first two parts, is the culmination of the book. Written in a fast-paced narrative style, it has the rhythm and scope of the great works of fiction. Thus, despite attesting Cunha's vast scientific knowledge, *Rebellion in the Backlands* is first and foremost the work of a literary master, one who does not hesitate to go beyond the strict confines of science to convey a personal vision. Nowhere is this more obvious than in the paradoxical depiction of the backlander. Although Cunha subscribed to the deterministic scientific theories of the time, according to which the population of the backlands was doomed to extinction by the weakening effects of miscegenation and harsh climate, he portrays the backlander as a brave survivor perfectly fitted to his harsh environment. By means of an original interweaving of scientific vocabulary with figurative language and myth, Cunha elevates the backlander to the status of hero and turns the conflict at Canudos into a battle of epic proportions.

Rebellion in the Backlands belongs to a long tradition of literary works dealing with the issue of national identity, one which dates to the Romantic period, when, in their effort to establish a separate identity from the Portuguese colonizers, Brazilians developed a mythical view of themselves as the harmonious synthesis of the white, black, and indigenous races that constituted their nationality. Cunha calls this myth into question by proposing an interpretation of Brazil that underscores the country's unresolvable differences.

Rebellion in the Backlands has been influential both inside and outside Brazil. Although it did not inaugurate the literary treatment of the backlands, it changed the representation of that region in a definitive way by stressing its harsh conditions of life and by turning it into a symbol of the "other" Brazil. Cunha's approach has inspired a number of Brazilian writers, particularly in the 1930's, as well as many of the young Brazilian filmmakers who created the New Cinema movement in the 1960's. Cunha's masterpiece has also been the source of important works outside Brazil, such as R. B. Cunninghame Graham's *A Brazilian Mystic: The Life and Miracles of Antônio Conselheiro* (1920), a study of the career of the Canudos leader, and Peruvian writer Mario Vargas Llosa's acclaimed novel *The War of the End of the World* (1981; English translation, 1984).

BIBLIOGRAPHICAL REFERENCES: Isaac Goldberg, *Brazilian Literature*, 1922, has an informative chapter on Euclides da Cunha which is one of the earliest studies of Cunha's work in English. Samuel Putnam, "Brazil's Greatest Book: A Translator's Introduction," included in his translation of *Rebellion in the Backlands*, 1944, is the best introduction to Euclides da Cunha in English. *Modern Latin American Literature*, 1975, edited by David William Foster and Virginia Ramos Foster, contains a useful selection of critical assessments of Cunha's work, some of which have been translated from the Portuguese by the editors. Waldo Frank, *South American Journey*, 1943, devotes about ten pages to Cunha and calls *Rebellion in the Backlands* "Brazil's greatest book"; David Brookshaw, *Race and Color in Brazilian Literature*, 1986, makes only passing references to *Rebellion in the Backlands* in the chapter "Post-Abolitionist Literature" but provides a very good study of the representation of racial issues in nineteenth and twentieth century Brazilian literature. See also Frederic Amory, "Euclydes da Cunha as Poet," *Luso-Brazilian Review*, XII (1975), 175-185; Sara Castro-Klaren, "Santos and Cangaceiros: Inscription Without Discourse in *Os sertões* and *La guerra del fin del mondo*," *Modern Language Notes*, CI (March, 1986), 366-388; Alfred J. MacAdam, "Mario Vargas Llosa and Euclides da Cunha: Some Problems of Intertextuality," in *Proceedings of the Tenth Congress of the International Comparative Literature Association*, III, 85-90; John Walker, "Canudos Revisited: Cunninghame-Graham, Vargas Llosa and the Messianic Tradition," *Symposium: A Quarterly Journal in Modern Foreign Literatures*, XLI, no. 4,

(1987/1988), 308-316; and Thomas E. Skidmore and Thomas H. Holloway, "New Light on Euclides da Cunha: Letters to Oliveira Lima, 1903-1909," *Luso-Brazilian Review*, LVIII (1971), 30-55.

Luiz Fernando Valente

DAVID DAICHES

Born: Sunderland, England
Date: September 2, 1912

PRINCIPAL WORKS

CRITICISM: *Literature and Society*, 1938; *The Novel and the Modern World*, 1939, revised 1960; *Poetry and the Modern World*, 1940; *Virginia Woolf*, 1942, revised 1963; *Robert Louis Stevenson*, 1947; *A Study of Literature for Readers and Critics*, 1948; *Robert Burns*, 1950, revised 1966; *Willa Cather: A Critical Introduction*, 1951; *Stevenson and the Art of Fiction*, 1951; *Walt Whitman: Man, Poet, Philosopher*, 1955; *Critical Approaches to Literature*, 1956; *Literary Essays*, 1956, 1957; *Milton*, 1957, revised 1966; *The Present Age in British Literature*, 1958; *A Critical History of English Literature*, 1960; *George Eliot: "Middlemarch,"* 1962, 1963; *English Literature*, 1964; *More Literary Essays*, 1967, 1968; *The Teaching of Literature in American Universities*, 1968; *Some Late Victorian Attitudes*, 1969; *Sir Walter Scott and His World*, 1971; *Robert Burns and His World*, 1971, 1972; *Robert Louis Stevenson and His World*, 1973; *James Boswell and His World*, 1975; *God and the Poets*, 1983.

RELIGION: *The King James Version of the English Bible: A Study of Its Sources and Development*, 1941; *Moses: The Man and His Vision*, 1976.

HISTORY: *The Paradox of Scottish Culture: The Eighteenth Century Experience*, 1964; *Scotch Whiskey: Its Past and Present*, 1969; *Was: A Pastime from Time Past*, 1975; *Scotland and the Union*, 1977; *Glasgow*, 1977; *Edinburgh*, 1978; *Literature and Gentility in Scotland*, 1982.

BIOGRAPHY: *The Last Stuart: The Life and Times of Bonnie Prince Charlie*, 1973; *Robert Ferguson*, 1982.

AUTOBIOGRAPHY: *Two Worlds: An Edinburgh Jewish Childhood*, 1956; *A Third World*, 1971.

TRAVEL SKETCH: *Literary Landscapes of the British Isles: A Narrative Atlas*, 1979 (with John Flowers).

EDITED TEXTS: *The Norton Anthology of English Literature*, 1962, 1984 (with others); *Robert Burns, Commonplace Book 1773-1785*, 1965; *The Idea of a New University: An Experiment in Sussex*, 1964, 1970; *Literature and Western Civilization*, 1972-1975 (with others); *Robert Burns: Selected Poems*, 1980; *A Companion to Scottish Culture*, 1981.

David Daiches is one of the prime examples of the old-fashioned humanist man of letters, a writer who considers that his primary duty is to illuminate his subject by unearthing all the information he can find and then arranging it in order. In doing so he acts under the direction of no particular critical theory other than the assumption that the historical context of the work considered has much to do with the ways in which it can be understood and appreciated.

Born on September 2, 1912, in Sunderland, England, Daiches was reared there and in Scotland, to which his parents moved after World War I. He attended the University of Edinburgh, where he earned both B.A. and M.A. degrees with first-class honors in 1934. He then attended the universities at Oxford and Cambridge, receiving doctorates from both in 1939. Daiches embarked on a teaching career that would take him to many universities in both the United States and England, ending at the University of Sussex, where he spent the years from 1961 to 1977. After his retirement, he settled in Edinburgh, Scotland.

Daiches' scholarly career began even before he had completed his graduate studies. At first he concentrated on general studies in the theory of literature, producing a series of books concerning the function of literature in society and attempting to establish basic principles for the study of literature. In these, especially in *Literature and Society*, he proves an able exponent of the so-called Genetic Criticism, which prevailed before the advent of the New Criticism. Certainly not doctrinaire, he simply argues persuasively that reading is an act of interpreting a text, that the author intended to communicate a meaning through the text, and that the best way to uncover that meaning is to learn as much as possible about the author and his times.

Daiches next began a series of what could be called practical applications, having settled the questions of general theory. The first of these was a literary study of the King James Bible, one of the central documents in the development of prose style in English. As could be predicted from the theoretical works, his object was to learn all he could about the translators, the circumstances of the translation, and what the translators believed they were doing. Other works on specific writers followed, of which *Virginia Woolf*, *Robert Louis Stevenson*, and *Robert Burns* are particularly noteworthy. The book on Woolf remains the single best introduction to her work; here Daiches for the first time entirely subordinates himself to his subject, so that his prose becomes an unobtrusive medium of revelation. The study of Stevenson has not been surpassed, perhaps because the subject is a writer most effectively read from the perspective of Daiches' theories. The masterpiece, however, is the study of Burns; Daiches' intellect burns away the fog left by previous commentators, and his prose illuminates his insights.

From 1951, when he began a residence at the University of Cambridge, Daiches continued to work in both general theory and particular illustration. These works were well received, though none was judged exceptional. His *Critical Approaches to Literature*, however, served as a bible to the generation of graduate students beginning work from the mid-1950's, and his introductions to twentieth century writers for the *Norton Anthology of English Literature* synthesized the basic facts and backgrounds for students whose literary studies began in the 1960's. At the same time, he published the first volume of his autobiography, *Two Worlds*, interesting in its own right but made even more fascinating by the simplicity, clarity, and directness of his prose style. Also during this period, when the study of literature was becoming increasingly compartmentalized, specialized, and theory-ridden, he presented his two-volume *A Critical History of English Literature*, easily the clearest, most balanced, and most successful of the spate of literary histories appearing at the time.

Thereafter, Daiches returned to his studies of individual writers, redoing several he had done previously and formulating his conclusions about teaching after twenty years' experience. He also wrote a fascinating and authoritative book on an unusual nonacademic subject: the history, technology, and art of distilling scotch whiskey. *Scotch Whiskey: Its Past and Present* would become one of his most popular works. In it, Daiches approached his subject exactly the way he approached a literary tradition: He aimed to disclose the continuing influence of the past on the present, to show exactly how past practice continues to interact with and inform life today.

Almost equally popular is Daiches' study of the Jacobite movement, *The Last Stuart: The Life and Times of Bonnie Prince Charlie*. Astonishingly, Daiches managed to write for the general reader while meeting the most exacting standards of specialist scholarships. He assembled all the relevant information, then coordinated it to show how it connects in the time and place of his subject. Daiches' attitude is impartial, magisterial; dealing with material often sentimentalized, he deflates the romance by revealing the often-grim realities. Yet somehow he managed to lose none of the excitement in the process. His account of Bonnie Prince Charlie's escape, for example, remains vivid years after reading. Clearly, Daiches' work is that of an accomplished, undistracted scholar.

BIBLIOGRAPHICAL REFERENCES: Few attempts have been made to provide a general account of Daiches' career as a whole; most criticism is in the form of reviews of single books. The only efforts at a synoptic view are Robert Alter, "Literary Essays," *Commentary*, XLVII (May, 1969), 94-97, and Gertrude M. White, "Don't Look Back: Something Might Be Gaining on You," *The Sewanee Review*, LXXXI (October, 1973), 870-874. For reviews of *Two Worlds*, see Francis Russell, *The Christian Science Monitor*, April 30, 1956, 9, and *The New Yorker*,

XXXII (March 24, 1956), 151. See also *The Washington Post*, March 30, 1979, for a review of *A Third World*.

James Livingston

GUY DAVENPORT

Born: Anderson, South Carolina
Date: November 23, 1927

PRINCIPAL WORKS

SHORT FICTION: *Tatlin!*, 1974; *Da Vinci's Bicycle*, 1979; *Eclogues*, 1981; *Apples and Pears and Other Stories*, 1984; *The Jules Verne Steam Balloon*, 1987.

POETRY: *Flowers and Leaves*, 1966; *Cydonia Florentia*, 1966.

ESSAYS: *The Geography of the Imagination*, 1981; *Every Force Evolves a Form*, 1987.

TRANSLATIONS: *Carmina Archilochi: The Fragments of Archilochos*, 1964; *Sappho: Songs and Fragments*, 1965; *Archilochos, Sappho, Alkman: Three Lyric Poets of the Late Greek Bronze Age*, 1980; *Herakleitos and Diogenes*, 1980; *The Mimes of Herondas*, 1981.

Few living writers command the diversity of Guy Mattison Davenport, Jr. He is accomplished as a short-story writer, essayist, and translator and is successful and appreciated as a critic, lecturer, editor, poet, and scholar. He also qualifies as an illustrator and draftsman and has written libretti. He was born in Anderson, South Carolina, on November 23, 1927, to Guy Mattison Davenport, an express agent, and his wife, Marie Fant Davenport. As a youth, he was studious and interested in classical literature. After completing a B.A. at Duke University in 1948, he was a Rhodes Scholar and earned a B.Litt. at the University of Oxford in 1950; he then served in the U.S. Army for two years, after which he taught English at Washington University in St. Louis. He received a Ph.D. from Harvard University in 1961 and began teaching at the University of Kentucky in 1963.

That Davenport has never owned or driven an automobile suggests his independence from prevailing norms—a quality that is evident in his writing as well. His most significant contribution to the arts is assuredly his short fiction. Despite the variegated nature of Davenport's fiction, his stories share certain common features: They are experimental, modernist, and learned. Davenport's stories dispense with much of the machinery of the traditional short story; often as not, the reader cannot initially discern who the speaker is, and there is little in the sense of action, character, or development that can be read as plot. A typical Davenport story might juxtapose narratives set in different centuries, with no explicit connection, asking the reader to intuit the relation between them. Such devices clearly identify Davenport as a modernist. At the same time, he fills his works with allusions from history, religion, art, and science—particularly classical ones—such that his scholarship is a bedrock of the fiction. Some reviewers have found fault with the conspicuous erudition of Davenport's stories, but this conclusion is presumptuous and lazy, for the learned nature of his stories provides the foundation which will sustain them.

Davenport himself has described his stories as "assemblages." What Davenport means by this term, adapted from modern art, is readily apparent: He assembles into a coherent whole a combination of story, essay, anecdote, and lecture (but mostly "story," though there are no plots); he assembles a number of characters from various backgrounds, eras, and professions, and he assembles various comments about life, morality, and human nature. Davenport's stories number a few dozen, and virtually any one of them can be used to demonstrate these assertions. In "The Richard Nixon Freischutz Rag," Nixon visits China and converses with Mao Tse-tung; Leonardo da Vinci is seen working and thinking in his shop; finally, Gertrude Stein and Alice B. Toklas make social comments while visiting Assisi. In "The Wooden Tower of Archytas," Archytas makes and flies a wooden dove powered by steam; in the same story, Native Americans in South Carolina sing for the soul of a dove: The setting is a slave dormitory.

Without question, Davenport's essays are more accessible than his stories. To begin with, he does focus on a single point, demonstrating it in a forthright manner, becoming a first-quality essayist in the traditional sense of that word. Like his fiction, his essays are always learned, full of allusions from history, science, and the arts; yet it is possible to determine quickly his point. He successfully blends personal anecdote, historical events, social commentary, and artistic criticism in a highly distinctive manner. One of his best-known essays is "Making It Uglier to the Airport," the opening of which illustrates his characteristic tone. This essay is typical of both his stories and essays. In it, Davenport proceeds to support his assertions that the buildings of America are all ugly, with specifics from Chicago, New York, and eventually his own Lexington, Kentucky, making a very persuasive case. The essay is sprinkled with information from and about the writings of Michelangelo; Ada Louise Huxtable, a journalist who writes about architecture; Manfredo a Tafuri, an architect and writer; and Daniel Defoe—and all of this within the first two pages. Davenport then shifts to a personal anecdote about being denied a passport at the Lexington post office because he does not have a driver's license; next he shows how everything said before applied to some dozen or so cities across the nation. By the time the reader reaches the conclusion, there is no escape from his claim that "the automobile and airplane have made us nomads again."

Davenport's career is not characterized by progression, growth, and development in the sense that these terms would be applied to most authors. He was forty-three years old before he published his first story, and his maturity as a scholar and writer was already established in other ways. He has produced translations, essays, stories, and some poetry in a prolific way throughout his adult life. There is no change in the substance of his work, thinking, and productivity; rather, there is to be found only elaboration upon ideas formed from the outset. In the course of exploring those insights, Davenport has produced one of the most significant bodies of work in contemporary American literature.

BIBLIOGRAPHICAL REFERENCES: A number of excellent critical articles and reviews have been written about the major collections of stories and essays. *Tatlin!* is best discussed by Richard Peaver in his article "*Tatlin!*: Or, The Limits of Fiction," *The Hudson Review*, XXVIII (1975), 141-146, and by George Kearns, "Guy Davenport in Harmony," *The Hudson Review*, XXXIII (1980), 449-454. A partial explanation of the stories in *Da Vinci's Bicycle* is provided by Davenport's friend Hugh Kenner in "Assemblages," *National Review*, XXXI (1979), 1238-1241. Readers should also study "A Guydebook to the Last Modernist: Davenport on Davenport and *Da Vinci's Bicycle*," *Journal of Narrative Technique*, XVI (1986), 148-161. A review of *Apples and Pears and Other Stories* is helpful in understanding this collection: Bob Halliday, "Guy Davenport's Terrestrial Paradise," *The Washington Post Book World*, January 20, 1985, 8. For an article on *The Jules Verne Steam Balloon*, see Joseph C. Schöpp, "Perfect Landscape with Pastoral Figures: Guy Davenport's Danish Eclogue à la Fourier," in *Facing Texts: Encounters Between Contemporary Writers and Critics*, 1988, edited by Heide Ziegler. Essays in *The Geography of the Imagination* have been carefully reviewed by William C. Waterson in "A Mapping of the Mind," *The New Leader*, LXIV (1981), 16-17. George Steiner provides a more succinct summary in "Rare Bird," *The New Yorker*, LVII (1981), 196. William Burton has published a bibliography of critical articles and reviews, "Guy Davenport: A Bibliographic Checklist," *American Book Collector*, V (1984), 37-46.

Carl Singleton

DONALD DAVIE

Born: Barnsley, Yorkshire, England
Date: July 17, 1922

Principal Works

POETRY: *Brides of Reason*, 1955; *A Winter Talent and Other Poems*, 1957; *The Forests of Lithuania*, 1959; *A Sequence for Francis Parkman*, 1961; *New and Selected Poems*, 1961; *Events and Wisdoms: Poems, 1957-1963*, 1964; *Essex Poems, 1963-1967*, 1969; *Collected Poems, 1950-1970*, 1972; *The Shires*, 1974; *In the Stopping Train and Other Poems*, 1977; "*Three for Water-Music*" and "*The Shires*," 1981; *Collected Poems, 1970-1983*, 1983; *To Scorch or Freeze: Poems About the Sacred*, 1988.

LITERARY CRITICISM: *The Purity of Diction in English Verse*, 1952; *Articulate Energy: An Enquiry into the Syntax of English Poetry*, 1955; *Ezra Pound: Poet as Sculptor*, 1964; *Pound*, 1975; *The Poet in the Imaginary Museum: Essays of Two Decades*, 1977; *Trying to Explain*, 1979.

MEMOIR: *These the Companions: Reflections*, 1983.

RELIGION: *A Gathered Church: The Literature of English Dissenting Interest, 1700-1930*, 1978; *Dissentient Voice: The Ward and Phillips Lectures for 1980 with Some Related Pieces*, 1982.

TRANSLATION: *The Poems of Dr. Zhivago*, 1965 (by Boris Pasternak).

Donald Alfred Davie is an English poet, critic, editor, and translator. He was born the son of George Clarke, a sergeant in a Scottish regiment, and Alice (Sugden) Davie, a schoolmistress who cultivated Davie's predisposition for literary criticism by insisting that he record the substance of every book he read. Davie attended the University of Cambridge and joined the Royal Navy upon graduation. Assigned to Arctic Russia in World War II, he combated loneliness by reading the works of Robert Burns, Lord Byron, and Russian authors in translation, a period later documented in *These the Companions*. Before going to India for the last months of the war, he was married to Doreen John in 1945.

After demobilization, Davie returned to Cambridge, where he began to learn the craft of poetry and corresponded with American critic Yvor Winters, from whom he learned much about poetic rhythms. His review of an anthology by Winters in *Poetry London* is often viewed as the beginning of the Movement in English poetry. The Movement, a reactionary group of university-trained poets whose preference was for metrical verse, challenged the elitism of British culture.

Thus Davie was an established critic before his first book of poems appeared. His first critical volume, *The Purity of Diction in English Verse*, draws parallels between the laws of syntax and the laws of society, maintaining that the poet bears responsibility for purifying and correcting the spoken language; he finds virtue in eighteenth century Augustan poetry's use of formal poetic structures and proselike syntax. In *Articulate Energy*, he argues the need for clarity, reason, and readability in modern verse, arguments consistent with those of other Movement poets in the 1950's, notably Kingsley Amis, Philip Larkin, and Thom Gunn. Because of his existing reputation as a critic, Davie soon became the Movement's most intellectual spokesman in calling for an improved social and moral content in poetry. Eschewing the symbolism and imagism characteristic of verse in the 1940's, Davie called for an intelligible, restrained poetry that employed traditional syntax and easily apprehended images.

Davie's most significant critical works are his two books on Ezra Pound, which praise Pound's rhythmical and linguistic talents. These methodological studies consider Pound's translations and their originals as well as difficult sections of Pound's *Cantos*, which he elucidates. Although Davie ranks Pound as one of the great world poets, he is no apologist for Pound's politics and the corrupting influence they brought to his work.

Davie began writing criticism in order to understand his own poems, and his early book of poetry, *Brides of Reason*, displays a classical formalism compatible with his criticism. Mainly metrical academic pieces typifying Davie's concern for aesthetic control, the poems emphasize the intellect over sensual experience. In 1950, Davie began a seven-year self-imposed exile in Dublin, and his perspective of an Englishman living in Ireland prefigures the sectarian violence of subsequent decades.

In 1957, Davie made the first of many trips to the United States, resulting in the publication of *A Sequence for Francis Parkman*. Like his friend Charles Tomlinson (whom he called the most accomplished British poet of his generation), Davie made trips to North America to broaden his knowledge of the English language rather than to escape the stultifying world of British letters. His kinship with the United States prompted him over the years to accept various teaching positions there, including ones at Stanford University and Vanderbilt University.

Returning to England by ocean liner, Davie penned *The Forests of Lithuania*, his version of Adam Mickiewicz's Polish romantic verse novel *Pan Tadeusz* (1834; English translation, 1917). Like Pound, Davie sought to condense a masterpiece worthy of emulation. Moreover, Pound had suggested that a poet should translate to improve his style; thus, to escape the rigors of metrical verse, Davie also translated the poems of Boris Pasternak.

Nostalgia and a sense of loss pervade *The Shires*, Davie's most condemned book of verse. A wistful collection of forty poems, one for each county in England, *The Shires* was a critical failure, and Davie bought up the remaining supply of books to keep it from being remaindered. His following volume *In the Stopping Train*, also privileges the England of yesteryear, but it displays a more relaxed, though still self-conscious, style. Its twenty-eight poems often employ a dialectical technique wherein Davie poses questions, then answers, then further questions and answers. The themes are fairly conventional, showing an academic awareness of John Keats's concept of negative capability, though his ear for language is not as keen.

In *A Gathered Church* and *Dissentient Voice*, Davie traces the literary and cultural implications of his religious dissent. In *These the Companions*, a personal literary memoir, he more clearly addresses the important influences on his literary career, particularly the influence of F. R. Leavis and Yvor Winters, whom he calls puritans, meaning persons of unwavering principle for whom matters of morality and intellect were absolute. In *The Poet in the Imaginary Museum*, Davie attempts to vindicate his aestheticism by claiming that the poet should be an artificer or maker rather than a prophet or creator. Yet as a clever metrical poet who rejects vulgarity and sensationalism, Davie has achieved only limited success. Those academics who would separate poetry and criticism have found his verses pretentious or banal, but he has been warmly received by those, especially fellow Movement poets, who appreciate his unwillingness to condescend to readers; for example, Thom Gunn called Davie one of the best three English poets of his generation. "If poems were made solely of ideas," John Lucas writes in *New Statesman*, "there would be few more interesting poets than Donald Davie."

BIBLIOGRAPHICAL REFERENCES: Donald Davie has written frequently about his literary life. His 1986 autobiographical entry in *Contemporary Authors, Autobiography Series*, Vol. 3, offers commentary beyond that previously available in his collections of essays and memoirs. Davie's interest in religious dissent is fundamental to Neal Powell, "Donald Davie, Dissentient Voice," *British Poetry Since 1970: A Critical Survey*, 1980 (edited by Peter Jones and Michael Schmidt), and Valentine Cunningham, "Dissenting Davie," *The Listener*, August 26, 1952. Christopher Ricks's essay "Davie's Pound," *New Statesman*, LXIX, April 16, 1965, and Martin Dodsworth's "Pound Revalued," *Encounter*, XXV, July, 1965, provide additional insights into Davie's admiration for Pound. For pertinent criticism of Davie the poet, see Thom Gunn, "Things, Voices, Minds," *The Yale Review*, LII (Autumn, 1962), 129-138; D. E. Richardson, "Donald Davie and the Escape from the Nineteenth Century," *The Sewanee Review*, LXXXVI (Fall, 1978), 577-581; Peter Levi, "Impresario of the Waves," *New Statesman*, June 6, 1980; and Michael Kirkhorn,

"English Poetry Since 1950," *The Sewanee Review*, LXXIX, Summer, 1981. See also *On Modern Poetry: Essays Presented to Donald Davie*, edited by Vereen Bell and Laurence Lerner, 1988.

Jerry Bradley

ROBERTSON DAVIES

Born: Thamesville, Canada
Date: August 28, 1913

PRINCIPAL WORKS

NOVELS: *Tempest-Tost*, 1951; *Leaven of Malice*, 1954; *A Mixture of Frailties*, 1958; *Fifth Business*, 1970; *The Manticore*, 1972; *World of Wonders*, 1975; *The Rebel Angels*, 1982; *What's Bred in the Bone*, 1985; *The Lyre of Orpheus*, 1989.

CRITICISM AND ESSAYS: *Shakespeare's Boy Actors*, 1939; *The Diary of Samuel Marchbanks*, 1947; *The Table Talk of Samuel Marchbanks*, 1949; *A Voice from the Attic*, 1960; *Samuel Marchbanks' Almanack*, 1967; *Stephen Leacock: Feast of Stephen*, 1970; *One Half of Robertson Davies*, 1977; *The Mirror of Nature*, 1983; *The Papers of Samuel Marchbanks*, 1985.

PLAYS: *Eros at Breakfast and Other Plays*, pb. 1949; *At My Heart's Core*, pr., pb. 1952; *Hunting Stuart and Other Plays*, pb. 1972; *Question Time*, pr., pb. 1975.

Although beginning his career as a novelist relatively late in life, at age thirty-eight, William Robertson Davies has become not only the best-known Canadian novelist of the twentieth century but indeed one of the leading writers of the world. He was born on August 28, 1913, in Thamesville, Ontario, a small town about midway between Windsor and London; his father, William Rupert Davies, was a prominent publisher. After attending various local schools, Davies entered Upper Canada College, Toronto, and Queen's University, Kingston, before taking a B.Litt. degree from Balliol College, University of Oxford, in 1938. Thereafter he joined the Old Vic Company in London as teacher and performer, leaving it to return to the publishing business in Canada in 1940. For two years he served as literary editor of *Saturday Night*, a leading literary magazine, in Toronto; then he became the publisher and editor of the Peterborough, Ontario, *Examiner* for twenty years. He also was active in drama, writing plays, directing theatrical productions, and working with Tyrone Guthrie and others to resuscitate Canadian theater and establish the Stratford Theatrical Festival. In 1951, he began publishing fiction. Named professor of English at the University of Toronto in 1960, he became master of Massey College there in 1962 and remained until retirement in 1981; he continued to reside in Toronto after retirement and to publish novels at regular intervals.

Tempest-Tost, the first novel of the Salterton Trilogy, begins Davies' presentation of life in a small Canadian university town. The choice of a Canadian setting is not accidental; from the onset of his career Davies has taken it as part of his vocation to correct the shortcomings of Canadian culture by gently ridiculing them. *Tempest-Tost* also draws on Davies' theatrical experience; its subject is the staging of William Shakespeare's *The Tempest* by a local amateur company. Typical small-town tensions and animosities threaten to undermine the production, but Shakespeare proves capable of transcending petty rivalries and trivial antagonisms and of elevating some of the participants to new heights of awareness. *Leaven of Malice* extends the satire by deepening it: Local antagonism here springs from evil impulses, desires to hurt, rather than being merely casual eccentricities. A false engagement announcement inserted in a local newspaper on a malicious whim leads to open hostility between two families. Strangely, love grows out of this conflict; the couple, indifferent to each other previously, eventually marry. *A Mixture of Frailties* takes a young female singer from small-town Canada to the sophisticated world of European opera; it suggests that exposure to the wide world, while bearing risks, is necessary for full human development.

The Salterton Trilogy gained international attention; the Deptford Trilogy raised Davies to the top rank of world authors. To the humor, deft characterization, and strong structure of the earlier set the successor added arcane anecdotal richness, religious mysticism, psychological depth, and expanded thematic range. These three novels all grow out of a single event.

During a snowball fight between two ten-year-olds, Dunstan Ramsey and Percy "Boy" Staunton, Staunton loads a snowball with a rock. Dunstan evades the missile, which hits Mrs. Mary Dempster in the head, triggering a premature childbirth and eventually causing a complete mental breakdown. Each of the novels centers on one of the three male participants in this accident.

In *Fifth Business*, taking responsibility for the accident because he dodged, Dunstan bears the burden of guilt. This guilt has driven him to religion for solace; he studies hagiography, the careers of saints, becoming the major Protestant authority on the subject. This study ultimately leads to his own salvation, obtained when Dunstan finally realizes that he was not intended to become a saint himself.

The same material appears from the point of view of Boy Staunton in *The Manticore*; it also is told in retrospect, following his mysterious death. He has been found in his car in Lake Ontario, his mouth stopped with the same rock that hit Mrs. Dempster. The novel traces the double mystery of the drowning and the rock. It leads to a performance by the illusionist Magnus Eisengrim (the stage name of Paul Dempster, the son born prematurely to Mrs. Dempster), during which a summoned brass head answers questions from the audience. Boy's son David asks who killed his father. This question disrupts the show, and David escapes in the confusion, but suffers a breakdown. Eventually he is sent for psychotherapy to Switzerland, where he comes to accept his father's life and death.

Paul Dempster takes center stage in *World of Wonders*. Kidnapped while a boy by a stage magician in a circuit carnival, he voluntarily joins the group to become a magician himself and to learn the secrets and the motives of his captor. After a sojourn in Europe as a stage double, he strikes out on his own as a master illusionist. In the course of these wanderings, he goes through several transformations of his own and ends with a transcendent comprehension of the way in which accident determines part of the purpose of human life. His experiences, paralleling in oblique ways the course of the protagonists of the other two novels, reveal the hidden affinities in the different yet related pilgrimages of three souls. He ends by gaining a superior understanding of the function of good and evil in developing the soul.

Davies' later novels build on the basis laid in the two trilogies. In *The Rebel Angels*, his most celebrated book, Davies takes as subject the academic world, specifically a college of the University of Toronto. Francis Cornish, an eccentric art collector, has named a number of professors as executors of his estate. A subplot traces the affair between one of these professors and his graduate assistant, a beautiful woman of Gypsy descent. Another subplot explores the research of another professor, an expert in human refuse, who develops a remarkable theory of filth therapy. A third examines the unsettling effects on the faculty of the return to campus of a brilliant but unprincipled professor who had been dismissed for unethical activities.

What's Bred in the Bone takes the form of a posthumous biography of Francis Cornish told by two angels, the Angel of Biography from the staff of the Recording Angel, called the Lesser Zadkiel, and Cornish's personal daimon, Maimas. Both shape and influence the life they recount; both, in fact, are necessary for Cornish to live a complete life. By the end of the novel, both are revealed as metaphors rather than actual spirits, emblems of the two spiritual forces implicit in the complete life. In general, Cornish's object is to preserve the inner vision of the great artists of the past in a world that has replaced it with spurious sensationalism or empty ratiocination. Like all Davies' works, this one abounds with incidental information on a cornucopia of topics.

BIBLIOGRAPHICAL REFERENCES: Bruce King presents a capable survey of Davies' career up to 1980 in "Canada: Robertson Davies and Identity," in *The New English Literatures: Cultural Nationalism in a Changing World*, 1980. David Stouck covers more in *Major Canadian Authors: A Critical Introduction*, 1984. The only detailed book-length study of Davies' work is Patricia Monk, *The Smaller Infinity: The Jungian Self in the Novels of Robertson Davies*, 1982; it offers much insight, but stops with the Deptford Trilogy. Robert G. Lawrence and Samuel L. Macey collect a number of useful essays in *Studies in Robertson Davies' Deptford Trilogy*, 1980. Early critical biographies are Patricia Morley, *Robertson Davies*, 1977; and Judith Skelton Grant, *Robertson Davies*, 1978. For a useful collection of interviews, see *Conversations with Robertson Davies*, 1989, edited by J. Madison Davis.

James Livingston